TRAUMA

188.21.224.34 - - [28/Jul/2010:12:13:41 +0200] "GET /Seiten/Forms
_and_Infos.html HTTP/1.1" 200 16472 "http://www.google.at/search?q
=Tips+and+tricks+on+how-to+enhance+bureaucratic+burdens+in+the+asy
lum+process+in+Austria+and+in+the+Schengen+Area&ie=utf-8&oe=utf-8&
aq=t&rls=org.mozilla:de:official&client=firefox-a" "Mozilla/5.0 (Wi
ndows; U; Windows NT 5.1; de; rv:1.9.2.3) Gecko/20100401 Firefox/3.
6.3 (.NET CLR 3.5.30729)"

88.116.224.102

```
inetnum:        88.116.224.100 - 88.116.224.103
netname:        BMF-HWY-AT
descr:          BM f. Landesverteidigung
descr:          Hetzgasse 2
descr:          1030 Wien
country:        AT
admin-c:        HMH25-RIPE
tech-c:         HMH25-RIPE
status:         ASSIGNED PA
mnt-by:         AS8447-MNT
mnt-lower:      AS8447-MNT
source:         RIPE # Filtered
```

UBERMORGEN.COM
AAbA
Logfile
Asylabwehramt
Asylum Defence Agency

Trauma Verlag Wien

Erstauflage 2011
First Edition 2011

http://www.asylabwehramt.at
http://www.asylabwehramt.at/index_e.html

ISBN: 978-3-9502910-8-7

no copyright UBERMORGEN.COM, 2011
Dieses Buch gibt es nur bei Trauma Wien im Online-Versand.
http://traumawien.at – verlag@traumawien.at
und als .PDF auf UBERMORGEN.COM

Dieses Buch wurde in Computer Modern gesetzt.
Cover: Luc Gross & Julian Palacz
Produktion: Julian Palacz
Edit: Luc Gross
Projekt: UBERMORGEN.COM
Coding: Michael Zeltner
Assistance: Philipp Teister

Für Billie & Lola
Lampedusa, Januar 2011

Inhaltsverzeichnis

1 Webserver Log

195.190.15.10[1] - - [04/Jun/2010:14:33:21 +0200] "GET /Seiten/Ueberuns.html HTTP/1.0" 302 340 "http://www.google.at/search?hl=de&source=hp&q=asylabwehramt&cts=1275654797936&aq=f&aqi=&oq=&gs_rfai=" "Mozilla/5.0 (Macintosh; U; Intel Mac OS X 10.4; de; rv:1.9.2.3) Gecko/20100401 Firefox/3.6.3"

195.190.15.10 - - [04/Jun/2010:14:33:54 +0200] "GET /Seiten/Ausseneinsaetze.html HTTP/1.0" 200 8817 "http://www.google.at/search?hl=de&source=hp&q=asylabwehramt&cts=1275654797936&aq=f&aqi=&oq=&gs_rfai=" "Mozilla/5.0 (Macintosh; U; Intel Mac OS X 10.4; de; rv:1.9.2.3) Gecko/20100401 Firefox/3.6.3"

195.190.15.10 - - [04/Jun/2010:14:33:55 +0200] "GET /favicon.ico HTTP/1.0" 302 340 "-" "Mozilla/5.0 (Macintosh; U; Intel Mac OS X 10.4; de; rv:1.9.2.3) Gecko/20100401 Firefox/3.6.3"

195.190.15.10 - - [04/Jun/2010:14:33:58 +0200] "GET /favicon.ico HTTP/1.0" 302 340 "-" "Mozilla/5.0 (Macintosh; U; Intel Mac OS X 10.4; de; rv:1.9.2.3) Gecko/20100401 Firefox/3.6.3"

195.190.15.10 - - [04/Jun/2010:14:34:07 +0200] "GET / HTTP/1.0" 200 11188 "http://www.asylabwehramt.at/Seiten/Ausseneinsaetze.html" "Mozilla/5.0 (Macintosh; U; Intel Mac OS X 10.4; de; rv:1.9.2.3) Gecko/20100401 Firefox/3.6.3"

195.190.15.10 - - [04/Jun/2010:14:34:33 +0200] "GET /Seiten/Aktuelles.html HTTP/1.0" 200 10909 "http://www.asylabwehramt.at/" "Mozilla/5.0 (Macintosh; U; Intel Mac OS X 10.4; de; rv:1.9.2.3) Gec

---

[1]WHOIS record on page 306

13

```
ko/20100401 Firefox/3.6.3"
195.190.15.10 - - [04/Jun/2010:14:34:54 +0200] "GET /Seiten/Bilder.html HTTP/1.0" 200 9059 "http://www.asylabwehramt.at/Seiten/Aktuelles.html" "Mozilla/5.0 (Macintosh; U; Intel Mac OS X 10.4; de; rv:1.9.2.3) Gecko/20100401 Firefox/3.6.3"
195.190.15.10 - - [04/Jun/2010:14:35:12 +0200] "GET /Seiten/Rundzeichen.html HTTP/1.0" 200 8459 "http://www.asylabwehramt.at/Seiten/Ausseneinsaetze.html" "Mozilla/5.0 (Macintosh; U; Intel Mac OS X 10.4; de; rv:1.9.2.3) Gecko/20100401 Firefox/3.6.3"
80.122.180.78[2] - - [05/Jun/2010:13:27:30 +0200] "GET /Bilder/flyer_nigeria_Internet.pdf HTTP/1.1" 200 702826 "-" "Mozilla/5.0 (Windows; U; Windows NT 6.0; de; rv:1.9.2.3) Gecko/20100401 Firefox/3.6.3 ( .NET CLR 3.5.30729)"
80.122.180.78 - - [05/Jun/2010:13:27:32 +0200] "GET /Bilder/flyer_nigeria_Internet.pdf HTTP/1.1" 206 4321 "-" "Mozilla/5.0 (Windows; U; Windows NT 6.0; de; rv:1.9.2.3) Gecko/20100401 Firefox/3.6.3 ( .NET CLR 3.5.30729)"
80.122.180.78 - - [05/Jun/2010:13:27:33 +0200] "GET /favicon.ico HTTP/1.1" 302 340 "-" "Mozilla/5.0 (Windows; U; Windows NT 6.0; de; rv:1.9.2.3) Gecko/20100401 Firefox/3.6.3 ( .NET CLR 3.5.30729)"
80.122.180.78 - - [05/Jun/2010:13:28:06 +0200] "GET / HTTP/1.1" 200 11188 "-" "Mozilla/5.0 (Windows; U; Windows NT 6.0; de; rv:1.9.2.3) Gecko/20100401 Firefox/3.6.3 ( .NET CLR 3.5.30729)"
80.122.180.78 - - [05/Jun/2010:13:29:03 +0200] "GET /Seiten/Aktuelles.html HTTP/1.1" 200 10909 "http://www.asylabwehramt.at/" "Mozilla/5.0 (Windows; U; Windows NT 6.0; de; rv:1.9.2.3) Gecko/20100401 Firefox/3.6.3 ( .NET CLR 3.5.30729)"
80.122.180.78 - - [05/Jun/2010:13:29:04 +0200] "GET /Bilder/leistung_2.jpg HTTP/1.1" 200 4918 "http://www.asylabwehramt.at/Seiten/Aktuelles.html" "Mozilla/5.0 (Windows; U; Windows NT 6.0; de; rv:1.9.2.3) Gecko/20100401 Firefox/3.6.3 ( .NET CLR 3.5.30729)"
80.122.180.78 - - [05/Jun/2010:13:29:25 +0200] "GET /Seiten/Bilder.html HTTP/1.1" 200 9059 "http://www.asylabwehramt.at/Seiten/Aktuelles.html" "Mozilla/5.0 (Windows; U; Windows NT 6.0; de; rv:1.
```

[2]WHOIS record on page 285

9.2.3) Gecko/20100401 Firefox/3.6.3 (.NET CLR 3.5.30729)"

80.122.180.78 - - [05/Jun/2010:13:29:44 +0200] "GET /Seiten/Ausseneinsaetze.html HTTP/1.1" 200 88
17 "http://www.asylabwehramt.at/Seiten/Bilder.html" "Mozilla/5.0 (Windows; U; Windows NT 6.0; de;
rv:1.9.2.3) Gecko/20100401 Firefox/3.6.3 (.NET CLR 3.5.30729)"

80.122.180.78 - - [05/Jun/2010:13:30:29 +0200] "GET /Seiten/Links.html HTTP/1.1" 200 10030 "http:
//www.asylabwehramt.at/" "Mozilla/5.0 (Windows; U; Windows NT 6.0; de; rv:1.9.2.3) Gecko/20100401
Firefox/3.6.3 (.NET CLR 3.5.30729)"

80.122.180.78 - - [05/Jun/2010:13:31:14 +0200] "GET /Seiten/Material.html HTTP/1.1" 200 9527 "htt
p://www.asylabwehramt.at/" "Mozilla/5.0 (Windows; U; Windows NT 6.0; de; rv:1.9.2.3) Gecko/201004
01 Firefox/3.6.3 (.NET CLR 3.5.30729)"

80.122.180.78 - - [05/Jun/2010:13:31:42 +0200] "GET /Bilder/flyer_nigeria_Internet.pdf HTTP/1.1"
206 571754 "http://www.asylabwehramt.at/Seiten/Material.html" "Mozilla/5.0 (Windows; U; Windows N
T 6.0; de; rv:1.9.2.3) Gecko/20100401 Firefox/3.6.3 (.NET CLR 3.5.30729)"

80.122.180.78 - - [05/Jun/2010:13:31:43 +0200] "GET /Bilder/flyer_nigeria_Internet.pdf HTTP/1.1"
206 4321 "-" "Mozilla/5.0 (Windows; U; Windows NT 6.0; de; rv:1.9.2.3) Gecko/20100401 Firefox/3.6
.3 (.NET CLR 3.5.30729)"

80.122.180.78 - - [05/Jun/2010:13:31:58 +0200] "GET /Bilder/IOM-Kosovo-Broschuere_Internet.pdf HT
TP/1.1" 200 728811 "http://www.asylabwehramt.at/Seiten/Material.html" "Mozilla/5.0 (Windows; U; W
indows NT 6.0; de; rv:1.9.2.3) Gecko/20100401 Firefox/3.6.3 (.NET CLR 3.5.30729)"

80.122.180.78 - - [05/Jun/2010:13:31:59 +0200] "GET /Bilder/IOM-Kosovo-Broschuere_Internet.pdf HT
TP/1.1" 206 4321 "-" "Mozilla/5.0 (Windows; U; Windows NT 6.0; de; rv:1.9.2.3) Gecko/20100401 Fir
efox/3.6.3 (.NET CLR 3.5.30729)"

80.122.180.78 - - [05/Jun/2010:13:33:09 +0200] "GET /Seiten/Ueberuns.html HTTP/1.1" 302 340 "http
://www.google.at/search?q=%22Andreas+Bichelbauer%22&ie=utf-8&oe=utf-8&aq=t&rls=org.mozilla:de:off
icial&client=firefox-a" "Mozilla/5.0 (Windows; U; Windows NT 6.0; de; rv:1.9.2.3) Gecko/20100401
Firefox/3.6.3 (.NET CLR 3.5.30729)"

80.122.180.78 - - [05/Jun/2010:13:33:47 +0200] "GET /Seiten/About.html HTTP/1.1" 302 340 "http://
www.google.at/search?q=%22Andreas+Bichelbauer%22&ie=utf-8&oe=utf-8&aq=t&rls=org.mozilla:de:offici

```
al&client=firefox-a" "Mozilla/5.0 (Windows; U; Windows NT 6.0; de; rv:1.9.2.3) Gecko/20100401 Fir
efox/3.6.3 ( .NET CLR 3.5.30729)"
80.120.179.10 [3] - - [07/Jun/2010:09:56:04 +0200] "GET / HTTP/1.1" 200 11827 "-" "Mozilla/4.0 (compa
tible; MSIE 7.0; Windows NT 5.1; Trident/4.0; .NET CLR 1.1.4322; InfoPath.1; MS-RTC LM 8)"
80.120.179.10 - - [07/Jun/2010:09:56:41 +0200] "GET /Seiten/Aktuelles.html HTTP/1.1" 200 12570 "h
ttp://www.asylabwehramt.at/" "Mozilla/4.0 (compatible; MSIE 7.0; Windows NT 5.1; Trident/4.0; .NE
T CLR 1.1.4322; InfoPath.1; MS-RTC LM 8)"
80.120.179.10 - - [07/Jun/2010:09:57:05 +0200] "GET /Seiten/Material.html HTTP/1.1" 200 11980 "ht
tp://www.asylabwehramt.at/Seiten/Aktuelles.html" "Mozilla/4.0 (compatible; MSIE 7.0; Windows NT 5
.1; Trident/4.0; .NET CLR 1.1.4322; InfoPath.1; MS-RTC LM 8)"
80.120.179.10 - - [07/Jun/2010:09:57:17 +0200] "GET /Material/Asyl_Jahresstatistik_2009.pdf HTTP/
1.1" 200 680643 "http://www.asylabwehramt.at/Seiten/Material.html" "Mozilla/4.0 (compatible; MSIE
7.0; Windows NT 5.1; Trident/4.0; .NET CLR 1.1.4322; InfoPath.1; MS-RTC LM 8)"
80.120.179.10 - - [07/Jun/2010:09:57:36 +0200] "GET /Seiten/Rundzeichen.html HTTP/1.1" 200 8837 "
http://www.asylabwehramt.at/Seiten/Material.html" "Mozilla/4.0 (compatible; MSIE 7.0; Windows NT
5.1; Trident/4.0; .NET CLR 1.1.4322; InfoPath.1; MS-RTC LM 8)"
80.120.179.10 - - [07/Jun/2010:09:57:40 +0200] "GET /Seiten/Bilder.html HTTP/1.1" 200 9571 "http:
//www.asylabwehramt.at/Seiten/Material.html" "Mozilla/4.0 (compatible; MSIE 7.0; Windows NT 5.1;
Trident/4.0; .NET CLR 1.1.4322; InfoPath.1; MS-RTC LM 8)"
80.120.179.10 - - [07/Jun/2010:09:57:58 +0200] "GET /Seiten/Links.html HTTP/1.1" 200 18362 "http:
//www.asylabwehramt.at/Seiten/Material.html" "Mozilla/4.0 (compatible; MSIE 7.0; Windows NT 5.1;
Trident/4.0; .NET CLR 1.1.4322; InfoPath.1; MS-RTC LM 8)"
80.120.179.10 - - [07/Jun/2010:09:57:59 +0200] "GET /Bilder/IBM.png HTTP/1.1" 200 8413 "http://ww
w.asylabwehramt.at/Seiten/Links.html" "Mozilla/4.0 (compatible; MSIE 7.0; Windows NT 5.1; Trident
/4.0; .NET CLR 1.1.4322; InfoPath.1; MS-RTC LM 8)"
80.120.179.10 - - [07/Jun/2010:09:58:34 +0200] "GET /Seiten/Press.html HTTP/1.1" 200 10955 "http:
```

---

[3]WHOIS record on page 320

//www.asylabwehramt.at/Seiten/Links.html" "Mozilla/4.0 (compatible; MSIE 7.0; Windows NT 5.1; Tri
dent/4.0; .NET CLR 1.1.4322; InfoPath.1; MS-RTC LM 8)"

80.120.179.10 - - [07/Jun/2010:10:07:16 +0200] "GET /favicon.ico HTTP/1.1" 302 340 "-" "Mozilla/4
.0 (compatible; MSIE 8.0; Windows NT 5.1; Trident/4.0; .NET CLR 1.1.4322; .NET CLR 2.0.50727; .NE
T CLR 3.0.04506.30; .NET CLR 3.0.04506.648; InfoPath.2)"

213.208.144.130 - - [07/Jun/2010:10:10:45 +0200] "GET /Seiten/Impressum.html HTTP/1.0" 200 11483
"http://www.google.at/search?hl=de&source=hp&q=asylabwehramt&aq=f&aqi=&oq=&gs_rfai=" "Mozill
a/4.0 (compatible; MSIE 7.0; Windows NT 5.2; .NET CLR 1.1.4322; InfoPath.1; .NET CLR 2.0.50727; .
NET CLR 3.0.4506.2152; .NET CLR 3.5.30729)"

213.208.144.130 - - [07/Jun/2010:10:11:36 +0200] "GET /index.html HTTP/1.0" 200 11827 "http://www
.asylabwehramt.at/Seiten/Impressum.html" "Mozilla/4.0 (compatible; MSIE 7.0; Windows NT 5.2; .NET
CLR 1.1.4322; InfoPath.1; .NET CLR 2.0.50727; .NET CLR 3.0.4506.2152; .NET CLR 3.5.30729)"

213.208.144.130 - - [07/Jun/2010:10:12:42 +0200] "GET /Seiten/Aktuelles.html HTTP/1.0" 200 12570
"http://www.asylabwehramt.at/index.html" "Mozilla/4.0 (compatible; MSIE 7.0; Windows NT 5.2; .NET
CLR 1.1.4322; InfoPath.1; .NET CLR 2.0.50727; .NET CLR 3.0.4506.2152; .NET CLR 3.5.30729)"

213.208.144.130 - - [07/Jun/2010:10:14:58 +0200] "GET / HTTP/1.0" 200 11827 "http://www.ubermorg
en.com/2010/" "Mozilla/4.0 (compatible; MSIE 7.0; Windows NT 5.2; .NET CLR 1.1.4322; InfoPath.1;
.NET CLR 2.0.50727; .NET CLR 3.0.4506.2152; .NET CLR 3.5.30729)"

213.208.144.130 - - [07/Jun/2010:10:15:41 +0200] "GET /Seiten/Aktuelles.html HTTP/1.0" 200 12570
"http://www.asylabwehramt.at/" "Mozilla/4.0 (compatible; MSIE 7.0; Windows NT 5.2; .NET CLR 1.1.4
322; InfoPath.1; .NET CLR 2.0.50727; .NET CLR 3.0.4506.2152; .NET CLR 3.5.30729)"

213.208.144.130 - - [07/Jun/2010:10:15:48 +0200] "GET /Seiten/Orgstrukt.html HTTP/1.0" 200 14086
"http://www.asylabwehramt.at/Seiten/Aktuelles.html" "Mozilla/4.0 (compatible; MSIE 7.0; Windows N
T 5.2; .NET CLR 1.1.4322; InfoPath.1; .NET CLR 2.0.50727; .NET CLR 3.0.4506.2152; .NET CLR 3.5.30
729)"

213.208.144.130 - - [07/Jun/2010:10:16:00 +0200] "GET /Seiten/Links.html HTTP/1.0" 200 18362 "htt

---

[4]WHOIS record on page 297

17

p://www.asylabwehramt.at/Seiten/Orgstrukt.html" "Mozilla/4.0 (compatible; MSIE 7.0; Windows NT 5.2; .NET CLR 1.1.4322; InfoPath.1; .NET CLR 2.0.50727; .NET CLR 3.0.4506.2152; .NET CLR 3.5.30729)"

213.208.144.130 - - [07/Jun/2010:10:16:05 +0200] "GET /Seiten/Press.html HTTP/1.0" 200 10955 "http://www.asylabwehramt.at/Seiten/Links.html" "Mozilla/4.0 (compatible; MSIE 7.0; Windows NT 5.2; .NET CLR 1.1.4322; InfoPath.1; .NET CLR 2.0.50727; .NET CLR 3.0.4506.2152; .NET CLR 3.5.30729)"

213.208.144.130 - - [07/Jun/2010:10:16:07 +0200] "GET /Seiten/Presse.html HTTP/1.0" 200 10956 "http://www.asylabwehramt.at/Seiten/Press.html" "Mozilla/4.0 (compatible; MSIE 7.0; Windows NT 5.2; .NET CLR 1.1.4322; InfoPath.1; .NET CLR 2.0.50727; .NET CLR 3.0.4506.2152; .NET CLR 3.5.30729)"

213.208.144.130 - - [07/Jun/2010:10:16:10 +0200] "GET /Seiten/Bilder.html HTTP/1.0" 200 9571 "http://www.asylabwehramt.at/Seiten/Press.html" "Mozilla/4.0 (compatible; MSIE 7.0; Windows NT 5.2; .NET CLR 1.1.4322; InfoPath.1; .NET CLR 2.0.50727; .NET CLR 3.0.4506.2152; .NET CLR 3.5.30729)"

213.208.144.130 - - [07/Jun/2010:10:16:18 +0200] "GET /Seiten/Seal.html HTTP/1.0" 200 8872 "http://www.asylabwehramt.at/Seiten/Bilder.html" "Mozilla/4.0 (compatible; MSIE 7.0; Windows NT 5.2; .NET CLR 1.1.4322; InfoPath.1; .NET CLR 2.0.50727; .NET CLR 3.5.30729)"

213.208.144.130 - - [07/Jun/2010:10:16:23 +0200] "GET /Seiten/Forms_and_Infos.html HTTP/1.0" 200 11046 "http://www.asylabwehramt.at/Seiten/Seal.html" "Mozilla/4.0 (compatible; MSIE 7.0; Windows NT 5.2; .NET CLR 1.1.4322; InfoPath.1; .NET CLR 2.0.50727; .NET CLR 3.0.4506.2152; .NET CLR 3.5.30729)"

213.208.144.130 - - [07/Jun/2010:10:16:24 +0200] "GET /Seiten/Material.html HTTP/1.0" 200 11980 "http://www.asylabwehramt.at/Seiten/Forms_and_Infos.html" "Mozilla/4.0 (compatible; MSIE 7.0; Windows NT 5.2; .NET CLR 3.0.4506.2152; .NET CLR 3.5.30729)"

213.208.144.130 - - [07/Jun/2010:10:16:27 +0200] "GET /Seiten/Latestnews.html HTTP/1.0" 200 12574 "http://www.asylabwehramt.at/Seiten/Material.html" "Mozilla/4.0 (compatible; MSIE 7.0; Windows NT 5.2; .NET CLR 3.0.4506.2152; .NET CLR 3.5.30729)"

213.208.144.130 - - [07/Jun/2010:10:17:10 +0200] "GET /index_e.html HTTP/1.0" 200 11855 "http://w

```
ww.asylabwehramt.at/Seiten/Aktuelles.html" "Mozilla/4.0 (compatible; MSIE 7.0; Windows NT 5.2; .NET CLR 1.1.4322; InfoPath.1; .NET CLR 2.0.50727; .NET CLR 3.0.4506.2152; .NET CLR 3.5.30729)"
80.120.179.10 - - [07/Jun/2010:10:17:35 +0200] "GET /favicon.ico HTTP/1.1" 302 340 "-" "Mozilla/4.0 (compatible; MSIE 8.0; Windows NT 5.1; Trident/4.0; .NET CLR 1.1.4322; .NET CLR 2.0.50727; .NET CLR 3.0.04506.30; .NET CLR 3.0.04506.648; InfoPath.2)"
213.208.144.130 - - [07/Jun/2010:10:18:05 +0200] "GET /Seiten/Rundzeichen.html HTTP/1.0" 200 8837 "http://www.asylabwehramt.at/Seiten/Aktuelles.html" "Mozilla/4.0 (compatible; MSIE 7.0; Windows NT 5.2; .NET CLR 1.1.4322; InfoPath.1; .NET CLR 2.0.50727; .NET CLR 3.0.4506.2152; .NET CLR 3.5.30729)"
213.208.144.130 - - [07/Jun/2010:10:18:17 +0200] "GET /index.html HTTP/1.0" 200 11827 "http://www.asylabwehramt.at/Seiten/Latestnews.html" "Mozilla/4.0 (compatible; MSIE 7.0; Windows NT 5.2; .NET CLR 1.1.4322; InfoPath.1; .NET CLR 2.0.50727; .NET CLR 3.0.4506.2152; .NET CLR 3.5.30729)"
80.120.179.10 - - [07/Jun/2010:10:19:13 +0200] "GET /Seiten/Seal.html HTTP/1.1" 200 8872 "http://www.asylabwehramt.at/Seiten/Aktuelles.html" "Mozilla/4.0 (compatible; MSIE 8.0; Windows NT 5.1; Trident/4.0; .NET CLR 1.1.4322; .NET CLR 2.0.50727; .NET CLR 3.0.04506.30; .NET CLR 3.0.04506.648; InfoPath.2)"
213.208.144.130 - - [07/Jun/2010:10:31:40 +0200] "GET /Seiten/Rundzeichen.html HTTP/1.0" 200 8837 "http://www.asylabwehramt.at/Seiten/Aktuelles.html" "Mozilla/4.0 (compatible; MSIE 7.0; Windows NT 5.2; .NET CLR 1.1.4322; InfoPath.1; .NET CLR 2.0.50727; .NET CLR 3.0.4506.2152; .NET CLR 3.5.30729)"
213.208.144.130 - - [07/Jun/2010:10:31:42 +0200] "GET /Seiten/Material.html HTTP/1.0" 200 11980 "http://www.asylabwehramt.at/Seiten/Rundzeichen.html" "Mozilla/4.0 (compatible; MSIE 7.0; Windows NT 5.2; .NET CLR 1.1.4322; InfoPath.1; .NET CLR 2.0.50727; .NET CLR 3.0.4506.2152; .NET CLR 3.5.30729)"
213.208.144.130 - - [07/Jun/2010:10:31:47 +0200] "GET /Material/Hotline_Franzoesisch.PDF HTTP/1.0" 200 515416 "http://www.asylabwehramt.at/Seiten/Material.html" "Mozilla/4.0 (compatible; MSIE 7.0; Windows NT 5.2; .NET CLR 1.1.4322; InfoPath.1; .NET CLR 2.0.50727; .NET CLR 3.0.4506.2152; .NET CLR 3.5.30729)"
```

```
213.208.144.130 - - [07/Jun/2010:10:32:10 +0200] "GET /Material/Hotline_Deutsch.pdf HTTP/1.0" 200
489465 "http://www.asylabwehramt.at/Seiten/Material.html" "Mozilla/4.0 (compatible; MSIE 7.0; Wi
ndows NT 5.2; .NET CLR 1.1.4322; InfoPath.1; .NET CLR 2.0.50727; .NET CLR 3.0.4506.2152; .NET CLR
3.5.30729)"
213.208.144.130 - - [07/Jun/2010:10:32:47 +0200] "GET /Material/Hotline_Englisch.PDF HTTP/1.0" 20
0 473359 "http://www.asylabwehramt.at/Seiten/Material.html" "Mozilla/4.0 (compatible; MSIE 7.0; W
indows NT 5.2; .NET CLR 1.1.4322; InfoPath.1; .NET CLR 2.0.50727; .NET CLR 3.0.4506.2152; .NET CL
R 3.5.30729)"
213.208.144.130 - - [07/Jun/2010:10:33:09 +0200] "GET /Material/Asyl_Jahresstatistik_2009.pdf HTT
P/1.0" 200 680643 "http://www.asylabwehramt.at/Seiten/Material.html" "Mozilla/4.0 (compatible; MS
IE 7.0; Windows NT 5.2; .NET CLR 1.1.4322; InfoPath.1; .NET CLR 2.0.50727; .NET CLR 3.0.4506.2152
; .NET CLR 3.5.30729)"
213.208.144.130 - - [07/Jun/2010:13:23:47 +0200] "GET / HTTP/1.0" 200 11827 "-" "Mozilla/4.0 (com
patible; MSIE 7.0; Windows NT 5.2; .NET CLR 1.1.4322; InfoPath.1; .NET CLR 2.0.50727; .NET CLR 3.
0.4506.2152; .NET CLR 3.5.30729)"
213.208.144.130 - - [07/Jun/2010:13:23:48 +0200] "GET /asyl.css HTTP/1.0" 304 - "http://www.asyla
bwehramt.at/" "Mozilla/4.0 (compatible; MSIE 7.0; Windows NT 5.2; .NET CLR 1.1.4322; InfoPath.1;
.NET CLR 2.0.50727; .NET CLR 3.0.4506.2152; .NET CLR 3.5.30729)"
213.208.144.130 - - [07/Jun/2010:13:25:29 +0200] "GET /Seiten/Rundzeichen.html HTTP/1.0" 304 - "h
ttp://www.asylabwehramt.at/" "Mozilla/4.0 (compatible; MSIE 7.0; Windows NT 5.2; .NET CLR 1.1.432
2; InfoPath.1; .NET CLR 2.0.50727; .NET CLR 3.0.4506.2152; .NET CLR 3.5.30729)"
213.208.144.130 - - [07/Jun/2010:13:25:34 +0200] "GET /Seiten/Bilder.html HTTP/1.0" 200 9571 "htt
p://www.asylabwehramt.at/Seiten/Rundzeichen.html" "Mozilla/4.0 (compatible; MSIE 7.0; Windows NT
5.2; .NET CLR 1.1.4322; InfoPath.1; .NET CLR 2.0.50727; .NET CLR 3.0.4506.2152; .NET CLR 3.5.3072
9)"
213.208.144.130 - - [07/Jun/2010:13:25:55 +0200] "GET /Seiten/Links.html HTTP/1.0" 200 18362 "htt
p://www.asylabwehramt.at/Seiten/Bilder.html" "Mozilla/4.0 (compatible; MSIE 7.0; Windows NT 5.2;
.NET CLR 1.1.4322; InfoPath.1; .NET CLR 2.0.50727; .NET CLR 3.0.4506.2152; .NET CLR 3.5.30729)"
```

80.120.179.10 - - [07/Jun/2010:15:05:29 +0200] "GET / HTTP/1.1" 304 - "http://www.google.at/searc
h?hl=de&source=hp&q=**asylabwehramt**&meta=&aq=f&aqi=&aql=&oq=&gs_rfai=" "Mozilla/4.0 (compatible; MS
IE 6.0; Windows NT 5.1; SV1; .NET CLR 1.1.4322)"

80.120.179.10 - - [07/Jun/2010:15:07:23 +0200] "GET /Seiten/Ausseneinsaetze.html HTTP/1.1" 200 91
90 "http://www.google.at/search?hl=de&source=hp&q=**asylabwehramt**&meta=&aq=f&aqi=&aql=&oq=&gs_rfai=
" "Mozilla/4.0 (compatible; MSIE 6.0; Windows NT 5.1; SV1; .NET CLR 1.1.4322)"

88.116.224.102[5] - - [07/Jun/2010:15:12:54 +0200] "GET / HTTP/1.1" 200 11827 "-" "Mozilla/5.0 (X11;
U; Linux i686; de; rv:1.9.0.18) Gecko/2010021501 Ubuntu/9.04 (jaunty) Firefox/3.0.18"

88.116.224.102 - - [07/Jun/2010:15:12:55 +0200] "GET /favicon.ico HTTP/1.1" 302 340 "-" "Mozilla/
5.0 (X11; U; Linux i686; de; rv:1.9.0.18) Gecko/2010021501 Ubuntu/9.04 (jaunty) Firefox/3.0.18"

88.116.224.102 - - [07/Jun/2010:15:15:02 +0200] "GET /Seiten/Orgstrukt.html HTTP/1.1" 200 14086 "
http://www.asylabwehramt.at/" "Mozilla/5.0 (X11; U; Linux i686; de; rv:1.9.0.18) Gecko/2010021501
Ubuntu/9.04 (jaunty) Firefox/3.0.18"

193.171.152.33[6] - - [07/Jun/2010:15:15:04 +0200] "GET / HTTP/1.1" 200 11827 "http://www.google.at/
search?hl=de&q=**asyl+abwehramt**&meta=" "Mozilla/4.0 (compatible; MSIE 8.0; Windows NT 5.1; Trident/
4.0; InfoPath.1; .NET CLR 1.1.4322; .NET CLR 2.0.50727; .NET CLR 3.0.04506.30; .NET CLR 3.0.04506
.648; .NET CLR 3.0.4506.2152; .NET CLR 3.5.30729)"

88.116.224.102 - - [07/Jun/2010:15:15:30 +0200] "GET /Seiten/Presse.html HTTP/1.1" 200 10956 "htt
p://www.asylabwehramt.at/Seiten/Orgstrukt.html" "Mozilla/5.0 (X11; U; Linux i686; de; rv:1.9.0.18
) Gecko/2010021501 Ubuntu/9.04 (jaunty) Firefox/3.0.18"

88.116.224.102 - - [07/Jun/2010:15:15:31 +0200] "GET /favicon.ico HTTP/1.1" 302 340 "-" "Mozilla/
5.0 (X11; U; Linux i686; de; rv:1.9.0.18) Gecko/2010021501 Ubuntu/9.04 (jaunty) Firefox/3.0.18"

213.208.144.130 - - [07/Jun/2010:15:15:44 +0200] "GET /Seiten/Aktuelles.html HTTP/1.0" 200 12570
"http://www.asylabwehramt.at/" "Mozilla/4.0 (compatible; MSIE 7.0; Windows NT 5.2; .NET CLR 1.1.4
322; InfoPath.1; .NET CLR 2.0.50727; .NET CLR 3.0.4506.2152; .NET CLR 3.5.30729)"

---

[5]WHOIS record on page 307
[6]WHOIS record on page 294

```
88.116.224.102 - - [07/Jun/2010:15:15:45 +0200] "GET /index.html HTTP/1.1" 200 11827 "http://www.asylabwehramt.at/Seiten/Presse.html" "Mozilla/5.0 (X11; U; Linux i686; de; rv:1.9.0.18) Gecko/2010021501 Ubuntu/9.04 (jaunty) Firefox/3.0.18"
88.116.224.102 - - [07/Jun/2010:15:15:46 +0200] "GET /favicon.ico HTTP/1.1" 302 340 "-" "Mozilla/5.0 (X11; U; Linux i686; de; rv:1.9.0.18) Gecko/2010021501 Ubuntu/9.04 (jaunty) Firefox/3.0.18"
88.116.224.102 - - [07/Jun/2010:15:15:47 +0200] "GET /Seiten/Aktuelles.html HTTP/1.1" 200 12570 "http://www.asylabwehramt.at/index.html" "Mozilla/5.0 (X11; U; Linux i686; de; rv:1.9.0.18) Gecko/2010021501 Ubuntu/9.04 (jaunty) Firefox/3.0.18"
88.116.224.102 - - [07/Jun/2010:15:15:48 +0200] "GET /Bilder/leistung_2.jpg HTTP/1.1" 200 4918 "http://www.asylabwehramt.at/Seiten/Aktuelles.html" "Mozilla/5.0 (X11; U; Linux i686; de; rv:1.9.0.18) Gecko/2010021501 Ubuntu/9.04 (jaunty) Firefox/3.0.18"
213.208.144.130 - - [07/Jun/2010:15:15:53 +0200] "GET /Seiten/Bilder.html HTTP/1.0" 200 9571 "http://www.asylabwehramt.at/Seiten/Material.html" "Mozilla/4.0 (compatible; MSIE 7.0; Windows NT 5.2; .NET CLR 1.1.4322; InfoPath.1; .NET CLR 2.0.50727; .NET CLR 3.0.4506.2152; .NET CLR 3.5.30729)"
88.116.224.102 - - [07/Jun/2010:15:16:02 +0200] "GET /favicon.ico HTTP/1.1" 302 340 "-" "Mozilla/5.0 (X11; U; Linux i686; de; rv:1.9.0.18) Gecko/2010021501 Ubuntu/9.04 (jaunty) Firefox/3.0.18"
213.208.144.130 - - [07/Jun/2010:15:17:26 +0200] "GET /favicon.ico HTTP/1.0" 302 340 "-" "Mozilla/4.0 (compatible; MSIE 7.0; Windows NT 5.2; .NET CLR 1.1.4322; InfoPath.1; .NET CLR 2.0.50727; .NET CLR 3.5.30729)"
213.208.144.130 - - [07/Jun/2010:15:17:32 +0200] "GET /Seite/Presse.html HTTP/1.0" 302 340 "http://www.asylabwehramt.at/" "Mozilla/4.0 (compatible; MSIE 7.0; Windows NT 5.2; .NET CLR 1.1.4322; InfoPath.1; .NET CLR 2.0.50727; .NET CLR 3.5.30729)"
213.208.144.130 - - [07/Jun/2010:15:17:51 +0200] "GET /Seiten/Orgstrukt.html HTTP/1.0" 200 14086 "http://www.asylabwehramt.at/" "Mozilla/4.0 (compatible; MSIE 7.0; Windows NT 5.2; .NET CLR 1.1.4322; InfoPath.1; .NET CLR 2.0.50727; .NET CLR 3.5.30729)"
213.208.144.130 - - [07/Jun/2010:15:18:00 +0200] "GET /favicon.ico HTTP/1.0" 302 340 "-" "Mozilla/4.0 (compatible; MSIE 7.0; Windows NT 5.2; .NET CLR 1.1.4322; InfoPath.1; .NET CLR 2.0.50727; .NET CLR 3.5.30729)"
```

```
88.116.224.102 - - [07/Jun/2010:15:18:06 +0200] "GET /favicon.ico HTTP/1.1" 302 340 "-" "Mozilla/
5.0 (X11; U; Linux i686; de; rv:1.9.0.18) Gecko/2010021501 Ubuntu/9.04 (jaunty) Firefox/3.0.18"
213.208.144.130 - - [07/Jun/2010:15:18:23 +0200] "GET /Seiten/Links.html HTTP/1.0" 200 18362 "htt
p://www.asylabwehramt.at/Seiten/Orgstrukt.html" "Mozilla/4.0 (compatible; MSIE 7.0; Windows NT 5.
2; .NET CLR 1.1.4322; InfoPath.1; .NET CLR 2.0.50727; .NET CLR 3.0.4506.2152; .NET CLR 3.5.30729)
"
213.208.144.130 - - [07/Jun/2010:15:18:31 +0200] "GET /Seiten/Press.html HTTP/1.0" 200 10955 "htt
p://www.asylabwehramt.at/Seiten/Aktuelles.html" "Mozilla/4.0 (compatible; MSIE 7.0; Windows NT 5.
2; .NET CLR 1.1.4322; InfoPath.1; .NET CLR 2.0.50727; .NET CLR 3.0.4506.2152; .NET CLR 3.5.30729)
"
193.171.152.33 - - [07/Jun/2010:15:19:21 +0200] "GET /Seiten/Bilder.html HTTP/1.1" 200 9571 "http
://www.asylabwehramt.at/" "Mozilla/4.0 (compatible; MSIE 8.0; Windows NT 5.1; Trident/4.0; InfoPa
th.1; .NET CLR 1.1.4322; .NET CLR 2.0.50727; .NET CLR 3.0.04506.30; .NET CLR 3.0.04506.648; .NET
CLR 3.0.4506.2152; .NET CLR 3.5.30729)"
193.171.152.33 - - [07/Jun/2010:15:19:46 +0200] "GET /Seiten/Orgstrukt.html HTTP/1.1" 200 14086 "
http://www.asylabwehramt.at/Seiten/Bilder.html" "Mozilla/4.0 (compatible; MSIE 8.0; Windows NT 5.
1; Trident/4.0; InfoPath.1; .NET CLR 1.1.4322; .NET CLR 2.0.50727; .NET CLR 3.0.04506.30; .NET CL
R 3.0.04506.648; .NET CLR 3.0.4506.2152; .NET CLR 3.5.30729)"
213.208.144.130 - - [07/Jun/2010:15:27:15 +0200] "GET /index.html HTTP/1.0" 200 11827 "http://www
.asylabwehramt.at/Seiten/Orgstrukt.html" "Mozilla/4.0 (compatible; MSIE 7.0; Windows NT 5.2; .NET
CLR 1.1.4322; InfoPath.1; .NET CLR 2.0.50727; .NET CLR 3.0.4506.2152; .NET CLR 3.5.30729)"
213.208.144.130 - - [07/Jun/2010:15:27:34 +0200] "GET /Seiten/Impressum.html HTTP/1.0" 200 11483
"http://www.asylabwehramt.at/index.html" "Mozilla/4.0 (compatible; MSIE 7.0; Windows NT 5.2; .NET
CLR 1.1.4322; InfoPath.1; .NET CLR 2.0.50727; .NET CLR 3.0.4506.2152; .NET CLR 3.5.30729)"
213.208.144.130 - - [07/Jun/2010:15:29:05 +0200] "GET /Seiten/Aktuelles.html HTTP/1.0" 200 12570
"http://www.asylabwehramt.at/index.html" "Mozilla/4.0 (compatible; MSIE 7.0; Windows NT 5.2; .NET
CLR 1.1.4322; InfoPath.1; .NET CLR 2.0.50727; .NET CLR 3.0.4506.2152; .NET CLR 3.5.30729)"
88.116.224.102 - - [07/Jun/2010:15:32:40 +0200] "GET /favicon.ico HTTP/1.1" 302 340 "-" "Mozilla/
```

```
88.116.224.102 - - [07/Jun/2010:15:32:47 +0200] "GET /Seiten/Bilder.html HTTP/1.1" 200 11980 "http://www.asylabwehramt.at/Seiten/Bilder.html" "Mozilla/5.0 (X11; U; Linux i686; de; rv:1.9.0.18) Gecko/2010021501 Ubuntu/9.04 (jaunty) Firefox/3.0.18"
88.116.224.102 - - [07/Jun/2010:15:32:57 +0200] "GET /Material/Hotline_Deutsch.pdf HTTP/1.1" 200 489465 "http://www.asylabwehramt.at/Seiten/Material.html" "Mozilla/5.0 (X11; U; Linux i686; de; rv:1.9.0.18) Gecko/2010021501 Ubuntu/9.04 (jaunty) Firefox/3.0.18"
88.116.224.102 - - [07/Jun/2010:15:32:58 +0200] "GET /favicon.ico HTTP/1.1" 302 340 "-" "Mozilla/5.0 (X11; U; Linux i686; de; rv:1.9.0.18) Gecko/2010021501 Ubuntu/9.04 (jaunty) Firefox/3.0.18"
88.116.224.102 - - [07/Jun/2010:15:34:00 +0200] "GET /Bilder/Ladung.png HTTP/1.1" 200 114658 "http://www.asylabwehramt.at/Seiten/Material.html" "Mozilla/5.0 (X11; U; Linux i686; de; rv:1.9.0.18) Gecko/2010021501 Ubuntu/9.04 (jaunty) Firefox/3.0.18"
88.116.224.102 - - [07/Jun/2010:15:35:04 +0200] "GET /favicon.ico HTTP/1.1" 302 340 "-" "Mozilla/5.0 (X11; U; Linux i686; de; rv:1.9.0.18) Gecko/2010021501 Ubuntu/9.04 (jaunty) Firefox/3.0.18"
88.116.224.102 - - [07/Jun/2010:15:35:07 +0200] "GET /Seiten/Rundzeichen.html HTTP/1.1" 200 8837 "http://www.asylabwehramt.at/Seiten/Material.html" "Mozilla/5.0 (X11; U; Linux i686; de; rv:1.9.0.18) Gecko/2010021501 Ubuntu/9.04 (jaunty) Firefox/3.0.18"
88.116.224.102 - - [07/Jun/2010:15:35:18 +0200] "GET /favicon.ico HTTP/1.1" 302 340 "-" "Mozilla/5.0 (X11; U; Linux i686; de; rv:1.9.0.18) Gecko/2010021501 Ubuntu/9.04 (jaunty) Firefox/3.0.18"
88.116.224.102 - - [07/Jun/2010:15:35:20 +0200] "GET /Seiten/Links.html HTTP/1.1" 200 18362 "http://www.asylabwehramt.at/Seiten/Rundzeichen.html" "Mozilla/5.0 (X11; U; Linux i686; de; rv:1.9.0.18) Gecko/2010021501 Ubuntu/9.04 (jaunty) Firefox/3.0.18"
88.116.224.102 - - [07/Jun/2010:15:35:21 +0200] "GET /Bilder/IBM.png HTTP/1.1" 200 8413 "http://www.asylabwehramt.at/Seiten/Links.html" "Mozilla/5.0 (X11; U; Linux i686; de; rv:1.9.0.18) Gecko/2010021501 Ubuntu/9.04 (jaunty) Firefox/3.0.18"
88.116.224.102 - - [07/Jun/2010:15:35:25 +0200] "GET /favicon.ico HTTP/1.1" 302 340 "-" "Mozilla/5.0 (X11; U; Linux i686; de; rv:1.9.0.18) Gecko/2010021501 Ubuntu/9.04 (jaunty) Firefox/3.0.18"
88.116.224.102 - - [07/Jun/2010:15:35:53 +0200] "GET /favicon.ico HTTP/1.1" 302 340 "-" "Mozilla/
```

88.116.224.102 - - [07/Jun/2010:15:36:08 +0200] "GET /Seiten/Latestnews.html HTTP/1.1" 200 12574 "http://www.asylabwehramt.at/Seiten/Aktuelles.html" "Mozilla/5.0 (X11; U; Linux i686; de; rv:1.9.0.18) Gecko/2010021501 Ubuntu/9.04 (jaunty) Firefox/3.0.18"

88.116.224.102 - - [07/Jun/2010:15:36:17 +0200] "GET /favicon.ico HTTP/1.1" 302 340 "-" "Mozilla/5.0 (X11; U; Linux i686; de; rv:1.9.0.18) Gecko/2010021501 Ubuntu/9.04 (jaunty) Firefox/3.0.18"

88.116.224.102 - - [07/Jun/2010:15:36:21 +0200] "GET /favicon.ico HTTP/1.1" 302 340 "-" "Mozilla/5.0 (X11; U; Linux i686; de; rv:1.9.0.18) Gecko/2010021501 Ubuntu/9.04 (jaunty) Firefox/3.0.18"

193.171.152.33 - - [07/Jun/2010:15:37:40 +0200] "GET /index_e.html HTTP/1.1" 200 11855 "http://www.asylabwehramt.at/" "Mozilla/4.0 (compatible; MSIE 8.0; Windows NT 5.1; Trident/4.0; InfoPath.1; .NET CLR 1.1.4322; .NET CLR 2.0.50727; .NET CLR 3.0.04506.30; .NET CLR 3.0.04506.648; .NET CLR 3.5.30729)"

193.171.152.33 - - [07/Jun/2010:15:37:44 +0200] "GET /index.html HTTP/1.1" 200 11827 "http://www.asylabwehramt.at/index_e.html" "Mozilla/4.0 (compatible; MSIE 8.0; Windows NT 5.1; Trident/4.0; InfoPath.1; .NET CLR 1.1.4322; .NET CLR 2.0.50727; .NET CLR 3.0.04506.30; .NET CLR 3.0.04506.648; .NET CLR 3.5.30729)"

193.171.152.33 - - [07/Jun/2010:15:37:55 +0200] "GET /Seiten/Aktuelles.html HTTP/1.1" 200 12570 "http://www.asylabwehramt.at/index.html" "Mozilla/4.0 (compatible; MSIE 8.0; Windows NT 5.1; Trident/4.0; InfoPath.1; .NET CLR 1.1.4322; .NET CLR 2.0.50727; .NET CLR 3.0.04506.30; .NET CLR 3.0.04506.648; .NET CLR 3.5.30729)"

213.208.144.130 - - [07/Jun/2010:15:38:23 +0200] "GET / HTTP/1.0" 200 11827 "-" "Mozilla/4.0 (compatible; MSIE 7.0; Windows NT 5.2; .NET CLR 1.1.4322; InfoPath.1; .NET CLR 2.0.50727; .NET CLR 3.0.4506.2152; .NET CLR 3.5.30729)"

213.208.144.130 - - [07/Jun/2010:15:38:41 +0200] "GET /Bilder/STRABAG.jpg HTTP/1.0" 200 39039 "http://www.asylabwehramt.at/Seiten/Aktuelles.html" "Mozilla/4.0 (compatible; MSIE 7.0; Windows NT 5.2; .NET CLR 1.1.4322; InfoPath.1; .NET CLR 2.0.50727; .NET CLR 3.0.4506.2152; .NET CLR 3.5.30729)"

213.208.144.130 - - [07/Jun/2010:15:39:07 +0200] "GET /Seiten/Bilder.html HTTP/1.0" 200 9571 "htt

```
p://www.asylabwehramt.at/Seiten/Aktuelles.html" "Mozilla/4.0 (compatible; MSIE 7.0; Windows NT 5.
2; .NET CLR 1.1.4322; InfoPath.1; .NET CLR 2.0.50727; .NET CLR 3.0.04506.2152; .NET CLR 3.5.30729)
"
193.171.152.33 - - [07/Jun/2010:15:39:51 +0200] "GET /Seiten/Impressum.html HTTP/1.1" 200 11483 "
http://www.asylabwehramt.at/Seiten/Aktuelles.html" "Mozilla/4.0 (compatible; MSIE 8.0; Windows NT
5.1; Trident/4.0; InfoPath.1; .NET CLR 3.0.4506.2152; .NET CLR 2.0.50727; .NET CLR 3.0.04506.30; .NET
CLR 3.0.04506.648; .NET CLR 3.0.4506.2152; .NET CLR 3.5.30729)"
193.171.152.33 - - [07/Jun/2010:15:41:13 +0200] "GET /Seiten/Material.html HTTP/1.1" 200 11980 "h
ttp://www.asylabwehramt.at/Seiten/Impressum.html" "Mozilla/4.0 (compatible; MSIE 8.0; Windows NT
5.1; Trident/4.0; InfoPath.1; .NET CLR 1.1.4322; .NET CLR 2.0.50727; .NET CLR 3.0.04506.30; .NET
CLR 3.0.04506.648; .NET CLR 3.0.4506.2152; .NET CLR 3.5.30729)"
193.171.152.33 - - [07/Jun/2010:15:41:26 +0200] "GET /Bilder/Ladung.png HTTP/1.1" 200 114658 "htt
p://www.asylabwehramt.at/Seiten/Material.html" "Mozilla/4.0 (compatible; MSIE 8.0; Windows NT 5.1
; Trident/4.0; InfoPath.1; .NET CLR 1.1.4322; .NET CLR 2.0.50727; .NET CLR 3.0.04506.30; .NET CLR
3.0.04506.648; .NET CLR 3.0.4506.2152; .NET CLR 3.5.30729)"
193.171.152.337 - - [07/Jun/2010:15:42:02 +0200] "GET /Seiten/Rundzeichen.html HTTP/1.1" 200 8837
"http://www.asylabwehramt.at/Seiten/Material.html" "Mozilla/4.0 (compatible; MSIE 8.0; Windows NT
5.1; Trident/4.0; InfoPath.1; .NET CLR 1.1.4322; .NET CLR 2.0.50727; .NET CLR 3.0.04506.30; .NET
CLR 3.0.04506.648; .NET CLR 3.0.4506.2152; .NET CLR 3.5.30729)"
193.171.152.33 - - [07/Jun/2010:15:42:22 +0200] "GET /Seiten/Links.html HTTP/1.1" 200 18362 "http
://www.asylabwehramt.at/Seiten/Bilder.html" "Mozilla/4.0 (compatible; MSIE 8.0; Windows NT 5.1; T
rident/4.0; InfoPath.1; .NET CLR 1.1.4322; .NET CLR 2.0.50727; .NET CLR 3.0.04506.30; .NET CLR 3.
0.04506.648; .NET CLR 3.0.4506.2152; .NET CLR 3.5.30729)"
193.171.152.33 - - [07/Jun/2010:15:42:58 +0200] "GET /Seiten/Press.html HTTP/1.1" 200 10955 "http
://www.asylabwehramt.at/Seiten/Bilder.html" "Mozilla/4.0 (compatible; MSIE 8.0; Windows NT 5.1; T
rident/4.0; InfoPath.1; .NET CLR 1.1.4322; .NET CLR 2.0.50727; .NET CLR 3.0.04506.30; .NET CLR 3.
0.04506.648; .NET CLR 3.0.4506.2152; .NET CLR 3.5.30729)"
193.171.152.33 - - [07/Jun/2010:15:43:45 +0200] "GET /Material/Asyl_Jahresstatistik_2009.pdf HTTP
```

/1.1" 200 680643 "http://www.asylabwehramt.at/Seiten/Material.html" "Mozilla/4.0 (compatible; MSIE 8.0; Windows NT 5.1; Trident/4.0; InfoPath.1; .NET CLR 1.1.4322; .NET CLR 2.0.50727; .NET CLR 3.0.04506.30; .NET CLR 3.0.04506.648; .NET CLR 3.5.30729)"

193.171.152.33 - - [07/Jun/2010:15:43:46 +0200] "GET /Material/Asyl_Jahresstatistik_2009.pdf HTTP/1.1" 206 4096 "_" "Mozilla/4.0 (compatible; MSIE 8.0; Windows NT 5.1; Trident/4.0; InfoPath.1; .NET CLR 1.1.4322; .NET CLR 2.0.50727; .NET CLR 3.0.04506.30; .NET CLR 3.0.04506.648; .NET CLR 3.0.4506.2152; .NET CLR 3.5.30729)"

193.171.152.33 - - [07/Jun/2010:15:43:47 +0200] "GET /Material/Asyl_Jahresstatistik_2009.pdf HTTP/1.1" 206 22679 "_" "Mozilla/4.0 (compatible; MSIE 8.0; Windows NT 5.1; Trident/4.0; InfoPath.1; .NET CLR 1.1.4322; .NET CLR 2.0.50727; .NET CLR 3.0.04506.30; .NET CLR 3.0.04506.648; .NET CLR 3.0.4506.2152; .NET CLR 3.5.30729)"

193.171.152.33 - - [07/Jun/2010:15:43:48 +0200] "GET /Material/Asyl_Jahresstatistik_2009.pdf HTTP/1.1" 206 26838 "_" "Mozilla/4.0 (compatible; MSIE 8.0; Windows NT 5.1; Trident/4.0; InfoPath.1; .NET CLR 1.1.4322; .NET CLR 2.0.50727; .NET CLR 3.0.04506.30; .NET CLR 3.0.04506.648; .NET CLR 3.0.4506.2152; .NET CLR 3.5.30729)"

193.171.152.33 - - [07/Jun/2010:15:43:49 +0200] "GET /Material/Asyl_Jahresstatistik_2009.pdf HTTP/1.1" 206 16089 "_" "Mozilla/4.0 (compatible; MSIE 8.0; Windows NT 5.1; Trident/4.0; InfoPath.1; .NET CLR 1.1.4322; .NET CLR 2.0.50727; .NET CLR 3.0.04506.30; .NET CLR 3.0.04506.648; .NET CLR 3.0.4506.2152; .NET CLR 3.5.30729)"

193.171.152.33 - - [07/Jun/2010:15:43:50 +0200] "GET /Material/Asyl_Jahresstatistik_2009.pdf HTTP/1.1" 206 16192 "_" "Mozilla/4.0 (compatible; MSIE 8.0; Windows NT 5.1; Trident/4.0; InfoPath.1; .NET CLR 1.1.4322; .NET CLR 2.0.50727; .NET CLR 3.0.04506.30; .NET CLR 3.0.04506.648; .NET CLR 3.0.4506.2152; .NET CLR 3.5.30729)"

193.171.152.33 - - [07/Jun/2010:15:43:51 +0200] "GET /Material/Asyl_Jahresstatistik_2009.pdf HTTP/1.1" 206 17376 "_" "Mozilla/4.0 (compatible; MSIE 8.0; Windows NT 5.1; Trident/4.0; InfoPath.1; .NET CLR 1.1.4322; .NET CLR 2.0.50727; .NET CLR 3.0.04506.30; .NET CLR 3.0.04506.648; .NET CLR 3.0.4506.2152; .NET CLR 3.5.30729)"

193.171.152.33 - - [07/Jun/2010:15:43:52 +0200] "GET /Material/Asyl_Jahresstatistik_2009.pdf HTTP

```
/1.1" 206 402501 "-" "Mozilla/4.0 (compatible; MSIE 8.0; Windows NT 5.1; Trident/4.0; InfoPath.1;
.NET CLR 1.1.4322; .NET CLR 2.0.50727; .NET CLR 3.0.04506.30; .NET CLR 3.0.04506.648; .NET CLR 3
.0.4506.2152; .NET CLR 3.5.30729)"
80.120.179.10 - - [07/Jun/2010:15:45:27 +0200] "GET /index.html HTTP/1.1" 200 11827 "-" "Mozilla/
4.0 (compatible; MSIE 8.0; Windows NT 5.1; Trident/4.0; .NET CLR 1.1.4322; .NET CLR 2.0.50727; .N
ET CLR 3.0.04506.30; .NET CLR 3.0.04506.648; InfoPath.2)"
80.120.179.10 - - [07/Jun/2010:15:47:36 +0200] "GET /Seiten/Aktuelles.html HTTP/1.1" 200 12570 "h
ttp://www.asylabwehramt.at/index.html" "Mozilla/4.0 (compatible; MSIE 8.0; Windows NT 5.1; Triden
t/4.0; .NET CLR 1.1.4322; .NET CLR 2.0.50727; .NET CLR 3.0.04506.30; .NET CLR 3.0.04506.648; Info
Path.2)"
80.120.179.10 - - [07/Jun/2010:15:47:52 +0200] "GET /Seiten/Material.html HTTP/1.1" 200 11980 "ht
tp://www.asylabwehramt.at/Seiten/Aktuelles.html" "Mozilla/4.0 (compatible; MSIE 8.0; Windows NT 5
.1; Trident/4.0; .NET CLR 1.1.4322; .NET CLR 2.0.50727; .NET CLR 3.0.04506.30; .NET CLR 3.0.04506
.648; InfoPath.2)"
80.120.179.10 - - [07/Jun/2010:15:47:57 +0200] "GET /Material/Hotline_Russisch.pdf HTTP/1.1" 200
239827 "http://www.asylabwehramt.at/Seiten/Material.html" "Mozilla/4.0 (compatible; MSIE 8.0; Win
dows NT 5.1; Trident/4.0; .NET CLR 1.1.4322; .NET CLR 2.0.50727; .NET CLR 3.0.04506.30; .NET CLR
3.0.04506.648; InfoPath.2)"
80.120.179.10 - - [07/Jun/2010:15:48:54 +0200] "GET /Material/Hotline_Englisch.PDF HTTP/1.1" 200
473359 "http://www.asylabwehramt.at/Seiten/Material.html" "Mozilla/4.0 (compatible; MSIE 8.0; Win
dows NT 5.1; Trident/4.0; .NET CLR 1.1.4322; .NET CLR 2.0.50727; .NET CLR 3.0.04506.30; .NET CLR
3.0.04506.648; InfoPath.2)"
80.120.179.10 - - [07/Jun/2010:15:49:09 +0200] "GET /Material/Asyl_Jahresstatistik_2009.pdf HTTP/
1.1" 200 680643 "http://www.asylabwehramt.at/Seiten/Material.html" "Mozilla/4.0 (compatible; MSIE
8.0; Windows NT 5.1; Trident/4.0; .NET CLR 1.1.4322; .NET CLR 2.0.50727; .NET CLR 3.0.04506.30;
.NET CLR 3.0.04506.648; InfoPath.2)"
80.120.179.10 - - [07/Jun/2010:15:51:49 +0200] "GET /Seiten/Bilder.html HTTP/1.1" 200 9571 "http:
//www.asylabwehramt.at/Seiten/Material.html" "Mozilla/4.0 (compatible; MSIE 8.0; Windows NT 5.1;
```

```
Trident/4.0; .NET CLR 1.1.4322; .NET CLR 2.0.50727; .NET CLR 3.0.04506.30; .NET CLR 3.0.04506.648
; InfoPath.2)"
80.120.179.10 - - [07/Jun/2010:15:52:04 +0200] "GET /Seiten/Links.html HTTP/1.1" 200 18362 "http:
//www.asylabwehramt.at/Seiten/Material.html" "Mozilla/4.0 (compatible; MSIE 8.0; Windows NT 5.1;
Trident/4.0; .NET CLR 1.1.4322; .NET CLR 2.0.50727; .NET CLR 3.0.04506.30; .NET CLR 3.0.04506.648
; InfoPath.2)"
80.120.179.10 - - [07/Jun/2010:15:55:07 +0200] "GET /Seiten/Presse.html HTTP/1.1" 200 10956 "http
://www.asylabwehramt.at/Seiten/Bilder.html" "Mozilla/4.0 (compatible; MSIE 8.0; Windows NT 5.1; T
rident/4.0; .NET CLR 1.1.4322; .NET CLR 2.0.50727; .NET CLR 3.0.04506.30; .NET CLR 3.0.04506.648;
InfoPath.2)"
80.120.179.10 - - [07/Jun/2010:16:01:06 +0200] "GET /favicon.ico HTTP/1.1" 302 340 "-" "Mozilla/4
.0 (compatible; MSIE 8.0; Windows NT 5.1; Trident/4.0; .NET CLR 1.1.4322; .NET CLR 2.0.50727; .NE
T CLR 3.0.04506.30; .NET CLR 3.0.04506.648; InfoPath.2)"
88.116.224.102 - - [07/Jun/2010:16:03:21 +0200] "GET / HTTP/1.1" 200 11827 "http://www.google.at/
search?hl=de&source=hp&q=asylabwehramt&cts=1275918962885&aq=f&aql=&oq=&gs_rfai=" "Mozilla/5.
0 (X11; U; Linux i686; de; rv:1.9.1.9) Gecko/20100401 Ubuntu/9.10 (karmic) Firefox/3.5.9"
88.116.224.102 - - [07/Jun/2010:16:03:22 +0200] "GET /favicon.ico HTTP/1.1" 302 340 "-" "Mozilla/
5.0 (X11; U; Linux i686; de; rv:1.9.1.9) Gecko/20100401 Ubuntu/9.10 (karmic) Firefox/3.5.9"
88.116.224.102 - - [07/Jun/2010:16:03:25 +0200] "GET /favicon.ico HTTP/1.1" 302 340 "-" "Mozilla/
5.0 (X11; U; Linux i686; de; rv:1.9.1.9) Gecko/20100401 Ubuntu/9.10 (karmic) Firefox/3.5.9"
193.171.152.33 - - [07/Jun/2010:16:03:36 +0200] "GET /favicon.ico HTTP/1.1" 302 340 "-" "Mozilla/
4.0 (compatible; MSIE 8.0; Windows NT 5.1; Trident/4.0; InfoPath.1; .NET CLR 1.1.4322; .NET CLR 2
.0.50727; .NET CLR 3.0.04506.30; .NET CLR 3.0.04506.648; .NET CLR 3.0.4506.2152; .NET CLR 3.5.307
29)"
88.116.224.102 - - [07/Jun/2010:16:04:25 +0200] "GET /Seiten/Rundzeichen.html HTTP/1.1" 200 8837
"http://www.asylabwehramt.at/" "Mozilla/5.0 (X11; U; Linux i686; de; rv:1.9.1.9) Gecko/20100401 U
buntu/9.10 (karmic) Firefox/3.5.9"
88.116.224.102 - - [07/Jun/2010:16:04:53 +0200] "GET /Seiten/Ausseneinsaetze.html HTTP/1.1" 200 9
```

190 "http://www.google.at/search?hl=de&source=hp&q=asylabwehramt&cts=1275189622885&aq=f&aqi=&aql=&oq=&gs_rfai=" "Mozilla/5.0 (X11; U; Linux i686; de; rv:1.9.1.9) Gecko/20100401 Ubuntu/9.10 (karmic) Firefox/3.5.9"

88.116.224.102 - - [07/Jun/2010:16:05:06 +0200] "GET /Seiten/Material.html HTTP/1.1" 200 11980 "http://www.asylabwehramt.at/Seiten/Ausseneinsaetze.html" "Mozilla/5.0 (X11; U; Linux i686; de; rv:1.9.1.9) Gecko/20100401 Ubuntu/9.10 (karmic) Firefox/3.5.9"

88.116.224.102 - - [07/Jun/2010:16:05:22 +0200] "GET /Seiten/Aktuelles.html HTTP/1.1" 200 12570 "http://www.asylabwehramt.at/Seiten/Material.html" "Mozilla/5.0 (X11; U; Linux i686; de; rv:1.9.1.9) Gecko/20100401 Ubuntu/9.10 (karmic) Firefox/3.5.9"

80.120.179.10 - - [07/Jun/2010:16:06:52 +0200] "GET / HTTP/1.1" 200 11827 "http://www.asylabwehramt.at/index.html" "Mozilla/4.0 (compatible; MSIE 6.0; Windows NT 5.1; SV1; .NET CLR 1.1.4322; .NET CLR 2.0.50727; .NET CLR 3.0.04506.30; .NET CLR 3.0.04506.648; InfoPath.2)"

80.120.179.10 - - [07/Jun/2010:16:06:56 +0200] "GET /Seiten/Orgstrukt.html HTTP/1.1" 200 14086 "http://www.asylabwehramt.at/" "Mozilla/4.0 (compatible; MSIE 6.0; Windows NT 5.1; SV1; .NET CLR 1.1.4322; .NET CLR 2.0.50727; .NET CLR 3.0.04506.30; .NET CLR 3.0.04506.648; InfoPath.2)"

80.120.179.10 - - [07/Jun/2010:16:07:39 +0200] "GET /Seiten/Rundzeichen.html HTTP/1.1" 200 8837 "http://www.asylabwehramt.at/Seiten/Aktuelles.html" "Mozilla/4.0 (compatible; MSIE 6.0; Windows NT 5.1; SV1; .NET CLR 1.1.4322; .NET CLR 2.0.50727; .NET CLR 3.0.04506.30; .NET CLR 3.0.04506.648; InfoPath.2)"

80.120.179.10 - - [07/Jun/2010:16:08:20 +0200] "GET /Seiten/Impressum.html HTTP/1.1" 200 11483 "http://www.asylabwehramt.at/Seiten/Links.html" "Mozilla/4.0 (compatible; MSIE 6.0; Windows NT 5.1; SV1; .NET CLR 1.1.4322; .NET CLR 2.0.50727; .NET CLR 3.0.04506.30; .NET CLR 3.0.04506.648; InfoPath.2)"

80.120.179.10 - - [07/Jun/2010:16:09:36 +0200] "GET /favicon.ico HTTP/1.1" 302 340 "-" "Mozilla/4.0 (compatible; MSIE 8.0; Windows NT 5.1; Trident/4.0; .NET CLR 1.1.4322; InfoPath.1)"

80.120.179.10 - - [07/Jun/2010:16:15:30 +0200] "GET /index_e.html HTTP/1.1" 200 11855 "http://www.asylabwehramt.at/index.html" "Mozilla/4.0 (compatible; MSIE 6.0; Windows NT 5.1; SV1; .NET CLR 1.1.4322; .NET CLR 2.0.50727; .NET CLR 3.0.04506.30; .NET CLR 3.0.04506.648; InfoPath.2)"

80.120.179.10 - - [07/Jun/2010:16:15:31 +0200] "GET /Seiten/Latestnews.html HTTP/1.1" 200 12574 " http://www.asylabwehramt.at/index_e.html" "Mozilla/4.0 (compatible; MSIE 6.0; Windows NT 5.1; SV1 ; .NET CLR 1.1.4322; .NET CLR 2.0.50727; .NET CLR 3.0.04506.30; .NET CLR 3.0.04506.648; InfoPath. 2)"

80.120.179.10 - - [07/Jun/2010:16:15:37 +0200] "GET /Seiten/Forms_and_Infos.html HTTP/1.1" 200 11 046 "http://www.asylabwehramt.at/Seiten/Latestnews.html" "Mozilla/4.0 (compatible; MSIE 6.0; Wind ows NT 5.1; SV1; .NET CLR 1.1.4322; .NET CLR 2.0.50727; .NET CLR 3.0.04506.30; .NET CLR 3.0.04506 .648; InfoPath.2)"

80.120.179.10 - - [07/Jun/2010:16:15:42 +0200] "GET /Seiten/Images.html HTTP/1.1" 200 9701 "http: //www.asylabwehramt.at/Seiten/Seal.html" "Mozilla/4.0 (compatible; MSIE 6.0; Windows NT 5.1; SV1; .NET CLR 1.1.4322; .NET CLR 2.0.50727; .NET CLR 3.0.04506.30; .NET CLR 3.0.04506.648; InfoPath.2)"

80.120.179.10 - - [07/Jun/2010:16:15:56 +0200] "GET /Seiten/Links_e.html HTTP/1.1" 200 18366 "htt p://www.asylabwehramt.at/Seiten/Images.html" "Mozilla/4.0 (compatible; MSIE 6.0; Windows NT 5.1; SV1; .NET CLR 1.1.4322; .NET CLR 2.0.50727; .NET CLR 3.0.04506.30; .NET CLR 3.0.04506.648; InfoPa th.2)"

80.120.179.10 - - [07/Jun/2010:16:22:08 +0200] "GET /Seiten/Bilder_buero.html HTTP/1.1" 200 11026 "http://www.asylabwehramt.at/Seiten/Bilder.html" "Mozilla/4.0 (compatible; MSIE 6.0; Windows NT 5.1; SV1; .NET CLR 1.1.4322; .NET CLR 2.0.50727; .NET CLR 3.0.04506.30; .NET CLR 3.0.04506.648; I nfoPath.2)"

80.120.179.10 - - [07/Jun/2010:16:22:09 +0200] "GET /Bilder/BAA_photos/IMG_0180.JPG HTTP/1.1" 200 112897 "http://www.asylabwehramt.at/Seiten/Bilder_buero.html" "Mozilla/4.0 (compatible; MSIE 6.0 ; Windows NT 5.1; SV1; .NET CLR 1.1.4322; .NET CLR 2.0.50727; .NET CLR 3.0.04506.30; .NET CLR 3.0 .04506.648; InfoPath.2)"

80.120.179.10 - - [07/Jun/2010:16:22:10 +0200] "GET /Bilder/BAA_photos/IMG_0196.JPG HTTP/1.1" 200 129278 "http://www.asylabwehramt.at/Seiten/Bilder_buero.html" "Mozilla/4.0 (compatible; MSIE 6.0 ; Windows NT 5.1; SV1; .NET CLR 1.1.4322; .NET CLR 2.0.50727; .NET CLR 3.0.04506.30; .NET CLR 3.0 .04506.648; InfoPath.2)"

```
80.120.179.10 - - [07/Jun/2010:16:33:12 +0200] "GET /Seite/Presse.html HTTP/1.1" 302 340 "http://www.asylabwehramt.at/index.html" "Mozilla/4.0 (compatible; MSIE 6.0; Windows NT 5.1; SV1; .NET CLR 1.1.4322; .NET CLR 2.0.50727; .NET CLR 3.0.04506.30; .NET CLR 3.0.04506.648; InfoPath.2)"

193.171.152.33 - - [07/Jun/2010:16:43:24 +0200] "GET /asyl.css HTTP/1.1" 304 - "http://www.asylabwehramt.at/" "Mozilla/4.0 (compatible; MSIE 8.0; Windows NT 5.1; Trident/4.0; InfoPath.1; .NET CLR 1.1.4322; .NET CLR 2.0.50727; .NET CLR 3.0.04506.30; .NET CLR 3.0.04506.648; .NET CLR 3.0.04506.2152; .NET CLR 3.5.30729)"

193.171.152.33 - - [07/Jun/2010:16:43:25 +0200] "GET /favicon.ico HTTP/1.1" 302 340 "-" "Mozilla/4.0 (compatible; MSIE 8.0; Windows NT 5.1; Trident/4.0; InfoPath.1; .NET CLR 1.1.4322; .NET CLR 2.0.50727; .NET CLR 3.0.04506.30; .NET CLR 3.0.04506.648; .NET CLR 3.0.04506.2152; .NET CLR 3.5.30729)"

88.116.224.102 - - [07/Jun/2010:16:47:17 +0200] "GET /favicon.ico HTTP/1.1" 302 340 "-" "Mozilla/5.0 (X11; U; Linux i686; de; rv:1.9.0.18) Gecko/2010021501 Ubuntu/9.04 (jaunty) Firefox/3.0.18"

88.116.224.102 - - [07/Jun/2010:16:47:31 +0200] "GET /favicon.ico HTTP/1.1" 302 340 "-" "Mozilla/5.0 (X11; U; Linux i686; de; rv:1.9.0.18) Gecko/2010021501 Ubuntu/9.04 (jaunty) Firefox/3.0.18"

88.116.224.102 - - [07/Jun/2010:16:47:45 +0200] "GET /Seiten/Bilder/Bilder_buero.html HTTP/1.1" 200 11026 "http://www.asylabwehramt.at/Seiten/Bilder.html" "Mozilla/5.0 (X11; U; Linux i686; de; rv:1.9.0.18) Gecko/2010021501 Ubuntu/9.04 (jaunty) Firefox/3.0.18"

88.116.224.102 - - [07/Jun/2010:16:47:49 +0200] "GET /Bilder/BAA_photos/IMG_0184.JPG HTTP/1.1" 200 125043 "http://www.asylabwehramt.at/Seiten/Bilder_buero.html" "Mozilla/5.0 (X11; U; Linux i686; de; rv:1.9.0.18) Gecko/2010021501 Ubuntu/9.04 (jaunty) Firefox/3.0.18"

88.116.224.102 - - [07/Jun/2010:16:47:50 +0200] "GET /Bilder/BAA_photos/IMG_0185.JPG HTTP/1.1" 200 98720 "http://www.asylabwehramt.at/Seiten/Bilder_buero.html" "Mozilla/5.0 (X11; U; Linux i686; de; rv:1.9.0.18) Gecko/2010021501 Ubuntu/9.04 (jaunty) Firefox/3.0.18"

88.116.224.102 - - [07/Jun/2010:16:47:59 +0200] "GET /Bilder/BAA_photos/IMG_0187.JPG HTTP/1.1" 200 191902 "http://www.asylabwehramt.at/Seiten/Bilder_buero.html" "Mozilla/5.0 (X11; U; Linux i686; de; rv:1.9.0.18) Gecko/2010021501 Ubuntu/9.04 (jaunty) Firefox/3.0.18"

88.116.224.102 - - [07/Jun/2010:16:48:03 +0200] "GET /Bilder/BAA_photos/IMG_0188.JPG HTTP/1.1" 20
```

```
200 179395 "http://www.asylabwehramt.at/Seiten/Bilder_buero.html" "Mozilla/5.0 (X11; U; Linux i686; de; rv:1.9.0.18) Gecko/2010021501 Ubuntu/9.04 (jaunty) Firefox/3.0.18"
88.116.224.102 - - [07/Jun/2010:16:48:07 +0200] "GET /Bilder/BAA_photos/IMG_0192.JPG HTTP/1.1" 200 109421 "http://www.asylabwehramt.at/Seiten/Bilder_buero.html" "Mozilla/5.0 (X11; U; Linux i686; de; rv:1.9.0.18) Gecko/2010021501 Ubuntu/9.04 (jaunty) Firefox/3.0.18"
88.116.224.102 - - [07/Jun/2010:16:48:08 +0200] "GET /Bilder/BAA_photos/IMG_0193.JPG HTTP/1.1" 200 128059 "http://www.asylabwehramt.at/Seiten/Bilder_buero.html" "Mozilla/5.0 (X11; U; Linux i686; de; rv:1.9.0.18) Gecko/2010021501 Ubuntu/9.04 (jaunty) Firefox/3.0.18"
88.116.224.102 - - [07/Jun/2010:16:48:12 +0200] "GET /Bilder/BAA_photos/IMG_0194.JPG HTTP/1.1" 200 181536 "http://www.asylabwehramt.at/Seiten/Bilder_buero.html" "Mozilla/5.0 (X11; U; Linux i686; de; rv:1.9.0.18) Gecko/2010021501 Ubuntu/9.04 (jaunty) Firefox/3.0.18"
88.116.224.102 - - [07/Jun/2010:16:48:13 +0200] "GET /Bilder/BAA_photos/IMG_0195.JPG HTTP/1.1" 200 122316 "http://www.asylabwehramt.at/Seiten/Bilder_buero.html" "Mozilla/5.0 (X11; U; Linux i686; de; rv:1.9.0.18) Gecko/2010021501 Ubuntu/9.04 (jaunty) Firefox/3.0.18"
88.116.224.102 - - [07/Jun/2010:16:48:15 +0200] "GET /Bilder/BAA_photos/IMG_0196.JPG HTTP/1.1" 200 129278 "http://www.asylabwehramt.at/Seiten/Bilder_buero.html" "Mozilla/5.0 (X11; U; Linux i686; de; rv:1.9.0.18) Gecko/2010021501 Ubuntu/9.04 (jaunty) Firefox/3.0.18"
80.120.179.10 - - [07/Jun/2010:16:48:18 +0200] "GET /Material/Hotline_Deutsch.pdf HTTP/1.1" 200 489465 "http://www.asylabwehramt.at/index.html" "Mozilla/4.0 (compatible; MSIE 8.0; Windows NT 5.1; Trident/4.0; .NET CLR 1.1.4322; InfoPath.1)"
88.116.224.102 - - [07/Jun/2010:16:48:20 +0200] "GET /Bilder/BAA_photos/IMG_0197.JPG HTTP/1.1" 200 110381 "http://www.asylabwehramt.at/Seiten/Bilder_buero.html" "Mozilla/5.0 (X11; U; Linux i686; de; rv:1.9.0.18) Gecko/2010021501 Ubuntu/9.04 (jaunty) Firefox/3.0.18"
88.116.224.102 - - [07/Jun/2010:16:48:24 +0200] "GET /Bilder/BAA_photos/IMG_0199.JPG HTTP/1.1" 200 90548 "http://www.asylabwehramt.at/Seiten/Bilder_buero.html" "Mozilla/5.0 (X11; U; Linux i686; de; rv:1.9.0.18) Gecko/2010021501 Ubuntu/9.04 (jaunty) Firefox/3.0.18"
88.116.224.102 - - [07/Jun/2010:16:48:25 +0200] "GET /Bilder/BAA_photos/IMG_0200.JPG HTTP/1.1" 200 82980 "http://www.asylabwehramt.at/Seiten/Bilder_buero.html" "Mozilla/5.0 (X11; U; Linux i686; de; rv:1.9.0.18) Gecko/2010021501 Ubuntu/9.04 (jaunty) Firefox/3.0.18"
```

```
de; rv:1.9.0.18) Gecko/2010021501 Ubuntu/9.04 (jaunty) Firefox/3.0.18"
88.116.224.102 - - [07/Jun/2010:16:48:27 +0200] "GET /Bilder/BAA_photos/IMG_0189.JPG HTTP/1.1" 20
0 163470 "http://www.asylabwehramt.at/Seiten/Bilder_buero.html" "Mozilla/5.0 (X11; U; Linux i686;
de; rv:1.9.0.18) Gecko/2010021501 Ubuntu/9.04 (jaunty) Firefox/3.0.18"
88.116.224.102 - - [07/Jun/2010:16:48:42 +0200] "GET /favicon.ico HTTP/1.1" 302 340 "-" "Mozilla/
5.0 (X11; U; Linux i686; de; rv:1.9.0.18) Gecko/2010021501 Ubuntu/9.04 (jaunty) Firefox/3.0.18"
88.116.224.102 - - [07/Jun/2010:16:49:53 +0200] "GET /favicon.ico HTTP/1.1" 302 340 "-" "Mozilla/
5.0 (X11; U; Linux i686; de; rv:1.9.0.18) Gecko/2010021501 Ubuntu/9.04 (jaunty) Firefox/3.0.18"
88.116.224.102 - - [07/Jun/2010:16:50:05 +0200] "GET /favicon.ico HTTP/1.1" 302 340 "-" "Mozilla/
5.0 (X11; U; Linux i686; de; rv:1.9.0.18) Gecko/2010021501 Ubuntu/9.04 (jaunty) Firefox/3.0.18"
88.116.224.102 - - [07/Jun/2010:16:50:09 +0200] "GET /favicon.ico HTTP/1.1" 302 340 "-" "Mozilla/
5.0 (X11; U; Linux i686; de; rv:1.9.0.18) Gecko/2010021501 Ubuntu/9.04 (jaunty) Firefox/3.0.18"
88.116.224.102 - - [07/Jun/2010:16:50:18 +0200] "GET /Seiten/Ausseneinsaetze.html HTTP/1.1" 200 9
190 "http://www.asylabwehramt.at/Seiten/Bilder.html" "Mozilla/5.0 (X11; U; Linux i686; de; rv:1.9
.0.18) Gecko/2010021501 Ubuntu/9.04 (jaunty) Firefox/3.0.18"
80.120.179.10 - - [07/Jun/2010:16:50:43 +0200] "GET /Seiten/Press.html HTTP/1.1" 200 10955 "http:
//www.asylabwehramt.at/Seiten/Bilder.html" "Mozilla/4.0 (compatible; MSIE 8.0; Windows NT 5.1; Tr
ident/4.0; .NET CLR 1.1.4322; InfoPath.1)"
88.116.224.102 - - [07/Jun/2010:16:50:57 +0200] "GET /favicon.ico HTTP/1.1" 302 340 "-" "Mozilla/
5.0 (X11; U; Linux i686; de; rv:1.9.0.18) Gecko/2010021501 Ubuntu/9.04 (jaunty) Firefox/3.0.18"
88.116.224.102 - - [07/Jun/2010:16:51:10 +0200] "GET /Seiten/Impressum.html HTTP/1.1" 200 11483 "
http://www.asylabwehramt.at/index.html" "Mozilla/5.0 (X11; U; Linux i686; de; rv:1.9.0.18) Gecko/
2010021501 Ubuntu/9.04 (jaunty) Firefox/3.0.18"
88.116.224.102 - - [07/Jun/2010:16:52:03 +0200] "GET /favicon.ico HTTP/1.1" 302 340 "-" "Mozilla/
5.0 (X11; U; Linux i686; de; rv:1.9.0.18) Gecko/2010021501 Ubuntu/9.04 (jaunty) Firefox/3.0.18"
88.116.224.102 - - [07/Jun/2010:16:52:12 +0200] "GET /index.html HTTP/1.1" 304 - "http://www.asyl
abwehramt.at/Seiten/Impressum.html" "Mozilla/5.0 (X11; U; Linux i686; de; rv:1.9.0.18) Gecko/2010
021501 Ubuntu/9.04 (jaunty) Firefox/3.0.18"
```

```
88.116.224.102 - - [07/Jun/2010:16:52:14 +0200] "GET /favicon.ico HTTP/1.1" 302 340 "-" "Mozilla/5.0 (X11; U; Linux i686; de; rv:1.9.0.18) Gecko/2010021501 Ubuntu/9.04 (jaunty) Firefox/3.0.18"
88.116.224.102 - - [07/Jun/2010:16:52:17 +0200] "GET /Seiten/Aktuelles.html HTTP/1.1" 304 - "http://www.asylabwehramt.at/index.html" "Mozilla/5.0 (X11; U; Linux i686; de; rv:1.9.0.18) Gecko/2010021501 Ubuntu/9.04 (jaunty) Firefox/3.0.18"
88.116.224.102 - - [07/Jun/2010:16:53:16 +0200] "GET /favicon.ico HTTP/1.1" 302 340 "-" "Mozilla/5.0 (X11; U; Linux i686; de; rv:1.9.0.18) Gecko/2010021501 Ubuntu/9.04 (jaunty) Firefox/3.0.18"
88.116.224.102 - - [07/Jun/2010:16:53:35 +0200] "GET /favicon.ico HTTP/1.1" 302 340 "-" "Mozilla/5.0 (X11; U; Linux i686; de; rv:1.9.0.18) Gecko/2010021501 Ubuntu/9.04 (jaunty) Firefox/3.0.18"
88.116.224.102 - - [07/Jun/2010:17:26:43 +0200] "GET / HTTP/1.1" 200 11827 "-" "Mozilla/4.0 (compatible; MSIE 8.0; Windows NT 6.0; Trident/4.0; GTB6.5; SLCC1; .NET CLR 2.0.50727; .NET CLR 3.5.21022; .NET CLR 3.5.30729; InfoPath.1; .NET CLR 3.0.30729; Tablet PC 2.0)"
88.116.224.102 - - [07/Jun/2010:17:27:13 +0200] "GET /Seiten/Latestnews.html HTTP/1.1" 200 12574 "http://www.asylabwehramt.at/" "Mozilla/4.0 (compatible; MSIE 8.0; Windows NT 6.0; Trident/4.0; GTB6.5; SLCC1; .NET CLR 2.0.50727; .NET CLR 3.5.21022; .NET CLR 3.5.30729; InfoPath.1; .NET CLR 3.0.30729; Tablet PC 2.0)"
88.116.224.102 - - [07/Jun/2010:17:27:26 +0200] "GET /Seiten/Links_e.html HTTP/1.1" 200 18366 "http://www.asylabwehramt.at/" "Mozilla/4.0 (compatible; MSIE 8.0; Windows NT 6.0; Trident/4.0; GTB6.5; SLCC1; .NET CLR 2.0.50727; .NET CLR 3.5.21022; .NET CLR 3.5.30729; InfoPath.1; .NET CLR 3.0.30729; Tablet PC 2.0)"
88.116.224.102 - - [07/Jun/2010:17:27:48 +0200] "GET /Seiten/Press.html HTTP/1.1" 200 10955 "http://www.asylabwehramt.at/Seiten/Links_e.html" "Mozilla/4.0 (compatible; MSIE 8.0; Windows NT 6.0; Trident/4.0; GTB6.5; SLCC1; .NET CLR 2.0.50727; .NET CLR 3.5.21022; .NET CLR 3.5.30729; InfoPath.1; .NET CLR 3.0.30729; Tablet PC 2.0)"
80.120.179.10 - - [07/Jun/2010:17:27:49 +0200] "GET /favicon.ico HTTP/1.1" 302 340 "-" "Mozilla/4.0 (compatible; MSIE 8.0; Windows NT 5.1; Trident/4.0; .NET CLR 1.1.4322; .NET CLR 2.0.50727; .NET CLR 3.0.04506.30; .NET CLR 3.0.04506.648; InfoPath.2)"
88.116.224.102 - - [07/Jun/2010:17:30:26 +0200] "GET /Seiten/Links.html HTTP/1.1" 200 18362 "http
```

```
://www.asylabwehramt.at/Seiten/Press.html" "Mozilla/4.0 (compatible; MSIE 8.0; Windows NT 6.0; Tr
ident/4.0; GTB6.5; SLCC1; .NET CLR 2.0.50727; .NET CLR 3.5.21022; .NET CLR 3.5.30729; InfoPath.1;
.NET CLR 3.0.30729; Tablet PC 2.0)"
213.208.144.130 - - [07/Jun/2010:17:32:42 +0200] "GET /favicon.ico HTTP/1.0" 302 340 "-" "Mozilla
/4.0 (compatible; MSIE 7.0; Windows NT 5.2; .NET CLR 1.1.4322; InfoPath.1; .NET CLR 2.0.50727; .N
ET CLR 3.0.4506.2152; .NET CLR 3.5.30729)"
91.112.214.67 - - [07/Jun/2010:18:32:08 +0200] "GET / HTTP/1.1" 200 11827 "http://www.google.at/u
rl?sa=t&source=web&cd=1&ved=0CBcQFjAA&url=http%3A%2F%2Fwww.asylabwehramt.at%2F&rct=j&q=Asylabwehr
amt&ei=BR8NT0HkDp-J0Lmf6NUP&usg=AFQjCNEy1zWC1vnxkLlPAGifRc344_0U4Q" "Mozilla/4.0 (compatible; MSI
E 8.0; Windows NT 5.1; Trident/4.0; .NET CLR 2.0.50727; InfoPath.2; .NET CLR 3.0.4506.2152; .NET
CLR 3.5.30729)"
91.112.214.67 - - [07/Jun/2010:18:32:58 +0200] "GET /Seiten/Aktuelles.html HTTP/1.1" 200 12570 "h
ttp://www.asylabwehramt.at/" "Mozilla/4.0 (compatible; MSIE 8.0; Windows NT 5.1; Trident/4.0; .NE
T CLR 2.0.50727; InfoPath.2; .NET CLR 3.0.4506.2152; .NET CLR 3.5.30729)"
91.112.214.67 - - [07/Jun/2010:18:35:23 +0200] "GET /favicon.ico HTTP/1.1" 302 340 "-" "Mozilla/4
.0 (compatible; MSIE 8.0; Windows NT 5.1; Trident/4.0; i0pus-I-M; .NET CLR 1.1.4322; .NET CLR 2.0
.50727; .NET CLR 3.0.4506.2152; .NET CLR 3.5.30729; InfoPath.2)"
91.112.214.67 - - [07/Jun/2010:18:35:39 +0200] "GET /Seiten/Bilder.html HTTP/1.1" 200 9571 "http:
//www.asylabwehramt.at/Seiten/Bilder.html" "Mozilla/4.0 (compatible; MSIE 8.0; Windows NT 5.1; Trident/4.0; i0pus-I
-M; .NET CLR 1.1.4322; .NET CLR 2.0.50727; .NET CLR 3.0.4506.2152; .NET CLR 3.5.30729; InfoPath.2
)"
91.112.214.67 - - [07/Jun/2010:18:35:40 +0200] "GET /Bilder/SCREEN_AAbA_Edutainment_Video.jpg HTT
P/1.1" 200 29259 "http://www.asylabwehramt.at/Seiten/Bilder.html" "Mozilla/4.0 (compatible; MSIE
8.0; Windows NT 5.1; Trident/4.0; i0pus-I-M; .NET CLR 1.1.4322; .NET CLR 2.0.50727; .NET CLR 3.0.
4506.2152; .NET CLR 3.5.30729; InfoPath.2)"
91.112.214.67 - - [07/Jun/2010:18:36:07 +0200] "GET /Seiten/Material.html HTTP/1.1" 200 11980 "ht
```

---

[7] WHOIS record on page 311

tp://www.asylabwehramt.at/" "Mozilla/4.0 (compatible; MSIE 8.0; Windows NT 5.1; Trident/4.0; i0pus-I-M; .NET CLR 1.1.4322; .NET CLR 2.0.50727; .NET CLR 3.0.4506.2152; .NET CLR 3.5.30729; InfoPath.2)"

91.112.214.67 - - [07/Jun/2010:18:36:12 +0200] "GET /Seiten/Rundzeichen.html HTTP/1.1" 200 8837 "http://www.asylabwehramt.at/Seiten/Material.html" "Mozilla/4.0 (compatible; MSIE 8.0; Windows NT 5.1; Trident/4.0; i0pus-I-M; .NET CLR 1.1.4322; .NET CLR 2.0.50727; .NET CLR 3.0.4506.2152; .NET CLR 3.5.30729; InfoPath.2)"

91.112.214.67 - - [07/Jun/2010:18:36:17 +0200] "GET /Seite/Press.html HTTP/1.1" 302 340 "http://www.asylabwehramt.at/index.html" "Mozilla/4.0 (compatible; MSIE 8.0; Windows NT 5.1; Trident/4.0; .NET CLR 2.0.50727; InfoPath.2; .NET CLR 3.0.4506.2152; .NET CLR 3.5.30729)"

91.112.214.67 - - [07/Jun/2010:18:36:22 +0200] "GET /Seiten/Orgstrukt.html HTTP/1.1" 200 14086 "http://www.asylabwehramt.at/Seiten/Rundzeichen.html" "Mozilla/4.0 (compatible; MSIE 8.0; Windows NT 5.1; Trident/4.0; i0pus-I-M; .NET CLR 1.1.4322; .NET CLR 2.0.50727; .NET CLR 3.0.4506.2152; .NET CLR 3.5.30729; InfoPath.2)"

91.112.214.67 - - [07/Jun/2010:18:45:50 +0200] "GET /Seiten/Ausseneinsaetze.html HTTP/1.1" 200 9190 "http://www.asylabwehramt.at/Seiten/Bilder.html" "Mozilla/4.0 (compatible; MSIE 8.0; Windows NT 5.1; Trident/4.0; i0pus-I-M; .NET CLR 1.1.4322; .NET CLR 2.0.50727; .NET CLR 3.0.4506.2152; .NET CLR 3.5.30729; InfoPath.2)"

91.112.214.67 - - [07/Jun/2010:18:45:51 +0200] "GET /Bilder/inventur.png HTTP/1.1" 200 848668 "http://www.asylabwehramt.at/Seiten/Ausseneinsaetze.html" "Mozilla/4.0 (compatible; MSIE 8.0; Windows NT 5.1; Trident/4.0; i0pus-I-M; .NET CLR 2.0.50727; .NET CLR 3.0.4506.2152; .NET CLR 3.5.30729; InfoPath.2)"

91.112.214.67 - - [07/Jun/2010:18:46:08 +0200] "GET /Seiten/Links.html HTTP/1.1" 200 18362 "http://www.asylabwehramt.at/Seiten/Ausseneinsaetze.html" "Mozilla/4.0 (compatible; MSIE 8.0; Windows NT 5.1; Trident/4.0; i0pus-I-M; .NET CLR 1.1.4322; .NET CLR 2.0.50727; .NET CLR 3.0.4506.2152; .NET CLR 3.5.30729; InfoPath.2)"

91.112.214.67 - - [07/Jun/2010:18:48:17 +0200] "GET /Seiten/Presse.html HTTP/1.1" 200 10956 "http://www.asylabwehramt.at/Seiten/Aktuelles.html" "Mozilla/4.0 (compatible; MSIE 8.0; Windows NT 5.1

```
; Trident/4.0; iOpus-I-M; .NET CLR 1.1.4322; .NET CLR 2.0.50727; .NET CLR 3.0.4506.2152; .NET CLR
  3.5.30729; InfoPath.2)"
91.112.214.67 - - [07/Jun/2010:18:48:26 +0200] "GET /OEFFENTLICHKEIT/07062010d.pdf HTTP/1.1" 200
  335529 "http://www.asylabwehramt.at/Seiten/Presse.html" "Mozilla/4.0 (compatible; MSIE 8.0; Windo
  ws NT 5.1; Trident/4.0; iOpus-I-M; .NET CLR 2.0.50727; .NET CLR 3.0.4506.2152;
  .NET CLR 3.5.30729; InfoPath.2)"
193.17.232.2[8] - - [07/Jun/2010:21:15:45 +0200] "GET / HTTP/1.0" 200 11827  "http://www.facebook.co
  m/l/0842c;www.asylabwehramt.at"  "Mozilla/5.0 (Windows; U; Windows NT 5.1; de; rv:1.9.1.2) Gecko/
  20090729 Firefox/3.5.2"
193.17.232.2 - - [07/Jun/2010:21:15:46 +0200] "GET /favicon.ico HTTP/1.0" 302 340 "-" "Mozilla/5.
  0 (Windows; U; Windows NT 5.1; de; rv:1.9.1.2) Gecko/20090729 Firefox/3.5.2"
193.17.232.2 - - [07/Jun/2010:21:16:05 +0200] "GET /Seiten/Bilder.html HTTP/1.0" 200 9571 "http:/
  /www.asylabwehramt.at/" "Mozilla/5.0 (Windows; U; Windows NT 5.1; de; rv:1.9.1.2) Gecko/20090729
  Firefox/3.5.2"
193.17.232.2 - - [07/Jun/2010:21:16:06 +0200] "GET /Bilder/SCREEN_AAbA_Edutainment_Video.jpg HTTP
  /1.0" 200 29259 "http://www.asylabwehramt.at/Seiten/Bilder.html" "Mozilla/5.0 (Windows; U; Window
  s NT 5.1; de; rv:1.9.1.2) Gecko/20090729 Firefox/3.5.2"
193.17.232.2 - - [07/Jun/2010:21:16:28 +0200] "GET /Seiten/Links.html HTTP/1.0" 200 18362 "http:/
  /www.asylabwehramt.at/Seiten/Bilder.html" "Mozilla/5.0 (Windows; U; Windows NT 5.1; de; rv:1.9.1.
  2) Gecko/20090729 Firefox/3.5.2"
80.120.179.10 - - [08/Jun/2010:06:54:32 +0200] "GET /index.html HTTP/1.1" 304 - "-" "Mozilla/4.0
  (compatible; MSIE 7.0; Windows NT 5.1; Trident/4.0; InfoPath.1; .NET CLR 1.1.4322; .NET CLR 2.0.5
  0727)"
80.120.179.10 - - [08/Jun/2010:06:54:33 +0200] "GET /favicon.ico HTTP/1.1" 302 340 "-" "Mozilla/4
  .0 (compatible; MSIE 8.0; Windows NT 5.1; Trident/4.0; InfoPath.1; .NET CLR 1.1.4322; .NET CLR 2.
  0.50727)"
```

8WHOIS record on page 317

80.120.179.10 - - [08/Jun/2010:06:54:37 +0200] "GET /Seiten/Impressum.html HTTP/1.1" 304 - "http://www.asylabwehramt.at/index.html" "Mozilla/4.0 (compatible; MSIE 8.0; Windows NT 5.1; Trident/4.0; InfoPath.1; .NET CLR 1.1.4322; .NET CLR 2.0.50727)"

91.112.214.67 - - [08/Jun/2010:07:46:48 +0200] "GET / HTTP/1.1" 304 - "-" "Mozilla/4.0 (compatible; MSIE 8.0; Windows NT 5.1; Trident/4.0; .NET CLR 1.1.4322; .NET CLR 2.0.50727; .NET CLR 3.0.450 6.2152; .NET CLR 3.5.30729)"

91.112.214.67 - - [08/Jun/2010:07:46:50 +0200] "GET /favicon.ico HTTP/1.1" 302 340 "-" "Mozilla/4.0 (compatible; MSIE 8.0; Windows NT 5.1; Trident/4.0; .NET CLR 1.1.4322; .NET CLR 2.0.50727; .NE T CLR 3.0.4506.2152; .NET CLR 3.5.30729)"

80.120.179.10 - - [08/Jun/2010:07:47:33 +0200] "GET / HTTP/1.1" 304 - "http://www.google.at/url?sa=t&source=web&cd=5&ved=0CDYQFjAE&url=http%3A%2F%2Fwww.asylabwehramt.at%2F&rct=j&q=asyl+verhinderung+beh%C3%B6rde&ei=bNkNTMaDGIuhOK2tz0gM&usg=AFQjCNEy1zWClvnxkLlPAGifRc344_0U4Q" "Mozilla/4.0 (compatible; MSIE 8.0; Windows NT 5.1; Trident/4.0; .NET CLR 1.1.4322; .NET CLR 2.0.50727; .NET CLR 3.0.04506.30; .NET CLR 3.0.4506.648; InfoPath.2; .NET CLR 3.0.4506.2152; .NET CLR 3.5.30729; MS-RTC LM 8)"

80.120.179.10 - - [08/Jun/2010:07:48:34 +0200] "GET /Seiten/Orgstrukt.html HTTP/1.1" 304 - "http://www.asylabwehramt.at/" "Mozilla/4.0 (compatible; MSIE 8.0; Windows NT 5.1; Trident/4.0; .NET CLR 1.1.4322; .NET CLR 2.0.50727; .NET CLR 3.0.04506.30; .NET CLR 3.0.4506.648; InfoPath.2; .NET CLR 3.0.4506.2152; .NET CLR 3.5.30729; MS-RTC LM 8)"

80.120.179.10 - - [08/Jun/2010:07:49:06 +0200] "GET /index.html HTTP/1.1" 200 11827 "http://www.asylabwehramt.at/Seiten/Orgstrukt.html" "Mozilla/4.0 (compatible; MSIE 8.0; Windows NT 5.1; Trident/4.0; .NET CLR 1.1.4322; .NET CLR 2.0.50727; .NET CLR 3.0.04506.30; .NET CLR 3.0.4506.648; InfoPath.2; .NET CLR 3.0.4506.2152; .NET CLR 3.5.30729; MS-RTC LM 8)"

80.120.179.10 - - [08/Jun/2010:07:49:08 +0200] "GET /index_e.html HTTP/1.1" 304 - "http://www.asylabwehramt.at/index.html" "Mozilla/4.0 (compatible; MSIE 8.0; Windows NT 5.1; Trident/4.0; .NET CLR 1.1.4322; .NET CLR 2.0.50727; .NET CLR 3.0.04506.30; .NET CLR 3.0.4506.648; InfoPath.2; .NET CLR 3.0.4506.2152; .NET CLR 3.5.30729; MS-RTC LM 8)"

```
80.120.179.10 - - [08/Jun/2010:07:49:12 +0200] "GET /Seiten/Aktuelles.html HTTP/1.1" 200 12570 "http://www.asylabwehramt.at/" "Mozilla/4.0 (compatible; MSIE 8.0; Windows NT 5.1; Trident/4.0; .NET CLR 2.0.50727; .NET CLR 3.0.04506.30; .NET CLR 3.0.04506.648; InfoPath.2; .NET CLR 1.1.4322; .NET CLR 3.0.4506.2152; .NET CLR 3.5.30729; MS-RTC LM 8)"
80.120.179.10 - - [08/Jun/2010:07:50:00 +0200] "GET /Seiten/Material.html HTTP/1.1" 200 11980 "http://www.asylabwehramt.at/Seiten/Aktuelles.html" "Mozilla/4.0 (compatible; MSIE 8.0; Windows NT 5.1; Trident/4.0; .NET CLR 1.1.4322; .NET CLR 2.0.50727; .NET CLR 3.0.04506.30; .NET CLR 3.0.04506.648; InfoPath.2; .NET CLR 3.0.4506.2152; .NET CLR 3.5.30729; MS-RTC LM 8)"
80.120.179.10 - - [08/Jun/2010:07:50:06 +0200] "GET /Bilder/Ladung.png HTTP/1.1" 200 114658 "http://www.asylabwehramt.at/Seiten/Material.html" "Mozilla/4.0 (compatible; MSIE 8.0; Windows NT 5.1; Trident/4.0; .NET CLR 1.1.4322; .NET CLR 2.0.50727; .NET CLR 3.0.04506.30; .NET CLR 3.0.04506.648; InfoPath.2; .NET CLR 3.0.4506.2152; .NET CLR 3.5.30729; MS-RTC LM 8)"
80.120.179.10 - - [08/Jun/2010:07:50:17 +0200] "GET /Seiten/Rundzeichen.html HTTP/1.1" 304 - "http://www.asylabwehramt.at/Seiten/Material.html" "Mozilla/4.0 (compatible; MSIE 8.0; Windows NT 5.1; Trident/4.0; .NET CLR 1.1.4322; .NET CLR 2.0.50727; .NET CLR 3.0.04506.30; .NET CLR 3.0.04506.648; InfoPath.2; .NET CLR 3.0.4506.2152; .NET CLR 3.5.30729; MS-RTC LM 8)"
80.120.179.10 - - [08/Jun/2010:07:50:23 +0200] "GET /Seiten/Bilder.html HTTP/1.1" 200 9571 "http://www.asylabwehramt.at/Seiten/Rundzeichen.html" "Mozilla/4.0 (compatible; MSIE 8.0; Windows NT 5.1; Trident/4.0; .NET CLR 1.1.4322; .NET CLR 2.0.50727; .NET CLR 3.0.04506.30; .NET CLR 3.0.04506.648; InfoPath.2; .NET CLR 3.0.4506.2152; .NET CLR 3.5.30729; MS-RTC LM 8)"
80.120.179.10 - - [08/Jun/2010:07:50:25 +0200] "GET /Seiten/Links.html HTTP/1.1" 200 18362 "http://www.asylabwehramt.at/Seiten/Bilder.html" "Mozilla/4.0 (compatible; MSIE 8.0; Windows NT 5.1; Trident/4.0; .NET CLR 1.1.4322; .NET CLR 2.0.50727; .NET CLR 3.0.04506.30; .NET CLR 3.0.04506.648; InfoPath.2; .NET CLR 3.0.4506.2152; .NET CLR 3.5.30729; MS-RTC LM 8)"
80.120.179.10 - - [08/Jun/2010:07:50:26 +0200] "GET /Bilder/IBM.png HTTP/1.1" 200 8413 "http://www.asylabwehramt.at/Seiten/Links.html" "Mozilla/4.0 (compatible; MSIE 8.0; Windows NT 5.1; Trident/4.0; .NET CLR 1.1.4322; .NET CLR 2.0.50727; .NET CLR 3.0.04506.30; .NET CLR 3.5.30729; MS-RTC LM 8)"
```

```
80.120.179.10 - - [08/Jun/2010:07:50:28 +0200] "GET /Bilder/omvlogo_3c.jpg HTTP/1.1" 200 22855 "h
ttp://www.asylabwehramt.at/Seiten/Links.html" "Mozilla/4.0 (compatible; MSIE 8.0; Windows NT 5.1;
Trident/4.0; .NET CLR 1.1.4322; .NET CLR 2.0.50727; .NET CLR 3.0.04506.30; .NET CLR 3.0.04506.64
8; InfoPath.2; .NET CLR 3.0.4506.2152; .NET CLR 3.5.30729; MS-RTC LM 8)"
80.120.179.10 - - [08/Jun/2010:07:51:14 +0200] "GET /Seiten/Press.html HTTP/1.1" 304 - "http://ww
w.asylabwehramt.at/Seiten/Links.html" "Mozilla/4.0 (compatible; MSIE 8.0; Windows NT 5.1; Trident
/4.0; .NET CLR 1.1.4322; .NET CLR 2.0.50727; .NET CLR 3.0.04506.30; .NET CLR 3.0.04506.648; InfoP
ath.2; .NET CLR 3.0.4506.2152; .NET CLR 3.5.30729; MS-RTC LM 8)"
91.112.214.67 - - [08/Jun/2010:07:54:55 +0200] "GET /Seiten/Orgstrukt.html HTTP/1.1" 304 - "http:
//www.asylabwehramt.at/" "Mozilla/4.0 (compatible; MSIE 8.0; Windows NT 5.1; Trident/4.0; .NET CL
R 1.1.4322; .NET CLR 2.0.50727; .NET CLR 3.0.4506.2152; .NET CLR 3.5.30729)"
80.120.179.10 - - [08/Jun/2010:08:24:25 +0200] "GET /favicon.ico HTTP/1.1" 302 340 "-" "Mozilla/4
.0 (compatible; MSIE 8.0; Windows NT 5.1; Trident/4.0; .NET CLR 1.1.4322; .NET CLR 2.0.50727; .NE
T CLR 3.0.04506.30; .NET CLR 3.0.04506.648; InfoPath.2)"
80.120.179.10 - - [08/Jun/2010:08:24:44 +0200] "GET /favicon.ico HTTP/1.1" 302 340 "-" "Mozilla/4
.0 (compatible; MSIE 7.0; Windows NT 5.1; .NET CLR 1.1.4322; .NET CLR 2.0.50727; .NET CLR 3.0.045
06.30; .NET CLR 3.0.04506.648; InfoPath.2; .NET CLR 3.0.4506.2152; .NET CLR 3.5.30729; MS-RTC LM
8)"
80.120.179.10 - - [08/Jun/2010:08:25:28 +0200] "GET /Seiten/Impressum.html HTTP/1.1" 200 11483 "h
ttp://www.asylabwehramt.at/Seiten/Aktuelles.html" "Mozilla/4.0 (compatible; MSIE 7.0; Windows NT
5.1; .NET CLR 1.1.4322; .NET CLR 2.0.50727; .NET CLR 3.0.04506.30; .NET CLR 3.0.04506.648; InfoPa
th.2; .NET CLR 3.0.4506.2152; .NET CLR 3.5.30729; MS-RTC LM 8)"
80.120.179.10 - - [08/Jun/2010:08:28:28 +0200] "GET /Seiten/Ausseneinsaetze.html HTTP/1.1" 200 91
90 "http://www.asylabwehramt.at/Seiten/Bilder.html" "Mozilla/4.0 (compatible; MSIE 7.0; Windows N
T 5.1; .NET CLR 1.1.4322; .NET CLR 2.0.50727; .NET CLR 3.0.04506.30; .NET CLR 3.0.04506.648; Info
Path.2; .NET CLR 3.0.4506.2152; .NET CLR 3.5.30729; MS-RTC LM 8)"
80.120.179.10 - - [08/Jun/2010:08:28:42 +0200] "GET /Seiten/Bilder_buero.html HTTP/1.1" 200 11026
"http://www.asylabwehramt.at/Seiten/Bilder.html" "Mozilla/4.0 (compatible; MSIE 7.0; Windows NT
```

```
5.1; .NET CLR 1.1.4322; .NET CLR 2.0.50727; .NET CLR 3.0.04506.30; .NET CLR 3.0.04506.648; InfoPath.2; .NET CLR 3.0.4506.2152; .NET CLR 3.5.30729; MS-RTC LM 8)"
80.120.179.10 - - [08/Jun/2010:08:28:43 +0200] "GET /Bilder/BAA_photos/IMG_0185.JPG HTTP/1.1" 200 98720 "http://www.asylabwehramt.at/Seiten/Bilder_buero.html" "Mozilla/4.0 (compatible; MSIE 7.0; Windows NT 5.1; .NET CLR 1.1.4322; .NET CLR 2.0.50727; .NET CLR 3.0.4506.2152; .NET CLR 3.5.30729; .NET CLR 3.0.04506.30; .NET CLR 3.0.04506.648; InfoPath.2;
80.120.179.10 - - [08/Jun/2010:08:28:44 +0200] "GET /Bilder/BAA_photos/IMG_0196.JPG HTTP/1.1" 200 129278 "http://www.asylabwehramt.at/Seiten/Bilder_buero.html" "Mozilla/4.0 (compatible; MSIE 7.0; Windows NT 5.1; .NET CLR 1.1.4322; .NET CLR 2.0.50727; .NET CLR 3.0.4506.2152; .NET CLR 3.5.30729; MS-RTC LM 8)"
80.120.179.10 - - [08/Jun/2010:08:30:35 +0200] "GET /Seiten/Links_e.html HTTP/1.1" 200 18366 "http://www.asylabwehramt.at/Seiten/Bilder.html" "Mozilla/4.0 (compatible; MSIE 7.0; Windows NT 5.1; .NET CLR 1.1.4322; .NET CLR 2.0.50727; .NET CLR 3.0.04506.30; .NET CLR 3.0.04506.648; InfoPath.2; .NET CLR 3.0.4506.2152; .NET CLR 3.5.30729; MS-RTC LM 8)"
80.120.179.10 - - [08/Jun/2010:08:33:16 +0200] "GET /Seiten/Presse.html HTTP/1.1" 200 10956 "http://www.asylabwehramt.at/Seiten/Impressum.html" "Mozilla/4.0 (compatible; MSIE 7.0; Windows NT 5.1; .NET CLR 1.1.4322; .NET CLR 2.0.50727; .NET CLR 3.5.30729; MS-RTC LM 8)"
80.120.179.10 - - [08/Jun/2010:08:33:20 +0200] "GET /OEFFENTLICHKEIT/07062010d.pdf HTTP/1.1" 200 335529 "http://www.asylabwehramt.at/Seiten/Presse.html" "Mozilla/4.0 (compatible; MSIE 7.0; Windows NT 5.1; .NET CLR 1.1.4322; .NET CLR 2.0.50727; .NET CLR 3.0.4506.2152; .NET CLR 3.5.30729; MS-RTC LM 8)"
193.171.152.33 - - [08/Jun/2010:08:45:21 +0200] "GET / HTTP/1.1" 304 - "-" "Mozilla/5.0 (X11; U; Linux i686; en-US) AppleWebKit/532.9 (KHTML, like Gecko) Chrome/5.0.307.11 Safari/532.9"
193.171.152.33 - - [08/Jun/2010:08:45:22 +0200] "GET /favicon.ico HTTP/1.1" 302 340 "-" "Mozilla/5.0 (X11; U; Linux i686; en-US) AppleWebKit/532.9 (KHTML, like Gecko) Chrome/5.0.307.11 Safari/532.9"
193.171.152.33 - - [08/Jun/2010:08:46:15 +0200] "GET /favicon.ico HTTP/1.1" 302 340 "-" "Mozilla/
```

```
5.0 (X11; U; Linux i686; en-US) AppleWebKit/532.9 (KHTML, like Gecko) Chrome/5.0.307.11 Safari/53
2.9"
193.171.152.33 - - [08/Jun/2010:08:46:17 +0200] "GET /Seiten/Aktuelles.html HTTP/1.1" 304 - "http
://www.asylabwehramt.at/" "Mozilla/5.0 (X11; U; Linux i686; en-US) AppleWebKit/532.9 (KHTML, like
Gecko) Chrome/5.0.307.11 Safari/532.9"
80.120.179.10 - - [08/Jun/2010:08:46:18 +0200] "GET /Seiten/Forms_and_Infos.html HTTP/1.1" 200 11
046 "http://www.asylabwehramt.at/index.html" "Mozilla/4.0 (compatible; MSIE 7.0; Windows NT 5.1;
.NET CLR 1.1.4322; .NET CLR 2.0.50727; .NET CLR 3.0.04506.30; .NET CLR 3.0.04506.648; InfoPath.2;
.NET CLR 3.0.4506.2152; .NET CLR 3.5.30729; MS-RTC LM 8)"
80.120.179.10 - - [08/Jun/2010:08:46:23 +0200] "GET /Material/Hotline_Deutsch.pdf HTTP/1.1" 200 4
89465 "http://www.asylabwehramt.at/Seiten/Forms_and_Infos.html" "Mozilla/4.0 (compatible; MSIE 7.
0; Windows NT 5.1; .NET CLR 1.1.4322; .NET CLR 2.0.50727; .NET CLR 3.0.04506.30; .NET CLR 3.0.045
06.648; InfoPath.2; .NET CLR 3.0.4506.2152; .NET CLR 3.5.30729; MS-RTC LM 8)"
193.171.152.33 - - [08/Jun/2010:08:46:30 +0200] "GET /Seiten/Orgstrukt.html HTTP/1.1" 304 - "http
://www.asylabwehramt.at/Seiten/Aktuelles.html" "Mozilla/5.0 (X11; U; Linux i686; en-US) AppleWebK
it/532.9 (KHTML, like Gecko) Chrome/5.0.307.11 Safari/532.9"
80.120.179.10 - - [08/Jun/2010:08:46:45 +0200] "GET /Material/Asyl_Jahresstatistik_2009.pdf HTTP/
1.1" 200 680643 "http://www.asylabwehramt.at/Seiten/Forms_and_Infos.html" "Mozilla/4.0 (compatibl
e; MSIE 7.0; Windows NT 5.1; .NET CLR 1.1.4322; .NET CLR 2.0.50727; .NET CLR 3.0.04506.30; .NET C
LR 3.0.04506.648; InfoPath.2; .NET CLR 3.0.4506.2152; .NET CLR 3.5.30729; MS-RTC LM 8)"
193.171.152.33 - - [08/Jun/2010:08:46:58 +0200] "GET /Seiten/Bilder.html HTTP/1.1" 304 - "http://
www.asylabwehramt.at/Seiten/Orgstrukt.html" "Mozilla/5.0 (X11; U; Linux i686; en-US) AppleWebKit/
532.9 (KHTML, like Gecko) Chrome/5.0.307.11 Safari/532.9"
193.171.152.33 - - [08/Jun/2010:08:46:59 +0200] "GET /Bilder/SCREEN_AAbA_Edutainment_Video.jpg HT
TP/1.1" 304 - "http://www.asylabwehramt.at/Seiten/Bilder.html" "Mozilla/5.0 (X11; U; Linux i686;
en-US) AppleWebKit/532.9 (KHTML, like Gecko) Chrome/5.0.307.11 Safari/532.9"
193.171.152.33 - - [08/Jun/2010:08:47:00 +0200] "GET /favicon.ico HTTP/1.1" 302 340 "-" "Mozilla/
5.0 (X11; U; Linux i686; en-US) AppleWebKit/532.9 (KHTML, like Gecko) Chrome/5.0.307.11 Safari/53
```

193.171.152.33 - - [08/Jun/2010:08:47:14 +0200] "GET /Seiten/Rundzeichen.html HTTP/1.1" 304 - "ht
tp://www.asylabwehramt.at/Seiten/Bilder.html" "Mozilla/5.0 (X11; U; Linux i686; en-US) AppleWebKi
t/532.9 (KHTML, like Gecko) Chrome/5.0.307.11 Safari/532.9"
193.171.152.33 - - [08/Jun/2010:08:47:21 +0200] "GET /favicon.ico HTTP/1.1" 302 340 "-" "Mozilla/
5.0 (X11; U; Linux i686; en-US) AppleWebKit/532.9 (KHTML, like Gecko) Chrome/5.0.307.11 Safari/53
2.9"
193.171.152.33 - - [08/Jun/2010:08:47:27 +0200] "GET /Seiten/Links.html HTTP/1.1" 304 - "http://w
ww.asylabwehramt.at/Seiten/Aktuelles.html" "Mozilla/5.0 (X11; U; Linux i686; en-US) AppleWebKit/5
32.9 (KHTML, like Gecko) Chrome/5.0.307.11 Safari/532.9"
193.171.152.33 - - [08/Jun/2010:08:47:28 +0200] "GET /favicon.ico HTTP/1.1" 302 340 "-" "Mozilla/
5.0 (X11; U; Linux i686; en-US) AppleWebKit/532.9 (KHTML, like Gecko) Chrome/5.0.307.11 Safari/53
2.9"
193.171.152.33 - - [08/Jun/2010:08:48:25 +0200] "GET / HTTP/1.1" 304 - "-" "Mozilla/5.0 (Windows;
U; Windows NT 5.1; de; rv:1.9.2.3) Gecko/20100401 Firefox/3.6.3"
193.171.152.33 - - [08/Jun/2010:08:48:28 +0200] "GET /favicon.ico HTTP/1.1" 302 340 "-" "Mozilla/
5.0 (Windows; U; Windows NT 5.1; de; rv:1.9.2.3) Gecko/20100401 Firefox/3.6.3"
193.171.152.33 - - [08/Jun/2010:08:48:47 +0200] "GET /favicon.ico HTTP/1.1" 302 340 "-" "Mozilla/
5.0 (X11; U; Linux i686; en-US) AppleWebKit/532.9 (KHTML, like Gecko) Chrome/5.0.307.11 Safari/53
2.9"
193.171.152.33 - - [08/Jun/2010:08:48:48 +0200] "GET /index.html HTTP/1.1" 304 - "http://www.asyl
abwehramt.at/Seiten/Aktuelles.html" "Mozilla/5.0 (X11; U; Linux i686; en-US) AppleWebKit/532.9 (K
HTML, like Gecko) Chrome/5.0.307.11 Safari/532.9"
193.171.152.33 - - [08/Jun/2010:08:49:04 +0200] "GET /Seiten/Orgstrukt.html HTTP/1.1" 304 - "http
://www.asylabwehramt.at/" "Mozilla/5.0 (Windows; U; Windows NT 5.1; de; rv:1.9.2.3) Gecko/2010040
1 Firefox/3.6.3"
193.171.152.33 - - [08/Jun/2010:08:49:05 +0200] "GET /asyl.css HTTP/1.1" 304 - "http://www.asylab
wehramt.at/Seiten/Orgstrukt.html" "Mozilla/5.0 (Windows; U; Windows NT 5.1; de; rv:1.9.2.3) Gecko

/20100401 Firefox/3.6.3"
193.171.152.33 - - [08/Jun/2010:08:49:07 +0200] "GET /Seiten/Impressum.html HTTP/1.1" 304 - "http://www.asylabwehramt.at/index.html" "Mozilla/5.0 (X11; U; Linux i686; en-US) AppleWebKit/532.9 (KHTML, like Gecko) Chrome/5.0.307.11 Safari/532.9"
193.171.152.33 - - [08/Jun/2010:08:49:47 +0200] "GET / HTTP/1.1" 304 - "-" "Mozilla/5.0 (X11; U; Linux i686; de; rv:1.9.0.15) Gecko/2009102815 Iceweasel/3.0.6 (Debian-3.0.6-3)"
193.171.152.33 - - [08/Jun/2010:08:49:48 +0200] "GET /favicon.ico HTTP/1.1" 302 340 "-" "Mozilla/5.0 (X11; U; Linux i686; de; rv:1.9.0.15) Gecko/2009102815 Iceweasel/3.0.6 (Debian-3.0.6-3)"
193.171.152.33 - - [08/Jun/2010:08:49:51 +0200] "GET /favicon.ico HTTP/1.1" 302 340 "-" "Mozilla/5.0 (X11; U; Linux i686; de; rv:1.9.0.15) Gecko/2009102815 Iceweasel/3.0.6 (Debian-3.0.6-3)"
193.171.152.33 - - [08/Jun/2010:08:50:00 +0200] "GET /favicon.ico HTTP/1.1" 302 340 "-" "Mozilla/5.0 (X11; U; Linux i686; en-US) AppleWebKit/532.9 (KHTML, like Gecko) Chrome/5.0.307.11 Safari/532.9"
193.171.152.33 - - [08/Jun/2010:08:50:07 +0200] "GET /Seiten/Rundzeichen.html HTTP/1.1" 304 - "http://www.asylabwehramt.at/Seiten/Orgstrukt.html" "Mozilla/5.0 (Windows; U; Windows NT 5.1; de; rv:1.9.2.3) Gecko/20100401 Firefox/3.6.3"
193.171.152.33 - - [08/Jun/2010:08:50:11 +0200] "GET /Seiten/Bilder.html HTTP/1.1" 304 - "http://www.asylabwehramt.at/Seiten/Rundzeichen.html" "Mozilla/5.0 (Windows; U; Windows NT 5.1; de; rv:1.9.2.3) Gecko/20100401 Firefox/3.6.3"
193.171.152.33 - - [08/Jun/2010:08:50:18 +0200] "GET / HTTP/1.1" 304 - "http://www.asylabwehramt.at/" "Mozilla/5.0 (X11; U; Linux i686; de; rv:1.9.0.15) Gecko/2009102815 Iceweasel/3.0.6 (Debian-3.0.6-3)"
193.171.152.33 - - [08/Jun/2010:08:50:23 +0200] "GET /Seiten/Aktuelles.html HTTP/1.1" 304 - "http://www.asylabwehramt.at/" "Mozilla/5.0 (X11; U; Linux i686; de; rv:1.9.0.15) Gecko/2009102815 Iceweasel/3.0.6 (Debian-3.0.6-3)"
193.171.152.33 - - [08/Jun/2010:08:50:24 +0200] "GET /Bilder/Header_AAbA.jpg HTTP/1.1" 304 - "http://www.asylabwehramt.at/Seiten/Aktuelles.html" "Mozilla/5.0 (X11; U; Linux i686; de; rv:1.9.0.15) Gecko/2009102815 Iceweasel/3.0.6 (Debian-3.0.6-3)"

```
193.171.152.33 - - [08/Jun/2010:08:50:41 +0200] "GET /Seiten/Material.html HTTP/1.1" 304 - "http:
//www.asylabwehramt.at/Seiten/Aktuelles.html" "Mozilla/5.0 (X11; U; Linux i686; de; rv:1.9.0.15)
Gecko/2009102815 Iceweasel/3.0.6 (Debian-3.0.6-3)"
88.116.224.102 - - [08/Jun/2010:12:53:28 +0200] "GET / HTTP/1.1" 200 11827  "http://eu.ixquick.co
m/do/metasearch.pl" "Mozilla/5.0 (X11; U; Linux i686; de; rv:1.9.1.9) Gecko/20100401 Ubuntu/9.10
(karmic) Firefox/3.5.9"
88.116.224.102 - - [08/Jun/2010:12:53:31 +0200] "GET /favicon.ico HTTP/1.1" 302 340 "-" "Mozilla/
5.0 (X11; U; Linux i686; de; rv:1.9.1.9) Gecko/20100401 Ubuntu/9.10 (karmic) Firefox/3.5.9"
88.116.224.102 - - [08/Jun/2010:12:53:40 +0200] "GET /Seiten/Impressum.html HTTP/1.1" 200 11483  "
http://www.asylabwehramt.at/" "Mozilla/5.0 (X11; U; Linux i686; de; rv:1.9.1.9) Gecko/20100401 Ub
untu/9.10 (karmic) Firefox/3.5.9"
88.116.224.102 - - [08/Jun/2010:12:55:27 +0200] "GET /Seiten/Rundzeichen.html HTTP/1.1" 200 8837
"http://www.asylabwehramt.at/" "Mozilla/5.0 (X11; U; Linux i686; de; rv:1.9.1.9) Gecko/20100401 U
buntu/9.10 (karmic) Firefox/3.5.9"
88.116.224.102 - - [08/Jun/2010:12:56:32 +0200] "GET /index.html HTTP/1.1" 200 11827 "http://www.
asylabwehramt.at/Seiten/Rundzeichen.html" "Mozilla/5.0 (X11; U; Linux i686; de; rv:1.9.1.9) Gecko
/20100401 Ubuntu/9.10 (karmic) Firefox/3.5.9"
91.112.214.67 - - [08/Jun/2010:13:25:37 +0200] "GET / HTTP/1.1" 304 - "-" "Mozilla/4.0 (compatibl
e; MSIE 8.0; Windows NT 5.1; Trident/4.0; .NET CLR 1.1.4322; .NET CLR 2.0.50727; .NET CLR 3.0.450
6.2152; .NET CLR 3.5.30729)"
91.112.214.67 - - [08/Jun/2010:13:25:51 +0200] "GET /Seiten/Impressum.html HTTP/1.1" 200 11483 "h
ttp://www.asylabwehramt.at/" "Mozilla/4.0 (compatible; MSIE 8.0; Windows NT 5.1; Trident/4.0; .NE
T CLR 1.1.4322; .NET CLR 2.0.50727; .NET CLR 3.0.4506.2152; .NET CLR 3.5.30729)"
91.112.214.67 - - [08/Jun/2010:13:26:02 +0200] "GET /index.html HTTP/1.1" 304 - "http://www.asyla
bwehramt.at/Seiten/Impressum.html" "Mozilla/4.0 (compatible; MSIE 8.0; Windows NT 5.1; Trident/4.
0; .NET CLR 1.1.4322; .NET CLR 2.0.50727; .NET CLR 3.0.4506.2152; .NET CLR 3.5.30729)"
91.112.214.67 - - [08/Jun/2010:13:26:36 +0200] "GET /index_e.html HTTP/1.1" 200 11855 "http://www
```

.asylabwehramt.at/" "Mozilla/4.0 (compatible; MSIE 8.0; Windows NT 5.1; Trident/4.0; .NET CLR 1.1.4322; .NET CLR 2.0.50727; .NET CLR 3.0.4506.2152; .NET CLR 3.5.30729)"
91.112.214.67 - - [08/Jun/2010:13:26:42 +0200] "GET /Seiten/Aktuelles.html HTTP/1.1" 304 - "http://www.asylabwehramt.at/" "Mozilla/4.0 (compatible; MSIE 8.0; Windows NT 5.1; Trident/4.0; .NET CLR 2.0.50727; .NET CLR 3.0.4506.2152; .NET CLR 3.5.30729)"
91.112.214.67 - - [08/Jun/2010:13:32:51 +0200] "GET /Seiten/Material.html HTTP/1.1" 304 - "http://www.asylabwehramt.at/Seiten/Aktuelles.html" "Mozilla/4.0 (compatible; MSIE 8.0; Windows NT 5.1; Trident/4.0; .NET CLR 1.1.4322; .NET CLR 2.0.50727; .NET CLR 3.0.4506.2152; .NET CLR 3.5.30729)"
91.112.214.67 - - [08/Jun/2010:13:34:31 +0200] "GET /Material/Asyl_Jahresstatistik_2009.pdf HTTP/1.1" 200 680643 "http://www.asylabwehramt.at/Seiten/Material.html" "Mozilla/4.0 (compatible; MSIE 8.0; Windows NT 5.1; Trident/4.0; .NET CLR 2.0.50727; .NET CLR 3.0.4506.2152; .NET CLR 3.5.30729)"
91.112.214.67 - - [08/Jun/2010:13:34:33 +0200] "GET /Material/Asyl_Jahresstatistik_2009.pdf HTTP/1.1" 206 4096 "-" "Mozilla/4.0 (compatible; MSIE 8.0; Windows NT 5.1; Trident/4.0; .NET CLR 1.1.4322; .NET CLR 2.0.50727; .NET CLR 3.0.4506.2152; .NET CLR 3.5.30729)"
91.112.214.67 - - [08/Jun/2010:13:34:34 +0200] "GET /Material/Asyl_Jahresstatistik_2009.pdf HTTP/1.1" 206 815 "-" "Mozilla/4.0 (compatible; MSIE 8.0; Windows NT 5.1; Trident/4.0; .NET CLR 1.1.4322; .NET CLR 2.0.50727; .NET CLR 3.0.4506.2152; .NET CLR 3.5.30729)"
91.112.214.67 - - [08/Jun/2010:13:34:35 +0200] "GET /Material/Asyl_Jahresstatistik_2009.pdf HTTP/1.1" 206 242018 "-" "Mozilla/4.0 (compatible; MSIE 8.0; Windows NT 5.1; Trident/4.0; .NET CLR 2.0.50727; .NET CLR 3.0.4506.2152; .NET CLR 3.5.30729)"
91.112.214.67 - - [08/Jun/2010:13:36:27 +0200] "GET /Seiten/Rundzeichen.html HTTP/1.1" 304 - "http://www.asylabwehramt.at/" "Mozilla/4.0 (compatible; MSIE 8.0; Windows NT 5.1; Trident/4.0; .NET CLR 1.1.4322; .NET CLR 2.0.50727; .NET CLR 3.0.4506.2152; .NET CLR 3.5.30729)"
91.112.214.67 - - [08/Jun/2010:13:36:41 +0200] "GET /Seiten/Bilder.html HTTP/1.1" 304 - "http://www.asylabwehramt.at/Seiten/Rundzeichen.html" "Mozilla/4.0 (compatible; MSIE 8.0; Windows NT 5.1; Trident/4.0; .NET CLR 2.0.50727; .NET CLR 3.0.4506.2152; .NET CLR 3.5.30729)"
91.112.214.67 - - [08/Jun/2010:13:37:07 +0200] "GET /Seiten/Links.html HTTP/1.1" 304 - "http://ww

```
w.asylabwehramt.at/Seiten/Bilder.html" "Mozilla/4.0 (compatible; MSIE 8.0; Windows NT 5.1; Triden
t/4.0; .NET CLR 2.0.50727; .NET CLR 3.0.4506.2152; .NET CLR 3.5.30729)"
91.112.214.67 - - [08/Jun/2010:13:39:44 +0200] "GET /Seiten/Press.html HTTP/1.1" 200 10955 "http:
//www.asylabwehramt.at/Seiten/Links.html" "Mozilla/4.0 (compatible; MSIE 8.0; Windows NT 5.1; Tri
dent/4.0; .NET CLR 1.1.4322; .NET CLR 2.0.50727; .NET CLR 3.0.4506.2152; .NET CLR 3.5.30729)"
91.112.214.67 - - [08/Jun/2010:13:39:48 +0200] "GET /Seiten/Presse.html HTTP/1.1" 304 - "http://w
ww.asylabwehramt.at/Seiten/Press.html" "Mozilla/4.0 (compatible; MSIE 8.0; Windows NT 5.1; Triden
t/4.0; .NET CLR 1.1.4322; .NET CLR 2.0.50727; .NET CLR 3.0.4506.2152; .NET CLR 3.5.30729)"
85.158.226.1 [9] - - [08/Jun/2010:15:06:23 +0200] "GET / HTTP/1.1" 200 11827 "http://www.google.at/ur
l?sa=t&source=web&cd=1&ved=0CBgQFjAA&url=http%3A%2F%2Fwww.asylabwehramt.at%2F&rct=j&q=asylabwehra
mt &ei=RUAOTJy6B4-V4gbfwLCtDA&usg=AFQjCNEy1zWC1vnxklIPAGifRc344_0U4Q" "Mozilla/4.0 (compatible; MS
IE 8.0; Windows NT 5.1; Trident/4.0; .NET CLR 1.1.4322; .NET CLR 2.0.50727)"
85.158.226.1 - - [08/Jun/2010:15:07:02 +0200] "GET /index.html HTTP/1.1" 200 11827 "http://www.as
ylabwehramt.at/" "Mozilla/4.0 (compatible; MSIE 8.0; Windows NT 5.1; Trident/4.0; .NET CLR 1.1.43
22; .NET CLR 2.0.50727)"
85.158.226.1 - - [08/Jun/2010:15:07:09 +0200] "GET /Seiten/Orgstrukt.html HTTP/1.1" 200 14086 "ht
tp://www.asylabwehramt.at/index.html" "Mozilla/4.0 (compatible; MSIE 8.0; Windows NT 5.1; Trident
/4.0; .NET CLR 1.1.4322; .NET CLR 2.0.50727)"
85.158.226.1 - - [08/Jun/2010:15:07:21 +0200] "GET /index_e.html HTTP/1.1" 200 11855 "http://www.
asylabwehramt.at/index.html" "Mozilla/4.0 (compatible; MSIE 8.0; Windows NT 5.1; Trident/4.0; .NE
T CLR 1.1.4322; .NET CLR 2.0.50727)"
85.158.226.1 - - [08/Jun/2010:15:07:26 +0200] "GET /Seiten/Aktuelles.html HTTP/1.1" 200 12570 "ht
tp://www.asylabwehramt.at/index_e.html" "Mozilla/4.0 (compatible; MSIE 8.0; Windows NT 5.1; Tride
nt/4.0; .NET CLR 1.1.4322; .NET CLR 2.0.50727)"
85.158.226.1 - - [08/Jun/2010:15:07:51 +0200] "GET /Seiten/Material.html HTTP/1.1" 200 11980 "htt
p://www.asylabwehramt.at/Seiten/Aktuelles.html" "Mozilla/4.0 (compatible; MSIE 8.0; Windows NT 5.
```

[9] WHOIS record on page 326

1; Trident/4.0; .NET CLR 1.1.4322; .NET CLR 2.0.50727)"

85.158.226.1 - - [08/Jun/2010:15:08:00 +0200] "GET /Seiten/Rundzeichen.html HTTP/1.1" 200 8837 "http://www.asylabwehramt.at/Seiten/Material.html" "Mozilla/4.0 (compatible; MSIE 8.0; Windows NT 5.1; Trident/4.0; .NET CLR 2.0.50727)"

85.158.226.1 - - [08/Jun/2010:15:08:13 +0200] "GET /Seiten/Bilder.html HTTP/1.1" 200 9571 "http://www.asylabwehramt.at/Seiten/Rundzeichen.html" "Mozilla/4.0 (compatible; MSIE 8.0; Windows NT 5.1; Trident/4.0; .NET CLR 2.0.50727)"

85.158.226.1 - - [08/Jun/2010:15:08:23 +0200] "GET /Seiten/Links.html HTTP/1.1" 200 18362 "http://www.asylabwehramt.at/Seiten/Bilder.html" "Mozilla/4.0 (compatible; MSIE 8.0; Windows NT 5.1; Trident/4.0; .NET CLR 1.1.4322; .NET CLR 2.0.50727)"

85.158.226.1 - - [08/Jun/2010:15:08:48 +0200] "GET /Seiten/Press.html HTTP/1.1" 200 10955 "http://www.asylabwehramt.at/Seiten/Links.html" "Mozilla/4.0 (compatible; MSIE 8.0; Windows NT 5.1; Trident/4.0; .NET CLR 1.1.4322; .NET CLR 2.0.50727)"

85.158.226.1 - - [08/Jun/2010:15:08:55 +0200] "GET /OEFFENTLICHKEIT/07062010d.pdf HTTP/1.1" 200 335529 "http://www.asylabwehramt.at/Seiten/Press.html" "Mozilla/4.0 (compatible; MSIE 8.0; Windows NT 5.1; Trident/4.0; .NET CLR 1.1.4322; .NET CLR 2.0.50727)"

195.190.15.10 - - [08/Jun/2010:15:56:29 +0200] "GET / HTTP/1.0" 200 11827 "http://www.google.at/search?hl=de&&sa=X&ei=CUw0TKCaKcO00Ne1tJAN&ved=0CBQQBSgA&q=asyl+abwehramt&spell=1" "Mozilla/5.0 (Macintosh; U; Intel Mac OS X 10_4_11; de-de) AppleWebKit/531.9 (KHTML, like Gecko) Version/4.0.3 Safari/531.9"

195.190.15.10 - - [08/Jun/2010:15:56:41 +0200] "GET /Seiten/Orgstrukt.html HTTP/1.0" 200 14086 "http://www.asylabwehramt.at/" "Mozilla/5.0 (Macintosh; U; Intel Mac OS X 10_4_11; de-de) AppleWebKit/531.9 (KHTML, like Gecko) Version/4.0.3 Safari/531.9"

195.190.15.10 - - [08/Jun/2010:15:56:58 +0200] "GET /index_e.html HTTP/1.0" 200 11855 "http://www.asylabwehramt.at/Seiten/Orgstrukt.html" "Mozilla/5.0 (Macintosh; U; Intel Mac OS X 10_4_11; de-de) AppleWebKit/531.9 (KHTML, like Gecko) Version/4.0.3 Safari/531.9"

195.190.15.10 - - [08/Jun/2010:15:57:04 +0200] "GET /Seiten/Bilder.html HTTP/1.0" 200 9571 "http://www.asylabwehramt.at/index_e.html" "Mozilla/5.0 (Macintosh; U; Intel Mac OS X 10_4_11; de-de) A

```
ppleWebKit/531.9 (KHTML, like Gecko) Version/4.0.3 Safari/531.9"
195.190.15.10 - - [08/Jun/2010:15:57:12 +0200] "GET /Seiten/Ausseneinsaetze.html HTTP/1.0" 200 91
90 "http://www.asylabwehramt.at/Seiten/Bilder.html" "Mozilla/5.0 (Macintosh; U; Intel Mac OS X 10
_4_11; de-de) AppleWebKit/531.9 (KHTML, like Gecko) Version/4.0.3 Safari/531.9"
195.190.15.10 - - [08/Jun/2010:15:57:18 +0200] "GET /Seiten/Press.html HTTP/1.0" 200 10955 "http:
//www.asylabwehramt.at/Seiten/Ausseneinsaetze.html" "Mozilla/5.0 (Macintosh; U; Intel Mac OS X 10
_4_11; de-de) AppleWebKit/531.9 (KHTML, like Gecko) Version/4.0.3 Safari/531.9"
195.190.15.10 - - [08/Jun/2010:15:57:23 +0200] "GET /OEFFENTLICHKEIT/07062010d.pdf HTTP/1.0" 200
335529 "http://www.asylabwehramt.at/Seiten/Press.html" "Mozilla/5.0 (Macintosh; U; Intel Mac OS X
10_4_11; de-de) AppleWebKit/531.9 (KHTML, like Gecko) Version/4.0.3 Safari/531.9"
80.120.179.10 - - [08/Jun/2010:16:01:26 +0200] "GET / HTTP/1.1" 200 11827 "-" "Mozilla/4.0 (compa
tible; MSIE 6.0; Windows NT 5.1; SV1; .NET CLR 1.1.4322; .NET CLR 2.0.50727; .NET CLR 3.0.04506.3
0; .NET CLR 3.0.04506.648; InfoPath.2)"
80.120.179.10 - - [08/Jun/2010:16:01:39 +0200] "GET /Seiten/Bilder.html HTTP/1.1" 200 9571 "http:
//www.asylabwehramt.at" "Mozilla/4.0 (compatible; MSIE 6.0; Windows NT 5.1; SV1; .NET CLR 1.1.432
2; .NET CLR 2.0.50727; .NET CLR 3.0.04506.30; .NET CLR 3.0.04506.648; InfoPath.2)"
80.120.179.10 - - [08/Jun/2010:16:01:42 +0200] "GET /Seiten/Bilder_buero.html HTTP/1.1" 200 11026
"http://www.asylabwehramt.at/Seiten/Bilder.html" "Mozilla/4.0 (compatible; MSIE 6.0; Windows NT
5.1; SV1; .NET CLR 1.1.4322; .NET CLR 2.0.50727; .NET CLR 3.0.04506.30; .NET CLR 3.0.04506.648; I
nfoPath.2)"
80.120.179.10 - - [08/Jun/2010:16:01:43 +0200] "GET /Bilder/BAA_photos/IMG_0193.JPG HTTP/1.1" 200
128059 "http://www.asylabwehramt.at/Seiten/Bilder_buero.html" "Mozilla/4.0 (compatible; MSIE 6.0
; Windows NT 5.1; SV1; .NET CLR 1.1.4322; .NET CLR 2.0.50727; .NET CLR 3.0.04506.30; .NET CLR 3.0
.04506.648; InfoPath.2)"
80.120.179.10 - - [08/Jun/2010:16:02:00 +0200] "GET /index.html HTTP/1.1" 200 11827 "http://www.a
sylabwehramt.at/Seiten/Bilder_buero.html" "Mozilla/4.0 (compatible; MSIE 6.0; Windows NT 5.1; SV1
; .NET CLR 1.1.4322; .NET CLR 2.0.50727; .NET CLR 3.0.04506.30; .NET CLR 3.0.04506.648; InfoPath.
2)"
```

```
80.120.179.10 - - [08/Jun/2010:16:02:03 +0200] "GET /Seiten/Orgstrukt.html HTTP/1.1" 200 14086 "http://www.asylabwehramt.at/index.html" "Mozilla/4.0 (compatible; MSIE 6.0; Windows NT 5.1; SV1; .NET CLR 1.1.4322; .NET CLR 2.0.50727; .NET CLR 3.0.04506.30; .NET CLR 3.0.04506.648; InfoPath.2)"
88.116.224.102 - - [09/Jun/2010:08:34:08 +0200] "GET / HTTP/1.1" 200 11827 "-" "Mozilla/4.0 (compatible; MSIE 8.0; Windows NT 5.1; Trident/4.0)"
88.116.224.102 - - [09/Jun/2010:08:34:09 +0200] "GET /favicon.ico HTTP/1.1" 302 340 "-" "Mozilla/4.0 (compatible; MSIE 8.0; Windows NT 5.1; Trident/4.0)"
88.116.224.102 - - [09/Jun/2010:08:34:59 +0200] "GET /Seiten/Orgstrukt.html HTTP/1.1" 200 14086 "http://www.asylabwehramt.at/" "Mozilla/4.0 (compatible; MSIE 8.0; Windows NT 5.1; Trident/4.0)"
80.120.179.10 - - [09/Jun/2010:10:25:49 +0200] "GET / HTTP/1.1" 200 11827 "-" "Mozilla/4.0 (compatible; MSIE 6.0; Windows NT 5.1; SV1; .NET CLR 1.1.4322; .NET CLR 2.0.50727; .NET CLR 3.0.04506.30; .NET CLR 3.0.04506.648; InfoPath.2)"
80.120.179.10 - - [09/Jun/2010:11:30:25 +0200] "GET /asyl.css HTTP/1.1" 200 860 "http://www.asylabwehramt.at/" "Mozilla/4.0 (compatible; MSIE 8.0; Windows NT 5.1; Trident/4.0; GTB6.3; .NET CLR 1.1.4322; .NET CLR 2.0.50727; .NET CLR 3.0.04506.648; InfoPath.2)"
80.120.179.10 - - [09/Jun/2010:11:37:57 +0200] "GET /favicon.ico HTTP/1.1" 302 340 "-" "Mozilla/4.0 (compatible; MSIE 8.0; Windows NT 5.1; Trident/4.0; InfoPath.1; .NET CLR 1.1.4322; .NET CLR 2.0.50727)"
80.120.179.10 - - [09/Jun/2010:11:38:46 +0200] "GET /Seiten/Aktuelles.html HTTP/1.1" 200 12570 "http://www.asylabwehramt.at/" "Mozilla/4.0 (compatible; MSIE 8.0; Windows NT 5.1; Trident/4.0; InfoPath.1; .NET CLR 1.1.4322; .NET CLR 2.0.50727)"
80.120.179.10 - - [09/Jun/2010:11:38:55 +0200] "GET /Seiten/Orgstrukt.html HTTP/1.1" 200 14086 "http://www.asylabwehramt.at/Seiten/Aktuelles.html" "Mozilla/4.0 (compatible; MSIE 8.0; Windows NT 5.1; Trident/4.0; InfoPath.1; .NET CLR 1.1.4322; .NET CLR 2.0.50727)"
80.120.179.10 - - [09/Jun/2010:11:39:15 +0200] "GET /Seiten/Latestnews.html HTTP/1.1" 200 12574 "http://www.asylabwehramt.at/Seiten/Orgstrukt.html" "Mozilla/4.0 (compatible; MSIE 8.0; Windows NT 5.1; Trident/4.0; InfoPath.1; .NET CLR 1.1.4322; .NET CLR 2.0.50727)"
80.120.179.10 - - [09/Jun/2010:11:39:21 +0200] "GET /Seiten/Forms_and_Infos.html HTTP/1.1" 200 11
```

```
046 "http://www.asylabwehramt.at/Seiten/Latestnews.html" "Mozilla/4.0 (compatible; MSIE 8.0; Windows NT 5.1; Trident/4.0; InfoPath.1; .NET CLR 1.1.4322; .NET CLR 2.0.50727)"
80.120.179.10 - - [09/Jun/2010:11:39:25 +0200] "GET /Material/Hotline_Russisch.pdf HTTP/1.1" 200 239827 "http://www.asylabwehramt.at/Seiten/Forms_and_Infos.html" "Mozilla/4.0 (compatible; MSIE 8.0; Windows NT 5.1; Trident/4.0; InfoPath.1; .NET CLR 1.1.4322; .NET CLR 2.0.50727)"
80.120.179.10 - - [09/Jun/2010:11:39:49 +0200] "GET /Seiten/Seal.html HTTP/1.1" 200 8872 "http://www.asylabwehramt.at/Seiten/Forms_and_Infos.html" "Mozilla/4.0 (compatible; MSIE 8.0; Windows NT 5.1; Trident/4.0; InfoPath.1; .NET CLR 1.1.4322; .NET CLR 2.0.50727)"
80.120.179.10 - - [09/Jun/2010:11:39:51 +0200] "GET /Seiten/Images.html HTTP/1.1" 200 9701 "http://www.asylabwehramt.at/Seiten/Seal.html" "Mozilla/4.0 (compatible; MSIE 8.0; Windows NT 5.1; Trident/4.0; InfoPath.1; .NET CLR 1.1.4322; .NET CLR 2.0.50727)"
80.120.179.10 - - [09/Jun/2010:11:40:01 +0200] "GET /Seiten/Links.html HTTP/1.1" 200 18362 "http://www.asylabwehramt.at/Seiten/Images.html" "Mozilla/4.0 (compatible; MSIE 8.0; Windows NT 5.1; Trident/4.0; InfoPath.1; .NET CLR 1.1.4322; .NET CLR 2.0.50727)"
80.120.179.10 - - [09/Jun/2010:11:40:11 +0200] "GET /Seiten/Press.html HTTP/1.1" 200 10955 "http://www.asylabwehramt.at/Seiten/Links.html" "Mozilla/4.0 (compatible; MSIE 8.0; Windows NT 5.1; Trident/4.0; InfoPath.1; .NET CLR 1.1.4322; .NET CLR 2.0.50727)"
88.116.224.102 - - [09/Jun/2010:12:18:42 +0200] "GET / HTTP/1.1" 200 11827 "-" "Opera/9.27 (Windows NT 5.1; U; de)"
88.116.224.102 - - [09/Jun/2010:12:18:52 +0200] "GET /asyl.css HTTP/1.1" 200 860 "http://www.asylabwehramt.at/" "Opera/9.27 (Windows NT 5.1; U; de)"
88.116.224.102 - - [09/Jun/2010:12:18:53 +0200] "GET /Bilder/Header_AAbA.jpg HTTP/1.1" 200 33599 "http://www.asylabwehramt.at/" "Opera/9.27 (Windows NT 5.1; U; de)"
88.116.224.102 - - [09/Jun/2010:12:19:08 +0200] "GET /favicon.ico HTTP/1.1" 302 340 "http://www.asylabwehramt.at/" "Opera/9.27 (Windows NT 5.1; U; de)"
88.116.224.102 - - [09/Jun/2010:12:21:50 +0200] "GET /Seiten/Aktuelles.html HTTP/1.1" 200 12570 "http://www.asylabwehramt.at/" "Opera/9.27 (Windows NT 5.1; U; de)"
88.116.224.102 - - [09/Jun/2010:12:22:09 +0200] "GET /Bilder/STRABAG.jpg HTTP/1.1" 200 39039 "htt
```

p://www.asylabwehramt.at/Seiten/Aktuelles.html" "Opera/9.27 (Windows NT 5.1; U; de)"

88.116.224.102 - - [09/Jun/2010:12:22:10 +0200] "GET /Bilder/leistung_2.jpg HTTP/1.1" 200 4918 "h ttp://www.asylabwehramt.at/Seiten/Aktuelles.html" "Opera/9.27 (Windows NT 5.1; U; de)"

194.153.217.248 [10] - - [09/Jun/2010:13:38:42 +0200] "GET /Bilder/Ladung.png HTTP/1.1" 200 114658 "-" "Mozilla/5.0 (X11; U; Linux x86_64; de; rv:1.9.2.3) Gecko/20100423 Ubuntu/10.04 (lucid) Firefox/ 3.6.3"

194.153.217.248 - - [09/Jun/2010:13:38:57 +0200] "GET / HTTP/1.1" 200 11827 "-" "Mozilla/5.0 (X11 ; U; Linux x86_64; de; rv:1.9.2.3) Gecko/20100423 Ubuntu/10.04 (lucid) Firefox/3.6.3"

194.153.217.248 - - [09/Jun/2010:13:38:58 +0200] "GET /favicon.ico HTTP/1.1" 302 340 "-" "Mozilla /5.0 (X11; U; Linux x86_64; de; rv:1.9.2.3) Gecko/20100423 Ubuntu/10.04 (lucid) Firefox/3.6.3"

194.153.217.248 - - [09/Jun/2010:13:39:01 +0200] "GET /favicon.ico HTTP/1.1" 302 340 "-" "Mozilla /5.0 (X11; U; Linux x86_64; de; rv:1.9.2.3) Gecko/20100423 Ubuntu/10.04 (lucid) Firefox/3.6.3"

194.153.217.248 - - [09/Jun/2010:13:39:23 +0200] "GET /Seiten/Aktuelles.html HTTP/1.1" 200 12570 "http://www.asylabwehramt.at/" "Mozilla/5.0 (X11; U; Linux x86_64; de; rv:1.9.2.3) Gecko/20100423 Ubuntu/10.04 (lucid) Firefox/3.6.3"

194.153.217.248 - - [09/Jun/2010:13:39:24 +0200] "GET /Bilder/Asylabwehramt_Seal_800x800.png HTTP /1.1" 200 269132 "http://www.asylabwehramt.at/Seiten/Aktuelles.html" "Mozilla/5.0 (X11; U; Linux x86_64; de; rv:1.9.2.3) Gecko/20100423 Ubuntu/10.04 (lucid) Firefox/3.6.3"

194.153.217.248 - - [09/Jun/2010:13:39:51 +0200] "GET /Seiten/Latestnews.html HTTP/1.1" 200 12574 "http://www.asylabwehramt.at/Seiten/Aktuelles.html" "Mozilla/5.0 (X11; U; Linux x86_64; de; rv:1 .9.2.3) Gecko/20100423 Ubuntu/10.04 (lucid) Firefox/3.6.3"

194.153.217.248 - - [09/Jun/2010:13:39:53 +0200] "GET /Seiten/Seal.html HTTP/1.1" 200 8872 "http: //www.asylabwehramt.at/Seiten/Latestnews.html" "Mozilla/5.0 (X11; U; Linux x86_64; de; rv:1.9.2.3) Gecko/20100423 Ubuntu/10.04 (lucid) Firefox/3.6.3"

194.153.217.248 - - [09/Jun/2010:13:39:59 +0200] "GET /Seiten/Images.html HTTP/1.1" 200 9701 "htt p://www.asylabwehramt.at/Seiten/Seal.html" "Mozilla/5.0 (X11; U; Linux x86_64; de; rv:1.9.2.3) Ge

---

[10]WHOIS record on page 295

53

```
cko/20100423 Ubuntu/10.04 (lucid) Firefox/3.6.3"
194.153.217.248 - - [09/Jun/2010:13:40:00 +0200] "GET /Bilder/BAA_photos/IMG_0198.JPG HTTP/1.1" 2
00 109214 "http://www.asylabwehramt.at/Seiten/Images.html" "Mozilla/5.0 (X11; U; Linux x86_64; de
; rv:1.9.2.3) Gecko/20100423 Ubuntu/10.04 (lucid) Firefox/3.6.3"
194.153.217.248 - - [09/Jun/2010:13:40:05 +0200] "GET /Seiten/Images_office.html HTTP/1.1" 200 11
084 "http://www.asylabwehramt.at/Seiten/Images.html" "Mozilla/5.0 (X11; U; Linux x86_64; de; rv:1
.9.2.3) Gecko/20100423 Ubuntu/10.04 (lucid) Firefox/3.6.3"
194.153.217.248 - - [09/Jun/2010:13:40:06 +0200] "GET /Bilder/BAA_photos/IMG_0179.JPG HTTP/1.1" 2
00 187140 "http://www.asylabwehramt.at/Seiten/Images_office.html" "Mozilla/5.0 (X11; U; Linux x86
_64; de; rv:1.9.2.3) Gecko/20100423 Ubuntu/10.04 (lucid) Firefox/3.6.3"
194.153.217.248 - - [09/Jun/2010:13:40:07 +0200] "GET /Bilder/BAA_photos/IMG_0191.JPG HTTP/1.1" 2
00 124240 "http://www.asylabwehramt.at/Seiten/Images_office.html" "Mozilla/5.0 (X11; U; Linux x86
_64; de; rv:1.9.2.3) Gecko/20100423 Ubuntu/10.04 (lucid) Firefox/3.6.3"
194.153.217.248 - - [09/Jun/2010:13:40:08 +0200] "GET /Bilder/BAA_photos/IMG_0199.JPG HTTP/1.1" 2
00 90548 "http://www.asylabwehramt.at/Seiten/Images_office.html" "Mozilla/5.0 (X11; U; Linux x86_
64; de; rv:1.9.2.3) Gecko/20100423 Ubuntu/10.04 (lucid) Firefox/3.6.3"
194.153.217.248 - - [09/Jun/2010:13:41:45 +0200] "GET /Seiten/Forms_and_Infos.html HTTP/1.1" 200
11046 "http://www.asylabwehramt.at/Seiten/Images.html" "Mozilla/5.0 (X11; U; Linux x86_64; de; rv
:1.9.2.3) Gecko/20100423 Ubuntu/10.04 (lucid) Firefox/3.6.3"
194.153.217.248 - - [09/Jun/2010:13:41:54 +0200] "GET /Seiten/Impressum.html HTTP/1.1" 200 11483
"http://www.asylabwehramt.at/Seiten/Forms_and_Infos.html" "Mozilla/5.0 (X11; U; Linux x86_64; de;
rv:1.9.2.3) Gecko/20100423 Ubuntu/10.04 (lucid) Firefox/3.6.3"
194.153.217.248 - - [09/Jun/2010:13:42:07 +0200] "GET /Seiten/Press.html HTTP/1.1" 200 10955 "htt
p://www.asylabwehramt.at/Seiten/Impressum.html" "Mozilla/5.0 (X11; U; Linux x86_64; de; rv:1.9.2.
3) Gecko/20100423 Ubuntu/10.04 (lucid) Firefox/3.6.3"
194.153.217.248 - - [09/Jun/2010:13:42:14 +0200] "GET /OEFFENTLICHKEIT/07062010d.pdf HTTP/1.1" 20
0 335529 "http://www.asylabwehramt.at/Seiten/Press.html" "Mozilla/5.0 (X11; U; Linux x86_64; de;
rv:1.9.2.3) Gecko/20100423 Ubuntu/10.04 (lucid) Firefox/3.6.3"
```

80.120.179.10 - - [10/Jun/2010:08:56:39 +0200] "GET / HTTP/1.1" 200 11828 "-" "Mozilla/4.0 (compatible; MSIE 8.0; Windows NT 5.1; Trident/4.0; .NET CLR 1.1.4322; .NET CLR 2.0.50727; .NET CLR 3.0.04506.30; .NET CLR 3.0.04506.648; InfoPath.2; .NET CLR 3.0.4506.2152; .NET CLR 3.5.30729; MS-RTC LM 8)"

78.41.144.41[11] - - [11/Jun/2010:10:43:17 +0200] "GET / HTTP/1.0" 200 11828 "http://www.google.at/search?hl=de&&sa=X&ei=EvcRTNaII9yXOKOKgIsI&ved=0CBQQBSgA&q=`asyl+abwehramt`&spell=1" "Mozilla/4.0 (compatible; MSIE 7.0; Windows NT 5.1; .NET CLR 2.0.50727; .NET CLR 1.1.4322; .NET CLR 3.0.04506.30; .NET CLR 3.0.04506.648; .NET CLR 3.0.4506.2152; .NET CLR 3.5.30729)"

78.41.144.41 - - [11/Jun/2010:10:43:18 +0200] "GET /favicon.ico HTTP/1.0" 302 340 "-" "Mozilla/4.0 (compatible; MSIE 7.0; Windows NT 5.1; .NET CLR 2.0.50727; .NET CLR 1.1.4322; .NET CLR 3.0.04506.30; .NET CLR 3.0.04506.648; .NET CLR 3.0.4506.2152; .NET CLR 3.5.30729)"

78.41.144.41 - - [11/Jun/2010:10:45:15 +0200] "GET /Seiten/Bilder.html HTTP/1.0" 200 9571 "http://www.asylabwehramt.at/" "Mozilla/4.0 (compatible; MSIE 7.0; Windows NT 5.1; .NET CLR 2.0.50727; .NET CLR 1.1.4322; .NET CLR 3.0.04506.30; .NET CLR 3.0.04506.648; .NET CLR 3.0.4506.2152; .NET CLR 3.5.30729)"

78.41.144.41 - - [11/Jun/2010:10:45:26 +0200] "GET /Seiten/Press.html HTTP/1.0" 200 10955 "http://www.asylabwehramt.at/Seiten/Bilder.html" "Mozilla/4.0 (compatible; MSIE 7.0; Windows NT 5.1; .NET CLR 2.0.50727; .NET CLR 1.1.4322; .NET CLR 3.0.04506.30; .NET CLR 3.0.04506.648; .NET CLR 3.0.4506.2152; .NET CLR 3.5.30729)"

78.41.144.41 - - [11/Jun/2010:10:45:29 +0200] "GET /Seiten/Links.html HTTP/1.0" 200 18362 "http://www.asylabwehramt.at/Seiten/Press.html" "Mozilla/4.0 (compatible; MSIE 7.0; Windows NT 5.1; .NET CLR 2.0.50727; .NET CLR 1.1.4322; .NET CLR 3.0.04506.30; .NET CLR 3.0.04506.648; .NET CLR 3.0.4506.2152; .NET CLR 3.5.30729)"

78.41.144.41 - - [11/Jun/2010:10:45:34 +0200] "GET /Seiten/Bilder_buero.html HTTP/1.0" 200 11026 "http://www.asylabwehramt.at/Seiten/Bilder.html" "Mozilla/4.0 (compatible; MSIE 7.0; Windows NT 5.1; .NET CLR 2.0.50727; .NET CLR 1.1.4322; .NET CLR 3.0.04506.30; .NET CLR 3.0.04506.648; .NET CL

---

[11] WHOIS record on page 298

```
R 3.0.4506.2152; .NET CLR 3.5.30729)"
78.41.144.41 - - [11/Jun/2010:10:45:35 +0200] "GET /Bilder/BAA_photos/IMG_0179.JPG HTTP/1.0" 200
187140 "http://www.asylabwehramt.at/Seiten/Bilder_buero.html" "Mozilla/4.0 (compatible; MSIE 7.0;
Windows NT 5.1; .NET CLR 2.0.50727; .NET CLR 1.1.4322; .NET CLR 3.0.04506.30; .NET CLR 3.0.04506
.648; .NET CLR 3.0.4506.2152; .NET CLR 3.5.30729)"
78.41.144.41 - - [11/Jun/2010:10:45:36 +0200] "GET /Bilder/BAA_photos/IMG_0195.JPG HTTP/1.0" 200
122316 "http://www.asylabwehramt.at/Seiten/Bilder_buero.html" "Mozilla/4.0 (compatible; MSIE 7.0;
Windows NT 5.1; .NET CLR 2.0.50727; .NET CLR 1.1.4322; .NET CLR 3.0.04506.30; .NET CLR 3.0.04506
.648; .NET CLR 3.0.4506.2152; .NET CLR 3.5.30729)"
78.41.144.41 - - [11/Jun/2010:10:47:04 +0200] "GET /Seiten/Rundzeichen.html HTTP/1.0" 200 8837 "h
ttp://www.asylabwehramt.at/Seiten/Bilder.html" "Mozilla/4.0 (compatible; MSIE 7.0; Windows NT 5.1
; .NET CLR 2.0.50727; .NET CLR 1.1.4322; .NET CLR 3.0.04506.30; .NET CLR 3.0.04506.648; .NET CLR
3.0.4506.2152; .NET CLR 3.5.30729)"
78.41.144.41 - - [11/Jun/2010:10:47:10 +0200] "GET / HTTP/1.0" 304 - "http://www.google.at/search
?hl=de&q=Suche&btnG=Suche&aq=f&aqi=&oq=&gs_rfai=" "Mozilla/4.0 (compatible; MSIE 7.0
; Windows NT 5.1; .NET CLR 2.0.50727; .NET CLR 1.1.4322; .NET CLR 3.0.04506.30; .NET CLR 3.0.0450
6.648; .NET CLR 3.0.4506.2152; .NET CLR 3.5.30729)"
78.41.144.41 - - [11/Jun/2010:10:47:15 +0200] "GET /Seiten/Material.html HTTP/1.0" 200 11980 "htt
p://www.asylabwehramt.at/Seiten/Rundzeichen.html" "Mozilla/4.0 (compatible; MSIE 7.0; Windows NT
5.1; .NET CLR 2.0.50727; .NET CLR 1.1.4322; .NET CLR 3.0.04506.30; .NET CLR 3.0.04506.648; .NET C
LR 3.0.4506.2152; .NET CLR 3.5.30729)"
78.41.144.41 - - [11/Jun/2010:10:47:22 +0200] "GET /Seiten/Aktuelles.html HTTP/1.0" 200 12570 "ht
tp://www.asylabwehramt.at/Seiten/Material.html" "Mozilla/4.0 (compatible; MSIE 7.0; Windows NT 5.
1; .NET CLR 2.0.50727; .NET CLR 1.1.4322; .NET CLR 3.0.04506.30; .NET CLR 3.0.04506.648; .NET CLR
3.0.4506.2152; .NET CLR 3.5.30729)"
78.41.144.41 - - [11/Jun/2010:10:47:26 +0200] "GET /index.html HTTP/1.0" 200 11828 "http://www.as
ylabwehramt.at/Seiten/Aktuelles.html" "Mozilla/4.0 (compatible; MSIE 7.0; Windows NT 5.1; .NET CL
R 2.0.50727; .NET CLR 1.1.4322; .NET CLR 3.0.04506.30; .NET CLR 3.0.04506.648; .NET CLR 3.0.4506.
```

```
2152; .NET CLR 3.5.30729)"
78.41.144.41 - - [11/Jun/2010:10:47:27 +0200] "GET /Seiten/Rundzeichen.html HTTP/1.0" 304 - "http
://www.asylabwehramt.at/" "Mozilla/4.0 (compatible; MSIE 7.0; Windows NT 5.1; .NET CLR 2.0.50727;
.NET CLR 1.1.4322; .NET CLR 3.0.04506.30; .NET CLR 3.0.04506.648; .NET CLR 2152; .NET C
LR 3.5.30729)"
78.41.144.41 - - [11/Jun/2010:10:47:31 +0200] "GET /Seiten/Bilder.html HTTP/1.0" 304 - "http://ww
w.asylabwehramt.at/Seiten/Rundzeichen.html" "Mozilla/4.0 (compatible; MSIE 7.0; Windows NT 5.1; .
NET CLR 2.0.50727; .NET CLR 1.1.4322; .NET CLR 3.0.04506.30; .NET CLR 3.0.04506.648; .NET CLR 3.0
.4506.2152; .NET CLR 3.5.30729)"
78.41.144.41 - - [11/Jun/2010:10:47:51 +0200] "GET /Seiten/Links.html HTTP/1.0" 304 - "http://www
.asylabwehramt.at/Seiten/Bilder.html" "Mozilla/4.0 (compatible; MSIE 7.0; Windows NT 5.1; .NET CL
R 2.0.50727; .NET CLR 1.1.4322; .NET CLR 3.0.04506.30; .NET CLR 3.0.04506.648; .NET CLR 3.0.4506.
2152; .NET CLR 3.5.30729)"
78.41.144.41 - - [11/Jun/2010:10:48:29 +0200] "GET /Seiten/Orgstrukt.html HTTP/1.0" 200 14086 "ht
tp://www.asylabwehramt.at/Seiten/Links.html" "Mozilla/4.0 (compatible; MSIE 7.0; Windows NT 5.1;
.NET CLR 2.0.50727; .NET CLR 1.1.4322; .NET CLR 3.0.04506.30; .NET CLR 3.0.04506.648; .NET CLR 3.
0.4506.2152; .NET CLR 3.5.30729)"
78.41.144.41 - - [11/Jun/2010:10:48:34 +0200] "GET /Seiten/Aktuelles.html HTTP/1.0" 304 - "http:/
/www.asylabwehramt.at/Seiten/Orgstrukt.html" "Mozilla/4.0 (compatible; MSIE 7.0; Windows NT 5.1;
.NET CLR 2.0.50727; .NET CLR 1.1.4322; .NET CLR 3.0.04506.30; .NET CLR 3.0.04506.648; .NET CLR 3.
0.4506.2152; .NET CLR 3.5.30729)"
78.41.144.41 - - [11/Jun/2010:10:48:42 +0200] "GET /Seiten/Material.html HTTP/1.0" 304 - "http://
www.asylabwehramt.at/Seiten/Aktuelles.html" "Mozilla/4.0 (compatible; MSIE 7.0; Windows NT 5.1; .
NET CLR 2.0.50727; .NET CLR 1.1.4322; .NET CLR 3.0.04506.30; .NET CLR 3.0.04506.648; .NET CLR 3.0
.4506.2152; .NET CLR 3.5.30729)"
78.41.144.41 - - [11/Jun/2010:10:48:48 +0200] "GET /Bilder/flyer_nigeria_Internet.pdf HTTP/1.0" 2
00 702826 "http://www.asylabwehramt.at/Seiten/Material.html" "Mozilla/4.0 (compatible; MSIE 7.0;
Windows NT 5.1; .NET CLR 2.0.50727; .NET CLR 1.1.4322; .NET CLR 3.0.04506.30; .NET CLR 3.0.04506.
```

```
648; .NET CLR 3.0.4506.2152; .NET CLR 3.5.30729)"
78.41.144.41 - - [11/Jun/2010:10:48:50 +0200] "GET /Bilder/flyer_nigeria_Internet.pdf HTTP/1.0" 2
06 4096 "-" "Mozilla/4.0 (compatible; MSIE 7.0; Windows NT 5.1; .NET CLR 2.0.50727; .NET CLR 1.1.
4322; .NET CLR 3.0.04506.30; .NET CLR 3.0.4506.648; .NET CLR 3.0.4506.2152; .NET CLR 3.5.30729)"
78.41.144.41 - - [11/Jun/2010:10:49:17 +0200] "GET /Bilder/IOM-Kosovo-Broschuere_Internet.pdf HTT
P/1.0" 200 728811 "http://www.asylabwehramt.at/Seiten/Material.html" "Mozilla/4.0 (compatible; MS
IE 7.0; Windows NT 5.1; .NET CLR 2.0.50727; .NET CLR 1.1.4322; .NET CLR 3.0.04506.30; .NET CLR 3.
0.04506.648; .NET CLR 3.0.4506.2152; .NET CLR 3.5.30729)"
78.41.144.41 - - [11/Jun/2010:10:49:18 +0200] "GET /Bilder/IOM-Kosovo-Broschuere_Internet.pdf HTT
P/1.0" 206 4096 "-" "Mozilla/4.0 (compatible; MSIE 7.0; Windows NT 5.1; .NET CLR 2.0.50727; .NET
CLR 1.1.4322; .NET CLR 3.0.04506.30; .NET CLR 3.0.4506.648; .NET CLR 3.0.4506.2152; .NET CLR 3.5
.30729)"
78.41.144.41 - - [11/Jun/2010:10:51:03 +0200] "GET /Material/Hotline_Russisch.pdf HTTP/1.0" 200 2
39827 "http://www.asylabwehramt.at/Seiten/Material.html" "Mozilla/4.0 (compatible; MSIE 7.0; Wind
ows NT 5.1; .NET CLR 2.0.50727; .NET CLR 1.1.4322; .NET CLR 3.0.04506.30; .NET CLR 3.0.04506.648;
.NET CLR 3.0.4506.2152; .NET CLR 3.5.30729)"
78.41.144.41 - - [11/Jun/2010:10:51:23 +0200] "GET /Seiten/Press.html HTTP/1.0" 304 - "http://www
.asylabwehramt.at/Seiten/Material.html" "Mozilla/4.0 (compatible; MSIE 7.0; Windows NT 5.1; .NET
CLR 2.0.50727; .NET CLR 1.1.4322; .NET CLR 3.0.04506.30; .NET CLR 3.0.04506.648; .NET CLR 3.0.450
6.2152; .NET CLR 3.5.30729)"
78.41.144.41 - - [11/Jun/2010:10:51:40 +0200] "GET /Seiten/Impressum.html HTTP/1.0" 200 11483 "ht
tp://www.asylabwehramt.at/Seiten/Press.html" "Mozilla/4.0 (compatible; MSIE 7.0; Windows NT 5.1;
.NET CLR 2.0.50727; .NET CLR 1.1.4322; .NET CLR 3.0.04506.30; .NET CLR 3.0.04506.648; .NET CLR 3.
0.4506.2152; .NET CLR 3.5.30729)"
78.41.144.41 - - [11/Jun/2010:10:52:56 +0200] "GET /index.html HTTP/1.0" 304 - "http://www.asylab
wehramt.at/Seiten/Impressum.html" "Mozilla/4.0 (compatible; MSIE 7.0; Windows NT 5.1; .NET CLR 2.
0.50727; .NET CLR 1.1.4322; .NET CLR 3.0.04506.648; .NET CLR 3.0.4506.2152
; .NET CLR 3.5.30729)"
```

```
78.41.144.41 - - [11/Jun/2010:10:53:06 +0200] "GET /Seiten/Presse.html HTTP/1.0" 200 10956 "http:
//www.asylabwehramt.at/index.html" "Mozilla/4.0 (compatible; MSIE 7.0; Windows NT 5.1; .NET CLR 2
.0.50727; .NET CLR 1.1.4322; .NET CLR 3.0.04506.30; .NET CLR 3.0.04506.648; .NET CLR 3.0.4506.215
2; .NET CLR 3.5.30729)"

78.41.144.41 - - [11/Jun/2010:10:53:07 +0200] "GET /index.html HTTP/1.0" 304 - "http://www.asylab
wehramt.at/Seiten/Presse.html" "Mozilla/4.0 (compatible; MSIE 7.0; Windows NT 5.1; .NET CLR 2.0.5
0727; .NET CLR 1.1.4322; .NET CLR 3.0.04506.30; .NET CLR 3.0.04506.648; .NET CLR 3.0.4506.2152; .
NET CLR 3.5.30729)"

78.41.144.41 - - [11/Jun/2010:10:53:09 +0200] "GET /Seiten/Aktuelles.html HTTP/1.0" 304 - "http:/
/www.asylabwehramt.at/index.html" "Mozilla/4.0 (compatible; MSIE 7.0; Windows NT 5.1; .NET CLR 2.
0.50727; .NET CLR 1.1.4322; .NET CLR 3.0.04506.30; .NET CLR 3.0.04506.648; .NET CLR 3.0.4506.2152
; .NET CLR 3.5.30729)"

78.41.144.41 - - [11/Jun/2010:10:53:18 +0200] "GET /index.html HTTP/1.0" 304 - "http://www.asylab
wehramt.at/Seiten/Aktuelles.html" "Mozilla/4.0 (compatible; MSIE 7.0; Windows NT 5.1; .NET CLR 2.
0.50727; .NET CLR 1.1.4322; .NET CLR 3.0.04506.30; .NET CLR 3.0.04506.648; .NET CLR 3.0.4506.2152
; .NET CLR 3.5.30729)"

78.41.144.41 - - [11/Jun/2010:10:54:18 +0200] "GET /index.html HTTP/1.0" 304 - "http://www.asylab
wehramt.at/Seiten/Impressum.html" "Mozilla/4.0 (compatible; MSIE 7.0; Windows NT 5.1; .NET CLR 2.
0.50727; .NET CLR 1.1.4322; .NET CLR 3.0.04506.30; .NET CLR 3.0.04506.648; .NET CLR 3.0.4506.2152
; .NET CLR 3.5.30729)"

78.41.144.41 - - [11/Jun/2010:10:55:48 +0200] "GET /Seiten/Bilder.html HTTP/1.0" 304 - "http://ww
w.asylabwehramt.at/index.html" "Mozilla/4.0 (compatible; MSIE 7.0; Windows NT 5.1; .NET CLR 2.0.5
0727; .NET CLR 1.1.4322; .NET CLR 3.0.04506.30; .NET CLR 3.0.04506.648; .NET CLR 3.0.4506.2152; .
NET CLR 3.5.30729)"

80.120.179.10 - - [11/Jun/2010:11:05:12 +0200] "GET / HTTP/1.1" 200 11828 "http://www.google.at/u
rl?sa=t&source=web&cd=1&ved=0CBcQFjAA&url=http%3A%2F%2Fwww.asylabwehramt.at%2F&rct=j&q=asylabwehr
amt&ei=0_wRTDKx0-WJOLve6KEI&usg=AFQjCNEy1zWClvnxkLlPAGifRc344_OU4Q" "Mozilla/4.0 (compatible; MSI
E 8.0; Windows NT 5.1; Trident/4.0; .NET CLR 1.1.4322; .NET CLR 2.0.50727; .NET CLR 3.0.04506.30;
```

```
80.120.179.10 - - [11/Jun/2010:11:05:25 +0200] "GET /Seiten/Orgstrukt.html HTTP/1.1" 200 14086 "http://www.asylabwehramt.at/" "Mozilla/4.0 (compatible; MSIE 8.0; Windows NT 5.1; Trident/4.0; .NET CLR 1.1.4322; .NET CLR 2.0.50727; .NET CLR 3.0.04506.30; .NET CLR 3.0.04506.648; InfoPath.2)"
80.120.179.10 - - [11/Jun/2010:11:13:27 +0200] "GET /Seiten/Impressum.html HTTP/1.1" 200 11483 "http://www.asylabwehramt.at/" "Mozilla/4.0 (compatible; MSIE 6.0; Windows NT 5.1; SV1; .NET CLR 1.1.4322; .NET CLR 2.0.50727; .NET CLR 3.0.04506.30; .NET CLR 3.0.04506.648; InfoPath.2)"
80.120.179.10 - - [11/Jun/2010:11:14:08 +0200] "GET /Seiten/Material.html HTTP/1.1" 200 11980 "http://www.asylabwehramt.at/Seiten/Impressum.html" "Mozilla/4.0 (compatible; MSIE 6.0; Windows NT 5.1; SV1; .NET CLR 1.1.4322; .NET CLR 2.0.50727; .NET CLR 3.0.04506.30; .NET CLR 3.0.04506.648; InfoPath.2)"
80.120.179.10 - - [11/Jun/2010:11:14:20 +0200] "GET /Bilder/flyer_nigeria_Internet.pdf HTTP/1.1" 200 702826 "http://www.asylabwehramt.at/Seiten/Material.html" "Mozilla/4.0 (compatible; MSIE 6.0; Windows NT 5.1; SV1; .NET CLR 1.1.4322; .NET CLR 2.0.50727; .NET CLR 3.0.04506.30; .NET CLR 3.0.04506.648; InfoPath.2)"
80.120.179.10 - - [11/Jun/2010:12:54:16 +0200] "GET /Seiten/Bilder.html HTTP/1.1" 200 9571 "http://www.asylabwehramt.at/Seiten/Orgstrukt.html" "Mozilla/4.0 (compatible; MSIE 6.0; Windows NT 5.1; SV1; .NET CLR 1.1.4322; .NET CLR 2.0.50727; .NET CLR 3.0.04506.30; .NET CLR 3.0.04506.648; InfoPath.2)"
80.120.179.10 - - [11/Jun/2010:12:54:33 +0200] "GET /Seiten/Seal.html HTTP/1.1" 200 8872 "http://www.asylabwehramt.at/Seiten/Bilder.html" "Mozilla/4.0 (compatible; MSIE 6.0; Windows NT 5.1; SV1; .NET CLR 1.1.4322; .NET CLR 2.0.50727; .NET CLR 3.0.04506.30; .NET CLR 3.0.04506.648; InfoPath.2)"
80.120.179.10 - - [11/Jun/2010:12:54:39 +0200] "GET /Seiten/Aktuelles.html HTTP/1.1" 200 12570 "http://www.asylabwehramt.at/Seiten/Seal.html" "Mozilla/4.0 (compatible; MSIE 6.0; Windows NT 5.1; SV1; .NET CLR 1.1.4322; .NET CLR 2.0.50727; .NET CLR 3.0.04506.30; .NET CLR 3.0.04506.648; InfoPath.2)"
80.120.179.10 - - [11/Jun/2010:12:54:56 +0200] "GET /index.html HTTP/1.1" 200 11828 "http://www.a
```

sylabwehramt.at/Seiten/Aktuelles.html" "Mozilla/4.0 (compatible; MSIE 6.0; Windows NT 5.1; SV1; .NET CLR 1.1.4322; .NET CLR 2.0.50727; .NET CLR 3.0.04506.30; .NET CLR 3.0.04506.648; InfoPath.2)"

80.120.179.10 - - [11/Jun/2010:13:29:58 +0200] "GET /favicon.ico HTTP/1.1" 302 340 "-" "Mozilla/4 .0 (compatible; MSIE 8.0; Windows NT 5.1; Trident/4.0; .NET CLR 1.1.4322; .NET CLR 2.0.50727; .NE T CLR 3.0.04506.30; .NET CLR 3.0.04506.648; InfoPath.2; .NET CLR 3.5.3072 9; MS-RTC LM 8)"

80.120.179.10 - - [11/Jun/2010:13:44:34 +0200] "GET /Material/Hotline_Deutsch.pdf HTTP/1.1" 200 4 89465 "http://www.asylabwehramt.at/Seiten/Material.html" "Mozilla/4.0 (compatible; MSIE 6.0; Wind ows NT 5.1; SV1; .NET CLR 1.1.4322; .NET CLR 2.0.50727; .NET CLR 3.0.04506.30; .NET CLR 3.0.04506 .648; InfoPath.2)"

80.120.179.10 - - [11/Jun/2010:13:45:20 +0200] "GET /Seiten/Presse.html HTTP/1.1" 200 10956 "http ://www.asylabwehramt.at/Seiten/Material.html" "Mozilla/4.0 (compatible; MSIE 6.0; Windows NT 5.1; SV1; .NET CLR 1.1.4322; .NET CLR 2.0.50727; .NET CLR 3.0.04506.30; .NET CLR 3.0.04506.648; InfoP ath.2)"

194.232.79.100 [12] - - [11/Jun/2010:15:17:47 +0200] "GET / HTTP/1.1" 200 11828 "http://www.google.at/ search?hl=de&q=asylabwehramt+wollzeile &meta=" "Mozilla/4.0 (compatible; MSIE 8.0; Windows NT 6.0; Trident/4.0; SLCC1; .NET CLR 2.0.50727; .NET CLR 3.5.30729; .NET CLR 3.0.30618)"

194.232.79.100 - - [11/Jun/2010:15:50:55 +0200] "GET / HTTP/1.1" 304 - "http://www.google.at/sear ch?hl=de&q=asylabwehramt+wollzeile &meta=" "Mozilla/4.0 (compatible; MSIE 8.0; Windows NT 6.0; Tri dent/4.0; SLCC1; .NET CLR 2.0.50727; .NET CLR 3.5.30729; .NET CLR 3.0.30618)"

194.232.79.100 - - [11/Jun/2010:15:56:39 +0200] "GET /favicon.ico HTTP/1.1" 302 340 "-" "Mozilla/ 4.0 (compatible; MSIE 8.0; Windows NT 6.0; Trident/4.0; SLCC1; .NET CLR 2.0.50727; .NET CLR 3.5.3 0729; .NET CLR 3.0.30618)"

194.232.79.100 - - [11/Jun/2010:15:56:48 +0200] "GET /Seiten/Aktuelles.html HTTP/1.1" 200 12570 " http://www.asylabwehramt.at/" "Mozilla/4.0 (compatible; MSIE 8.0; Windows NT 6.0; Trident/4.0; SL CC1; .NET CLR 2.0.50727; .NET CLR 3.5.30729; .NET CLR 3.0.30618)"

---

[12] WHOIS record on page 301

```
194.232.79.100 - - [11/Jun/2010:15:56:49 +0200] "GET /Bilder/leistung_2.jpg HTTP/1.1" 200 4918 "http://www.asylabwehramt.at/Seiten/Aktuelles.html" "Mozilla/4.0 (compatible; MSIE 8.0; Windows NT 6.0; Trident/4.0; SLCC1; .NET CLR 2.0.50727; .NET CLR 3.5.30729; .NET CLR 3.0.30618)"
194.232.79.100 - - [11/Jun/2010:15:57:26 +0200] "GET /Seiten/Orgstrukt.html HTTP/1.1" 200 14086 "http://www.asylabwehramt.at/" "Mozilla/4.0 (compatible; MSIE 8.0; Windows NT 6.0; Trident/4.0; SLCC1; .NET CLR 2.0.50727; .NET CLR 3.5.30729; .NET CLR 3.0.30618)"
194.232.79.100 - - [11/Jun/2010:15:58:16 +0200] "GET /Seiten/Press.html HTTP/1.1" 200 10955 "http://www.asylabwehramt.at/" "Mozilla/4.0 (compatible; MSIE 8.0; Windows NT 6.0; Trident/4.0; SLCC1; .NET CLR 2.0.50727; .NET CLR 3.5.30729; .NET CLR 3.0.30618)"
194.232.79.100 - - [11/Jun/2010:15:58:24 +0200] "GET /OEFFENTLICHKEIT/07062010d.pdf HTTP/1.1" 200 333788 "http://www.asylabwehramt.at/Seiten/Press.html" "Mozilla/4.0 (compatible; MSIE 8.0; Windows NT 6.0; Trident/4.0; SLCC1; .NET CLR 2.0.50727; .NET CLR 3.5.30729; .NET CLR 3.0.30618)"
80.120.179.10 - - [11/Jun/2010:15:59:05 +0200] "GET /Material/Asyl_Jahresstatistik_2009.pdf HTTP/1.1" 200 680643 "http://www.asylabwehramt.at/Seiten/Material.html" "Mozilla/4.0 (compatible; MSIE 8.0; Windows NT 5.1; Trident/4.0; InfoPath.1; .NET CLR 1.1.4322; .NET CLR 2.0.50727)"
194.232.79.100 - - [11/Jun/2010:16:00:26 +0200] "GET /Seiten/Bilder.html HTTP/1.1" 200 9571 "http://www.asylabwehramt.at/Seiten/Press.html" "Mozilla/4.0 (compatible; MSIE 8.0; Windows NT 6.0; Trident/4.0; SLCC1; .NET CLR 2.0.50727; .NET CLR 3.5.30729; .NET CLR 3.0.30618)"
194.232.79.100 - - [11/Jun/2010:16:00:27 +0200] "GET /Bilder/SCREEN_AAbA_Edutainment_Video.jpg HTTP/1.1" 200 29259 "http://www.asylabwehramt.at/Seiten/Bilder.html" "Mozilla/4.0 (compatible; MSIE 8.0; Windows NT 6.0; Trident/4.0; SLCC1; .NET CLR 2.0.50727; .NET CLR 3.5.30729; .NET CLR 3.0.30618)"
194.232.79.100 - - [11/Jun/2010:16:00:35 +0200] "GET /Seiten/Seal.html HTTP/1.1" 200 8872 "http://www.asylabwehramt.at/Seiten/Bilder.html" "Mozilla/4.0 (compatible; MSIE 8.0; Windows NT 6.0; Trident/4.0; SLCC1; .NET CLR 2.0.50727; .NET CLR 3.5.30729; .NET CLR 3.0.30618)"
194.232.79.100 - - [11/Jun/2010:16:00:41 +0200] "GET /index.html HTTP/1.1" 200 11828 "http://www.asylabwehramt.at/Seiten/Seal.html" "Mozilla/4.0 (compatible; MSIE 8.0; Windows NT 6.0; Trident/4.0; SLCC1; .NET CLR 2.0.50727; .NET CLR 3.5.30729; .NET CLR 3.0.30618)"
```

```
80.120.179.10 - - [11/Jun/2010:16:01:49 +0200] "GET /Seiten/Latestnews.html HTTP/1.1" 200 12574 "http://www.asylabwehramt.at/Seiten/Aktuelles.html" "Mozilla/4.0 (compatible; MSIE 8.0; Windows NT 5.1; Trident/4.0; .NET CLR 1.1.4322; .NET CLR 2.0.50727; .NET CLR 3.0.04506.648; InfoPath.2)"
80.120.179.10 - - [11/Jun/2010:16:01:53 +0200] "GET /Seiten/Forms_and_Infos.html HTTP/1.1" 200 11046 "http://www.asylabwehramt.at/Seiten/Latestnews.html" "Mozilla/4.0 (compatible; MSIE 8.0; Windows NT 5.1; Trident/4.0; .NET CLR 1.1.4322; .NET CLR 2.0.50727; .NET CLR 3.0.04506.648; InfoPath.2)"
80.120.179.10 - - [11/Jun/2010:16:02:01 +0200] "GET /Material/Hotline_Georgisch.PDF HTTP/1.1" 200 822080 "http://www.asylabwehramt.at/Seiten/Forms_and_Infos.html" "Mozilla/4.0 (compatible; MSIE 8.0; Windows NT 5.1; Trident/4.0; .NET CLR 1.1.4322; .NET CLR 2.0.50727; .NET CLR 3.0.04506.30; .NET CLR 3.0.04506.648; InfoPath.2)"
80.120.179.10 - - [11/Jun/2010:16:04:31 +0200] "GET /Seiten/Links.html HTTP/1.1" 200 18362 "http://www.asylabwehramt.at/Seiten/Bilder.html" "Mozilla/4.0 (compatible; MSIE 8.0; Windows NT 5.1; Trident/4.0; .NET CLR 1.1.4322; .NET CLR 2.0.50727; .NET CLR 3.0.04506.30; .NET CLR 3.0.04506.648; InfoPath.2)"
80.120.179.10 - - [11/Jun/2010:16:04:32 +0200] "GET /Bilder/BMDI.png HTTP/1.1" 200 8268 "http://www.asylabwehramt.at/Seiten/Links.html" "Mozilla/4.0 (compatible; MSIE 8.0; Windows NT 5.1; Trident/4.0; .NET CLR 2.0.50727; .NET CLR 3.0.04506.30; .NET CLR 3.0.04506.648; InfoPath.2)"
80.120.179.10 - - [11/Jun/2010:16:05:31 +0200] "GET /Seiten/Press.html HTTP/1.1" 200 10955 "http://www.asylabwehramt.at/index.html" "Mozilla/4.0 (compatible; MSIE 8.0; Windows NT 5.1; Trident/4.0; .NET CLR 1.1.4322; .NET CLR 2.0.50727; .NET CLR 3.0.04506.30; .NET CLR 3.0.04506.648; InfoPath.2)"
80.120.179.10 - - [14/Jun/2010:07:30:41 +0200] "GET / HTTP/1.1" 200 11828 "-" "Mozilla/4.0 (compatible; MSIE 6.0; Windows NT 5.1; SV1; .NET CLR 1.1.4322; .NET CLR 2.0.50727; .NET CLR 3.0.04506.30; .NET CLR 3.0.04506.648; InfoPath.2; .NET CLR 3.0.4506.2152; .NET CLR 3.5.30729; MS-RTC LM 8)"
80.120.179.10 - - [14/Jun/2010:07:31:21 +0200] "GET /Seiten/Aktuelles.html HTTP/1.1" 200 12570 "h
```

```
ttp://www.asylabwehramt.at/" "Mozilla/4.0 (compatible; MSIE 6.0; Windows NT 5.1; SV1; .NET CLR 1.1.4322; .NET CLR 2.0.50727; .NET CLR 3.0.04506.30; .NET CLR 3.0.04506.648; InfoPath.2; .NET CLR 3.0.4506.2152; .NET CLR 3.5.30729; MS-RTC LM 8)"

80.120.179.10 - - [14/Jun/2010:07:31:22 +0200] "GET /Bilder/56.jpg HTTP/1.1" 200 4494 "http://www.asylabwehramt.at/Seiten/Aktuelles.html" "Mozilla/4.0 (compatible; MSIE 6.0; Windows NT 5.1; SV1; .NET CLR 1.1.4322; .NET CLR 2.0.50727; .NET CLR 3.0.04506.30; .NET CLR 3.0.04506.648; InfoPath.2; .NET CLR 3.0.4506.2152; .NET CLR 3.5.30729; MS-RTC LM 8)"

88.116.224.102 - - [14/Jun/2010:10:49:39 +0200] "GET / HTTP/1.1" 200 11828 "-" "Mozilla/5.0 (X11; U; Linux i686; de; rv:1.9.0.15) Gecko/2009102815 Ubuntu/9.04 (jaunty) Firefox/3.0.15 (.NET CLR 3.5.30729)"

88.116.224.102 - - [14/Jun/2010:10:49:40 +0200] "GET /favicon.ico HTTP/1.1" 302 340 "-" "Mozilla/5.0 (X11; U; Linux i686; de; rv:1.9.0.15) Gecko/2009102815 Ubuntu/9.04 (jaunty) Firefox/3.0.15 (.NET CLR 3.5.30729)"

88.116.224.102 - - [14/Jun/2010:10:49:43 +0200] "GET /favicon.ico HTTP/1.1" 302 340 "-" "Mozilla/5.0 (X11; U; Linux i686; de; rv:1.9.0.15) Gecko/2009102815 Ubuntu/9.04 (jaunty) Firefox/3.0.15 (.NET CLR 3.5.30729)"

88.116.224.102 - - [14/Jun/2010:10:53:39 +0200] "GET /Seiten/Impressum.html HTTP/1.1" 200 11505 "http://www.asylabwehramt.at/" "Mozilla/5.0 (X11; U; Linux i686; de; rv:1.9.0.15) Gecko/2009102815 Ubuntu/9.04 (jaunty) Firefox/3.0.15 (.NET CLR 3.5.30729)"

88.116.224.102 - - [14/Jun/2010:10:56:12 +0200] "GET /Seiten/Aktuelles.html HTTP/1.1" 200 12570 "http://www.asylabwehramt.at/Seiten/Impressum.html" "Mozilla/5.0 (X11; U; Linux i686; de; rv:1.9.0.15) Gecko/2009102815 Ubuntu/9.04 (jaunty) Firefox/3.0.15 (.NET CLR 3.5.30729)"

88.116.224.102 - - [14/Jun/2010:10:56:13 +0200] "GET /Bilder/leistung_2.jpg HTTP/1.1" 200 4918 "http://www.asylabwehramt.at/Seiten/Aktuelles.html" "Mozilla/5.0 (X11; U; Linux i686; de; rv:1.9.0.15) Gecko/2009102815 Ubuntu/9.04 (jaunty) Firefox/3.0.15 (.NET CLR 3.5.30729)"

88.116.224.102 - - [14/Jun/2010:10:57:30 +0200] "GET /Seiten/Latestnews.html HTTP/1.1" 200 12574 "http://www.asylabwehramt.at/Seiten/Aktuelles.html" "Mozilla/5.0 (X11; U; Linux i686; de; rv:1.9.0.15) Gecko/2009102815 Ubuntu/9.04 (jaunty) Firefox/3.0.15 (.NET CLR 3.5.30729)"
```

```
88.116.224.102 - - [14/Jun/2010:10:57:34 +0200] "GET /Seiten/Material.html HTTP/1.1" 200 11980 "h
ttp://www.asylabwehramt.at/Seiten/Latestnews.html" "Mozilla/5.0 (X11; U; Linux i686; de; rv:1.9.0
.15) Gecko/2009102815 Ubuntu/9.04 (jaunty) Firefox/3.0.15 (.NET CLR 3.5.30729)"
88.116.224.102 - - [14/Jun/2010:10:58:06 +0200] "GET /Material/Asyl_Jahresstatistik_2009.pdf HTTP
/1.1" 200 680643 "http://www.asylabwehramt.at/Seiten/Material.html" "Mozilla/5.0 (X11; U; Linux i
686; de; rv:1.9.0.15) Gecko/2009102815 Ubuntu/9.04 (jaunty) Firefox/3.0.15 (.NET CLR 3.5.30729)"
88.116.224.102 - - [14/Jun/2010:10:58:25 +0200] "GET /Seiten/Rundzeichen.html HTTP/1.1" 200 8837
"http://www.asylabwehramt.at/Seiten/Material.html" "Mozilla/5.0 (X11; U; Linux i686; de; rv:1.9.0
.15) Gecko/2009102815 Ubuntu/9.04 (jaunty) Firefox/3.0.15 (.NET CLR 3.5.30729)"
88.116.224.102 - - [14/Jun/2010:10:58:32 +0200] "GET /Seiten/Seal.html HTTP/1.1" 200 8872 "http:/
/www.asylabwehramt.at/Seiten/Rundzeichen.html" "Mozilla/5.0 (X11; U; Linux i686; de; rv:1.9.0.15)
Gecko/2009102815 Ubuntu/9.04 (jaunty) Firefox/3.0.15 (.NET CLR 3.5.30729)"
88.116.224.102 - - [14/Jun/2010:10:58:36 +0200] "GET /Seiten/Bilder.html HTTP/1.1" 200 9571 "http
://www.asylabwehramt.at/Seiten/Seal.html" "Mozilla/5.0 (X11; U; Linux i686; de; rv:1.9.0.15) Geck
o/2009102815 Ubuntu/9.04 (jaunty) Firefox/3.0.15 (.NET CLR 3.5.30729)"
88.116.224.102 - - [14/Jun/2010:11:00:54 +0200] "GET /Seiten/Links_e.html HTTP/1.1" 200 18366 "ht
tp://www.asylabwehramt.at/Seiten/Bilder.html" "Mozilla/5.0 (X11; U; Linux i686; de; rv:1.9.0.15)
Gecko/2009102815 Ubuntu/9.04 (jaunty) Firefox/3.0.15 (.NET CLR 3.5.30729)"
88.116.224.102 - - [14/Jun/2010:11:02:22 +0200] "GET /index.html HTTP/1.1" 200 11828 "http://www.
asylabwehramt.at/Seiten/Links_e.html" "Mozilla/5.0 (X11; U; Linux i686; de; rv:1.9.0.15) Gecko/20
09102815 Ubuntu/9.04 (jaunty) Firefox/3.0.15 (.NET CLR 3.5.30729)"
80.120.179.10 - - [14/Jun/2010:12:45:08 +0200] "GET /favicon.ico HTTP/1.1" 302 340 "-" "Mozilla/4
.0 (compatible; MSIE 8.0; Windows NT 5.1; Trident/4.0; SV1; .NET CLR 1.1.4322; .NET CLR 2.0.50727
; .NET CLR 3.0.04506.30; .NET CLR 3.0.04506.648; InfoPath.2)"
80.120.179.10 - - [14/Jun/2010:12:45:31 +0200] "GET /Seiten/Bilder.html HTTP/1.1" 200 9571 "http:
//www.asylabwehramt.at/Seiten/Aktuelles.html" "Mozilla/4.0 (compatible; MSIE 8.0; Windows NT 5.1;
Trident/4.0; SV1; .NET CLR 1.1.4322; .NET CLR 2.0.50727; .NET CLR 3.0.04506.30; .NET CLR 3.0.045
06.648; InfoPath.2)"
```

```
80.120.179.10 - - [14/Jun/2010:12:46:27 +0200] "GET /Seiten/Material.html HTTP/1.1" 200 11980 "http://www.asylabwehramt.at/Seiten/Aktuelles.html" "Mozilla/4.0 (compatible; MSIE 8.0; Windows NT 5.1; Trident/4.0; SV1; .NET CLR 1.1.4322; .NET CLR 2.0.50727; .NET CLR 3.0.04506.30; .NET CLR 3.0.04506.648; InfoPath.2)"
80.120.179.10 - - [14/Jun/2010:12:46:32 +0200] "GET /Bilder/flyer_nigeria_Internet.pdf HTTP/1.1" 200 702826 "http://www.asylabwehramt.at/Seiten/Material.html" "Mozilla/4.0 (compatible; MSIE 8.0; Windows NT 5.1; Trident/4.0; SV1; .NET CLR 1.1.4322; .NET CLR 2.0.50727; .NET CLR 3.0.04506.30; .NET CLR 3.0.04506.648; InfoPath.2)"
80.120.179.10 - - [14/Jun/2010:12:47:09 +0200] "GET /Material/Asyl_Jahresstatistik_2009.pdf HTTP/1.1" 200 680643 "http://www.asylabwehramt.at/Seiten/Material.html" "Mozilla/4.0 (compatible; MSIE 8.0; Windows NT 5.1; Trident/4.0; SV1; .NET CLR 1.1.4322; .NET CLR 2.0.50727; .NET CLR 3.0.04506.30; .NET CLR 3.0.04506.648; InfoPath.2)"
193.171.152.33 - - [14/Jun/2010:18:02:10 +0200] "GET /Bilder/Header_AAbA.jpg HTTP/1.1" 304 - - "-" "Mozilla/4.0 (compatible;)"
193.171.152.33 - - [15/Jun/2010:00:32:46 +0200] "GET /asyl.css HTTP/1.1" 304 - - "-" "Mozilla/4.0 (compatible;)"
193.171.152.33 - - [15/Jun/2010:07:26:05 +0200] "GET / HTTP/1.1" 200 11828 "http://www.google.at/url?sa=t&source=web&cd=1&ved=0CBcQFjAA&url=http%3A%2F%2Fwww.asylabwehramt.at%2F&rct=j&q=asylabwehramt&ei=3A4XTOGMDIKt0O66vJkL&usg=AFQjCNEy1zWClvnxkLlPAGifRc344_OU4Q" "Mozilla/4.0 (compatible; MSIE 8.0; Windows NT 5.1; Trident/4.0; InfoPath.1; .NET CLR 1.1.4322; .NET CLR 2.0.50727; .NET CLR 3.0.04506.648; .NET CLR 3.0.4506.2152; .NET CLR 3.5.30729)"
193.171.152.33 - - [15/Jun/2010:07:26:06 +0200] "GET /favicon.ico HTTP/1.1" 302 340 "-" "Mozilla/4.0 (compatible; MSIE 8.0; Windows NT 5.1; Trident/4.0; InfoPath.1; .NET CLR 1.1.4322; .NET CLR 2.0.50727; .NET CLR 3.0.04506.648; .NET CLR 3.0.4506.2152; .NET CLR 3.5.307 29)"
80.120.179.10 - - [15/Jun/2010:08:21:18 +0200] "GET /Seiten/Orgstrukt.html HTTP/1.1" 200 14086 "http://derstandard.at/1276413064470/Fall-Zogaj-Der-Staerkere-gibt-niemals-nach" "Mozilla/4.0 (co
```

```
mpatible; MSIE 8.0; Windows NT 5.1; Trident/4.0; .NET CLR 2.0.50727; .NET CLR 3.0.4506.2152; .NET CLR 3.5.30729; InfoPath.1)"
80.120.179.10 - - [15/Jun/2010:08:21:19 +0200] "GET /favicon.ico HTTP/1.1" 302 340 "-" "Mozilla/4.0 (compatible; MSIE 8.0; Windows NT 5.1; Trident/4.0; .NET CLR 2.0.50727; .NET CLR 3.0.4506.2152; .NET CLR 3.5.30729; InfoPath.1)"
194.153.217.248 - - [15/Jun/2010:09:06:05 +0200] "GET / HTTP/1.1" 200 11828 "http://derstandard.at/1276413064470/Fall-Zogaj-Der-Staerkere-gibt-niemals-nach" "Mozilla/5.0 (Windows; U; Windows NT 5.1; de; rv:1.9.1.4) Gecko/20091016 Firefox/3.5.4 ( .NET CLR 3.5.30729)"
194.153.217.248 - - [15/Jun/2010:09:06:09 +0200] "GET /favicon.ico HTTP/1.1" 302 340 "-" "Mozilla/5.0 (Windows; U; Windows NT 5.1; de; rv:1.9.1.4) Gecko/20091016 Firefox/3.5.307 29)"
80.120.179.10 - - [15/Jun/2010:09:55:03 +0200] "GET / HTTP/1.1" 200 11828 "http://www.google.at/search?hl=de&source=hp&q=Asylabwehr&btnG=Google-Suche&meta=cr%3DcountryAT&aq=f&aql=&oq=&gs_rfai=" "Mozilla/4.0 (compatible; MSIE 6.0; Windows NT 5.1; SV1; .NET CLR 1.1.4322; .NET CLR 2.0.507 27; .NET CLR 3.0.04506.648; InfoPath.2)"
80.120.179.10 - - [15/Jun/2010:09:55:54 +0200] "GET /Seiten/Aktuelles.html HTTP/1.1" 200 12570 "http://www.asylabwehramt.at/" "Mozilla/4.0 (compatible; MSIE 6.0; Windows NT 5.1; SV1; .NET CLR 1.1.4322; .NET CLR 2.0.50727; .NET CLR 3.0.04506.30; InfoPath.2)"
80.120.179.10 - - [15/Jun/2010:09:55:55 +0200] "GET /Bilder/Asylabwehramt_Seal_800x800.png HTTP/1.1" 200 269132 "http://www.asylabwehramt.at/Seiten/Aktuelles.html" "Mozilla/4.0 (compatible; MSIE 6.0; Windows NT 5.1; SV1; .NET CLR 1.1.4322; .NET CLR 2.0.50727; .NET CLR 3.0.04506.30; .NET CLR 3.0.04506.648; InfoPath.2)"
80.120.179.10 - - [15/Jun/2010:09:56:04 +0200] "GET /Seiten/Material.html HTTP/1.1" 200 11980 "http://www.asylabwehramt.at/Seiten/Aktuelles.html" "Mozilla/4.0 (compatible; MSIE 6.0; Windows NT 5.1; SV1; .NET CLR 1.1.4322; .NET CLR 2.0.50727; .NET CLR 3.0.04506.30; .NET CLR 3.0.04506.648; In foPath.2)"
80.120.179.10 - - [15/Jun/2010:09:56:09 +0200] "GET /Bilder/flyer_nigeria_Internet.pdf HTTP/1.1"
```

```
200 702826 "http://www.asylabwehramt.at/Seiten/Material.html" "Mozilla/4.0 (compatible; MSIE 6.0;
Windows NT 5.1; SV1; .NET CLR 1.1.4322; .NET CLR 2.0.50727; .NET CLR 3.0.04506.30; .NET CLR 3.0.
04506.648; InfoPath.2)"
80.120.179.10 - - [15/Jun/2010:09:57:39 +0200] "GET /index.html HTTP/1.1" 200 11828 "http://www.a
sylabwehramt.at/Seiten/Orgstrukt.html" "Mozilla/4.0 (compatible; MSIE 6.0; Windows NT 5.1; SV1; .
NET CLR 1.1.4322; .NET CLR 2.0.50727; .NET CLR 3.0.04506.30; .NET CLR 3.0.04506.648; InfoPath.2)"
193.186.185.101[13] - - [15/Jun/2010:10:13:29 +0200] "GET / HTTP/1.1" 200 11828 "http://derstandard.
at/1276413064470/Fall-Zogaj-Der-Staerkere-gibt-niemals-nach" "Mozilla/4.0 (compatible; MSIE 6.0;
Windows NT 5.1; SV1; InfoPath.1; .NET CLR 1.1.4322; .NET CLR 3.0.4506.2152;
.NET CLR 3.5.30729)"
193.186.185.101 - - [15/Jun/2010:10:13:30 +0200] "GET /asyl.css HTTP/1.1" 200 860 "http://www.asy
labwehramt.at/" "Mozilla/4.0 (compatible; MSIE 6.0; Windows NT 5.1; SV1; InfoPath.1; .NET CLR 2.0
.50727; .NET CLR 3.0.4506.2152; .NET CLR 3.5.30729)"
193.186.185.101 - - [15/Jun/2010:10:14:26 +0200] "GET /Seiten/Bilder.html HTTP/1.1" 200 9571 "htt
p://www.asylabwehramt.at/" "Mozilla/4.0 (compatible; MSIE 6.0; Windows NT 5.1; SV1; InfoPath.1; .
NET CLR 2.0.50727; .NET CLR 1.1.4322; .NET CLR 3.0.4506.2152; .NET CLR 3.5.30729)"
193.186.185.101 - - [15/Jun/2010:10:14:38 +0200] "GET /Seiten/Impressum.html HTTP/1.1" 200 11505
"http://www.asylabwehramt.at/" "Mozilla/4.0 (compatible; MSIE 6.0; Windows NT 5.1; SV1; InfoPath.
1; .NET CLR 2.0.50727; .NET CLR 1.1.4322; .NET CLR 3.0.4506.2152; .NET CLR 3.5.30729)"
193.186.185.101 - - [15/Jun/2010:10:15:10 +0200] "GET /Seiten/Orgstrukt.html HTTP/1.1" 200 14086
"http://derstandard.at/1276413064470/Fall-Zogaj-Der-Staerkere-gibt-niemals-nach" "Mozilla/4.0 (
compatible; MSIE 6.0; Windows NT 5.1; SV1; InfoPath.1; .NET CLR 2.0.50727; .NET CLR 1.1.4322; .NE
T CLR 3.0.4506.2152; .NET CLR 3.5.30729)"
85.158.226.103[14] - - [15/Jun/2010:10:18:09 +0200] "GET / HTTP/1.1" 200 11828 "http://derstandard.a
t/1276413064470/Fall-Zogaj-Der-Staerkere-gibt-niemals-nach" "Mozilla/4.0 (compatible; MSIE 8.0;
```

[13]WHOIS record on page 287
[14]WHOIS record on page 296

```
Windows NT 6.0; Trident/4.0; SLCC1; .NET CLR 2.0.50727; InfoPath.2; .NET CLR 3.5.30729; .NET CLR 3.0.30729)"
85.158.226.103 - - [15/Jun/2010:10:18:21 +0200] "GET /Seiten/Aktuelles.html HTTP/1.1" 200 12570 "http://www.asylabwehramt.at/" "Mozilla/4.0 (compatible; MSIE 8.0; Windows NT 6.0; Trident/4.0; SLCC1; .NET CLR 2.0.50727; InfoPath.2; .NET CLR 3.5.30729; .NET CLR 3.0.30729)"
85.158.226.103 - - [15/Jun/2010:10:18:36 +0200] "GET /index.html HTTP/1.1" 200 11828 "http://www.asylabwehramt.at/Seiten/Aktuelles.html" "Mozilla/4.0 (compatible; MSIE 8.0; Windows NT 6.0; Trident/4.0; SLCC1; .NET CLR 2.0.50727; InfoPath.2; .NET CLR 3.5.30729; .NET CLR 3.0.30729)"
194.232.79.193 [15] - - [15/Jun/2010:10:21:16 +0200] "GET / HTTP/1.1" 200 11828 "http://derstandard.at/1276413064470/Fall-Zogaj-Der-Staerkere-gibt-niemals-nach" "Mozilla/4.0 (compatible; MSIE 8.0; Windows NT 5.1; Trident/4.0; .NET CLR 1.1.4322; .NET CLR 2.0.50727; .NET CLR 3.0.4506.2152; .NET CLR 3.5.30729)"
194.232.79.193 - - [15/Jun/2010:10:21:38 +0200] "GET /Seiten/Aktuelles.html HTTP/1.1" 200 12570 "http://www.asylabwehramt.at/" "Mozilla/4.0 (compatible; MSIE 8.0; Windows NT 5.1; Trident/4.0; .NET CLR 1.1.4322; .NET CLR 2.0.50727; .NET CLR 3.0.4506.2152; .NET CLR 3.5.30729)"
194.232.79.193 - - [15/Jun/2010:10:22:40 +0200] "GET /Seiten/Material.html HTTP/1.1" 200 11980 "http://www.asylabwehramt.at/Seiten/Aktuelles.html" "Mozilla/4.0 (compatible; MSIE 8.0; Windows NT 5.1; Trident/4.0; .NET CLR 1.1.4322; .NET CLR 2.0.50727; .NET CLR 3.0.4506.2152; .NET CLR 3.5.30729)"
194.232.79.193 - - [15/Jun/2010:10:22:49 +0200] "GET /Material/Hotline_Deutsch.pdf HTTP/1.1" 200 489465 "http://www.asylabwehramt.at/Seiten/Material.html" "Mozilla/4.0 (compatible; MSIE 8.0; Windows NT 5.1; Trident/4.0; .NET CLR 1.1.4322; .NET CLR 2.0.50727; .NET CLR 3.0.4506.2152; .NET CLR 3.5.30729)"
194.232.79.193 - - [15/Jun/2010:10:23:36 +0200] "GET /Seiten/Rundzeichen.html HTTP/1.1" 200 8837 "http://www.asylabwehramt.at/Seiten/Material.html" "Mozilla/4.0 (compatible; MSIE 8.0; Windows NT 5.1; Trident/4.0; .NET CLR 2.0.50727; .NET CLR 3.0.4506.2152; .NET CLR 3.5.30
```

[15]WHOIS record on page 319

```
729)"
194.232.79.193 - - [15/Jun/2010:10:23:50 +0200] "GET /Seiten/Bilder.html HTTP/1.1" 200 9571 "http
://www.asylabwehramt.at/Seiten/Rundzeichen.html" "Mozilla/4.0 (compatible; MSIE 8.0; Windows NT 5
.1; Trident/4.0; .NET CLR 1.1.4322; .NET CLR 2.0.50727; .NET CLR 3.0.4506.2152; .NET CLR 3.5.3072
9)"
194.232.79.193 - - [15/Jun/2010:10:24:04 +0200] "GET /Seiten/Bilder_buero.html HTTP/1.1" 200 1102
6 "http://www.asylabwehramt.at/Seiten/Bilder.html" "Mozilla/4.0 (compatible; MSIE 8.0; Windows NT
5.1; Trident/4.0; .NET CLR 1.1.4322; .NET CLR 2.0.50727; .NET CLR 3.0.4506.2152; .NET CLR 3.5.30
729)"
194.232.79.193 - - [15/Jun/2010:10:24:05 +0200] "GET /Bilder/BAA_photos/IMG_0186.JPG HTTP/1.1" 20
0 103810 "http://www.asylabwehramt.at/Seiten/Bilder_buero.html" "Mozilla/4.0 (compatible; MSIE 8.
0; Windows NT 5.1; Trident/4.0; .NET CLR 1.1.4322; .NET CLR 2.0.50727; .NET CLR 3.0.4506.2152; .N
ET CLR 3.5.30729)"
194.232.79.193 - - [15/Jun/2010:10:24:06 +0200] "GET /Bilder/BAA_photos/IMG_0195.JPG HTTP/1.1" 20
0 122316 "http://www.asylabwehramt.at/Seiten/Bilder_buero.html" "Mozilla/4.0 (compatible; MSIE 8.
0; Windows NT 5.1; Trident/4.0; .NET CLR 1.1.4322; .NET CLR 2.0.50727; .NET CLR 3.0.4506.2152; .N
ET CLR 3.5.30729)"
194.232.79.193 - - [15/Jun/2010:10:24:07 +0200] "GET /Bilder/BAA_photos/IMG_0191.JPG HTTP/1.1" 20
0 124240 "http://www.asylabwehramt.at/Seiten/Bilder_buero.html" "Mozilla/4.0 (compatible; MSIE 8.
0; Windows NT 5.1; Trident/4.0; .NET CLR 1.1.4322; .NET CLR 2.0.50727; .NET CLR 3.0.4506.2152; .N
ET CLR 3.5.30729)"
194.232.79.193 - - [15/Jun/2010:10:25:18 +0200] "GET /Seiten/Images.html HTTP/1.1" 200 9701 "http
://www.asylabwehramt.at/Seiten/Bilder.html" "Mozilla/4.0 (compatible; MSIE 8.0; Windows NT 5.1; T
rident/4.0; .NET CLR 1.1.4322; .NET CLR 2.0.50727; .NET CLR 3.0.4506.2152; .NET CLR 3.5.30729)"
194.232.79.193 - - [15/Jun/2010:10:25:22 +0200] "GET /Seiten/Links_e.html HTTP/1.1" 200 18366 "ht
tp://www.asylabwehramt.at/Seiten/Images.html" "Mozilla/4.0 (compatible; MSIE 8.0; Windows NT 5.1;
Trident/4.0; .NET CLR 1.1.4322; .NET CLR 2.0.50727; .NET CLR 3.0.4506.2152; .NET CLR 3.5.30729)"
194.232.79.193 - - [15/Jun/2010:10:25:44 +0200] "GET /Seiten/Presse.html HTTP/1.1" 200 10956 "htt
```

194.232.79.193 - - [15/Jun/2010:10:25:47 +0200] "GET /OEFFENTLICHKEIT/07062010d.pdf HTTP/1.1" 200 333788 "http://www.asylabwehramt.at/Seiten/Presse.html" "Mozilla/4.0 (compatible; MSIE 8.0; Windows NT 5.1; Trident/4.0; .NET CLR 2.0.50727; .NET CLR 3.0.4506.2152; .NET CLR 3.5.30729)"

194.232.79.193 - - [15/Jun/2010:10:27:21 +0200] "GET /Seiten/Press.html HTTP/1.1" 200 10955 "http://www.asylabwehramt.at/Seiten/Presse.html" "Mozilla/4.0 (compatible; MSIE 8.0; Windows NT 5.1; Trident/4.0; .NET CLR 2.0.50727; .NET CLR 3.0.4506.2152; .NET CLR 3.5.30729)"

194.232.79.193 - - [15/Jun/2010:10:27:31 +0200] "GET /index.html HTTP/1.1" 200 11828 "http://www.asylabwehramt.at/Seiten/Links_e.html" "Mozilla/4.0 (compatible; MSIE 8.0; Windows NT 5.1; Trident/4.0; .NET CLR 2.0.50727; .NET CLR 3.0.4506.2152; .NET CLR 3.5.30729)"

194.232.79.193 - - [15/Jun/2010:10:28:08 +0200] "GET /index_e.html HTTP/1.1" 200 11855 "http://www.asylabwehramt.at/index.html" "Mozilla/4.0 (compatible; MSIE 8.0; Windows NT 5.1; Trident/4.0; .NET CLR 2.0.50727; .NET CLR 3.0.4506.2152; .NET CLR 3.5.30729)"

194.232.79.193 - - [15/Jun/2010:10:28:14 +0200] "GET /Seiten/Orgstrukt.html HTTP/1.1" 200 14086 "http://www.asylabwehramt.at/index.html" "Mozilla/4.0 (compatible; MSIE 8.0; Windows NT 5.1; Trident/4.0; .NET CLR 2.0.50727; .NET CLR 3.0.4506.2152; .NET CLR 3.5.30729)"

194.232.79.193 - - [15/Jun/2010:10:28:39 +0200] "GET /Seiten/Latestnews.html HTTP/1.1" 200 12574 "http://www.asylabwehramt.at/Seiten/Orgstrukt.html" "Mozilla/4.0 (compatible; MSIE 8.0; Windows NT 5.1; Trident/4.0; .NET CLR 2.0.50727; .NET CLR 3.0.4506.2152; .NET CLR 3.5.30729)"

194.232.79.193 - - [15/Jun/2010:10:29:16 +0200] "GET /Seiten/Impressum.html HTTP/1.1" 200 11505 "http://www.asylabwehramt.at/Seiten/Aktuelles.html" "Mozilla/4.0 (compatible; MSIE 8.0; Windows NT 5.1; Trident/4.0; .NET CLR 2.0.50727; .NET CLR 3.0.4506.2152; .NET CLR 3.5.30729)"

194.232.79.193 - - [15/Jun/2010:10:30:49 +0200] "GET /Bilder/Ladung.png HTTP/1.1" 200 114658 "http://www.asylabwehramt.at/Seiten/Material.html" "Mozilla/4.0 (compatible; MSIE 8.0; Windows NT 5.1

; Trident/4.0; .NET CLR 1.1.4322; .NET CLR 2.0.50727; .NET CLR 3.0.4506.2152; .NET CLR 3.5.30729)
"

194.232.79.100 - - [15/Jun/2010:11:39:02 +0200] "GET / HTTP/1.1" 200 11828 "http://www.google.at/search?hl=de&q=**asylabwehramt**&meta=" "Mozilla/4.0 (compatible; MSIE 8.0; Windows NT 6.0; Trident/4.0; SLCC1; .NET CLR 2.0.50727; .NET CLR 3.5.30729; .NET CLR 3.0.30618)"

194.232.79.100 - - [15/Jun/2010:11:41:56 +0200] "GET / HTTP/1.1" 200 11828 "http://www.google.at/search?hl=de&source=hp&q=**asyl+abwehramt**&aq=f&aqi=&aql=&oq=&gs_rfai=" "Mozilla/4.0 (compatible; MSIE 7.0; Windows NT 6.0; SLCC1; .NET CLR 2.0.50727; .NET CLR 3.5.30729; .NET CLR 3.0.30618)"

194.232.79.100 - - [15/Jun/2010:11:42:56 +0200] "GET /Seiten/Aktuelles.html HTTP/1.1" 200 12570 "http://www.asylabwehramt.at/" "Mozilla/4.0 (compatible; MSIE 7.0; Windows NT 6.0; SLCC1; .NET CLR 2.0.50727; .NET CLR 3.5.30729; .NET CLR 3.0.30618)"

194.232.79.100 - - [15/Jun/2010:11:43:32 +0200] "GET /Seiten/Material.html HTTP/1.1" 200 11980 "http://www.asylabwehramt.at/Seiten/Aktuelles.html" "Mozilla/4.0 (compatible; MSIE 7.0; Windows NT 6.0; SLCC1; .NET CLR 2.0.50727; .NET CLR 3.5.30729; .NET CLR 3.0.30618)"

194.232.79.100 - - [15/Jun/2010:11:43:37 +0200] "GET /Seiten/Rundzeichen.html HTTP/1.1" 200 8837 "http://www.asylabwehramt.at/Seiten/Material.html" "Mozilla/4.0 (compatible; MSIE 7.0; Windows NT 6.0; SLCC1; .NET CLR 2.0.50727; .NET CLR 3.5.30729; .NET CLR 3.0.30618)"

194.232.79.100 - - [15/Jun/2010:11:43:41 +0200] "GET /Seiten/Bilder.html HTTP/1.1" 200 9571 "http://www.asylabwehramt.at/Seiten/Rundzeichen.html" "Mozilla/4.0 (compatible; MSIE 7.0; Windows NT 6.0; SLCC1; .NET CLR 2.0.50727; .NET CLR 3.5.30729; .NET CLR 3.0.30618)"

194.232.79.100 - - [15/Jun/2010:11:43:52 +0200] "GET /Seiten/Bilder.html HTTP/1.1" 200 9571 "http://www.asylabwehramt.at/" "Mozilla/4.0 (compatible; MSIE 8.0; Windows NT 6.0; Trident/4.0; SLCC1; .NET CLR 2.0.50727; .NET CLR 3.5.30729; .NET CLR 3.0.30618)"

194.232.79.100 - - [15/Jun/2010:11:43:54 +0200] "GET /Seiten/Links.html HTTP/1.1" 200 18362 "http://www.asylabwehramt.at/Seiten/Bilder.html" "Mozilla/4.0 (compatible; MSIE 7.0; Windows NT 6.0; SLCC1; .NET CLR 2.0.50727; .NET CLR 3.5.30729; .NET CLR 3.0.30618)"

194.232.79.100 - - [15/Jun/2010:11:43:59 +0200] "GET /Seiten/Press.html HTTP/1.1" 200 10955 "http://www.asylabwehramt.at/Seiten/Links.html" "Mozilla/4.0 (compatible; MSIE 7.0; Windows NT 6.0; SL

```
CC1; .NET CLR 2.0.50727; .NET CLR 3.5.30729; .NET CLR 3.0.30618)"

194.232.79.100 - - [15/Jun/2010:11:44:08 +0200] "GET / HTTP/1.1" 200 11828 "-" "Mozilla/4.0 (compatible; MSIE 8.0; Windows NT 5.1; Trident/4.0; .NET CLR 1.1.4322; .NET CLR 3.0.04506.30; .NET CLR 2.0.50727; InfoPath.1; .NET CLR 3.5.30729)"

194.232.79.100 - - [15/Jun/2010:11:44:09 +0200] "GET /favicon.ico HTTP/1.1" 302 340 "-" "Mozilla/5.0 (compatible; Google Desktop/5.9.911.3589; http://desktop.google.com/)"

194.232.79.100 - - [15/Jun/2010:11:44:19 +0200] "GET /Seiten/Impressum.html HTTP/1.1" 200 11505 "http://www.asylabwehramt.at/Seiten/Press.html" "Mozilla/4.0 (compatible; MSIE 7.0; Windows NT 6.0; SLCC1; .NET CLR 2.0.50727; .NET CLR 3.5.30729; .NET CLR 3.0.30618)"

194.232.79.100 - - [15/Jun/2010:11:44:41 +0200] "GET /Seiten/Aktuelles.html HTTP/1.1" 200 12570 "http://www.asylabwehramt.at/" "Mozilla/4.0 (compatible; MSIE 8.0; Windows NT 5.1; Trident/4.0; .NET CLR 3.0.04506.30; .NET CLR 2.0.50727; InfoPath.1; .NET CLR 3.0.4506.2152; .NET CLR 1.1.4322; .NET CLR 3.5.30729)"

194.232.79.100 - - [15/Jun/2010:11:44:52 +0200] "GET /index.html HTTP/1.1" 200 11828 "http://www.asylabwehramt.at/Seiten/Impressum.html" "Mozilla/4.0 (compatible; MSIE 7.0; Windows NT 6.0; SLCC1; .NET CLR 2.0.50727; .NET CLR 3.5.30729; .NET CLR 3.0.30618)"

80.120.179.10 - - [15/Jun/2010:11:58:50 +0200] "GET /favicon.ico HTTP/1.1" 302 340 "-" "Mozilla/4.0 (compatible; MSIE 8.0; Windows NT 5.1; Trident/4.0; .NET CLR 1.1.4322; InfoPath.1)"

80.120.179.10 - - [15/Jun/2010:11:59:34 +0200] "GET /Seiten/Links.html HTTP/1.1" 200 18362 "http://www.asylabwehramt.at/index.html" "Mozilla/4.0 (compatible; MSIE 8.0; Windows NT 5.1; Trident/4.0; .NET CLR 1.1.4322; InfoPath.1)"

80.120.179.10 - - [15/Jun/2010:11:59:38 +0200] "GET /Seiten/Press.html HTTP/1.1" 200 10955 "http://www.asylabwehramt.at/Seiten/Links.html" "Mozilla/4.0 (compatible; MSIE 8.0; Windows NT 5.1; Trident/4.0; .NET CLR 1.1.4322; InfoPath.1)"

91.112.214.67 - - [15/Jun/2010:12:03:14 +0200] "GET / HTTP/1.1" 200 11828 "-" "Mozilla/4.0 (compatible; MSIE 8.0; Windows NT 5.1; Trident/4.0; .NET CLR 2.0.50727; InfoPath.2; .NET CLR 3.0.4506.2152; .NET CLR 3.5.30729)"

88.116.224.102 - - [15/Jun/2010:12:19:54 +0200] "GET / HTTP/1.1" 200 11828 "-" "Mozilla/4.0 (comp
```

```
atible; MSIE 8.0; Windows NT 6.0; Trident/4.0; GTB0.0; SLCC1; .NET CLR 2.0.50727; .NET CLR 3.5.21
022; .NET CLR 3.5.30729; InfoPath.1; .NET CLR 3.0.30729; Tablet PC 2.0)"
193.104.125.4^16 - - [15/Jun/2010:12:42:15 +0200] "GET /Seiten/Orgstrukt.html HTTP/1.1" 200 14086 "-
" "Mozilla/4.0 (compatible; MSIE 7.0; Windows NT 5.1; .NET CLR 2.0.50727; .NET CLR 3.0.4506.2152;
.NET CLR 3.5.30729)"
193.104.125.4 - - [15/Jun/2010:12:42:28 +0200] "GET /index.html HTTP/1.1" 200 11828 "http://www.a
sylabwehramt.at/Seiten/Orgstrukt.html" "Mozilla/4.0 (compatible; MSIE 7.0; Windows NT 5.1; .NET C
LR 2.0.50727; .NET CLR 3.0.4506.2152; .NET CLR 3.5.30729)"
193.104.125.4 - - [15/Jun/2010:12:42:35 +0200] "GET /Seiten/Material.html HTTP/1.1" 200 11980 "ht
tp://www.asylabwehramt.at/index.html" "Mozilla/4.0 (compatible; MSIE 7.0; Windows NT 5.1; .NET CL
R 2.0.50727; .NET CLR 3.0.4506.2152; .NET CLR 3.5.30729)"
193.104.125.4 - - [15/Jun/2010:12:42:40 +0200] "GET /Seiten/Rundzeichen.html HTTP/1.1" 200 8837 "
http://www.asylabwehramt.at/Seiten/Material.html" "Mozilla/4.0 (compatible; MSIE 7.0; Windows NT
5.1; .NET CLR 2.0.50727; .NET CLR 3.0.4506.2152; .NET CLR 3.5.30729)"
193.104.125.4 - - [15/Jun/2010:12:42:41 +0200] "GET /Bilder/Asylabwehramt_Seal_800x800.png HTTP/1
.1" 200 269132 "http://www.asylabwehramt.at/Seiten/Rundzeichen.html" "Mozilla/4.0 (compatible; MS
IE 7.0; Windows NT 5.1; .NET CLR 2.0.50727; .NET CLR 3.0.4506.2152; .NET CLR 3.5.30729)"
193.104.125.4 - - [15/Jun/2010:12:42:52 +0200] "GET /Seiten/Links.html HTTP/1.1" 200 18362 "http:
//www.asylabwehramt.at/Seiten/Rundzeichen.html" "Mozilla/4.0 (compatible; MSIE 7.0; Windows NT 5.
1; .NET CLR 2.0.50727; .NET CLR 3.0.4506.2152; .NET CLR 3.5.30729)"
193.104.125.4 - - [15/Jun/2010:12:43:26 +0200] "GET /Seiten/Press.html HTTP/1.1" 200 10955 "http:
//www.asylabwehramt.at/Seiten/Links.html" "Mozilla/4.0 (compatible; MSIE 7.0; Windows NT 5.1; .NE
T CLR 2.0.50727; .NET CLR 3.0.4506.2152; .NET CLR 3.5.30729)"
193.104.125.4 - - [15/Jun/2010:12:43:37 +0200] "GET /Seiten/Impressum.html HTTP/1.1" 200 11505 "h
ttp://www.asylabwehramt.at/Seiten/Press.html" "Mozilla/4.0 (compatible; MSIE 7.0; Windows NT 5.1;
.NET CLR 2.0.50727; .NET CLR 3.0.4506.2152; .NET CLR 3.5.30729)"
```

---

[16] WHOIS record on page 305

```
193.104.125.4 - - [15/Jun/2010:12:43:57 +0200] "GET /Seiten/Images.html HTTP/1.1" 200 9701 "http:
//www.asylabwehramt.at/Seiten/Impressum.html" "Mozilla/4.0 (compatible; MSIE 7.0; Windows NT 5.1;
.NET CLR 2.0.50727; .NET CLR 3.0.4506.2152; .NET CLR 3.5.30729)"
193.104.125.4 - - [15/Jun/2010:12:44:03 +0200] "GET /Seiten/Ausseneinsaetze.html HTTP/1.1" 200 91
90 "http://www.asylabwehramt.at/Seiten/Images.html" "Mozilla/4.0 (compatible; MSIE 7.0; Windows N
T 5.1; .NET CLR 2.0.50727; .NET CLR 3.0.4506.2152; .NET CLR 3.5.30729)"
80.120.179.10 - - [15/Jun/2010:13:26:35 +0200] "GET /Material/Hotline_Deutsch.pdf HTTP/1.1" 200 4
89465 "http://www.asylabwehramt.at/" "Mozilla/4.0 (compatible; MSIE 6.0; Windows NT 5.1; SV1; .NE
T CLR 1.1.4322; .NET CLR 2.0.50727; .NET CLR 3.0.04506.30; .NET CLR 3.0.04506.648; InfoPath.2)"
80.120.179.10 - - [15/Jun/2010:13:32:03 +0200] "GET /Seiten/Bilder.html HTTP/1.1" 200 9571 "http:
//www.asylabwehramt.at/" "Mozilla/4.0 (compatible; MSIE 6.0; Windows NT 5.1; SV1; .NET CLR 1.1.43
22)"
80.120.179.10 - - [15/Jun/2010:13:32:19 +0200] "GET /Seiten/Ausseneinsaetze.html HTTP/1.1" 200 91
90 "http://www.asylabwehramt.at/Seiten/Bilder.html" "Mozilla/4.0 (compatible; MSIE 6.0; Windows N
T 5.1; SV1; .NET CLR 1.1.4322)"
80.120.179.10 - - [15/Jun/2010:13:32:27 +0200] "GET /Seiten/Rundzeichen.html HTTP/1.1" 200 8837 "
http://www.asylabwehramt.at/Seiten/Ausseneinsaetze.html" "Mozilla/4.0 (compatible; MSIE 6.0; Wind
ows NT 5.1; SV1; .NET CLR 1.1.4322)"
80.120.179.10 - - [15/Jun/2010:13:34:42 +0200] "GET /OEFFENTLICHKEIT/07062010d.pdf HTTP/1.1" 200
333788 "http://www.asylabwehramt.at/Seiten/Press.html" "Mozilla/4.0 (compatible; MSIE 6.0; Window
s NT 5.1; SV1; .NET CLR 1.1.4322)"
194.232.79.100 - - [15/Jun/2010:13:35:22 +0200] "GET / HTTP/1.1" 200 11828 "http://www.google.at/
search?q=asylabwehramt&ie=utf-8&oe=utf-8&aq=t&rls=org.mozilla:de:official&client=firefox-a" "Mozi
lla/5.0 (Windows; U; Windows NT 6.0; de; rv:1.9.0.6) Gecko/2009011913 Firefox/3.6 (.NET CLR 3.5
.30729)"
194.232.79.100 - - [15/Jun/2010:13:35:23 +0200] "GET /favicon.ico HTTP/1.1" 302 340 "-" "Mozilla/
5.0 (Windows; U; Windows NT 6.0; de; rv:1.9.0.6) Gecko/2009011913 Firefox/3.6 (.NET CLR 3.5.307
29)"
```

```
194.232.79.100 - - [15/Jun/2010:13:35:24 +0200] "GET /favicon.ico HTTP/1.1" 302 340 "-" "Mozilla/5.0 (Windows; U; Windows NT 6.0; de; rv:1.9.0.6) Gecko/2009011913 Firefox/3.0.6 (.NET CLR 3.5.307 29)"
194.232.79.100 - - [15/Jun/2010:13:36:55 +0200] "GET /Seiten/Aktuelles.html HTTP/1.1" 200 12570 "http://www.asylabwehramt.at/" "Mozilla/5.0 (Windows; U; Windows NT 6.0; de; rv:1.9.0.6) Gecko/2009011913 Firefox/3.0.6 (.NET CLR 3.5.30729)"
194.232.79.100 - - [15/Jun/2010:13:38:49 +0200] "GET /Seiten/Rundzeichen.html HTTP/1.1" 200 8837 "http://www.asylabwehramt.at/Seiten/Aktuelles.html" "Mozilla/5.0 (Windows; U; Windows NT 6.0; de; rv:1.9.0.6) Gecko/2009011913 Firefox/3.0.6 (.NET CLR 3.5.30729)"
194.232.79.100 - - [15/Jun/2010:13:38:58 +0200] "GET /Seiten/Bilder.html HTTP/1.1" 200 9571 "http://www.asylabwehramt.at/Seiten/Rundzeichen.html" "Mozilla/5.0 (Windows; U; Windows NT 6.0; de; rv:1.9.0.6) Gecko/2009011913 Firefox/3.0.6 (.NET CLR 3.5.30729)"
194.232.79.100 - - [15/Jun/2010:13:40:23 +0200] "GET /index.html HTTP/1.1" 200 11828 "http://www.asylabwehramt.at/Seiten/Bilder.html" "Mozilla/5.0 (Windows; U; Windows NT 6.0; de; rv:1.9.0.6) Gecko/2009011913 Firefox/3.0.6 (.NET CLR 3.5.30729)"
80.120.179.10 - - [15/Jun/2010:14:04:20 +0200] "GET /Bilder/Ladung.png HTTP/1.1" 200 114658 "http://www.asylabwehramt.at/Seiten/Material.html" "Mozilla/4.0 (compatible; MSIE 6.0; Windows NT 5.1; SV1; .NET CLR 1.1.4322; .NET CLR 2.0.50727; .NET CLR 3.0.4506.2152; .NET CLR 3.5.30729; MS-RTC LM 8)"
80.120.179.10 - - [15/Jun/2010:14:15:47 +0200] "GET /index_e.html HTTP/1.1" 200 11855 "http://www.asylabwehramt.at/" "Mozilla/4.0 (compatible; MSIE 6.0; Windows NT 5.1; SV1; .NET CLR 1.1.4322; .NET CLR 2.0.50727; .NET CLR 3.0.04506.30; .NET CLR 3.0.04506.648; InfoPath.2)"
80.120.179.10 - - [15/Jun/2010:14:15:49 +0200] "GET /Seiten/Latestnews.html HTTP/1.1" 200 12574 "http://www.asylabwehramt.at/index_e.html" "Mozilla/4.0 (compatible; MSIE 6.0; Windows NT 5.1; SV1; .NET CLR 1.1.4322; .NET CLR 2.0.50727; .NET CLR 3.0.04506.30; .NET CLR 3.0.04506.648; InfoPath.2)"
80.120.179.10 - - [15/Jun/2010:14:16:03 +0200] "GET /Seiten/Impressum.html HTTP/1.1" 200 11505 "http://www.asylabwehramt.at/Seiten/Latestnews.html" "Mozilla/4.0 (compatible; MSIE 6.0; Windows NT 2)"
```

5.1; SV1; .NET CLR 1.1.4322; .NET CLR 2.0.50727; .NET CLR 3.0.04506.648; InfoPath.2)"

80.120.179.10 - - [15/Jun/2010:14:23:33 +0200] "GET /Seiten/Bilder_buero.html HTTP/1.1" 200 11026 "http://www.asylabwehramt.at/Seiten/Bilder.html" "Mozilla/4.0 (compatible; MSIE 6.0; Windows NT 5.1; SV1; .NET CLR 1.1.4322; .NET CLR 2.0.50727; .NET CLR 3.0.04506.30; .NET CLR 3.0.04506.648; InfoPath.2)"

80.120.179.10 - - [15/Jun/2010:14:23:34 +0200] "GET /Bilder/BAA_photos/IMG_0188.JPG HTTP/1.1" 200 179395 "http://www.asylabwehramt.at/Seiten/Bilder_buero.html" "Mozilla/4.0 (compatible; MSIE 6.0; Windows NT 5.1; SV1; .NET CLR 1.1.4322; .NET CLR 2.0.50727; .NET CLR 3.0.04506.30; .NET CLR 3.0.04506.648; InfoPath.2)"

80.120.179.10 - - [15/Jun/2010:14:27:39 +0200] "GET /Material/Asyl_Jahresstatistik_2009.pdf HTTP/1.1" 200 680643 "http://www.asylabwehramt.at/Seiten/Material.html" "Mozilla/4.0 (compatible; MSIE 6.0; Windows NT 5.1; SV1; .NET CLR 1.1.4322; .NET CLR 2.0.50727; .NET CLR 3.0.04506.30; .NET CLR 3.0.04506.648; InfoPath.2)"

80.120.179.10 - - [15/Jun/2010:14:27:52 +0200] "GET /Seiten/Orgstrukt.html HTTP/1.1" 200 14086 "http://www.asylabwehramt.at/index.html" "Mozilla/4.0 (compatible; MSIE 6.0; Windows NT 5.1; SV1; .NET CLR 1.1.4322; .NET CLR 2.0.50727; .NET CLR 3.0.04506.30; .NET CLR 3.0.04506.648; InfoPath.2)"

88.116.224.102 - - [15/Jun/2010:15:13:22 +0200] "GET / HTTP/1.1" 304 - "http://www.google.at/search?sourceid=navclient&hl=de&ie=UTF-8&rlz=1T4SUNC_deAT356AT356&q=asylabwehramt" "Mozilla/4.0 (compatible; MSIE 8.0; Windows NT 6.0; Trident/4.0; GTB0.0; SLCC1; .NET CLR 2.0.50727; .NET CLR 3.5.21022; .NET CLR 3.5.30729; InfoPath.1; .NET CLR 3.0.30729; Tablet PC 2.0)"&

88.116.224.102 - - [15/Jun/2010:15:13:23 +0200] "GET /Bilder/Header_AAbA.jpg HTTP/1.1" 304 - "http://www.asylabwehramt.at/" "Mozilla/4.0 (compatible; MSIE 8.0; Windows NT 6.0; Trident/4.0; GTB0.0; SLCC1; .NET CLR 2.0.50727; .NET CLR 3.5.21022; .NET CLR 3.5.30729; InfoPath.1; .NET CLR 3.0.30729; Tablet PC 2.0)"

194.232.79.100 - - [15/Jun/2010:16:26:16 +0200] "GET / HTTP/1.1" 200 11828 "-" "Mozilla/4.0 (compatible; MSIE 7.0; Windows NT 5.1; GTB6.5; .NET CLR 1.1.4322; .NET CLR 2.0.50727; .NET CLR 3.0.045

06.30; .NET CLR 3.0.4506.2152; .NET CLR 3.5.30729)"

194.232.79.100 - - [15/Jun/2010:16:26:24 +0200] "GET /Seiten/Aktuelles.html HTTP/1.1" 200 12570 "http://asylabwehramt.at/" "Mozilla/4.0 (compatible; MSIE 7.0; Windows NT 5.1; GTB6.5; .NET CLR 2.0.50727; .NET CLR 1.1.4322; .NET CLR 3.0.4506.2152; .NET CLR 3.5.30729)"

194.232.79.100 - - [15/Jun/2010:16:26:25 +0200] "GET /Bilder/leistung_2.jpg HTTP/1.1" 200 4918 "http://asylabwehramt.at/Seiten/Aktuelles.html" "Mozilla/4.0 (compatible; MSIE 7.0; Windows NT 5.1; GTB6.5; .NET CLR 2.0.50727; .NET CLR 1.1.4322; .NET CLR 3.0.4506.2152; .NET CLR 3.5.30729)"

194.232.79.100 - - [15/Jun/2010:16:26:50 +0200] "GET /Seiten/Rundzeichen.html HTTP/1.1" 200 8837 "http://asylabwehramt.at/Seiten/Aktuelles.html" "Mozilla/4.0 (compatible; MSIE 7.0; Windows NT 5.1; GTB6.5; .NET CLR 2.0.50727; .NET CLR 1.1.4322; .NET CLR 3.0.4506.2152; .NET CLR 3.5.30729)"

194.232.79.100 - - [15/Jun/2010:16:26:55 +0200] "GET /Seiten/Material.html HTTP/1.1" 200 11980 "http://asylabwehramt.at/Seiten/Rundzeichen.html" "Mozilla/4.0 (compatible; MSIE 7.0; Windows NT 5.1; GTB6.5; .NET CLR 2.0.50727; .NET CLR 1.1.4322; .NET CLR 3.0.4506.2152; .NET CLR 3.5.30729)"

194.232.79.100 - - [15/Jun/2010:16:26:59 +0200] "GET /Bilder/flyer_nigeria_Internet.pdf HTTP/1.1" 200 702826 "http://asylabwehramt.at/Seiten/Material.html" "Mozilla/4.0 (compatible; MSIE 7.0; Windows NT 5.1; GTB6.5; .NET CLR 2.0.50727; .NET CLR 1.1.4322; .NET CLR 3.0.04506.30; .NET CLR 3.5.30729)"

194.232.79.100 - - [15/Jun/2010:16:27:01 +0200] "GET /Bilder/flyer_nigeria_Internet.pdf HTTP/1.1" 206 414331 "-" "Mozilla/4.0 (compatible; MSIE 7.0; Windows NT 5.1; GTB6.5; .NET CLR 2.0.50727; .NET CLR 1.1.4322; .NET CLR 3.0.04506.30; .NET CLR 3.5.30729)"

194.232.79.100 - - [15/Jun/2010:16:27:33 +0200] "GET /Bilder/Ladung.png HTTP/1.1" 200 114658 "http://asylabwehramt.at/Seiten/Material.html" "Mozilla/4.0 (compatible; MSIE 7.0; Windows NT 5.1; GTB6.5; .NET CLR 2.0.50727; .NET CLR 1.1.4322; .NET CLR 3.0.04506.30; .NET CLR 3.5.30729)"

194.232.79.100 - - [15/Jun/2010:16:27:50 +0200] "GET /Material/Hotline_Deutsch.pdf HTTP/1.1" 200

489465 "http://asylabwehramt.at/Seiten/Material.html" "Mozilla/4.0 (compatible; MSIE 7.0; Windows NT 5.1; GTB6.5; .NET CLR 2.0.50727; .NET CLR 1.1.4322; .NET CLR 3.0.04506.30; .NET CLR 3.0.4506.2152; .NET CLR 3.5.30729)"

194.232.79.100 - - [15/Jun/2010:16:28:20 +0200] "GET /Material/Hotline_Franzoesisch.PDF HTTP/1.1" 200 515416 "http://asylabwehramt.at/Seiten/Material.html" "Mozilla/4.0 (compatible; MSIE 7.0; Windows NT 5.1; GTB6.5; .NET CLR 2.0.50727; .NET CLR 1.1.4322; .NET CLR 3.0.04506.30; .NET CLR 3.0.4506.2152; .NET CLR 3.5.30729)"

80.120.179.10 - - [15/Jun/2010:17:12:37 +0200] "GET / HTTP/1.1" 200 11828 "http://www.google.at/url?sa=t&source=web&cd=1&ved=0CBUQFjAA&url=http%3A%2F%2Fwww.asylabwehramt.at%2F&rct=j&q=`asyl+abweh ramt`&ei=Y5gXTKqvO0dKMOPDLvYkL&usg=AFQjCNEy1zWClvnxklPAGifRc344_OU4Q" "Mozilla/4.0 (compatible; MSIE 8.0; Windows NT 5.1; Trident/4.0; .NET CLR 1.1.4322; InfoPath.1)"

80.120.179.10 - - [15/Jun/2010:17:12:38 +0200] "GET /favicon.ico HTTP/1.1" 302 340 "-" "Mozilla/4.0 (compatible; MSIE 8.0; Windows NT 5.1; Trident/4.0; .NET CLR 1.1.4322; InfoPath.1)"

80.120.179.10 - - [15/Jun/2010:17:14:12 +0200] "GET /Seiten/Aktuelles.html HTTP/1.1" 200 12570 "http://www.asylabwehramt.at/Seiten/Orgstrukt.html" "Mozilla/4.0 (compatible; MSIE 8.0; Windows NT 5.1; Trident/4.0; .NET CLR 1.1.4322; InfoPath.1)"

80.120.179.10 - - [15/Jun/2010:17:14:23 +0200] "GET /Seiten/Material.html HTTP/1.1" 200 11980 "http://www.asylabwehramt.at/Seiten/Aktuelles.html" "Mozilla/4.0 (compatible; MSIE 8.0; Windows NT 5.1; Trident/4.0; .NET CLR 1.1.4322; InfoPath.1)"

80.120.179.10 - - [15/Jun/2010:17:17:09 +0200] "GET /index.html HTTP/1.1" 200 11828 "http://www.asylabwehramt.at/Seiten/Links.html" "Mozilla/4.0 (compatible; MSIE 8.0; Windows NT 5.1; Trident/4.0; .NET CLR 1.1.4322; InfoPath.1)"

80.120.179.10 - - [16/Jun/2010:01:28:26 +0200] "GET /Seiten/Press.html HTTP/1.1" 200 10955 "http://www.asylabwehramt.at/Seiten/Aktuelles.html" "Mozilla/4.0 (compatible; MSIE 6.0; Windows NT 5.1; SV1; .NET CLR 1.1.4322; InfoPath.1)"

80.120.179.10 - - [16/Jun/2010:01:28:35 +0200] "GET /OEFFENTLICHKEIT/07062010d.pdf HTTP/1.1" 200 333788 "http://www.asylabwehramt.at/Seiten/Press.html" "Mozilla/4.0 (compatible; MSIE 6.0; Windows NT 5.1; SV1; .NET CLR 1.1.4322; InfoPath.1)"

79

```
78.41.144.41 - - [16/Jun/2010:06:57:41 +0200] "GET /index.html HTTP/1.0" 200 11828 "-" "Mozilla/4
.0 (compatible; MSIE 7.0; Windows NT 5.1)"
78.41.144.41 - - [16/Jun/2010:06:57:42 +0200] "GET /asyl.css HTTP/1.0" 200 860 "http://www.asylab
wehramt.at/index.html" "Mozilla/4.0 (compatible; MSIE 7.0; Windows NT 5.1)"
85.158.226.32 [17] - - [16/Jun/2010:07:52:59 +0200] "GET / HTTP/1.1" 200 11828 "-" "Mozilla/4.0 (compa
tible; MSIE 7.0; Windows NT 5.1; .NET CLR 1.1.4322; .NET CLR 2.0.50727; .NET CLR 3.0.4506.2152; .
NET CLR 3.5.30729)"
85.158.226.32 - - [16/Jun/2010:07:53:00 +0200] "GET /favicon.ico HTTP/1.1" 302 340 "-" "Mozilla/4
.0 (compatible; MSIE 7.0; Windows NT 5.1; .NET CLR 1.1.4322; .NET CLR 2.0.50727; .NET CLR 3.0.450
6.2152; .NET CLR 3.5.30729)"
85.158.226.32 - - [16/Jun/2010:07:54:36 +0200] "GET /Seiten/Bilder.html HTTP/1.1" 200 9571 "http:
//www.asylabwehramt.at/" "Mozilla/4.0 (compatible; MSIE 7.0; Windows NT 5.1; .NET CLR 1.1.4322; .
NET CLR 2.0.50727; .NET CLR 3.0.4506.2152; .NET CLR 3.5.30729)"
85.158.226.32 - - [16/Jun/2010:07:54:45 +0200] "GET /Seiten/Aktuelles.html HTTP/1.1" 200 12570 "h
ttp://www.asylabwehramt.at/Seiten/Bilder.html" "Mozilla/4.0 (compatible; MSIE 7.0; Windows NT 5.1
; .NET CLR 1.1.4322; .NET CLR 2.0.50727; .NET CLR 3.0.4506.2152; .NET CLR 3.5.30729)"
85.158.226.32 - - [16/Jun/2010:07:54:46 +0200] "GET /Bilder/fitnesscenter_traiskirchen.jpg HTTP/1
.1" 200 5721 "http://www.asylabwehramt.at/Seiten/Aktuelles.html" "Mozilla/4.0 (compatible; MSIE 7
.0; Windows NT 5.1; .NET CLR 1.1.4322; .NET CLR 2.0.50727; .NET CLR 3.0.4506.2152; .NET CLR 3.5.3
0729)"
85.158.226.32 - - [16/Jun/2010:07:56:14 +0200] "GET /Seiten/Press.html HTTP/1.1" 200 10955 "http:
//www.asylabwehramt.at/Seiten/Aktuelles.html" "Mozilla/4.0 (compatible; MSIE 7.0; Windows NT 5.1;
.NET CLR 1.1.4322; .NET CLR 2.0.50727; .NET CLR 3.0.4506.2152; .NET CLR 3.5.30729)"
80.120.179.10 - - [16/Jun/2010:08:11:58 +0200] "GET /Material/Hotline_Deutsch.pdf HTTP/1.1" 200 4
89465 "http://www.asylabwehramt.at/" "Mozilla/4.0 (compatible; MSIE 6.0; Windows NT 5.1; SV1; .NE
T CLR 1.1.4322; .NET CLR 2.0.50727; .NET CLR 3.0.04506.30; .NET CLR 3.0.04506.648; InfoPath.2)"
```

---

[17]WHOIS record on page 304

```
80.120.179.10 - - [16/Jun/2010:08:14:33 +0200] "GET /Seiten/Rundzeichen.html HTTP/1.1" 200 8837 "
http://www.asylabwehramt.at/Seiten/Material.html" "Mozilla/4.0 (compatible; MSIE 6.0; Windows NT
5.1; SV1; .NET CLR 1.1.4322; .NET CLR 2.0.50727; .NET CLR 3.0.04506.30; .NET CLR 3.0.04506.648; I
nfoPath.2)"

80.120.179.10 - - [16/Jun/2010:08:14:35 +0200] "GET /Seiten/Bilder.html HTTP/1.1" 200 9571 "http:
//www.asylabwehramt.at/Seiten/Rundzeichen.html" "Mozilla/4.0 (compatible; MSIE 6.0; Windows NT 5.
1; SV1; .NET CLR 1.1.4322; .NET CLR 2.0.50727; .NET CLR 3.0.04506.30; .NET CLR 3.0.04506.648; Inf
oPath.2)"

80.120.179.10 - - [16/Jun/2010:08:14:46 +0200] "GET /Seiten/Links.html HTTP/1.1" 200 18362 "http:
//www.asylabwehramt.at/Seiten/Bilder.html" "Mozilla/4.0 (compatible; MSIE 6.0; Windows NT 5.1; SV
1; .NET CLR 1.1.4322; .NET CLR 2.0.50727; .NET CLR 3.0.04506.30; .NET CLR 3.0.04506.648; InfoPath
.2)"

80.120.179.10 - - [16/Jun/2010:08:14:47 +0200] "GET /Bilder/IBM.png HTTP/1.1" 200 8413 "http://ww
w.asylabwehramt.at/Seiten/Links.html" "Mozilla/4.0 (compatible; MSIE 6.0; Windows NT 5.1; SV1; .N
ET CLR 1.1.4322; .NET CLR 2.0.50727; .NET CLR 3.0.04506.30; .NET CLR 3.0.04506.648; InfoPath.2)"

88.116.224.102 - - [16/Jun/2010:08:32:52 +0200] "GET / HTTP/1.1" 304 - "http://www.google.at/sear
ch?sourceid=navclient&aq=3h&oq=&hl=de&ie=UTF-8&rlz=1T4SUNC_deAT356AT356&q=asylabwehramt" "Mozilla
/4.0 (compatible; MSIE 8.0; Windows NT 6.0; Trident/4.0; GTB0.0; SLCC1; .NET CLR 2.0.50727; .NET
CLR 3.5.21022; .NET CLR 3.5.30729; InfoPath.1; .NET CLR 3.0.30729; Tablet PC 2.0)"

88.116.224.102 - - [16/Jun/2010:08:33:13 +0200] "GET /Seiten/Rundzeichen.html HTTP/1.1" 200 8837
"http://www.asylabwehramt.at/" "Mozilla/4.0 (compatible; MSIE 8.0; Windows NT 6.0; Trident/4.0; G
TB0.0; SLCC1; .NET CLR 2.0.50727; .NET CLR 3.5.21022; .NET CLR 3.5.30729; InfoPath.1; .NET CLR 3.
0.30729; Tablet PC 2.0)"

88.116.224.102 - - [16/Jun/2010:08:33:14 +0200] "GET /Bilder/Asylabwehramt_Seal_800x800.png HTTP/
1.1" 304 - "http://www.asylabwehramt.at/Seiten/Rundzeichen.html" "Mozilla/4.0 (compatible; MSIE 8
.0; Windows NT 6.0; Trident/4.0; GTB0.0; SLCC1; .NET CLR 2.0.50727; .NET CLR 3.5.21022; .NET CLR
3.5.30729; InfoPath.1; .NET CLR 3.0.30729; Tablet PC 2.0)"
```

```
88.116.224.102 - - [16/Jun/2010:08:33:33 +0200] "GET /Seiten/Links.html HTTP/1.1" 304 - "http://w
ww.asylabwehramt.at/Seiten/Rundzeichen.html" "Mozilla/4.0 (compatible; MSIE 8.0; Windows NT 6.0;
Trident/4.0; GTB0.0; SLCC1; .NET CLR 2.0.50727; .NET CLR 3.5.21022; .NET CLR 3.5.30729; InfoPath.
1; .NET CLR 3.0.30729; Tablet PC 2.0)"
88.116.224.102 - - [16/Jun/2010:08:34:19 +0200] "GET /Seiten/Aktuelles.html HTTP/1.1" 200 12570 "
http://www.asylabwehramt.at/Seiten/Links.html" "Mozilla/4.0 (compatible; MSIE 8.0; Windows NT 6.0
; Trident/4.0; GTB0.0; SLCC1; .NET CLR 2.0.50727; .NET CLR 3.5.21022; .NET CLR 3.5.30729; InfoPat
h.1; .NET CLR 3.0.30729; Tablet PC 2.0)"
80.120.179.10 - - [16/Jun/2010:08:49:32 +0200] "GET /asyl.css HTTP/1.1" 304 - "http://www.asylabw
ehramt.at/" "Mozilla/4.0 (compatible; MSIE 8.0; Windows NT 5.1; Trident/4.0; .NET CLR 1.1.4322; I
nfoPath.1; MS-RTC LM 8)"
80.120.179.10 - - [16/Jun/2010:08:49:33 +0200] "GET /Bilder/Header_AAbA.jpg HTTP/1.1" 304 - "http
://www.asylabwehramt.at/" "Mozilla/4.0 (compatible; MSIE 8.0; Windows NT 5.1; Trident/4.0; .NET C
LR 1.1.4322; InfoPath.1; MS-RTC LM 8)"
80.120.179.10 - - [16/Jun/2010:08:51:26 +0200] "GET /Seiten/Impressum.html HTTP/1.1" 200 11505 "h
ttp://www.asylabwehramt.at/" "Mozilla/4.0 (compatible; MSIE 8.0; Windows NT 5.1; Trident/4.0; .NE
T CLR 1.1.4322; InfoPath.1; MS-RTC LM 8)"
80.120.179.10 - - [16/Jun/2010:08:51:54 +0200] "GET /Bilder/Ladung.png HTTP/1.1" 200 114658 "http
://www.asylabwehramt.at/Seiten/Material.html" "Mozilla/4.0 (compatible; MSIE 8.0; Windows NT 5.1;
Trident/4.0; .NET CLR 1.1.4322; InfoPath.1; MS-RTC LM 8)"
80.120.179.10 - - [16/Jun/2010:08:52:07 +0200] "GET /Bilder/flyer_nigeria_Internet.pdf HTTP/1.1"
200 702826 "http://www.asylabwehramt.at/Seiten/Material.html" "Mozilla/4.0 (compatible; MSIE 8.0;
Windows NT 5.1; Trident/4.0; .NET CLR 1.1.4322; InfoPath.1; MS-RTC LM 8)"
80.120.179.10 - - [16/Jun/2010:08:52:16 +0200] "GET /Material/Asyl_Jahresstatistik_2009.pdf HTTP/
1.1" 200 680643 "http://www.asylabwehramt.at/Seiten/Material.html" "Mozilla/4.0 (compatible; MSIE
8.0; Windows NT 5.1; Trident/4.0; .NET CLR 1.1.4322; InfoPath.1; MS-RTC LM 8)"
80.120.179.10 - - [16/Jun/2010:08:52:56 +0200] "GET /Seiten/Presse.html HTTP/1.1" 200 10956 "http
://www.asylabwehramt.at/Seiten/Links.html" "Mozilla/4.0 (compatible; MSIE 8.0; Windows NT 5.1; Tr
```

ident/4.0; .NET CLR 1.1.4322; InfoPath.1; MS-RTC LM 8)"
193.171.152.33 - - [16/Jun/2010:08:53:01 +0200] "GET / HTTP/1.1" 304 - "-" "Mozilla/4.0 (compatible; MSIE 7.0; Windows NT 5.1; GTB6.5; InfoPath.1)"
193.171.152.33 - - [16/Jun/2010:08:53:02 +0200] "GET /Bilder/Header_AAbA.jpg HTTP/1.1" 304 - "http://www.asylabwehramt.at/" "Mozilla/4.0 (compatible; MSIE 7.0; Windows NT 5.1; GTB6.5; InfoPath.1)"
193.171.152.33 - - [16/Jun/2010:08:54:27 +0200] "GET /Seiten/Presse.html HTTP/1.1" 200 10956 "http://www.asylabwehramt.at/" "Mozilla/4.0 (compatible; MSIE 7.0; Windows NT 5.1; GTB6.5; InfoPath.1)"
193.171.152.33 - - [16/Jun/2010:08:55:01 +0200] "GET /Seiten/Bilder.html HTTP/1.1" 200 9571 "http://www.asylabwehramt.at/Seiten/Presse.html" "Mozilla/4.0 (compatible; MSIE 7.0; Windows NT 5.1; GTB6.5; InfoPath.1)"
193.171.152.33 - - [16/Jun/2010:08:55:02 +0200] "GET /asyl.css HTTP/1.1" 304 - "http://www.asylabwehramt.at/Seiten/Bilder.html" "Mozilla/4.0 (compatible; MSIE 7.0; Windows NT 5.1; GTB6.5; InfoPath.1)"
193.171.152.33 - - [16/Jun/2010:08:55:39 +0200] "GET /Seiten/Links.html HTTP/1.1" 200 18362 "http://www.asylabwehramt.at/Seiten/Presse.html" "Mozilla/4.0 (compatible; MSIE 7.0; Windows NT 5.1; GTB6.5; InfoPath.1)"
193.171.152.33 - - [16/Jun/2010:09:09:31 +0200] "GET / HTTP/1.1" 304 - "http://www.google.at/search?hl=de&q=asylabwehramt &meta=" "Mozilla/4.0 (compatible; MSIE 8.0; Windows NT 5.1; Trident/4.0; InfoPath.1; .NET CLR 1.1.4322; .NET CLR 2.0.50727; .NET CLR 3.0.04506.648; .NET CLR 3.0.4506.2152; .NET CLR 3.5.30729)"
193.171.152.33 - - [16/Jun/2010:09:09:33 +0200] "GET /favicon.ico HTTP/1.1" 302 340 "-" "Mozilla/4.0 (compatible; MSIE 8.0; Windows NT 5.1; Trident/4.0; InfoPath.1; .NET CLR 1.1.4322; .NET CLR 2.0.50727; .NET CLR 3.0.04506.30; .NET CLR 3.0.04506.648; .NET CLR 3.0.4506.2152; .NET CLR 3.5.30729)"
193.171.152.33 - - [16/Jun/2010:09:09:42 +0200] "GET /Seiten/Impressum.html HTTP/1.1" 200 11505 "http://www.asylabwehramt.at/" "Mozilla/4.0 (compatible; MSIE 8.0; Windows NT 5.1; Trident/4.0; In

```
foPath.1; .NET CLR 1.1.4322; .NET CLR 2.0.50727; .NET CLR 3.0.04506.30; .NET CLR 3.0.04506.648; .NET CLR 3.0.4506.2152; .NET CLR 3.5.30729)"
193.171.152.33 - - [16/Jun/2010:09:10:06 +0200] "GET /Seiten/Seal.html HTTP/1.1" 200 8872 "http://www.asylabwehramt.at/" "Mozilla/4.0 (compatible; MSIE 8.0; Windows NT 5.1; Trident/4.0; InfoPath.1; .NET CLR 1.1.4322; .NET CLR 2.0.50727; .NET CLR 3.0.04506.648; .NET CLR 3.0.04506.30; .NET CLR 3.0.4506.2152; .NET CLR 3.5.30729)"
193.171.152.33 - - [16/Jun/2010:09:10:11 +0200] "GET /Seiten/Links_e.html HTTP/1.1" 200 18366 "http://www.asylabwehramt.at/Seiten/Seal.html" "Mozilla/4.0 (compatible; MSIE 8.0; Windows NT 5.1; Trident/4.0; InfoPath.1; .NET CLR 1.1.4322; .NET CLR 2.0.50727; .NET CLR 3.0.04506.30; .NET CLR 3.0.04506.648; .NET CLR 3.0.4506.2152; .NET CLR 3.5.30729)"
193.171.152.33 - - [16/Jun/2010:09:10:17 +0200] "GET /Seiten/Latestnews.html HTTP/1.1" 200 12574 "http://www.asylabwehramt.at/Seiten/Links_e.html" "Mozilla/4.0 (compatible; MSIE 8.0; Windows NT 5.1; Trident/4.0; InfoPath.1; .NET CLR 1.1.4322; .NET CLR 2.0.50727; .NET CLR 3.0.04506.30; .NET CLR 3.0.04506.648; .NET CLR 3.0.4506.2152; .NET CLR 3.5.30729)"
193.171.152.33 - - [16/Jun/2010:09:10:21 +0200] "GET /index.html HTTP/1.1" 200 11828 "http://www.asylabwehramt.at/Seiten/Latestnews.html" "Mozilla/4.0 (compatible; MSIE 8.0; Windows NT 5.1; Trident/4.0; InfoPath.1; .NET CLR 1.1.4322; .NET CLR 2.0.50727; .NET CLR 3.0.04506.30; .NET CLR 3.0.04506.648; .NET CLR 3.0.4506.2152; .NET CLR 3.5.30729)"
193.171.152.33 - - [16/Jun/2010:09:10:23 +0200] "GET /index_e.html HTTP/1.1" 200 11855 "http://www.asylabwehramt.at/index.html" "Mozilla/4.0 (compatible; MSIE 8.0; Windows NT 5.1; Trident/4.0; InfoPath.1; .NET CLR 1.1.4322; .NET CLR 2.0.50727; .NET CLR 3.0.04506.30; .NET CLR 3.0.04506.648; .NET CLR 3.0.4506.2152; .NET CLR 3.5.30729)"
193.171.152.33 - - [16/Jun/2010:09:10:25 +0200] "GET /Seiten/Aktuelles.html HTTP/1.1" 200 12570 "http://www.asylabwehramt.at/Seiten/Latestnews.html" "Mozilla/4.0 (compatible; MSIE 8.0; Windows NT 5.1; Trident/4.0; InfoPath.1; .NET CLR 1.1.4322; .NET CLR 2.0.50727; .NET CLR 3.5.30729)"
193.171.152.33 - - [16/Jun/2010:09:10:31 +0200] "GET /Seiten/Forms_and_Infos.html HTTP/1.1" 200 1046 "http://www.asylabwehramt.at/Seiten/Aktuelles.html" "Mozilla/4.0 (compatible; MSIE 8.0; Wind
```

```
ows NT 5.1; Trident/4.0; InfoPath.1; .NET CLR 1.1.4322; .NET CLR 2.0.50727; .NET CLR 3.0.04506.30
; .NET CLR 3.0.04506.648; .NET CLR 3.0.4506.2152; .NET CLR 3.5.30729)"
193.171.152.33 - - [16/Jun/2010:09:10:37 +0200] "GET /Seiten/Rundzeichen.html HTTP/1.1" 200 8837
"http://www.asylabwehramt.at/Seiten/Aktuelles.html" "Mozilla/4.0 (compatible; MSIE 8.0; Windows N
T 5.1; Trident/4.0; InfoPath.1; .NET CLR 1.1.4322; .NET CLR 2.0.50727; .NET CLR 3.0.04506.30; .NE
T CLR 3.0.04506.648; .NET CLR 3.0.4506.2152; .NET CLR 3.5.30729)"
193.171.152.33 - - [16/Jun/2010:09:10:39 +0200] "GET /Seiten/Images.html HTTP/1.1" 200 9701 "http
://www.asylabwehramt.at/Seiten/Seal.html" "Mozilla/4.0 (compatible; MSIE 8.0; Windows NT 5.1; Tri
dent/4.0; InfoPath.1; .NET CLR 1.1.4322; .NET CLR 2.0.50727; .NET CLR 3.0.04506.30; .NET CLR 3.0.
04506.648; .NET CLR 3.0.4506.2152; .NET CLR 3.5.30729)"
193.171.152.33 - - [16/Jun/2010:09:10:48 +0200] "GET /Seiten/Bilder_buero.html HTTP/1.1" 200 1102
6 "http://www.asylabwehramt.at/Seiten/Images.html" "Mozilla/4.0 (compatible; MSIE 8.0; Windows NT
5.1; Trident/4.0; InfoPath.1; .NET CLR 1.1.4322; .NET CLR 2.0.50727; .NET CLR 3.0.04506.30; .NET
CLR 3.0.04506.648; .NET CLR 3.0.4506.2152; .NET CLR 3.5.30729)"
193.171.152.33 - - [16/Jun/2010:09:10:49 +0200] "GET /Bilder/BAA_photos/IMG_0187.JPG HTTP/1.1" 20
0 191902 "http://www.asylabwehramt.at/Seiten/Bilder_buero.html" "Mozilla/4.0 (compatible; MSIE 8.
0; Windows NT 5.1; Trident/4.0; InfoPath.1; .NET CLR 1.1.4322; .NET CLR 3.0.4506.2152; .NET CLR 3.5.30729)"
4506.30; .NET CLR 3.0.04506.648; .NET CLR 3.0.4506.2152; .NET CLR 3.5.30729)"
193.171.152.33 - - [16/Jun/2010:09:10:50 +0200] "GET /Bilder/BAA_photos/IMG_0189.JPG HTTP/1.1" 20
0 163470 "http://www.asylabwehramt.at/Seiten/Bilder_buero.html" "Mozilla/4.0 (compatible; MSIE 8.
0; Windows NT 5.1; Trident/4.0; InfoPath.1; .NET CLR 1.1.4322; .NET CLR 3.0.4506.2152; .NET CLR 3.5.30729)"
4506.30; .NET CLR 3.0.04506.648; .NET CLR 3.0.4506.2152; .NET CLR 3.5.30729)"
193.171.152.33 - - [16/Jun/2010:09:10:51 +0200] "GET /Bilder/BAA_photos/IMG_0191.JPG HTTP/1.1" 20
0 124240 "http://www.asylabwehramt.at/Seiten/Bilder_buero.html" "Mozilla/4.0 (compatible; MSIE 8.
0; Windows NT 5.1; Trident/4.0; InfoPath.1; .NET CLR 1.1.4322; .NET CLR 3.0.4506.2152; .NET CLR 3.5.30729)"
4506.30; .NET CLR 3.0.04506.648; .NET CLR 3.0.4506.2152; .NET CLR 3.5.30729)"
193.171.152.33 - - [16/Jun/2010:09:10:52 +0200] "GET /Bilder/BAA_photos/IMG_0195.JPG HTTP/1.1" 20
0 122316 "http://www.asylabwehramt.at/Seiten/Bilder_buero.html" "Mozilla/4.0 (compatible; MSIE 8.
```

```
0; Windows NT 5.1; Trident/4.0; InfoPath.1; .NET CLR 1.1.4322; .NET CLR 2.0.50727; .NET CLR 3.0.0
4506.30; .NET CLR 3.0.04506.648; .NET CLR 3.0.4506.2152; .NET CLR 3.5.30729)"
193.171.152.33 - - [16/Jun/2010:09:12:32 +0200] "GET /Seiten/Ausseneinsaetze.html HTTP/1.1" 200 9
190 "http://www.asylabwehramt.at/Seiten/Images.html" "Mozilla/4.0 (compatible; MSIE 8.0; Windows
NT 5.1; Trident/4.0; InfoPath.1; .NET CLR 1.1.4322; .NET CLR 2.0.50727; .NET CLR 3.0.04506.30; .N
ET CLR 3.0.04506.648; .NET CLR 3.0.4506.2152; .NET CLR 3.5.30729)"
193.171.152.33 - - [16/Jun/2010:09:12:55 +0200] "GET /Seiten/Press.html HTTP/1.1" 200 10955 "http
://www.asylabwehramt.at/Seiten/Links.html" "Mozilla/4.0 (compatible; MSIE 8.0; Windows NT 5.1; Tr
ident/4.0; InfoPath.1; .NET CLR 1.1.4322; .NET CLR 2.0.50727; .NET CLR 3.0.04506.30; .NET CLR 3.0
.04506.648; .NET CLR 3.0.4506.2152; .NET CLR 3.5.30729)"
193.171.152.33 - - [16/Jun/2010:09:12:58 +0200] "GET /OEFFENTLICHKEIT/07062010d.pdf HTTP/1.1" 200
333788 "http://www.asylabwehramt.at/Seiten/Press.html" "Mozilla/4.0 (compatible; MSIE 8.0; Windo
ws NT 5.1; Trident/4.0; InfoPath.1; .NET CLR 1.1.4322; .NET CLR 2.0.50727; .NET CLR 3.0.04506.30;
.NET CLR 3.0.04506.648; .NET CLR 3.0.4506.2152; .NET CLR 3.5.30729)"
193.171.152.33 - - [16/Jun/2010:09:14:14 +0200] "GET /asyl.css HTTP/1.1" 304 - "http://www.asylab
wehramt.at/index.html" "Mozilla/4.0 (compatible; MSIE 8.0; Windows NT 5.1; Trident/4.0; InfoPath.
1; .NET CLR 1.1.4322; .NET CLR 2.0.50727; .NET CLR 3.0.04506.30; .NET CLR 3.0.04506.648; .NET CLR
3.0.4506.2152; .NET CLR 3.5.30729)"
193.171.152.33 - - [16/Jun/2010:09:17:52 +0200] "GET /Bilder/Header_AAbA.jpg HTTP/1.1" 304 - "htt
p://www.asylabwehramt.at/Seiten/Presse.html" "Mozilla/4.0 (compatible; MSIE 8.0; Windows NT 5.1;
Trident/4.0; InfoPath.1; .NET CLR 1.1.4322; .NET CLR 2.0.50727; .NET CLR 3.0.04506.30; .NET CLR 3
.0.04506.648; .NET CLR 3.0.4506.2152; .NET CLR 3.5.30729)"
80.120.179.10 - - [16/Jun/2010:09:22:55 +0200] "GET /Seiten/Seal.html HTTP/1.1" 200 8872 "http://
www.asylabwehramt.at/Seiten/Rundzeichen.html" "Mozilla/4.0 (compatible; MSIE 6.0; Windows NT 5.1;
SV1; .NET CLR 1.1.4322)"
80.120.179.10 - - [16/Jun/2010:09:22:59 +0200] "GET /Seiten/Forms_and_Infos.html HTTP/1.1" 200 11
046 "http://www.asylabwehramt.at/Seiten/Seal.html" "Mozilla/4.0 (compatible; MSIE 6.0; Windows NT
5.1; SV1; .NET CLR 1.1.4322)"
```

193.171.152.33 - - [16/Jun/2010:09:24:54 +0200] "GET /asyl.css HTTP/1.1" 304 - "http://www.asylab
wehramt.at/index.html" "Mozilla/4.0 (compatible; MSIE 7.0; Windows NT 5.1; GTB6.5; InfoPath.1)"
193.171.152.33 - - [16/Jun/2010:09:24:55 +0200] "GET /Seiten/Material.html HTTP/1.1" 200 11980 "h
ttp://www.asylabwehramt.at/index.html" "Mozilla/4.0 (compatible; MSIE 7.0; Windows NT 5.1; GTB6.5
; InfoPath.1)"
78.41.144.41 - - [16/Jun/2010:09:37:41 +0200] "GET / HTTP/1.0" 200 11828 "-" "Mozilla/4.0 (compat
ible; MSIE 7.0; Windows NT 5.1; .NET CLR 2.0.50727; .NET CLR 1.1.4322; .NET CLR 3.0.04506.30; .NE
T CLR 3.0.04506.648; .NET CLR 3.0.4506.2152; .NET CLR 3.5.30729)"
78.41.144.41 - - [16/Jun/2010:09:37:42 +0200] "GET /favicon.ico HTTP/1.0" 302 340 "-" "Mozilla/4.
0 (compatible; MSIE 7.0; Windows NT 5.1; .NET CLR 2.0.50727; .NET CLR 1.1.4322; .NET CLR 3.0.0450
6.30; .NET CLR 3.0.04506.648; .NET CLR 3.0.4506.2152; .NET CLR 3.5.30729)"
78.41.144.41 - - [16/Jun/2010:09:38:05 +0200] "GET /Seiten/Bilder.html HTTP/1.0" 200 9571 "http:/
/www.asylabwehramt.at/" "Mozilla/4.0 (compatible; MSIE 7.0; Windows NT 5.1; .NET CLR 2.0.50727; .
NET CLR 1.1.4322; .NET CLR 3.0.04506.30; .NET CLR 3.0.04506.648; .NET CLR 3.0.4506.2152; .NET CLR
3.5.30729)"
78.41.144.41 - - [16/Jun/2010:09:38:13 +0200] "GET /Seiten/Aktuelles.html HTTP/1.0" 200 12570 "ht
tp://www.asylabwehramt.at/Seiten/Bilder.html" "Mozilla/4.0 (compatible; MSIE 7.0; Windows NT 5.1;
.NET CLR 2.0.50727; .NET CLR 1.1.4322; .NET CLR 3.0.04506.30; .NET CLR 3.0.04506.648; .NET CLR 3
.0.4506.2152; .NET CLR 3.5.30729)"
78.41.144.41 - - [16/Jun/2010:09:58:59 +0200] "GET / HTTP/1.0" 304 - "-" "Mozilla/4.0 (compatible
; MSIE 7.0; Windows NT 5.1; .NET CLR 2.0.50727; .NET CLR 1.1.4322; .NET CLR 3.0.04506.30; .NET CL
R 3.0.04506.648; .NET CLR 3.0.4506.2152; .NET CLR 3.5.30729)"
78.41.144.41 - - [16/Jun/2010:09:59:03 +0200] "GET /Seiten/Orgstrukt.html HTTP/1.0" 200 14086 "ht
tp://www.asylabwehramt.at/" "Mozilla/4.0 (compatible; MSIE 7.0; Windows NT 5.1; .NET CLR 2.0.5072
7; .NET CLR 1.1.4322; .NET CLR 3.0.04506.30; .NET CLR 3.0.04506.648; .NET CLR 3.0.4506.2152; .NET
CLR 3.5.30729)"
78.41.144.41 - - [16/Jun/2010:09:59:37 +0200] "GET /Seiten/Material.html HTTP/1.0" 200 11980 "htt
p://www.asylabwehramt.at/Seiten/Orgstrukt.html" "Mozilla/4.0 (compatible; MSIE 7.0; Windows NT 5.

```
1; .NET CLR 2.0.50727; .NET CLR 1.1.4322; .NET CLR 3.0.04506.648; .NET CLR
3.0.4506.2152; .NET CLR 3.5.30729)"
78.41.144.41 - - [16/Jun/2010:09:59:42 +0200] "GET /Bilder/Ladung.png HTTP/1.0" 200 114658 "http:
//www.asylabwehramt.at/Seiten/Material.html" "Mozilla/4.0 (compatible; MSIE 7.0; Windows NT 5.1;
.NET CLR 2.0.50727; .NET CLR 1.1.4322; .NET CLR 3.0.04506.648; .NET CLR 3.
0.4506.2152; .NET CLR 3.5.30729)"
78.41.144.41 - - [16/Jun/2010:09:59:59 +0200] "GET /Bilder/IOM-Kosovo-Broschuere_Internet.pdf HTT
P/1.0" 200 728811 "http://www.asylabwehramt.at/Seiten/Material.html" "Mozilla/4.0 (compatible; MS
IE 7.0; Windows NT 5.1; .NET CLR 2.0.50727; .NET CLR 1.1.4322; .NET CLR 3.0.04506.30; .NET CLR 3.
0.04506.648; .NET CLR 3.0.4506.2152; .NET CLR 3.5.30729)"
78.41.144.41 - - [16/Jun/2010:10:00:02 +0200] "GET /Bilder/IOM-Kosovo-Broschuere_Internet.pdf HTT
P/1.0" 206 4096 "-" "Mozilla/4.0 (compatible; MSIE 7.0; Windows NT 5.1; .NET CLR 2.0.50727; .NET
CLR 1.1.4322; .NET CLR 3.0.04506.30; .NET CLR 3.0.04506.648; .NET CLR 3.0.4506.2152; .NET CLR 3.5
.30729)"
78.41.144.41 - - [16/Jun/2010:10:00:48 +0200] "GET /Material/Hotline_Deutsch.pdf HTTP/1.0" 200 48
9465 "http://www.asylabwehramt.at/Seiten/Material.html" "Mozilla/4.0 (compatible; MSIE 7.0; Windo
ws NT 5.1; .NET CLR 2.0.50727; .NET CLR 1.1.4322; .NET CLR 3.0.04506.30; .NET CLR 3.0.04506.648;
.NET CLR 3.0.4506.2152; .NET CLR 3.5.30729)"
78.41.144.41 - - [16/Jun/2010:10:01:08 +0200] "GET /Material/Hotline_Englisch.PDF HTTP/1.0" 200 4
73359 "http://www.asylabwehramt.at/Seiten/Material.html" "Mozilla/4.0 (compatible; MSIE 7.0; Wind
ows NT 5.1; .NET CLR 2.0.50727; .NET CLR 1.1.4322; .NET CLR 3.0.04506.30; .NET CLR 3.0.04506.648;
.NET CLR 3.0.4506.2152; .NET CLR 3.5.30729)"
78.41.144.41 - - [16/Jun/2010:10:01:19 +0200] "GET /Seiten/Rundzeichen.html HTTP/1.0" 200 8837 "h
ttp://www.asylabwehramt.at/Seiten/Material.html" "Mozilla/4.0 (compatible; MSIE 7.0; Windows NT 5
.1; .NET CLR 2.0.50727; .NET CLR 1.1.4322; .NET CLR 3.0.04506.30; .NET CLR 3.0.04506.648; .NET CL
R 3.0.4506.2152; .NET CLR 3.5.30729)"
78.41.144.41 - - [16/Jun/2010:10:01:25 +0200] "GET /Seiten/Bilder.html HTTP/1.0" 304 - "http://ww
w.asylabwehramt.at/Seiten/Rundzeichen.html" "Mozilla/4.0 (compatible; MSIE 7.0; Windows NT 5.1; .
```

NET CLR 2.0.50727; .NET CLR 1.1.4322; .NET CLR 3.0.04506.30; .NET CLR 3.0.04506.648; .NET CLR 3.0.4506.2152; .NET CLR 3.5.30729)"

78.41.144.41 - - [16/Jun/2010:10:01:36 +0200] "GET /Seiten/Ausseneinsaetze.html HTTP/1.0" 200 9190 "http://www.asylabwehramt.at/Seiten/Bilder.html" "Mozilla/4.0 (compatible; MSIE 7.0; Windows NT 5.1; .NET CLR 2.0.50727; .NET CLR 1.1.4322; .NET CLR 3.0.04506.30; .NET CLR 3.0.04506.648; .NET CLR 3.0.4506.2152; .NET CLR 3.5.30729)"

78.41.144.41 - - [16/Jun/2010:10:01:45 +0200] "GET /Seiten/Links.html HTTP/1.0" 200 18362 "http://www.asylabwehramt.at/Seiten/Ausseneinsaetze.html" "Mozilla/4.0 (compatible; MSIE 7.0; Windows NT 5.1; .NET CLR 2.0.50727; .NET CLR 1.1.4322; .NET CLR 3.0.04506.30; .NET CLR 3.0.04506.648; .NET CLR 3.0.4506.2152; .NET CLR 3.5.30729)"

78.41.144.41 - - [16/Jun/2010:10:01:46 +0200] "GET /Bilder/STRABAG.jpg HTTP/1.0" 304 - "http://www.asylabwehramt.at/Seiten/Links.html" "Mozilla/4.0 (compatible; MSIE 7.0; Windows NT 5.1; .NET CLR 2.0.50727; .NET CLR 1.1.4322; .NET CLR 3.0.04506.30; .NET CLR 3.0.04506.648; .NET CLR 3.0.4506.2152; .NET CLR 3.5.30729)"

78.41.144.41 - - [16/Jun/2010:10:02:17 +0200] "GET /Seiten/Press.html HTTP/1.0" 200 10955 "http://www.asylabwehramt.at/Seiten/Links.html" "Mozilla/4.0 (compatible; MSIE 7.0; Windows NT 5.1; .NET CLR 2.0.50727; .NET CLR 1.1.4322; .NET CLR 3.0.04506.30; .NET CLR 3.0.04506.648; .NET CLR 3.0.4506.2152; .NET CLR 3.5.30729)"

78.41.144.41 - - [16/Jun/2010:10:02:33 +0200] "GET /OEFFENTLICHKEIT/07062010d.pdf HTTP/1.0" 200 333788 "http://www.asylabwehramt.at/Seiten/Press.html" "Mozilla/4.0 (compatible; MSIE 7.0; Windows NT 5.1; .NET CLR 2.0.50727; .NET CLR 1.1.4322; .NET CLR 3.0.04506.30; .NET CLR 3.0.04506.648; .NET CLR 3.0.4506.2152; .NET CLR 3.5.30729)"

78.41.144.41 - - [16/Jun/2010:10:04:23 +0200] "GET / HTTP/1.0" 304 - "-" "Mozilla/4.0 (compatible; MSIE 7.0; Windows NT 5.1; .NET CLR 2.0.50727; .NET CLR 1.1.4322; .NET CLR 3.0.04506.30; .NET CLR 3.0.04506.648; .NET CLR 3.0.4506.2152; .NET CLR 3.5.30729)"

78.41.144.41 - - [16/Jun/2010:10:04:24 +0200] "GET /asyl.css HTTP/1.0" 304 - "http://www.asylabwehramt.at/" "Mozilla/4.0 (compatible; MSIE 7.0; Windows NT 5.1; .NET CLR 2.0.50727; .NET CLR 1.1.4322; .NET CLR 3.0.04506.30; .NET CLR 3.0.04506.648; .NET CLR 3.0.4506.2152; .NET CLR 3.5.30729)"

```
78.41.144.41 - - [16/Jun/2010:10:04:31 +0200] "GET /Seiten/Material.html HTTP/1.0" 304 - "http://
www.asylabwehramt.at/" "Mozilla/4.0 (compatible; MSIE 7.0; Windows NT 5.1; .NET CLR 2.0.50727; .N
ET CLR 1.1.4322; .NET CLR 3.0.4506.30; .NET CLR 3.0.04506.648; .NET CLR 3.0.4506.2152; .NET CLR
3.5.30729)"
78.41.144.41 - - [16/Jun/2010:10:04:35 +0200] "GET /Bilder/flyer_nigeria_Internet.pdf HTTP/1.0" 2
00 702826 "http://www.asylabwehramt.at/Seiten/Material.html" "Mozilla/4.0 (compatible; MSIE 7.0;
Windows NT 5.1; .NET CLR 2.0.50727; .NET CLR 1.1.4322; .NET CLR 3.0.04506.30; .NET CLR 3.0.04506.
648; .NET CLR 3.0.4506.2152; .NET CLR 3.5.30729)"
78.41.144.41 - - [16/Jun/2010:10:04:36 +0200] "GET /Bilder/flyer_nigeria_Internet.pdf HTTP/1.0" 2
06 888 "-" "Mozilla/4.0 (compatible; MSIE 7.0; Windows NT 5.1; .NET CLR 2.0.50727; .NET CLR 1.1.4
322; .NET CLR 3.0.04506.30; .NET CLR 3.0.04506.648; .NET CLR 3.0.4506.2152; .NET CLR 3.5.30729)"
80.120.179.10 - - [16/Jun/2010:10:06:11 +0200] "GET /favicon.ico HTTP/1.1" 302 340 "-" "Mozilla/4
.0 (compatible; MSIE 8.0; Windows NT 5.1; Trident/4.0; InfoPath.1; .NET CLR 1.1.4322; .NET CLR 2.
0.50727; MS-RTC LM 8)"
80.120.179.10 - - [16/Jun/2010:10:08:19 +0200] "GET /favicon.ico HTTP/1.1" 302 340 "-" "Mozilla/4
.0 (compatible; MSIE 8.0; Windows NT 5.1; Trident/4.0; .NET CLR 1.1.4322; .NET CLR 2.0.50727; .NE
T CLR 3.0.04506.30; .NET CLR 3.0.04506.648; InfoPath.2)"
78.41.144.41 - - [16/Jun/2010:10:08:55 +0200] "GET /Material/Asyl_Jahresstatistik_2009.pdf HTTP/1
.0" 200 680643 "http://www.asylabwehramt.at/Seiten/Material.html" "Mozilla/4.0 (compatible; MSIE
7.0; Windows NT 5.1; .NET CLR 2.0.50727; .NET CLR 1.1.4322; .NET CLR 3.0.04506.30; .NET CLR 3.0.0
4506.648; .NET CLR 3.0.4506.2152; .NET CLR 3.5.30729)"
78.41.144.41 - - [16/Jun/2010:10:09:35 +0200] "GET /Material/Asyl_Jahresstatistik_2009.pdf HTTP/1
.0" 206 4096 "-" "Mozilla/4.0 (compatible; MSIE 7.0; Windows NT 5.1; .NET CLR 2.0.50727; .NET CLR
1.1.4322; .NET CLR 3.0.04506.30; .NET CLR 3.0.04506.648; .NET CLR 3.0.4506.2152; .NET CLR 3.5.30
729)"
78.41.144.41 - - [16/Jun/2010:10:09:36 +0200] "GET /Material/Asyl_Jahresstatistik_2009.pdf HTTP/1
.0" 206 268465 "-" "Mozilla/4.0 (compatible; MSIE 7.0; Windows NT 5.1; .NET CLR 2.0.50727; .NET C
LR 1.1.4322; .NET CLR 3.0.04506.30; .NET CLR 3.0.04506.648; .NET CLR 3.0.4506.2152; .NET CLR 3.5.
```

30729)"

80.120.179.10 - - [16/Jun/2010:11:08:05 +0200] "GET /favicon.ico HTTP/1.1" 302 340 "-" "Mozilla/4.0 (compatible; MSIE 8.0; Windows NT 5.1; Trident/4.0; .NET CLR 1.1.4322; InfoPath.1)"

80.120.179.10 - - [16/Jun/2010:12:32:14 +0200] "GET /favicon.ico HTTP/1.1" 302 340 "-" "Mozilla/4.0 (compatible; MSIE 8.0; Windows NT 5.1; Trident/4.0; .NET CLR 1.1.4322; .NET CLR 2.0.50727; .NET CLR 3.0.04506.30; .NET CLR 3.0.04506.648; InfoPath.2)"

78.41.144.41 - - [16/Jun/2010:12:59:13 +0200] "GET / HTTP/1.0" 304 - "-" "Mozilla/4.0 (compatible; MSIE 7.0; Windows NT 5.1; .NET CLR 2.0.50727; .NET CLR 1.1.4322; .NET CLR 3.0.04506.30; .NET CLR 3.0.04506.648; .NET CLR 3.5.30729)"

78.41.144.41 - - [16/Jun/2010:12:59:14 +0200] "GET /favicon.ico HTTP/1.0" 302 340 "-" "Mozilla/4.0 (compatible; MSIE 7.0; Windows NT 5.1; .NET CLR 2.0.50727; .NET CLR 1.1.4322; .NET CLR 3.0.04506.30; .NET CLR 3.0.04506.648; .NET CLR 3.0.04506.2152; .NET CLR 3.5.30729)"

78.41.144.41 - - [16/Jun/2010:12:59:35 +0200] "GET / HTTP/1.0" 304 - "http://www.asylabwehramt.at/" "Mozilla/4.0 (compatible; MSIE 7.0; Windows NT 5.1; .NET CLR 2.0.50727; .NET CLR 1.1.4322; .NET CLR 3.0.04506.30; .NET CLR 3.0.04506.648; .NET CLR 3.0.04506.2152; .NET CLR 3.5.30729)"

78.41.144.41 - - [16/Jun/2010:12:59:37 +0200] "GET /index_e.html HTTP/1.0" 200 11855 "http://www.asylabwehramt.at/" "Mozilla/4.0 (compatible; MSIE 7.0; Windows NT 5.1; .NET CLR 2.0.50727; .NET CLR 1.1.4322; .NET CLR 3.0.04506.30; .NET CLR 3.0.04506.648; .NET CLR 3.0.04506.2152; .NET CLR 3.5.30729)"

78.41.144.41 - - [16/Jun/2010:12:59:55 +0200] "GET / HTTP/1.0" 304 - "http://www.asylabwehramt.at/index_e.html" "Mozilla/4.0 (compatible; MSIE 7.0; Windows NT 5.1; .NET CLR 2.0.50727; .NET CLR 1.1.4322; .NET CLR 3.0.04506.30; .NET CLR 3.0.04506.648; .NET CLR 3.0.04506.2152; .NET CLR 3.5.3072 9)"

78.41.144.41 - - [16/Jun/2010:13:00:35 +0200] "GET /Material/Hotline_Deutsch.pdf HTTP/1.0" 304 - "http://www.asylabwehramt.at/" "Mozilla/4.0 (compatible; MSIE 7.0; Windows NT 5.1; .NET CLR 2.0.50727; .NET CLR 3.0.04506.30; .NET CLR 3.0.04506.648; .NET CLR 3.0.04506.2152; .NET CLR 3.5.30729)"

78.41.144.41 - - [16/Jun/2010:13:01:12 +0200] "GET /Material/Hotline_Deutsch.pdf HTTP/1.0" 304 -

91

```
"http://www.asylabwehramt.at/" "Mozilla/4.0 (compatible; MSIE 7.0; Windows NT 5.1; .NET CLR 2.0.5
0727; .NET CLR 1.1.4322; .NET CLR 3.0.04506.30; .NET CLR 3.0.04506.648; .NET CLR 3.0.4506.2152; .
NET CLR 3.5.30729)"
78.41.144.41 - - [16/Jun/2010:13:01:22 +0200] "GET /Seiten/Aktuelles.html HTTP/1.0" 304 - "http:/
/www.asylabwehramt.at/" "Mozilla/4.0 (compatible; MSIE 7.0; Windows NT 5.1; .NET CLR 2.0.50727; .
NET CLR 1.1.4322; .NET CLR 3.0.04506.30; .NET CLR 3.0.04506.648; .NET CLR 3.0.4506.2152; .NET CLR
3.5.30729)"
78.41.144.41 - - [16/Jun/2010:13:02:22 +0200] "GET /Seiten/Bilder.html HTTP/1.0" 304 - "http://ww
w.asylabwehramt.at/Seiten/Aktuelles.html" "Mozilla/4.0 (compatible; MSIE 7.0; Windows NT 5.1; .NE
T CLR 2.0.50727; .NET CLR 1.1.4322; .NET CLR 3.0.04506.30; .NET CLR 3.0.04506.648; .NET CLR 3.0.4
506.2152; .NET CLR 3.5.30729)"
78.41.144.41 - - [16/Jun/2010:13:02:44 +0200] "GET /Seiten/Links.html HTTP/1.0" 304 - "http://www
.asylabwehramt.at/Seiten/Bilder.html" "Mozilla/4.0 (compatible; MSIE 7.0; Windows NT 5.1; .NET CL
R 2.0.50727; .NET CLR 1.1.4322; .NET CLR 3.0.04506.30; .NET CLR 3.0.04506.648; .NET CLR 3.0.4506.
2152; .NET CLR 3.5.30729)"
78.41.144.41 - - [16/Jun/2010:13:02:55 +0200] "GET / HTTP/1.0" 304 - "-" "Mozilla/4.0 (compatible
; MSIE 7.0; Windows NT 5.1; .NET CLR 2.0.50727; .NET CLR 1.1.4322; .NET CLR 3.0.04506.30; .NET CL
R 3.0.04506.648; .NET CLR 3.0.4506.2152; .NET CLR 3.5.30729)"
78.41.144.41 - - [16/Jun/2010:13:03:17 +0200] "GET /Seiten/Images.html HTTP/1.0" 200 9701 "http:/
/www.asylabwehramt.at/" "Mozilla/4.0 (compatible; MSIE 7.0; Windows NT 5.1; .NET CLR 2.0.50727; .
NET CLR 1.1.4322; .NET CLR 3.0.04506.30; .NET CLR 3.0.04506.648; .NET CLR 3.0.4506.2152; .NET CLR
3.5.30729)"
78.41.144.41 - - [16/Jun/2010:13:03:28 +0200] "GET /Seiten/Links_e.html HTTP/1.0" 200 18366 "http
://www.asylabwehramt.at/Seiten/Images.html" "Mozilla/4.0 (compatible; MSIE 7.0; Windows NT 5.1; .
NET CLR 2.0.50727; .NET CLR 1.1.4322; .NET CLR 3.0.04506.30; .NET CLR 3.0.04506.648; .NET CLR 3.0
.4506.2152; .NET CLR 3.5.30729)"
78.41.144.41 - - [16/Jun/2010:13:03:35 +0200] "GET /Seiten/Latestnews.html HTTP/1.0" 200 12574 "h
ttp://www.asylabwehramt.at/Seiten/Links_e.html" "Mozilla/4.0 (compatible; MSIE 7.0; Windows NT 5.
```

1; .NET CLR 2.0.50727; .NET CLR 1.1.4322; .NET CLR 3.0.4506.30; .NET CLR 3.0.4506.648; .NET CLR 3.0.4506.2152; .NET CLR 3.5.30729)"

78.41.144.41 - - [16/Jun/2010:13:03:39 +0200] "GET /Seiten/Press.html HTTP/1.0" 304 - "http://www.asylabwehramt.at/Seiten/Links.html" "Mozilla/4.0 (compatible; MSIE 7.0; Windows NT 5.1; .NET CLR 2.0.50727; .NET CLR 1.1.4322; .NET CLR 3.0.4506.30; .NET CLR 3.0.4506.648; .NET CLR 3.0.4506.2152; .NET CLR 3.5.30729)"

78.41.144.41 - - [16/Jun/2010:13:03:45 +0200] "GET /Seiten/Orgstrukt.html HTTP/1.0" 304 - "http://www.asylabwehramt.at/Seiten/Press.html" "Mozilla/4.0 (compatible; MSIE 7.0; Windows NT 5.1; .NET CLR 2.0.50727; .NET CLR 1.1.4322; .NET CLR 3.0.04506.30; .NET CLR 3.0.04506.648; .NET CLR 3.0.4506.2152; .NET CLR 3.5.30729)"

78.41.144.41 - - [16/Jun/2010:13:03:54 +0200] "GET /index.html HTTP/1.0" 304 - "http://www.asylabwehramt.at/Seiten/Latestnews.html" "Mozilla/4.0 (compatible; MSIE 7.0; Windows NT 5.1; .NET CLR 2.0.50727; .NET CLR 1.1.4322; .NET CLR 3.0.04506.30; .NET CLR 3.0.04506.648; .NET CLR 3.0.4506.2152; .NET CLR 3.5.30729)"

80.120.179.10 - - [16/Jun/2010:13:03:55 +0200] "GET /favicon.ico HTTP/1.1" 302 340 "-" "Mozilla/4.0 (compatible; MSIE 8.0; Windows NT 5.1; Trident/4.0; .NET CLR 1.1.4322; .NET CLR 2.0.50727; .NET CLR 3.0.04506.30; .NET CLR 3.0.04506.648; InfoPath.2)"

78.41.144.41 - - [16/Jun/2010:13:03:56 +0200] "GET /Seiten/Rundzeichen.html HTTP/1.0" 304 - "http://www.asylabwehramt.at/index.html" "Mozilla/4.0 (compatible; MSIE 7.0; Windows NT 5.1; .NET CLR 2.0.50727; .NET CLR 1.1.4322; .NET CLR 3.0.04506.30; .NET CLR 3.0.04506.648; .NET CLR 3.0.4506.2152; .NET CLR 3.5.30729)"

78.41.144.41 - - [16/Jun/2010:13:04:01 +0200] "GET /index.html HTTP/1.0" 304 - "http://www.asylabwehramt.at/Seiten/Orgstrukt.html" "Mozilla/4.0 (compatible; MSIE 7.0; Windows NT 5.1; .NET CLR 2.0.50727; .NET CLR 1.1.4322; .NET CLR 3.0.04506.30; .NET CLR 3.0.04506.648; .NET CLR 3.0.4506.2152; .NET CLR 3.5.30729)"

78.41.144.41 - - [16/Jun/2010:13:04:03 +0200] "GET /Seiten/Orgstrukt.html HTTP/1.0" 304 - "http://www.asylabwehramt.at/index.html" "Mozilla/4.0 (compatible; MSIE 7.0; Windows NT 5.1; .NET CLR 2.0.50727; .NET CLR 1.1.4322; .NET CLR 3.0.04506.30; .NET CLR 3.0.04506.648; .NET CLR 3.0.4506.2152

```
78.41.144.41 - - [16/Jun/2010:13:04:10 +0200] "GET /index.html HTTP/1.0" 304 - "http://www.asylab
wehramt.at/Seiten/Orgstrukt.html" "Mozilla/4.0 (compatible; MSIE 7.0; Windows NT 5.1; .NET CLR 2.
0.50727; .NET CLR 1.1.4322; .NET CLR 3.0.04506.648; .NET CLR 3.0.04506.2152
; .NET CLR 3.5.30729)"
78.41.144.41 - - [16/Jun/2010:13:04:13 +0200] "GET /Seiten/Aktuelles.html HTTP/1.0" 304 - "http:/
/www.asylabwehramt.at/index.html" "Mozilla/4.0 (compatible; MSIE 7.0; Windows NT 5.1; .NET CLR 2.
0.50727; .NET CLR 1.1.4322; .NET CLR 3.0.04506.648; .NET CLR 3.0.04506.2152
; .NET CLR 3.5.30729)"
78.41.144.41 - - [16/Jun/2010:13:04:14 +0200] "GET /Seiten/Latestnews.html HTTP/1.0" 304 - "http:
//www.asylabwehramt.at/Seiten/Aktuelles.html" "Mozilla/4.0 (compatible; MSIE 7.0; Windows NT 5.1;
.NET CLR 2.0.50727; .NET CLR 1.1.4322; .NET CLR 3.0.04506.30; .NET CLR 3.0.04506.648; .NET CLR 3
.0.4506.2152; .NET CLR 3.5.30729)"
78.41.144.41 - - [16/Jun/2010:13:04:18 +0200] "GET /Seiten/Forms_and_Infos.html HTTP/1.0" 200 110
46 "http://www.asylabwehramt.at/Seiten/Latestnews.html" "Mozilla/4.0 (compatible; MSIE 7.0; Windo
ws NT 5.1; .NET CLR 2.0.50727; .NET CLR 1.1.4322; .NET CLR 3.0.04506.30; .NET CLR 3.0.04506.648;
.NET CLR 3.0.4506.2152; .NET CLR 3.5.30729)"
78.41.144.41 - - [16/Jun/2010:13:04:25 +0200] "GET /Bilder/flyer_nigeria_Internet.pdf HTTP/1.0" 3
04 - "http://www.asylabwehramt.at/Seiten/Forms_and_Infos.html" "Mozilla/4.0 (compatible; MSIE 7.0
; Windows NT 5.1; .NET CLR 2.0.50727; .NET CLR 1.1.4322; .NET CLR 3.0.04506.30; .NET CLR 3.0.0450
6.648; .NET CLR 3.0.4506.2152; .NET CLR 3.5.30729)"
78.41.144.41 - - [16/Jun/2010:13:04:26 +0200] "GET /Bilder/flyer_nigeria_Internet.pdf HTTP/1.0" 2
06 4096 "-" "Mozilla/4.0 (compatible; MSIE 7.0; Windows NT 5.1; .NET CLR 2.0.50727; .NET CLR 1.1.
4322; .NET CLR 3.0.04506.30; .NET CLR 3.0.04506.648; .NET CLR 3.0.4506.2152; .NET CLR 3.5.30729)"
78.41.144.41 - - [16/Jun/2010:13:04:53 +0200] "GET /Bilder/Ladung.png HTTP/1.0" 304 - "http://www
.asylabwehramt.at/Seiten/Forms_and_Infos.html" "Mozilla/4.0 (compatible; MSIE 7.0; Windows NT 5.1
; .NET CLR 2.0.50727; .NET CLR 1.1.4322; .NET CLR 3.0.04506.648; .NET CLR
3.0.4506.2152; .NET CLR 3.5.30729)"
```

78.41.144.41 - - [16/Jun/2010:13:05:02 +0200] "GET /Material/Asyl_Jahresstatistik_2009.pdf HTTP/1.0" 304 - "http://www.asylabwehramt.at/Seiten/Forms_and_Infos.html" "Mozilla/4.0 (compatible; MSIE 7.0; Windows NT 5.1; .NET CLR 2.0.50727; .NET CLR 1.1.4322; .NET CLR 3.0.04506.30; .NET CLR 3.0.04506.648; .NET CLR 3.0.4506.2152; .NET CLR 3.5.30729)"

80.120.179.10 - - [16/Jun/2010:13:05:22 +0200] "GET /Bilder/flyer_nigeria_Internet.pdf HTTP/1.1" 200 702826 "-" "Mozilla/4.0 (compatible; MSIE 8.0; Windows NT 5.1; Trident/4.0; .NET CLR 1.1.4322; .NET CLR 2.0.50727; .NET CLR 3.0.04506.30; .NET CLR 3.0.04506.648; InfoPath.2)"

78.41.144.41 - - [16/Jun/2010:13:05:29 +0200] "GET /Material/Asyl_Jahresstatistik_2009.pdf HTTP/1.0" 206 4096 "-" "Mozilla/4.0 (compatible; MSIE 7.0; Windows NT 5.1; .NET CLR 2.0.50727; .NET CLR 1.1.4322; .NET CLR 3.0.04506.30; .NET CLR 3.0.04506.648; .NET CLR 3.0.4506.2152; .NET CLR 3.5.30729)"

78.41.144.41 - - [16/Jun/2010:13:05:30 +0200] "GET /Material/Asyl_Jahresstatistik_2009.pdf HTTP/1.0" 206 179 "-" "Mozilla/4.0 (compatible; MSIE 7.0; Windows NT 5.1; .NET CLR 2.0.50727; .NET CLR 1.1.4322; .NET CLR 3.0.04506.30; .NET CLR 3.0.04506.648; .NET CLR 3.0.4506.2152; .NET CLR 3.5.30729)"

78.41.144.41 - - [16/Jun/2010:13:05:31 +0200] "GET /Material/Asyl_Jahresstatistik_2009.pdf HTTP/1.0" 206 10875 "-" "Mozilla/4.0 (compatible; MSIE 7.0; Windows NT 5.1; .NET CLR 2.0.50727; .NET CLR 1.1.4322; .NET CLR 3.0.04506.30; .NET CLR 3.0.04506.648; .NET CLR 3.0.4506.2152; .NET CLR 3.5.30729)"

78.41.144.41 - - [16/Jun/2010:13:05:32 +0200] "GET /Material/Asyl_Jahresstatistik_2009.pdf HTTP/1.0" 206 403796 "-" "Mozilla/4.0 (compatible; MSIE 7.0; Windows NT 5.1; .NET CLR 2.0.50727; .NET CLR 1.1.4322; .NET CLR 3.0.04506.30; .NET CLR 3.0.04506.648; .NET CLR 3.0.4506.2152; .NET CLR 3.5.30729)"

78.41.144.41 - - [16/Jun/2010:13:06:35 +0200] "GET /Seiten/Forms_and_Infos.html HTTP/1.0" 304 - "http://www.asylabwehramt.at/Seiten/Latestnews.html" "Mozilla/4.0 (compatible; MSIE 7.0; Windows NT 5.1; .NET CLR 2.0.50727; .NET CLR 1.1.4322; .NET CLR 3.0.04506.30; .NET CLR 3.0.04506.648; .NET CLR 3.0.4506.2152; .NET CLR 3.5.30729)"

78.41.144.41 - - [16/Jun/2010:13:06:43 +0200] "GET /Material/Hotline_Russisch.pdf HTTP/1.0" 200 2

```
39827 "http://www.asylabwehramt.at/Seiten/Forms_and_Infos.html" "Mozilla/4.0 (compatible; MSIE 7.
0; Windows NT 5.1; .NET CLR 2.0.50727; .NET CLR 1.1.4322; .NET CLR 3.0.04506.30; .NET CLR 3.0.045
06.648; .NET CLR 3.0.4506.2152; .NET CLR 3.5.30729)"
78.41.144.41 - - [16/Jun/2010:13:06:49 +0200] "GET /Bilder/IOM-Kosovo-Broschuere_Internet.pdf HTT
P/1.0" 304 - "http://www.asylabwehramt.at/Seiten/Forms_and_Infos.html" "Mozilla/4.0 (compatible;
MSIE 7.0; Windows NT 5.1; .NET CLR 2.0.50727; .NET CLR 1.1.4322; .NET CLR 3.0.04506.30; .NET CLR
3.0.04506.648; .NET CLR 3.0.4506.2152; .NET CLR 3.5.30729)"
78.41.144.41 - - [16/Jun/2010:13:06:50 +0200] "GET /Bilder/IOM-Kosovo-Broschuere_Internet.pdf HTT
P/1.0" 206 4096 "-" "Mozilla/4.0 (compatible; MSIE 7.0; Windows NT 5.1; .NET CLR 2.0.50727; .NET
CLR 1.1.4322; .NET CLR 3.0.04506.30; .NET CLR 3.0.04506.648; .NET CLR 3.0.4506.2152; .NET CLR 3.5
.30729)"
78.41.144.41 - - [16/Jun/2010:13:06:58 +0200] "GET / HTTP/1.0" 304 - "-" "Mozilla/4.0 (compatible
; MSIE 7.0; Windows NT 5.1; .NET CLR 2.0.50727; .NET CLR 1.1.4322; .NET CLR 3.0.04506.30; .NET CL
R 3.0.04506.648; .NET CLR 3.0.4506.2152; .NET CLR 3.5.30729)"
78.41.144.41 - - [16/Jun/2010:13:07:01 +0200] "GET /Material/Hotline_Franzoesisch.PDF HTTP/1.0" 2
00 515416 "http://www.asylabwehramt.at/Seiten/Forms_and_Infos.html" "Mozilla/4.0 (compatible; MSI
E 7.0; Windows NT 5.1; .NET CLR 2.0.50727; .NET CLR 1.1.4322; .NET CLR 3.0.04506.30; .NET CLR 3.0
.04506.648; .NET CLR 3.0.4506.2152; .NET CLR 3.5.30729)"
78.41.144.41 - - [16/Jun/2010:13:07:02 +0200] "GET /Material/Hotline_Franzoesisch.PDF HTTP/1.0" 2
06 4096 "-" "Mozilla/4.0 (compatible; MSIE 7.0; Windows NT 5.1; .NET CLR 2.0.50727; .NET CLR 1.1.
4322; .NET CLR 3.0.04506.30; .NET CLR 3.0.04506.648; .NET CLR 3.0.4506.2152; .NET CLR 3.5.30729)"
78.41.144.41 - - [16/Jun/2010:13:07:26 +0200] "GET /Material/Hotline_Englisch.PDF HTTP/1.0" 304 -
"http://www.asylabwehramt.at/Seiten/Forms_and_Infos.html" "Mozilla/4.0 (compatible; MSIE 7.0; Wi
ndows NT 5.1; .NET CLR 2.0.50727; .NET CLR 1.1.4322; .NET CLR 3.0.04506.30; .NET CLR 3.0.04506.64
8; .NET CLR 3.0.4506.2152; .NET CLR 3.5.30729)"
78.41.144.41 - - [16/Jun/2010:13:07:27 +0200] "GET /Seiten/Material.html HTTP/1.0" 304 - "http://
www.asylabwehramt.at/" "Mozilla/4.0 (compatible; MSIE 7.0; Windows NT 5.1; .NET CLR 2.0.50727; .N
ET CLR 1.1.4322; .NET CLR 3.0.04506.30; .NET CLR 3.0.4506.2152; .NET CLR
```

```
3.5.30729"
78.41.144.41 - - [16/Jun/2010:13:07:30 +0200] "GET /Bilder/flyer_nigeria_Internet.pdf HTTP/1.0" 3
04 - "http://www.asylabwehramt.at/Seiten/Material.html" "Mozilla/4.0 (compatible; MSIE 7.0; Windo
ws NT 5.1; .NET CLR 2.0.50727; .NET CLR 1.1.4322; .NET CLR 3.0.04506.30; .NET CLR 3.0.04506.648;
.NET CLR 3.0.4506.2152; .NET CLR 3.5.30729)"
78.41.144.41 - - [16/Jun/2010:13:07:31 +0200] "GET /Bilder/flyer_nigeria_Internet.pdf HTTP/1.0" 2
06 4096 "-" "Mozilla/4.0 (compatible; MSIE 7.0; Windows NT 5.1; .NET CLR 2.0.50727; .NET CLR 1.1.
4322; .NET CLR 3.0.04506.30; .NET CLR 3.0.04506.648; .NET CLR 3.0.4506.2152; .NET CLR 3.5.30729)"
78.41.144.41 - - [16/Jun/2010:13:07:32 +0200] "GET /Seiten/Links_e.html HTTP/1.0" 304 - "http://w
ww.asylabwehramt.at/Seiten/Forms_and_Infos.html" "Mozilla/4.0 (compatible; MSIE 7.0; Windows NT 5
.1; .NET CLR 2.0.50727; .NET CLR 1.1.4322; .NET CLR 3.0.04506.30; .NET CLR 3.0.04506.648; .NET CL
R 3.0.4506.2152; .NET CLR 3.5.30729)"
78.41.144.41 - - [16/Jun/2010:13:07:55 +0200] "GET /Seiten/Images.html HTTP/1.0" 304 - "http://ww
w.asylabwehramt.at/Seiten/Material.html" "Mozilla/4.0 (compatible; MSIE 7.0; Windows NT 5.1; .NET
CLR 2.0.50727; .NET CLR 1.1.4322; .NET CLR 3.0.04506.30; .NET CLR 3.0.04506.648; .NET CLR 3.0.45
06.2152; .NET CLR 3.5.30729)"
78.41.144.41 - - [16/Jun/2010:13:08:09 +0200] "GET /Seiten/Rundzeichen.html HTTP/1.0" 304 - "http
://www.asylabwehramt.at/Seiten/Images.html" "Mozilla/4.0 (compatible; MSIE 7.0; Windows NT 5.1; .
NET CLR 2.0.50727; .NET CLR 1.1.4322; .NET CLR 3.0.04506.30; .NET CLR 3.0.04506.648; .NET CLR 3.0
.4506.2152; .NET CLR 3.5.30729)"
78.41.144.41 - - [16/Jun/2010:13:08:12 +0200] "GET /Seiten/Forms_and_Infos.html HTTP/1.0" 304 - "
http://www.asylabwehramt.at/Seiten/Rundzeichen.html" "Mozilla/4.0 (compatible; MSIE 7.0; Windows
NT 5.1; .NET CLR 2.0.50727; .NET CLR 1.1.4322; .NET CLR 3.0.04506.30; .NET CLR 3.0.04506.648; .NE
T CLR 3.0.4506.2152; .NET CLR 3.5.30729)"
78.41.144.41 - - [16/Jun/2010:13:14:27 +0200] "GET / HTTP/1.0" 304 - "-" "Mozilla/4.0 (compatible
; MSIE 7.0; Windows NT 5.1; .NET CLR 2.0.50727; .NET CLR 1.1.4322; .NET CLR 3.0.04506.30; .NET CL
R 3.0.4506.648; .NET CLR 3.0.04506.648; .NET CLR 3.0.4506.2152; .NET CLR 3.5.30729)"
80.120.179.10 - - [16/Jun/2010:13:35:19 +0200] "GET /favicon.ico HTTP/1.1" 302 340 "-" "Mozilla/4
```

```
mail.1f-law.at - - [16/Jun/2010:13:36:12 +0200] "GET / HTTP/1.1" 200 11828 "http://diepre
sse.com/home/panorama/oesterreich/573975/index.do?direct=573454&_vl_backlink=/home/index.do&selCh
annel=119" "Mozilla/4.0 (compatible; MSIE 8.0; Windows NT 5.1; Trident/4.0; .NET CLR 1.1.4322; .NET CLR 2.0.50727; .NE
T CLR 3.0.04506.30; .NET CLR 3.0.04506.648; InfoPath.2)"
NET CLR 2.0.50727; .NET CLR 3.0.04506.2152; .NET CLR 3.5.30729)"
80.120.179.10 - - [16/Jun/2010:13:52:15 +0200] "GET /favicon.ico HTTP/1.1" 302 340 "-" "Mozilla/4
.0 (compatible; MSIE 8.0; Windows NT 5.1; Trident/4.0; .NET CLR 1.1.4322; InfoPath.1)"
78.41.144.41 - - [16/Jun/2010:14:05:49 +0200] "GET / HTTP/1.0" 304 - "-" "Mozilla/4.0 (compatible
; MSIE 7.0; Windows NT 5.1; .NET CLR 2.0.50727; .NET CLR 1.1.4322; .NET CLR 3.0.04506.30; .NET CL
R 3.0.04506.648; .NET CLR 3.0.04506.2152; .NET CLR 3.5.30729)"
193.171.152.33 - - [16/Jun/2010:14:51:08 +0200] "GET / HTTP/1.1" 304 - "-" "Mozilla/4.0 (compatib
le; MSIE 6.0; Windows NT 5.1; InfoPath.1)"
193.171.152.33 - - [16/Jun/2010:14:52:56 +0200] "GET /Bilder/56.jpg HTTP/1.1" 304 - "http://www.a
sylabwehramt.at/Seiten/Aktuelles.html" "Mozilla/4.0 (compatible; MSIE 6.0; Windows NT 5.1; InfoPa
th.1)"
193.171.152.33 - - [16/Jun/2010:14:54:43 +0200] "GET / HTTP/1.1" 304 - "-" "Mozilla/5.0 (Windows;
U; Windows NT 5.1; de; rv:1.9.0.10) Gecko/2009042316 Firefox/3.0.10 (.NET CLR 3.5.30729)"
193.171.152.33 - - [16/Jun/2010:14:54:44 +0200] "GET /asyl.css HTTP/1.1" 304 - "http://www.asylab
wehramt.at/" "Mozilla/5.0 (Windows; U; Windows NT 5.1; de; rv:1.9.0.10) Gecko/2009042316 Firefox/
3.0.10 (.NET CLR 3.5.30729)"
193.171.152.33 - - [16/Jun/2010:14:54:45 +0200] "GET /favicon.ico HTTP/1.1" 302 340 "-" "Mozilla/
5.0 (Windows; U; Windows NT 5.1; de; rv:1.9.0.10) Gecko/2009042316 Firefox/3.0.10 (.NET CLR 3.5.3
0729)"
193.171.152.33 - - [16/Jun/2010:14:54:48 +0200] "GET /favicon.ico HTTP/1.1" 302 340 "-" "Mozilla/
5.0 (Windows; U; Windows NT 5.1; de; rv:1.9.0.10) Gecko/2009042316 Firefox/3.0.10 (.NET CLR 3.5.3
0729)"
```

```
193.171.152.33 - - [16/Jun/2010:14:55:14 +0200] "GET /Bilder/BAA_photos/IMG_0198.JPG HTTP/1.1" 200 109214 "http://www.asylabwehramt.at/Seiten/Bilder.html" "Mozilla/5.0 (Windows; U; Windows NT 5.1; de; rv:1.9.0.10) Gecko/2009042316 Firefox/3.0.10 (.NET CLR 3.5.30729)"
193.171.152.33 - - [16/Jun/2010:14:55:37 +0200] "GET /Bilder/STRABAG.jpg HTTP/1.1" 304 - "http://www.asylabwehramt.at/Seiten/Links.html" "Mozilla/5.0 (Windows; U; Windows NT 5.1; de; rv:1.9.0.10) Gecko/2009042316 Firefox/3.0.10 (.NET CLR 3.5.30729)"
194.232.79.100 - - [16/Jun/2010:15:04:44 +0200] "GET / HTTP/1.1" 200 11828 "http://diepresse.com/home/panorama/oesterreich/573975/index.do?_vl_backlink=/home/panorama/oesterreich/573454/index.do&direct=573454" "Mozilla/5.0 (Windows; U; Windows NT 5.0 (Windows; U; Windows NT 6.0; de; rv:1.9.2.3) Gecko/20100401 Firefox/3.6.3 (.NET CLR 3.5.30729)"
194.232.79.100 - - [16/Jun/2010:15:04:45 +0200] "GET /favicon.ico HTTP/1.1" 302 340 "-" "Mozilla/5.0 (Windows; U; Windows NT 6.0; de; rv:1.9.2.3) Gecko/20100401 Firefox/3.6.3 (.NET CLR 3.5.30729)"
194.232.79.100 - - [16/Jun/2010:15:04:48 +0200] "GET /favicon.ico HTTP/1.1" 302 340 "-" "Mozilla/5.0 (Windows; U; Windows NT 6.0; de; rv:1.9.2.3) Gecko/20100401 Firefox/3.6.3 (.NET CLR 3.5.30729)"
194.232.79.100 - - [16/Jun/2010:15:05:02 +0200] "GET /Seiten/Aktuelles.html HTTP/1.1" 200 12570 "http://www.asylabwehramt.at/" "Mozilla/5.0 (Windows; U; Windows NT 6.0; de; rv:1.9.2.3) Gecko/20100401 Firefox/3.6.3 (.NET CLR 3.5.30729)"
80.120.179.10 - - [16/Jun/2010:15:09:07 +0200] "GET / HTTP/1.1" 200 11828 "-" "Mozilla/4.0 (compatible; MSIE 7.0; Windows NT 5.1; Trident/4.0; .NET CLR 1.1.4322; .NET CLR 2.0.50727; .NET CLR 3.0.04506.30; .NET CLR 3.0.04506.648; InfoPath.2)"
80.120.179.10 - - [16/Jun/2010:15:09:26 +0200] "GET /Seiten/Aktuelles.html HTTP/1.1" 200 12570 "http://www.asylabwehramt.at/" "Mozilla/4.0 (compatible; MSIE 7.0; Windows NT 5.1; Trident/4.0; .NET CLR 1.1.4322; .NET CLR 2.0.50727; .NET CLR 3.0.04506.30; .NET CLR 3.0.04506.648; InfoPath.2)"
80.120.179.10 - - [16/Jun/2010:15:09:36 +0200] "GET /Seiten/Links.html HTTP/1.1" 200 18362 "http://www.asylabwehramt.at/Seiten/Aktuelles.html" "Mozilla/4.0 (compatible; MSIE 7.0; Windows NT 5.1;
```

```
Trident/4.0; .NET CLR 1.1.4322; .NET CLR 2.0.50727; .NET CLR 3.0.04506.30; .NET CLR 3.0.04506.64
8; InfoPath.2)"
80.120.179.10 - - [16/Jun/2010:15:09:41 +0200] "GET /Seiten/Press.html HTTP/1.1" 200 10955 "http:
//www.asylabwehramt.at/Seiten/Links.html" "Mozilla/4.0 (compatible; MSIE 7.0; Windows NT 5.1; Tri
dent/4.0; .NET CLR 1.1.4322; .NET CLR 2.0.50727; .NET CLR 3.0.04506.30; .NET CLR 3.0.04506.648; I
nfoPath.2)"
80.120.179.10 - - [16/Jun/2010:15:09:45 +0200] "GET /index.html HTTP/1.1" 200 11828 "http://www.a
sylabwehramt.at/Seiten/Press.html" "Mozilla/4.0 (compatible; MSIE 7.0; Windows NT 5.1; Trident/4.
0; .NET CLR 1.1.4322; .NET CLR 2.0.50727; .NET CLR 3.0.04506.30; .NET CLR 3.0.04506.648; InfoPath
.2)"
80.120.179.10 - - [16/Jun/2010:15:10:24 +0200] "GET /index_e.html HTTP/1.1" 200 11855 "http://www
.asylabwehramt.at/index.html" "Mozilla/4.0 (compatible; MSIE 7.0; Windows NT 5.1; Trident/4.0; .N
ET CLR 1.1.4322; .NET CLR 2.0.50727; .NET CLR 3.0.04506.30; .NET CLR 3.0.04506.648; InfoPath.2)"
80.120.179.10 - - [16/Jun/2010:15:10:37 +0200] "GET /Seiten/Material.html HTTP/1.1" 200 11980 "ht
tp://www.asylabwehramt.at/Seiten/Aktuelles.html" "Mozilla/4.0 (compatible; MSIE 7.0; Windows NT 5
.1; Trident/4.0; .NET CLR 1.1.4322; .NET CLR 2.0.50727; .NET CLR 3.0.04506.30; .NET CLR 3.0.04506
.648; InfoPath.2)"
80.120.179.10 - - [16/Jun/2010:15:10:45 +0200] "GET /Seiten/Rundzeichen.html HTTP/1.1" 200 8837 "
http://www.asylabwehramt.at/Seiten/Material.html" "Mozilla/4.0 (compatible; MSIE 7.0; Windows NT
5.1; Trident/4.0; .NET CLR 1.1.4322; .NET CLR 2.0.50727; .NET CLR 3.0.04506.30; .NET CLR 3.0.0450
6.648; InfoPath.2)"
80.120.179.10 - - [16/Jun/2010:15:10:55 +0200] "GET /Seiten/Bilder.html HTTP/1.1" 200 9571 "http:
//www.asylabwehramt.at/Seiten/Rundzeichen.html" "Mozilla/4.0 (compatible; MSIE 7.0; Windows NT 5.
1; Trident/4.0; .NET CLR 1.1.4322; .NET CLR 2.0.50727; .NET CLR 3.0.04506.30; .NET CLR 3.0.04506.
648; InfoPath.2)"
80.120.179.10 - - [16/Jun/2010:15:10:56 +0200] "GET /Bilder/SCREEN_AAbA_Edutainment_Video.jpg HTT
P/1.1" 200 29259 "http://www.asylabwehramt.at/Seiten/Bilder.html" "Mozilla/4.0 (compatible; MSIE
7.0; Windows NT 5.1; Trident/4.0; .NET CLR 1.1.4322; .NET CLR 2.0.50727; .NET CLR 3.0.04506.30; .
```

NET CLR 3.0.04506.648; InfoPath.2)"

78.41.144.41 - - [16/Jun/2010:15:12:33 +0200] "GET / HTTP/1.0" 304 - "-" "Mozilla/4.0 (compatible; MSIE 7.0; Windows NT 5.1; .NET CLR 2.0.50727; .NET CLR 1.1.4322; .NET CLR 3.0.04506.30; .NET CLR 3.0.04506.648; .NET CLR 3.5.30729)"

78.41.144.41 - - [16/Jun/2010:15:12:45 +0200] "GET /Seiten/Links_e.html HTTP/1.0" 304 - "http://www.asylabwehramt.at/" "Mozilla/4.0 (compatible; MSIE 7.0; Windows NT 5.1; .NET CLR 2.0.50727; .NET CLR 1.1.4322; .NET CLR 3.0.04506.30; .NET CLR 3.0.04506.648; .NET CLR 3.0.04506.2152; .NET CLR 3.5.30729)"

80.120.179.10 - - [16/Jun/2010:15:16:01 +0200] "GET /favicon.ico HTTP/1.1" 302 340 "-" "Mozilla/4.0 (compatible; MSIE 8.0; Windows NT 5.1; Trident/4.0; InfoPath.1; .NET CLR 1.1.4322; .NET CLR 2.0.50727)"

80.120.179.10 - - [16/Jun/2010:15:16:27 +0200] "GET /Seiten/Ausseneinsaetze.html HTTP/1.1" 200 9190 "http://www.asylabwehramt.at/Seiten/Bilder.html" "Mozilla/4.0 (compatible; MSIE 8.0; Windows NT 5.1; Trident/4.0; InfoPath.1; .NET CLR 1.1.4322; .NET CLR 2.0.50727)"

80.120.179.10 - - [16/Jun/2010:15:16:36 +0200] "GET /Seiten/Latestnews.html HTTP/1.1" 200 12574 "http://www.asylabwehramt.at/Seiten/Ausseneinsaetze.html" "Mozilla/4.0 (compatible; MSIE 8.0; Windows NT 5.1; Trident/4.0; InfoPath.1; .NET CLR 1.1.4322; .NET CLR 2.0.50727)"

80.120.179.10 - - [16/Jun/2010:15:17:07 +0200] "GET /Seiten/Presse.html HTTP/1.1" 200 10956 "http://www.asylabwehramt.at/index.html" "Mozilla/4.0 (compatible; MSIE 8.0; Windows NT 5.1; Trident/4.0; InfoPath.1; .NET CLR 1.1.4322; .NET CLR 2.0.50727)"

80.120.179.10 - - [16/Jun/2010:15:17:20 +0200] "GET /Seiten/Impressum.html HTTP/1.1" 200 11505 "http://www.asylabwehramt.at/Seiten/Presse.html" "Mozilla/4.0 (compatible; MSIE 8.0; Windows NT 5.1; Trident/4.0; InfoPath.1; .NET CLR 1.1.4322; .NET CLR 2.0.50727)"

80.120.179.10 - - [16/Jun/2010:15:17:57 +0200] "GET /Seiten/Images.html HTTP/1.1" 200 9701 "http://www.asylabwehramt.at/index.html" "Mozilla/4.0 (compatible; MSIE 8.0; Windows NT 5.1; Trident/4.0; InfoPath.1; .NET CLR 1.1.4322; .NET CLR 2.0.50727)"

80.120.179.10 - - [16/Jun/2010:15:18:07 +0200] "GET /Seiten/Forms_and_Infos.html HTTP/1.1" 200 11046 "http://www.asylabwehramt.at/Seiten/Rundzeichen.html" "Mozilla/4.0 (compatible; MSIE 8.0; Win

```
dows NT 5.1; Trident/4.0; InfoPath.1; .NET CLR 1.1.4322; .NET CLR 2.0.50727)"
80.120.179.10 - - [16/Jun/2010:15:18:15 +0200] "GET /Material/Hotline_Deutsch.pdf HTTP/1.1" 200 4
89465 "http://www.asylabwehramt.at/Seiten/Forms_and_Infos.html" "Mozilla/4.0 (compatible; MSIE 8.
0; Windows NT 5.1; Trident/4.0; InfoPath.1; .NET CLR 1.1.4322; .NET CLR 2.0.50727)"
85.158.226.1 - - [17/Jun/2010:07:53:42 +0200] "GET / HTTP/1.1" 200 11828 "http://www.google.at/ur
l?sa=t&source=web&cd=2&ved=0CB8QFjAB&url=http%3A%2F%2Fwww.asylabwehramt.at%2F&rct=j&q=asylabwehra
mt&ei=TbgZTM_hGNDKONPH7LIK&usg=AFQjCNEy1zWClvnxkLlPAGifRc344_0U4Q" "Mozilla/4.0 (compatible; MSIE
8.0; Windows NT 5.1; Trident/4.0; .NET CLR 1.1.4322; .NET CLR 2.0.50727)"
193.187.212.100[18] - - [17/Jun/2010:08:52:08 +0200] "GET /index.html HTTP/1.1" 200 11828 "-" "Mozill
a/4.0 (compatible; MSIE 8.0; Windows NT 5.1; Trident/4.0)"
193.187.212.100 - - [17/Jun/2010:08:52:09 +0200] "GET /favicon.ico HTTP/1.1" 302 340 "-" "Mozilla
/4.0 (compatible; MSIE 8.0; Windows NT 5.1; Trident/4.0)"
193.187.212.100 - - [17/Jun/2010:08:54:09 +0200] "GET / HTTP/1.1" 200 11828 "http://www.asylabweh
ramt.at/index.html" "Mozilla/4.0 (compatible; MSIE 8.0; Windows NT 5.1; Trident/4.0)"
193.187.212.100 - - [17/Jun/2010:08:54:21 +0200] "GET /Seiten/Aktuelles.html HTTP/1.1" 200 12570
"http://www.asylabwehramt.at/" "Mozilla/4.0 (compatible; MSIE 8.0; Windows NT 5.1; Trident/4.0)"
193.187.212.100 - - [17/Jun/2010:08:54:31 +0200] "GET /Seiten/Material.html HTTP/1.1" 200 11980 "
http://www.asylabwehramt.at/Seiten/Aktuelles.html" "Mozilla/4.0 (compatible; MSIE 8.0; Windows NT
5.1; Trident/4.0)"
193.187.212.100 - - [17/Jun/2010:08:54:47 +0200] "GET /Seiten/Rundzeichen.html HTTP/1.1" 200 8837
"http://www.asylabwehramt.at/Seiten/Material.html" "Mozilla/4.0 (compatible; MSIE 8.0; Windows N
T 5.1; Trident/4.0)"
193.187.212.100 - - [17/Jun/2010:08:54:50 +0200] "GET /Seiten/Bilder.html HTTP/1.1" 200 9571 "htt
p://www.asylabwehramt.at/Seiten/Rundzeichen.html" "Mozilla/4.0 (compatible; MSIE 8.0; Windows NT
5.1; Trident/4.0)"
193.187.212.100 - - [17/Jun/2010:08:55:01 +0200] "GET /Seiten/Links.html HTTP/1.1" 200 18362 "htt
```

[18] WHOIS record on page 308

```
p://www.asylabwehramt.at/Seiten/Bilder.html" "Mozilla/4.0 (compatible; MSIE 8.0; Windows NT 5.1; Trident/4.0)"
193.187.212.100 - - [17/Jun/2010:08:55:04 +0200] "GET /Seiten/Press.html HTTP/1.1" 200 10955 "htt p://www.asylabwehramt.at/Seiten/Links.html" "Mozilla/4.0 (compatible; MSIE 8.0; Windows NT 5.1; T rident/4.0)"
78.41.144.41 - - [17/Jun/2010:09:26:05 +0200] "GET / HTTP/1.0" 304 - "http://www.dasweissehaus.a t/wwwnew/de/ausstellungencontent.html" "Mozilla/4.0 (compatible; MSIE 7.0; Windows NT 5.1; .NET CLR 2.0.50727; .NET CLR 1.1.4322; .NET CLR 3.0.04506.648; .NET CLR 3.0.450 6.2152; .NET CLR 3.5.30729)"
78.41.144.41 - - [17/Jun/2010:09:26:34 +0200] "GET /Seiten/Aktuelles.html HTTP/1.0" 304 - "http:/ /www.asylabwehramt.at/" "Mozilla/4.0 (compatible; MSIE 7.0; Windows NT 5.1; .NET CLR 2.0.50727; . NET CLR 1.1.4322; .NET CLR 3.0.04506.30; .NET CLR 3.0.4506.2152; .NET CLR 3.5.30729)"
78.41.144.41 - - [17/Jun/2010:09:26:53 +0200] "GET /Seiten/Orgstrukt.html HTTP/1.0" 304 - "http:/ /www.asylabwehramt.at/Seiten/Aktuelles.html" "Mozilla/4.0 (compatible; MSIE 7.0; Windows NT 5.1; .NET CLR 2.0.50727; .NET CLR 1.1.4322; .NET CLR 3.0.04506.30; .NET CLR 3. 0.4506.2152; .NET CLR 3.5.30729)"
78.41.144.41 - - [17/Jun/2010:09:27:53 +0200] "GET /Seiten/Material.html HTTP/1.0" 304 - "http:// www.asylabwehramt.at/Seiten/Orgstrukt.html" "Mozilla/4.0 (compatible; MSIE 7.0; Windows NT 5.1; . NET CLR 2.0.50727; .NET CLR 1.1.4322; .NET CLR 3.0.04506.30; .NET CLR 3.0.4506.2152; .NET CLR 3.5.30729)"
78.41.144.41 - - [17/Jun/2010:09:27:59 +0200] "GET /Bilder/flyer_nigeria_Internet.pdf HTTP/1.0" 3 04 - "http://www.asylabwehramt.at/Seiten/Material.html" "Mozilla/4.0 (compatible; MSIE 7.0; Windo ws NT 5.1; .NET CLR 2.0.50727; .NET CLR 1.1.4322; .NET CLR 3.0.04506.30; .NET CLR 3.0.04506.648; .NET CLR 3.0.4506.2152; .NET CLR 3.5.30729)"
78.41.144.41 - - [17/Jun/2010:09:28:01 +0200] "GET /Bilder/flyer_nigeria_Internet.pdf HTTP/1.0" 2 06 4096 "-" "Mozilla/4.0 (compatible; MSIE 7.0; Windows NT 5.1; .NET CLR 2.0.50727; .NET CLR 1.1. 4322; .NET CLR 3.0.04506.648; .NET CLR 3.0.4506.2152; .NET CLR 3.5.30729)"
```

```
78.41.144.41 - - [17/Jun/2010:09:28:36 +0200] "GET /Seiten/Rundzeichen.html HTTP/1.0" 304 - "http
://www.asylabwehramt.at/Seiten/Material.html" "Mozilla/4.0 (compatible; MSIE 7.0; Windows NT 5.1;
.NET CLR 2.0.50727; .NET CLR 1.1.4322; .NET CLR 3.0.04506.30; .NET CLR 3
.0.4506.2152; .NET CLR 3.5.30729)"
78.41.144.41 - - [17/Jun/2010:09:28:43 +0200] "GET /Seiten/Bilder.html HTTP/1.0" 304 - "http://ww
w.asylabwehramt.at/Seiten/Rundzeichen.html" "Mozilla/4.0 (compatible; MSIE 7.0; Windows NT 5.1; .
NET CLR 2.0.50727; .NET CLR 1.1.4322; .NET CLR 3.0.04506.30; .NET CLR 3.0
.4506.2152; .NET CLR 3.5.30729)"
78.41.144.41 - - [17/Jun/2010:09:28:57 +0200] "GET /Seiten/Ausseneinsaetze.html HTTP/1.0" 304 - "
http://www.asylabwehramt.at/Seiten/Bilder.html" "Mozilla/4.0 (compatible; MSIE 7.0; Windows NT 5.
1; .NET CLR 2.0.50727; .NET CLR 1.1.4322; .NET CLR 3.0.04506.30; .NET CLR
3.0.4506.2152; .NET CLR 3.5.30729)"
78.41.144.41 - - [17/Jun/2010:09:29:04 +0200] "GET /Seiten/Press.html HTTP/1.0" 304 - "http://www
.asylabwehramt.at/Seiten/Ausseneinsaetze.html" "Mozilla/4.0 (compatible; MSIE 7.0; Windows NT 5.1
; .NET CLR 2.0.50727; .NET CLR 1.1.4322; .NET CLR 3.0.04506.30; .NET CLR
3.0.4506.2152; .NET CLR 3.5.30729)"
78.41.144.41 - - [17/Jun/2010:09:29:34 +0200] "GET / HTTP/1.0" 304 - "-" "Mozilla/4.0 (compatible
; MSIE 7.0; Windows NT 5.1; .NET CLR 2.0.50727; .NET CLR 1.1.4322; .NET CLR 3.0.04506.30; .NET CL
R 3.0.04506.648; .NET CLR 3.0.4506.2152; .NET CLR 3.5.30729)"
78.41.144.41 - - [17/Jun/2010:09:29:35 +0200] "GET /favicon.ico HTTP/1.0" 302 340 "-" "Mozilla/4.
0 (compatible; MSIE 7.0; Windows NT 5.1; .NET CLR 2.0.50727; .NET CLR 1.1.4322; .NET CLR 3.0.0450
6.30; .NET CLR 3.0.04506.648; .NET CLR 3.0.4506.2152; .NET CLR 3.5.30729)"
78.41.144.41 - - [17/Jun/2010:09:33:49 +0200] "GET /index_e.html HTTP/1.0" 304 - "http://www.asyl
abwehramt.at/Seiten/Press.html" "Mozilla/4.0 (compatible; MSIE 7.0; Windows NT 5.1; .NET CLR 2.0.
50727; .NET CLR 1.1.4322; .NET CLR 3.0.04506.30; .NET CLR 3.0.04506.648; .NET CLR 3.0.4506.2152;
.NET CLR 3.5.30729)"
78.41.144.41 - - [17/Jun/2010:09:33:54 +0200] "GET /Seiten/Links_e.html HTTP/1.0" 304 - "http://w
ww.asylabwehramt.at/index_e.html" "Mozilla/4.0 (compatible; MSIE 7.0; Windows NT 5.1; .NET CLR 2.
```

```
0.50727; .NET CLR 1.1.4322; .NET CLR 3.0.04506.30; .NET CLR 3.0.4506.2152; .NET CLR 3.5.30729)"

80.120.179.10 - - [17/Jun/2010:09:42:14 +0200] "GET / HTTP/1.1" 200 11828 "http://www.google.at/url?sa=t&source=web&cd=2&ved=0CB8QFjAB&url=http%3A%2F%2Fwww.asylabwehramt.at%2F&rct=j&q=Asylabwehramt&ei=wdEZTP2YFIiKOJz2oIwK&usg=AFQjCNEy1zWClvnxkLlPAGifRc344_0U4Q" "Mozilla/4.0 (compatible; MSIE 8.0; Windows NT 5.1; Trident/4.0; .NET CLR 1.1.4322; .NET CLR 2.0.50727; .NET CLR 3.0.04506.30; .NET CLR 3.0.04506.648; InfoPath.2)"

78.41.144.41 - - [17/Jun/2010:10:48:39 +0200] "GET /Material/Hotline_Deutsch.pdf HTTP/1.0" 304 - "http://www.asylabwehramt.at/" "Mozilla/4.0 (compatible; MSIE 7.0; Windows NT 5.1; .NET CLR 2.0.50727; .NET CLR 1.1.4322; .NET CLR 3.0.04506.30; .NET CLR 3.0.04506.648; .NET CLR 3.0.4506.2152; .NET CLR 3.5.30729)"

78.41.144.41 - - [17/Jun/2010:10:48:49 +0200] "GET / HTTP/1.0" 304 - "-" "Mozilla/4.0 (compatible; MSIE 7.0; Windows NT 5.1; .NET CLR 2.0.50727; .NET CLR 1.1.4322; .NET CLR 3.0.04506.30; .NET CLR 3.0.04506.648; .NET CLR 3.0.4506.2152; .NET CLR 3.5.30729)"

78.41.144.41 - - [17/Jun/2010:10:48:51 +0200] "GET /Seiten/Aktuelles.html HTTP/1.0" 304 - "http://www.asylabwehramt.at/" "Mozilla/4.0 (compatible; MSIE 7.0; Windows NT 5.1; .NET CLR 2.0.50727; .NET CLR 1.1.4322; .NET CLR 3.0.04506.30; .NET CLR 3.0.04506.648; .NET CLR 3.0.4506.2152; .NET CLR 3.5.30729)"

78.41.144.41 - - [17/Jun/2010:10:49:48 +0200] "GET /Seiten/Rundzeichen.html HTTP/1.0" 304 - "http://www.asylabwehramt.at/Seiten/Aktuelles.html" "Mozilla/4.0 (compatible; MSIE 7.0; Windows NT 5.1; .NET CLR 2.0.50727; .NET CLR 1.1.4322; .NET CLR 3.0.04506.30; .NET CLR 3.0.04506.648; .NET CLR 3.0.4506.2152; .NET CLR 3.5.30729)"

78.41.144.41 - - [17/Jun/2010:10:49:51 +0200] "GET /Seiten/Bilder.html HTTP/1.0" 304 - "http://www.asylabwehramt.at/Seiten/Rundzeichen.html" "Mozilla/4.0 (compatible; MSIE 7.0; Windows NT 5.1; .NET CLR 2.0.50727; .NET CLR 1.1.4322; .NET CLR 3.0.04506.30; .NET CLR 3.0.04506.648; .NET CLR 3.0.4506.2152; .NET CLR 3.5.30729)"

78.41.144.41 - - [17/Jun/2010:10:49:58 +0200] "GET /Seiten/Bilder_buero.html HTTP/1.0" 200 11026 "http://www.asylabwehramt.at/Seiten/Bilder.html" "Mozilla/4.0 (compatible; MSIE 7.0; Windows NT 5
```

```
.1; .NET CLR 2.0.50727; .NET CLR 1.1.4322; .NET CLR 3.0.04506.30; .NET CLR 3.0.04506.648; .NET CL
R 3.0.4506.2152; .NET CLR 3.5.30729)"
78.41.144.41 - - [17/Jun/2010:10:49:59 +0200] "GET /Bilder/BAA_photos/IMG_0184.JPG HTTP/1.0" 200
125043 "http://www.asylabwehramt.at/Seiten/Bilder_buero.html" "Mozilla/4.0 (compatible; MSIE 7.0;
Windows NT 5.1; .NET CLR 2.0.50727; .NET CLR 1.1.4322; .NET CLR 3.0.04506.30; .NET CLR 3.0.04506
.648; .NET CLR 3.0.4506.2152; .NET CLR 3.5.30729)"
78.41.144.41 - - [17/Jun/2010:10:50:00 +0200] "GET /Bilder/BAA_photos/IMG_0194.JPG HTTP/1.0" 200
181536 "http://www.asylabwehramt.at/Seiten/Bilder_buero.html" "Mozilla/4.0 (compatible; MSIE 7.0;
Windows NT 5.1; .NET CLR 2.0.50727; .NET CLR 1.1.4322; .NET CLR 3.0.04506.30; .NET CLR 3.0.04506
.648; .NET CLR 3.0.4506.2152; .NET CLR 3.5.30729)"
78.41.144.41 - - [17/Jun/2010:10:53:09 +0200] "GET /index.html HTTP/1.0" 304 - "http://www.asylab
wehramt.at/Seiten/Bilder_buero.html" "Mozilla/4.0 (compatible; MSIE 7.0; Windows NT 5.1; .NET CLR
2.0.50727; .NET CLR 1.1.4322; .NET CLR 3.0.04506.30; .NET CLR 3.0.04506.648; .NET CLR 3.0.4506.2
152; .NET CLR 3.5.30729)"
78.41.144.41 - - [17/Jun/2010:10:53:22 +0200] "GET /Seiten/Aktuelles.html HTTP/1.0" 304 - "http:/
/www.asylabwehramt.at/index.html" "Mozilla/4.0 (compatible; MSIE 7.0; Windows NT 5.1; .NET CLR 2.
0.50727; .NET CLR 1.1.4322; .NET CLR 3.0.04506.30; .NET CLR 3.0.04506.648; .NET CLR 3.0.4506.2152
; .NET CLR 3.5.30729)"
78.41.144.41 - - [17/Jun/2010:10:53:23 +0200] "GET /Seiten/Material.html HTTP/1.0" 304 - "http://
www.asylabwehramt.at/Seiten/Aktuelles.html" "Mozilla/4.0 (compatible; MSIE 7.0; Windows NT 5.1; .
NET CLR 2.0.50727; .NET CLR 1.1.4322; .NET CLR 3.0.04506.30; .NET CLR 3.0.04506.648; .NET CLR 3.0
.4506.2152; .NET CLR 3.5.30729)"
78.41.144.41 - - [17/Jun/2010:10:53:27 +0200] "GET /Bilder/Ladung.png HTTP/1.0" 304 - "http://www
.asylabwehramt.at/Seiten/Material.html" "Mozilla/4.0 (compatible; MSIE 7.0; Windows NT 5.1; .NET
CLR 2.0.50727; .NET CLR 1.1.4322; .NET CLR 3.0.04506.30; .NET CLR 3.0.04506.648; .NET CLR 3.0.450
6.2152; .NET CLR 3.5.30729)"
78.41.144.41 - - [17/Jun/2010:10:53:38 +0200] "GET /Bilder/flyer_nigeria_Internet.pdf HTTP/1.0" 3
04 - "http://www.asylabwehramt.at/Seiten/Material.html" "Mozilla/4.0 (compatible; MSIE 7.0; Windo
```

ws NT 5.1; .NET CLR 2.0.50727; .NET CLR 1.1.4322; .NET CLR 3.0.4506.30; .NET CLR 3.0.4506.2152; .NET CLR 3.5.30729)"

78.41.144.41 - - [17/Jun/2010:10:53:39 +0200] "GET /Bilder/flyer_nigeria_Internet.pdf HTTP/1.0" 2 06 4096 "-" "Mozilla/4.0 (compatible; MSIE 7.0; Windows NT 5.1; .NET CLR 2.0.50727; .NET CLR 1.1. 4322; .NET CLR 3.0.04506.30; .NET CLR 3.0.04506.648; .NET CLR 3.0.4506.2152; .NET CLR 3.5.30729)"

78.41.144.41 - - [17/Jun/2010:10:54:02 +0200] "GET /Bilder/IOM-Kosovo-Broschuere_Internet.pdf HTT P/1.0" 304 - "http://www.asylabwehramt.at/Seiten/Material.html" "Mozilla/4.0 (compatible; MSIE 7. 0; Windows NT 5.1; .NET CLR 2.0.50727; .NET CLR 1.1.4322; .NET CLR 3.0.04506.30; .NET CLR 3.0.045 06.648; .NET CLR 3.0.4506.2152; .NET CLR 3.5.30729)"

78.41.144.41 - - [17/Jun/2010:10:54:03 +0200] "GET /Bilder/IOM-Kosovo-Broschuere_Internet.pdf HTT P/1.0" 206 4096 "-" "Mozilla/4.0 (compatible; MSIE 7.0; Windows NT 5.1; .NET CLR 2.0.50727; .NET CLR 1.1.4322; .NET CLR 3.0.04506.30; .NET CLR 3.0.04506.648; .NET CLR 3.0.4506.2152; .NET CLR 3.5 .30729)"

78.41.144.41 - - [17/Jun/2010:10:54:25 +0200] "GET /Seiten/Bilder.html HTTP/1.0" 304 - "http://ww w.asylabwehramt.at/Seiten/Material.html" "Mozilla/4.0 (compatible; MSIE 7.0; Windows NT 5.1; .NET CLR 2.0.50727; .NET CLR 1.1.4322; .NET CLR 3.0.04506.30; .NET CLR 3.0.04506.648; .NET CLR 3.0.45 06.2152; .NET CLR 3.5.30729)"

78.41.144.41 - - [17/Jun/2010:10:54:33 +0200] "GET /Seiten/Ausseneinsaetze.html HTTP/1.0" 304 - " http://www.asylabwehramt.at/Seiten/Bilder.html" "Mozilla/4.0 (compatible; MSIE 7.0; Windows NT 5. 1; .NET CLR 2.0.50727; .NET CLR 1.1.4322; .NET CLR 3.0.04506.30; .NET CLR 3.0.04506.648; .NET CLR 3.0.4506.2152; .NET CLR 3.5.30729)"

78.41.144.41 - - [17/Jun/2010:10:54:38 +0200] "GET /Seiten/Links.html HTTP/1.0" 304 - "http://www .asylabwehramt.at/Seiten/Ausseneinsaetze.html" "Mozilla/4.0 (compatible; MSIE 7.0; Windows NT 5.1 ; .NET CLR 2.0.50727; .NET CLR 1.1.4322; .NET CLR 3.0.04506.30; .NET CLR 3.0.04506.648; .NET CLR 3.0.4506.2152; .NET CLR 3.5.30729)"

78.41.144.41 - - [17/Jun/2010:10:58:50 +0200] "GET / HTTP/1.0" 304 - "-" "Mozilla/4.0 (compatible ; MSIE 7.0; Windows NT 5.1; .NET CLR 2.0.50727; .NET CLR 1.1.4322; .NET CLR 3.0.04506.30; .NET CL R 3.0.04506.648; .NET CLR 3.0.4506.2152; .NET CLR 3.5.30729)"

```
78.41.144.41 - - [17/Jun/2010:10:58:52 +0200] "GET /Seiten/Links.html HTTP/1.0" 304 - "http://www
.asylabwehramt.at/" "Mozilla/4.0 (compatible; MSIE 7.0; Windows NT 5.1; .NET CLR 2.0.50727; .NET
CLR 1.1.4322; .NET CLR 3.0.04506.30; .NET CLR 3.0.4506.648; .NET CLR 3.0.4506.2152; .NET CLR 3.5
.30729)"
78.41.144.41 - - [17/Jun/2010:10:58:53 +0200] "GET /Bilder/BMI.png HTTP/1.0" 304 - "http://www.as
ylabwehramt.at/Seiten/Links.html" "Mozilla/4.0 (compatible; MSIE 7.0; Windows NT 5.1; .NET CLR 2.
0.50727; .NET CLR 1.1.4322; .NET CLR 3.0.04506.30; .NET CLR 3.0.04506.648; .NET CLR 3.0.4506.2152
; .NET CLR 3.5.30729)"
80.120.179.10 - - [17/Jun/2010:13:13:25 +0200] "GET /Seiten/Rundzeichen.html HTTP/1.1" 200 8837 "
http://www.asylabwehramt.at/" "Mozilla/4.0 (compatible; MSIE 6.0; Windows NT 5.1; SV1; .NET CLR 1
.1.4322)"
80.120.179.10 - - [17/Jun/2010:13:13:26 +0200] "GET /Bilder/Asylabwehramt_Seal_800x800.png HTTP/1
.1" 200 269132 "http://www.asylabwehramt.at/Seiten/Rundzeichen.html" "Mozilla/4.0 (compatible; MS
IE 6.0; Windows NT 5.1; SV1; .NET CLR 1.1.4322)"
80.120.179.10 - - [17/Jun/2010:13:13:30 +0200] "GET /Seiten/Aktuelles.html HTTP/1.1" 200 12570 "h
ttp://www.asylabwehramt.at/Seiten/Rundzeichen.html" "Mozilla/4.0 (compatible; MSIE 6.0; Windows N
T 5.1; SV1; .NET CLR 1.1.4322)"
80.120.179.10 - - [17/Jun/2010:13:13:37 +0200] "GET /Seiten/Links.html HTTP/1.1" 200 18362 "http:
//www.asylabwehramt.at/Seiten/Aktuelles.html" "Mozilla/4.0 (compatible; MSIE 6.0; Windows NT 5.1;
SV1; .NET CLR 1.1.4322)"
80.120.179.10 - - [17/Jun/2010:13:14:43 +0200] "GET /Seiten/Material.html HTTP/1.1" 200 11980 "ht
tp://www.asylabwehramt.at/Seiten/Links.html" "Mozilla/4.0 (compatible; MSIE 6.0; Windows NT 5.1;
SV1; .NET CLR 1.1.4322)"
80.120.179.10 - - [17/Jun/2010:13:14:58 +0200] "GET /index.html HTTP/1.1" 200 11828 "http://www.a
sylabwehramt.at/Seiten/Aktuelles.html" "Mozilla/4.0 (compatible; MSIE 6.0; Windows NT 5.1; SV1; .
NET CLR 1.1.4322)"
80.120.179.10 - - [17/Jun/2010:13:15:03 +0200] "GET /Seiten/Bilder.html HTTP/1.1" 200 9571 "http:
//www.asylabwehramt.at/index.html" "Mozilla/4.0 (compatible; MSIE 6.0; Windows NT 5.1; SV1; .NET
```

```
CLR 1.1.4322)"
80.120.179.10 - - [17/Jun/2010:13:15:36 +0200] "GET /Seiten/Press.html HTTP/1.1" 200 10955 "http:
//www.asylabwehramt.at/Seiten/Links.html" "Mozilla/4.0 (compatible; MSIE 6.0; Windows NT 5.1; SV1
; .NET CLR 1.1.4322)"
80.120.179.10 - - [17/Jun/2010:13:16:02 +0200] "GET /Seiten/Orgstrukt.html HTTP/1.1" 200 14086 "h
ttp://www.asylabwehramt.at/Seiten/Aktuelles.html" "Mozilla/4.0 (compatible; MSIE 6.0; Windows NT
5.1; SV1; .NET CLR 1.1.4322)"
80.120.179.10 - - [17/Jun/2010:13:17:13 +0200] "GET /Seiten/Impressum.html HTTP/1.1" 200 11505 "h
ttp://www.asylabwehramt.at/Seiten/Aktuelles.html" "Mozilla/4.0 (compatible; MSIE 6.0; Windows NT
5.1; SV1; .NET CLR 1.1.4322)"
193.171.152.33 - - [17/Jun/2010:13:29:21 +0200] "GET / HTTP/1.1" 304 - "-" "Mozilla/5.0 (Windows;
U; Windows NT 5.1; de; rv:1.9.0.10) Gecko/2009042316 Firefox/3.0.10 (.NET CLR 3.5.30729)"
193.171.152.33 - - [17/Jun/2010:13:29:22 +0200] "GET /asyl.css HTTP/1.1" 304 - "http://www.asylab
wehramt.at/" "Mozilla/5.0 (Windows; U; Windows NT 5.1; de; rv:1.9.0.10) Gecko/2009042316 Firefox/
3.0.10 (.NET CLR 3.5.30729)"
193.171.152.33 - - [17/Jun/2010:13:29:24 +0200] "GET /favicon.ico HTTP/1.1" 302 340 "-" "Mozilla/
5.0 (Windows; U; Windows NT 5.1; de; rv:1.9.0.10) Gecko/2009042316 Firefox/3.0.10 (.NET CLR 3.5.3
0729)"
193.171.152.33 - - [17/Jun/2010:13:29:35 +0200] "GET / HTTP/1.1" 304 - "http://www.google.at/url?
sa=t&source=web&cd=1&ved=0CBcQFjAA&url=http%3A%2F%2Fwww.asylabwehramt.at%2F&rct=j&q=asylabwehramt
&ei=GgcaTMmH086h0On8idAK&usg=AFQjCNEy1zWClvnxkLlPAGifRc344_0U4Q" "Mozilla/5.0 (Windows; U; Window
s NT 5.1; de; rv:1.9.2.3) Gecko/20100401 Firefox/3.6.3"
193.171.152.33 - - [17/Jun/2010:13:29:36 +0200] "GET /Bilder/Header_AAbA.jpg HTTP/1.1" 304 - "htt
p://www.asylabwehramt.at/" "Mozilla/5.0 (Windows; U; Windows NT 5.1; de; rv:1.9.2.3) Gecko/201004
01 Firefox/3.6.3"
193.171.152.33 - - [17/Jun/2010:13:29:39 +0200] "GET /favicon.ico HTTP/1.1" 302 340 "-" "Mozilla/
5.0 (Windows; U; Windows NT 5.1; de; rv:1.9.2.3) Gecko/20100401 Firefox/3.6.3"
193.171.152.33 - - [17/Jun/2010:13:29:40 +0200] "GET /Seiten/Orgstrukt.html HTTP/1.1" 200 14086 "
```

```
http://www.asylabwehramt.at/" "Mozilla/5.0 (Windows; U; Windows NT 5.1; de; rv:1.9.0.10) Gecko/2009042316 Firefox/3.0.10 (.NET CLR 3.5.30729)"
193.171.152.33 - - [17/Jun/2010:13:29:45 +0200] "GET /Seiten/Bilder.html HTTP/1.1" 304 - "http://www.asylabwehramt.at/" "Mozilla/5.0 (Windows; U; Windows NT 5.1; de; rv:1.9.2.3) Gecko/20100401 Firefox/3.6.3"
193.171.152.33 - - [17/Jun/2010:13:30:02 +0200] "GET /Seiten/Bilder.html HTTP/1.1" 304 - "http://www.asylabwehramt.at/Seiten/Orgstrukt.html" "Mozilla/5.0 (Windows; U; Windows NT 5.1; de; rv:1.9.0.10) Gecko/2009042316 Firefox/3.0.10 (.NET CLR 3.5.30729)"
193.171.152.33 - - [17/Jun/2010:13:30:03 +0200] "GET /Seiten/Rundzeichen.html HTTP/1.1" 304 - "http://www.asylabwehramt.at/Seiten/Bilder.html" "Mozilla/5.0 (Windows; U; Windows NT 5.1; de; rv:1.9.2.3) Gecko/20100401 Firefox/3.6.3"
193.171.152.33 - - [17/Jun/2010:13:30:09 +0200] "GET /index.html HTTP/1.1" 304 - "http://www.asylabwehramt.at/Seiten/Rundzeichen.html" "Mozilla/5.0 (Windows; U; Windows NT 5.1; de; rv:1.9.2.3) Gecko/20100401 Firefox/3.6.3"
193.171.152.33 - - [17/Jun/2010:13:30:21 +0200] "GET /Seiten/Links.html HTTP/1.1" 304 - "http://www.asylabwehramt.at/Seiten/Bilder.html" "Mozilla/5.0 (Windows; U; Windows NT 5.1; de; rv:1.9.0.10) Gecko/2009042316 Firefox/3.0.10 (.NET CLR 3.5.30729)"
193.171.152.33 - - [17/Jun/2010:13:30:22 +0200] "GET /Bilder/frontex.png HTTP/1.1" 304 - "http://www.asylabwehramt.at/Seiten/Links.html" "Mozilla/5.0 (Windows; U; Windows NT 5.1; de; rv:1.9.0.10) Gecko/2009042316 Firefox/3.0.10 (.NET CLR 3.5.30729)"
193.171.152.33 - - [17/Jun/2010:13:30:57 +0200] "GET /index.html HTTP/1.1" 304 - "http://www.asylabwehramt.at/Seiten/Links.html" "Mozilla/5.0 (Windows; U; Windows NT 5.1; de; rv:1.9.0.10) Gecko/2009042316 Firefox/3.0.10 (.NET CLR 3.5.30729)"
193.171.152.33 - - [17/Jun/2010:13:31:33 +0200] "GET /Seiten/Aktuelles.html HTTP/1.1" 304 - "http://www.asylabwehramt.at/index.html" "Mozilla/5.0 (Windows; U; Windows NT 5.1; de; rv:1.9.2.3) Gecko/20100401 Firefox/3.6.3"
193.171.152.33 - - [17/Jun/2010:13:31:34 +0200] "GET /Bilder/fitnesscenter_traiskirchen.jpg HTTP/1.1" 304 - "http://www.asylabwehramt.at/Seiten/Aktuelles.html" "Mozilla/5.0 (Windows; U; Windows
```

NT 5.1; de; rv:1.9.2.3) Gecko/20100401 Firefox/3.6.3"
193.171.152.33 - - [17/Jun/2010:13:33:44 +0200] "GET /Seiten/Links.html HTTP/1.1" 304 - "http://www.asylabwehramt.at/Seiten/Aktuelles.html" "Mozilla/5.0 (Windows; U; Windows NT 5.1; de; rv:1.9.2.3) Gecko/20100401 Firefox/3.6.3"
193.171.152.33 - - [17/Jun/2010:13:34:28 +0200] "GET /Seiten/Press.html HTTP/1.1" 304 - "http://www.asylabwehramt.at/Seiten/Links.html" "Mozilla/5.0 (Windows; U; Windows NT 5.1; de; rv:1.9.2.3) Gecko/20100401 Firefox/3.6.3"
193.171.152.33 - - [17/Jun/2010:13:34:33 +0200] "GET /OEFFENTLICHKEIT/07062010d.pdf HTTP/1.1" 304 - "http://www.asylabwehramt.at/Seiten/Press.html" "Mozilla/5.0 (Windows; U; Windows NT 5.1; de; rv:1.9.2.3) Gecko/20100401 Firefox/3.6.3"
78.41.144.41 - - [17/Jun/2010:13:56:44 +0200] "GET / HTTP/1.0" 304 - "http://www.google.at/search?hl=de&source=hp&q=asylabwehramt&aq=f&aqi=&aql=&oq=&gs_rfai=" "Mozilla/4.0 (compatible; MSIE 7.0; Windows NT 5.1; .NET CLR 2.0.50727; .NET CLR 1.1.4322; .NET CLR 3.0.04506.30; .NET CLR 3.0.04506.648; .NET CLR 3.0.4506.2152; .NET CLR 3.5.30729)"
78.41.144.41 - - [17/Jun/2010:13:57:04 +0200] "GET /Seiten/Orgstrukt.html HTTP/1.0" 304 - "http://www.asylabwehramt.at/" "Mozilla/4.0 (compatible; MSIE 7.0; Windows NT 5.1; .NET CLR 2.0.50727; .NET CLR 1.1.4322; .NET CLR 3.0.04506.30; .NET CLR 3.0.04506.648; .NET CLR 3.0.4506.2152; .NET CLR 3.5.30729)"
78.41.144.41 - - [17/Jun/2010:13:57:14 +0200] "GET /Seiten/Material.html HTTP/1.0" 304 - "http://www.asylabwehramt.at/Seiten/Orgstrukt.html" "Mozilla/4.0 (compatible; MSIE 7.0; Windows NT 5.1; .NET CLR 2.0.50727; .NET CLR 1.1.4322; .NET CLR 3.0.04506.30; .NET CLR 3.0.04506.648; .NET CLR 3.0.4506.2152; .NET CLR 3.5.30729)"
78.41.144.41 - - [17/Jun/2010:13:57:19 +0200] "GET /Bilder/flyer_nigeria_Internet.pdf HTTP/1.0" 304 - "http://www.asylabwehramt.at/Seiten/Material.html" "Mozilla/4.0 (compatible; MSIE 7.0; Windows NT 5.1; .NET CLR 2.0.50727; .NET CLR 1.1.4322; .NET CLR 3.0.04506.30; .NET CLR 3.0.04506.648; .NET CLR 3.0.4506.2152; .NET CLR 3.5.30729)"
78.41.144.41 - - [17/Jun/2010:13:57:20 +0200] "GET /Bilder/flyer_nigeria_Internet.pdf HTTP/1.0" 206 4096 "-" "Mozilla/4.0 (compatible; MSIE 7.0; Windows NT 5.1; .NET CLR 1.1.

```
4322; .NET CLR 3.0.04506.30; .NET CLR 3.0.04506.648; .NET CLR 3.0.4506.2152; .NET CLR 3.5.30729)"
78.41.144.41 - - [17/Jun/2010:13:57:36 +0200] "GET /index.html HTTP/1.0" 304 - "http://www.asylab
wehramt.at/Seiten/Material.html" "Mozilla/4.0 (compatible; MSIE 7.0; Windows NT 5.1; .NET CLR 2.0
.50727; .NET CLR 1.1.4322; .NET CLR 3.0.04506.30; .NET CLR 3.0.04506.648; .NET CLR 3.0.4506.2152;
.NET CLR 3.5.30729)"
78.41.144.41 - - [17/Jun/2010:13:57:52 +0200] "GET /Seiten/Material.html HTTP/1.0" 304 - "http://
www.asylabwehramt.at/index.html" "Mozilla/4.0 (compatible; MSIE 7.0; Windows NT 5.1; .NET CLR 2.0
.50727; .NET CLR 1.1.4322; .NET CLR 3.0.04506.30; .NET CLR 3.0.04506.648; .NET CLR 3.0.4506.2152;
.NET CLR 3.5.30729)"
80.120.179.10 - - [17/Jun/2010:14:18:09 +0200] "GET /favicon.ico HTTP/1.1" 302 340 "-" "Mozilla/4
.0 (compatible; MSIE 8.0; Windows NT 5.1; Trident/4.0; .NET CLR 1.1.4322; .NET CLR 2.0.50727; .NE
T CLR 3.0.04506.30; .NET CLR 3.0.04506.648; InfoPath.2; MS-RTC LM 8)"
80.120.179.10 - - [17/Jun/2010:14:18:17 +0200] "GET /favicon.ico HTTP/1.1" 302 340 "-" "Mozilla/4
.0 (compatible; MSIE 8.0; Windows NT 5.1; Trident/4.0; .NET CLR 1.1.4322; .NET CLR 2.0.50727; .NE
T CLR 3.0.04506.30; .NET CLR 3.0.04506.648; InfoPath.2; MS-RTC LM 8)"
80.120.179.10 - - [17/Jun/2010:14:20:27 +0200] "GET /Bilder/Ladung.png HTTP/1.1" 200 114658 "http
://www.asylabwehramt.at/Seiten/Material.html" "Mozilla/4.0 (compatible; MSIE 8.0; Windows NT 5.1;
Trident/4.0; .NET CLR 1.1.4322; .NET CLR 2.0.50727; .NET CLR 3.0.04506.30; .NET CLR 3.0.04506.64
8; InfoPath.2; MS-RTC LM 8)"
80.120.179.10 - - [17/Jun/2010:14:20:44 +0200] "GET /Bilder/flyer_nigeria_Internet.pdf HTTP/1.1"
200 702826 "http://www.asylabwehramt.at/Seiten/Material.html" "Mozilla/4.0 (compatible; MSIE 8.0;
Windows NT 5.1; Trident/4.0; .NET CLR 1.1.4322; .NET CLR 2.0.50727; .NET CLR 3.0.04506.30; .NET
CLR 3.0.04506.648; InfoPath.2; MS-RTC LM 8)"
80.120.179.10 - - [17/Jun/2010:14:22:08 +0200] "GET /index_e.html HTTP/1.1" 200 11855 "http://www
.asylabwehramt.at/Seiten/Press.html" "Mozilla/4.0 (compatible; MSIE 8.0; Windows NT 5.1; Trident/
4.0; .NET CLR 1.1.4322; .NET CLR 2.0.50727; .NET CLR 3.0.04506.30; .NET CLR 3.0.04506.648; InfoPa
th.2; MS-RTC LM 8)"
80.120.179.10 - - [17/Jun/2010:14:22:11 +0200] "GET /Seiten/Latestnews.html HTTP/1.1" 200 12574 "
```

http://www.asylabwehramt.at/index_e.html" "Mozilla/4.0 (compatible; MSIE 8.0; Windows NT 5.1; Trident/4.0; .NET CLR 1.1.4322; .NET CLR 2.0.50727; .NET CLR 3.0.04506.30; .NET CLR 3.0.04506.648; InfoPath.2; MS-RTC LM 8)"

80.120.179.10 - - [17/Jun/2010:14:25:54 +0200] "GET /Material/Hotline_Russisch.pdf HTTP/1.1" 200 239827 "http://www.asylabwehramt.at/Seiten/Material.html" "Mozilla/4.0 (compatible; MSIE 8.0; Windows NT 5.1; Trident/4.0; .NET CLR 1.1.4322; .NET CLR 2.0.50727; .NET CLR 3.0.04506.30; .NET CLR 3.0.04506.648; InfoPath.2; MS-RTC LM 8)"

193.187.212.100 - - [17/Jun/2010:14:43:38 +0200] "GET /index.html HTTP/1.1" 304 - "-" "Mozilla/4.0 (compatible; MSIE 8.0; Windows NT 5.1; Trident/4.0)"

80.120.179.10 - - [17/Jun/2010:15:18:20 +0200] "GET / HTTP/1.1" 200 11828 "-" "Mozilla/4.0 (compatible; MSIE 8.0; Windows NT 5.1; Trident/4.0; .NET CLR 1.1.4322; .NET CLR 2.0.50727; .NET CLR 3.0.04506.30; .NET CLR 3.0.04506.648; InfoPath.2)"

78.41.144.41 - - [17/Jun/2010:15:18:33 +0200] "GET / HTTP/1.0" 304 - "-" "Mozilla/4.0 (compatible; MSIE 7.0; Windows NT 5.1; .NET CLR 2.0.50727; .NET CLR 1.1.4322; .NET CLR 3.0.04506.30; .NET CLR 3.0.04506.648; .NET CLR 3.0.04506.2152; .NET CLR 3.5.30729)"

78.41.144.41 - - [17/Jun/2010:15:18:34 +0200] "GET /favicon.ico HTTP/1.0" 302 340 "-" "Mozilla/4.0 (compatible; MSIE 7.0; Windows NT 5.1; .NET CLR 2.0.50727; .NET CLR 1.1.4322; .NET CLR 3.0.04506.30; .NET CLR 3.0.04506.648; .NET CLR 3.0.04506.2152; .NET CLR 3.5.30729)"

80.120.179.10 - - [17/Jun/2010:15:18:54 +0200] "GET /asyl.css HTTP/1.1" 200 860 "http://www.asylabwehramt.at/" "Mozilla/4.0 (compatible; MSIE 8.0; Windows NT 5.1; Trident/4.0; .NET CLR 1.1.4322; .NET CLR 2.0.50727; .NET CLR 3.0.04506.30; .NET CLR 3.0.04506.648; InfoPath.2)"

80.120.179.10 - - [17/Jun/2010:15:18:56 +0200] "GET /favicon.ico HTTP/1.1" 302 340 "-" "Mozilla/4.0 (compatible; MSIE 8.0; Windows NT 5.1; Trident/4.0; .NET CLR 1.1.4322; .NET CLR 2.0.50727; .NET CLR 3.0.04506.30; .NET CLR 3.0.04506.648; InfoPath.2)"

78.41.144.41 - - [17/Jun/2010:15:22:02 +0200] "GET / HTTP/1.0" 304 - "-" "Mozilla/4.0 (compatible; MSIE 7.0; Windows NT 5.1; .NET CLR 2.0.50727; .NET CLR 3.0.04506.30; .NET CLR 3.0.04506.648; .NET CLR 3.0.04506.2152; .NET CLR 3.5.21022; .NET CLR 3.5.30729)"

78.41.144.41 - - [17/Jun/2010:15:27:44 +0200] "GET / HTTP/1.0" 304 - "http://www.asylabwehramt.at

```
/" "Mozilla/4.0 (compatible; MSIE 7.0; Windows NT 5.1; .NET CLR 2.0.50727; .NET CLR 1.1.4322; .NE
T CLR 3.0.04506.30; .NET CLR 3.0.04506.648; .NET CLR 3.0.4506.2152; .NET CLR 3.5.30729)"
78.41.144.41 - - [17/Jun/2010:15:27:46 +0200] "GET /Seiten/Aktuelles.html HTTP/1.0" 304 - "http:/
/www.asylabwehramt.at/" "Mozilla/4.0 (compatible; MSIE 7.0; Windows NT 5.1; .NET CLR 2.0.50727; .
NET CLR 1.1.4322; .NET CLR 3.0.04506.30; .NET CLR 3.0.04506.648; .NET CLR 3.0.4506.2152; .NET CLR
3.5.30729)"
78.41.144.41 - - [17/Jun/2010:15:27:47 +0200] "GET /Bilder/56.jpg HTTP/1.0" 304 - "http://www.asy
labwehramt.at/Seiten/Aktuelles.html" "Mozilla/4.0 (compatible; MSIE 7.0; Windows NT 5.1; .NET CLR
2.0.50727; .NET CLR 1.1.4322; .NET CLR 3.0.04506.30; .NET CLR 3.0.04506.648; .NET CLR 3.0.4506.2
152; .NET CLR 3.5.30729)"
78.41.144.41 - - [17/Jun/2010:15:28:30 +0200] "GET /Seiten/Material.html HTTP/1.0" 304 - "http://
www.asylabwehramt.at/Seiten/Aktuelles.html" "Mozilla/4.0 (compatible; MSIE 7.0; Windows NT 5.1; .
NET CLR 2.0.50727; .NET CLR 1.1.4322; .NET CLR 3.0.04506.30; .NET CLR 3.0.04506.648; .NET CLR 3.0
.4506.2152; .NET CLR 3.5.30729)"
78.41.144.41 - - [17/Jun/2010:15:28:33 +0200] "GET /Bilder/flyer_nigeria_Internet.pdf HTTP/1.0" 3
04 - "http://www.asylabwehramt.at/Seiten/Material.html" "Mozilla/4.0 (compatible; MSIE 7.0; Windo
ws NT 5.1; .NET CLR 2.0.50727; .NET CLR 1.1.4322; .NET CLR 3.0.04506.30; .NET CLR 3.0.04506.648;
.NET CLR 3.0.4506.2152; .NET CLR 3.5.30729)"
78.41.144.41 - - [17/Jun/2010:15:28:34 +0200] "GET /Bilder/flyer_nigeria_Internet.pdf HTTP/1.0" 2
06 4096 "-" "Mozilla/4.0 (compatible; MSIE 7.0; Windows NT 5.1; .NET CLR 2.0.50727; .NET CLR 1.1.
4322; .NET CLR 3.0.04506.30; .NET CLR 3.0.04506.648; .NET CLR 3.0.4506.2152; .NET CLR 3.5.30729)"
78.41.144.41 - - [17/Jun/2010:15:28:48 +0200] "GET /Bilder/IOM-Kosovo-Broschuere_Internet.pdf HTT
P/1.0" 304 - "http://www.asylabwehramt.at/Seiten/Material.html" "Mozilla/4.0 (compatible; MSIE 7.
0; Windows NT 5.1; .NET CLR 2.0.50727; .NET CLR 1.1.4322; .NET CLR 3.0.04506.30; .NET CLR 3.0.045
06.648; .NET CLR 3.0.4506.2152; .NET CLR 3.5.30729)"
78.41.144.41 - - [17/Jun/2010:15:28:49 +0200] "GET /Bilder/IOM-Kosovo-Broschuere_Internet.pdf HTT
P/1.0" 206 4096 "-" "Mozilla/4.0 (compatible; MSIE 7.0; Windows NT 5.1; .NET CLR 2.0.50727; .NET
CLR 1.1.4322; .NET CLR 3.0.04506.30; .NET CLR 3.0.04506.648; .NET CLR 3.5
```

```
.30729)"
78.41.144.41 - - [17/Jun/2010:15:29:12 +0200] "GET /Material/Hotline_DariFarsiPersisch.pdf HTTP/1.0" 200 143251 "http://www.asylabwehramt.at/Seiten/Material.html" "Mozilla/4.0 (compatible; MSIE 7.0; Windows NT 5.1; .NET CLR 2.0.50727; .NET CLR 1.1.4322; .NET CLR 3.0.4506.30; .NET CLR 3.0.0 4506.648; .NET CLR 3.0.4506.2152; .NET CLR 3.5.30729)"
80.120.179.10 - - [17/Jun/2010:15:29:15 +0200] "GET /favicon.ico HTTP/1.1" 302 340 "-" "Mozilla/4.0 (compatible; MSIE 8.0; Windows NT 5.1; Trident/4.0; .NET CLR 1.1.4322; InfoPath.1)"
78.41.144.41 - - [17/Jun/2010:15:29:22 +0200] "GET /Material/Asyl_Jahresstatistik_2009.pdf HTTP/1.0" 304 - "http://www.asylabwehramt.at/Seiten/Material.html" "Mozilla/4.0 (compatible; MSIE 7.0; Windows NT 5.1; .NET CLR 2.0.50727; .NET CLR 1.1.4322; .NET CLR 3.0.04506.30; .NET CLR 3.0.04506. 648; .NET CLR 3.0.4506.2152; .NET CLR 3.5.30729)"
78.41.144.41 - - [17/Jun/2010:15:29:28 +0200] "GET /Seiten/Images.html HTTP/1.0" 304 - "http://ww w.asylabwehramt.at/Seiten/Material.html" "Mozilla/4.0 (compatible; MSIE 7.0; Windows NT 5.1; .NET CLR 2.0.50727; .NET CLR 1.1.4322; .NET CLR 3.0.04506.30; .NET CLR 3.0.04506.648; .NET CLR 3.0.45 06.2152; .NET CLR 3.5.30729)"
78.41.144.41 - - [17/Jun/2010:15:29:29 +0200] "GET /Bilder/SCREEN_AAbA_Edutainment_Video.jpg HTTP /1.0" 304 - "http://www.asylabwehramt.at/Seiten/Images.html" "Mozilla/4.0 (compatible; MSIE 7.0; Windows NT 5.1; .NET CLR 2.0.50727; .NET CLR 1.1.4322; .NET CLR 3.0.04506.30; .NET CLR 3.0.04506. 648; .NET CLR 3.0.4506.2152; .NET CLR 3.5.30729)"
78.41.144.41 - - [17/Jun/2010:15:29:35 +0200] "GET /Seiten/Ausseneinsaetze.html HTTP/1.0" 304 - " http://www.asylabwehramt.at/Seiten/Images.html" "Mozilla/4.0 (compatible; MSIE 7.0; Windows NT 5. 1; .NET CLR 2.0.50727; .NET CLR 1.1.4322; .NET CLR 3.0.04506.30; .NET CLR 3.0.04506.648; .NET CLR 3.0.4506.2152; .NET CLR 3.5.30729)"
78.41.144.41 - - [17/Jun/2010:15:29:46 +0200] "GET /Seiten/Bilder_buero.html HTTP/1.0" 304 - "htt p://www.asylabwehramt.at/Seiten/Images.html" "Mozilla/4.0 (compatible; MSIE 7.0; Windows NT 5.1; .NET CLR 2.0.50727; .NET CLR 1.1.4322; .NET CLR 3.0.04506.30; .NET CLR 3.0.04506.648; .NET CLR 3. 0.4506.2152; .NET CLR 3.5.30729)"
78.41.144.41 - - [17/Jun/2010:15:29:47 +0200] "GET /Bilder/BAA_photos/IMG_0182.JPG HTTP/1.0" 304
```

```
78.41.144.41 - - [17/Jun/2010:15:29:49 +0200] "GET /Bilder/BAA_photos/IMG_0187.JPG HTTP/1.0" 304 - "http://www.asylabwehramt.at/Seiten/Bilder_buero.html" "Mozilla/4.0 (compatible; MSIE 7.0; Windows NT 5.1; .NET CLR 2.0.50727; .NET CLR 1.1.4322; .NET CLR 3.0.4506.2152; .NET CLR 3.0.04506.30; .NET CLR 3.0.04506.648; .NET CLR 3.5.30729)"
78.41.144.41 - - [17/Jun/2010:15:29:50 +0200] "GET /Bilder/BAA_photos/IMG_0189.JPG HTTP/1.0" 304 - "http://www.asylabwehramt.at/Seiten/Bilder_buero.html" "Mozilla/4.0 (compatible; MSIE 7.0; Windows NT 5.1; .NET CLR 2.0.50727; .NET CLR 1.1.4322; .NET CLR 3.0.4506.2152; .NET CLR 3.0.04506.30; .NET CLR 3.0.04506.648; .NET CLR 3.5.30729)"
78.41.144.41 - - [17/Jun/2010:15:29:51 +0200] "GET /Bilder/BAA_photos/IMG_0196.JPG HTTP/1.0" 304 - "http://www.asylabwehramt.at/Seiten/Bilder_buero.html" "Mozilla/4.0 (compatible; MSIE 7.0; Windows NT 5.1; .NET CLR 2.0.50727; .NET CLR 1.1.4322; .NET CLR 3.0.4506.2152; .NET CLR 3.0.04506.30; .NET CLR 3.0.04506.648; .NET CLR 3.5.30729)"
78.41.144.41 - - [17/Jun/2010:15:30:55 +0200] "GET /Seiten/Links_e.html HTTP/1.0" 304 - "http://www.asylabwehramt.at/Seiten/Images.html" "Mozilla/4.0 (compatible; MSIE 7.0; Windows NT 5.1; .NET CLR 2.0.50727; .NET CLR 1.1.4322; .NET CLR 3.0.04506.30; .NET CLR 3.0.04506.648; .NET CLR 3.0.450 6.2152; .NET CLR 3.5.30729)"
80.120.179.10 - - [17/Jun/2010:15:31:48 +0200] "GET /Material/Hotline_Deutsch.pdf HTTP/1.1" 200 4 89465 "http://www.asylabwehramt.at/" "Mozilla/4.0 (compatible; MSIE 8.0; Windows NT 5.1; Trident/ 4.0; .NET CLR 1.1.4322; InfoPath.1)"
78.41.144.41 - - [17/Jun/2010:15:31:57 +0200] "GET /Seiten/Presse.html HTTP/1.0" 200 10956 "http://www.asylabwehramt.at/Seiten/Links_e.html" "Mozilla/4.0 (compatible; MSIE 7.0; Windows NT 5.1; .NET CLR 2.0.50727; .NET CLR 1.1.4322; .NET CLR 3.0.04506.30; .NET CLR 3.0.04506.648; .NET CLR 3.0.4506.2152; .NET CLR 3.5.30729)"
78.41.144.41 - - [17/Jun/2010:15:31:59 +0200] "GET /OEFFENTLICHKEIT/07062010d.pdf HTTP/1.0" 304 - "http://www.asylabwehramt.at/Seiten/Presse.html" "Mozilla/4.0 (compatible; MSIE 7.0; Windows NT
```

```
5.1; .NET CLR 2.0.50727; .NET CLR 1.1.4322; .NET CLR 3.0.04506.30; .NET CLR 3.0.04506.648; .NET C
LR 3.0.4506.2152; .NET CLR 3.5.30729)"
78.41.144.41 - - [17/Jun/2010:15:32:34 +0200] "GET /Seiten/Press.html HTTP/1.0" 304 - "http://www
.asylabwehramt.at/Seiten/Presse.html" "Mozilla/4.0 (compatible; MSIE 7.0; Windows NT 5.1; .NET CL
R 2.0.50727; .NET CLR 1.1.4322; .NET CLR 3.0.04506.30; .NET CLR 3.0.04506.648; .NET CLR 3.0.4506.
2152; .NET CLR 3.5.30729)"
80.120.179.10 - - [17/Jun/2010:17:21:16 +0200] "GET /Material/Asyl_Jahresstatistik_2009.pdf HTTP/
1.1" 200 680643 "http://www.asylabwehramt.at/Seiten/Material.html" "Mozilla/4.0 (compatible; MSIE
6.0; Windows NT 5.1; SV1; .NET CLR 1.1.4322; .NET CLR 2.0.50727; .NET CLR 3.0.04506.30; .NET CLR
3.0.04506.648; InfoPath.2)"
88.116.224.102 - - [17/Jun/2010:23:12:06 +0200] "GET / HTTP/1.1" 200 11828 "http://diepresse.com
/home/panorama/oesterreich/574454/index.do?offset=1325&page=28" "Mozilla/5.0 (X11; U; Linux i686
; de; rv:1.9.0.18) Gecko/2010021501 Ubuntu/9.04 (jaunty) Firefox/3.0.18"
88.116.224.102 - - [17/Jun/2010:23:12:07 +0200] "GET /favicon.ico HTTP/1.1" 302 340 "-" "Mozilla/
5.0 (X11; U; Linux i686; de; rv:1.9.0.18) Gecko/2010021501 Ubuntu/9.04 (jaunty) Firefox/3.0.18"
88.116.224.102 - - [17/Jun/2010:23:13:21 +0200] "GET /Seiten/Orgstrukt.html HTTP/1.1" 200 14086 "
$http://diepresse.com/home/panorama/oesterreich/574454/index.do?offset=1325&page=28" "Mozilla/5.
0 (X11; U; Linux i686; de; rv:1.9.0.18) Gecko/2010021501 Ubuntu/9.04 (jaunty) Firefox/3.0.18"
88.116.224.102 - - [17/Jun/2010:23:13:22 +0200] "GET /favicon.ico HTTP/1.1" 302 340 "-" "Mozilla/
5.0 (X11; U; Linux i686; de; rv:1.9.0.18) Gecko/2010021501 Ubuntu/9.04 (jaunty) Firefox/3.0.18"
88.116.224.102 - - [17/Jun/2010:23:13:25 +0200] "GET /favicon.ico HTTP/1.1" 302 340 "-" "Mozilla/
5.0 (X11; U; Linux i686; de; rv:1.9.0.18) Gecko/2010021501 Ubuntu/9.04 (jaunty) Firefox/3.0.18"
88.116.224.102 - - [17/Jun/2010:23:15:09 +0200] "GET /index.html HTTP/1.1" 200 11828 "http://www.
asylabwehramt.at/Seiten/Orgstrukt.html" "Mozilla/5.0 (X11; U; Linux i686; de; rv:1.9.0.18) Gecko/
2010021501 Ubuntu/9.04 (jaunty) Firefox/3.0.18"
88.116.224.102 - - [17/Jun/2010:23:15:11 +0200] "GET /Seiten/Aktuelles.html HTTP/1.1" 200 12570 "
http://www.asylabwehramt.at/index.html" "Mozilla/5.0 (X11; U; Linux i686; de; rv:1.9.0.18) Gecko/
```

```
2010021501 Ubuntu/9.04 (jaunty) Firefox/3.0.18"
88.116.224.102 - - [17/Jun/2010:23:15:12 +0200] "GET /Bilder/leistung_2.jpg HTTP/1.1" 200 4918 "http://www.asylabwehramt.at/Seiten/Aktuelles.html" "Mozilla/5.0 (X11; U; Linux i686; de; rv:1.9.0.18) Gecko/2010021501 Ubuntu/9.04 (jaunty) Firefox/3.0.18"
88.116.224.102 - - [17/Jun/2010:23:15:29 +0200] "GET /favicon.ico HTTP/1.1" 302 340 "-" "Mozilla/5.0 (X11; U; Linux i686; de; rv:1.9.0.18) Gecko/2010021501 Ubuntu/9.04 (jaunty) Firefox/3.0.18"
88.116.224.102 - - [17/Jun/2010:23:15:30 +0200] "GET /Bilder/Asylabwehramt_Seal_800x800.png HTTP/1.1" 206 59506 "http://www.asylabwehramt.at/Seiten/Rundzeichen.html" "Mozilla/5.0 (X11; U; Linux i686; de; rv:1.9.0.18) Gecko/2010021501 Ubuntu/9.04 (jaunty) Firefox/3.0.18"
88.116.224.102 - - [17/Jun/2010:23:15:32 +0200] "GET /favicon.ico HTTP/1.1" 302 340 "-" "Mozilla/5.0 (X11; U; Linux i686; de; rv:1.9.0.18) Gecko/2010021501 Ubuntu/9.04 (jaunty) Firefox/3.0.18"
88.116.224.102 - - [17/Jun/2010:23:15:41 +0200] "GET /Seiten/Links.html HTTP/1.1" 200 18362 "http://www.asylabwehramt.at/Seiten/Rundzeichen.html" "Mozilla/5.0 (X11; U; Linux i686; de; rv:1.9.0.18) Gecko/2010021501 Ubuntu/9.04 (jaunty) Firefox/3.0.18"
88.116.224.102 - - [17/Jun/2010:23:15:47 +0200] "GET /favicon.ico HTTP/1.1" 302 340 "-" "Mozilla/5.0 (X11; U; Linux i686; de; rv:1.9.0.18) Gecko/2010021501 Ubuntu/9.04 (jaunty) Firefox/3.0.18"
88.116.224.102 - - [17/Jun/2010:23:16:22 +0200] "GET /Seiten/Impressum.html HTTP/1.1" 200 11505 "http://www.asylabwehramt.at/Seiten/Links.html" "Mozilla/5.0 (X11; U; Linux i686; de; rv:1.9.0.18) Gecko/2010021501 Ubuntu/9.04 (jaunty) Firefox/3.0.18"
88.116.224.102 - - [17/Jun/2010:23:19:05 +0200] "GET /favicon.ico HTTP/1.1" 302 340 "-" "Mozilla/5.0 (X11; U; Linux i686; de; rv:1.9.0.18) Gecko/2010021501 Ubuntu/9.04 (jaunty) Firefox/3.0.18"
88.116.224.102 - - [17/Jun/2010:23:19:21 +0200] "GET /favicon.ico HTTP/1.1" 302 340 "-" "Mozilla/5.0 (X11; U; Linux i686; de; rv:1.9.0.18) Gecko/2010021501 Ubuntu/9.04 (jaunty) Firefox/3.0.18"
88.116.224.102 - - [17/Jun/2010:23:19:55 +0200] "GET /favicon.ico HTTP/1.1" 302 340 "-" "Mozilla/5.0 (X11; U; Linux i686; de; rv:1.9.0.18) Gecko/2010021501 Ubuntu/9.04 (jaunty) Firefox/3.0.18"
88.116.224.102 - - [17/Jun/2010:23:20:41 +0200] "GET /favicon.ico HTTP/1.1" 302 340 "-" "Mozilla/5.0 (X11; U; Linux i686; de; rv:1.9.0.18) Gecko/2010021501 Ubuntu/9.04 (jaunty) Firefox/3.0.18"
88.116.224.102 - - [17/Jun/2010:23:21:29 +0200] "GET /favicon.ico HTTP/1.1" 302 340 "-" "Mozilla/5.0 (X11; U; Linux i686; de; rv:1.9.0.18) Gecko/2010021501 Ubuntu/9.04 (jaunty) Firefox/3.0.18"
```

5.0 (X11; U; Linux i686; de; rv:1.9.0.18) Gecko/2010021501 Ubuntu/9.04 (jaunty) Firefox/3.0.18"
193.171.152.33 - - [17/Jun/2010:23:22:03 +0200] "GET / HTTP/1.1" 304 - "-" "Mozilla/4.0 (compatib
le; MSIE 8.0; Windows NT 5.1; Trident/4.0; InfoPath.1; .NET CLR 1.1.4322; .NET CLR 2.0.50727; .NE
T CLR 3.0.04506.30; .NET CLR 3.0.04506.648; .NET CLR 3.0.4506.2152; .NET CLR 3.5.30729)"
193.171.152.33 - - [17/Jun/2010:23:22:11 +0200] "GET /Seiten/Impressum.html HTTP/1.1" 304 - "http
://www.asylabwehramt.at/" "Mozilla/4.0 (compatible; MSIE 8.0; Windows NT 5.1; Trident/4.0; InfoPa
th.1; .NET CLR 1.1.4322; .NET CLR 2.0.50727; .NET CLR 3.0.04506.30; .NET CLR 3.0.04506.648; .NET
CLR 3.0.4506.2152; .NET CLR 3.5.30729)"
193.171.152.33 - - [18/Jun/2010:05:34:40 +0200] "GET /index.html HTTP/1.1" 304 - "http://www.asyl
abwehramt.at/Seiten/Orgstrukt.html" "Mozilla/4.0 (compatible; MSIE 8.0; Windows NT 5.1; Trident/4
.0; InfoPath.1; .NET CLR 1.1.4322; .NET CLR 2.0.50727; .NET CLR 3.0.04506.30; .NET CLR 3.0.04506.
648; .NET CLR 3.0.4506.2152; .NET CLR 3.5.30729)"
193.171.152.33 - - [18/Jun/2010:05:37:42 +0200] "GET /Material/Hotline_Deutsch.pdf HTTP/1.1" 200
489465 "http://www.asylabwehramt.at/index.html" "Mozilla/4.0 (compatible; MSIE 8.0; Windows NT 5.
1; Trident/4.0; InfoPath.1; .NET CLR 1.1.4322; .NET CLR 2.0.50727; .NET CLR 3.0.04506.30; .NET CL
R 3.0.04506.648; .NET CLR 3.0.4506.2152; .NET CLR 3.5.30729)"
193.171.152.33 - - [18/Jun/2010:05:39:04 +0200] "GET /Seiten/Aktuelles.html HTTP/1.1" 304 - "http
://www.asylabwehramt.at/index.html" "Mozilla/4.0 (compatible; MSIE 8.0; Windows NT 5.1; Trident/4
.0; InfoPath.1; .NET CLR 1.1.4322; .NET CLR 2.0.50727; .NET CLR 3.0.04506.30; .NET CLR 3.0.04506.
648; .NET CLR 3.0.4506.2152; .NET CLR 3.5.30729)"
193.171.152.33 - - [18/Jun/2010:05:40:32 +0200] "GET /Seiten/Rundzeichen.html HTTP/1.1" 304 - "ht
tp://www.asylabwehramt.at/Seiten/Impressum.html" "Mozilla/4.0 (compatible; MSIE 8.0; Windows NT 5
.1; Trident/4.0; InfoPath.1; .NET CLR 1.1.4322; .NET CLR 2.0.50727; .NET CLR 3.0.04506.30; .NET C
LR 3.0.04506.648; .NET CLR 3.0.4506.2152; .NET CLR 3.5.30729)"
193.171.152.33 - - [18/Jun/2010:05:40:50 +0200] "GET /Seiten/Bilder.html HTTP/1.1" 304 - "http://
www.asylabwehramt.at/Seiten/Rundzeichen.html" "Mozilla/4.0 (compatible; MSIE 8.0; Windows NT 5.1;
Trident/4.0; InfoPath.1; .NET CLR 1.1.4322; .NET CLR 2.0.50727; .NET CLR 3.0.04506.30; .NET CLR
3.0.04506.648; .NET CLR 3.0.4506.2152; .NET CLR 3.5.30729)"

```
193.171.152.33 - - [18/Jun/2010:05:41:10 +0200] "GET /Seiten/Ausseneinsaetze.html HTTP/1.1" 304 -
"http://www.asylabwehramt.at/Seiten/Bilder.html" "Mozilla/4.0 (compatible; MSIE 8.0; Windows NT
5.1; Trident/4.0; InfoPath.1; .NET CLR 1.1.4322; .NET CLR 2.0.50727; .NET CLR 3.0.04506.30; .NET
CLR 3.0.04506.648; .NET CLR 3.0.4506.2152; .NET CLR 3.5.30729)"
193.171.152.33 - - [18/Jun/2010:05:41:31 +0200] "GET /Seiten/Links.html HTTP/1.1" 304 - "http://w
ww.asylabwehramt.at/Seiten/Ausseneinsaetze.html" "Mozilla/4.0 (compatible; MSIE 8.0; Windows NT 5
.1; Trident/4.0; InfoPath.1; .NET CLR 1.1.4322; .NET CLR 2.0.50727; .NET CLR 3.0.04506.30; .NET C
LR 3.0.04506.648; .NET CLR 3.0.4506.2152; .NET CLR 3.5.30729)"
193.171.152.33 - - [18/Jun/2010:05:41:32 +0200] "GET /Bilder/BMI.png HTTP/1.1" 304 - "http://www.
asylabwehramt.at/Seiten/Links.html" "Mozilla/4.0 (compatible; MSIE 8.0; Windows NT 5.1; Trident/4
.0; InfoPath.1; .NET CLR 1.1.4322; .NET CLR 2.0.50727; .NET CLR 3.0.04506.30; .NET CLR 3.0.04506.
648; .NET CLR 3.0.4506.2152; .NET CLR 3.5.30729)"
88.116.224.102 - - [18/Jun/2010:06:28:48 +0200] "GET / HTTP/1.1" 200 11828 "http://www.google.at/
url?sa=t&source=web&cd=1&ved=0CBcQFjAA&url=http%3A%2F%2Fwww.asylabwehramt.at%2F&rct=j&q= asylabweh
ramt &ei=8vUaTK6pNZCmOK30yJ8K&usg=AFQjCNEy1zWClvnxklLlPAGifRc344_OU4Q" "Mozilla/5.0 (X11; U; Linux
i686; de; rv:1.9.1.7) Gecko/20100106 Ubuntu/9.10 (karmic) Firefox/3.5.7"
88.116.224.102 - - [18/Jun/2010:06:28:49 +0200] "GET /Bilder/Header_AAbA.jpg HTTP/1.1" 200 33599
"http://www.asylabwehramt.at/" "Mozilla/5.0 (X11; U; Linux i686; de; rv:1.9.1.7) Gecko/20100106 U
buntu/9.10 (karmic) Firefox/3.5.7"
88.116.224.102 - - [18/Jun/2010:06:30:57 +0200] "GET /Material/Hotline_Deutsch.pdf HTTP/1.1" 200
489465 "http://www.asylabwehramt.at/" "Mozilla/5.0 (X11; U; Linux i686; de; rv:1.9.1.7) Gecko/201
00106 Ubuntu/9.10 (karmic) Firefox/3.5.7"
88.116.224.102 - - [18/Jun/2010:06:31:28 +0200] "GET /Seiten/Aktuelles.html HTTP/1.1" 200 12570 "
http://www.asylabwehramt.at/" "Mozilla/5.0 (X11; U; Linux i686; de; rv:1.9.1.7) Gecko/20100106 Ub
untu/9.10 (karmic) Firefox/3.5.7"
88.116.224.102 - - [18/Jun/2010:06:32:00 +0200] "GET /Seiten/Material.html HTTP/1.1" 200 11980 "h
ttp://www.asylabwehramt.at/Seiten/Aktuelles.html" "Mozilla/5.0 (X11; U; Linux i686; de; rv:1.9.1.
7) Gecko/20100106 Ubuntu/9.10 (karmic) Firefox/3.5.7"
```

```
88.116.224.102 - - [18/Jun/2010:06:32:10 +0200] "GET /Bilder/IOM-Kosovo-Broschuere_Internet.pdf HTTP/1.1" 200 728811 "http://www.asylabwehramt.at/Seiten/Material.html" "Mozilla/5.0 (X11; U; Linux i686; de; rv:1.9.1.7) Gecko/20100106 Ubuntu/9.10 (karmic) Firefox/3.5.7"
88.116.224.102 - - [18/Jun/2010:06:34:08 +0200] "GET /Seiten/Bilder.html HTTP/1.1" 200 9571 "http://www.asylabwehramt.at/Seiten/Material.html" "Mozilla/5.0 (X11; U; Linux i686; de; rv:1.9.1.7) Gecko/20100106 Ubuntu/9.10 (karmic) Firefox/3.5.7"
88.116.224.102 - - [18/Jun/2010:06:34:09 +0200] "GET /Bilder/BAA_photos/IMG_0198.JPG HTTP/1.1" 200 109214 "http://www.asylabwehramt.at/Seiten/Bilder.html" "Mozilla/5.0 (X11; U; Linux i686; de; rv:1.9.1.7) Gecko/20100106 Ubuntu/9.10 (karmic) Firefox/3.5.7"
88.116.224.102 - - [18/Jun/2010:06:34:53 +0200] "GET /Seiten/Press.html HTTP/1.1" 200 10955 "http://www.asylabwehramt.at/Seiten/Material.html" "Mozilla/5.0 (X11; U; Linux i686; de; rv:1.9.1.7) Gecko/20100106 Ubuntu/9.10 (karmic) Firefox/3.5.7"
80.120.179.10 - - [18/Jun/2010:08:45:42 +0200] "GET /favicon.ico HTTP/1.1" 302 340 "-" "Mozilla/4.0 (compatible; MSIE 8.0; Windows NT 5.1; Trident/4.0; InfoPath.1; .NET CLR 1.1.4322; .NET CLR 2.0.50727; MS-RTC LM 8)"
80.120.179.10 - - [18/Jun/2010:08:46:13 +0200] "GET /Seiten/Bilder.html HTTP/1.1" 200 9571 "http://www.asylabwehramt.at/" "Mozilla/4.0 (compatible; MSIE 8.0; Windows NT 5.1; Trident/4.0; InfoPath.1; .NET CLR 1.1.4322; .NET CLR 2.0.50727; MS-RTC LM 8)"
80.120.179.10 - - [18/Jun/2010:08:46:49 +0200] "GET /index.html HTTP/1.1" 200 11828 "http://www.asylabwehramt.at/Seiten/Bilder.html" "Mozilla/4.0 (compatible; MSIE 8.0; Windows NT 5.1; Trident/4.0; InfoPath.1; .NET CLR 2.0.50727; MS-RTC LM 8)"
80.120.179.10 - - [18/Jun/2010:08:47:05 +0200] "GET /Seiten/Press.html HTTP/1.1" 200 10955 "http://www.asylabwehramt.at/index.html" "Mozilla/4.0 (compatible; MSIE 8.0; Windows NT 5.1; Trident/4.0; InfoPath.1; .NET CLR 2.0.50727; MS-RTC LM 8)"
80.120.179.10 - - [18/Jun/2010:08:47:20 +0200] "GET /Seiten/Rundzeichen.html HTTP/1.1" 200 8837 "http://www.asylabwehramt.at/Seiten/Press.html" "Mozilla/4.0 (compatible; MSIE 8.0; Windows NT 5.1; Trident/4.0; InfoPath.1; .NET CLR 1.1.4322; .NET CLR 2.0.50727; MS-RTC LM 8)"
80.120.179.10 - - [18/Jun/2010:08:47:30 +0200] "GET /Seiten/Material.html HTTP/1.1" 200 11980 "ht
```

tp://www.asylabwehramt.at/Seiten/Rundzeichen.html" "Mozilla/4.0 (compatible; MSIE 8.0; Windows NT 5.1; Trident/4.0; InfoPath.1; .NET CLR 1.1.4322; .NET CLR 2.0.50727; MS-RTC LM 8)"
80.120.179.10 - - [18/Jun/2010:08:47:37 +0200] "GET /Seiten/Aktuelles.html HTTP/1.1" 200 12570 "h
ttp://www.asylabwehramt.at/Seiten/Material.html" "Mozilla/4.0 (compatible; MSIE 8.0; Windows NT 5
.1; Trident/4.0; InfoPath.1; .NET CLR 1.1.4322; .NET CLR 2.0.50727; MS-RTC LM 8)"
80.120.179.10 - - [18/Jun/2010:08:48:09 +0200] "GET /Seiten/Links.html HTTP/1.1" 200 18362 "http:
//www.asylabwehramt.at/Seiten/Material.html" "Mozilla/4.0 (compatible; MSIE 8.0; Windows NT 5.1;
Trident/4.0; InfoPath.1; .NET CLR 1.1.4322; .NET CLR 2.0.50727; MS-RTC LM 8)"
80.120.179.10 - - [18/Jun/2010:10:39:03 +0200] "GET / HTTP/1.1" 304 - "http://www.google.at/searc
h?hl=de&source=hp&q=asylabwehramt&meta=&aq=f&aqi=&aql=&oq=&gs_rfai=" "Mozilla/4.0 (compatible; MS
IE 6.0; Windows NT 5.1; SV1; .NET CLR 1.1.4322; .NET CLR 3.0.4506.2152; .NET
CLR 3.5.30729)"
193.171.152.33 - - [18/Jun/2010:10:48:26 +0200] "GET / HTTP/1.1" 304 - "http://www.google.at/url?
sa=t&source=web&cd=1&ved=0CBUQhgIwAA&url=http%3A%2F%2Fwww.asylabwehramt.at%2F&rct=j&q=asylabwehr&
ei=1zIbTMi3A8maON7vxKcK&usg=AFQjCNEy1zWClvnxklIPAGifRc344_0U4Q" "Mozilla/5.0 (Windows; U; Windows
NT 5.1; de; rv:1.9.0.10) Gecko/2009042316 Firefox/3.0.10 (.NET CLR 3.5.30729)"
193.171.152.33 - - [18/Jun/2010:10:48:27 +0200] "GET /favicon.ico HTTP/1.1" 302 340 "-" "Mozilla/
5.0 (Windows; U; Windows NT 5.1; de; rv:1.9.0.10) Gecko/2009042316 Firefox/3.0.10 (.NET CLR 3.5.3
0729)"
193.171.152.33 - - [18/Jun/2010:10:48:29 +0200] "GET /favicon.ico HTTP/1.1" 302 340 "-" "Mozilla/
5.0 (Windows; U; Windows NT 5.1; de; rv:1.9.0.10) Gecko/2009042316 Firefox/3.0.10 (.NET CLR 3.5.3
0729)"
193.171.152.33 - - [18/Jun/2010:10:48:38 +0200] "GET /Seiten/Aktuelles.html HTTP/1.1" 304 - "http
://www.asylabwehramt.at/" "Mozilla/5.0 (Windows; U; Windows NT 5.1; de; rv:1.9.0.10) Gecko/2009042316 Firefox/3.0.10 (.NET CLR 3.5.30729)"
193.171.152.33 - - [18/Jun/2010:10:48:39 +0200] "GET /Bilder/56.jpg HTTP/1.1" 304 - "http://www.a
sylabwehramt.at/Seiten/Aktuelles.html" "Mozilla/5.0 (Windows; U; Windows NT 5.1; de; rv:1.9.0.10)
Gecko/2009042316 Firefox/3.0.10 (.NET CLR 3.5.30729)"

80.120.179.10 - - [18/Jun/2010:10:49:41 +0200] "GET /favicon.ico HTTP/1.1" 302 340 "-" "Mozilla/4.0 (compatible; MSIE 8.0; Windows NT 6.1; WOW64; Trident/4.0; SLCC2; .NET CLR 2.0.50727; .NET CLR 3.5.30729; .NET CLR 3.0.30729)"

80.120.179.10 - - [18/Jun/2010:12:25:52 +0200] "GET /favicon.ico HTTP/1.1" 302 340 "-" "Mozilla/4.0 (compatible; MSIE 8.0; Windows NT 5.1; Trident/4.0; .NET CLR 1.1.4322; InfoPath.1)"

80.120.179.10 - - [18/Jun/2010:13:17:13 +0200] "GET /favicon.ico HTTP/1.1" 302 340 "-" "Mozilla/4.0 (compatible; MSIE 8.0; Windows NT 5.1; Trident/4.0; .NET CLR 2.0.50727; .NET CLR 3.0.04506.30; .NET CLR 3.0.04506.648; InfoPath.2; MS-RTC LM 8)"

80.120.179.10 - - [18/Jun/2010:13:20:11 +0200] "GET /Seiten/Impressum.html HTTP/1.1" 200 11505 "http://www.asylabwehramt.at/Seiten/Aktuelles.html" "Mozilla/4.0 (compatible; MSIE 8.0; Windows NT 5.1; Trident/4.0; .NET CLR 1.1.4322; .NET CLR 2.0.50727; .NET CLR 3.0.04506.30; .NET CLR 3.0.04506.648; InfoPath.2; MS-RTC LM 8)"

80.120.179.10 - - [18/Jun/2010:13:20:51 +0200] "GET /Material/Hotline_Georgisch.PDF HTTP/1.1" 200 822080 "http://www.asylabwehramt.at/Seiten/Material.html" "Mozilla/4.0 (compatible; MSIE 8.0; Windows NT 5.1; Trident/4.0; .NET CLR 1.1.4322; .NET CLR 2.0.50727; .NET CLR 3.0.04506.30; .NET CLR 3.0.04506.648; InfoPath.2; MS-RTC LM 8)"

80.120.179.10 - - [18/Jun/2010:13:22:26 +0200] "GET /Seiten/Orgstrukt.html HTTP/1.1" 200 14086 "http://www.asylabwehramt.at/index.html" "Mozilla/4.0 (compatible; MSIE 8.0; Windows NT 5.1; Trident/4.0; .NET CLR 1.1.4322; .NET CLR 2.0.50727; .NET CLR 3.0.04506.30; .NET CLR 3.0.04506.648; InfoPath.2; MS-RTC LM 8)"

80.120.179.10 - - [18/Jun/2010:13:24:58 +0200] "GET /Seiten/Seal.html HTTP/1.1" 200 8872 "http://www.asylabwehramt.at/Seiten/Orgstrukt.html" "Mozilla/4.0 (compatible; MSIE 8.0; Windows NT 5.1; Trident/4.0; .NET CLR 1.1.4322; .NET CLR 2.0.50727; .NET CLR 3.0.04506.30; .NET CLR 3.0.04506.648; InfoPath.2; MS-RTC LM 8)"

80.120.179.10 - - [18/Jun/2010:13:26:59 +0200] "GET /Seiten/Forms_and_Infos.html HTTP/1.1" 200 11046 "http://www.asylabwehramt.at/index.html" "Mozilla/4.0 (compatible; MSIE 8.0; Windows NT 5.1; Trident/4.0; .NET CLR 1.1.4322; .NET CLR 2.0.50727; .NET CLR 3.0.04506.30; .NET CLR 3.0.04506.648; InfoPath.2; MS-RTC LM 8)"

```
80.120.179.10 - - [18/Jun/2010:14:19:44 +0200] "GET /favicon.ico HTTP/1.1" 302 340 "-" "Mozilla/4
.0 (compatible; MSIE 8.0; Windows NT 5.1; Trident/4.0; .NET CLR 2.0.50727; .NE
T CLR 3.0.04506.30; .NET CLR 3.0.04506.648; InfoPath.2)"
80.120.179.10 - - [18/Jun/2010:14:42:57 +0200] "GET /Material/Hotline_Deutsch.pdf HTTP/1.1" 200 4
89465 "http://www.asylabwehramt.at/" "Mozilla/4.0 (compatible; MSIE 6.0; Windows NT 5.1; SV1; .NE
T CLR 1.1.4322; .NET CLR 2.0.50727; .NET CLR 3.0.04506.30; .NET CLR 3.0.04506.648; InfoPath.2; .N
ET CLR 3.0.4506.2152; .NET CLR 3.5.30729; MS-RTC LM 8)"
193.171.152.33 - - [21/Jun/2010:04:25:40 +0200] "GET /Bilder/56.jpg HTTP/1.1" 304 - "-" "Mozilla/
4.0 (compatible;)"
193.171.152.33 - - [21/Jun/2010:10:23:30 +0200] "GET / HTTP/1.1" 304 - "http://www.google.at/url?
sa=t&source=web&cd=1&ved=0CBcQFjAA&url=http%3A%2F%2Fwww.asylabwehramt.at%2F&rct=j&q=Asylabwehramt
&ei=fCEfTKHPAtWSOJKN-ewL&usg=AFQjCNEy1zWClvnxKllPAGifRc344_0U4Q" "Mozilla/4.0 (compatible; MSIE 8
.0; Windows NT 5.1; Trident/4.0; InfoPath.1; .NET CLR 1.1.4322; .NET CLR 2.0.50727; .NET CLR 3.0.
04506.30; .NET CLR 3.0.04506.648; .NET CLR 3.0.4506.2152; .NET CLR 3.5.30729)"
193.171.152.33 - - [21/Jun/2010:10:23:38 +0200] "GET /Seiten/Orgstrukt.html HTTP/1.1" 304 - "http
://www.asylabwehramt.at/" "Mozilla/4.0 (compatible; MSIE 8.0; Windows NT 5.1; Trident/4.0; InfoPa
th.1; .NET CLR 1.1.4322; .NET CLR 2.0.50727; .NET CLR 3.0.04506.30; .NET CLR 3.0.04506.648; .NET
CLR 3.0.4506.2152; .NET CLR 3.5.30729)"
193.171.152.33 - - [21/Jun/2010:10:25:45 +0200] "GET /Seiten/Bilder.html HTTP/1.1" 304 - "http://
www.asylabwehramt.at/" "Mozilla/4.0 (compatible; MSIE 8.0; Windows NT 5.1; Trident/4.0; InfoPath.
1; .NET CLR 1.1.4322; .NET CLR 2.0.50727; .NET CLR 3.0.04506.30; .NET CLR 3.0.04506.648; .NET CLR
3.0.4506.2152; .NET CLR 3.5.30729)"
193.171.152.33 - - [21/Jun/2010:10:25:59 +0200] "GET /Seiten/Images.html HTTP/1.1" 304 - "http://
www.asylabwehramt.at/Seiten/Bilder.html" "Mozilla/4.0 (compatible; MSIE 8.0; Windows NT 5.1; Trid
ent/4.0; InfoPath.1; .NET CLR 1.1.4322; .NET CLR 2.0.50727; .NET CLR 3.0.04506.30; .NET CLR 3.0.0
4506.648; .NET CLR 3.0.4506.2152; .NET CLR 3.5.30729)"
193.171.152.33 - - [21/Jun/2010:10:26:21 +0200] "GET /Seiten/Bilder_buero.html HTTP/1.1" 200 1102
6 "http://www.asylabwehramt.at/Seiten/Images.html" "Mozilla/4.0 (compatible; MSIE 8.0; Windows NT
```

```
5.1; Trident/4.0; InfoPath.1; .NET CLR 1.1.4322; .NET CLR 2.0.50727; .NET CLR 3.0.04506.30; .NET
CLR 3.0.04506.648; .NET CLR 3.0.4506.2152; .NET CLR 3.5.30729)"
193.171.152.33 - - [21/Jun/2010:10:26:22 +0200] "GET /Bilder/BAA_photos/IMG_0179.JPG HTTP/1.1" 30
4 - "http://www.asylabwehramt.at/Seiten/Bilder_buero.html" "Mozilla/4.0 (compatible; MSIE 8.0; Wi
ndows NT 5.1; Trident/4.0; InfoPath.1; .NET CLR 1.1.4322; .NET CLR 2.0.50727; .NET CLR 3.0.04506.
30; .NET CLR 3.0.04506.648; .NET CLR 3.0.4506.2152; .NET CLR 3.5.30729)"
193.171.152.33 - - [21/Jun/2010:10:26:24 +0200] "GET /Bilder/BAA_photos/IMG_0184.JPG HTTP/1.1" 30
4 - "http://www.asylabwehramt.at/Seiten/Bilder_buero.html" "Mozilla/4.0 (compatible; MSIE 8.0; Wi
ndows NT 5.1; Trident/4.0; InfoPath.1; .NET CLR 1.1.4322; .NET CLR 2.0.50727; .NET CLR 3.0.04506.
30; .NET CLR 3.0.04506.648; .NET CLR 3.0.4506.2152; .NET CLR 3.5.30729)"
193.171.152.33 - - [21/Jun/2010:10:26:26 +0200] "GET /Bilder/BAA_photos/IMG_0185.JPG HTTP/1.1" 30
4 - "http://www.asylabwehramt.at/Seiten/Bilder_buero.html" "Mozilla/4.0 (compatible; MSIE 8.0; Wi
ndows NT 5.1; Trident/4.0; InfoPath.1; .NET CLR 1.1.4322; .NET CLR 2.0.50727; .NET CLR 3.0.04506.
30; .NET CLR 3.0.04506.648; .NET CLR 3.0.4506.2152; .NET CLR 3.5.30729)"
193.171.152.33 - - [21/Jun/2010:10:26:27 +0200] "GET /Bilder/BAA_photos/IMG_0189.JPG HTTP/1.1" 30
4 - "http://www.asylabwehramt.at/Seiten/Bilder_buero.html" "Mozilla/4.0 (compatible; MSIE 8.0; Wi
ndows NT 5.1; Trident/4.0; InfoPath.1; .NET CLR 1.1.4322; .NET CLR 2.0.50727; .NET CLR 3.0.04506.
30; .NET CLR 3.0.04506.648; .NET CLR 3.0.4506.2152; .NET CLR 3.5.30729)"
193.171.152.33 - - [21/Jun/2010:10:26:28 +0200] "GET /Bilder/BAA_photos/IMG_0191.JPG HTTP/1.1" 30
4 - "http://www.asylabwehramt.at/Seiten/Bilder_buero.html" "Mozilla/4.0 (compatible; MSIE 8.0; Wi
ndows NT 5.1; Trident/4.0; InfoPath.1; .NET CLR 1.1.4322; .NET CLR 2.0.50727; .NET CLR 3.0.04506.
30; .NET CLR 3.0.04506.648; .NET CLR 3.0.4506.2152; .NET CLR 3.5.30729)"
193.171.152.33 - - [21/Jun/2010:10:26:30 +0200] "GET /Bilder/BAA_photos/IMG_0193.JPG HTTP/1.1" 30
4 - "http://www.asylabwehramt.at/Seiten/Bilder_buero.html" "Mozilla/4.0 (compatible; MSIE 8.0; Wi
ndows NT 5.1; Trident/4.0; InfoPath.1; .NET CLR 1.1.4322; .NET CLR 3.0.4506.2152; .NET CLR 3.5.30729)"
30; .NET CLR 3.0.04506.648; .NET CLR 3.0.4506.2152; .NET CLR 3.5.30729)"
193.171.152.33 - - [21/Jun/2010:10:26:31 +0200] "GET /Bilder/BAA_photos/IMG_0194.JPG HTTP/1.1" 30
4 - "http://www.asylabwehramt.at/Seiten/Bilder_buero.html" "Mozilla/4.0 (compatible; MSIE 8.0; Wi
```

```
ndows NT 5.1; Trident/4.0; InfoPath.1; .NET CLR 1.1.4322; .NET CLR 2.0.50727; .NET CLR 3.0.04506.
30; .NET CLR 3.0.04506.648; .NET CLR 3.0.4506.2152; .NET CLR 3.5.30729)"
193.171.152.33 - - [21/Jun/2010:10:26:32 +0200] "GET /Bilder/BAA_photos/IMG_0195.JPG HTTP/1.1" 30
4 - "http://www.asylabwehramt.at/Seiten/Bilder_buero.html" "Mozilla/4.0 (compatible; MSIE 8.0; Wi
ndows NT 5.1; Trident/4.0; InfoPath.1; .NET CLR 1.1.4322; .NET CLR 2.0.50727; .NET CLR 3.0.04506.
30; .NET CLR 3.0.04506.648; .NET CLR 3.0.4506.2152; .NET CLR 3.5.30729)"
193.171.152.33 - - [21/Jun/2010:10:26:33 +0200] "GET /Bilder/BAA_photos/IMG_0200.JPG HTTP/1.1" 30
4 - "http://www.asylabwehramt.at/Seiten/Bilder_buero.html" "Mozilla/4.0 (compatible; MSIE 8.0; Wi
ndows NT 5.1; Trident/4.0; InfoPath.1; .NET CLR 1.1.4322; .NET CLR 2.0.50727; .NET CLR 3.0.04506.
30; .NET CLR 3.0.04506.648; .NET CLR 3.0.4506.2152; .NET CLR 3.5.30729)"
193.171.152.33 - - [21/Jun/2010:10:27:32 +0200] "GET /index.html HTTP/1.1" 304 - "http://www.asyl
abwehramt.at/Seiten/Bilder.html" "Mozilla/4.0 (compatible; MSIE 8.0; Windows NT 5.1; Trident/4.0;
InfoPath.1; .NET CLR 1.1.4322; .NET CLR 2.0.50727; .NET CLR 3.0.04506.30; .NET CLR 3.0.04506.648
; .NET CLR 3.0.4506.2152; .NET CLR 3.5.30729)"
80.120.179.10 - - [21/Jun/2010:11:23:40 +0200] "GET / HTTP/1.1" 200 11828 "-" "Mozilla/4.0 (compa
tible; MSIE 8.0; Windows NT 5.1; Trident/4.0; InfoPath.1; .NET CLR 1.1.4322; .NET CLR 2.0.50727;
MS-RTC LM 8)"
80.120.179.10 - - [21/Jun/2010:11:23:41 +0200] "GET /asyl.css HTTP/1.1" 200 860 "http://www.asyla
bwehramt.at/" "Mozilla/4.0 (compatible; MSIE 8.0; Windows NT 5.1; Trident/4.0; InfoPath.1; .NET C
LR 1.1.4322; .NET CLR 2.0.50727; MS-RTC LM 8)"
80.120.179.10 - - [21/Jun/2010:11:24:10 +0200] "GET /Seiten/Bilder.html HTTP/1.1" 200 9571 "http:
//www.asylabwehramt.at/" "Mozilla/4.0 (compatible; MSIE 8.0; Windows NT 5.1; Trident/4.0; InfoPat
h.1; .NET CLR 1.1.4322; .NET CLR 2.0.50727; MS-RTC LM 8)"
80.120.179.10 - - [21/Jun/2010:11:24:11 +0200] "GET /Bilder/BAA_photos/IMG_0198.JPG HTTP/1.1" 200
109214 "http://www.asylabwehramt.at/Seiten/Bilder.html" "Mozilla/4.0 (compatible; MSIE 8.0; Wind
ows NT 5.1; Trident/4.0; InfoPath.1; .NET CLR 1.1.4322; .NET CLR 2.0.50727; MS-RTC LM 8)"
80.120.179.10 - - [21/Jun/2010:11:25:02 +0200] "GET /index.html HTTP/1.1" 200 11828 "http://www.a
sylabwehramt.at/Seiten/Bilder.html" "Mozilla/4.0 (compatible; MSIE 8.0; Windows NT 5.1; Trident/4
```

```
.0; InfoPath.1; .NET CLR 1.1.4322; .NET CLR 2.0.50727; MS-RTC LM 8)"
80.120.179.10 - - [21/Jun/2010:11:28:16 +0200] "GET /favicon.ico HTTP/1.1" 302 340 "-" "Mozilla/4.0 (compatible; MSIE 8.0; Windows NT 5.1; Trident/4.0; .NET CLR 1.1.4322; .NET CLR 2.0.50727; MS-RTC LM 8)"
80.120.179.10 - - [21/Jun/2010:11:28:29 +0200] "GET /Seiten/Ausseneinsaetze.html HTTP/1.1" 200 9190 "http://www.asylabwehramt.at/Seiten/Bilder.html" "Mozilla/4.0 (compatible; MSIE 8.0; Windows NT 5.1; Trident/4.0; InfoPath.1; .NET CLR 1.1.4322; .NET CLR 2.0.50727; MS-RTC LM 8)"
80.120.179.10 - - [21/Jun/2010:11:28:39 +0200] "GET /Seiten/Aktuelles.html HTTP/1.1" 200 12570 "http://www.asylabwehramt.at/Seiten/Bilder.html" "Mozilla/4.0 (compatible; MSIE 8.0; Windows NT 5.1; Trident/4.0; InfoPath.1; .NET CLR 1.1.4322; .NET CLR 2.0.50727; MS-RTC LM 8)"
80.120.179.10 - - [21/Jun/2010:11:29:49 +0200] "GET /Seiten/Links.html HTTP/1.1" 200 18362 "http://www.asylabwehramt.at/" "Mozilla/4.0 (compatible; MSIE 8.0; Windows NT 5.1; Trident/4.0; InfoPath.1; .NET CLR 1.1.4322; .NET CLR 2.0.50727; MS-RTC LM 8)"
80.120.179.10 - - [21/Jun/2010:11:29:50 +0200] "GET /Bilder/BMDI.png HTTP/1.1" 200 8268 "http://www.asylabwehramt.at/Seiten/Links.html" "Mozilla/4.0 (compatible; MSIE 8.0; Windows NT 5.1; Trident/4.0; InfoPath.1; .NET CLR 1.1.4322; .NET CLR 2.0.50727; MS-RTC LM 8)"
80.120.179.10 - - [21/Jun/2010:11:30:16 +0200] "GET /Seiten/Press.html HTTP/1.1" 200 10955 "http://www.asylabwehramt.at/Seiten/Links.html" "Mozilla/4.0 (compatible; MSIE 8.0; Windows NT 5.1; Trident/4.0; InfoPath.1; .NET CLR 1.1.4322; .NET CLR 2.0.50727; MS-RTC LM 8)"
80.120.179.10 - - [21/Jun/2010:11:30:22 +0200] "GET /OEFFENTLICHKEIT/07062010d.pdf HTTP/1.1" 200 333788 "http://www.asylabwehramt.at/Seiten/Press.html" "Mozilla/4.0 (compatible; MSIE 8.0; Windows NT 5.1; Trident/4.0; InfoPath.1; .NET CLR 1.1.4322; .NET CLR 2.0.50727; MS-RTC LM 8)"
78.41.144.41 - - [21/Jun/2010:12:09:46 +0200] "GET /index.html HTTP/1.0" 304 - "-" "Mozilla/4.0 (compatible; MSIE 7.0; Windows NT 5.1; .NET CLR 2.0.50727; .NET CLR 1.1.4322; .NET CLR 3.0.04506.30; .NET CLR 3.0.04506.648; .NET CLR 3.0.4506.2152; .NET CLR 3.5.30729)"
80.120.179.10 - - [21/Jun/2010:12:20:16 +0200] "GET /favicon.ico HTTP/1.1" 302 340 "-" "Mozilla/4.0 (compatible; MSIE 8.0; Windows NT 5.1; Trident/4.0; .NET CLR 1.1.4322; .NET CLR 2.0.50727; MS-RTC LM 8)"
T CLR 3.0.04506.30; .NET CLR 3.0.04506.648; InfoPath.2; MS-RTC LM 8)"
```

```
80.120.179.10 - - [21/Jun/2010:12:41:22 +0200] "GET /Seiten/Orgstrukt.html HTTP/1.1" 200 14086 "h
ttp://www.asylabwehramt.at/" "Mozilla/4.0 (compatible; MSIE 6.0; Windows NT 5.1; SV1; .NET CLR 1.
1.4322; .NET CLR 2.0.50727; .NET CLR 3.0.04506.648; InfoPath.2)"
80.120.179.10 - - [21/Jun/2010:12:42:37 +0200] "GET /Seiten/Material.html HTTP/1.1" 200 11980 "ht
tp://www.asylabwehramt.at/" "Mozilla/4.0 (compatible; MSIE 6.0; Windows NT 5.1; SV1; .NET CLR 1.1
.4322; .NET CLR 2.0.50727; .NET CLR 3.0.04506.648; InfoPath.2)"
80.120.179.10 - - [21/Jun/2010:12:42:42 +0200] "GET /Material/Hotline_Arabisch.PDF HTTP/1.1" 200
684897 "http://www.asylabwehramt.at/Seiten/Material.html" "Mozilla/4.0 (compatible; MSIE 6.0; Win
dows NT 5.1; SV1; .NET CLR 1.1.4322; .NET CLR 2.0.50727; .NET CLR 3.0.04506.30; .NET CLR 3.0.0450
6.648; InfoPath.2)"
80.120.179.10 - - [21/Jun/2010:12:44:26 +0200] "GET /Seiten/Latestnews.html HTTP/1.1" 200 12574 "
http://www.asylabwehramt.at/Seiten/Links.html" "Mozilla/4.0 (compatible; MSIE 6.0; Windows NT 5.1
; SV1; .NET CLR 1.1.4322; .NET CLR 2.0.50727; .NET CLR 3.0.04506.648; .NET CLR 3.0.04506.30; Info
Path.2)"
80.120.179.10 - - [21/Jun/2010:12:44:31 +0200] "GET /Seiten/Images.html HTTP/1.1" 200 9701 "http:
//www.asylabwehramt.at/Seiten/Latestnews.html" "Mozilla/4.0 (compatible; MSIE 6.0; Windows NT 5.1
; SV1; .NET CLR 1.1.4322; .NET CLR 2.0.50727; .NET CLR 3.0.04506.648; .NET CLR 3.0.04506.30; Info
Path.2)"
80.120.179.10 - - [21/Jun/2010:12:45:16 +0200] "GET /Seiten/Links_e.html HTTP/1.1" 200 18366 "htt
p://www.asylabwehramt.at/Seiten/Images.html" "Mozilla/4.0 (compatible; MSIE 6.0; Windows NT 5.1;
SV1; .NET CLR 1.1.4322; .NET CLR 2.0.50727; .NET CLR 3.0.04506.30; .NET CLR 3.0.04506.648; InfoPa
th.2)"
80.120.179.10 - - [21/Jun/2010:12:45:48 +0200] "GET /Seiten/Forms_and_Infos.html HTTP/1.1" 200 11
046 "http://www.asylabwehramt.at/Seiten/Links_e.html" "Mozilla/4.0 (compatible; MSIE 6.0; Windows
NT 5.1; SV1; .NET CLR 1.1.4322; .NET CLR 2.0.50727; .NET CLR 3.0.04506.30; .NET CLR 3.0.04506.64
8; InfoPath.2)"
80.120.179.10 - - [21/Jun/2010:12:45:50 +0200] "GET /Material/Hotline_Russisch.pdf HTTP/1.1" 200
239827 "http://www.asylabwehramt.at/Seiten/Forms_and_Infos.html" "Mozilla/4.0 (compatible; MSIE 6
```

```
.0; Windows NT 5.1; SV1; .NET CLR 1.1.4322; .NET CLR 2.0.50727; .NET CLR 3
.0.04506.648; InfoPath.2)"
80.120.179.10 - - [21/Jun/2010:12:46:02 +0200] "GET /Material/Asyl_Jahresstatistik_2009.pdf HTTP/
1.1" 200 680643 "http://www.asylabwehramt.at/Seiten/Forms_and_Infos.html" "Mozilla/4.0 (compatibl
e; MSIE 6.0; Windows NT 5.1; SV1; .NET CLR 1.1.4322; .NET CLR 2.0.50727; .NET CLR 3.0.04506.30; .
NET CLR 3.0.04506.648; InfoPath.2)"
80.120.179.10 - - [21/Jun/2010:12:46:38 +0200] "GET /Bilder/Ladung.png HTTP/1.1" 200 114658 "http
://www.asylabwehramt.at/Seiten/Material.html" "Mozilla/4.0 (compatible; MSIE 6.0; Windows NT 5.1;
SV1; .NET CLR 1.1.4322; .NET CLR 2.0.50727; .NET CLR 3.0.04506.30; .NET CLR 3.0.04506.648; InfoP
ath.2)"
80.120.179.10 - - [21/Jun/2010:12:46:56 +0200] "GET /Seiten/Presse.html HTTP/1.1" 200 10956 "http
://www.asylabwehramt.at/Seiten/Material.html" "Mozilla/4.0 (compatible; MSIE 6.0; Windows NT 5.1;
SV1; .NET CLR 1.1.4322; .NET CLR 2.0.50727; .NET CLR 3.0.04506.30; .NET CLR 3.0.04506.648; InfoP
ath.2)"
80.120.179.10 - - [21/Jun/2010:12:49:07 +0200] "GET /Seiten/Rundzeichen.html HTTP/1.1" 200 8837 "
http://www.asylabwehramt.at/Seiten/Bilder.html" "Mozilla/4.0 (compatible; MSIE 6.0; Windows NT 5.
1; SV1; .NET CLR 1.1.4322; .NET CLR 2.0.50727; .NET CLR 3.0.04506.30; .NET CLR 3.0.04506.648; Inf
oPath.2)"
80.120.179.10 - - [21/Jun/2010:12:49:18 +0200] "GET /Bilder/flyer_nigeria_Internet.pdf HTTP/1.1"
200 702826 "http://www.asylabwehramt.at/Seiten/Material.html" "Mozilla/4.0 (compatible; MSIE 6.0;
Windows NT 5.1; SV1; .NET CLR 1.1.4322; .NET CLR 2.0.50727; .NET CLR 3.0.04506.30; .NET CLR 3.0.
04506.648; InfoPath.2)"
80.120.179.10 - - [21/Jun/2010:12:49:38 +0200] "GET /Material/Hotline_Deutsch.pdf HTTP/1.1" 200 4
89465 "http://www.asylabwehramt.at/Seiten/Material.html" "Mozilla/4.0 (compatible; MSIE 6.0; Wind
ows NT 5.1; SV1; .NET CLR 1.1.4322; .NET CLR 2.0.50727; .NET CLR 3.0.04506.30; .NET CLR 3.0.04506
.648; InfoPath.2)"
80.120.179.10 - - [21/Jun/2010:12:50:00 +0200] "GET /favicon.ico HTTP/1.1" 302 340 "-" "Mozilla/4
.0 (compatible; MSIE 8.0; Windows NT 5.1; Trident/4.0; .NET CLR 1.1.4322; .NET CLR 2.0.50727; .NE
```

```
80.120.179.10 - - [21/Jun/2010:13:35:19 +0200] "GET /favicon.ico HTTP/1.1" 302 340 "-" "Mozilla/4.0 (compatible; MSIE 8.0; Windows NT 5.1; Trident/4.0; InfoPath.2; .NET CLR 3.0.04506.30; .NET CLR 3.0.04506.648; InfoPath.2; MS-RTC LM 8)"
80.120.179.10 - - [21/Jun/2010:13:51:27 +0200] "GET /Material/Hotline_Tuerkisch.PDF HTTP/1.1" 200 553151 "http://www.asylabwehramt.at/Seiten/Material.html" "Mozilla/4.0 (compatible; MSIE 6.0; Windows NT 5.1; SV1; .NET CLR 1.1.4322)"
80.120.179.10 - - [21/Jun/2010:13:57:01 +0200] "GET /_vti_bin/owssvr.dll?UL=1&ACT=4&BUILD=8164&STRMVER=4&CAPREQ=0 HTTP/1.1" 302 340 "-" "Mozilla/4.0 (compatible; MSIE 7.0; Windows NT 5.1; .NET CLR 1.1.4322; .NET CLR 2.0.50727; .NET CLR 3.0.04506.648; InfoPath.2)"
80.120.179.10 - - [21/Jun/2010:14:33:17 +0200] "GET /favicon.ico HTTP/1.1" 302 340 "-" "Mozilla/4.0 (compatible; MSIE 8.0; Windows NT 5.1; Trident/4.0; InfoPath.2; .NET CLR 3.0.04506.30; .NET CLR 3.0.04506.648; InfoPath.2)"
80.120.179.10 - - [22/Jun/2010:06:32:05 +0200] "GET / HTTP/1.1" 200 11828 "-" "Mozilla/4.0 (compatible; MSIE 6.0; Windows NT 5.1; SV1; .NET CLR 1.1.4322; .NET CLR 2.0.50727; .NET CLR 3.0.04506.30; .NET CLR 3.0.04506.648; InfoPath.2)"
80.120.179.10 - - [22/Jun/2010:06:32:06 +0200] "GET /asyl.css HTTP/1.1" 200 860 "http://www.asylabwehramt.at/" "Mozilla/4.0 (compatible; MSIE 6.0; Windows NT 5.1; SV1; .NET CLR 2.0.50727; .NET CLR 3.0.04506.30; .NET CLR 3.0.04506.648; InfoPath.2)"
85.158.226.1 - - [22/Jun/2010:12:27:17 +0200] "GET / HTTP/1.1" 304 - "-" "Mozilla/4.0 (compatible; MSIE 8.0; Windows NT 5.1; Trident/4.0; .NET CLR 2.0.50727)"
85.158.226.1 - - [22/Jun/2010:12:27:18 +0200] "GET /asyl.css HTTP/1.1" 200 860 "http://www.asylabwehramt.at/" "Mozilla/4.0 (compatible; MSIE 8.0; Windows NT 5.1; Trident/4.0; .NET CLR 1.1.4322; .NET CLR 2.0.50727)"
85.158.226.1 - - [22/Jun/2010:12:27:19 +0200] "GET /favicon.ico HTTP/1.1" 302 340 "-" "Mozilla/4.0 (compatible; MSIE 8.0; Windows NT 5.1; Trident/4.0; .NET CLR 1.1.4322; .NET CLR 2.0.50727)"
85.158.226.1 - - [22/Jun/2010:12:33:34 +0200] "GET / HTTP/1.1" 304 - "-" "Mozilla/4.0 (compatible; MSIE 8.0; Windows NT 5.1; Trident/4.0; .NET CLR 1.1.4322; .NET CLR 2.0.50727)"
80.120.179.10 - - [23/Jun/2010:09:35:20 +0200] "GET / HTTP/1.1" 200 11828 "http://www.google.at/u
```

```
rl?sa=t&source=web&cd=2&ved=0CBsQFjAB&url=http%3A%2F%2Fwww.asylabwehramt.at%2F&rct=j&q=asylabwehr
amt&ei=JbkhTNv7Ho6ION38uTo&usg=AFQjCNEy1zWClvmxklPAGifRc344_0U4Q" "Mozilla/4.0 (compatible; MSIE
8.0; Windows NT 5.1; Trident/4.0; .NET CLR 1.1.4322; .NET CLR 2.0.50727; .NET CLR 3.0.04506.30;
.NET CLR 3.0.04506.648; InfoPath.2; MS-RTC LM 8)"

80.120.179.10 - - [23/Jun/2010:11:15:28 +0200] "GET /asyl.css HTTP/1.1" 200 860 "http://www.asyla
bwehramt.at/" "Mozilla/4.0 (compatible; MSIE 8.0; Windows NT 5.1; Trident/4.0; .NET CLR 1.1.4322;
.NET CLR 2.0.50727; .NET CLR 3.0.04506.30; .NET CLR 3.0.04506.648; InfoPath.2; MS-RTC LM 8)"

88.116.224.102 - - [23/Jun/2010:15:53:38 +0200] "GET / HTTP/1.1" 200 11828 "http://www.google.at/
search?hl=de&q=asyl+abwa&btnG=Google-Suche&meta=cr%3DcountryAT&aq=f&oq=" "Opera/9.80 (Windows NT
5.1; U; de) Presto/2.2.15 Version/10.00"

88.116.224.102 - - [23/Jun/2010:15:53:54 +0200] "GET /Seiten/Aktuelles.html HTTP/1.1" 200 12570 "
http://www.asylabwehramt.at/" "Opera/9.80 (Windows NT 5.1; U; de) Presto/2.2.15 Version/10.00"

88.116.224.102 - - [23/Jun/2010:15:54:01 +0200] "GET /Seiten/Rundzeichen.html HTTP/1.1" 200 8837
"http://www.asylabwehramt.at/Seiten/Aktuelles.html" "Opera/9.80 (Windows NT 5.1; U; de) Presto/2.
2.15 Version/10.00"

88.116.224.102 - - [23/Jun/2010:15:54:03 +0200] "GET /Bilder/Asylabwehramt_Seal_800x800.png HTTP/
1.1" 200 269132 "http://www.asylabwehramt.at/Seiten/Rundzeichen.html" "Opera/9.80 (Windows NT 5.1
; U; de) Presto/2.2.15 Version/10.00"

88.116.224.102 - - [23/Jun/2010:15:54:13 +0200] "GET /Seiten/Rundzeichen.html HTTP/1.1" 200 8837
"http://www.asylabwehramt.at/Seiten/Aktuelles.html" "Opera/9.80 (Windows NT 5.1; U; de) Presto/2.
2.15 Version/10.00"

88.116.224.102 - - [23/Jun/2010:15:54:14 +0200] "GET /asyl.css HTTP/1.1" 304 - "http://www.asylab
wehramt.at/Seiten/Rundzeichen.html" "Opera/9.80 (Windows NT 5.1; U; de) Presto/2.2.15 Version/10.
00"

88.116.224.102 - - [23/Jun/2010:15:54:32 +0200] "GET /Bilder/Asylabwehramt_Seal_800x800.png HTTP/
1.1" 200 269132 "http://www.asylabwehramt.at/Seiten/Rundzeichen.html" "Opera/9.80 (Windows NT 5.1
; U; de) Presto/2.2.15 Version/10.00"

88.116.224.102 - - [23/Jun/2010:15:54:43 +0200] "GET /Seiten/Material.html HTTP/1.1" 200 11980 "h
```

```
ttp://www.asylabwehramt.at/Seiten/Rundzeichen.html" "Opera/9.80 (Windows NT 5.1; U; de) Presto/2.2.15 Version/10.00"
88.116.224.102 - - [23/Jun/2010:15:54:48 +0200] "GET /Material/Hotline_Deutsch.pdf HTTP/1.1" 200 489465 "http://www.asylabwehramt.at/Seiten/Material.html" "Opera/9.80 (Windows NT 5.1; U; de) Presto/2.2.15 Version/10.00"
193.5.216.100 [19] - - [23/Jun/2010:17:50:15 +0200] "GET / HTTP/1.0" 200 11828 "http://www.ubermorgen.com/2010/" "Mozilla/4.0 (compatible; MSIE 7.0; Windows NT 5.1; .NET CLR 1.1.4322; .NET CLR 2.0.50727; .NET CLR 3.0.4506.2152; .NET CLR 3.5.30729; EIE6)"
193.5.216.100 - - [23/Jun/2010:17:50:16 +0200] "GET /asyl.css HTTP/1.0" 200 860 "http://www.asylabwehramt.at/" "Mozilla/4.0 (compatible; MSIE 7.0; Windows NT 5.1; .NET CLR 1.1.4322; .NET CLR 2.0.50727; .NET CLR 3.0.4506.2152; .NET CLR 3.5.30729; EIE6)"
80.120.179.10 - - [24/Jun/2010:08:09:11 +0200] "GET / HTTP/1.1" 200 11828 "-" "Mozilla/4.0 (compatible; MSIE 6.0; Windows NT 5.1; SV1; .NET CLR 1.1.4322)"
80.120.179.10 - - [24/Jun/2010:10:56:37 +0200] "GET /index.html HTTP/1.1" 200 11828 "-" "Mozilla/4.0 (compatible; MSIE 8.0; Windows NT 5.1; Trident/4.0; .NET CLR 1.1.4322; .NET CLR 2.0.50727; .NET CLR 3.0.04506.30; .NET CLR 3.0.04506.648; InfoPath.2)"
80.120.179.10 - - [24/Jun/2010:10:56:51 +0200] "GET /Seiten/Aktuelles.html HTTP/1.1" 200 12570 "http://www.asylabwehramt.at/index.html" "Mozilla/4.0 (compatible; MSIE 8.0; Windows NT 5.1; Trident/4.0; .NET CLR 1.1.4322; .NET CLR 2.0.50727; .NET CLR 3.0.04506.648; InfoPath.2)"
80.120.179.10 - - [24/Jun/2010:10:56:52 +0200] "GET /Bilder/leistung_2.jpg HTTP/1.1" 200 4918 "http://www.asylabwehramt.at/Seiten/Aktuelles.html" "Mozilla/4.0 (compatible; MSIE 8.0; Windows NT 5.1; Trident/4.0; .NET CLR 2.0.50727; .NET CLR 3.0.04506.30; .NET CLR 3.0.04506.648; InfoPath.2)"
80.120.179.10 - - [24/Jun/2010:10:57:14 +0200] "GET /Seiten/Links.html HTTP/1.1" 200 18362 "http://www.asylabwehramt.at/Seiten/Aktuelles.html" "Mozilla/4.0 (compatible; MSIE 8.0; Windows NT 5.1;
```

---

[19] WHOIS record on page 325

```
Trident/4.0; .NET CLR 1.1.4322; .NET CLR 2.0.50727; .NET CLR 3.0.04506.30; .NET CLR 3.0.04506.64
8; InfoPath.2)"
80.120.179.10 - - [24/Jun/2010:11:06:04 +0200] "GET /index_e.html HTTP/1.1" 200 11855 "http://www
.asylabwehramt.at/" "Mozilla/4.0 (compatible; MSIE 6.0; Windows NT 5.1; SV1; InfoPath.1; .NET CLR
1.1.4322; .NET CLR 2.0.50727)"
80.120.179.10 - - [24/Jun/2010:11:07:52 +0200] "GET /Seiten/Orgstrukt.html HTTP/1.1" 200 14086 "h
ttp://www.asylabwehramt.at/" "Mozilla/4.0 (compatible; MSIE 6.0; Windows NT 5.1; SV1; InfoPath.1;
.NET CLR 1.1.4322; .NET CLR 2.0.50727)"
80.120.179.10 - - [24/Jun/2010:11:08:17 +0200] "GET /Seiten/Bilder.html HTTP/1.1" 200 9571 "http:
//www.asylabwehramt.at/Seiten/Orgstrukt.html" "Mozilla/4.0 (compatible; MSIE 6.0; Windows NT 5.1;
SV1; InfoPath.1; .NET CLR 1.1.4322; .NET CLR 2.0.50727)"
80.120.179.10 - - [24/Jun/2010:11:08:18 +0200] "GET /Bilder/SCREEN_AAbA_Edutainment_Video.jpg HTT
P/1.1" 200 29259 "http://www.asylabwehramt.at/Seiten/Bilder.html" "Mozilla/4.0 (compatible; MSIE
6.0; Windows NT 5.1; SV1; InfoPath.1; .NET CLR 1.1.4322; .NET CLR 2.0.50727)"
80.120.179.10 - - [24/Jun/2010:11:13:11 +0200] "GET /Seiten/Impressum.html HTTP/1.1" 200 11628 "h
ttp://www.asylabwehramt.at/Seiten/Aktuelles.html" "Mozilla/4.0 (compatible; MSIE 6.0; Windows NT
5.1; SV1; .NET CLR 1.1.4322; .NET CLR 2.0.50727; .NET CLR 3.0.04506.30; .NET CLR 3.0.04506.648; I
nfoPath.2)"
80.120.179.10 - - [24/Jun/2010:11:23:16 +0200] "GET /Seiten/Rundzeichen.html HTTP/1.1" 200 8837 "
http://www.asylabwehramt.at/Seiten/Aktuelles.html" "Mozilla/4.0 (compatible; MSIE 6.0; Windows NT
5.1; SV1; .NET CLR 1.1.4322; .NET CLR 2.0.50727; .NET CLR 3.0.04506.30; .NET CLR 3.0.04506.648;
InfoPath.2)"
193.171.152.33 - - [25/Jun/2010:13:43:27 +0200] "GET /Seiten/Impressum.html HTTP/1.1" 200 11628 "
http://www.google.at/search?q=asylabwehramt.at&ie=utf-8&oe=utf-8&aq=t&rls=org.mozilla:de:official
&client=firefox-a" "Mozilla/5.0 (Windows; U; Windows NT 5.1; de; rv:1.9.0.10) Gecko/2009042316 Fi
refox/3.0.10 (.NET CLR 3.5.30729)"
193.171.152.33 - - [25/Jun/2010:13:43:28 +0200] "GET /favicon.ico HTTP/1.1" 302 340 "-" "Mozilla/
5.0 (Windows; U; Windows NT 5.1; de; rv:1.9.0.10) Gecko/2009042316 Firefox/3.0.10 (.NET CLR 3.5.3
```

```
0729)"
193.171.152.33 - - [25/Jun/2010:13:43:31 +0200] "GET /favicon.ico HTTP/1.1" 302 340 "-" "Mozilla/
5.0 (Windows; U; Windows NT 5.1; de; rv:1.9.0.10) Gecko/2009042316 Firefox/3.0.10 (.NET CLR 3.5.3
0729)"
193.171.152.33 - - [25/Jun/2010:13:43:50 +0200] "GET /index.html HTTP/1.1" 304 - "http://www.asyl
abwehramt.at/Seiten/Impressum.html" "Mozilla/5.0 (Windows; U; Windows NT 5.1; de; rv:1.9.0.10) Ge
cko/2009042316 Firefox/3.0.10 (.NET CLR 3.5.30729)"
193.171.152.33 - - [25/Jun/2010:13:43:52 +0200] "GET /Seiten/Aktuelles.html HTTP/1.1" 200 12570 "
http://www.asylabwehramt.at/index.html" "Mozilla/5.0 (Windows; U; Windows NT 5.1; de; rv:1.9.0.10
) Gecko/2009042316 Firefox/3.0.10 (.NET CLR 3.5.30729)"
193.171.152.33 - - [25/Jun/2010:13:43:57 +0200] "GET /Seiten/Material.html HTTP/1.1" 200 11980 "h
ttp://www.asylabwehramt.at/Seiten/Aktuelles.html" "Mozilla/5.0 (Windows; U; Windows NT 5.1; de; r
v:1.9.0.10) Gecko/2009042316 Firefox/3.0.10 (.NET CLR 3.5.30729)"
193.171.152.33 - - [25/Jun/2010:13:44:03 +0200] "GET /Seiten/Rundzeichen.html HTTP/1.1" 304 - "ht
tp://www.asylabwehramt.at/Seiten/Material.html" "Mozilla/5.0 (Windows; U; Windows NT 5.1; de; rv:
1.9.0.10) Gecko/2009042316 Firefox/3.0.10 (.NET CLR 3.5.30729)"
193.171.152.33 - - [25/Jun/2010:13:44:06 +0200] "GET /Seiten/Bilder.html HTTP/1.1" 304 - "http://
www.asylabwehramt.at/Seiten/Rundzeichen.html" "Mozilla/5.0 (Windows; U; Windows NT 5.1; de; rv:1.
9.0.10) Gecko/2009042316 Firefox/3.0.10 (.NET CLR 3.5.30729)"
193.171.152.33 - - [25/Jun/2010:13:44:31 +0200] "GET /Seiten/Orgstrukt.html HTTP/1.1" 200 14086 "
http://www.asylabwehramt.at/index.html" "Mozilla/5.0 (Windows; U; Windows NT 5.1; de; rv:1.9.0.10
) Gecko/2009042316 Firefox/3.0.10 (.NET CLR 3.5.30729)"
193.171.152.33 - - [27/Jun/2010:17:45:20 +0200] "GET / HTTP/1.1" 304 - "-" "Mozilla/4.0 (compatib
le;)"
80.120.179.10 - - [28/Jun/2010:08:41:56 +0200] "GET / HTTP/1.1" 200 11828 "http://www.google.at/u
rl?sa=t&source=web&cd=1&ved=0CCkQFjAA&url=http%3A%2F%2Fwww.asylabwehramt.at%2F&rct=j&q=█asylabwehr
█amt█&ei=MUQoTJ-MBoq1sQaSkv3DBA&usg=AFQjCNEy1zWC1vnxklPAGifRc344_0U4Q" "Mozilla/4.0 (compatible; M
SIE 8.0; Windows NT 5.1; Trident/4.0; .NET CLR 1.1.4322; .NET CLR 2.0.50727; .NET CLR 3.0.04506.3
```

134

0; .NET CLR 3.0.04506.648; InfoPath.2)"

194.138.12.170[20] - - [28/Jun/2010:09:03:01 +0200] "GET / HTTP/1.1" 200 11828 "-" "Mozilla/4.0 (compatible; MSIE 7.0; Windows NT 6.0; Windows NT 5.1; SV1) ; .NET CLR 1.0.3705; .NET CLR 2.0.50727; .NET CLR 3.0.04506.30; .NET CLR 1.1.4322; InfoPath.1; .NET CLR 3.0.4506.2152; .NET CLR 3.5.30729; MS-RTC LM 8)"

194.138.12.170 - - [28/Jun/2010:09:03:27 +0200] "GET /Seiten/Aktuelles.html HTTP/1.1" 200 12570 " http://www.asylabwehramt.at/" "Mozilla/4.0 (compatible; MSIE 7.0; Windows NT 5.1; Mozilla/4.0 (compatible; MSIE 6.0; Windows NT 5.1; SV1) ; .NET CLR 1.0.3705; .NET CLR 2.0.50727; .NET CLR 3.0.04 506.30; .NET CLR 1.1.4322; InfoPath.1; .NET CLR 3.0.4506.2152; .NET CLR 3.5.30729; MS-RTC LM 8)"

194.138.12.170 - - [28/Jun/2010:09:03:28 +0200] "GET /Bilder/leistung_2.jpg HTTP/1.1" 200 4918 "h ttp://www.asylabwehramt.at/Seiten/Aktuelles.html" "Mozilla/4.0 (compatible; MSIE 7.0; Windows NT 5.1; Mozilla/4.0 (compatible; MSIE 6.0; Windows NT 5.1; SV1) ; .NET CLR 1.0.3705; .NET CLR 2.0.50 727; .NET CLR 3.0.04506.30; .NET CLR 1.1.4322; InfoPath.1; .NET CLR 3.0.4506.2152; .NET CLR 3.5.3 0729; MS-RTC LM 8)"

194.138.12.170 - - [28/Jun/2010:09:03:41 +0200] "GET /Seiten/Material.html HTTP/1.1" 200 11980 "h ttp://www.asylabwehramt.at/Seiten/Aktuelles.html" "Mozilla/4.0 (compatible; MSIE 7.0; Windows NT 5.1; Mozilla/4.0 (compatible; MSIE 6.0; Windows NT 5.1; SV1) ; .NET CLR 1.0.3705; .NET CLR 2.0.50 727; .NET CLR 3.0.04506.30; .NET CLR 1.1.4322; InfoPath.1; .NET CLR 3.0.4506.2152; .NET CLR 3.5.3 0729; MS-RTC LM 8)"

194.138.12.170 - - [28/Jun/2010:09:03:47 +0200] "GET /Seiten/Rundzeichen.html HTTP/1.1" 200 8837 "http://www.asylabwehramt.at/Seiten/Material.html" "Mozilla/4.0 (compatible; MSIE 7.0; Windows NT 5.1; Mozilla/4.0 (compatible; MSIE 6.0; Windows NT 5.1; SV1) ; .NET CLR 1.0.3705; .NET CLR 2.0.5 0727; .NET CLR 3.0.04506.30; .NET CLR 1.1.4322; InfoPath.1; .NET CLR 3.0.4506.2152; .NET CLR 3.5. 30729; MS-RTC LM 8)"

194.138.12.170 - - [28/Jun/2010:09:03:48 +0200] "GET /Seiten/Bilder.html HTTP/1.1" 200 9571 "http ://www.asylabwehramt.at/Seiten/Rundzeichen.html" "Mozilla/4.0 (compatible; MSIE 7.0; Windows NT 5

[20]WHOIS record on page 321

```
.1; Mozilla/4.0 (compatible; MSIE 6.0; Windows NT 5.1; SV1) ; .NET CLR 1.0.3705; .NET CLR 2.0.507
27; .NET CLR 3.0.04506.30; .NET CLR 1.1.4322; InfoPath.1; .NET CLR 3.0.4506.2152; .NET CLR 3.5.30
729; MS-RTC LM 8)"
194.138.12.170 - - [28/Jun/2010:09:03:54 +0200] "GET /Seiten/Links.html HTTP/1.1" 200 18362 "http
://www.asylabwehramt.at/Seiten/Bilder.html" "Mozilla/4.0 (compatible; MSIE 7.0; Windows NT 5.1; M
ozilla/4.0 (compatible; MSIE 6.0; Windows NT 5.1; SV1) ; .NET CLR 1.0.3705; .NET CLR 2.0.50727; .
NET CLR 3.0.04506.30; .NET CLR 1.1.4322; InfoPath.1; .NET CLR 3.0.4506.2152; .NET CLR 3.5.30729;
MS-RTC LM 8)"
80.120.179.10 - - [28/Jun/2010:10:01:02 +0200] "GET /Seiten/Aktuelles.html HTTP/1.1" 200 12570 "h
ttp://www.asylabwehramt.at/" "Mozilla/4.0 (compatible; MSIE 6.0; Windows NT 5.1; SV1; .NET CLR 1.
1.4322; .NET CLR 2.0.50727; .NET CLR 3.0.04506.30; .NET CLR 3.0.04506.648; InfoPath.2)"
80.120.179.10 - - [28/Jun/2010:10:02:32 +0200] "GET /Seiten/Bilder.html HTTP/1.1" 200 9571 "http:
//www.asylabwehramt.at/Seiten/Aktuelles.html" "Mozilla/4.0 (compatible; MSIE 6.0; Windows NT 5.1;
SV1; .NET CLR 1.1.4322; .NET CLR 2.0.50727; .NET CLR 3.0.04506.30; .NET CLR 3.0.04506.648; InfoP
ath.2)"
80.120.179.10 - - [28/Jun/2010:10:02:33 +0200] "GET /Bilder/ausseneinsatz.png HTTP/1.1" 200 12409
24 "http://www.asylabwehramt.at/Seiten/Bilder.html" "Mozilla/4.0 (compatible; MSIE 6.0; Windows N
T 5.1; SV1; .NET CLR 1.1.4322; .NET CLR 2.0.50727; .NET CLR 3.0.04506.30; .NET CLR 3.0.04506.648;
InfoPath.2)"
80.120.179.10 - - [28/Jun/2010:10:02:46 +0200] "GET /Seiten/Links.html HTTP/1.1" 200 18362 "http:
//www.asylabwehramt.at/Seiten/Bilder.html" "Mozilla/4.0 (compatible; MSIE 6.0; Windows NT 5.1; SV
1; .NET CLR 1.1.4322; .NET CLR 2.0.50727; .NET CLR 3.0.04506.30; .NET CLR 3.0.04506.648; InfoPath
.2)"
194.138.12.170 - - [28/Jun/2010:11:12:40 +0200] "GET / HTTP/1.1" 200 11828 "-" "Mozilla/4.0 (comp
atible; MSIE 6.0; Windows NT 5.1; Mozilla/4.0 (compatible; MSIE 6.0; Windows NT 5.1; SV1) ; .NET
CLR 1.0.3705; .NET CLR 2.0.50727; .NET CLR 3.0.04506.30; .NET CLR 1.1.4322; InfoPath.1; .NET CLR
3.0.4506.2152; .NET CLR 3.5.30729; MS-RTC LM 8)"
194.138.12.170 - - [28/Jun/2010:11:12:45 +0200] "GET /Seiten/Links.html HTTP/1.1" 200 18362 "http
```

```
://www.asylabwehramt.at/" "Mozilla/4.0 (compatible; MSIE 7.0; Windows NT 5.1; Mozilla/4.0 (compat
ible; MSIE 6.0; Windows NT 5.1; SV1) ; .NET CLR 1.0.3705; .NET CLR 2.0.50727; .NET CLR 3.0.04506.
30; .NET CLR 1.1.4322; InfoPath.1; .NET CLR 3.0.4506.2152; .NET CLR 3.5.30729; MS-RTC LM 8)"
194.138.12.170 - - [28/Jun/2010:11:12:46 +0200] "GET /Seiten/Material.html HTTP/1.1" 200 11980 "h
ttp://www.asylabwehramt.at/Seiten/Links.html" "Mozilla/4.0 (compatible; MSIE 7.0; Windows NT 5.1;
Mozilla/4.0 (compatible; MSIE 6.0; Windows NT 5.1; SV1) ; .NET CLR 1.0.3705; .NET CLR 2.0.50727;
.NET CLR 3.0.04506.30; .NET CLR 1.1.4322; InfoPath.1; .NET CLR 3.0.4506.2152; .NET CLR 3.5.30729
; MS-RTC LM 8)"
194.138.12.170 - - [28/Jun/2010:11:12:53 +0200] "GET /Bilder/Ladung.png HTTP/1.1" 200 114658 "htt
p://www.asylabwehramt.at/Seiten/Material.html" "Mozilla/4.0 (compatible; MSIE 7.0; Windows NT 5.1
; Mozilla/4.0 (compatible; MSIE 6.0; Windows NT 5.1; SV1) ; .NET CLR 1.0.3705; .NET CLR 2.0.50727
; .NET CLR 3.0.04506.30; .NET CLR 1.1.4322; InfoPath.1; .NET CLR 3.0.4506.2152; .NET CLR 3.5.3072
9; MS-RTC LM 8)"
194.138.12.170 - - [28/Jun/2010:11:13:32 +0200] "GET /Material/Hotline_Albanisch.PDF HTTP/1.1" 20
0 644638 "http://www.asylabwehramt.at/Seiten/Material.html" "Mozilla/4.0 (compatible; MSIE 7.0; W
indows NT 5.1; Mozilla/4.0 (compatible; MSIE 6.0; Windows NT 5.1; SV1) ; .NET CLR 1.0.3705; .NET
CLR 2.0.50727; .NET CLR 3.0.04506.30; .NET CLR 1.1.4322; InfoPath.1; .NET CLR 3.0.4506.2152; .NET
CLR 3.5.30729; MS-RTC LM 8)"
194.138.12.170 - - [28/Jun/2010:11:13:39 +0200] "GET /Material/Hotline_Albanisch.PDF HTTP/1.1" 20
6 510121 "-" "Mozilla/4.0 (compatible; MSIE 7.0; Windows NT 5.1; Mozilla/4.0 (compatible; MSIE 6.
0; Windows NT 5.1; SV1) ; .NET CLR 1.0.3705; .NET CLR 2.0.50727; .NET CLR 3.0.04506.30; .NET CLR
1.1.4322; InfoPath.1; .NET CLR 3.0.4506.2152; .NET CLR 3.5.30729; MS-RTC LM 8)"
194.138.12.170 - - [28/Jun/2010:11:38:55 +0200] "GET /index.html HTTP/1.1" 200 11828 "http://www.
asylabwehramt.at/Seiten/Material.html" "Mozilla/4.0 (compatible; MSIE 7.0; Windows NT 5.1; Mozill
a/4.0 (compatible; MSIE 6.0; Windows NT 5.1; SV1) ; .NET CLR 1.0.3705; .NET CLR 2.0.50727; .NET C
LR 3.0.04506.30; .NET CLR 1.1.4322; InfoPath.1; .NET CLR 3.0.4506.2152; .NET CLR 3.5.30729; MS-RT
C LM 8)"
194.138.12.170 - - [28/Jun/2010:11:39:30 +0200] "GET /Seiten/Impressum.html HTTP/1.1" 200 11628 "
```

137

```
http://www.asylabwehramt.at/index.html" "Mozilla/4.0 (compatible; MSIE 7.0; Windows NT 5.1; Mozilla/4.0 (compatible; MSIE 6.0; Windows NT 5.1; SV1) ; .NET CLR 1.0.3705; .NET CLR 2.0.50727; .NET CLR 3.0.04506.30; .NET CLR 1.1.4322; InfoPath.1; .NET CLR 3.0.4506.2152; .NET CLR 3.5.30729; MS-RTC LM 8)"

213.208.144.130 - - [28/Jun/2010:12:18:41 +0200] "GET / HTTP/1.0" 200 11828 "http://www.google.at/search?hl=de&source=hp&q=asylabwehramt&aq=f&aqi=&aql=&oq=&gs_rfai=" "Mozilla/4.0 (compatible; MSIE 7.0; Windows NT 5.2; .NET CLR 1.1.4322; InfoPath.1; .NET CLR 2.0.50727; .NET CLR 3.0.4506.2152; .NET CLR 3.5.30729)"

194.138.12.170 - - [28/Jun/2010:12:19:05 +0200] "GET / HTTP/1.1" 200 11828 "-" "Mozilla/5.0 (Windows; U; Windows NT 5.1; de; rv:1.9.0.19) Gecko/2010031422 Firefox/3.0.19 (.NET CLR 3.5.30729)"

194.138.12.170 - - [28/Jun/2010:12:19:07 +0200] "GET /favicon.ico HTTP/1.1" 302 336 "-" "Mozilla/5.0 (Windows; U; Windows NT 5.1; de; rv:1.9.0.19) Gecko/2010031422 Firefox/3.0.19 (.NET CLR 3.5.30729)"

194.138.12.170 - - [28/Jun/2010:12:19:08 +0200] "GET /favicon.ico HTTP/1.1" 302 336 "-" "Mozilla/5.0 (Windows; U; Windows NT 5.1; de; rv:1.9.0.19) Gecko/2010031422 Firefox/3.0.19 (.NET CLR 3.5.30729)"

213.208.144.130 - - [28/Jun/2010:12:19:17 +0200] "GET /Seiten/Rundzeichen.html HTTP/1.0" 200 8837 "http://www.asylabwehramt.at/" "Mozilla/4.0 (compatible; MSIE 7.0; Windows NT 5.2; .NET CLR 1.1.4322; InfoPath.1; .NET CLR 2.0.50727; .NET CLR 3.0.4506.2152; .NET CLR 3.5.30729)"

213.208.144.130 - - [28/Jun/2010:12:19:18 +0200] "GET /Bilder/Asylabwehramt_Seal_800x800.png HTTP/1.0" 200 269132 "http://www.asylabwehramt.at/Seiten/Rundzeichen.html" "Mozilla/4.0 (compatible; MSIE 7.0; Windows NT 5.2; .NET CLR 1.1.4322; InfoPath.1; .NET CLR 2.0.50727; .NET CLR 3.0.4506.21 52; .NET CLR 3.5.30729)"

213.208.144.130 - - [28/Jun/2010:12:19:21 +0200] "GET /Seiten/Material.html HTTP/1.0" 200 11980 "http://www.asylabwehramt.at/Seiten/Rundzeichen.html" "Mozilla/4.0 (compatible; MSIE 7.0; Windows NT 5.2; .NET CLR 1.1.4322; InfoPath.1; .NET CLR 2.0.50727; .NET CLR 3.0.4506.2152; .NET CLR 3.5.30729)"

213.208.144.130 - - [28/Jun/2010:12:19:25 +0200] "GET /Material/Hotline_Deutsch.pdf HTTP/1.0" 200
```

489465 "http://www.asylabwehramt.at/Seiten/Material.html" "Mozilla/4.0 (compatible; MSIE 7.0; Wi
ndows NT 5.2; .NET CLR 1.1.4322; InfoPath.1; .NET CLR 2.0.50727; .NET CLR 3.0.4506.2152; .NET CLR
3.5.30729)"

213.208.144.130 - - [28/Jun/2010:12:19:58 +0200] "GET /Seiten/Bilder.html HTTP/1.0" 200 9571 "htt
p://www.asylabwehramt.at/Seiten/Rundzeichen.html" "Mozilla/4.0 (compatible; MSIE 7.0; Windows NT
5.2; .NET CLR 1.1.4322; InfoPath.1; .NET CLR 2.0.50727; .NET CLR 3.0.4506.2152; .NET CLR 3.5.3072
9)"

213.208.144.130 - - [28/Jun/2010:12:20:02 +0200] "GET /Seiten/Bilder_buero.html HTTP/1.0" 200 110
26 "http://www.asylabwehramt.at/Seiten/Bilder.html" "Mozilla/4.0 (compatible; MSIE 7.0; Windows N
T 5.2; .NET CLR 1.1.4322; InfoPath.1; .NET CLR 2.0.50727; .NET CLR 3.0.4506.2152; .NET CLR 3.5.30
729)"

213.208.144.130 - - [28/Jun/2010:12:20:03 +0200] "GET /Bilder/BAA_photos/IMG_0184.JPG HTTP/1.0" 2
00 125043 "http://www.asylabwehramt.at/Seiten/Bilder_buero.html" "Mozilla/4.0 (compatible; MSIE 7
.0; Windows NT 5.2; .NET CLR 1.1.4322; InfoPath.1; .NET CLR 2.0.50727; .NET CLR 3.0.4506.2152; .N
ET CLR 3.5.30729)"

213.208.144.130 - - [28/Jun/2010:12:25:50 +0200] "GET /Seiten/Images.html HTTP/1.0" 200 9701 "htt
p://www.asylabwehramt.at/Seiten/Bilder.html" "Mozilla/4.0 (compatible; MSIE 7.0; Windows NT 5.2;
.NET CLR 1.1.4322; InfoPath.1; .NET CLR 2.0.50727; .NET CLR 3.0.4506.2152; .NET CLR 3.5.30729)"

213.208.144.130 - - [28/Jun/2010:12:25:52 +0200] "GET /Seiten/Links_e.html HTTP/1.0" 200 18366 "h
ttp://www.asylabwehramt.at/Seiten/Images.html" "Mozilla/4.0 (compatible; MSIE 7.0; Windows NT 5.2
; .NET CLR 1.1.4322; InfoPath.1; .NET CLR 2.0.50727; .NET CLR 3.0.4506.2152; .NET CLR 3.5.30729)"

213.208.144.130 - - [28/Jun/2010:12:25:54 +0200] "GET /Seiten/Links.html HTTP/1.0" 200 18362 "htt
p://www.asylabwehramt.at/Seiten/Links_e.html" "Mozilla/4.0 (compatible; MSIE 7.0; Windows NT 5.2;
.NET CLR 1.1.4322; InfoPath.1; .NET CLR 2.0.50727; .NET CLR 3.0.4506.2152; .NET CLR 3.5.30729)"

213.208.144.130 - - [28/Jun/2010:12:25:56 +0200] "GET /Seiten/Press.html HTTP/1.0" 200 11777 "htt
p://www.asylabwehramt.at/Seiten/Links.html" "Mozilla/4.0 (compatible; MSIE 7.0; Windows NT 5.2; .
NET CLR 1.1.4322; InfoPath.1; .NET CLR 2.0.50727; .NET CLR 3.0.4506.2152; .NET CLR 3.5.30729)"

213.208.144.130 - - [28/Jun/2010:12:25:59 +0200] "GET /OEFFENTLICHKEIT/media/Leporello_17062010.M

```
P3 HTTP/1.0" 200 5791744 "http://www.asylabwehramt.at/Seiten/Press.html" "Mozilla/4.0 (compatible
; MSIE 7.0; Windows NT 5.2; .NET CLR 1.1.4322; InfoPath.1; .NET CLR 2.0.50727; .NET CLR 3.0.4506.
2152; .NET CLR 3.5.30729)"
213.208.144.130 - - [28/Jun/2010:12:26:00 +0200] "GET /OEFFENTLICHKEIT/media/Leporello_17062010.M
P3 HTTP/1.0" 200 5791744 "-" "NSPlayer/10.0.0.4007 WMFSDK/10.0"
194.138.12.170 - - [28/Jun/2010:15:05:42 +0200] "GET / HTTP/1.1" 200 11828 "-" "Mozilla/5.0 (Wind
ows; U; Windows NT 5.1; de; rv:1.9.0.19) Gecko/2010031422 Firefox/3.0.19 (.NET CLR 3.5.30729)"
194.232.79.100 - - [28/Jun/2010:15:19:03 +0200] "GET / HTTP/1.1" 200 11828 "http://www.google.at/
search?hl=de&q=asylabwehramt&meta=" "Mozilla/4.0 (compatible; MSIE 8.0; Windows NT 6.0; Trident/4
.0; SLCC1; .NET CLR 2.0.50727; .NET CLR 3.5.30729; .NET CLR 3.0.30618)"
194.232.79.100 - - [28/Jun/2010:15:19:45 +0200] "GET / HTTP/1.1" 304 - "http://www.google.at/sear
ch?hl=de&q=asylabwehramt&meta=" "Mozilla/4.0 (compatible; MSIE 8.0; Windows NT 6.0; Trident/4.0;
SLCC1; .NET CLR 2.0.50727; .NET CLR 3.5.30729; .NET CLR 3.0.30618)"
194.232.79.100 - - [28/Jun/2010:15:19:46 +0200] "GET / HTTP/1.1" 304 - "http://www.google.at/sear
ch?hl=de&q=asylabwehramt&meta=" "Mozilla/4.0 (compatible; MSIE 8.0; Windows NT 6.0; Trident/4.0;
SLCC1; .NET CLR 2.0.50727; .NET CLR 3.5.30729; .NET CLR 3.0.30618)"
194.232.79.100 - - [28/Jun/2010:15:19:47 +0200] "GET / HTTP/1.1" 304 - "http://www.google.at/sear
ch?hl=de&q=asylabwehramt&meta=" "Mozilla/4.0 (compatible; MSIE 8.0; Windows NT 6.0; Trident/4.0;
SLCC1; .NET CLR 2.0.50727; .NET CLR 3.5.30729; .NET CLR 3.0.30618)"
194.138.12.170 - - [28/Jun/2010:16:32:52 +0200] "GET / HTTP/1.1" 304 - "-" "Mozilla/4.0 (compatib
le; MSIE 7.0; Windows NT 5.1; Mozilla/4.0 (compatible; MSIE 6.0; Windows NT 5.1; SV1) ; .NET CLR
1.0.3705; .NET CLR 2.0.50727; .NET CLR 3.0.04506.30; .NET CLR 1.1.4322; InfoPath.1; .NET CLR 3.0.
4506.2152; .NET CLR 3.5.30729; MS-RTC LM 8)"
194.138.12.171[21] - - [29/Jun/2010:09:12:42 +0200] "GET /Bilder/Header_AAbA.jpg HTTP/1.1" 304 - "htt
p://asylabwehramt.at/" "Mozilla/5.0 (Windows; U; Windows NT 5.1; de; rv:1.9.0.19) Gecko/201003142
2 Firefox/3.0.19 (.NET CLR 3.5.30729)"
```

```
194.138.12.171 - - [29/Jun/2010:09:12:45 +0200] "GET /favicon.ico HTTP/1.1" 302 336 "-" "Mozilla/
5.0 (Windows; U; Windows NT 5.1; de; rv:1.9.0.19) Gecko/2010031422 Firefox/3.0.19 (.NET CLR 3.5.3
0729)"
194.138.12.171 - - [29/Jun/2010:09:12:58 +0200] "GET /Seiten/Impressum.html HTTP/1.1" 200 11628 "
http://asylabwehramt.at/" "Mozilla/5.0 (Windows; U; Windows NT 5.1; de; rv:1.9.0.19) Gecko/201003
1422 Firefox/3.0.19 (.NET CLR 3.5.30729)"
80.120.179.10 - - [29/Jun/2010:11:14:34 +0200] "GET / HTTP/1.1" 200 11828 "-" "Mozilla/4.0 (compa
tible; MSIE 6.0; Windows NT 5.1; SV1; .NET CLR 1.1.4322)"
194.138.12.171 - - [29/Jun/2010:14:03:56 +0200] "GET / HTTP/1.1" 200 11828 "-" "Mozilla/5.0 (Wind
ows; U; Windows NT 5.1; de; rv:1.9.0.19) Gecko/2010031422 Firefox/3.0.19 (.NET CLR 3.5.30729)"
194.138.12.171 - - [29/Jun/2010:14:20:26 +0200] "GET /Seiten/Links.html HTTP/1.1" 200 18362 "http
://asylabwehramt.at/" "Mozilla/5.0 (Windows; U; Windows NT 5.1; de; rv:1.9.0.19) Gecko/2010031422
Firefox/3.0.19 (.NET CLR 3.5.30729)"
194.138.12.171 - - [29/Jun/2010:14:20:27 +0200] "GET /Bilder/BMI.png HTTP/1.1" 200 55823 "http://
asylabwehramt.at/Seiten/Links.html" "Mozilla/5.0 (Windows; U; Windows NT 5.1; de; rv:1.9.0.19) Ge
cko/2010031422 Firefox/3.0.19 (.NET CLR 3.5.30729)"
194.138.12.171 - - [29/Jun/2010:14:21:20 +0200] "GET /Seiten/Bilder.html HTTP/1.1" 200 9985 "http
://asylabwehramt.at/Seiten/Links.html" "Mozilla/5.0 (Windows; U; Windows NT 5.1; de; rv:1.9.0.19)
Gecko/2010031422 Firefox/3.0.19 (.NET CLR 3.5.30729)"
194.138.12.171 - - [29/Jun/2010:14:21:40 +0200] "GET /Seiten/Rundzeichen.html HTTP/1.1" 200 8837
"http://asylabwehramt.at/Seiten/Bilder.html" "Mozilla/5.0 (Windows; U; Windows NT 5.1; de; rv:1.9
.0.19) Gecko/2010031422 Firefox/3.0.19 (.NET CLR 3.5.30729)"
194.138.12.171 - - [29/Jun/2010:14:21:43 +0200] "GET /Seiten/Aktuelles.html HTTP/1.1" 200 12570 "
http://asylabwehramt.at/Seiten/Material.html" "Mozilla/5.0 (Windows; U; Windows NT 5.1; de; rv:1.
9.0.19) Gecko/2010031422 Firefox/3.0.19 (.NET CLR 3.5.30729)"
194.138.12.171 - - [29/Jun/2010:14:21:44 +0200] "GET /Bilder/leistung_2.jpg HTTP/1.1" 200 4918 "h
ttp://asylabwehramt.at/Seiten/Aktuelles.html" "Mozilla/5.0 (Windows; U; Windows NT 5.1; de; rv:1.
9.0.19) Gecko/2010031422 Firefox/3.0.19 (.NET CLR 3.5.30729)"
```

```
78.41.144.41 - - [29/Jun/2010:16:01:19 +0200] "GET / HTTP/1.0" 200 11833 "http://www.google.at/se
arch?hl=de&&sa=X&ei=qvwpTMmZG8-MOMX13bID&ved=0CBoQBSgA&q=asyl+abwehramt&spell=1" "Mozilla/4.0 (co
mpatible; MSIE 7.0; Windows NT 5.1; .NET CLR 2.0.50727; .NET CLR 1.1.4322; .NET CLR 3.0.04506.30;
 .NET CLR 3.0.04506.648; .NET CLR 3.0.4506.2152; .NET CLR 3.5.30729)"
78.41.144.41 - - [29/Jun/2010:16:02:28 +0200] "GET /Seiten/Aktuelles.html HTTP/1.0" 200 12600 "ht
tp://www.asylabwehramt.at/" "Mozilla/4.0 (compatible; MSIE 7.0; Windows NT 5.1; .NET CLR 2.0.5072
7; .NET CLR 1.1.4322; .NET CLR 3.0.04506.30; .NET CLR 3.0.04506.648; .NET CLR 3.0.4506.2152; .NET
 CLR 3.5.30729)"
78.41.144.41 - - [29/Jun/2010:16:02:29 +0200] "GET /Bilder/fitnesscenter_traiskirchen.jpg HTTP/1.
0" 200 5721 "http://www.asylabwehramt.at/Seiten/Aktuelles.html" "Mozilla/4.0 (compatible; MSIE 7.
0; Windows NT 5.1; .NET CLR 2.0.50727; .NET CLR 1.1.4322; .NET CLR 3.0.04506.30; .NET CLR 3.0.045
06.648; .NET CLR 3.0.4506.2152; .NET CLR 3.5.30729)"
78.41.144.41 - - [29/Jun/2010:16:02:55 +0200] "GET /Seiten/Rundzeichen.html HTTP/1.0" 200 8867 "h
ttp://www.asylabwehramt.at/Seiten/Aktuelles.html" "Mozilla/4.0 (compatible; MSIE 7.0; Windows NT
5.1; .NET CLR 2.0.50727; .NET CLR 1.1.4322; .NET CLR 3.0.04506.30; .NET CLR 3.0.04506.648; .NET C
LR 3.0.4506.2152; .NET CLR 3.5.30729)"
78.41.144.41 - - [29/Jun/2010:16:03:00 +0200] "GET /Seiten/Bilder.html HTTP/1.0" 200 10015 "http:
//www.asylabwehramt.at/Seiten/Rundzeichen.html" "Mozilla/4.0 (compatible; MSIE 7.0; Windows NT 5.
1; .NET CLR 2.0.50727; .NET CLR 1.1.4322; .NET CLR 3.0.04506.30; .NET CLR 3.0.04506.648; .NET CLR
3.0.4506.2152; .NET CLR 3.5.30729)"
78.41.144.41 - - [29/Jun/2010:16:03:16 +0200] "GET /Seiten/Ausseneinsaetze.html HTTP/1.0" 200 922
0 "http://www.asylabwehramt.at/Seiten/Bilder.html" "Mozilla/4.0 (compatible; MSIE 7.0; Windows NT
5.1; .NET CLR 2.0.50727; .NET CLR 1.1.4322; .NET CLR 3.0.04506.30; .NET CLR 3.0.04506.648; .NET
CLR 3.0.4506.2152; .NET CLR 3.5.30729)"
78.41.144.41 - - [29/Jun/2010:16:03:23 +0200] "GET /Seiten/Images.html HTTP/1.0" 200 10187 "http:
//www.asylabwehramt.at/Seiten/Ausseneinsaetze.html" "Mozilla/4.0 (compatible; MSIE 7.0; Windows N
T 5.1; .NET CLR 2.0.50727; .NET CLR 1.1.4322; .NET CLR 3.0.04506.30; .NET CLR 3.0.04506.648; .NET
 CLR 3.0.4506.2152; .NET CLR 3.5.30729)"
```

78.41.144.41 - - [29/Jun/2010:16:03:29 +0200] "GET /Seiten/Presse.html HTTP/1.0" 200 11788 "http://www.asylabwehramt.at/Seiten/Images.html" "Mozilla/4.0 (compatible; MSIE 7.0; Windows NT 5.1; .NET CLR 2.0.50727; .NET CLR 1.1.4322; .NET CLR 3.0.04506.30; .NET CLR 3.0.04506.648; .NET CLR 3.0.4506.2152; .NET CLR 3.5.30729)"

78.41.144.41 - - [29/Jun/2010:16:04:04 +0200] "GET /Seiten/Forms_and_Infos.html HTTP/1.0" 200 11108 "http://www.asylabwehramt.at/Seiten/Rundzeichen.html" "Mozilla/4.0 (compatible; MSIE 7.0; Windows NT 5.1; .NET CLR 2.0.50727; .NET CLR 1.1.4322; .NET CLR 3.0.04506.30; .NET CLR 3.0.04506.648; .NET CLR 3.0.4506.2152; .NET CLR 3.5.30729)"

78.41.144.41 - - [29/Jun/2010:16:04:14 +0200] "GET /Material/Hotline_Deutsch.pdf HTTP/1.0" 200 489465 "http://www.asylabwehramt.at/Seiten/Forms_and_Infos.html" "Mozilla/4.0 (compatible; MSIE 7.0; Windows NT 5.1; .NET CLR 2.0.50727; .NET CLR 1.1.4322; .NET CLR 3.0.04506.30; .NET CLR 3.0.04506.648; .NET CLR 3.0.04506.2152; .NET CLR 3.5.30729)"

78.41.144.41 - - [29/Jun/2010:16:04:33 +0200] "GET /Seiten/Seal.html HTTP/1.0" 200 8905 "http://www.asylabwehramt.at/Seiten/Forms_and_Infos.html" "Mozilla/4.0 (compatible; MSIE 7.0; Windows NT 5.1; .NET CLR 2.0.50727; .NET CLR 1.1.4322; .NET CLR 3.0.04506.30; .NET CLR 3.0.04506.648; .NET CLR 3.0.4506.2152; .NET CLR 3.5.30729)"

78.41.144.41 - - [29/Jun/2010:16:04:35 +0200] "GET /Seiten/Material.html HTTP/1.0" 200 12010 "http://www.asylabwehramt.at/Seiten/Seal.html" "Mozilla/4.0 (compatible; MSIE 7.0; Windows NT 5.1; .NET CLR 2.0.50727; .NET CLR 1.1.4322; .NET CLR 3.0.04506.30; .NET CLR 3.0.04506.648; .NET CLR 3.0.4506.2152; .NET CLR 3.5.30729)"

78.41.144.41 - - [29/Jun/2010:16:04:39 +0200] "GET /Seiten/Presse.html HTTP/1.0" 200 11788 "http://www.asylabwehramt.at/Seiten/Material.html" "Mozilla/4.0 (compatible; MSIE 7.0; Windows NT 5.1; .NET CLR 2.0.50727; .NET CLR 1.1.4322; .NET CLR 3.0.04506.30; .NET CLR 3.0.04506.648; .NET CLR 3.0.4506.2152; .NET CLR 3.5.30729)"

78.41.144.41 - - [30/Jun/2010:11:31:44 +0200] "GET / HTTP/1.0" 200 11984 "-" "Mozilla/4.0 (compatible; MSIE 7.0; Windows NT 5.1)"

78.41.144.41 - - [30/Jun/2010:11:31:47 +0200] "GET /Seiten/Material.html HTTP/1.0" 200 12038 "http://www.asylabwehramt.at/" "Mozilla/4.0 (compatible; MSIE 7.0; Windows NT 5.1)"

```
78.41.144.41 - - [30/Jun/2010:11:31:55 +0200] "GET /index.html HTTP/1.0" 200 11984 "http://www.as
ylabwehramt.at/Seiten/Material.html" "Mozilla/4.0 (compatible; MSIE 7.0; Windows NT 5.1)"
78.41.144.41 - - [30/Jun/2010:11:32:03 +0200] "GET /index_e.html HTTP/1.0" 200 12016 "http://www.
asylabwehramt.at/" "Mozilla/4.0 (compatible; MSIE 7.0; Windows NT 5.1)"
78.41.144.41 - - [30/Jun/2010:11:32:07 +0200] "GET /Seiten/Latestnews.html HTTP/1.0" 200 12721 "h
ttp://www.asylabwehramt.at/index_e.html" "Mozilla/4.0 (compatible; MSIE 7.0; Windows NT 5.1)"
78.41.144.41 - - [30/Jun/2010:11:32:12 +0200] "GET /Seiten/Aktuelles.html HTTP/1.0" 200 12690 "ht
tp://www.asylabwehramt.at/Seiten/Latestnews.html" "Mozilla/4.0 (compatible; MSIE 7.0; Windows NT
5.1)"
78.41.144.41 - - [30/Jun/2010:11:32:16 +0200] "GET /Seiten/Forms_and_Infos.html HTTP/1.0" 200 111
36 "http://www.asylabwehramt.at/Seiten/Material.html" "Mozilla/4.0 (compatible; MSIE 7.0; Windows
NT 5.1)"
78.41.144.41 - - [30/Jun/2010:11:32:20 +0200] "GET /Seiten/Seal.html HTTP/1.0" 200 8933 "http://w
ww.asylabwehramt.at/Seiten/Forms_and_Infos.html" "Mozilla/4.0 (compatible; MSIE 7.0; Windows NT 5
.1)"
78.41.144.41 - - [30/Jun/2010:11:32:23 +0200] "GET /Seiten/Bilder.html HTTP/1.0" 200 10043 "http:
//www.asylabwehramt.at/Seiten/Rundzeichen.html" "Mozilla/4.0 (compatible; MSIE 7.0; Windows NT 5.
1)"
78.41.144.41 - - [30/Jun/2010:11:32:25 +0200] "GET /Seiten/Images.html HTTP/1.0" 200 10215 "http:
//www.asylabwehramt.at/Seiten/Bilder.html" "Mozilla/4.0 (compatible; MSIE 7.0; Windows NT 5.1)"
78.41.144.41 - - [30/Jun/2010:11:32:26 +0200] "GET /Bilder/IBM.png HTTP/1.0" 200 8413 "http://www
.asylabwehramt.at/Seiten/Links_e.html" "Mozilla/4.0 (compatible; MSIE 7.0; Windows NT 5.1)"
78.41.144.41 - - [30/Jun/2010:11:32:27 +0200] "GET /Seiten/Links.html HTTP/1.0" 200 18420 "http:/
/www.asylabwehramt.at/Seiten/Links_e.html" "Mozilla/4.0 (compatible; MSIE 7.0; Windows NT 5.1)"
78.41.144.41 - - [30/Jun/2010:11:32:28 +0200] "GET /Seiten/Press.html HTTP/1.0" 200 11867 "http:/
/www.asylabwehramt.at/Seiten/Links.html" "Mozilla/4.0 (compatible; MSIE 7.0; Windows NT 5.1)"
194.138.12.170 - - [30/Jun/2010:12:13:33 +0200] "GET / HTTP/1.1" 200 11984 "-" "Mozilla/5.0 (Wind
ows; U; Windows NT 5.1; de; rv:1.9.0.19) Gecko/2010031422 Firefox/3.0.19 (.NET CLR 3.5.30729)"
```

194.138.12.170 - - [30/Jun/2010:12:13:34 +0200] "GET /favicon.ico HTTP/1.1" 302 336 "-" "Mozilla/5.0 (Windows; U; Windows NT 5.1; de; rv:1.9.0.19) Gecko/2010031422 Firefox/3.0.19 (.NET CLR 3.5.3 0729)"

194.138.12.170 - - [30/Jun/2010:12:13:37 +0200] "GET /favicon.ico HTTP/1.1" 302 336 "-" "Mozilla/5.0 (Windows; U; Windows NT 5.1; de; rv:1.9.0.19) Gecko/2010031422 Firefox/3.0.19 (.NET CLR 3.5.3 0729)"

194.138.12.170 - - [30/Jun/2010:12:14:01 +0200] "GET /Seiten/Impressum.html HTTP/1.1" 200 11684 " http://asylabwehramt.at/" "Mozilla/5.0 (Windows; U; Windows NT 5.1; de; rv:1.9.0.19) Gecko/201003 1422 Firefox/3.0.19 (.NET CLR 3.5.30729)"

193.5.216.100 - - [01/Jul/2010:07:32:22 +0200] "GET / HTTP/1.0" 200 11992 "http://www.google.ch/s earch?hl=de&&sa=X&ei=YygsTI6fCsiOOMj8mbIJ&ved=0CAUQBSgA&q=asyl+abwehramt&spell=1" "Mozilla/4.0 (c ompatible; MSIE 6.0; Windows NT 5.2; SV1; .NET CLR 1.1.4322; .NET CLR 2.0.50727; .NET CLR 3.0.045 06.648; .NET CLR 3.5.21022; .NET CLR 3.0.4506.2152; .NET CLR 3.5.30729)"

193.5.216.100 - - [01/Jul/2010:07:32:59 +0200] "GET /Seiten/Bilder.html HTTP/1.0" 200 10043 "http ://www.asylabwehramt.at/" "Mozilla/4.0 (compatible; MSIE 6.0; Windows NT 5.2; SV1; .NET CLR 1.1.4 322; .NET CLR 2.0.50727; .NET CLR 3.0.04506.648; .NET CLR 3.5.21022; .NET CLR 3.0.4506.2152; .NET CLR 3.5.30729)"

194.138.12.170 - - [01/Jul/2010:09:58:23 +0200] "GET / HTTP/1.1" 200 11992 "-" "Mozilla/5.0 (Wind ows; U; Windows NT 5.1; de; rv:1.9.0.19) Gecko/2010031422 Firefox/3.0.19 (.NET CLR 3.5.30729)"

193.171.152.33 - - [01/Jul/2010:12:16:01 +0200] "GET / HTTP/1.1" 200 11992 "http://www.google.at/ search?hl=de&q=Asylabwehramt&btnG=Google-Suche&meta=" "Mozilla/4.0 (compatible; MSIE 8.0; Windows NT 5.1; Trident/4.0; InfoPath.1; .NET CLR 2.0.50727; OfficeLiveConnector.1.3; OfficeLivePatch.0. 0)"

193.171.152.33 - - [01/Jul/2010:12:16:02 +0200] "GET /favicon.ico HTTP/1.1" 302 340 "-" "Mozilla/4.0 (compatible; MSIE 8.0; Windows NT 5.1; Trident/4.0; InfoPath.1; .NET CLR 2.0.50727; OfficeLiv eConnector.1.3; OfficeLivePatch.0.0)"

193.171.152.33 - - [01/Jul/2010:12:16:09 +0200] "GET /Seiten/Orgstrukt.html HTTP/1.1" 200 14119 " http://www.asylabwehramt.at/" "Mozilla/4.0 (compatible; MSIE 8.0; Windows NT 5.1; Trident/4.0; In

```
193.171.152.33 - - [01/Jul/2010:12:16:29 +0200] "GET /Seiten/Links.html HTTP/1.1" 200 18479 "http://www.asylabwehramt.at/Seiten/Orgstrukt.html" "Mozilla/4.0 (compatible; MSIE 8.0; Windows NT 5.1; Trident/4.0; InfoPath.1; .NET CLR 2.0.50727; OfficeLiveConnector.1.3; OfficeLivePatch.0.0)"
193.171.152.33 - - [01/Jul/2010:12:16:44 +0200] "GET /Seiten/Press.html HTTP/1.1" 200 11867 "http://www.asylabwehramt.at/Seiten/Links.html" "Mozilla/4.0 (compatible; MSIE 8.0; Windows NT 5.1; Trident/4.0; InfoPath.1; .NET CLR 2.0.50727; OfficeLiveConnector.1.3; OfficeLivePatch.0.0)"
193.171.152.33 - - [01/Jul/2010:12:17:36 +0200] "GET /Seiten/Aktuelles.html HTTP/1.1" 200 12690 "http://www.asylabwehramt.at/Seiten/Press.html" "Mozilla/4.0 (compatible; MSIE 8.0; Windows NT 5.1; Trident/4.0; InfoPath.1; .NET CLR 2.0.50727; OfficeLiveConnector.1.3; OfficeLivePatch.0.0)"
193.171.152.33 - - [01/Jul/2010:12:17:37 +0200] "GET /Bilder/leistung_2.jpg HTTP/1.1" 304 - "http://www.asylabwehramt.at/Seiten/Aktuelles.html" "Mozilla/4.0 (compatible; MSIE 8.0; Windows NT 5.1; Trident/4.0; InfoPath.1; .NET CLR 2.0.50727; OfficeLiveConnector.1.3; OfficeLivePatch.0.0)"
193.171.152.33 - - [01/Jul/2010:12:18:06 +0200] "GET /Seiten/Bilder.html HTTP/1.1" 200 10043 "http://www.asylabwehramt.at/Seiten/Aktuelles.html" "Mozilla/4.0 (compatible; MSIE 8.0; Windows NT 5.1; Trident/4.0; InfoPath.1; .NET CLR 2.0.50727; OfficeLiveConnector.1.3; OfficeLivePatch.0.0)"
193.171.152.33 - - [01/Jul/2010:12:18:46 +0200] "GET /Seiten/Rundzeichen.html HTTP/1.1" 200 8895 "http://www.asylabwehramt.at/Seiten/Bilder.html" "Mozilla/4.0 (compatible; MSIE 8.0; Windows NT 5.1; Trident/4.0; InfoPath.1; .NET CLR 2.0.50727; OfficeLiveConnector.1.3; OfficeLivePatch.0.0)"
193.171.152.33 - - [01/Jul/2010:12:18:54 +0200] "GET /index.html HTTP/1.1" 200 11992 "http://www.asylabwehramt.at/Seiten/Rundzeichen.html" "Mozilla/4.0 (compatible; MSIE 8.0; Windows NT 5.1; Trident/4.0; InfoPath.1; .NET CLR 2.0.50727; OfficeLiveConnector.1.3; OfficeLivePatch.0.0)"
193.171.152.33 - - [01/Jul/2010:12:20:08 +0200] "GET /index_e.html HTTP/1.1" 200 12025 "http://www.asylabwehramt.at/index.html" "Mozilla/4.0 (compatible; MSIE 8.0; Windows NT 5.1; Trident/4.0; InfoPath.1; .NET CLR 2.0.50727; OfficeLiveConnector.1.3; OfficeLivePatch.0.0)"
80.120.179.10 - - [07/Jul/2010:11:17:58 +0200] "GET / HTTP/1.1" 200 11992 "-" "Mozilla/4.0 (compatible; MSIE 6.0; Windows NT 5.1; SV1; InfoPath.1; .NET CLR 1.1.4322; .NET CLR 2.0.50727)"
88.116.224.102 - - [07/Jul/2010:19:55:49 +0200] "GET / HTTP/1.1" 200 11992 "-" "Mozilla/5.0 (X11;
```

```
U; Linux i686; de; rv:1.9.2.6) Gecko/20100628 Ubuntu/10.04 (lucid) Firefox/3.6.6"
88.116.224.102 - - [07/Jul/2010:19:56:14 +0200] "GET /Seiten/Aktuelles.html HTTP/1.1" 200 12690 "
http://www.asylabwehramt.at/" "Mozilla/5.0 (X11; U; Linux i686; de; rv:1.9.2.6) Gecko/20100628 Ub
untu/10.04 (lucid) Firefox/3.6.6"
88.116.224.102 - - [07/Jul/2010:19:56:48 +0200] "GET /Seiten/Rundzeichen.html HTTP/1.1" 200 8895
"http://www.asylabwehramt.at/Seiten/Aktuelles.html" "Mozilla/5.0 (X11; U; Linux i686; de; rv:1.9.
2.6) Gecko/20100628 Ubuntu/10.04 (lucid) Firefox/3.6.6"
88.116.224.102 - - [07/Jul/2010:19:56:52 +0200] "GET /Seiten/Forms_and_Infos.html HTTP/1.1" 200 1
5692 "http://www.asylabwehramt.at/Seiten/Rundzeichen.html" "Mozilla/5.0 (X11; U; Linux i686; de;
rv:1.9.2.6) Gecko/20100628 Ubuntu/10.04 (lucid) Firefox/3.6.6"
88.116.224.102 - - [07/Jul/2010:19:56:58 +0200] "GET /Seiten/Seal.html HTTP/1.1" 200 8933 "http:/
/www.asylabwehramt.at/Seiten/Forms_and_Infos.html" "Mozilla/5.0 (X11; U; Linux i686; de; rv:1.9.2
.6) Gecko/20100628 Ubuntu/10.04 (lucid) Firefox/3.6.6"
88.116.224.102 - - [07/Jul/2010:19:57:03 +0200] "GET /Seiten/Material.html HTTP/1.1" 200 16558 "h
ttp://www.asylabwehramt.at/Seiten/Seal.html" "Mozilla/5.0 (X11; U; Linux i686; de; rv:1.9.2.6) Ge
cko/20100628 Ubuntu/10.04 (lucid) Firefox/3.6.6"
88.116.224.102 - - [07/Jul/2010:19:57:19 +0200] "GET /Seiten/Press.html HTTP/1.1" 200 11867 "http
://www.asylabwehramt.at/Seiten/Aktuelles.html" "Mozilla/5.0 (X11; U; Linux i686; de; rv:1.9.2.6)
Gecko/20100628 Ubuntu/10.04 (lucid) Firefox/3.6.6"
88.116.224.102 - - [07/Jul/2010:19:57:21 +0200] "GET /Seiten/Presse.html HTTP/1.1" 200 11816 "htt
p://www.asylabwehramt.at/Seiten/Press.html" "Mozilla/5.0 (X11; U; Linux i686; de; rv:1.9.2.6) Gec
ko/20100628 Ubuntu/10.04 (lucid) Firefox/3.6.6"
88.116.224.102 - - [07/Jul/2010:19:57:34 +0200] "GET /index.html HTTP/1.1" 200 11992 "http://www.
asylabwehramt.at/Seiten/Presse.html" "Mozilla/5.0 (X11; U; Linux i686; de; rv:1.9.2.6) Gecko/2010
0628 Ubuntu/10.04 (lucid) Firefox/3.6.6"
193.171.152.33 - - [08/Jul/2010:00:53:46 +0200] "GET /asyl.css HTTP/1.1" 304 - "-" "Mozilla/4.0 (
compatible;)"
```

193.134.242.12[22] - - [08/Jul/2010:10:22:39 +0200] "GET / HTTP/1.0" 200 11992 "http://www.zeit.de/2010/28/A-Asylabwehramt" "Mozilla/5.0 (Windows; U; Windows NT 5.1; en-GB; rv:1.9.2.6) Gecko/20100625 Firefox/3.6.6"

193.134.242.12 - - [08/Jul/2010:10:22:40 +0200] "GET /asyl.css HTTP/1.0" 200 860 "http://www.asylabwehramt.at/" "Mozilla/5.0 (Windows; U; Windows NT 5.1; en-GB; rv:1.9.2.6) Gecko/20100625 Firefox/3.6.6"

193.134.242.12 - - [08/Jul/2010:10:22:42 +0200] "GET /favicon.ico HTTP/1.0" 302 340 "-" "Mozilla/5.0 (Windows; U; Windows NT 5.1; en-GB; rv:1.9.2.6) Gecko/20100625 Firefox/3.6.6"

193.134.242.12 - - [08/Jul/2010:10:22:45 +0200] "GET /favicon.ico HTTP/1.0" 302 340 "-" "Mozilla/5.0 (Windows; U; Windows NT 5.1; en-GB; rv:1.9.2.6) Gecko/20100625 Firefox/3.6.6"

193.134.242.12 - - [08/Jul/2010:10:24:46 +0200] "GET /Seiten/Bilder.html HTTP/1.0" 200 10043 "http://www.asylabwehramt.at/" "Mozilla/5.0 (Windows; U; Windows NT 5.1; en-GB; rv:1.9.2.6) Gecko/20100625 Firefox/3.6.6"

193.134.242.12 - - [08/Jul/2010:10:24:47 +0200] "GET /Bilder/Ausstellung_weisses_haus_wien_esel_fotos/eSeL_UBERMORGEN_asylabwehramt_dasweissehaus_453_thumb.jpg HTTP/1.0" 200 47504 "http://www.asylabwehramt.at/Seiten/Bilder.html" "Mozilla/5.0 (Windows; U; Windows NT 5.1; en-GB; rv:1.9.2.6) Gecko/20100625 Firefox/3.6.6"

193.134.242.12 - - [08/Jul/2010:10:25:19 +0200] "GET /Seiten/Ausseneinsaetze.html HTTP/1.0" 200 9381 "http://www.asylabwehramt.at/Seiten/Bilder.html" "Mozilla/5.0 (Windows; U; Windows NT 5.1; en-GB; rv:1.9.2.6) Gecko/20100625 Firefox/3.6.6"

193.134.242.12 - - [08/Jul/2010:10:25:20 +0200] "GET /Bilder/inventur.png HTTP/1.0" 200 848668 "http://www.asylabwehramt.at/Seiten/Ausseneinsaetze.html" "Mozilla/5.0 (Windows; U; Windows NT 5.1; en-GB; rv:1.9.2.6) Gecko/20100625 Firefox/3.6.6"

193.134.242.12 - - [08/Jul/2010:10:27:20 +0200] "GET /Seiten/Material.html HTTP/1.0" 200 16558 "http://www.asylabwehramt.at/Seiten/Ausseneinsaetze.html" "Mozilla/5.0 (Windows; U; Windows NT 5.1; en-GB; rv:1.9.2.6) Gecko/20100625 Firefox/3.6.6"

[22]WHOIS record on page 288

193.134.242.12 - - [08/Jul/2010:10:27:44 +0200] "GET /Bilder/Ladung.png HTTP/1.0" 200 114658 "htt
p://www.asylabwehramt.at/Seiten/Material.html" "Mozilla/5.0 (Windows; U; Windows NT 5.1; en-GB; r
v:1.9.2.6) Gecko/20100625 Firefox/3.6.6"

193.134.242.12 - - [08/Jul/2010:10:27:57 +0200] "GET /Material/Hotline_Georgisch.PDF HTTP/1.0" 20
0 822080 "http://www.asylabwehramt.at/Seiten/Material.html" "Mozilla/5.0 (Windows; U; Windows NT
5.1; en-GB; rv:1.9.2.6) Gecko/20100625 Firefox/3.6.6"

193.134.242.12 - - [08/Jul/2010:10:28:22 +0200] "GET /Seiten/Links.html HTTP/1.0" 200 18864 "http
://www.asylabwehramt.at/Seiten/Material.html" "Mozilla/5.0 (Windows; U; Windows NT 5.1; en-GB; rv
:1.9.2.6) Gecko/20100625 Firefox/3.6.6"

193.134.242.12 - - [08/Jul/2010:10:32:32 +0200] "GET /favicon.ico HTTP/1.0" 302 340 "-" "Mozilla/
5.0 (Windows; U; Windows NT 5.1; en-GB; rv:1.9.2.6) Gecko/20100625 Firefox/3.6.6 GTB7.0"

193.134.242.12 - - [08/Jul/2010:10:32:35 +0200] "GET /favicon.ico HTTP/1.0" 302 340 "-" "Mozilla/
5.0 (Windows; U; Windows NT 5.1; en-GB; rv:1.9.2.6) Gecko/20100625 Firefox/3.6.6 GTB7.0"

193.134.242.12 - - [08/Jul/2010:10:36:59 +0200] "GET /Material/Hotline_Deutsch.pdf HTTP/1.0" 200
489465 "http://www.asylabwehramt.at/Seiten/Material.html" "Mozilla/5.0 (Windows; U; Windows NT 5.
1; en-GB; rv:1.9.2.6) Gecko/20100625 Firefox/3.6.6"

193.134.242.12 - - [08/Jul/2010:10:37:34 +0200] "GET /Seiten/Orgstrukt.html HTTP/1.0" 200 14119 "
http://www.asylabwehramt.at/Seiten/Material.html" "Mozilla/5.0 (Windows; U; Windows NT 5.1; en-GB
; rv:1.9.2.6) Gecko/20100625 Firefox/3.6.6"

193.134.242.12 - - [08/Jul/2010:10:38:17 +0200] "GET /index.html HTTP/1.0" 200 11992 "http://www.
asylabwehramt.at/Seiten/Orgstrukt.html" "Mozilla/5.0 (Windows; U; Windows NT 5.1; en-GB; rv:1.9.2
.6) Gecko/20100625 Firefox/3.6.6"

193.41.228.76 [23] - - [08/Jul/2010:11:01:23 +0200] "GET /favicon.ico HTTP/1.1" 302 340 "-" "Mozilla/4
.0 (compatible; MSIE 7.0; Windows NT 5.1; .NET CLR 2.0.50727; .NET CLR 3.0.04506.648; .NET CLR 3.
5.21022; InfoPath.1)"

193.41.228.76 - - [08/Jul/2010:11:01:24 +0200] "GET /Bilder/Header_AAbA_anim.gif HTTP/1.1" 200 19

---

[23] WHOIS record on page 300

```
997 "http://www.asylabwehramt.at/" "Mozilla/4.0 (compatible; MSIE 7.0; Windows NT 5.1; .NET CLR 2
.0.50727; .NET CLR 3.0.04506.648; .NET CLR 3.5.21022; InfoPath.1)"
193.41.228.76 - - [08/Jul/2010:11:01:31 +0200] "GET /Seiten/Bilder.html HTTP/1.1" 200 10043 "http
://www.asylabwehramt.at/" "Mozilla/4.0 (compatible; MSIE 7.0; Windows NT 5.1; .NET CLR 2.0.50727;
.NET CLR 3.0.04506.648; .NET CLR 3.5.21022; InfoPath.1)"
193.134.242.12 - - [08/Jul/2010:11:16:36 +0200] "GET /favicon.ico HTTP/1.0" 302 340 "-" "Mozilla/
5.0 (Windows; U; Windows NT 5.1; en-GB; rv:1.9.2.6) Gecko/20100625 Firefox/3.6.6 GTB7.0"
193.134.242.12 - - [08/Jul/2010:11:16:39 +0200] "GET /favicon.ico HTTP/1.0" 302 340 "-" "Mozilla/
5.0 (Windows; U; Windows NT 5.1; en-GB; rv:1.9.2.6) Gecko/20100625 Firefox/3.6.6 GTB7.0"
193.134.242.12 - - [08/Jul/2010:11:16:51 +0200] "GET /Material/Hotline_Franzoesisch.PDF HTTP/1.0"
200 515416 "http://www.asylabwehramt.at/Seiten/Material.html" "Mozilla/5.0 (Windows; U; Windows
NT 5.1; en-GB; rv:1.9.2.6) Gecko/20100625 Firefox/3.6.6 GTB7.0"
193.41.228.76 - - [08/Jul/2010:11:45:27 +0200] "GET /favicon.ico HTTP/1.1" 302 340 "-" "Mozilla/4
.0 (compatible; MSIE 7.0; Windows NT 5.1; .NET CLR 2.0.50727; .NET CLR 3.0.04506.648; .NET CLR 3.
5.21022; InfoPath.1)"
193.41.228.76 - - [08/Jul/2010:11:45:36 +0200] "GET /Seiten/Rundzeichen.html HTTP/1.1" 200 8895 "
http://www.asylabwehramt.at/" "Mozilla/4.0 (compatible; MSIE 7.0; Windows NT 5.1; .NET CLR 2.0.50
727; .NET CLR 3.0.04506.648; .NET CLR 3.5.21022; InfoPath.1)"
193.41.228.76 - - [08/Jul/2010:11:46:09 +0200] "GET /Seiten/Aktuelles.html HTTP/1.1" 200 12690 "h
ttp://www.asylabwehramt.at/Seiten/Bilder.html" "Mozilla/4.0 (compatible; MSIE 7.0; Windows NT 5.1
; .NET CLR 2.0.50727; .NET CLR 3.0.04506.648; .NET CLR 3.5.21022; InfoPath.1)"
193.41.228.76 - - [08/Jul/2010:11:46:10 +0200] "GET /Bilder/leistung_2.jpg HTTP/1.1" 200 4918 "ht
tp://www.asylabwehramt.at/Seiten/Aktuelles.html" "Mozilla/4.0 (compatible; MSIE 7.0; Windows NT 5
.1; .NET CLR 2.0.50727; .NET CLR 3.0.04506.648; .NET CLR 3.5.21022; InfoPath.1)"
193.41.228.76 - - [08/Jul/2010:11:46:46 +0200] "GET /Seiten/Material.html HTTP/1.1" 200 16558 "ht
tp://www.asylabwehramt.at/Seiten/Aktuelles.html" "Mozilla/4.0 (compatible; MSIE 7.0; Windows NT 5
.1; .NET CLR 2.0.50727; .NET CLR 3.0.04506.648; .NET CLR 3.5.21022; InfoPath.1)"
193.41.228.76 - - [08/Jul/2010:11:46:50 +0200] "GET /Bilder/Ladung.png HTTP/1.1" 200 114658 "http
```

```
://www.asylabwehramt.at/Seiten/Material.html" "Mozilla/4.0 (compatible; MSIE 7.0; Windows NT 5.1;
.NET CLR 2.0.50727; .NET CLR 3.0.04506.648; .NET CLR 3.5.21022; InfoPath.1)"
193.134.242.12 - - [08/Jul/2010:12:15:21 +0200] "GET /favicon.ico HTTP/1.0" 302 340 "-" "Mozilla/
5.0 (Windows; U; Windows NT 5.1; en-GB; rv:1.9.2.6) Gecko/20100625 Firefox/3.6.6 GTB7.1"
193.134.242.12 - - [08/Jul/2010:12:15:24 +0200] "GET /favicon.ico HTTP/1.0" 302 340 "-" "Mozilla/
5.0 (Windows; U; Windows NT 5.1; en-GB; rv:1.9.2.6) Gecko/20100625 Firefox/3.6.6 GTB7.1"
193.134.242.12 - - [08/Jul/2010:12:15:42 +0200] "GET /Seiten/Aktuelles.html HTTP/1.0" 200 12690 "
http://www.asylabwehramt.at/" "Mozilla/5.0 (Windows; U; Windows NT 5.1; en-GB; rv:1.9.2.6) Gecko/
20100625 Firefox/3.6.6 GTB7.1"
193.134.242.12 - - [08/Jul/2010:12:15:43 +0200] "GET /Bilder/56.jpg HTTP/1.0" 200 4494 "http://ww
w.asylabwehramt.at/Seiten/Aktuelles.html" "Mozilla/5.0 (Windows; U; Windows NT 5.1; en-GB; rv:1.9
.2.6) Gecko/20100625 Firefox/3.6.6 GTB7.1"
193.134.242.12 - - [08/Jul/2010:12:16:20 +0200] "GET /Seiten/Rundzeichen.html HTTP/1.0" 200 8895
"http://www.asylabwehramt.at/Seiten/Material.html" "Mozilla/5.0 (Windows; U; Windows NT 5.1; en-G
B; rv:1.9.2.6) Gecko/20100625 Firefox/3.6.6 GTB7.1"
193.134.242.12 - - [08/Jul/2010:12:17:05 +0200] "GET /Seiten/Press.html HTTP/1.0" 200 11867 "http
://www.asylabwehramt.at/Seiten/Links.html" "Mozilla/5.0 (Windows; U; Windows NT 5.1; en-GB; rv:1.
9.2.6) Gecko/20100625 Firefox/3.6.6 GTB7.1"
193.247.39.154[24] - - [08/Jul/2010:15:02:54 +0200] "GET / HTTP/1.0" 200 11992 "http://www.zeit.de/2
010/28/A-Asylabwehramt?page=1" "Mozilla/4.0 (compatible; MSIE 7.0; Windows NT 5.1; .NET CLR 1.1.
4322; .NET CLR 2.0.50727; .NET CLR 3.0.04506.648; .NET CLR 3.5.21022; InfoPath.1; .NET CLR 3.0.45
06.2152; .NET CLR 3.5.30729)"
193.247.39.154 - - [08/Jul/2010:15:03:53 +0200] "GET /Material/Hotline_Deutsch.pdf HTTP/1.0" 200
489465 "http://www.asylabwehramt.at/" "Mozilla/4.0 (compatible; MSIE 7.0; Windows NT 5.1; .NET CL
R 1.1.4322; .NET CLR 2.0.50727; .NET CLR 3.0.04506.648; .NET CLR 3.5.21022; InfoPath.1; .NET CLR
3.0.4506.2152; .NET CLR 3.5.30729)"
```

---

[24] WHOIS record on page 293

151

```
193.247.39.154 - - [08/Jul/2010:15:04:17 +0200] "GET /Seiten/Material.html HTTP/1.0" 200 16558 "h
ttp://www.asylabwehramt.at/" "Mozilla/4.0 (compatible; MSIE 7.0; Windows NT 5.1; .NET CLR 1.1.432
2; .NET CLR 2.0.50727; .NET CLR 3.0.04506.648; .NET CLR 3.5.21022; InfoPath.1; .NET CLR 3.0.4506.
2152; .NET CLR 3.5.30729)"
193.247.39.154 - - [08/Jul/2010:15:04:22 +0200] "GET /Bilder/flyer_nigeria_Internet.pdf HTTP/1.0"
200 702826 "http://www.asylabwehramt.at/Seiten/Material.html" "Mozilla/4.0 (compatible; MSIE 7.0
; Windows NT 5.1; .NET CLR 1.1.4322; .NET CLR 2.0.50727; .NET CLR 3.0.04506.648; .NET CLR 3.5.210
22; InfoPath.1; .NET CLR 3.0.4506.2152; .NET CLR 3.5.30729)"
193.247.39.154 - - [08/Jul/2010:15:06:30 +0200] "GET /favicon.ico HTTP/1.0" 302 340 "-" "Mozilla/
4.0 (compatible; MSIE 7.0; Windows NT 5.1; .NET CLR 1.1.4322; .NET CLR 2.0.50727; .NET CLR 3.0.04
506.648; .NET CLR 3.5.21022; InfoPath.1; .NET CLR 3.0.4506.2152; .NET CLR 3.5.30729)"
193.247.39.154 - - [08/Jul/2010:15:06:33 +0200] "GET /Seiten/Aktuelles.html HTTP/1.0" 200 12690 "
http://www.asylabwehramt.at/" "Mozilla/4.0 (compatible; MSIE 7.0; Windows NT 5.1; .NET CLR 1.1.43
22; .NET CLR 2.0.50727; .NET CLR 3.0.04506.648; .NET CLR 3.5.21022; InfoPath.1; .NET CLR 3.0.4506
.2152; .NET CLR 3.5.30729)"
193.247.39.154 - - [08/Jul/2010:15:07:18 +0200] "GET /Seiten/Bilder.html HTTP/1.0" 200 10043 "htt
p://www.asylabwehramt.at/Seiten/Material.html" "Mozilla/4.0 (compatible; MSIE 7.0; Windows NT 5.1
; .NET CLR 1.1.4322; .NET CLR 2.0.50727; .NET CLR 3.0.04506.648; .NET CLR 3.5.21022; InfoPath.1;
.NET CLR 3.0.4506.2152; .NET CLR 3.5.30729)"
193.247.39.154 - - [08/Jul/2010:15:07:42 +0200] "GET /Seiten/Links.html HTTP/1.0" 200 18864 "http
://www.asylabwehramt.at/Seiten/Bilder.html" "Mozilla/4.0 (compatible; MSIE 7.0; Windows NT 5.1; .
NET CLR 1.1.4322; .NET CLR 2.0.50727; .NET CLR 3.0.04506.648; .NET CLR 3.5.21022; InfoPath.1; .NE
T CLR 3.0.4506.2152; .NET CLR 3.5.30729)"
193.247.39.154 - - [08/Jul/2010:15:07:43 +0200] "GET /Bilder/frontex.png HTTP/1.0" 200 22383 "htt
p://www.asylabwehramt.at/Seiten/Links.html" "Mozilla/4.0 (compatible; MSIE 7.0; Windows NT 5.1; .
NET CLR 1.1.4322; .NET CLR 2.0.50727; .NET CLR 3.0.04506.648; .NET CLR 3.5.21022; InfoPath.1; .NE
T CLR 3.0.4506.2152; .NET CLR 3.5.30729)"
88.116.224.102 - - [08/Jul/2010:15:25:15 +0200] "GET / HTTP/1.1" 200 11992 "http://www.zeit.de/2
```

`010/28/A-Asylabwehramt` " "Mozilla/5.0 (Windows; U; Windows NT 5.1; de; rv:1.9.2.6) Gecko/20100625 Firefox/3.6.6"

88.116.224.102 - - [08/Jul/2010:15:26:40 +0200] "GET /Seiten/Impressum.html HTTP/1.1" 200 11684 " http://www.asylabwehramt.at/" "Mozilla/5.0 (Windows; U; Windows NT 5.1; de; rv:1.9.2.6) Gecko/201 00625 Firefox/3.6.6"

88.116.224.102 - - [08/Jul/2010:15:27:15 +0200] "GET /index.html HTTP/1.1" 200 11992 "http://www. asylabwehramt.at/Seiten/Impressum.html" "Mozilla/5.0 (Windows; U; Windows NT 5.1; de; rv:1.9.2.6) Gecko/20100625 Firefox/3.6.6"

88.116.224.102 - - [08/Jul/2010:15:27:18 +0200] "GET /Seiten/Aktuelles.html HTTP/1.1" 200 12690 " http://www.asylabwehramt.at/index.html" "Mozilla/5.0 (Windows; U; Windows NT 5.1; de; rv:1.9.2.6) Gecko/20100625 Firefox/3.6.6"

88.116.224.102 - - [08/Jul/2010:15:28:03 +0200] "GET /Seiten/Rundzeichen.html HTTP/1.1" 200 8895 "http://www.asylabwehramt.at/Seiten/Aktuelles.html" "Mozilla/5.0 (Windows; U; Windows NT 5.1; de; rv:1.9.2.6) Gecko/20100625 Firefox/3.6.6"

88.116.224.102 - - [08/Jul/2010:15:28:15 +0200] "GET /Seiten/Bilder.html HTTP/1.1" 200 10043 "htt p://www.asylabwehramt.at/Seiten/Rundzeichen.html" "Mozilla/5.0 (Windows; U; Windows NT 5.1; de; r v:1.9.2.6) Gecko/20100625 Firefox/3.6.6"

88.116.224.102 - - [08/Jul/2010:15:29:14 +0200] "GET /Seiten/Links.html HTTP/1.1" 200 18864 "http ://www.asylabwehramt.at/Seiten/Bilder.html" "Mozilla/5.0 (Windows; U; Windows NT 5.1; de; rv:1.9. 2.6) Gecko/20100625 Firefox/3.6.6"

`62.154.194.53`[25] - - [09/Jul/2010:06:56:39 +0200] "GET / HTTP/1.1" 200 11992 "-" "Mozilla/4.0 (compa tible; MSIE 5.5; Windows NT 5.0)"

80.120.179.10 - - [09/Jul/2010:08:35:57 +0200] "GET /Seiten/Bilder_Ausstellung.html HTTP/1.1" 200 16437 "-" "Mozilla/4.0 (compatible; MSIE 6.0; Windows NT 5.1; SV1; .NET CLR 1.1.4322)"

80.120.179.10 - - [09/Jul/2010:08:35:58 +0200] "GET /Bilder/Ausstellung_weisses_haus_wien_esel_fo tos/eSeL_UBERMORGEN_asylabwehramt_dasweissehaus_463_thumb.jpg HTTP/1.1" 200 25117 "http://asylabw

---

25 WHOIS record on page 310

153

```
ehramt.at/Seiten/Bilder_Ausstellung.html" "Mozilla/4.0 (compatible; MSIE 6.0; Windows NT 5.1; SV1; .NET CLR 1.1.4322)"
80.120.179.10 - - [09/Jul/2010:08:35:59 +0200] "GET /Bilder/Ausstellung_weisses_haus_wien_esel_fotos/eSeL_UBERMORGEN_asylabwehramt_dasweissehaus_514_thumb.jpg HTTP/1.1" 200 58758 "http://asylabwehramt.at/Seiten/Bilder_Ausstellung.html" "Mozilla/4.0 (compatible; MSIE 6.0; Windows NT 5.1; SV1; .NET CLR 1.1.4322)"
80.120.179.10 - - [09/Jul/2010:08:36:08 +0200] "GET /index.html HTTP/1.1" 200 11992 "http://asylabwehramt.at/Seiten/Bilder_Ausstellung.html" "Mozilla/4.0 (compatible; MSIE 6.0; Windows NT 5.1; SV1; .NET CLR 1.1.4322)"
80.120.179.10 - - [09/Jul/2010:08:36:49 +0200] "GET /Seiten/Material.html HTTP/1.1" 200 16558 "http://asylabwehramt.at/index.html" "Mozilla/4.0 (compatible; MSIE 6.0; Windows NT 5.1; SV1; .NET CLR 1.1.4322)"
80.120.179.10 - - [09/Jul/2010:08:36:59 +0200] "GET /Bilder/flyer_nigeria_Internet.pdf HTTP/1.1" 200 702826 "http://asylabwehramt.at/Seiten/Material.html" "Mozilla/4.0 (compatible; MSIE 6.0; Windows NT 5.1; SV1; .NET CLR 1.1.4322)"
80.120.179.10 - - [09/Jul/2010:08:38:09 +0200] "GET /Bilder/Ausstellung_weisses_haus_wien_esel_fotos/eSeL_UBERMORGEN_asylabwehramt_dasweissehaus_456_thumb.jpg HTTP/1.1" 200 28685 "http://asylabwehramt.at/Seiten/Bilder_Ausstellung.html" "Mozilla/4.0 (compatible; MSIE 6.0; Windows NT 5.1; SV1; .NET CLR 1.1.4322)"
80.120.179.10 - - [09/Jul/2010:08:38:26 +0200] "GET /Seiten/Orgstrukt.html HTTP/1.1" 200 14119 "-" "Mozilla/4.0 (compatible; MSIE 6.0; Windows NT 5.1; SV1; .NET CLR 1.1.4322)"
80.120.179.10 - - [09/Jul/2010:08:58:36 +0200] "GET /Bilder/Ausstellung_weisses_haus_wien_esel_fotos/eSeL_UBERMORGEN_asylabwehramt_dasweissehaus_456_thumb.jpg HTTP/1.1" 200 28685 "http://asylabwehramt.at/Seiten/Bilder_Ausstellung.html" "Mozilla/4.0 (compatible; MSIE 6.0; Windows NT 5.1; SV1; .NET CLR 1.1.4322)"
80.120.179.10 - - [09/Jul/2010:08:58:44 +0200] "GET /Seiten/Aktuelles.html HTTP/1.1" 200 12690 "http://asylabwehramt.at/Seiten/Bilder_Ausstellung.html" "Mozilla/4.0 (compatible; MSIE 6.0; Windows s NT 5.1; SV1; .NET CLR 1.1.4322)"
```

```
80.120.179.10 - - [09/Jul/2010:08:59:00 +0200] "GET /Bilder/Ladung.png HTTP/1.1" 200 114658 "http://asylabwehramt.at/Seiten/Material.html" "Mozilla/4.0 (compatible; MSIE 6.0; Windows NT 5.1; SV1; .NET CLR 1.1.4322)"
80.120.179.10 - - [09/Jul/2010:09:00:33 +0200] "GET /Material/Asyl_Jahresstatistik_2009.pdf HTTP/1.1" 200 680643 "http://asylabwehramt.at/Seiten/Material.html" "Mozilla/4.0 (compatible; MSIE 6.0; Windows NT 5.1; SV1; .NET CLR 1.1.4322)"
80.120.179.10 - - [09/Jul/2010:09:01:04 +0200] "GET /Material/Hotline_Deutsch.pdf HTTP/1.1" 200 489465 "http://asylabwehramt.at/Seiten/Material.html" "Mozilla/4.0 (compatible; MSIE 6.0; Windows NT 5.1; SV1; .NET CLR 1.1.4322)"
80.120.179.10 - - [09/Jul/2010:10:08:25 +0200] "GET /Seiten/Bilder.html HTTP/1.1" 200 10043 "http://asylabwehramt.at/Seiten/Bilder.html" "Mozilla/4.0 (compatible; MSIE 6.0; Windows NT 5.1; SV1; .NET CLR 1.1.4322)"
80.120.179.10 - - [09/Jul/2010:10:08:26 +0200] "GET /Bilder/SCREEN_AAbA_Edutainment_Video.jpg HTTP/1.1" 200 29259 "http://asylabwehramt.at/Seiten/Bilder.html" "Mozilla/4.0 (compatible; MSIE 6.0; Windows NT 5.1; SV1; .NET CLR 1.1.4322)"
80.120.179.10 - - [09/Jul/2010:10:08:52 +0200] "GET /Seiten/Press.html HTTP/1.1" 200 12186 "http://asylabwehramt.at/Seiten/Bilder.html" "Mozilla/4.0 (compatible; MSIE 6.0; Windows NT 5.1; SV1; .NET CLR 1.1.4322)"
193.171.152.33 - - [09/Jul/2010:11:02:14 +0200] "GET / HTTP/1.1" 304 - "-" "Mozilla/4.0 (compatible; MSIE 8.0; Windows NT 5.1; Trident/4.0; InfoPath.1)"
193.171.152.33 - - [09/Jul/2010:11:02:51 +0200] "GET /Seiten/Aktuelles.html HTTP/1.1" 200 12690 "http://www.asylabwehramt.at/" "Mozilla/4.0 (compatible; MSIE 8.0; Windows NT 5.1; Trident/4.0; InfoPath.1)"
193.171.152.33 - - [09/Jul/2010:11:03:11 +0200] "GET /Seiten/Material.html HTTP/1.1" 200 16558 "http://www.asylabwehramt.at/Seiten/Aktuelles.html" "Mozilla/4.0 (compatible; MSIE 8.0; Windows NT 5.1; Trident/4.0; InfoPath.1)"
193.171.152.33 - - [09/Jul/2010:11:03:20 +0200] "GET /Seiten/Rundzeichen.html HTTP/1.1" 200 8895 "http://www.asylabwehramt.at/Seiten/Material.html" "Mozilla/4.0 (compatible; MSIE 8.0; Windows NT
```

5.1; Trident/4.0; InfoPath.1)"
193.171.152.33 - - [09/Jul/2010:11:03:27 +0200] "GET /Seiten/Bilder.html HTTP/1.1" 200 10043 "htt
p://www.asylabwehramt.at/Seiten/Rundzeichen.html" "Mozilla/4.0 (compatible; MSIE 8.0; Windows NT
5.1; Trident/4.0; InfoPath.1)"
193.171.152.33 - - [09/Jul/2010:11:03:51 +0200] "GET /Seiten/Links.html HTTP/1.1" 200 18864 "http
://www.asylabwehramt.at/Seiten/Bilder.html" "Mozilla/4.0 (compatible; MSIE 8.0; Windows NT 5.1; T
rident/4.0; InfoPath.1)"
193.171.152.33 - - [09/Jul/2010:11:04:09 +0200] "GET /Seiten/Press.html HTTP/1.1" 200 12186 "http
://www.asylabwehramt.at/Seiten/Links.html" "Mozilla/4.0 (compatible; MSIE 8.0; Windows NT 5.1; Tr
ident/4.0; InfoPath.1)"
78.41.144.41 - - [09/Jul/2010:12:51:25 +0200] "GET / HTTP/1.0" 200 11992 "-" "Mozilla/4.0 (compat
ible; MSIE 7.0; Windows NT 5.1; .NET CLR 2.0.50727; .NET CLR 1.1.4322; .NET CLR 3.0.04506.30; .NE
T CLR 3.0.04506.648; .NET CLR 3.0.4506.2152; .NET CLR 3.5.30729)"
78.41.144.41 - - [09/Jul/2010:12:51:26 +0200] "GET /asyl.css HTTP/1.0" 304 - "http://www.asylabwe
hramt.at/" "Mozilla/4.0 (compatible; MSIE 7.0; Windows NT 5.1; .NET CLR 2.0.50727; .NET CLR 1.1.4
322; .NET CLR 3.0.04506.30; .NET CLR 3.0.04506.648; .NET CLR 3.0.4506.2152; .NET CLR 3.5.30729)"
88.116.224.102 - - [09/Jul/2010:13:48:07 +0200] "GET / HTTP/1.1" 200 11992 "http://www.google.at/
search?hl=de&source=hp&q=**asylabwehramt**&meta=&aq=f&aqi=&aql=&oq=&gs_rfai=" "Mozilla/4.0 (compatibl
e; MSIE 6.0; Windows NT 5.1; SV1; InfoPath.1)"
88.116.224.102 - - [09/Jul/2010:13:48:08 +0200] "GET /asyl.css HTTP/1.1" 200 860 "http://www.asyl
abwehramt.at/" "Mozilla/4.0 (compatible; MSIE 6.0; Windows NT 5.1; SV1; InfoPath.1)"
88.116.224.102 - - [09/Jul/2010:13:49:04 +0200] "GET /Seiten/Rundzeichen.html HTTP/1.1" 200 8895
"http://www.asylabwehramt.at/" "Mozilla/4.0 (compatible; MSIE 6.0; Windows NT 5.1; SV1; InfoPath.
1)"
88.116.224.102 - - [09/Jul/2010:13:49:11 +0200] "GET /Seiten/Links.html HTTP/1.1" 200 18864 "http
://www.asylabwehramt.at/Seiten/Rundzeichen.html" "Mozilla/4.0 (compatible; MSIE 6.0; Windows NT 5
.1; SV1; InfoPath.1)"
88.116.224.102 - - [09/Jul/2010:13:49:12 +0200] "GET /Bilder/IBM.png HTTP/1.1" 200 8413 "http://w

```
ww.asylabwehramt.at/Seiten/Links.html" "Mozilla/4.0 (compatible; MSIE 6.0; Windows NT 5.1; SV1; I
nfoPath.1)"
88.116.224.102 - - [09/Jul/2010:13:49:22 +0200] "GET /Seiten/Seal.html HTTP/1.1" 200 8933 "http:/
/www.asylabwehramt.at/Seiten/Links.html" "Mozilla/4.0 (compatible; MSIE 6.0; Windows NT 5.1; SV1;
InfoPath.1)"
88.116.224.102 - - [09/Jul/2010:13:49:23 +0200] "GET /asyl.css HTTP/1.1" 304 - "http://www.asylab
wehramt.at/Seiten/Seal.html" "Mozilla/4.0 (compatible; MSIE 6.0; Windows NT 5.1; SV1; InfoPath.1)
"
88.116.224.102 - - [09/Jul/2010:13:49:25 +0200] "GET /Seiten/Forms_and_Infos.html HTTP/1.1" 200 1
5692 "http://www.asylabwehramt.at/Seiten/Seal.html" "Mozilla/4.0 (compatible; MSIE 6.0; Windows N
T 5.1; SV1; InfoPath.1)"
88.116.224.102 - - [09/Jul/2010:13:49:33 +0200] "GET /index.html HTTP/1.1" 200 11992 "http://www.
asylabwehramt.at/Seiten/Forms_and_Infos.html" "Mozilla/4.0 (compatible; MSIE 6.0; Windows NT 5.1;
SV1; InfoPath.1)"
88.116.224.102 - - [09/Jul/2010:13:49:36 +0200] "GET /Seiten/Material.html HTTP/1.1" 200 16558 "h
ttp://www.asylabwehramt.at/index.html" "Mozilla/4.0 (compatible; MSIE 6.0; Windows NT 5.1; SV1; I
nfoPath.1)"
88.116.224.102 - - [09/Jul/2010:13:49:57 +0200] "GET /Material/Hotline_Deutsch.pdf HTTP/1.1" 200
489465 "http://www.asylabwehramt.at/Seiten/Material.html" "Mozilla/4.0 (compatible; MSIE 6.0; Win
dows NT 5.1; SV1; InfoPath.1)"
88.116.224.102 - - [09/Jul/2010:13:49:58 +0200] "GET /Material/Hotline_Deutsch.pdf HTTP/1.1" 206
485425 "-" "Mozilla/4.0 (compatible; MSIE 6.0; Windows NT 5.1; SV1; InfoPath.1)"
88.116.224.102 - - [09/Jul/2010:13:50:06 +0200] "GET /Material/Hotline_Deutsch.pdf HTTP/1.1" 206
440478 "-" "Mozilla/4.0 (compatible; MSIE 6.0; Windows NT 5.1; SV1; InfoPath.1)"
88.116.224.102 - - [09/Jul/2010:13:50:43 +0200] "GET /Seiten/Bilder.html HTTP/1.1" 200 10043 "htt
p://www.asylabwehramt.at/Seiten/Material.html" "Mozilla/4.0 (compatible; MSIE 6.0; Windows NT 5.1
; SV1; InfoPath.1)"
88.116.224.102 - - [09/Jul/2010:13:50:44 +0200] "GET /Bilder/BAA_photos/IMG_0198.JPG HTTP/1.1" 20
```

```
0 109214 "http://www.asylabwehramt.at/Seiten/Bilder.html" "Mozilla/4.0 (compatible; MSIE 6.0; Win
dows NT 5.1; SV1; InfoPath.1)"
88.116.224.102 - - [09/Jul/2010:13:51:16 +0200] "GET /Seiten/Bilder_Ausstellung.html HTTP/1.1" 20
0 16437 "http://www.asylabwehramt.at/Seiten/Bilder.html" "Mozilla/4.0 (compatible; MSIE 6.0; Wind
ows NT 5.1; SV1; InfoPath.1)"
88.116.224.102 - - [09/Jul/2010:13:51:17 +0200] "GET /Bilder/Ausstellung_weisses_haus_wien_esel_f
otos/eSeL_UBERMORGEN_asylabwehramt_dasweissehaus_456_thumb.jpg HTTP/1.1" 200 28685 "http://www.as
ylabwehramt.at/Seiten/Bilder_Ausstellung.html" "Mozilla/4.0 (compatible; MSIE 6.0; Windows NT 5.1
; SV1; InfoPath.1)"
88.116.224.102 - - [09/Jul/2010:13:51:18 +0200] "GET /Bilder/Ausstellung_weisses_haus_wien_esel_f
otos/eSeL_UBERMORGEN_asylabwehramt_dasweissehaus_472_thumb.jpg HTTP/1.1" 200 62552 "http://www.as
ylabwehramt.at/Seiten/Bilder_Ausstellung.html" "Mozilla/4.0 (compatible; MSIE 6.0; Windows NT 5.1
; SV1; InfoPath.1)"
88.116.224.102 - - [09/Jul/2010:13:51:19 +0200] "GET /Bilder/Ausstellung_weisses_haus_wien_esel_f
otos/eSeL_UBERMORGEN_asylabwehramt_dasweissehaus_502_thumb.jpg HTTP/1.1" 200 46872 "http://www.as
ylabwehramt.at/Seiten/Bilder_Ausstellung.html" "Mozilla/4.0 (compatible; MSIE 6.0; Windows NT 5.1
; SV1; InfoPath.1)"
88.116.224.102 - - [09/Jul/2010:13:51:20 +0200] "GET /Bilder/Ausstellung_weisses_haus_wien_esel_f
otos/eSeL_UBERMORGEN_asylabwehramt_dasweissehaus_512_thumb.jpg HTTP/1.1" 200 40860 "http://www.as
ylabwehramt.at/Seiten/Bilder_Ausstellung.html" "Mozilla/4.0 (compatible; MSIE 6.0; Windows NT 5.1
; SV1; InfoPath.1)"
88.116.224.102 - - [09/Jul/2010:13:51:22 +0200] "GET /Bilder/Ausstellung_weisses_haus_wien_esel_f
otos/eSeL_UBERMORGEN_asylabwehramt_dasweissehaus_520_thumb.jpg HTTP/1.1" 200 77245 "http://www.as
ylabwehramt.at/Seiten/Bilder_Ausstellung.html" "Mozilla/4.0 (compatible; MSIE 6.0; Windows NT 5.1
; SV1; InfoPath.1)"
88.116.224.102 - - [09/Jul/2010:13:51:23 +0200] "GET /Seiten/Aktuelles.html HTTP/1.1" 200 12690 "
http://www.asylabwehramt.at/Seiten/Bilder_Ausstellung.html" "Mozilla/4.0 (compatible; MSIE 6.0; W
indows NT 5.1; SV1; InfoPath.1)"
```

```
88.116.224.102 - - [09/Jul/2010:13:51:28 +0200] "GET /Seiten/Links.html HTTP/1.1" 304 - "http://w
ww.asylabwehramt.at/Seiten/Aktuelles.html" "Mozilla/4.0 (compatible; MSIE 6.0; Windows NT 5.1; SV
1; InfoPath.1)"
88.116.224.102 - - [09/Jul/2010:13:51:30 +0200] "GET /Seiten/Press.html HTTP/1.1" 200 12186 "http
://www.asylabwehramt.at/Seiten/Links.html" "Mozilla/4.0 (compatible; MSIE 6.0; Windows NT 5.1; SV
1; InfoPath.1)"
193.134.242.12 - - [09/Jul/2010:14:44:54 +0200] "GET / HTTP/1.0" 304 - "http://www.zeit.de/2010/
28/A-Asylabwehramt" "Mozilla/5.0 (Windows; U; Windows NT 5.1; en-GB; rv:1.9.2.6) Gecko/20100625
Firefox/3.6.6"
193.134.242.12 - - [09/Jul/2010:14:44:55 +0200] "GET /Bilder/Header_AAbA_anim.gif HTTP/1.0" 304 -
"http://www.asylabwehramt.at/" "Mozilla/5.0 (Windows; U; Windows NT 5.1; en-GB; rv:1.9.2.6) Geck
o/20100625 Firefox/3.6.6"
193.134.242.12 - - [09/Jul/2010:14:44:58 +0200] "GET /favicon.ico HTTP/1.0" 302 340 "-" "Mozilla/
5.0 (Windows; U; Windows NT 5.1; en-GB; rv:1.9.2.6) Gecko/20100625 Firefox/3.6.6"
193.134.242.12 - - [09/Jul/2010:14:47:29 +0200] "GET /Seiten/Aktuelles.html HTTP/1.0" 304 - "http
://www.asylabwehramt.at/" "Mozilla/5.0 (Windows; U; Windows NT 5.1; en-GB; rv:1.9.2.6) Gecko/2010
0625 Firefox/3.6.6"
193.134.242.12 - - [09/Jul/2010:14:47:59 +0200] "GET /Seiten/Bilder_Ausstellung.html HTTP/1.0" 20
0 16437 "http://www.asylabwehramt.at/Seiten/Aktuelles.html" "Mozilla/5.0 (Windows; U; Windows NT
5.1; en-GB; rv:1.9.2.6) Gecko/20100625 Firefox/3.6.6"
193.134.242.12 - - [09/Jul/2010:14:48:01 +0200] "GET /Bilder/Ausstellung_weisses_haus_wien_esel_f
otos/eSeL_UBERMORGEN_asylabwehramt_dasweissehaus_476_thumb.jpg HTTP/1.0" 200 46505 "http://www.as
ylabwehramt.at/Seiten/Bilder_Ausstellung.html" "Mozilla/5.0 (Windows; U; Windows NT 5.1; en-GB; r
v:1.9.2.6) Gecko/20100625 Firefox/3.6.6"
193.134.242.12 - - [09/Jul/2010:14:48:02 +0200] "GET /Bilder/Ausstellung_weisses_haus_wien_esel_f
otos/eSeL_UBERMORGEN_asylabwehramt_dasweissehaus_481_thumb.jpg HTTP/1.0" 200 25101 "http://www.as
ylabwehramt.at/Seiten/Bilder_Ausstellung.html" "Mozilla/5.0 (Windows; U; Windows NT 5.1; en-GB; r
```

```
193.134.242.12 - - [09/Jul/2010:14:48:04 +0200] "GET /Bilder/Ausstellung_weisses_haus_wien_esel_fotos/eSeL_UBERMORGEN_asylabwehramt_dasweissehaus_507_thumb.jpg HTTP/1.0" 200 40356 "http://www.asylabwehramt.at/Seiten/Bilder_Ausstellung.html" "Mozilla/5.0 (Windows; U; Windows NT 5.1; en-GB; rv:1.9.2.6) Gecko/20100625 Firefox/3.6.6"
193.134.242.12 - - [09/Jul/2010:14:48:05 +0200] "GET /Bilder/Ausstellung_weisses_haus_wien_esel_fotos/eSeL_UBERMORGEN_asylabwehramt_dasweissehaus_516_thumb.jpg HTTP/1.0" 200 43027 "http://www.asylabwehramt.at/Seiten/Bilder_Ausstellung.html" "Mozilla/5.0 (Windows; U; Windows NT 5.1; en-GB; rv:1.9.2.6) Gecko/20100625 Firefox/3.6.6"
193.134.242.12 - - [09/Jul/2010:14:48:06 +0200] "GET /Bilder/Ausstellung_weisses_haus_wien_esel_fotos/eSeL_UBERMORGEN_asylabwehramt_dasweissehaus_517_thumb.jpg HTTP/1.0" 200 75254 "http://www.asylabwehramt.at/Seiten/Bilder_Ausstellung.html" "Mozilla/5.0 (Windows; U; Windows NT 5.1; en-GB; rv:1.9.2.6) Gecko/20100625 Firefox/3.6.6"
193.134.242.12 - - [09/Jul/2010:14:48:07 +0200] "GET /Bilder/Ausstellung_weisses_haus_wien_esel_fotos/eSeL_UBERMORGEN_asylabwehramt_dasweissehaus_520_thumb.jpg HTTP/1.0" 200 77245 "http://www.asylabwehramt.at/Seiten/Bilder_Ausstellung.html" "Mozilla/5.0 (Windows; U; Windows NT 5.1; en-GB; rv:1.9.2.6) Gecko/20100625 Firefox/3.6.6"
193.134.242.12 - - [09/Jul/2010:14:48:27 +0200] "GET /Seiten/Press.html HTTP/1.0" 200 12186 "http://www.asylabwehramt.at/Seiten/Aktuelles.html" "Mozilla/5.0 (Windows; U; Windows NT 5.1; en-GB; rv:1.9.2.6) Gecko/20100625 Firefox/3.6.6"
193.134.242.12 - - [09/Jul/2010:14:49:59 +0200] "GET /Bilder/Ausstellung_weisses_haus_wien_esel_fotos/eSeL_UBERMORGEN_asylabwehramt_dasweissehaus_481.jpg HTTP/1.0" 200 273732 "http://www.asylabwehramt.at/Seiten/Bilder_Ausstellung.html" "Mozilla/5.0 (Windows; U; Windows NT 5.1; en-GB; rv:1.9.2.6) Gecko/20100625 Firefox/3.6.6"
193.134.242.12 - - [09/Jul/2010:14:50:53 +0200] "GET /Seiten/Impressum.html HTTP/1.0" 200 11684 "http://www.asylabwehramt.at/Seiten/Bilder_Ausstellung.html" "Mozilla/5.0 (Windows; U; Windows NT 5.1; en-GB; rv:1.9.2.6) Gecko/20100625 Firefox/3.6.6"
193.134.242.12 - - [09/Jul/2010:14:52:12 +0200] "GET /Seiten/Latestnews.html HTTP/1.0" 200 12721
```

```
"http://www.asylabwehramt.at/Seiten/Impressum.html" "Mozilla/5.0 (Windows; U; Windows NT 5.1; en-GB; rv:1.9.2.6) Gecko/20100625 Firefox/3.6.6"
193.134.242.12 - - [09/Jul/2010:14:52:15 +0200] "GET /Seiten/Seal.html HTTP/1.0" 200 8933 "http://www.asylabwehramt.at/Seiten/Latestnews.html" "Mozilla/5.0 (Windows; U; Windows NT 5.1; en-GB; rv:1.9.2.6) Gecko/20100625 Firefox/3.6.6"
193.134.242.12 - - [09/Jul/2010:14:52:24 +0200] "GET /Seiten/Images.html HTTP/1.0" 200 10215 "http://www.asylabwehramt.at/Seiten/Seal.html" "Mozilla/5.0 (Windows; U; Windows NT 5.1; en-GB; rv:1.9.2.6) Gecko/20100625 Firefox/3.6.6"
193.134.242.12 - - [09/Jul/2010:14:52:29 +0200] "GET /Seiten/Rundzeichen.html HTTP/1.0" 304 - "http://www.asylabwehramt.at/Seiten/Images.html" "Mozilla/5.0 (Windows; U; Windows NT 5.1; en-GB; rv:1.9.2.6) Gecko/20100625 Firefox/3.6.6"
193.134.242.12 - - [09/Jul/2010:15:00:30 +0200] "GET /Seiten/Bilder_buero.html HTTP/1.0" 200 11084 "http://www.asylabwehramt.at/Seiten/Images.html" "Mozilla/5.0 (Windows; U; Windows NT 5.1; en-GB; rv:1.9.2.6) Gecko/20100625 Firefox/3.6.6"
193.134.242.12 - - [09/Jul/2010:15:00:34 +0200] "GET /Bilder/BAA_photos/IMG_0185.JPG HTTP/1.0" 200 98720 "http://www.asylabwehramt.at/Seiten/Bilder_buero.html" "Mozilla/5.0 (Windows; U; Windows NT 5.1; en-GB; rv:1.9.2.6) Gecko/20100625 Firefox/3.6.6"
193.134.242.12 - - [09/Jul/2010:15:00:38 +0200] "GET /Bilder/BAA_photos/IMG_0186.JPG HTTP/1.0" 200 103810 "http://www.asylabwehramt.at/Seiten/Bilder_buero.html" "Mozilla/5.0 (Windows; U; Windows NT 5.1; en-GB; rv:1.9.2.6) Gecko/20100625 Firefox/3.6.6"
193.134.242.12 - - [09/Jul/2010:15:00:39 +0200] "GET /Bilder/BAA_photos/IMG_0187.JPG HTTP/1.0" 200 191902 "http://www.asylabwehramt.at/Seiten/Bilder_buero.html" "Mozilla/5.0 (Windows; U; Windows NT 5.1; en-GB; rv:1.9.2.6) Gecko/20100625 Firefox/3.6.6"
193.134.242.12 - - [09/Jul/2010:15:00:40 +0200] "GET /Bilder/BAA_photos/IMG_0188.JPG HTTP/1.0" 200 179395 "http://www.asylabwehramt.at/Seiten/Bilder_buero.html" "Mozilla/5.0 (Windows; U; Windows NT 5.1; en-GB; rv:1.9.2.6) Gecko/20100625 Firefox/3.6.6"
193.134.242.12 - - [09/Jul/2010:15:00:41 +0200] "GET /Bilder/BAA_photos/IMG_0189.JPG HTTP/1.0" 200 163470 "http://www.asylabwehramt.at/Seiten/Bilder_buero.html" "Mozilla/5.0 (Windows; U; Windows NT 5.1; en-GB; rv:1.9.2.6) Gecko/20100625 Firefox/3.6.6"
```

```
193.134.242.12 - - [09/Jul/2010:15:00:44 +0200] "GET /Bilder/BAA_photos/IMG_0191.JPG HTTP/1.0" 200 124240 "http://www.asylabwehramt.at/Seiten/Bilder_buero.html" "Mozilla/5.0 (Windows; U; Windows NT 5.1; en-GB; rv:1.9.2.6) Gecko/20100625 Firefox/3.6.6"
193.134.242.12 - - [09/Jul/2010:15:00:45 +0200] "GET /Bilder/BAA_photos/IMG_0193.JPG HTTP/1.0" 200 128059 "http://www.asylabwehramt.at/Seiten/Bilder_buero.html" "Mozilla/5.0 (Windows; U; Windows NT 5.1; en-GB; rv:1.9.2.6) Gecko/20100625 Firefox/3.6.6"
193.134.242.12 - - [09/Jul/2010:15:00:49 +0200] "GET /Bilder/BAA_photos/IMG_0194.JPG HTTP/1.0" 200 181536 "http://www.asylabwehramt.at/Seiten/Bilder_buero.html" "Mozilla/5.0 (Windows; U; Windows NT 5.1; en-GB; rv:1.9.2.6) Gecko/20100625 Firefox/3.6.6"
193.134.242.12 - - [09/Jul/2010:15:00:50 +0200] "GET /Bilder/BAA_photos/IMG_0195.JPG HTTP/1.0" 200 122316 "http://www.asylabwehramt.at/Seiten/Bilder_buero.html" "Mozilla/5.0 (Windows; U; Windows NT 5.1; en-GB; rv:1.9.2.6) Gecko/20100625 Firefox/3.6.6"
193.134.242.12 - - [09/Jul/2010:15:00:52 +0200] "GET /Bilder/BAA_photos/IMG_0196.JPG HTTP/1.0" 200 129278 "http://www.asylabwehramt.at/Seiten/Bilder_buero.html" "Mozilla/5.0 (Windows; U; Windows NT 5.1; en-GB; rv:1.9.2.6) Gecko/20100625 Firefox/3.6.6"
193.134.242.12 - - [09/Jul/2010:15:00:54 +0200] "GET /Bilder/BAA_photos/IMG_0200.JPG HTTP/1.0" 200 82980 "http://www.asylabwehramt.at/Seiten/Bilder_buero.html" "Mozilla/5.0 (Windows; U; Windows NT 5.1; en-GB; rv:1.9.2.6) Gecko/20100625 Firefox/3.6.6"
193.134.242.12 - - [09/Jul/2010:15:09:41 +0200] "GET /favicon.ico HTTP/1.0" 302 340 "-" "Mozilla/5.0 (Windows; U; Windows NT 5.1; en-GB; rv:1.9.2.6) Gecko/20100625 Firefox/3.6.6 GTB7.0"
193.134.242.12 - - [09/Jul/2010:15:27:24 +0200] "GET /favicon.ico HTTP/1.0" 302 340 "-" "Mozilla/5.0 (Windows; U; Windows NT 5.1; en-GB; rv:1.9.2.6) Gecko/20100625 Firefox/3.6.6 GTB7.1"
88.116.224.102 - - [09/Jul/2010:15:36:52 +0200] "GET / HTTP/1.1" 200 11992 "http://eu.ixquick.com/do/metasearch.pl" "Mozilla/5.0 (X11; U; Linux i686; de; rv:1.9.1.9) Gecko/20100401 Ubuntu/9.10 (karmic) Firefox/3.5.9"
88.116.224.102 - - [09/Jul/2010:15:36:55 +0200] "GET /favicon.ico HTTP/1.1" 302 340 "-" "Mozilla/
```

5.0 (X11; U; Linux i686; de; rv:1.9.1.9) Gecko/20100401 Ubuntu/9.10 (karmic) Firefox/3.5.9"

88.116.224.102 - - [09/Jul/2010:15:36:57 +0200] "GET /Seiten/Bilder.html HTTP/1.1" 200 10043 "http://www.asylabwehramt.at/" "Mozilla/5.0 (X11; U; Linux i686; de; rv:1.9.1.9) Gecko/20100401 Ubuntu/9.10 (karmic) Firefox/3.5.9"

194.232.79.193 - - [09/Jul/2010:15:37:05 +0200] "GET / HTTP/1.1" 200 11992 "-" "Mozilla/4.0 (compatible; MSIE 8.0; Windows NT 5.1; Trident/4.0; .NET CLR 2.0.50727; .NET CLR 3.0.4506.2152; .NET CLR 3.5.30729)"

194.232.79.193 - - [09/Jul/2010:15:37:06 +0200] "GET /favicon.ico HTTP/1.1" 302 340 "-" "Mozilla/4.0 (compatible; MSIE 8.0; Windows NT 5.1; Trident/4.0; .NET CLR 2.0.50727; .NET CLR 3.0.4506.2152; .NET CLR 3.5.30729)"

194.232.79.193 - - [09/Jul/2010:15:37:46 +0200] "GET /Seiten/Orgstrukt.html HTTP/1.1" 200 14119 "http://www.asylabwehramt.at/" "Mozilla/4.0 (compatible; MSIE 8.0; Windows NT 5.1; Trident/4.0; .NET CLR 1.1.4322; .NET CLR 2.0.50727; .NET CLR 3.0.4506.2152; .NET CLR 3.5.30729)"

88.116.224.102 - - [09/Jul/2010:15:37:47 +0200] "GET /Seiten/Ausseneinsaetze.html HTTP/1.1" 200 9381 "http://www.asylabwehramt.at/Seiten/Bilder.html" "Mozilla/5.0 (X11; U; Linux i686; de; rv:1.9.1.9) Gecko/20100401 Ubuntu/9.10 (karmic) Firefox/3.5.9"

194.232.79.193 - - [09/Jul/2010:15:37:58 +0200] "GET /index.html HTTP/1.1" 200 11992 "http://www.asylabwehramt.at/Seiten/Orgstrukt.html" "Mozilla/4.0 (compatible; MSIE 8.0; Windows NT 5.1; .NET CLR 3.0.4506.2152; .NET CLR 3.5.30729)"

194.232.79.193 - - [09/Jul/2010:15:38:00 +0200] "GET /Seiten/Aktuelles.html HTTP/1.1" 200 12690 "http://www.asylabwehramt.at/index.html" "Mozilla/4.0 (compatible; MSIE 8.0; Windows NT 5.1; Trident/4.0; .NET CLR 2.0.50727; .NET CLR 3.0.4506.2152; .NET CLR 3.5.30729)"

88.116.224.102 - - [09/Jul/2010:15:38:15 +0200] "GET /Seiten/Aktuelles.html HTTP/1.1" 200 12690 "http://www.asylabwehramt.at/Seiten/Ausseneinsaetze.html" "Mozilla/5.0 (X11; U; Linux i686; de; rv:1.9.1.9) Gecko/20100401 Ubuntu/9.10 (karmic) Firefox/3.5.9"

88.116.224.102 - - [09/Jul/2010:15:38:46 +0200] "GET /Seiten/Material.html HTTP/1.1" 200 16558 "http://www.asylabwehramt.at/Seiten/Aktuelles.html" "Mozilla/5.0 (X11; U; Linux i686; de; rv:1.9.1.9) Gecko/20100401 Ubuntu/9.10 (karmic) Firefox/3.5.9"

```
88.116.224.102 - - [09/Jul/2010:15:39:04 +0200] "GET /Seiten/Rundzeichen.html HTTP/1.1" 200 8895
"http://www.asylabwehramt.at/Seiten/Material.html" "Mozilla/5.0 (X11; U; Linux i686; de; rv:1.9.1
.9) Gecko/20100401 Ubuntu/9.10 (karmic) Firefox/3.5.9"
88.116.224.102 - - [09/Jul/2010:15:39:12 +0200] "GET /Seiten/Links.html HTTP/1.1" 200 18864 "http
://www.asylabwehramt.at/Seiten/Rundzeichen.html" "Mozilla/5.0 (X11; U; Linux i686; de; rv:1.9.1.9
) Gecko/20100401 Ubuntu/9.10 (karmic) Firefox/3.5.9"
88.116.224.102 - - [09/Jul/2010:15:39:45 +0200] "GET /Seiten/Press.html HTTP/1.1" 200 12186 "http
://www.asylabwehramt.at/Seiten/Links.html" "Mozilla/5.0 (X11; U; Linux i686; de; rv:1.9.1.9) Geck
o/20100401 Ubuntu/9.10 (karmic) Firefox/3.5.9"
88.116.224.102 - - [09/Jul/2010:15:42:10 +0200] "GET /Seiten/Orgstruct.html HTTP/1.1" 200 14398 "
http://www.asylabwehramt.at/Seiten/Press.html" "Mozilla/5.0 (X11; U; Linux i686; de; rv:1.9.1.9)
Gecko/20100401 Ubuntu/9.10 (karmic) Firefox/3.5.9"
195.190.15.10 - - [09/Jul/2010:22:16:33 +0200] "GET / HTTP/1.0" 200 11992 "http://www.facebook.c
om/l.php?u=http%3A%2F%2Fwww.asylabwehramt.at%2F&h=29624v3-W72rsQUshaGzz1VRaVw" "Mozilla/5.0 (Win
dows; U; Windows NT 5.1; de; rv:1.8.1.11) Gecko/20071127 Firefox/2.0.0.11 GTB7.0 (.NET CLR 3.5.30
729)"
62.154.194.53 - - [10/Jul/2010:05:43:33 +0200] "GET / HTTP/1.1" 200 11992 "-" "Mozilla/4.0 (compa
tible; MSIE 5.5; Windows NT 5.0)"
213.208.144.130 - - [11/Jul/2010:05:40:46 +0200] "GET / HTTP/1.0" 200 11992 "http://by149w.bay14
9.mail.live.com/mail/InboxLight.aspx?FolderID=00000000-0000-0000-0000-000000000001&InboxSortAscen
ding=False&InboxSortBy=Date&n=108055512" "Mozilla/4.0 (compatible; MSIE 7.0; Windows NT 5.2; .NE
T CLR 1.1.4322; InfoPath.1; .NET CLR 2.0.50727; .NET CLR 3.0.04506.648; .NET CLR 3.5.21022)"
62.154.194.53 - - [11/Jul/2010:05:43:27 +0200] "GET / HTTP/1.1" 200 11992 "-" "Mozilla/4.0 (compa
tible; MSIE 5.5; Windows NT 5.0)"
78.41.144.41 - - [11/Jul/2010:18:21:04 +0200] "GET / HTTP/1.0" 304 - "-" "Mozilla/4.0 (compatible
; MSIE 7.0; Windows NT 5.2; .NET CLR 1.1.4322; .NET CLR 2.0.50727; .NET CLR 3.0.4506.2152; .NET C
LR 3.5.30729)"
```

78.41.144.41 - - [11/Jul/2010:18:21:05 +0200] "GET /favicon.ico HTTP/1.0" 302 340 "-" "Mozilla/4.0 (compatible; MSIE 7.0; Windows NT 5.2; .NET CLR 1.1.4322; .NET CLR 2.0.50727; .NET CLR 3.0.4506.2152; .NET CLR 3.5.30729)"

62.154.194.53 - - [12/Jul/2010:07:33:57 +0200] "GET / HTTP/1.1" 200 11992 "-" "Mozilla/4.0 (compatible; MSIE 5.5; Windows NT 5.0)"

195.245.92.74 [26] - - [12/Jul/2010:08:44:22 +0200] "GET /favicon.ico HTTP/1.0" 302 340 "-" "Mozilla/4.0 (compatible; MSIE 7.0; Windows NT 5.1; .NET CLR 1.1.4322; .NET CLR 2.0.50727; .NET CLR 3.0.4506.2152; .NET CLR 3.5.30729)"

195.245.92.74 - - [12/Jul/2010:08:44:41 +0200] "GET /Seiten/Links.html HTTP/1.0" 200 18864 "http://www.asylabwehramt.at/index.html" "Mozilla/4.0 (compatible; MSIE 7.0; Windows NT 5.1; .NET CLR 1.1.4322; .NET CLR 2.0.50727; .NET CLR 3.0.4506.2152; .NET CLR 3.5.30729)"

195.245.92.74 - - [12/Jul/2010:08:44:42 +0200] "GET /Bilder/omvlogo_3c.jpg HTTP/1.0" 200 22855 "http://www.asylabwehramt.at/Seiten/Links.html" "Mozilla/4.0 (compatible; MSIE 7.0; Windows NT 5.1; .NET CLR 1.1.4322; .NET CLR 2.0.50727; .NET CLR 3.0.4506.2152; .NET CLR 3.5.30729)"

195.245.92.74 - - [12/Jul/2010:08:45:01 +0200] "GET /Seiten/Impressum.html HTTP/1.0" 200 11684 "http://www.asylabwehramt.at/Seiten/Links.html" "Mozilla/4.0 (compatible; MSIE 7.0; Windows NT 5.1; .NET CLR 1.1.4322; .NET CLR 2.0.50727; .NET CLR 3.0.4506.2152; .NET CLR 3.5.30729)"

195.245.92.74 - - [12/Jul/2010:08:45:22 +0200] "GET /Seiten/Orgstrukt.html HTTP/1.0" 200 14119 "http://www.asylabwehramt.at/Seiten/Impressum.html" "Mozilla/4.0 (compatible; MSIE 7.0; Windows NT 5.1; .NET CLR 1.1.4322; .NET CLR 2.0.50727; .NET CLR 3.0.4506.2152; .NET CLR 3.5.30729)"

195.245.92.74 - - [12/Jul/2010:08:45:27 +0200] "GET /Seiten/Aktuelles.html HTTP/1.0" 200 12690 "http://www.asylabwehramt.at/index.html" "Mozilla/4.0 (compatible; MSIE 7.0; Windows NT 5.1; .NET CLR 1.1.4322; .NET CLR 2.0.50727; .NET CLR 3.0.4506.2152; .NET CLR 3.5.30729)"

195.245.92.74 - - [12/Jul/2010:08:45:28 +0200] "GET /Bilder/56.jpg HTTP/1.0" 200 4494 "http://www.asylabwehramt.at/Seiten/Aktuelles.html" "Mozilla/4.0 (compatible; MSIE 7.0; Windows NT 5.1; .NET CLR 1.1.4322; .NET CLR 2.0.50727; .NET CLR 3.0.4506.2152; .NET CLR 3.5.30729)"

---

[26] WHOIS record on page 290

```
195.245.92.74 - - [12/Jul/2010:08:45:49 +0200] "GET /Seiten/Material.html HTTP/1.0" 200 16806 "ht
tp://www.asylabwehramt.at/Seiten/Aktuelles.html" "Mozilla/4.0 (compatible; MSIE 7.0; Windows NT 5
.1; .NET CLR 1.1.4322; .NET CLR 2.0.50727; .NET CLR 3.0.4506.2152; .NET CLR 3.5.30729)"
195.245.92.74 - - [12/Jul/2010:08:45:51 +0200] "GET /Seiten/Rundzeichen.html HTTP/1.0" 200 8895 "
http://www.asylabwehramt.at/Seiten/Material.html" "Mozilla/4.0 (compatible; MSIE 7.0; Windows NT
5.1; .NET CLR 1.1.4322; .NET CLR 2.0.50727; .NET CLR 3.0.4506.2152; .NET CLR 3.5.30729)"
195.245.92.74 - - [12/Jul/2010:08:46:04 +0200] "GET /Material/Asyl_Jahresstatistik_2009.pdf HTTP/
1.0" 200 680643 "http://www.asylabwehramt.at/Seiten/Material.html" "Mozilla/4.0 (compatible; MSIE
7.0; Windows NT 5.1; .NET CLR 1.1.4322; .NET CLR 2.0.50727; .NET CLR 3.0.4506.2152; .NET CLR 3.5
.30729)"
195.245.92.74 - - [12/Jul/2010:08:46:05 +0200] "GET /Material/Asyl_Jahresstatistik_2009.pdf HTTP/
1.0" 206 20 "-" "Mozilla/4.0 (compatible; MSIE 7.0; Windows NT 5.1; .NET CLR 1.1.4322; .NET CLR 2
.0.50727; .NET CLR 3.0.4506.2152; .NET CLR 3.5.30729)"
195.245.92.74 - - [12/Jul/2010:08:46:06 +0200] "GET /Material/Asyl_Jahresstatistik_2009.pdf HTTP/
1.0" 206 29238 "-" "Mozilla/4.0 (compatible; MSIE 7.0; Windows NT 5.1; .NET CLR 1.1.4322; .NET CL
R 2.0.50727; .NET CLR 3.0.4506.2152; .NET CLR 3.5.30729)"
195.245.92.74 - - [12/Jul/2010:08:46:07 +0200] "GET /Material/Asyl_Jahresstatistik_2009.pdf HTTP/
1.0" 206 49826 "-" "Mozilla/4.0 (compatible; MSIE 7.0; Windows NT 5.1; .NET CLR 1.1.4322; .NET CL
R 2.0.50727; .NET CLR 3.0.4506.2152; .NET CLR 3.5.30729)"
195.245.92.74 - - [12/Jul/2010:08:46:08 +0200] "GET /Material/Asyl_Jahresstatistik_2009.pdf HTTP/
1.0" 206 49246 "-" "Mozilla/4.0 (compatible; MSIE 7.0; Windows NT 5.1; .NET CLR 1.1.4322; .NET CL
R 2.0.50727; .NET CLR 3.0.4506.2152; .NET CLR 3.5.30729)"
195.245.92.74 - - [12/Jul/2010:08:46:09 +0200] "GET /Material/Asyl_Jahresstatistik_2009.pdf HTTP/
1.0" 206 16089 "-" "Mozilla/4.0 (compatible; MSIE 7.0; Windows NT 5.1; .NET CLR 1.1.4322; .NET CL
R 2.0.50727; .NET CLR 3.0.4506.2152; .NET CLR 3.5.30729)"
195.245.92.74 - - [12/Jul/2010:08:46:10 +0200] "GET /Material/Asyl_Jahresstatistik_2009.pdf HTTP/
1.0" 206 14304 "-" "Mozilla/4.0 (compatible; MSIE 7.0; Windows NT 5.1; .NET CLR 1.1.4322; .NET CL
R 2.0.50727; .NET CLR 3.0.4506.2152; .NET CLR 3.5.30729)"
```

```
195.245.92.74 - - [12/Jul/2010:08:46:11 +0200] "GET /Material/Asyl_Jahresstatistik_2009.pdf HTTP/
1.0" 206 17376 "-" "Mozilla/4.0 (compatible; MSIE 7.0; Windows NT 5.1; .NET CLR 1.1.4322; .NET CL
R 2.0.50727; .NET CLR 3.0.4506.2152; .NET CLR 3.5.30729)"
80.120.179.10 - - [12/Jul/2010:10:50:07 +0200] "GET / HTTP/1.1" 200 11992 "-" "Mozilla/4.0 (compa
tible; MSIE 6.0; Windows NT 5.1; SV1; .NET CLR 1.1.4322; .NET CLR 2.0.50727; .NET CLR 3.0.04506.3
0; .NET CLR 3.0.04506.648; InfoPath.2)"
80.120.179.10 - - [12/Jul/2010:10:50:08 +0200] "GET /asyl.css HTTP/1.1" 200 860 "http://www.asyla
bwehramt.at/" "Mozilla/4.0 (compatible; MSIE 6.0; Windows NT 5.1; SV1; .NET CLR 1.1.4322; .NET CL
R 2.0.50727; .NET CLR 3.0.04506.30; .NET CLR 3.0.04506.648; InfoPath.2)"
80.120.179.10 - - [12/Jul/2010:10:50:22 +0200] "GET /Seiten/Latestnews.html HTTP/1.1" 200 12721 "
http://www.asylabwehramt.at/" "Mozilla/4.0 (compatible; MSIE 6.0; Windows NT 5.1; SV1; .NET CLR 1
.1.4322; .NET CLR 2.0.50727; .NET CLR 3.0.04506.30; .NET CLR 3.0.04506.648; InfoPath.2)"
80.120.179.10 - - [12/Jul/2010:10:54:26 +0200] "GET /Seiten/Material.html HTTP/1.1" 200 16806 "ht
tp://www.asylabwehramt.at/" "Mozilla/4.0 (compatible; MSIE 6.0; Windows NT 5.1; SV1; .NET CLR 1.1
.4322; .NET CLR 2.0.50727; .NET CLR 3.0.04506.30; .NET CLR 3.0.04506.648; InfoPath.2)"
80.120.179.10 - - [12/Jul/2010:10:54:35 +0200] "GET /Material/Flyer_Volksschutz_Praevention_Aufkl
aerung_FPOE.pdf HTTP/1.1" 200 661529 "http://www.asylabwehramt.at/Seiten/Material.html" "Mozilla/
4.0 (compatible; MSIE 6.0; Windows NT 5.1; SV1; .NET CLR 1.1.4322; .NET CLR 2.0.50727; .NET CLR 3
.0.04506.30; .NET CLR 3.0.04506.648; InfoPath.2)"
80.120.179.10 - - [12/Jul/2010:11:11:47 +0200] "GET /Bilder/Ladung.png HTTP/1.1" 200 114658 "http
://www.asylabwehramt.at/Seiten/Material.html" "Mozilla/4.0 (compatible; MSIE 6.0; Windows NT 5.1;
SV1; .NET CLR 1.1.4322; .NET CLR 2.0.50727; .NET CLR 3.0.04506.30; .NET CLR 3.0.04506.648; InfoP
ath.2)"
80.120.179.10 - - [12/Jul/2010:11:12:12 +0200] "GET /Material/Hotline_Deutsch.pdf HTTP/1.1" 200 4
89465 "http://www.asylabwehramt.at/Seiten/Material.html" "Mozilla/4.0 (compatible; MSIE 6.0; Wind
ows NT 5.1; SV1; .NET CLR 1.1.4322; .NET CLR 2.0.50727; .NET CLR 3.0.04506.30; .NET CLR 3.0.04506
.648; InfoPath.2)"
80.120.179.10 - - [12/Jul/2010:11:12:49 +0200] "GET /Material/Asyl_Jahresstatistik_2009.pdf HTTP/
```

```
1.1" 200 680643 "http://www.asylabwehramt.at/Seiten/Material.html" "Mozilla/4.0 (compatible; MSIE 6.0; Windows NT 5.1; SV1; .NET CLR 1.1.4322; .NET CLR 2.0.50727; .NET CLR 3.0.04506.648; InfoPath.2)"
78.41.144.41 - - [12/Jul/2010:15:22:19 +0200] "GET / HTTP/1.0" 304 - "-" "Mozilla/4.0 (compatible; MSIE 7.0; Windows NT 5.1; .NET CLR 2.0.50727; .NET CLR 3.0.04506.30; .NET CLR 3.5.21022; .NET CLR 3.0.4506.2152; .NET CLR 3.5.30729)"
78.41.144.41 - - [12/Jul/2010:15:23:36 +0200] "GET /Bilder/Header_AAbA_anim.gif HTTP/1.0" 304 - "http://www.facebook.com/" "Mozilla/4.0 (compatible; MSIE 7.0; Windows NT 5.1; .NET CLR 2.0.5072 7; .NET CLR 3.0.04506.30; .NET CLR 3.0.4506.2152; .NET CLR 3.5.30729)"
78.41.144.41 - - [12/Jul/2010:15:25:01 +0200] "GET / HTTP/1.0" 304 - "http://www.asylabwehramt.at /" "Mozilla/4.0 (compatible; MSIE 7.0; Windows NT 5.1; .NET CLR 2.0.50727; .NET CLR 3.0.04506.30; .NET CLR 3.0.04506.648; .NET CLR 3.5.21022; .NET CLR 3.0.4506.2152; .NET CLR 3.5.30729)"
78.41.144.41 - - [12/Jul/2010:15:25:03 +0200] "GET /Seiten/Aktuelles.html HTTP/1.0" 200 13367 "http://www.asylabwehramt.at/" "Mozilla/4.0 (compatible; MSIE 7.0; Windows NT 5.1; .NET CLR 2.0.5072 7; .NET CLR 3.0.04506.30; .NET CLR 3.0.4506.2152; .NET CLR 3.5.30729)"
78.41.144.41 - - [12/Jul/2010:15:25:59 +0200] "GET /Seiten/Material.html HTTP/1.0" 200 17073 "http://www.asylabwehramt.at/Seiten/Aktuelles.html" "Mozilla/4.0 (compatible; MSIE 7.0; Windows NT 5.1; .NET CLR 2.0.50727; .NET CLR 3.0.04506.30; .NET CLR 3.5.21022; .NET CLR 3.0.4506.2152; .NET CLR 3.5.30729)"
78.41.144.41 - - [12/Jul/2010:15:26:35 +0200] "GET /Bilder/IOM-Kosovo-Broschuere_Internet.pdf HTTP/1.0" 200 728811 "http://www.asylabwehramt.at/Seiten/Material.html" "Mozilla/4.0 (compatible; MSIE 7.0; Windows NT 5.1; .NET CLR 2.0.50727; .NET CLR 3.0.04506.30; .NET CLR 3.0.04506.648; .NET CLR 3.5.21022; .NET CLR 3.0.4506.2152; .NET CLR 3.5.30729)"
78.41.144.41 - - [12/Jul/2010:15:26:36 +0200] "GET /Bilder/IOM-Kosovo-Broschuere_Internet.pdf HTTP/1.0" 206 4096 "-" "Mozilla/4.0 (compatible; MSIE 7.0; Windows NT 5.1; .NET CLR 2.0.50727; .NET CLR 3.0.04506.30; .NET CLR 3.0.04506.648; .NET CLR 3.5.21022; .NET CLR 3.0.4506.2152; .NET CLR 3.
```

```
5.30729)"
78.41.144.41 - - [12/Jul/2010:15:27:39 +0200] "GET /Bilder/flyer_nigeria_Internet.pdf HTTP/1.0" 200 702826 "http://www.asylabwehramt.at/Seiten/Material.html" "Mozilla/4.0 (compatible; MSIE 7.0; Windows NT 5.1; .NET CLR 2.0.50727; .NET CLR 3.0.04506.30; .NET CLR 3.0.04506.648; .NET CLR 3.5.21022; .NET CLR 3.0.4506.2152; .NET CLR 3.5.30729)"
78.41.144.41 - - [12/Jul/2010:15:28:22 +0200] "GET /Seiten/Impressum.html HTTP/1.0" 200 11684 "http://www.asylabwehramt.at/Seiten/Material.html" "Mozilla/4.0 (compatible; MSIE 7.0; Windows NT 5.1; .NET CLR 2.0.50727; .NET CLR 3.0.04506.30; .NET CLR 3.0.04506.648; .NET CLR 3.5.21022; .NET CLR 3.0.4506.2152; .NET CLR 3.5.30729)"
78.41.144.41 - - [12/Jul/2010:15:28:28 +0200] "GET /Seiten/Rundzeichen.html HTTP/1.0" 200 8895 "http://www.asylabwehramt.at/Seiten/Impressum.html" "Mozilla/4.0 (compatible; MSIE 7.0; Windows NT 5.1; .NET CLR 2.0.50727; .NET CLR 3.0.04506.30; .NET CLR 3.0.04506.648; .NET CLR 3.5.21022; .NET CLR 3.0.4506.2152; .NET CLR 3.5.30729)"
78.41.144.41 - - [12/Jul/2010:15:28:35 +0200] "GET /Seiten/Bilder.html HTTP/1.0" 200 10043 "http://www.asylabwehramt.at/Seiten/Rundzeichen.html" "Mozilla/4.0 (compatible; MSIE 7.0; Windows NT 5.1; .NET CLR 2.0.50727; .NET CLR 3.0.04506.30; .NET CLR 3.0.04506.648; .NET CLR 3.5.21022; .NET CLR 3.0.4506.2152; .NET CLR 3.5.30729)"
78.41.144.41 - - [12/Jul/2010:15:30:48 +0200] "GET /Seiten/Press.html HTTP/1.0" 200 12186 "http://www.asylabwehramt.at/Seiten/Bilder.html" "Mozilla/4.0 (compatible; MSIE 7.0; Windows NT 5.1; .NET CLR 2.0.50727; .NET CLR 3.0.04506.30; .NET CLR 3.0.04506.648; .NET CLR 3.5.21022; .NET CLR 3.0.4506.2152; .NET CLR 3.5.30729)"
78.41.144.41 - - [12/Jul/2010:15:31:16 +0200] "GET /OEFFENTLICHKEIT/media/Leporello_17062010.MP3 HTTP/1.0" 200 5791744 "http://www.asylabwehramt.at/Seiten/Press.html" "Mozilla/4.0 (compatible; MSIE 7.0; Windows NT 5.1; .NET CLR 2.0.50727; .NET CLR 3.0.04506.30; .NET CLR 3.5.21022; .NET CLR 3.0.04506.648; .NET CLR 3.5.21022; .NET CLR 3.0.4506.2152; .NET CLR 3.5.30729)"
62.154.194.53 - - [13/Jul/2010:06:55:42 +0200] "GET / HTTP/1.1" 200 11992 "-" "Mozilla/4.0 (compatible; MSIE 5.5; Windows NT 5.0)"
213.208.144.130 - - [13/Jul/2010:09:36:23 +0200] "GET / HTTP/1.0" 200 11992 "-" "Mozilla/4.0 (com
```

```
patible; MSIE 7.0; Windows NT 5.2; .NET CLR 1.1.4322; InfoPath.1; .NET CLR 2.0.50727; .NET CLR 3.
0.4506.2152; .NET CLR 3.5.30729)"
213.208.144.130 - - [13/Jul/2010:09:36:45 +0200] "GET /Seiten/Aktuelles.html HTTP/1.0" 200 13367
"http://www.asylabwehramt.at/" "Mozilla/4.0 (compatible; MSIE 7.0; Windows NT 5.2; .NET CLR 1.1.4
322; InfoPath.1; .NET CLR 2.0.50727; .NET CLR 3.5.30729)"
213.208.144.130 - - [13/Jul/2010:09:37:10 +0200] "GET /Seiten/Press.html HTTP/1.0" 200 12186 "htt
p://www.asylabwehramt.at/Seiten/Aktuelles.html" "Mozilla/4.0 (compatible; MSIE 7.0; Windows NT 5.
2; .NET CLR 1.1.4322; InfoPath.1; .NET CLR 2.0.50727; .NET CLR 3.5.30729)"

213.208.144.130 - - [13/Jul/2010:09:37:20 +0200] "GET /Seiten/Latestnews.html HTTP/1.0" 200 13371
"http://www.asylabwehramt.at/Seiten/Press.html" "Mozilla/4.0 (compatible; MSIE 7.0; Windows NT 5
.2; .NET CLR 1.1.4322; InfoPath.1; .NET CLR 2.0.50727; .NET CLR 3.0.4506.2152; .NET CLR 3.5.30729
)"
213.208.144.130 - - [13/Jul/2010:09:37:21 +0200] "GET /Seiten/Orgstruct.html HTTP/1.0" 200 14226
"http://www.asylabwehramt.at/Seiten/Latestnews.html" "Mozilla/4.0 (compatible; MSIE 7.0; Windows
NT 5.2; .NET CLR 1.1.4322; InfoPath.1; .NET CLR 2.0.50727; .NET CLR 3.0.4506.2152; .NET CLR 3.5.3
0729)"
194.153.217.248 - - [13/Jul/2010:11:33:10 +0200] "GET / HTTP/1.1" 200 11992 "http://www.zeit.de/
2010/28/A-Asylabwehramt" "Mozilla/5.0 (Windows; U; Windows NT 5.1; de; rv:1.9.1.10) Gecko/201005
04 Firefox/3.5.10"
194.153.217.248 - - [13/Jul/2010:11:33:11 +0200] "GET /favicon.ico HTTP/1.1" 302 340 "-" "Mozilla
/5.0 (Windows; U; Windows NT 5.1; de; rv:1.9.1.10) Gecko/20100504 Firefox/3.5.10"
194.153.217.248 - - [13/Jul/2010:11:33:13 +0200] "GET /favicon.ico HTTP/1.1" 302 340 "-" "Mozilla
/5.0 (Windows; U; Windows NT 5.1; de; rv:1.9.1.10) Gecko/20100504 Firefox/3.5.10"
213.208.144.130 - - [13/Jul/2010:12:30:33 +0200] "GET / HTTP/1.0" 200 11992 "-" "Mozilla/4.0 (com
patible; MSIE 7.0; Windows NT 5.2; .NET CLR 1.1.4322; InfoPath.1; .NET CLR 2.0.50727; .NET CLR 3.
0.4506.2152; .NET CLR 3.5.30729)"
```

213.208.144.130 - - [13/Jul/2010:12:30:35 +0200] "GET /asyl.css HTTP/1.0" 200 860 "http://www.asylabwehramt.at/" "Mozilla/4.0 (compatible; MSIE 7.0; Windows NT 5.2; .NET CLR 1.1.4322; InfoPath.1; .NET CLR 2.0.50727; .NET CLR 3.0.4506.2152; .NET CLR 3.5.30729)"

213.208.144.130 - - [13/Jul/2010:12:34:03 +0200] "GET /index_e.html HTTP/1.0" 200 12025 "http://www.asylabwehramt.at/" "Mozilla/4.0 (compatible; MSIE 7.0; Windows NT 5.2; .NET CLR 1.1.4322; InfoPath.1; .NET CLR 2.0.50727; .NET CLR 3.0.4506.2152; .NET CLR 3.5.30729)"

213.208.144.130 - - [13/Jul/2010:12:34:09 +0200] "GET /Seiten/Latestnews.html HTTP/1.0" 200 13371 "http://www.asylabwehramt.at/index_e.html" "Mozilla/4.0 (compatible; MSIE 7.0; Windows NT 5.2; .NET CLR 1.1.4322; InfoPath.1; .NET CLR 2.0.50727; .NET CLR 3.0.4506.2152; .NET CLR 3.5.30729)"

213.208.144.130 - - [13/Jul/2010:12:34:20 +0200] "GET /Bilder/leistung_2.jpg HTTP/1.0" 200 4918 "http://www.asylabwehramt.at/Seiten/Latestnews.html" "Mozilla/4.0 (compatible; MSIE 7.0; Windows NT 5.2; .NET CLR 1.1.4322; InfoPath.1; .NET CLR 2.0.50727; .NET CLR 3.0.4506.2152; .NET CLR 3.5.30729)"

213.208.144.130 - - [13/Jul/2010:13:54:27 +0200] "GET / HTTP/1.0" 200 11992 "-" "Mozilla/4.0 (compatible; MSIE 7.0; Windows NT 5.2; .NET CLR 1.1.4322; InfoPath.1; .NET CLR 2.0.50727; .NET CLR 3.0.4506.2152; .NET CLR 3.5.30729)"

213.208.144.130 - - [13/Jul/2010:13:54:38 +0200] "GET /Seiten/Links.html HTTP/1.0" 200 18864 "http://www.asylabwehramt.at/" "Mozilla/4.0 (compatible; MSIE 7.0; Windows NT 5.2; .NET CLR 1.1.4322; InfoPath.1; .NET CLR 2.0.50727; .NET CLR 3.0.4506.2152; .NET CLR 3.5.30729)"

213.208.144.130 - - [13/Jul/2010:13:55:27 +0200] "GET /Seiten/Material.html HTTP/1.0" 200 17073 "http://www.asylabwehramt.at/Seiten/Links.html" "Mozilla/4.0 (compatible; MSIE 7.0; Windows NT 5.2; .NET CLR 1.1.4322; InfoPath.1; .NET CLR 2.0.50727; .NET CLR 3.0.4506.2152; .NET CLR 3.5.30729)"

213.208.144.130 - - [13/Jul/2010:13:55:34 +0200] "GET /Material/Hotline_Englisch.PDF HTTP/1.0" 200 473359 "http://www.asylabwehramt.at/Seiten/Material.html" "Mozilla/4.0 (compatible; MSIE 7.0; Windows NT 5.2; .NET CLR 1.1.4322; InfoPath.1; .NET CLR 2.0.50727; .NET CLR 3.0.4506.2152; .NET CLR 3.5.30729)"

213.208.144.130 - - [13/Jul/2010:13:56:03 +0200] "GET /favicon.ico HTTP/1.0" 302 340 "-" "Mozilla/4.0 (compatible; MSIE 7.0; Windows NT 5.2; .NET CLR 1.1.4322; InfoPath.1; .NET CLR 2.0.50727)"

```
213.208.144.130 - - [13/Jul/2010:13:58:22 +0200] "GET /Bilder/IOM-Kosovo-Broschuere_Internet.pdf
HTTP/1.0" 200 728811 "http://www.asylabwehramt.at/Seiten/Material.html" "Mozilla/4.0 (compatible;
MSIE 7.0; Windows NT 5.2; .NET CLR 1.1.4322; InfoPath.1; .NET CLR 2.0.50727; .NET CLR 3.0.4506.2
152; .NET CLR 3.5.30729)"
213.208.144.130 - - [13/Jul/2010:13:58:32 +0200] "GET /Bilder/flyer_nigeria_Internet.pdf HTTP/1.0
" 200 702826 "http://www.asylabwehramt.at/Seiten/Material.html" "Mozilla/4.0 (compatible; MSIE 7.
0; Windows NT 5.2; .NET CLR 1.1.4322; InfoPath.1; .NET CLR 2.0.50727; .NET CLR 3.0.4506.2152; .NE
T CLR 3.5.30729)"
213.208.144.130 - - [13/Jul/2010:13:58:33 +0200] "GET /Bilder/flyer_nigeria_Internet.pdf HTTP/1.0
" 206 410499 "-" "Mozilla/4.0 (compatible; MSIE 7.0; Windows NT 5.2; .NET CLR 1.1.4322; InfoPath.
1; .NET CLR 2.0.50727; .NET CLR 3.0.4506.2152; .NET CLR 3.5.30729)"
213.208.144.130 - - [13/Jul/2010:13:59:08 +0200] "GET /Seiten/Aktuelles.html HTTP/1.0" 200 13367
"http://www.asylabwehramt.at/Seiten/Material.html" "Mozilla/4.0 (compatible; MSIE 7.0; Windows NT
5.2; .NET CLR 1.1.4322; InfoPath.1; .NET CLR 2.0.50727; .NET CLR 3.0.4506.2152; .NET CLR 3.5.307
29)"
213.208.144.130 - - [13/Jul/2010:13:59:09 +0200] "GET /Bilder/leistung_2.jpg HTTP/1.0" 200 4918 "
http://www.asylabwehramt.at/Seiten/Aktuelles.html" "Mozilla/4.0 (compatible; MSIE 7.0; Windows NT
5.2; .NET CLR 1.1.4322; InfoPath.1; .NET CLR 2.0.50727; .NET CLR 3.0.4506.2152; .NET CLR 3.5.307
29)"
213.208.144.130 - - [13/Jul/2010:13:59:43 +0200] "GET /Seiten/Rundzeichen.html HTTP/1.0" 200 8895
"http://www.asylabwehramt.at/Seiten/Aktuelles.html" "Mozilla/4.0 (compatible; MSIE 7.0; Windows
NT 5.2; .NET CLR 1.1.4322; InfoPath.1; .NET CLR 2.0.50727; .NET CLR 3.0.4506.2152; .NET CLR 3.5.3
0729)"
213.208.144.130 - - [13/Jul/2010:13:59:49 +0200] "GET /Seiten/Bilder.html HTTP/1.0" 200 10043 "ht
tp://www.asylabwehramt.at/Seiten/Rundzeichen.html" "Mozilla/4.0 (compatible; MSIE 7.0; Windows NT
5.2; .NET CLR 1.1.4322; InfoPath.1; .NET CLR 2.0.50727; .NET CLR 3.0.4506.2152; .NET CLR 3.5.307
29)"
213.208.144.130 - - [13/Jul/2010:14:00:09 +0200] "GET /Seiten/Bilder_Ausstellung.html HTTP/1.0" 2
```

00 16437 "http://www.asylabwehramt.at/Seiten/Bilder.html" "Mozilla/4.0 (compatible; MSIE 7.0; Windows NT 5.2; .NET CLR 1.1.4322; InfoPath.1; .NET CLR 2.0.50727; .NET CLR 3.0.4506.2152; .NET CLR 3.5.30729)"

213.208.144.130 - - [13/Jul/2010:14:01:36 +0200] "GET /Seiten/Press.html HTTP/1.0" 200 12186 "http://www.asylabwehramt.at/Seiten/Links.html" "Mozilla/4.0 (compatible; MSIE 7.0; Windows NT 5.2; .NET CLR 1.1.4322; InfoPath.1; .NET CLR 2.0.50727; .NET CLR 3.0.4506.2152; .NET CLR 3.5.30729)"

213.208.144.130 - - [13/Jul/2010:14:01:49 +0200] "GET /Seiten/Orgstruct.html HTTP/1.0" 200 14226 "http://www.asylabwehramt.at/Seiten/Press.html" "Mozilla/4.0 (compatible; MSIE 7.0; Windows NT 5.2; .NET CLR 1.1.4322; InfoPath.1; .NET CLR 2.0.50727; .NET CLR 3.0.4506.2152; .NET CLR 3.5.30729)"

213.208.144.130 - - [13/Jul/2010:15:55:27 +0200] "GET / HTTP/1.0" 200 11992 "-" "Mozilla/4.0 (compatible; MSIE 7.0; Windows NT 5.2; .NET CLR 1.1.4322; InfoPath.1; .NET CLR 2.0.50727; .NET CLR 3.0.4506.2152; .NET CLR 3.5.30729)"

213.208.144.130 - - [13/Jul/2010:17:48:27 +0200] "GET / HTTP/1.0" 200 11992 "-" "Mozilla/4.0 (compatible; MSIE 7.0; Windows NT 5.2; .NET CLR 1.1.4322; InfoPath.1; .NET CLR 2.0.50727; .NET CLR 3.5.21022)"

62.154.194.53 - - [14/Jul/2010:07:32:38 +0200] "GET / HTTP/1.1" 200 11992 "-" "Mozilla/4.0 (compatible; MSIE 5.5; Windows NT 5.0)"

85.158.227.72[27] - - [14/Jul/2010:08:17:54 +0200] "GET / HTTP/1.1" 200 11992 "-" "Mozilla/5.0 (Windows; U; Windows NT 5.1; de; rv:1.9.1.10) Gecko/20100504 Firefox/3.5.10"

85.158.227.72 - - [14/Jul/2010:08:17:57 +0200] "GET /favicon.ico HTTP/1.1" 302 340 "-" "Mozilla/5.0 (Windows; U; Windows NT 5.1; de; rv:1.9.1.10) Gecko/20100504 Firefox/3.5.10"

85.158.227.72 - - [14/Jul/2010:08:18:28 +0200] "GET /index.html HTTP/1.1" 200 11992 "http://www.asylabwehramt.at/" "Mozilla/5.0 (Windows; U; Windows NT 5.1; de; rv:1.9.1.10) Gecko/20100504 Firefox/3.5.10"

85.158.227.72 - - [14/Jul/2010:08:18:31 +0200] "GET /Seiten/Orgstrukt.html HTTP/1.1" 200 14119 "h

---

[27]WHOIS record on page 322

173

```
ttp://www.asylabwehramt.at/index.html" "Mozilla/5.0 (Windows; U; Windows NT 5.1; de; rv:1.9.1.10)
Gecko/20100504 Firefox/3.5.10"
85.158.227.72 - - [14/Jul/2010:08:18:55 +0200] "GET /Seiten/Material.html HTTP/1.1" 200 17073 "ht
tp://www.asylabwehramt.at/index.html" "Mozilla/5.0 (Windows; U; Windows NT 5.1; de; rv:1.9.1.10)
Gecko/20100504 Firefox/3.5.10"
213.208.144.130 - - [14/Jul/2010:08:24:52 +0200] "GET / HTTP/1.0" 200 11992 "-" "Mozilla/4.0 (com
patible; MSIE 7.0; Windows NT 5.2; .NET CLR 1.1.4322; InfoPath.1; .NET CLR 2.0.50727; .NET CLR 3.
0.4506.2152; .NET CLR 3.5.30729)"
213.208.144.130 - - [14/Jul/2010:08:25:43 +0200] "GET /Seiten/Material.html HTTP/1.0" 200 17073 "
http://www.asylabwehramt.at/" "Mozilla/4.0 (compatible; MSIE 7.0; Windows NT 5.2; .NET CLR 1.1.43
22; InfoPath.1; .NET CLR 2.0.50727; .NET CLR 3.0.4506.2152; .NET CLR 3.5.30729)"
213.208.144.130 - - [14/Jul/2010:08:25:50 +0200] "GET /Seiten/Rundzeichen.html HTTP/1.0" 200 8895
"http://www.asylabwehramt.at/Seiten/Material.html" "Mozilla/4.0 (compatible; MSIE 7.0; Windows N
T 5.2; .NET CLR 1.1.4322; InfoPath.1; .NET CLR 2.0.50727; .NET CLR 3.0.4506.2152; .NET CLR 3.5.30
729)"
213.208.144.130 - - [14/Jul/2010:08:25:57 +0200] "GET /Seiten/Bilder.html HTTP/1.0" 200 10043 "ht
tp://www.asylabwehramt.at/Seiten/Rundzeichen.html" "Mozilla/4.0 (compatible; MSIE 7.0; Windows NT
5.2; InfoPath.1; .NET CLR 1.1.4322; .NET CLR 2.0.50727; .NET CLR 3.0.4506.2152; .NET CLR 3.5.307
29)"
80.120.179.10 - - [14/Jul/2010:08:34:06 +0200] "GET / HTTP/1.1" 200 11992 "http://www.google.at/s
earch?hl=de&source=hp&q=asylabwehramt&btnG=Google-Suche&meta=&aq=o&aqi=&aql=&oq=&gs_rfai=" "Mozil
la/4.0 (compatible; MSIE 6.0; Windows NT 5.1; SV1; .NET CLR 1.1.4322)"
80.120.179.10 - - [14/Jul/2010:08:34:35 +0200] "GET /Seiten/Aktuelles.html HTTP/1.1" 200 13367 "h
ttp://www.asylabwehramt.at/" "Mozilla/4.0 (compatible; MSIE 6.0; Windows NT 5.1; SV1; .NET CLR 1.
1.4322)"
80.120.179.10 - - [14/Jul/2010:08:34:36 +0200] "GET /Bilder/leistung_2.jpg HTTP/1.1" 200 4918 "ht
tp://www.asylabwehramt.at/Seiten/Aktuelles.html" "Mozilla/4.0 (compatible; MSIE 6.0; Windows NT 5
.1; SV1; .NET CLR 1.1.4322)"
```

80.120.179.10 - - [14/Jul/2010:08:34:42 +0200] "GET /Seiten/Material.html HTTP/1.1" 200 17073 "ht
tp://www.asylabwehramt.at/Seiten/Aktuelles.html" "Mozilla/4.0 (compatible; MSIE 6.0; Windows NT 5
.1; SV1; .NET CLR 1.1.4322)"
80.120.179.10 - - [14/Jul/2010:08:34:47 +0200] "GET /Bilder/Ladung.png HTTP/1.1" 200 114658 "http
://www.asylabwehramt.at/Seiten/Material.html" "Mozilla/4.0 (compatible; MSIE 6.0; Windows NT 5.1;
SV1; .NET CLR 1.1.4322)"
80.120.179.10 - - [14/Jul/2010:08:35:01 +0200] "GET /Bilder/flyer_nigeria_Internet.pdf HTTP/1.1"
200 702826 "http://www.asylabwehramt.at/Seiten/Material.html" "Mozilla/4.0 (compatible; MSIE 6.0;
Windows NT 5.1; SV1; .NET CLR 1.1.4322)"
91.204.193.192[28] - - [14/Jul/2010:08:56:48 +0200] "GET / HTTP/1.1" 200 11992 "http://www.google.de/
search?hl=de&&sa=X&ei=q189TMjCM5-y0gTEx5TTCA&ved=0CB0QBSgA&q=www.asylabwehramt.at&spell=1" "Mozil
la/4.0 (compatible; MSIE 7.0; Windows NT 5.1; .NET CLR 1.1.4322; .NET CLR 2.0.50727; .NET CLR 3.0
.04506.30; .NET CLR 3.0.4506.2152; .NET CLR 3.5.30729)"
91.204.193.192 - - [14/Jul/2010:08:57:22 +0200] "GET /Seiten/Orgstrukt.html HTTP/1.1" 200 14119 "
http://www.asylabwehramt.at/" "Mozilla/4.0 (compatible; MSIE 7.0; Windows NT 5.1; .NET CLR 1.1.43
22; .NET CLR 2.0.50727; .NET CLR 3.0.04506.30; .NET CLR 3.0.4506.2152; .NET CLR 3.5.30729)"
91.204.193.192 - - [14/Jul/2010:08:57:49 +0200] "GET /Seiten/Aktuelles.html HTTP/1.1" 200 13367 "
http://www.asylabwehramt.at/Seiten/Orgstrukt.html" "Mozilla/4.0 (compatible; MSIE 7.0; Windows NT
5.1; .NET CLR 1.1.4322; .NET CLR 2.0.50727; .NET CLR 3.0.04506.30; .NET CLR 3.0.4506.2152; .NET
CLR 3.5.30729)"
91.204.193.192 - - [14/Jul/2010:08:58:05 +0200] "GET /Seiten/Material.html HTTP/1.1" 200 17073 "h
ttp://www.asylabwehramt.at/Seiten/Aktuelles.html" "Mozilla/4.0 (compatible; MSIE 7.0; Windows NT
5.1; .NET CLR 1.1.4322; .NET CLR 2.0.50727; .NET CLR 3.0.04506.30; .NET CLR 3.0.4506.2152; .NET C
LR 3.5.30729)"
91.204.193.192 - - [14/Jul/2010:08:58:15 +0200] "GET /Material/Hotline_Albanisch.PDF HTTP/1.1" 20
0 644638 "http://www.asylabwehramt.at/Seiten/Material.html" "Mozilla/4.0 (compatible; MSIE 7.0; W

---

[28]WHOIS record on page 303

175

indows NT 5.1; .NET CLR 1.1.4322; .NET CLR 2.0.50727; .NET CLR 3.0.04506.30; .NET CLR 3.0.4506.21
52; .NET CLR 3.5.30729)"
91.204.193.192 - - [14/Jul/2010:08:58:16 +0200] "GET /Material/Hotline_Albanisch.PDF HTTP/1.1" 20
6 4096 "-" "Mozilla/4.0 (compatible; MSIE 7.0; Windows NT 5.1; .NET CLR 1.1.4322; .NET CLR 2.0.50
727; .NET CLR 3.0.04506.30; .NET CLR 3.0.4506.2152; .NET CLR 3.5.30729)"
91.204.193.192 - - [14/Jul/2010:08:58:29 +0200] "GET /Bilder/Ladung.png HTTP/1.1" 200 114658 "htt
p://www.asylabwehramt.at/Seiten/Material.html" "Mozilla/4.0 (compatible; MSIE 7.0; Windows NT 5.1
; .NET CLR 1.1.4322; .NET CLR 2.0.50727; .NET CLR 3.0.04506.30; .NET CLR 3.0.4506.2152; .NET CLR
3.5.30729)"
91.204.193.192 - - [14/Jul/2010:08:58:40 +0200] "GET /Seiten/Rundzeichen.html HTTP/1.1" 200 8895
"http://www.asylabwehramt.at/Seiten/Material.html" "Mozilla/4.0 (compatible; MSIE 7.0; Windows NT
5.1; .NET CLR 1.1.4322; .NET CLR 2.0.50727; .NET CLR 3.0.04506.30; .NET CLR 3.0.4506.2152; .NET
CLR 3.5.30729)"
91.204.193.192 - - [14/Jul/2010:08:58:45 +0200] "GET /Seiten/Seal.html HTTP/1.1" 200 8933 "http:/
/www.asylabwehramt.at/Seiten/Rundzeichen.html" "Mozilla/4.0 (compatible; MSIE 7.0; Windows NT 5.1
; .NET CLR 1.1.4322; .NET CLR 2.0.50727; .NET CLR 3.0.04506.30; .NET CLR 3.0.4506.2152; .NET CLR
3.5.30729)"
91.204.193.192 - - [14/Jul/2010:08:58:47 +0200] "GET /Seiten/Images.html HTTP/1.1" 200 10215 "htt
p://www.asylabwehramt.at/Seiten/Seal.html" "Mozilla/4.0 (compatible; MSIE 7.0; Windows NT 5.1; .N
ET CLR 1.1.4322; .NET CLR 2.0.50727; .NET CLR 3.0.04506.30; .NET CLR 3.0.4506.2152; .NET CLR 3.5.
30729)"
91.204.193.192 - - [14/Jul/2010:08:59:06 +0200] "GET /Seiten/Links_e.html HTTP/1.1" 200 18884 "ht
tp://www.asylabwehramt.at/Seiten/Images.html" "Mozilla/4.0 (compatible; MSIE 7.0; Windows NT 5.1;
.NET CLR 1.1.4322; .NET CLR 2.0.50727; .NET CLR 3.0.04506.30; .NET CLR 3.0.4506.2152; .NET CLR 3
.5.30729)"
91.204.193.192 - - [14/Jul/2010:08:59:46 +0200] "GET /Seiten/Links_e.html HTTP/1.1" 304 - "http:/
/www.asylabwehramt.at/Seiten/Links_e.html" "Mozilla/4.0 (compatible; MSIE 7.0; Windows NT 5.1; .N
ET CLR 1.1.4322; .NET CLR 2.0.50727; .NET CLR 3.0.04506.30; .NET CLR 3.0.4506.2152; .NET CLR 3.5.

30729)"

91.204.193.192 - - [14/Jul/2010:08:59:47 +0200] "GET /Seiten/Presse.html HTTP/1.1" 200 12135 "htt
p://www.asylabwehramt.at/Seiten/Links_e.html" "Mozilla/4.0 (compatible; MSIE 7.0; Windows NT 5.1;
.NET CLR 1.1.4322; .NET CLR 2.0.50727; .NET CLR 3.0.4506.30; .NET CLR 3.0.4506.2152; .NET CLR 3
.5.30729)"

91.204.193.192 - - [14/Jul/2010:08:59:55 +0200] "GET /OEFFENTLICHKEIT/media/ZEIT.pdf HTTP/1.1" 20
0 484489 "http://www.asylabwehramt.at/Seiten/Presse.html" "Mozilla/4.0 (compatible; MSIE 7.0; Win
dows NT 5.1; .NET CLR 1.1.4322; .NET CLR 2.0.50727; .NET CLR 3.0.04506.30; .NET CLR 3.0.4506.2152
; .NET CLR 3.5.30729)"

85.158.227.72 - - [14/Jul/2010:09:16:18 +0200] "GET / HTTP/1.1" 200 11992 "-" "Mozilla/5.0 (Windo
ws; U; Windows NT 5.1; de; rv:1.9.2.6) Gecko/20100625 Firefox/3.6.6"

85.158.227.72 - - [14/Jul/2010:09:16:21 +0200] "GET /favicon.ico HTTP/1.1" 302 340 "-" "Mozilla/5
.0 (Windows; U; Windows NT 5.1; de; rv:1.9.2.6) Gecko/20100625 Firefox/3.6.6"

85.158.227.72 - - [14/Jul/2010:09:16:35 +0200] "GET /Seiten/Impressum.html HTTP/1.1" 200 11684 "h
ttp://www.asylabwehramt.at/" "Mozilla/5.0 (Windows; U; Windows NT 5.1; de; rv:1.9.2.6) Gecko/2010
0625 Firefox/3.6.6"

85.158.227.72 - - [14/Jul/2010:09:16:47 +0200] "GET /index.html HTTP/1.1" 200 11992 "http://www.a
sylabwehramt.at/" "Mozilla/5.0 (Windows; U; Windows NT 5.1; de; rv:1.9.2.6) Gecko/20100625 Firefo
x/3.6.6"

85.158.227.72 - - [14/Jul/2010:09:17:18 +0200] "GET /Seiten/Bilder.html HTTP/1.1" 200 10043 "http
://www.asylabwehramt.at/index.html" "Mozilla/5.0 (Windows; U; Windows NT 5.1; de; rv:1.9.2.6) Gec
ko/20100625 Firefox/3.6.6"

85.158.227.72 - - [14/Jul/2010:09:17:48 +0200] "GET /Seiten/Material.html HTTP/1.1" 200 17073 "ht
tp://www.asylabwehramt.at/Seiten/Bilder.html" "Mozilla/5.0 (Windows; U; Windows NT 5.1; de; rv:1.
9.2.6) Gecko/20100625 Firefox/3.6.6"

85.158.227.72 - - [14/Jul/2010:09:18:07 +0200] "GET /Seiten/Rundzeichen.html HTTP/1.1" 200 8895 "
http://www.asylabwehramt.at/Seiten/Material.html" "Mozilla/5.0 (Windows; U; Windows NT 5.1; de; r
v:1.9.2.6) Gecko/20100625 Firefox/3.6.6"

```
85.158.227.72 - - [14/Jul/2010:10:18:45 +0200] "GET / HTTP/1.1" 200 11992 "-" "Mozilla/5.0 (Windows; U; Windows NT 5.1; de; rv:1.9.2.6) Gecko/20100625 Firefox/3.6.6"
85.158.227.72 - - [14/Jul/2010:10:18:48 +0200] "GET /favicon.ico HTTP/1.1" 302 340 "-" "Mozilla/5.0 (Windows; U; Windows NT 5.1; de; rv:1.9.2.6) Gecko/20100625 Firefox/3.6.6"
85.158.227.72 - - [14/Jul/2010:10:20:24 +0200] "GET / HTTP/1.1" 200 11992 "-" "Mozilla/5.0 (Windows; U; Windows NT 5.1; de; rv:1.9.1.2) Gecko/20090729 Firefox/3.5.2"
85.158.227.72 - - [14/Jul/2010:10:20:25 +0200] "GET /favicon.ico HTTP/1.1" 302 340 "-" "Mozilla/5.0 (Windows; U; Windows NT 5.1; de; rv:1.9.1.2) Gecko/20090729 Firefox/3.5.2"
85.158.227.72 - - [14/Jul/2010:10:20:27 +0200] "GET /favicon.ico HTTP/1.1" 302 340 "-" "Mozilla/5.0 (Windows; U; Windows NT 5.1; de; rv:1.9.1.2) Gecko/20090729 Firefox/3.5.2"
85.158.227.72 - - [14/Jul/2010:10:20:39 +0200] "GET /Seiten/Aktuelles.html HTTP/1.1" 200 13367 "http://www.asylabwehramt.at/" "Mozilla/5.0 (Windows; U; Windows NT 5.1; de; rv:1.9.1.2) Gecko/20090729 Firefox/3.5.2"
85.158.227.72 - - [14/Jul/2010:10:22:38 +0200] "GET /index.html HTTP/1.1" 200 11992 "http://www.asylabwehramt.at/Seiten/Aktuelles.html" "Mozilla/5.0 (Windows; U; Windows NT 5.1; de; rv:1.9.1.2) Gecko/20090729 Firefox/3.5.2"
85.158.227.72 - - [14/Jul/2010:10:22:46 +0200] "GET /Seiten/Orgstrukt.html HTTP/1.1" 200 14119 "http://www.asylabwehramt.at/index.html" "Mozilla/5.0 (Windows; U; Windows NT 5.1; de; rv:1.9.1.2) Gecko/20090729 Firefox/3.5.2"
85.158.227.72 - - [14/Jul/2010:10:26:29 +0200] "GET /Material/Hotline_Deutsch.pdf HTTP/1.1" 200 489465 "http://www.asylabwehramt.at/index.html" "Mozilla/5.0 (Windows; U; Windows NT 5.1; de; rv:1.9.1.2) Gecko/20090729 Firefox/3.5.2"
85.158.227.72 - - [14/Jul/2010:10:26:31 +0200] "GET /Material/Hotline_Deutsch.pdf HTTP/1.1" 206 456919 "-" "Mozilla/5.0 (Windows; U; Windows NT 5.1; de; rv:1.9.1.2) Gecko/20090729 Firefox/3.5.2"
85.158.227.72 - - [14/Jul/2010:10:27:24 +0200] "GET /Material/Hotline_Deutsch.pdf HTTP/1.1" 206 423929 "http://www.asylabwehramt.at/index.html" "Mozilla/5.0 (Windows; U; Windows NT 5.1; de; rv:1.9.1.2) Gecko/20090729 Firefox/3.5.2"
85.158.227.72 - - [14/Jul/2010:10:27:25 +0200] "GET /Material/Hotline_Deutsch.pdf HTTP/1.1" 206 4
```

```
23286 "-" "Mozilla/5.0 (Windows; U; Windows NT 5.1; de; rv:1.9.1.2) Gecko/20090729 Firefox/3.5.2"
85.158.227.72 - - [14/Jul/2010:10:28:25 +0200] "GET /Seiten/Bilder_Ausstellung.html HTTP/1.1" 200 16685 "http://www.asylabwehramt.at/Seiten/Aktuelles.html" "Mozilla/5.0 (Windows; U; Windows NT 5.1; de; rv:1.9.1.2) Gecko/20090729 Firefox/3.5.2"
85.158.227.72 - - [14/Jul/2010:10:28:26 +0200] "GET /Bilder/Ausstellung_weisses_haus_wien_esel_fotos/eSeL_UBERMORGEN_asylabwehramt_dasweissehaus_466_thumb.jpg HTTP/1.1" 200 76077 "http://www.asylabwehramt.at/Seiten/Bilder_Ausstellung.html" "Mozilla/5.0 (Windows; U; Windows NT 5.1; de; rv:1.9.1.2) Gecko/20090729 Firefox/3.5.2"
85.158.227.72 - - [14/Jul/2010:10:28:27 +0200] "GET /Bilder/Ausstellung_weisses_haus_wien_esel_fotos/eSeL_UBERMORGEN_asylabwehramt_dasweissehaus_484_thumb.jpg HTTP/1.1" 200 48099 "http://www.asylabwehramt.at/Seiten/Bilder_Ausstellung.html" "Mozilla/5.0 (Windows; U; Windows NT 5.1; de; rv:1.9.1.2) Gecko/20090729 Firefox/3.5.2"
85.158.227.72 - - [14/Jul/2010:10:28:28 +0200] "GET /Bilder/Ausstellung_weisses_haus_wien_esel_fotos/eSeL_UBERMORGEN_asylabwehramt_dasweissehaus_510_thumb.jpg HTTP/1.1" 200 49505 "http://www.asylabwehramt.at/Seiten/Bilder_Ausstellung.html" "Mozilla/5.0 (Windows; U; Windows NT 5.1; de; rv:1.9.1.2) Gecko/20090729 Firefox/3.5.2"
85.158.227.72 - - [14/Jul/2010:10:30:20 +0200] "GET /Seiten/Aktuelles.html HTTP/1.1" 200 13367 "http://www.asylabwehramt.at/" "Mozilla/5.0 (Windows; U; Windows NT 5.1; de; rv:1.9.2.6) Gecko/20100625 Firefox/3.6.6"
85.158.227.72 - - [14/Jul/2010:10:30:23 +0200] "GET /Bilder/leistung_2.jpg HTTP/1.1" 200 4918 "http://www.asylabwehramt.at/Seiten/Aktuelles.html" "Mozilla/5.0 (Windows; U; Windows NT 5.1; de; rv:1.9.2.6) Gecko/20100625 Firefox/3.6.6"
85.158.227.72 - - [14/Jul/2010:10:30:43 +0200] "GET /Seiten/Material.html HTTP/1.1" 200 17073 "http://www.asylabwehramt.at/Seiten/Aktuelles.html" "Mozilla/5.0 (Windows; U; Windows NT 5.1; de; rv:1.9.2.6) Gecko/20100625 Firefox/3.6.6"
85.158.227.72 - - [14/Jul/2010:10:31:08 +0200] "GET /Seiten/Rundzeichen.html HTTP/1.1" 200 8895 "http://www.asylabwehramt.at/Seiten/Material.html" "Mozilla/5.0 (Windows; U; Windows NT 5.1; de; rv:1.9.2.6) Gecko/20100625 Firefox/3.6.6"
```

```
85.158.227.72 - - [14/Jul/2010:10:31:14 +0200] "GET /Seiten/Bilder.html HTTP/1.1" 200 10043 "http
://www.asylabwehramt.at/Seiten/Rundzeichen.html" "Mozilla/5.0 (Windows; U; Windows NT 5.1; de; rv
:1.9.2.6) Gecko/20100625 Firefox/3.6.6"
85.158.227.72 - - [14/Jul/2010:10:31:27 +0200] "GET /Seiten/Links.html HTTP/1.1" 200 18864 "http:
//www.asylabwehramt.at/Seiten/Bilder.html" "Mozilla/5.0 (Windows; U; Windows NT 5.1; de; rv:1.9.2
.6) Gecko/20100625 Firefox/3.6.6"
85.158.227.72 - - [14/Jul/2010:10:31:30 +0200] "GET /Bilder/IBM.png HTTP/1.1" 200 8413 "http://ww
w.asylabwehramt.at/Seiten/Links.html" "Mozilla/5.0 (Windows; U; Windows NT 5.1; de; rv:1.9.2.6) G
ecko/20100625 Firefox/3.6.6"
85.158.227.72 - - [14/Jul/2010:10:31:31 +0200] "GET /Seiten/Material.html HTTP/1.1" 200 17073 "ht
tp://www.asylabwehramt.at/Seiten/Bilder_Ausstellung.html" "Mozilla/5.0 (Windows; U; Windows NT 5.
1; de; rv:1.9.1.2) Gecko/20090729 Firefox/3.5.2"
85.158.227.72 - - [14/Jul/2010:10:31:33 +0200] "GET /Bilder/Ladung.png HTTP/1.1" 200 114658 "http
://www.asylabwehramt.at/Seiten/Material.html" "Mozilla/5.0 (Windows; U; Windows NT 5.1; de; rv:1.
9.1.2) Gecko/20090729 Firefox/3.5.2"
85.158.227.72 - - [14/Jul/2010:10:31:40 +0200] "GET /Material/Flyer_Volksschutz_Praevention_Aufkl
aerung_FPOE.pdf HTTP/1.1" 200 661529 "http://www.asylabwehramt.at/Seiten/Material.html" "Mozilla/
5.0 (Windows; U; Windows NT 5.1; de; rv:1.9.1.2) Gecko/20090729 Firefox/3.5.2"
85.158.227.72 - - [14/Jul/2010:10:31:43 +0200] "GET /Seiten/Press.html HTTP/1.1" 200 12186 "http:
//www.asylabwehramt.at/Seiten/Links.html" "Mozilla/5.0 (Windows; U; Windows NT 5.1; de; rv:1.9.2.
6) Gecko/20100625 Firefox/3.6.6"
85.158.227.72 - - [14/Jul/2010:10:31:52 +0200] "GET /Bilder/flyer_nigeria_Internet.pdf HTTP/1.1"
200 702826 "http://www.asylabwehramt.at/Seiten/Material.html" "Mozilla/5.0 (Windows; U; Windows N
T 5.1; de; rv:1.9.1.2) Gecko/20090729 Firefox/3.5.2"
85.158.227.72 - - [14/Jul/2010:10:32:21 +0200] "GET /Material/Hotline_Russisch.pdf HTTP/1.1" 200
239827 "http://www.asylabwehramt.at/Seiten/Material.html" "Mozilla/5.0 (Windows; U; Windows NT 5.
1; de; rv:1.9.1.2) Gecko/20090729 Firefox/3.5.2"
85.158.227.72 - - [14/Jul/2010:10:32:35 +0200] "GET /Material/Hotline_Deutsch.pdf HTTP/1.1" 206 4
```

19284 "http://www.asylabwehramt.at/Seiten/Material.html" "Mozilla/5.0 (Windows; U; Windows NT 5.1; de; rv:1.9.1.2) Gecko/20090729 Firefox/3.5.2"
85.158.227.72 - - [14/Jul/2010:10:32:50 +0200] "GET /Seiten/Images.html HTTP/1.1" 200 10215 "http://www.asylabwehramt.at/Seiten/Material.html" "Mozilla/5.0 (Windows; U; Windows NT 5.1; de; rv:1.9.1.2) Gecko/20090729 Firefox/3.5.2"
85.158.227.72 - - [14/Jul/2010:10:32:51 +0200] "GET /Bilder/SCREEN_AAbA_Edutainment_Video.jpg HTTP/1.1" 200 29259 "http://www.asylabwehramt.at/Seiten/Images.html" "Mozilla/5.0 (Windows; U; Windows NT 5.1; de; rv:1.9.1.2) Gecko/20090729 Firefox/3.5.2"
85.158.227.72 - - [14/Jul/2010:10:33:04 +0200] "GET /Seiten/Links_e.html HTTP/1.1" 200 18884 "http://www.asylabwehramt.at/Seiten/Images.html" "Mozilla/5.0 (Windows; U; Windows NT 5.1; de; rv:1.9.1.2) Gecko/20090729 Firefox/3.5.2"
85.158.227.72 - - [14/Jul/2010:10:33:05 +0200] "GET /Bilder/dasweissehauslogo.png HTTP/1.1" 200 19920 "http://www.asylabwehramt.at/Seiten/Links_e.html" "Mozilla/5.0 (Windows; U; Windows NT 5.1; de; rv:1.9.1.2) Gecko/20090729 Firefox/3.5.2"
85.158.227.72 - - [14/Jul/2010:10:33:07 +0200] "GET /Bilder/IBM.png HTTP/1.1" 200 8413 "http://www.asylabwehramt.at/Seiten/Links_e.html" "Mozilla/5.0 (Windows; U; Windows NT 5.1; de; rv:1.9.1.2) Gecko/20090729 Firefox/3.5.2"
85.158.227.72 - - [14/Jul/2010:10:33:14 +0200] "GET /Bilder/frontex.png HTTP/1.1" 200 22383 "http://www.asylabwehramt.at/Seiten/Links_e.html" "Mozilla/5.0 (Windows; U; Windows NT 5.1; de; rv:1.9.1.2) Gecko/20090729 Firefox/3.5.2"
85.158.227.72 - - [14/Jul/2010:10:34:09 +0200] "GET /Seiten/Presse.html HTTP/1.1" 200 12135 "http://www.asylabwehramt.at/Seiten/Links_e.html" "Mozilla/5.0 (Windows; U; Windows NT 5.1; de; rv:1.9.1.2) Gecko/20090729 Firefox/3.5.2"
85.158.227.72 - - [14/Jul/2010:10:39:58 +0200] "GET /Material/Hotline_Deutsch.pdf HTTP/1.1" 206 414638 "-" "Mozilla/5.0 (Windows; U; Windows NT 5.1; de; rv:1.9.1.2) Gecko/20090729 Firefox/3.5.2"
85.158.227.72 - - [14/Jul/2010:10:40:00 +0200] "GET /Material/Hotline_Deutsch.pdf HTTP/1.1" 206 473303 "-" "Mozilla/5.0 (Windows; U; Windows NT 5.1; de; rv:1.9.1.2) Gecko/20090729 Firefox/3.5.2"

217.13.180.202 [29] - - [14/Jul/2010:12:07:33 +0200] "GET /OEFFENTLICHKEIT/media/ZEIT.pdf HTTP/1.1" 20
0 484489 "http://www.google.at/url?sa=t&source=web&cd=2&ved=0CBgQFjAB&url=http%3A%2F%2Fasylabwehr
amt.at%2FOEFFENTLICHKEIT%2Fmedia%2FZEIT.pdf&rct=j&q= asyl%20abwehramt &ei=Xow9TMTKGpO1OPjn3PEO&usg=
AFQjCNGV1D_w7_ftdD3VaxechL6E_oPsnQ" "Mozilla/4.0 (compatible; MSIE 8.0; Windows NT 5.2; Trident/4
.0; .NET CLR 1.1.4322; .NET CLR 2.0.50727; .NET CLR 3.0.4506.2152; .NET CLR 3.5.30729)"

217.13.180.202 - - [14/Jul/2010:12:09:10 +0200] "GET /OEFFENTLICHKEIT/media/ZEIT.pdf HTTP/1.1" 30
4 - "http://www.google.at/url?sa=t&source=web&cd=2&ved=0CBgQFjAB&url=http%3A%2F%2Fasylabwehramt.a
t%2FOEFFENTLICHKEIT%2Fmedia%2FZEIT.pdf&rct=j&q= asyl%20abwehramt &ei=Xow9TMTKGpO1OPjn3PEO&usg=AFQjC
NGV1D_w7_ftdD3VaxechL6E_oPsnQ" "Mozilla/4.0 (compatible; MSIE 8.0; Windows NT 5.2; Trident/4.0; .
NET CLR 1.1.4322; .NET CLR 2.0.50727; .NET CLR 3.0.4506.2152; .NET CLR 3.5.30729)"

217.13.180.202 - - [14/Jul/2010:12:10:40 +0200] "GET / HTTP/1.1" 200 11992 "http://www.google.at/
url?sa=t&source=web&cd=1&ved=0CBUQFjAA&url=http%3A%2F%2Fwww.asylabwehramt.at%2F&rct=j&q= asyl%20ab
wehramt &ei=Xow9TMTKGpO1OPjn3PEO&usg=AFQjCNEy1zWClvnxkl1PAGifRc344_OU4Q" "Mozilla/4.0 (compatible;
MSIE 8.0; Windows NT 5.2; Trident/4.0; .NET CLR 1.1.4322; .NET CLR 2.0.50727; .NET CLR 3.0.4506.
2152; .NET CLR 3.5.30729)"

217.13.180.202 - - [14/Jul/2010:12:10:42 +0200] "GET /Seiten/Rundzeichen.html HTTP/1.1" 200 8895
"http://www.asylabwehramt.at/" "Mozilla/4.0 (compatible; MSIE 8.0; Windows NT 5.2; Trident/4.0; .
NET CLR 1.1.4322; .NET CLR 2.0.50727; .NET CLR 3.0.4506.2152; .NET CLR 3.5.30729)"

217.13.180.202 - - [14/Jul/2010:12:10:47 +0200] "GET /Seiten/Orgstrukt.html HTTP/1.1" 200 14119 "
http://www.asylabwehramt.at/Seiten/Rundzeichen.html" "Mozilla/4.0 (compatible; MSIE 8.0; Windows
NT 5.2; Trident/4.0; .NET CLR 1.1.4322; .NET CLR 2.0.50727; .NET CLR 3.0.4506.2152; .NET CLR 3.5.
30729)"

217.13.180.202 - - [14/Jul/2010:12:11:05 +0200] "GET /asyl.css HTTP/1.1" 304 - "-" "Mozilla/4.0 (
compatible; MSIE 8.0; Windows NT 5.2; Trident/4.0; .NET CLR 1.1.4322; .NET CLR 2.0.50727; .NET CL
R 3.0.4506.2152; .NET CLR 3.5.30729)"

217.13.180.202 - - [14/Jul/2010:12:11:27 +0200] "GET /Bilder/Header_AAbA_anim.gif HTTP/1.1" 304 -

[29]WHOIS record on page 322

```
"-" "Mozilla/4.0 (compatible; MSIE 8.0; Windows NT 5.2; Trident/4.0; .NET CLR 1.1.4322; .NET CLR
2.0.50727; .NET CLR 3.0.4506.2152; .NET CLR 3.5.30729)"
62.154.194.53 - - [15/Jul/2010:07:32:28 +0200] "GET / HTTP/1.1" 200 11992 "-" "Mozilla/4.0 (compa
tible; MSIE 5.5; Windows NT 5.0)"
80.120.179.10 - - [15/Jul/2010:09:28:15 +0200] "GET / HTTP/1.1" 200 11992 "http://www.google.at/s
earch?hl=de&q=asyl%20abwehramt &num=1&ie=UTF-8&sa=N&tab=iw" "Mozilla/4.0 (compatible; MSIE 8.0; Win
dows NT 5.1; Trident/4.0; .NET CLR 1.1.4322; .NET CLR 2.0.50727; .NET CLR 3.0.04506.30; .NET CLR
3.0.04506.648; InfoPath.2)"
80.120.179.10 - - [15/Jul/2010:09:28:55 +0200] "GET /Seiten/Aktuelles.html HTTP/1.1" 200 13367 "h
ttp://www.asylabwehramt.at/" "Mozilla/4.0 (compatible; MSIE 8.0; Windows NT 5.1; Trident/4.0; .NE
T CLR 1.1.4322; .NET CLR 2.0.50727; .NET CLR 3.0.04506.30; .NET CLR 3.0.04506.648; InfoPath.2)"
80.120.179.10 - - [15/Jul/2010:09:29:04 +0200] "GET /Seiten/Material.html HTTP/1.1" 200 17073 "ht
tp://www.asylabwehramt.at/Seiten/Aktuelles.html" "Mozilla/4.0 (compatible; MSIE 8.0; Windows NT 5
.1; Trident/4.0; .NET CLR 1.1.4322; .NET CLR 2.0.50727; .NET CLR 3.0.04506.30; .NET CLR 3.0.04506
.648; InfoPath.2)"
80.120.179.10 - - [15/Jul/2010:09:29:11 +0200] "GET /Bilder/flyer_nigeria_Internet.pdf HTTP/1.1"
200 702826 "http://www.asylabwehramt.at/Seiten/Material.html" "Mozilla/4.0 (compatible; MSIE 8.0;
Windows NT 5.1; Trident/4.0; .NET CLR 1.1.4322; .NET CLR 2.0.50727; .NET CLR 3.0.04506.30; .NET
CLR 3.0.04506.648; InfoPath.2)"
213.208.144.130 - - [15/Jul/2010:10:02:42 +0200] "GET / HTTP/1.0" 200 11992 "-" "Mozilla/4.0 (com
patible; MSIE 7.0; Windows NT 5.2; InfoPath.1; .NET CLR 1.1.4322; .NET CLR 2.0.50727; .NET CLR 3.
0.4506.2152; .NET CLR 3.5.30729)"
213.208.144.130 - - [15/Jul/2010:10:09:35 +0200] "GET /Material/Hotline_Deutsch.pdf HTTP/1.0" 200
489465 "http://www.asylabwehramt.at/" "Mozilla/4.0 (compatible; MSIE 7.0; Windows NT 5.2; .NET C
LR 1.1.4322; InfoPath.1; .NET CLR 2.0.50727; .NET CLR 3.0.4506.2152; .NET CLR 3.5.30729)"
213.208.144.130 - - [15/Jul/2010:10:10:14 +0200] "GET / HTTP/1.0" 304 - "-" "Mozilla/4.0 (compati
ble; MSIE 7.0; Windows NT 5.2; .NET CLR 1.1.4322; InfoPath.1; .NET CLR 2.0.50727; .NET CLR 3.0.45
06.2152; .NET CLR 3.5.30729)"
```

183

```
213.208.144.130 - - [15/Jul/2010:10:10:19 +0200] "GET /Seiten/Aktuelles.html HTTP/1.0" 200 13367 "http://www.asylabwehramt.at/" "Mozilla/4.0 (compatible; MSIE 7.0; Windows NT 5.2; .NET CLR 3.5.30729)" 322; InfoPath.1; .NET CLR 2.0.50727; .NET CLR 3.0.4506.2152; .NET CLR 1.1.4
213.208.144.130 - - [15/Jul/2010:10:10:20 +0200] "GET /Bilder/leistung_2.jpg HTTP/1.0" 200 4918 "http://www.asylabwehramt.at/Seiten/Aktuelles.html" "Mozilla/4.0 (compatible; MSIE 7.0; Windows NT 5.2; .NET CLR 1.1.4322; InfoPath.1; .NET CLR 2.0.50727; .NET CLR 3.0.4506.2152; .NET CLR 3.5.307 29)"
213.208.144.130 - - [15/Jul/2010:10:10:30 +0200] "GET /Seiten/Material.html HTTP/1.0" 200 17073 "http://www.asylabwehramt.at/Seiten/Aktuelles.html" "Mozilla/4.0 (compatible; MSIE 7.0; Windows NT 5.2; .NET CLR 1.1.4322; InfoPath.1; .NET CLR 2.0.50727; .NET CLR 3.0.4506.2152; .NET CLR 3.5.307 29)"
213.208.144.130 - - [15/Jul/2010:10:42:45 +0200] "GET / HTTP/1.0" 200 11992 "-" "Mozilla/4.0 (com patible; MSIE 7.0; Windows NT 5.2; .NET CLR 1.1.4322; InfoPath.1; .NET CLR 2.0.50727)"
213.208.144.130 - - [15/Jul/2010:10:44:52 +0200] "GET /Seiten/Bilder.html HTTP/1.0" 200 10043 "ht tp://www.asylabwehramt.at/" "Mozilla/4.0 (compatible; MSIE 7.0; Windows NT 5.2; .NET CLR 1.1.4322 ; InfoPath.1; .NET CLR 2.0.50727)"
213.208.144.130 - - [15/Jul/2010:10:44:54 +0200] "GET /Bilder/Ausstellung_weisses_haus_wien_esel_ fotos/eSeL_UBERMORGEN_asylabwehramt_dasweissehaus_453_thumb.jpg HTTP/1.0" 200 47504 "http://www.a sylabwehramt.at/Seiten/Bilder.html" "Mozilla/4.0 (compatible; MSIE 7.0; Windows NT 5.2; .NET CLR 1.1.4322; InfoPath.1; .NET CLR 2.0.50727)"
213.208.144.130 - - [15/Jul/2010:10:45:08 +0200] "GET /index.html HTTP/1.0" 200 11992 "http://www .asylabwehramt.at/Seiten/Bilder.html" "Mozilla/4.0 (compatible; MSIE 7.0; Windows NT 5.2; .NET CL R 1.1.4322; InfoPath.1; .NET CLR 2.0.50727)"
213.208.144.130 - - [15/Jul/2010:11:00:02 +0200] "GET /Seiten/Press.html HTTP/1.0" 200 12186 "htt p://www.asylabwehramt.at/Seiten/Aktuelles.html" "Mozilla/4.0 (compatible; MSIE 7.0; Windows NT 5. 2; .NET CLR 1.1.4322; InfoPath.1; .NET CLR 2.0.50727)"
```

`194.232.11.80`[30] - - [15/Jul/2010:13:32:34 +0200] "GET / HTTP/1.1" 200 11992 "-" "Mozilla/4.0 (compatible; MSIE 7.0; Windows NT 5.1; .NET CLR 1.1.4322; InfoPath.1; .NET CLR 2.0.50727; .NET CLR 3.0.04506.30; .NET CLR 3.0.4506.2152; .NET CLR 3.5.30729; MOSER HOLDING Aktiengesellschaft; MOSER HOLDING Aktiengesellschaft)"

194.232.11.80 - - [15/Jul/2010:13:32:57 +0200] "GET /Seiten/Impressum.html HTTP/1.1" 200 11684 "http://www.asylabwehramt.at/" "Mozilla/4.0 (compatible; MSIE 7.0; Windows NT 5.1; .NET CLR 1.1.4322; InfoPath.1; .NET CLR 2.0.50727; .NET CLR 3.0.04506.30; .NET CLR 3.0.4506.2152; .NET CLR 3.5.30729; MOSER HOLDING Aktiengesellschaft; MOSER HOLDING Aktiengesellschaft)"

194.232.11.80 - - [15/Jul/2010:13:33:51 +0200] "GET /Seiten/Impressum.html HTTP/1.1" 304 - "http://www.asylabwehramt.at/Seiten/Impressum.html" "Mozilla/4.0 (compatible; MSIE 7.0; Windows NT 5.1; .NET CLR 1.1.4322; InfoPath.1; .NET CLR 2.0.50727; .NET CLR 3.0.04506.30; .NET CLR 3.0.4506.2152; .NET CLR 3.5.30729; MOSER HOLDING Aktiengesellschaft; MOSER HOLDING Aktiengesellschaft)"

194.232.11.80 - - [15/Jul/2010:13:33:56 +0200] "GET /index.html HTTP/1.1" 200 11992 "http://www.asylabwehramt.at/Seiten/Impressum.html" "Mozilla/4.0 (compatible; MSIE 7.0; Windows NT 5.1; .NET CLR 1.1.4322; InfoPath.1; .NET CLR 2.0.50727; .NET CLR 3.0.04506.30; .NET CLR 3.0.4506.2152; .NET CLR 3.5.30729; MOSER HOLDING Aktiengesellschaft; MOSER HOLDING Aktiengesellschaft)"

194.232.11.80 - - [15/Jul/2010:13:34:24 +0200] "GET /Seiten/Aktuelles.html HTTP/1.1" 200 13367 "http://www.asylabwehramt.at/index.html" "Mozilla/4.0 (compatible; MSIE 7.0; Windows NT 5.1; .NET CLR 1.1.4322; InfoPath.1; .NET CLR 2.0.50727; .NET CLR 3.0.04506.30; .NET CLR 3.0.4506.2152; .NET CLR 3.5.30729; MOSER HOLDING Aktiengesellschaft; MOSER HOLDING Aktiengesellschaft)"

194.232.11.80 - - [15/Jul/2010:13:36:19 +0200] "GET /Seiten/Bilder_Ausstellung.html HTTP/1.1" 200 16685 "http://www.asylabwehramt.at/Seiten/Aktuelles.html" "Mozilla/4.0 (compatible; MSIE 7.0; Windows NT 5.1; .NET CLR 1.1.4322; InfoPath.1; .NET CLR 2.0.50727; .NET CLR 3.0.04506.30; .NET CLR 3.5.30729; MOSER HOLDING Aktiengesellschaft; MOSER HOLDING Aktiengesellschaft)"

194.232.11.80 - - [15/Jul/2010:13:36:20 +0200] "GET /Bilder/Ausstellung_weisses_haus_wien_esel_fo

---

[30]WHOIS record on page 310

```
tos/eSeL_UBERMORGEN_asylabwehramt_dasweissehaus_456_thumb.jpg HTTP/1.1" 200 28685 "http://www.asylabwehramt.at/Seiten/Bilder_Ausstellung.html" "Mozilla/4.0 (compatible; MSIE 7.0; Windows NT 5.1; .NET CLR 2.0.50727; .NET CLR 3.0.04506.30; .NET CLR 3.0.4506.2152; .NET CLR 3.5.30729; MOSER HOLDING Aktiengesellschaft)"
194.232.11.80 - - [15/Jul/2010:13:36:21 +0200] "GET /Bilder/Ausstellung_weisses_haus_wien_esel_fotos/eSeL_UBERMORGEN_asylabwehramt_dasweissehaus_478_thumb.jpg HTTP/1.1" 200 54914 "http://www.asylabwehramt.at/Seiten/Bilder_Ausstellung.html" "Mozilla/4.0 (compatible; MSIE 7.0; Windows NT 5.1; .NET CLR 2.0.50727; .NET CLR 3.0.04506.30; .NET CLR 3.0.4506.2152; .NET CLR 3.5.30729; MOSER HOLDING Aktiengesellschaft)"
194.232.11.80 - - [15/Jul/2010:13:36:22 +0200] "GET /Bilder/Ausstellung_weisses_haus_wien_esel_fotos/eSeL_UBERMORGEN_asylabwehramt_dasweissehaus_520_thumb.jpg HTTP/1.1" 200 77245 "http://www.asylabwehramt.at/Seiten/Bilder_Ausstellung.html" "Mozilla/4.0 (compatible; MSIE 7.0; Windows NT 5.1; .NET CLR 2.0.50727; .NET CLR 3.0.04506.30; .NET CLR 3.0.4506.2152; .NET CLR 3.5.30729; MOSER HOLDING Aktiengesellschaft)"
194.232.11.80 - - [15/Jul/2010:13:37:03 +0200] "GET /Bilder/Ausstellung_weisses_haus_wien_esel_fotos/eSeL_UBERMORGEN_asylabwehramt_dasweissehaus_468.jpg HTTP/1.1" 200 331348 "http://www.asylabwehramt.at/Seiten/Bilder_Ausstellung.html" "Mozilla/4.0 (compatible; MSIE 7.0; Windows NT 5.1; .NET CLR 2.0.50727; .NET CLR 3.0.04506.30; .NET CLR 3.0.4506.2152; .NET CLR 3.5.30729; MOSER HOLDING Aktiengesellschaft)"
194.232.11.80 - - [15/Jul/2010:13:37:49 +0200] "GET /Seiten/Aktuelles.html HTTP/1.1" 304 - "http://www.asylabwehramt.at/Seiten/Bilder_Ausstellung.html" "Mozilla/4.0 (compatible; MSIE 7.0; Windows NT 5.1; .NET CLR 2.0.50727; .NET CLR 3.0.04506.30; .NET CLR 3.0.4506.2152; .NET CLR 3.5.30729; MOSER HOLDING Aktiengesellschaft)"
194.232.11.80 - - [15/Jul/2010:13:37:50 +0200] "GET /Seiten/Material.html HTTP/1.1" 200 17073 "http://www.asylabwehramt.at/Seiten/Aktuelles.html" "Mozilla/4.0 (compatible; MSIE 7.0; Windows NT 5.1; .NET CLR 2.0.50727; .NET CLR 3.0.04506.30; .NET CLR 3.0.4506.2152; .NET CLR 3.5.30729; MOSER HOLDING Aktiengesellschaft)"
```

80.120.179.10 - - [16/Jul/2010:09:09:13 +0200] "GET /Bilder/Header_AAbA_anim.gif HTTP/1.1" 200 19
997 "http://www.asylabwehramt.at/" "Mozilla/4.0 (compatible; MSIE 6.0; Windows NT 5.1; SV1; .NET
CLR 1.1.4322; .NET CLR 2.0.50727; .NET CLR 3.0.04506.30; .NET CLR 3.0.04506.648; InfoPath.2)"
mail.rechtens.at - - [16/Jul/2010:10:26:01 +0200] "GET / HTTP/1.1" 200 11992 "http://www.g
oogle.at/url?sa=t&source=web&cd=1&ved=0CBoQFjAA&url=http%3A%2F%2Fwww.asylabwehramt.at%2F&rct=j&q=
Asylabwehramt&ei=jRdATOXJNIWCOKrrhOcM&usg=AFQjCNEy1zWC1vnxkl1PAGifRc344_OU4Q" "Mozilla/5.0 (Windo
ws; U; Windows NT 5.1; de; rv:1.9.1.10) Gecko/20100504 Firefox/3.5.10 GTB7.1 (.NET CLR 3.5.30729)
"
mail.rechtens.at - - [16/Jul/2010:10:26:02 +0200] "GET /asyl.css HTTP/1.1" 200 860 "http:/
/www.asylabwehramt.at/" "Mozilla/5.0 (Windows; U; Windows NT 5.1; de; rv:1.9.1.10) Gecko/20100504
Firefox/3.5.10 GTB7.1 (.NET CLR 3.5.30729)"
mail.rechtens.at - - [16/Jul/2010:10:26:05 +0200] "GET /favicon.ico HTTP/1.1" 302 340 "-"
"Mozilla/5.0 (Windows; U; Windows NT 5.1; de; rv:1.9.1.10) Gecko/20100504 Firefox/3.5.10 GTB7.1 (
.NET CLR 3.5.30729)"
mail.rechtens.at - - [16/Jul/2010:10:27:44 +0200] "GET /Seiten/Bilder.html HTTP/1.1" 200 1
0043 "http://www.asylabwehramt.at/" "Mozilla/5.0 (Windows; U; Windows NT 5.1; de; rv:1.9.1.10) Ge
cko/20100504 Firefox/3.5.10 GTB7.1 (.NET CLR 3.5.30729)"
mail.rechtens.at - - [16/Jul/2010:10:27:45 +0200] "GET /Bilder/SCREEN_AAbA_Edutainment_Vid
eo.jpg HTTP/1.1" 200 29259 "http://www.asylabwehramt.at/Seiten/Bilder.html" "Mozilla/5.0 (Windows
; U; Windows NT 5.1; de; rv:1.9.1.10) Gecko/20100504 Firefox/3.5.10 GTB7.1 (.NET CLR 3.5.30729)"
217.13.180.202 - - [16/Jul/2010:14:06:38 +0200] "GET / HTTP/1.1" 200 11992 "http://www.google.at/
url?sa=t&source=web&cd=1&ved=0CBoQFjAA&url=http%3A%2F%2Fwww.asylabwehramt.at%2F&rct=j&q=asylabweh
ramt&ei=S0tATMOPLKOeONntwfAM&usg=AFQjCNEy1zWC1vnxkl1PAGifRc344_OU4Q" "Mozilla/4.0 (compatible; MS
IE 8.0; Windows NT 5.2; Trident/4.0; .NET CLR 1.1.4322; .NET CLR 2.0.50727; .NET CLR 3.0.4506.215
2; .NET CLR 3.5.30729)"
194.232.11.100[31] - - [16/Jul/2010:14:34:55 +0200] "GET /Seiten/Press.html HTTP/1.1" 200 12186 "http

---

://www.google.at/url?sa=t&source=web&cd=3&ved=0CBsQFjAC&url=http%3A%2F%2Fwww.asylabwehramt.at%2FS
eiten%2FPress.html&rct=j&q=zeit%20asylabwehramt&ei=blFATL6xGNOWOODeuNgM&usg=AFQjCNFfilLFGAepZdJ4k
almufF0f7qhjg" "Mozilla/4.0 (compatible; MSIE 8.0; Windows NT 5.1; Trident/4.0; .NET CLR 1.1.4322
; InfoPath.1; .NET CLR 2.0.50727; .NET CLR 3.0.4506.2152; .NET CLR 3.5.30729; MOSER HOLDING Aktie
ngesellschaft)"

194.232.11.100 - - [16/Jul/2010:14:34:56 +0200] "GET /favicon.ico HTTP/1.1" 302 340 "-" "Mozilla/
4.0 (compatible; MSIE 8.0; Windows NT 5.1; Trident/4.0; .NET CLR 1.1.4322; InfoPath.1; .NET CLR 2
.0.50727; .NET CLR 3.0.4506.2152; .NET CLR 3.5.30729; MOSER HOLDING Aktiengesellschaft)"

194.232.11.100 - - [16/Jul/2010:14:35:19 +0200] "GET /asyl.css HTTP/1.1" 304 - "-" "Mozilla/4.0 (
compatible; MSIE 8.0; Windows NT 5.1; Trident/4.0; .NET CLR 1.1.4322; InfoPath.1; .NET CLR 2.0.50
727; .NET CLR 3.0.4506.2152; .NET CLR 3.5.30729; MOSER HOLDING Aktiengesellschaft)"

194.232.11.100 - - [16/Jul/2010:14:35:29 +0200] "GET /asyl.css HTTP/1.1" 304 - "-" "Mozilla/4.0 (
compatible; MSIE 8.0; Windows NT 5.1; Trident/4.0; .NET CLR 1.1.4322; InfoPath.1; .NET CLR 2.0.50
727; .NET CLR 3.0.4506.2152; .NET CLR 3.5.30729; MOSER HOLDING Aktiengesellschaft)"

194.232.11.100 - - [16/Jul/2010:14:35:31 +0200] "GET /asyl.css HTTP/1.1" 304 - "-" "Mozilla/4.0 (
compatible; MSIE 8.0; Windows NT 5.1; Trident/4.0; .NET CLR 1.1.4322; InfoPath.1; .NET CLR 2.0.50
727; .NET CLR 3.0.4506.2152; .NET CLR 3.5.30729; MOSER HOLDING Aktiengesellschaft)"

194.232.11.100 - - [16/Jul/2010:14:35:32 +0200] "GET /Seiten/Aktuelles.html HTTP/1.1" 200 13367 "
http://www.asylabwehramt.at/Seiten/Press.html" "Mozilla/4.0 (compatible; MSIE 8.0; Windows NT 5.1
; Trident/4.0; .NET CLR 1.1.4322; InfoPath.1; .NET CLR 2.0.50727; .NET CLR 3.0.4506.2152; .NET CL
R 3.5.30729; MOSER HOLDING Aktiengesellschaft)"

194.232.11.100 - - [16/Jul/2010:14:35:33 +0200] "GET /asyl.css HTTP/1.1" 304 - "http://www.asylab
wehramt.at/Seiten/Aktuelles.html" "Mozilla/4.0 (compatible; MSIE 8.0; Windows NT 5.1; Trident/4.0
; .NET CLR 1.1.4322; InfoPath.1; .NET CLR 2.0.50727; .NET CLR 3.0.4506.2152; .NET CLR 3.5.30729;
MOSER HOLDING Aktiengesellschaft)"

194.232.11.100 - - [16/Jul/2010:14:35:56 +0200] "GET /Seiten/Bilder.html HTTP/1.1" 200 10043 "htt
p://www.asylabwehramt.at/Seiten/Aktuelles.html" "Mozilla/4.0 (compatible; MSIE 8.0; Windows NT 5.
1; Trident/4.0; .NET CLR 1.1.4322; InfoPath.1; .NET CLR 2.0.50727; .NET CLR 3.0.4506.2152; .NET C

LR 3.5.30729; MOSER HOLDING Aktiengesellschaft)"

194.232.11.100 - - [16/Jul/2010:14:36:04 +0200] "GET /Seiten/Press.html HTTP/1.1" 304 - "http://www.asylabwehramt.at/Seiten/Bilder.html" "Mozilla/4.0 (compatible; MSIE 8.0; Windows NT 5.1; Trident/4.0; .NET CLR 1.1.4322; InfoPath.1; .NET CLR 3.0.4506.2152; .NET CLR 3.5.30729; MOSER HOLDING Aktiengesellschaft)"

194.232.11.100 - - [16/Jul/2010:14:36:21 +0200] "GET /Seiten/Rundzeichen.html HTTP/1.1" 200 8895 "http://www.asylabwehramt.at/Seiten/Press.html" "Mozilla/4.0 (compatible; MSIE 8.0; Windows NT 5.1; Trident/4.0; .NET CLR 1.1.4322; InfoPath.1; .NET CLR 2.0.50727; .NET CLR 3.0.4506.2152; .NET CLR 3.5.30729; MOSER HOLDING Aktiengesellschaft)"

194.232.11.100 - - [16/Jul/2010:14:36:24 +0200] "GET /Seiten/Material.html HTTP/1.1" 200 17073 "http://www.asylabwehramt.at/Seiten/Rundzeichen.html" "Mozilla/4.0 (compatible; MSIE 8.0; Windows NT 5.1; Trident/4.0; .NET CLR 1.1.4322; InfoPath.1; .NET CLR 2.0.50727; .NET CLR 3.0.4506.2152; .NET CLR 3.5.30729; MOSER HOLDING Aktiengesellschaft)"

194.232.11.100 - - [16/Jul/2010:14:36:41 +0200] "GET /Seiten/Aktuelles.html HTTP/1.1" 304 - "http://www.asylabwehramt.at/Seiten/Material.html" "Mozilla/4.0 (compatible; MSIE 8.0; Windows NT 5.1; Trident/4.0; .NET CLR 1.1.4322; InfoPath.1; .NET CLR 2.0.50727; .NET CLR 3.0.4506.2152; .NET CLR 3.5.30729; MOSER HOLDING Aktiengesellschaft)"

194.232.11.100 - - [16/Jul/2010:14:36:43 +0200] "GET /index.html HTTP/1.1" 200 11992 "http://www.asylabwehramt.at/Seiten/Aktuelles.html" "Mozilla/4.0 (compatible; MSIE 8.0; Windows NT 5.1; Trident/4.0; .NET CLR 1.1.4322; InfoPath.1; .NET CLR 2.0.50727; .NET CLR 3.0.4506.2152; .NET CLR 3.5.30729; MOSER HOLDING Aktiengesellschaft)"

194.232.11.100 - - [16/Jul/2010:14:37:04 +0200] "GET /Seiten/Links.html HTTP/1.1" 200 18864 "http://www.asylabwehramt.at/index.html" "Mozilla/4.0 (compatible; MSIE 8.0; Windows NT 5.1; Trident/4.0; .NET CLR 1.1.4322; InfoPath.1; .NET CLR 2.0.50727; .NET CLR 3.0.4506.2152; .NET CLR 3.5.30729; MOSER HOLDING Aktiengesellschaft)"

194.232.11.100 - - [16/Jul/2010:14:37:19 +0200] "GET /index.html HTTP/1.1" 304 - "http://www.asylabwehramt.at/Seiten/Links.html" "Mozilla/4.0 (compatible; MSIE 8.0; Windows NT 5.1; Trident/4.0; .NET CLR 1.1.4322; .NET CLR 3.0.4506.2152; .NET CLR 3.5.30729; MO

```
SER HOLDING Aktiengesellschaft)"
194.232.11.100 - - [16/Jul/2010:14:37:23 +0200] "GET /Seiten/Aktuelles.html HTTP/1.1" 304 - "http
://www.asylabwehramt.at/index.html" "Mozilla/4.0 (compatible; MSIE 8.0; Windows NT 5.1; Trident/4
.0; .NET CLR 1.1.4322; InfoPath.1; .NET CLR 2.0.50727; .NET CLR 3.0.4506.2152; .NET CLR 3.5.30729
; MOSER HOLDING Aktiengesellschaft)"
194.232.11.100 - - [16/Jul/2010:14:37:24 +0200] "GET /Bilder/STRABAG.jpg HTTP/1.1" 304 - "http://
www.asylabwehramt.at/Seiten/Aktuelles.html" "Mozilla/4.0 (compatible; MSIE 8.0; Windows NT 5.1; T
rident/4.0; .NET CLR 1.1.4322; InfoPath.1; .NET CLR 2.0.50727; .NET CLR 3.0.4506.2152; .NET CLR 3
.5.30729; MOSER HOLDING Aktiengesellschaft)"
194.232.11.100 - - [16/Jul/2010:14:37:41 +0200] "GET /Seiten/Material.html HTTP/1.1" 304 - "http:
//www.asylabwehramt.at/Seiten/Aktuelles.html" "Mozilla/4.0 (compatible; MSIE 8.0; Windows NT 5.1;
Trident/4.0; .NET CLR 1.1.4322; InfoPath.1; .NET CLR 2.0.50727; .NET CLR 3.0.4506.2152; .NET CLR
3.5.30729; MOSER HOLDING Aktiengesellschaft)"
194.232.11.100 - - [16/Jul/2010:14:37:48 +0200] "GET /Bilder/Ladung.png HTTP/1.1" 200 114658 "htt
p://www.asylabwehramt.at/Seiten/Material.html" "Mozilla/4.0 (compatible; MSIE 8.0; Windows NT 5.1
; Trident/4.0; .NET CLR 1.1.4322; InfoPath.1; .NET CLR 2.0.50727; .NET CLR 3.0.4506.2152; .NET CL
R 3.5.30729; MOSER HOLDING Aktiengesellschaft)"
194.232.11.100 - - [16/Jul/2010:14:38:01 +0200] "GET /index.html HTTP/1.1" 304 - "http://www.asyl
abwehramt.at/Seiten/Material.html" "Mozilla/4.0 (compatible; MSIE 8.0; Windows NT 5.1; Trident/4.
0; .NET CLR 1.1.4322; InfoPath.1; .NET CLR 2.0.50727; .NET CLR 3.0.4506.2152; .NET CLR 3.5.30729;
MOSER HOLDING Aktiengesellschaft)"
194.232.11.100 - - [16/Jul/2010:14:38:06 +0200] "GET /Seiten/Aktuelles.html HTTP/1.1" 304 - "http
://www.asylabwehramt.at/index.html" "Mozilla/4.0 (compatible; MSIE 8.0; Windows NT 5.1; Trident/4
.0; .NET CLR 1.1.4322; InfoPath.1; .NET CLR 2.0.50727; .NET CLR 3.0.4506.2152; .NET CLR 3.5.30729
; MOSER HOLDING Aktiengesellschaft)"
194.232.11.100 - - [16/Jul/2010:14:38:10 +0200] "GET /Seiten/Material.html HTTP/1.1" 304 - "http:
//www.asylabwehramt.at/Seiten/Aktuelles.html" "Mozilla/4.0 (compatible; MSIE 8.0; Windows NT 5.1;
Trident/4.0; .NET CLR 1.1.4322; InfoPath.1; .NET CLR 2.0.50727; .NET CLR 3.0.4506.2152; .NET CLR
```

3.5.30729; MOSER HOLDING Aktiengesellschaft)"

194.232.11.100 - - [16/Jul/2010:14:38:12 +0200] "GET /Seiten/Rundzeichen.html HTTP/1.1" 304 - "http://www.asylabwehramt.at/Seiten/Material.html" "Mozilla/4.0 (compatible; MSIE 8.0; Windows NT 5.1; Trident/4.0; .NET CLR 1.1.4322; InfoPath.1; .NET CLR 2.0.50727; .NET CLR 3.0.4506.2152; .NET CLR 3.5.30729; MOSER HOLDING Aktiengesellschaft)"

194.232.11.100 - - [16/Jul/2010:14:38:13 +0200] "GET /Seiten/Bilder.html HTTP/1.1" 304 - "http://www.asylabwehramt.at/Seiten/Rundzeichen.html" "Mozilla/4.0 (compatible; MSIE 8.0; Windows NT 5.1; Trident/4.0; .NET CLR 1.1.4322; InfoPath.1; .NET CLR 2.0.50727; .NET CLR 3.0.4506.2152; .NET CLR 3.5.30729; MOSER HOLDING Aktiengesellschaft)"

194.232.11.100 - - [16/Jul/2010:14:38:14 +0200] "GET /Seiten/Links.html HTTP/1.1" 304 - "http://www.asylabwehramt.at/Seiten/Bilder.html" "Mozilla/4.0 (compatible; MSIE 8.0; Windows NT 5.1; Trident/4.0; .NET CLR 1.1.4322; InfoPath.1; .NET CLR 2.0.50727; .NET CLR 3.0.4506.2152; .NET CLR 3.5.30729; MOSER HOLDING Aktiengesellschaft)"

194.232.11.100 - - [16/Jul/2010:14:38:15 +0200] "GET /Bilder/STRABAG.jpg HTTP/1.1" 304 - "http://www.asylabwehramt.at/Seiten/Links.html" "Mozilla/4.0 (compatible; MSIE 8.0; Windows NT 5.1; Trident/4.0; .NET CLR 1.1.4322; InfoPath.1; .NET CLR 2.0.50727; .NET CLR 3.0.4506.2152; .NET CLR 3.5.30729; MOSER HOLDING Aktiengesellschaft)"

194.232.11.100 - - [16/Jul/2010:14:38:16 +0200] "GET /Seiten/Press.html HTTP/1.1" 304 - "http://www.asylabwehramt.at/Seiten/Links.html" "Mozilla/4.0 (compatible; MSIE 8.0; Windows NT 5.1; Trident/4.0; .NET CLR 1.1.4322; InfoPath.1; .NET CLR 2.0.50727; .NET CLR 3.0.4506.2152; .NET CLR 3.5.30729; MOSER HOLDING Aktiengesellschaft)"

194.232.11.100 - - [16/Jul/2010:14:38:20 +0200] "GET /OEFFENTLICHKEIT/07062010d.pdf HTTP/1.1" 200 333788 "http://www.asylabwehramt.at/Seiten/Press.html" "Mozilla/4.0 (compatible; MSIE 8.0; Windows NT 5.1; Trident/4.0; .NET CLR 1.1.4322; InfoPath.1; .NET CLR 2.0.50727; .NET CLR 3.0.4506.2152; .NET CLR 3.5.30729; MOSER HOLDING Aktiengesellschaft)"

194.232.11.100 - - [16/Jul/2010:14:49:05 +0200] "GET / HTTP/1.1" 200 11992 "http://www.google.at/url?sa=t&source=web&cd=1&ved=0CBoQFjAA&url=http%3A%2F%2Fwww.asylabwehramt.at%2F&rct=j&q=asylabwehramt&ei=P1VATNyAPKOHONapsY4N&usg=AFQjCNEy1zWClvnxkLlPAGifRc344_OU4Q" "Mozilla/4.0 (compatible; MS

```
IE 8.0; Windows NT 5.1; Trident/4.0; .NET CLR 1.1.4322; InfoPath.1; .NET CLR 2.0.50727; .NET CLR 3.0.4506.2152; .NET CLR 3.5.30729; MOSER HOLDING Aktiengesellschaft)"
194.232.11.100 - - [16/Jul/2010:14:49:06 +0200] "GET /favicon.ico HTTP/1.1" 302 340 "-" "Mozilla/4.0 (compatible; MSIE 8.0; Windows NT 5.1; Trident/4.0; .NET CLR 1.1.4322; InfoPath.1; .NET CLR 2.0.50727; .NET CLR 3.0.4506.2152; .NET CLR 3.5.30729; MOSER HOLDING Aktiengesellschaft)"
194.232.11.100 - - [16/Jul/2010:14:49:11 +0200] "GET /Seiten/Presse.html HTTP/1.1" 200 12135 "http://www.asylabwehramt.at/" "Mozilla/4.0 (compatible; MSIE 8.0; Windows NT 5.1; Trident/4.0; .NET CLR 1.1.4322; InfoPath.1; .NET CLR 2.0.50727; .NET CLR 3.0.4506.2152; .NET CLR 3.5.30729; MOSER HOLDING Aktiengesellschaft)"
194.232.11.100 - - [16/Jul/2010:14:50:21 +0200] "GET /Seiten/Bilder.html HTTP/1.1" 200 10043 "http://www.asylabwehramt.at/Seiten/Presse.html" "Mozilla/4.0 (compatible; MSIE 8.0; Windows NT 5.1; Trident/4.0; .NET CLR 1.1.4322; InfoPath.1; .NET CLR 2.0.50727; .NET CLR 3.0.4506.2152; .NET CLR 3.5.30729; MOSER HOLDING Aktiengesellschaft)"
194.232.11.100 - - [16/Jul/2010:14:50:22 +0200] "GET /Bilder/ausseneinsatz.png HTTP/1.1" 200 1240924 "http://www.asylabwehramt.at/Seiten/Bilder.html" "Mozilla/4.0 (compatible; MSIE 8.0; Windows NT 5.1; Trident/4.0; .NET CLR 1.1.4322; InfoPath.1; .NET CLR 2.0.50727; .NET CLR 3.0.4506.2152; .
194.232.11.100 - - [16/Jul/2010:14:50:31 +0200] "GET /Seiten/Bilder_Ausstellung.html HTTP/1.1" 200 16685 "http://www.asylabwehramt.at/Seiten/Bilder.html" "Mozilla/4.0 (compatible; MSIE 8.0; Windows NT 5.1; Trident/4.0; .NET CLR 1.1.4322; InfoPath.1; .NET CLR 2.0.50727; .NET CLR 3.0.4506.215 2; .NET CLR 3.5.30729; MOSER HOLDING Aktiengesellschaft)"
194.232.11.100 - - [16/Jul/2010:14:50:37 +0200] "GET /Bilder/Ausstellung_weisses_haus_wien_esel_fotos/eSeL_UBERMORGEN_asylabwehramt_dasweissehaus_453.jpg HTTP/1.1" 200 298009 "-" "Mozilla/4.0 (compatible; MSIE 8.0; Windows NT 5.1; Trident/4.0; .NET CLR 1.1.4322; InfoPath.1; .NET CLR 2.0.507 27; .NET CLR 3.0.4506.2152; .NET CLR 3.5.30729; MOSER HOLDING Aktiengesellschaft)"
194.232.11.100 - - [16/Jul/2010:14:52:20 +0200] "GET /Bilder/Ausstellung_weisses_haus_wien_esel_fotos/eSeL_UBERMORGEN_asylabwehramt_dasweissehaus_505.jpg HTTP/1.1" 200 455529 "-" "Mozilla/4.0 (compatible; MSIE 8.0; Windows NT 5.1; Trident/4.0; .NET CLR 1.1.4322; InfoPath.1; .NET CLR 2.0.507
```

27; .NET CLR 3.0.4506.2152; .NET CLR 3.5.30729; MOSER HOLDING Aktiengesellschaft)"

194.232.11.100 - - [16/Jul/2010:14:52:35 +0200] "GET /Bilder/Ausstellung_weisses_haus_wien_esel_f
otos/eSeL_UEBERMORGEN_asylabwehramt_dasweissehaus_481.jpg HTTP/1.1" 200 273732 "-" "Mozilla/4.0 (c
ompatible; MSIE 8.0; Windows NT 5.1; Trident/4.0; .NET CLR 1.1.4322; InfoPath.1; .NET CLR 2.0.507
27; .NET CLR 3.0.4506.2152; .NET CLR 3.5.30729; MOSER HOLDING Aktiengesellschaft)"

62.154.194.53 - - [17/Jul/2010:11:11:30 +0200] "GET / HTTP/1.1" 200 11992 "-" "Mozilla/4.0 (compa
tible; MSIE 5.5; Windows NT 5.0)"

62.154.194.53 - - [18/Jul/2010:09:03:40 +0200] "GET / HTTP/1.1" 200 11992 "-" "Mozilla/4.0 (compa
tible; MSIE 5.5; Windows NT 5.0)"

62.154.194.53 - - [19/Jul/2010:06:53:23 +0200] "GET / HTTP/1.1" 200 11992 "-" "Mozilla/4.0 (compa
tible; MSIE 5.5; Windows NT 5.0)"

193.171.152.33 - - [19/Jul/2010:09:36:20 +0200] "GET / HTTP/1.1" 200 11992 "http://www.google.at/
url?sa=t&source=web&cd=1&ved=0CBUQFjAA&url=http%3A%2F%2Fwww.asylabwehramt.at%2F&rct=j&q=asyl%20ab
wehramt&ei=cABETOW1At6kOMrmxIoN&usg=AFQjCNEy1zWClvnxkLlPAGifRc344_0U4Q" "Mozilla/5.0 (Windows; U;
Windows NT 5.1; de; rv:1.9.2.6) Gecko/20100625 Firefox/3.6.6 (.NET CLR 3.5.30729)"

193.171.152.33 - - [19/Jul/2010:09:36:21 +0200] "GET /asyl.css HTTP/1.1" 304 - "http://www.asylab
wehramt.at/" "Mozilla/5.0 (Windows; U; Windows NT 5.1; de; rv:1.9.2.6) Gecko/20100625 Firefox/3.6
.6 (.NET CLR 3.5.30729)"

193.171.152.33 - - [19/Jul/2010:09:37:21 +0200] "GET /Seiten/Impressum.html HTTP/1.1" 200 11684 "
http://www.asylabwehramt.at/" "Mozilla/5.0 (Windows; U; Windows NT 5.1; de; rv:1.9.2.6) Gecko/201
00625 Firefox/3.6.6 (.NET CLR 3.5.30729)"

193.171.152.33 - - [19/Jul/2010:09:37:37 +0200] "GET /Seiten/Aktuelles.html HTTP/1.1" 200 13367 "
http://www.asylabwehramt.at/Seiten/Impressum.html" "Mozilla/5.0 (Windows; U; Windows NT 5.1; de;
rv:1.9.2.6) Gecko/20100625 Firefox/3.6.6 (.NET CLR 3.5.30729)"

193.171.152.33 - - [19/Jul/2010:09:37:53 +0200] "GET /Seiten/Material.html HTTP/1.1" 200 17073 "h
ttp://www.asylabwehramt.at/Seiten/Aktuelles.html" "Mozilla/5.0 (Windows; U; Windows NT 5.1; de; r
v:1.9.2.6) Gecko/20100625 Firefox/3.6.6 (.NET CLR 3.5.30729)"

```
193.171.152.33 - - [19/Jul/2010:09:38:23 +0200] "GET /Seiten/Rundzeichen.html HTTP/1.1" 200 8895
"http://www.asylabwehramt.at/Seiten/Material.html" "Mozilla/5.0 (Windows; U; Windows NT 5.1; de;
rv:1.9.2.6) Gecko/20100625 Firefox/3.6.6 (.NET CLR 3.5.30729)"
193.171.152.33 - - [19/Jul/2010:09:38:29 +0200] "GET /Seiten/Bilder.html HTTP/1.1" 304 - "http://
www.asylabwehramt.at/Seiten/Rundzeichen.html" "Mozilla/5.0 (Windows; U; Windows NT 5.1; de; rv:1.
9.2.6) Gecko/20100625 Firefox/3.6.6 (.NET CLR 3.5.30729)"
193.171.152.33 - - [19/Jul/2010:09:38:50 +0200] "GET /Seiten/Links.html HTTP/1.1" 304 - "http://w
ww.asylabwehramt.at/Seiten/Bilder.html" "Mozilla/5.0 (Windows; U; Windows NT 5.1; de; rv:1.9.2.6)
Gecko/20100625 Firefox/3.6.6 (.NET CLR 3.5.30729)"
193.171.152.33 - - [19/Jul/2010:09:38:51 +0200] "GET /Bilder/BMDI.png HTTP/1.1" 200 8268 "http://
www.asylabwehramt.at/Seiten/Links.html" "Mozilla/5.0 (Windows; U; Windows NT 5.1; de; rv:1.9.2.6)
Gecko/20100625 Firefox/3.6.6 (.NET CLR 3.5.30729)"
193.171.152.33 - - [19/Jul/2010:09:39:12 +0200] "GET /Seiten/Press.html HTTP/1.1" 200 12186 "http
://www.asylabwehramt.at/Seiten/Links.html" "Mozilla/5.0 (Windows; U; Windows NT 5.1; de; rv:1.9.2
.6) Gecko/20100625 Firefox/3.6.6 (.NET CLR 3.5.30729)"
193.171.152.33 - - [19/Jul/2010:09:39:23 +0200] "GET /index.html HTTP/1.1" 200 11992 "http://www.
asylabwehramt.at/Seiten/Press.html" "Mozilla/5.0 (Windows; U; Windows NT 5.1; de; rv:1.9.2.6) Gec
ko/20100625 Firefox/3.6.6 (.NET CLR 3.5.30729)"
188.45.254.94 - - [19/Jul/2010:14:03:59 +0200] "GET / HTTP/1.1" 200 11992 "http://webmail.carita
s-wien.at/mail/kabram.nsf/iNotes/Mail/?OpenDocument&ui=dwa_frame&l=de&gz&CR&MX&TS=20100719T020449
,12Z&charset=ISO-8859-1&charset=ISO-8859-1&ua=gecko" "Mozilla/5.0 (Windows; U; Windows NT 5.1; d
e; rv:1.9.0.19) Gecko/2010031422 Firefox/3.0.19 (.NET CLR 3.5.30729)"
62.154.194.53 - - [20/Jul/2010:06:44:03 +0200] "GET / HTTP/1.1" 200 11992 "-" "Mozilla/4.0 (compa
tible; MSIE 5.5; Windows NT 5.0)"
85.158.226.32 - - [20/Jul/2010:08:54:54 +0200] "GET / HTTP/1.1" 200 11992 "http://www.austroweb.a
t/webTeaser.do?q=Abwehramt&locale=de&c=3" "Mozilla/4.0 (compatible; MSIE 7.0; Windows NT 5.1; .NE
T CLR 1.1.4322; .NET CLR 2.0.50727; .NET CLR 3.0.4506.2152; .NET CLR 3.5.30729)"
```

```
85.158.226.32 - - [20/Jul/2010:08:55:04 +0200] "GET /Seiten/Material.html HTTP/1.1" 200 17073 "ht
tp://asylabwehramt.at/" "Mozilla/4.0 (compatible; MSIE 7.0; Windows NT 5.1; .NET CLR 1.1.4322; .N
ET CLR 2.0.50727; .NET CLR 3.0.4506.2152; .NET CLR 3.5.30729)"

62.154.194.53 - - [21/Jul/2010:06:52:40 +0200] "GET / HTTP/1.1" 200 11992 "-" "Mozilla/4.0 (compa
tible; MSIE 5.5; Windows NT 5.0)"

80.120.179.10 - - [21/Jul/2010:11:01:32 +0200] "GET / HTTP/1.1" 200 11992 "-" "Mozilla/4.0 (compa
tible; MSIE 6.0; Windows NT 5.1; SV1; .NET CLR 1.1.4322)"

80.120.179.10 - - [21/Jul/2010:11:01:39 +0200] "GET /Seiten/Orgstrukt.html HTTP/1.1" 200 14119 "h
ttp://www.asylabwehramt.at" "Mozilla/4.0 (compatible; MSIE 6.0; Windows NT 5.1; SV1; .NET CLR 1.1
.4322)"

80.120.179.10 - - [21/Jul/2010:11:02:07 +0200] "GET /index.html HTTP/1.1" 200 11992 "http://www.a
sylabwehramt.at/Seiten/Orgstrukt.html" "Mozilla/4.0 (compatible; MSIE 6.0; Windows NT 5.1; SV1; .
NET CLR 1.1.4322)"

80.120.179.10 - - [21/Jul/2010:11:02:09 +0200] "GET /Seiten/Aktuelles.html HTTP/1.1" 200 14343 "h
ttp://www.asylabwehramt.at/index.html" "Mozilla/4.0 (compatible; MSIE 6.0; Windows NT 5.1; SV1; .
NET CLR 1.1.4322)"

80.120.179.10 - - [21/Jul/2010:11:02:18 +0200] "GET /Seiten/Material.html HTTP/1.1" 200 17335 "ht
tp://www.asylabwehramt.at/Seiten/Aktuelles.html" "Mozilla/4.0 (compatible; MSIE 6.0; Windows NT 5
.1; SV1; .NET CLR 1.1.4322)"

80.120.179.10 - - [21/Jul/2010:11:02:33 +0200] "GET /Material/Hotline_Deutsch.pdf HTTP/1.1" 200 4
89465 "http://www.asylabwehramt.at/Seiten/Material.html" "Mozilla/4.0 (compatible; MSIE 6.0; Wind
ows NT 5.1; SV1; .NET CLR 1.1.4322)"

80.120.179.10 - - [21/Jul/2010:11:02:44 +0200] "GET /Material/Asyl_Jahresstatistik_2009.pdf HTTP/
1.1" 200 680643 "http://www.asylabwehramt.at/Seiten/Material.html" "Mozilla/4.0 (compatible; MSIE
6.0; Windows NT 5.1; SV1; .NET CLR 1.1.4322)"

80.120.179.10 - - [21/Jul/2010:11:03:39 +0200] "GET /Seiten/Rundzeichen.html HTTP/1.1" 200 8895 "
http://www.asylabwehramt.at/" "Mozilla/4.0 (compatible; MSIE 6.0; Windows NT 5.1; SV1; .NET CLR 1
.1.4322)"
```

```
80.120.179.10 - - [21/Jul/2010:11:06:08 +0200] "GET /Seiten/Bilder.html HTTP/1.1" 200 10043 "http
://www.asylabwehramt.at/Seiten/Rundzeichen.html" "Mozilla/4.0 (compatible; MSIE 6.0; Windows NT 5
.1; SV1; .NET CLR 1.1.4322)"
80.120.179.10 - - [21/Jul/2010:11:06:26 +0200] "GET /Seiten/Links.html HTTP/1.1" 200 19047 "http:
//www.asylabwehramt.at/Seiten/Bilder.html" "Mozilla/4.0 (compatible; MSIE 6.0; Windows NT 5.1; SV
1; .NET CLR 1.1.4322)"
80.120.179.10 - - [21/Jul/2010:11:06:27 +0200] "GET /Bilder/BMI.png HTTP/1.1" 200 55823 "http://w
ww.asylabwehramt.at/Seiten/Links.html" "Mozilla/4.0 (compatible; MSIE 6.0; Windows NT 5.1; SV1; .
NET CLR 1.1.4322)"
80.120.179.10 - - [21/Jul/2010:11:06:57 +0200] "GET /Seiten/Press.html HTTP/1.1" 200 12186 "http:
//www.asylabwehramt.at/Seiten/Links.html" "Mozilla/4.0 (compatible; MSIE 6.0; Windows NT 5.1; SV1
; .NET CLR 1.1.4322)"
80.120.179.10 - - [21/Jul/2010:11:07:05 +0200] "GET /OEFFENTLICHKEIT/07062010d.pdf HTTP/1.1" 200
333788 "http://www.asylabwehramt.at/Seiten/Press.html" "Mozilla/4.0 (compatible; MSIE 6.0; Window
s NT 5.1; SV1; .NET CLR 1.1.4322)"
80.120.179.10 - - [21/Jul/2010:11:12:05 +0200] "GET /Seiten/Links_e.html HTTP/1.1" 200 19073 "htt
p://www.asylabwehramt.at/" "Mozilla/4.0 (compatible; MSIE 6.0; Windows NT 5.1; SV1; InfoPath.1; .
NET CLR 1.1.4322; .NET CLR 2.0.50727)"
80.120.179.10 - - [21/Jul/2010:11:12:43 +0200] "GET /Seiten/Impressum.html HTTP/1.1" 200 11939 "h
ttp://www.asylabwehramt.at/Seiten/Links_e.html" "Mozilla/4.0 (compatible; MSIE 6.0; Windows NT 5.
1; SV1; InfoPath.1; .NET CLR 1.1.4322; .NET CLR 2.0.50727)"
80.120.179.10 - - [21/Jul/2010:11:16:53 +0200] "GET /Seiten/Ausseneinsaetze.html HTTP/1.1" 200 93
81 "http://www.asylabwehramt.at/Seiten/Bilder.html" "Mozilla/4.0 (compatible; MSIE 6.0; Windows N
T 5.1; SV1; InfoPath.1; .NET CLR 1.1.4322; .NET CLR 2.0.50727)"
80.120.179.10 - - [21/Jul/2010:11:23:15 +0200] "GET /index_e.html HTTP/1.1" 200 12025 "http://www
.asylabwehramt.at/" "Mozilla/4.0 (compatible; MSIE 6.0; Windows NT 5.1; SV1; .NET CLR 1.1.4322; .
NET CLR 2.0.50727; .NET CLR 3.0.04506.30; .NET CLR 3.0.04506.648; InfoPath.2)"
80.120.179.10 - - [21/Jul/2010:11:24:15 +0200] "GET /Seiten/Images.html HTTP/1.1" 200 10215 "http
```

://www.asylabwehramt.at/Seiten/Ausseneinsaetze.html" "Mozilla/4.0 (compatible; MSIE 6.0; Windows NT 5.1; SV1; InfoPath.1; .NET CLR 1.1.4322; .NET CLR 2.0.50727)"
80.120.179.10 - - [21/Jul/2010:11:25:06 +0200] "GET /Seiten/Latestnews.html HTTP/1.1" 200 14563 "http://www.asylabwehramt.at/index_e.html" "Mozilla/4.0 (compatible; MSIE 6.0; Windows NT 5.1; SV1 ; .NET CLR 1.1.4322; .NET CLR 2.0.50727; .NET CLR 3.0.04506.30; .NET CLR 3.0.04506.648; InfoPath. 2)"

194.232.11.100 - - [21/Jul/2010:12:00:00 +0200] "GET / HTTP/1.1" 200 11992 "http://www.google.at/ url?sa=t&source=web&cd=1&ved=0CBUQFjAA&url=http%3A%2F%2Fwww.asylabwehramt.at%2F&rct=j&q=asyl%20ab wehramt &ei=HcVGTOKTJMOj4QaurcH7CQ&usg=AFQjCNEy1zWClvnxkLlPAGifRc344_0U4Q" "Mozilla/4.0 (compatibl e; MSIE 8.0; Windows NT 5.1; Trident/4.0; .NET CLR 1.1.4322; InfoPath.1; .NET CLR 2.0.50727; .NET CLR 3.0.4506.2152; .NET CLR 3.5.30729; MOSER HOLDING Aktiengesellschaft)"
194.232.11.100 - - [21/Jul/2010:12:00:04 +0200] "GET /Seiten/Press.html HTTP/1.1" 200 12186 "http ://www.asylabwehramt.at/" "Mozilla/4.0 (compatible; MSIE 8.0; Windows NT 5.1; Trident/4.0; .NET C LR 1.1.4322; InfoPath.1; .NET CLR 2.0.50727; .NET CLR 3.0.4506.2152; .NET CLR 3.5.30729; MOSER HO LDING Aktiengesellschaft)"
194.232.11.100 - - [21/Jul/2010:12:00:05 +0200] "GET /Bilder/Header_AAbA_anim.gif HTTP/1.1" 304 - "http://www.asylabwehramt.at/Seiten/Press.html" "Mozilla/4.0 (compatible; MSIE 8.0; Windows NT 5 .1; Trident/4.0; .NET CLR 1.1.4322; InfoPath.1; .NET CLR 2.0.50727; .NET CLR 3.0.4506.2152; .NET CLR 3.5.30729; MOSER HOLDING Aktiengesellschaft)"
194.232.11.100 - - [21/Jul/2010:12:00:11 +0200] "GET /Seiten/Press.html HTTP/1.1" 304 - "http://w ww.asylabwehramt.at/Seiten/Press.html" "Mozilla/4.0 (compatible; MSIE 8.0; Windows NT 5.1; Triden t/4.0; .NET CLR 1.1.4322; InfoPath.1; .NET CLR 2.0.50727; .NET CLR 3.0.4506.2152; .NET CLR 3.5.30 729; MOSER HOLDING Aktiengesellschaft)"
194.232.11.100 - - [21/Jul/2010:12:00:12 +0200] "GET /asyl.css HTTP/1.1" 304 - "http://www.asylab wehramt.at/Seiten/Press.html" "Mozilla/4.0 (compatible; MSIE 8.0; Windows NT 5.1; Trident/4.0; .N ET CLR 1.1.4322; InfoPath.1; .NET CLR 2.0.50727; .NET CLR 3.0.4506.2152; .NET CLR 3.5.30729; MOSE R HOLDING Aktiengesellschaft)"

```
194.232.11.100 - - [21/Jul/2010:12:00:13 +0200] "GET /Seiten/Bilder.html HTTP/1.1" 200 10043 "htt
p://www.asylabwehramt.at/Seiten/Press.html" "Mozilla/4.0 (compatible; MSIE 8.0; Windows NT 5.1; T
rident/4.0; .NET CLR 1.1.4322; InfoPath.1; .NET CLR 2.0.50727; .NET CLR 3.0.4506.2152; .NET CLR 3
.5.30729; MOSER HOLDING Aktiengesellschaft)"
194.232.11.100 - - [21/Jul/2010:12:00:33 +0200] "GET /Seiten/Bilder.html HTTP/1.1" 304 - "http://
www.asylabwehramt.at/Seiten/Bilder.html" "Mozilla/4.0 (compatible; MSIE 8.0; Windows NT 5.1; Trid
ent/4.0; .NET CLR 1.1.4322; InfoPath.1; .NET CLR 2.0.50727; .NET CLR 3.0.4506.2152; .NET CLR 3.5.
30729; MOSER HOLDING Aktiengesellschaft)"
194.232.11.100 - - [21/Jul/2010:12:00:46 +0200] "GET /Seiten/Bilder_Ausstellung.html HTTP/1.1" 20
0 16685 "http://www.asylabwehramt.at/Seiten/Bilder.html" "Mozilla/4.0 (compatible; MSIE 8.0; Wind
ows NT 5.1; Trident/4.0; .NET CLR 1.1.4322; InfoPath.1; .NET CLR 2.0.50727; .NET CLR 3.0.4506.215
2; .NET CLR 3.5.30729; MOSER HOLDING Aktiengesellschaft)"
80.120.179.10 - - [21/Jul/2010:12:43:34 +0200] "GET /Seiten/Bilder_Ausstellung.html HTTP/1.1" 200
16685 "http://www.asylabwehramt.at/Seiten/Bilder.html" "Mozilla/4.0 (compatible; MSIE 6.0; Windo
ws NT 5.1; SV1; .NET CLR 1.1.4322)"
80.120.179.10 - - [21/Jul/2010:12:43:35 +0200] "GET /Bilder/Ausstellung_weisses_haus_wien_esel_fo
tos/eSeL_UBERMORGEN_asylabwehramt_dasweissehaus_518_thumb.jpg HTTP/1.1" 200 72634 "http://www.asy
labwehramt.at/Seiten/Bilder_Ausstellung.html" "Mozilla/4.0 (compatible; MSIE 6.0; Windows NT 5.1;
SV1; .NET CLR 1.1.4322)"
80.120.179.10 - - [21/Jul/2010:12:43:36 +0200] "GET /Bilder/Ausstellung_weisses_haus_wien_esel_fo
tos/eSeL_UBERMORGEN_asylabwehramt_dasweissehaus_520_thumb.jpg HTTP/1.1" 200 77245 "http://www.asy
labwehramt.at/Seiten/Bilder_Ausstellung.html" "Mozilla/4.0 (compatible; MSIE 6.0; Windows NT 5.1;
SV1; .NET CLR 1.1.4322)"
80.120.179.10 - - [21/Jul/2010:12:43:41 +0200] "GET /Material/Flyer_Volksschutz_Praevention_Aufkl
aerung_FPOE.pdf HTTP/1.1" 200 661529 "http://www.asylabwehramt.at/Seiten/Material.html" "Mozilla/
4.0 (compatible; MSIE 6.0; Windows NT 5.1; SV1; .NET CLR 1.1.4322)"
80.120.179.10 - - [21/Jul/2010:13:38:10 +0200] "GET /Seiten/Links.html HTTP/1.1" 200 19139 "http:
//www.asylabwehramt.at/Seiten/Orgstrukt.html" "Mozilla/4.0 (compatible; MSIE 6.0; Windows NT 5.1;
```

```
SV1; .NET CLR 1.1.4322)"
80.120.179.10 - - [21/Jul/2010:17:52:15 +0200] "GET /asyl.css HTTP/1.1" 200 860 "http://www.asyla
bwehramt.at/" "Mozilla/4.0 (compatible; MSIE 6.0; Windows NT 5.1; SV1; .NET CLR 1.1.4322)"
80.120.179.10 - - [22/Jul/2010:06:48:38 +0200] "GET / HTTP/1.1" 200 11992 "-" "Mozilla/4.0 (compa
tible; MSIE 6.0; Windows NT 5.1; SV1; .NET CLR 1.1.4322; .NET CLR 2.0.50727; .NET CLR 3.0.04506.3
0; .NET CLR 3.0.04506.648; InfoPath.2)"
62.154.194.53 - - [22/Jul/2010:06:53:29 +0200] "GET / HTTP/1.1" 200 11992 "-" "Mozilla/4.0 (compa
tible; MSIE 5.5; Windows NT 5.0)"
213.208.144.130 - - [22/Jul/2010:15:37:22 +0200] "GET / HTTP/1.0" 200 11992 "-" "Mozilla/4.0 (com
patible; MSIE 7.0; Windows NT 5.2; .NET CLR 1.1.4322; InfoPath.1; .NET CLR 2.0.50727; .NET CLR 3.
0.4506.2152; .NET CLR 3.5.30729)"
213.208.144.130 - - [22/Jul/2010:15:37:25 +0200] "GET /Seiten/Aktuelles.html HTTP/1.0" 200 14343
"http://www.asylabwehramt.at/" "Mozilla/4.0 (compatible; MSIE 7.0; Windows NT 5.2; .NET CLR 1.1.4
322; InfoPath.1; .NET CLR 2.0.50727; .NET CLR 3.0.4506.2152; .NET CLR 3.5.30729)"
213.208.144.130 - - [22/Jul/2010:15:37:59 +0200] "GET /Seiten/Bilder.html HTTP/1.0" 200 10043 "ht
tp://www.asylabwehramt.at/Seiten/Aktuelles.html" "Mozilla/4.0 (compatible; MSIE 7.0; Windows NT 5
.2; .NET CLR 1.1.4322; InfoPath.1; .NET CLR 2.0.50727; .NET CLR 3.0.4506.2152; .NET CLR 3.5.30729
)"
213.208.144.130 - - [22/Jul/2010:15:38:03 +0200] "GET /Seiten/Presse.html HTTP/1.0" 200 12320 "ht
tp://www.asylabwehramt.at/Seiten/Bilder.html" "Mozilla/4.0 (compatible; MSIE 7.0; Windows NT 5.2;
.NET CLR 1.1.4322; InfoPath.1; .NET CLR 2.0.50727; .NET CLR 3.0.4506.2152; .NET CLR 3.5.30729)"
62.154.194.53 - - [23/Jul/2010:07:41:39 +0200] "GET / HTTP/1.1" 200 11992 "-" "Mozilla/4.0 (compa
tible; MSIE 5.5; Windows NT 5.0)"
80.120.179.10 - - [23/Jul/2010:09:02:05 +0200] "GET / HTTP/1.1" 200 11992 "-" "Mozilla/4.0 (compa
tible; MSIE 7.0; Windows NT 5.1; SV1; .NET CLR 1.1.4322; .NET CLR 2.0.50727; InfoPath.2)"
80.120.179.10 - - [23/Jul/2010:09:02:13 +0200] "GET /Seiten/Bilder.html HTTP/1.1" 200 10043 "http
://www.asylabwehramt.at/" "Mozilla/4.0 (compatible; MSIE 7.0; Windows NT 5.1; SV1; .NET CLR 1.1.4
322; .NET CLR 2.0.50727; InfoPath.2)"
```

```
80.120.179.10 - - [23/Jul/2010:09:02:56 +0200] "GET /Seiten/Seal.html HTTP/1.1" 200 8933 "http://www.asylabwehramt.at/Seiten/Bilder.html" "Mozilla/4.0 (compatible; MSIE 7.0; Windows NT 5.1; SV1; .NET CLR 1.1.4322; .NET CLR 2.0.50727; InfoPath.2)"
80.120.179.10 - - [23/Jul/2010:09:03:00 +0200] "GET /Seiten/Forms_and_Infos.html HTTP/1.1" 200 16472 "http://www.asylabwehramt.at/Seiten/Seal.html" "Mozilla/4.0 (compatible; MSIE 7.0; Windows NT 5.1; SV1; .NET CLR 1.1.4322; .NET CLR 2.0.50727; InfoPath.2)"
80.120.179.10 - - [23/Jul/2010:09:03:09 +0200] "GET /Bilder/Ladung.png HTTP/1.1" 200 114658 "http://www.asylabwehramt.at/Seiten/Forms_and_Infos.html" "Mozilla/4.0 (compatible; MSIE 7.0; Windows NT 5.1; SV1; .NET CLR 1.1.4322; .NET CLR 2.0.50727; InfoPath.2)"
80.120.179.10 - - [23/Jul/2010:09:03:31 +0200] "GET /Material/Flyer_Volksschutz_Praevention_Aufklaerung_FPOE.pdf HTTP/1.1" 200 661529 "http://www.asylabwehramt.at/Seiten/Forms_and_Infos.html" "Mozilla/4.0 (compatible; MSIE 7.0; Windows NT 5.1; SV1; .NET CLR 1.1.4322; .NET CLR 2.0.50727; InfoPath.2)"
80.120.179.10 - - [23/Jul/2010:09:03:43 +0200] "GET /Material/Hotline_Russisch.pdf HTTP/1.1" 200 239827 "http://www.asylabwehramt.at/Seiten/Forms_and_Infos.html" "Mozilla/4.0 (compatible; MSIE 7.0; Windows NT 5.1; SV1; .NET CLR 1.1.4322; .NET CLR 2.0.50727; InfoPath.2)"
194.232.11.100 - - [23/Jul/2010:18:31:40 +0200] "GET / HTTP/1.1" 200 11992 "http://www.google.at/url?sa=t&source=web&cd=1&ved=0CBoQFjAA&url=http%3A%2F%2Fwww.asylabwehramt.at%2F&rct=j&q=asylabwehramt&ei=2sNJTPvFAcqKOlb_2ZYD&usg=AFQjCNEy1zWClvnxkLlPAGifRc344_OU4Q" "Mozilla/4.0 (compatible; MSIE 8.0; Windows NT 5.1; Trident/4.0; .NET CLR 1.1.4322; InfoPath.1; .NET CLR 2.0.50727; .NET CLR 3.0.4506.2152; .NET CLR 3.5.30729; MOSER HOLDING Aktiengesellschaft)"
194.232.11.100 - - [23/Jul/2010:18:31:43 +0200] "GET /Seiten/Presse.html HTTP/1.1" 200 12320 "http://www.asylabwehramt.at/" "Mozilla/4.0 (compatible; MSIE 8.0; Windows NT 5.1; Trident/4.0; .NET CLR 1.1.4322; InfoPath.1; .NET CLR 2.0.50727; .NET CLR 3.0.4506.2152; .NET CLR 3.5.30729; MOSER HOLDING Aktiengesellschaft)"
194.232.11.100 - - [23/Jul/2010:22:38:42 +0200] "GET /Seiten/Material.html HTTP/1.1" 200 17335 "http://www.asylabwehramt.at/Seiten/Presse.html" "Mozilla/4.0 (compatible; MSIE 8.0; Windows NT 5.1; Trident/4.0; .NET CLR 1.1.4322; InfoPath.1; .NET CLR 2.0.50727; .NET CLR 3.0.4506.2152; .NET CL
```

R 3.5.30729; MOSER HOLDING Aktiengesellschaft)"

194.232.11.100 - - [23/Jul/2010:22:40:43 +0200] "GET /Seiten/Aktuelles.html HTTP/1.1" 200 14343 "http://www.asylabwehramt.at/Seiten/Material.html" "Mozilla/4.0 (compatible; MSIE 8.0; Windows NT 5.1; Trident/4.0; .NET CLR 1.1.4322; InfoPath.1; .NET CLR 2.0.50727; .NET CLR 3.0.4506.2152; .NET CLR 3.5.30729; MOSER HOLDING Aktiengesellschaft)"

194.232.11.100 - - [23/Jul/2010:22:40:51 +0200] "GET /Seiten/Aktuelles.html HTTP/1.1" 304 - "http://www.asylabwehramt.at/Seiten/Aktuelles.html" "Mozilla/4.0 (compatible; MSIE 8.0; Windows NT 5.1; Trident/4.0; .NET CLR 1.1.4322; InfoPath.1; .NET CLR 2.0.50727; .NET CLR 3.0.4506.2152; .NET CL R 3.5.30729; MOSER HOLDING Aktiengesellschaft)"

194.232.11.100 - - [23/Jul/2010:22:40:54 +0200] "GET /Seiten/Material.html HTTP/1.1" 304 - "http://www.asylabwehramt.at/Seiten/Aktuelles.html" "Mozilla/4.0 (compatible; MSIE 8.0; Windows NT 5.1; Trident/4.0; .NET CLR 1.1.4322; InfoPath.1; .NET CLR 2.0.50727; .NET CLR 3.0.4506.2152; .NET CLR 3.5.30729; MOSER HOLDING Aktiengesellschaft)"

194.232.11.100 - - [23/Jul/2010:22:41:38 +0200] "GET /Material/Asyl_Jahresstatistik_2009.pdf HTTP/1.1" 200 680643 "http://www.asylabwehramt.at/Seiten/Material.html" "Mozilla/4.0 (compatible; MSI E 8.0; Windows NT 5.1; Trident/4.0; .NET CLR 1.1.4322; InfoPath.1; .NET CLR 2.0.50727; .NET CLR 3 .0.4506.2152; .NET CLR 3.5.30729; MOSER HOLDING Aktiengesellschaft)"

194.232.11.100 - - [23/Jul/2010:22:43:31 +0200] "GET /Bilder/Ladung.png HTTP/1.1" 200 114658 "htt p://www.asylabwehramt.at/Seiten/Material.html" "Mozilla/4.0 (compatible; MSIE 8.0; Windows NT 5.1 ; Trident/4.0; .NET CLR 1.1.4322; InfoPath.1; .NET CLR 2.0.50727; .NET CLR 3.0.4506.2152; .NET CL R 3.5.30729; MOSER HOLDING Aktiengesellschaft)"

194.232.11.100 - - [23/Jul/2010:22:43:55 +0200] "GET /index.html HTTP/1.1" 200 11992 "http://www. asylabwehramt.at/Seiten/Material.html" "Mozilla/4.0 (compatible; MSIE 8.0; Windows NT 5.1; Triden t/4.0; .NET CLR 1.1.4322; InfoPath.1; .NET CLR 2.0.50727; .NET CLR 3.0.4506.2152; .NET CLR 3.5.30 729; MOSER HOLDING Aktiengesellschaft)"

194.232.11.100 - - [23/Jul/2010:22:45:23 +0200] "GET /Seiten/Material.html HTTP/1.1" 304 - "http://www.asylabwehramt.at/index.html" "Mozilla/4.0 (compatible; MSIE 8.0; Windows NT 5.1; Trident/4. 0; .NET CLR 1.1.4322; InfoPath.1; .NET CLR 2.0.50727; .NET CLR 3.0.4506.2152; .NET CLR 3.5.30729;

```
MOSER HOLDING Aktiengesellschaft)"
194.232.11.100 - - [23/Jul/2010:22:45:27 +0200] "GET /Material/Asyl_Jahresstatistik_2009.pdf HTTP
/1.1" 304 - "http://www.asylabwehramt.at/Seiten/Material.html" "Mozilla/4.0 (compatible; MSIE 8.0
; Windows NT 5.1; Trident/4.0; .NET CLR 1.1.4322; InfoPath.1; .NET CLR 2.0.50727; .NET CLR 3.0.45
06.2152; .NET CLR 3.5.30729; MOSER HOLDING Aktiengesellschaft)"
62.154.194.53 - - [24/Jul/2010:07:23:31 +0200] "GET / HTTP/1.1" 200 11992 "-" "Mozilla/4.0 (compa
tible; MSIE 5.5; Windows NT 5.0)"
80.120.179.10 - - [24/Jul/2010:11:39:51 +0200] "GET / HTTP/1.1" 200 11992 "-" "Mozilla/4.0 (compa
tible; MSIE 6.0; Windows NT 5.1; SV1; InfoPath.1; .NET CLR 1.1.4322; .NET CLR 2.0.50727)"
62.154.194.53 - - [25/Jul/2010:10:59:11 +0200] "GET / HTTP/1.1" 200 11992 "-" "Mozilla/4.0 (compa
tible; MSIE 5.5; Windows NT 5.0)"
62.154.194.53 - - [26/Jul/2010:06:52:26 +0200] "GET / HTTP/1.1" 200 11992 "-" "Mozilla/4.0 (compa
tible; MSIE 5.5; Windows NT 5.0)"
193.5.216.100 - - [26/Jul/2010:12:45:01 +0200] "GET / HTTP/1.0" 200 11992 "http://www.google.ch/s
earch?hl=de&source=hp&q=asylabwehramt&meta=&btnG=Google-Suche" "Mozilla/5.0 (X11; U; SunOS sun4u;
en-US; rv:1.9.1.6) Gecko/20091202 Firefox/3.5.6"
193.5.216.100 - - [26/Jul/2010:12:45:02 +0200] "GET /Bilder/Header_AAbA_anim.gif HTTP/1.0" 200 19
997 "http://www.asylabwehramt.at/" "Mozilla/5.0 (X11; U; SunOS sun4u; en-US; rv:1.9.1.6) Gecko/20
091202 Firefox/3.5.6"
193.5.216.100 - - [26/Jul/2010:12:45:04 +0200] "GET /favicon.ico HTTP/1.0" 302 340 "-" "Mozilla/5
.0 (X11; U; SunOS sun4u; en-US; rv:1.9.1.6) Gecko/20091202 Firefox/3.5.6"
193.5.216.100 - - [26/Jul/2010:12:45:47 +0200] "GET /Seiten/Aktuelles.html HTTP/1.0" 200 14343 "h
ttp://www.asylabwehramt.at/" "Mozilla/5.0 (X11; U; SunOS sun4u; en-US; rv:1.9.1.6) Gecko/20091202
Firefox/3.5.6"
193.5.216.100 - - [26/Jul/2010:12:46:26 +0200] "GET /Seiten/Material.html HTTP/1.0" 200 17335 "ht
tp://www.asylabwehramt.at/Seiten/Aktuelles.html" "Mozilla/5.0 (X11; U; SunOS sun4u; en-US; rv:1.9
.1.6) Gecko/20091202 Firefox/3.5.6"
193.5.216.100 - - [26/Jul/2010:12:46:37 +0200] "GET /Bilder/Ladung.png HTTP/1.0" 200 114658 "http
```

```
://www.asylabwehramt.at/Seiten/Material.html" "Mozilla/5.0 (X11; U; SunOS sun4u; en-US; rv:1.9.1.
6) Gecko/20091202 Firefox/3.5.6"
193.5.216.100 - - [26/Jul/2010:12:46:48 +0200] "GET /Material/Flyer_Volksschutz_Praevention_Aufkl
aerung_FPOE.pdf HTTP/1.0" 200 661529 "http://www.asylabwehramt.at/Seiten/Material.html" "Mozilla/
5.0 (X11; U; SunOS sun4u; en-US; rv:1.9.1.6) Gecko/20091202 Firefox/3.5.6"
193.5.216.100 - - [26/Jul/2010:12:47:04 +0200] "GET /Bilder/flyer_nigeria_Internet.pdf HTTP/1.0"
200 702826 "http://www.asylabwehramt.at/Seiten/Material.html" "Mozilla/5.0 (X11; U; SunOS sun4u;
en-US; rv:1.9.1.6) Gecko/20091202 Firefox/3.5.6"
193.5.216.100 - - [26/Jul/2010:12:47:49 +0200] "GET /Seiten/Rundzeichen.html HTTP/1.0" 200 8895 "
http://www.asylabwehramt.at/Seiten/Material.html" "Mozilla/5.0 (X11; U; SunOS sun4u; en-US; rv:1.
9.1.6) Gecko/20091202 Firefox/3.5.6"
193.5.216.100 - - [26/Jul/2010:12:47:53 +0200] "GET /Seiten/Press.html HTTP/1.0" 200 12374 "http:
//www.asylabwehramt.at/Seiten/Rundzeichen.html" "Mozilla/5.0 (X11; U; SunOS sun4u; en-US; rv:1.9.
1.6) Gecko/20091202 Firefox/3.5.6"
62.178.220.154 - - [27/Jul/2010:01:23:57 +0200] "GET / HTTP/1.1" 200 11992 "http://www.google.at/
search?hl=de&q=asylantrag+%C3%B6sterreich+im+ausland+stellen&cts=1280186425442&aq=f&aqi=&aql=&oq=
&gs_rfai=" "Mozilla/5.0 (Windows; U; Windows NT 5.1; de; rv:1.9.1.11) Gecko/20100701 Firefox/3.5.
11 ( .NET CLR 3.5.30729)"
62.154.194.53 - - [27/Jul/2010:06:46:12 +0200] "GET / HTTP/1.1" 200 11992 "-" "Mozilla/4.0 (compa
tible; MSIE 5.5; Windows NT 5.0)"
80.120.179.10 - - [27/Jul/2010:12:09:39 +0200] "GET / HTTP/1.1" 200 11992 "-" "Mozilla/4.0 (compa
tible; MSIE 6.0; Windows NT 5.1; SV1; .NET CLR 1.1.4322)"
80.120.179.10 - - [27/Jul/2010:12:09:57 +0200] "GET /Seiten/Press.html HTTP/1.1" 200 12374 "http:
//www.asylabwehramt.at/" "Mozilla/4.0 (compatible; MSIE 6.0; Windows NT 5.1; SV1; .NET CLR 1.1.43
22)"
80.120.179.10 - - [27/Jul/2010:12:10:01 +0200] "GET /OEFFENTLICHKEIT/07062010d.pdf HTTP/1.1" 200
333788 "http://www.asylabwehramt.at/Seiten/Press.html" "Mozilla/4.0 (compatible; MSIE 6.0; Window
s NT 5.1; SV1; .NET CLR 1.1.4322)"
```

```
80.120.179.10 - - [27/Jul/2010:12:11:03 +0200] "GET /Seiten/Aktuelles.html HTTP/1.1" 200 14343 "http://www.asylabwehramt.at/Seiten/Press.html" "Mozilla/4.0 (compatible; MSIE 6.0; Windows NT 5.1; SV1; .NET CLR 1.1.4322)"
80.120.179.10 - - [27/Jul/2010:12:11:04 +0200] "GET /Bilder/leistung_2.jpg HTTP/1.1" 200 4918 "http://www.asylabwehramt.at/Seiten/Aktuelles.html" "Mozilla/4.0 (compatible; MSIE 6.0; Windows NT 5.1; SV1; .NET CLR 1.1.4322)"
80.120.179.10 - - [27/Jul/2010:12:11:12 +0200] "GET /Bilder/PLakat_Mustafa_Nase.JPG HTTP/1.1" 200 359029 "http://www.asylabwehramt.at/Seiten/Aktuelles.html" "Mozilla/4.0 (compatible; MSIE 6.0; Windows NT 5.1; SV1; .NET CLR 1.1.4322)"
80.120.179.10 - - [27/Jul/2010:12:26:56 +0200] "GET /favicon.ico HTTP/1.1" 302 340 "-" "Mozilla/5.0 (Windows; U; Windows NT 5.1; de; rv:1.9.2.3) Gecko/20100401 Firefox/3.6.3"
80.120.179.10 - - [27/Jul/2010:12:26:57 +0200] "GET /favicon.ico HTTP/1.1" 302 340 "-" "Mozilla/5.0 (Windows; U; Windows NT 5.1; de; rv:1.9.2.3) Gecko/20100401 Firefox/3.6.3"
80.120.179.10 - - [27/Jul/2010:12:27:00 +0200] "GET /Seiten/Orgstrukt.html HTTP/1.1" 200 14119 "http://www.asylabwehramt.at/" "Mozilla/5.0 (Windows; U; Windows NT 5.1; de; rv:1.9.2.3) Gecko/20100401 Firefox/3.6.3"
80.120.179.10 - - [27/Jul/2010:12:27:27 +0200] "GET /index.html HTTP/1.1" 200 11992 "http://www.asylabwehramt.at/Seiten/Orgstrukt.html" "Mozilla/5.0 (Windows; U; Windows NT 5.1; de; rv:1.9.2.3) Gecko/20100401 Firefox/3.6.3"
80.120.179.10 - - [27/Jul/2010:12:27:39 +0200] "GET /Seiten/Bilder.html HTTP/1.1" 200 10043 "http://www.asylabwehramt.at/index.html" "Mozilla/5.0 (Windows; U; Windows NT 5.1; de; rv:1.9.2.3) Gecko/20100401 Firefox/3.6.3"
80.120.179.10 - - [27/Jul/2010:12:27:40 +0200] "GET /Bilder/Ausstellung_weisses_haus_wien_esel_fotos/eSeL_UBERMORGEN_asylabwehramt_dasweisseshaus_453_thumb.jpg HTTP/1.1" 200 47504 "http://www.asylabwehramt.at/Seiten/Bilder.html" "Mozilla/5.0 (Windows; U; Windows NT 5.1; de; rv:1.9.2.3) Gecko/20100401 Firefox/3.6.3"
80.120.179.10 - - [27/Jul/2010:12:28:04 +0200] "GET /Seiten/Bilder_Ausstellung.html HTTP/1.1" 200 16685 "http://www.asylabwehramt.at/Seiten/Bilder.html" "Mozilla/5.0 (Windows; U; Windows NT 5.1;
```

de; rv:1.9.2.3) Gecko/20100401 Firefox/3.6.3"

80.120.179.10 - - [27/Jul/2010:12:28:05 +0200] "GET /Bilder/Ausstellung_weisses_haus_wien_esel_fo
tos/eSeL_UBERMORGEN_asylabwehramt_dasweissehaus_468_thumb.jpg HTTP/1.1" 200 32572 "http://www.asy
labwehramt.at/Seiten/Bilder_Ausstellung.html" "Mozilla/5.0 (Windows; U; Windows NT 5.1; de; rv:1.
9.2.3) Gecko/20100401 Firefox/3.6.3"

62.154.194.53 - - [28/Jul/2010:07:33:28 +0200] "GET / HTTP/1.1" 200 11992 "-" "Mozilla/4.0 (compa
tible; MSIE 5.5; Windows NT 5.0)"

80.120.179.10 - - [28/Jul/2010:11:31:31 +0200] "GET / HTTP/1.1" 200 11992 "-" "Mozilla/4.0 (compa
tible; MSIE 6.0; Windows NT 5.1; SV1; .NET CLR 1.1.4322; .NET CLR 2.0.50727; .NET CLR 3.0.04506.3
0; .NET CLR 3.0.04506.648; InfoPath.2)"

80.120.179.10 - - [28/Jul/2010:11:31:36 +0200] "GET /asyl.css HTTP/1.1" 200 860 "http://www.asyla
bwehramt.at/" "Mozilla/4.0 (compatible; MSIE 6.0; Windows NT 5.1; SV1; .NET CLR 1.1.4322; .NET CL
R 2.0.50727; .NET CLR 3.0.04506.30; .NET CLR 3.0.04506.648; InfoPath.2)"

188.21.224.34[32] - - [28/Jul/2010:12:13:41 +0200] "GET /Seiten/Forms_and_Infos.html HTTP/1.1" 200 16
472 "http://www.google.at/search?q=Tips+and+tricks+on+how-to+enhance+bureaucratic+burdens+in+the+
asylum+process+in+Austria+and+in+the+Schengen+Area&ie=utf-8&oe=utf-8&aq=t&rls=org.mozilla:de:offi
cial&client=firefox-a" "Mozilla/5.0 (Windows; U; Windows NT 5.1; de; rv:1.9.2.3) Gecko/20100401 F
irefox/3.6.3 (.NET CLR 3.5.30729)"

62.154.194.53 - - [29/Jul/2010:06:40:48 +0200] "GET / HTTP/1.1" 200 11992 "-" "Mozilla/4.0 (compa
tible; MSIE 5.5; Windows NT 5.0)"

194.232.79.193 - - [29/Jul/2010:10:26:20 +0200] "GET / HTTP/1.1" 200 11992 "http://www.google.at/
url?sa=t&source=web&cd=1&ved=0CBUQFjAA&url=http%3A%2F%2Fwww.asylabwehramt.at%2F&rct=j&q=asyl%20ab
wehramt&ei=ITtRTIyJMtKZOLqdweUU&usg=AFQjCNEylzWClvmxklPAGifRc344_0U4Q" "Mozilla/4.0 (compatible;
MSIE 8.0; Windows NT 5.1; Trident/4.0; .NET CLR 1.1.4322; .NET CLR 2.0.50727; .NET CLR 3.0.4506.
2152; .NET CLR 3.5.30729)"

194.232.79.193 - - [29/Jul/2010:10:26:50 +0200] "GET /Seiten/Aktuelles.html HTTP/1.1" 200 14343 "

[32]WHOIS record on page 289

```
http://www.asylabwehramt.at/" "Mozilla/4.0 (compatible; MSIE 8.0; Windows NT 5.1; Trident/4.0; .NET CLR 1.1.4322; .NET CLR 3.0.4506.2152; .NET CLR 3.5.30729)"
194.232.79.193 - - [29/Jul/2010:10:26:51 +0200] "GET /Bilder/56.jpg HTTP/1.1" 200 4494 "http://www.asylabwehramt.at/Seiten/Aktuelles.html" "Mozilla/4.0 (compatible; MSIE 8.0; Windows NT 5.1; Trident/4.0; .NET CLR 1.1.4322; .NET CLR 2.0.50727; .NET CLR 3.0.4506.2152; .NET CLR 3.5.30729)"
194.232.79.193 - - [29/Jul/2010:10:26:52 +0200] "GET /Bilder/fitnesscenter_traiskirchen.jpg HTTP/1.1" 200 5721 "http://www.asylabwehramt.at/Seiten/Aktuelles.html" "Mozilla/4.0 (compatible; MSIE 8.0; Windows NT 5.1; Trident/4.0; .NET CLR 1.1.4322; .NET CLR 2.0.50727; .NET CLR 3.0.4506.2152; .NET CLR 3.5.30729)"
194.232.79.193 - - [29/Jul/2010:10:26:57 +0200] "GET /Seiten/Material.html HTTP/1.1" 200 17335 "http://www.asylabwehramt.at/Seiten/Aktuelles.html" "Mozilla/4.0 (compatible; MSIE 8.0; Windows NT 5.1; Trident/4.0; .NET CLR 1.1.4322; .NET CLR 2.0.50727; .NET CLR 3.0.4506.2152; .NET CLR 3.5.30729)"
194.232.79.193 - - [29/Jul/2010:10:27:04 +0200] "GET /Seiten/Rundzeichen.html HTTP/1.1" 200 8895 "http://www.asylabwehramt.at/Seiten/Material.html" "Mozilla/4.0 (compatible; MSIE 8.0; Windows NT 5.1; Trident/4.0; .NET CLR 1.1.4322; .NET CLR 2.0.50727; .NET CLR 3.0.4506.2152; .NET CLR 3.5.30729)"
194.232.79.193 - - [29/Jul/2010:10:27:12 +0200] "GET /Seiten/Bilder.html HTTP/1.1" 200 10043 "http://www.asylabwehramt.at/Seiten/Rundzeichen.html" "Mozilla/4.0 (compatible; MSIE 8.0; Windows NT 5.1; Trident/4.0; .NET CLR 1.1.4322; .NET CLR 2.0.50727; .NET CLR 3.0.4506.2152; .NET CLR 3.5.30729)"
194.232.79.193 - - [29/Jul/2010:10:27:20 +0200] "GET /Seiten/Bilder_Ausstellung.html HTTP/1.1" 200 16685 "http://www.asylabwehramt.at/Seiten/Bilder.html" "Mozilla/4.0 (compatible; MSIE 8.0; Windows NT 5.1; Trident/4.0; .NET CLR 1.1.4322; .NET CLR 2.0.50727; .NET CLR 3.0.4506.2152; .NET CLR 3.5.30729)"
194.232.79.193 - - [29/Jul/2010:10:27:21 +0200] "GET /Bilder/Ausstellung_weisses_haus_wien_esel_fotos/eSeL_UBERMORGEN_asylabwehramt_dasweissehaus_476_thumb.jpg HTTP/1.1" 200 46505 "http://www.asylabwehramt.at/Seiten/Bilder_Ausstellung.html" "Mozilla/4.0 (compatible; MSIE 8.0; Windows NT 5.1
```

```
; Trident/4.0; .NET CLR 1.1.4322; .NET CLR 2.0.50727; .NET CLR 3.0.4506.2152; .NET CLR 3.5.30729)"

194.232.79.193 - - [29/Jul/2010:10:27:22 +0200] "GET /Bilder/Ausstellung_weisses_haus_wien_esel_fotos/eSeL_UBERMORGEN_asylabwehramt_dasweissehaus_484_thumb.jpg HTTP/1.1" 200 48099 "http://www.asylabwehramt.at/Seiten/Bilder_Ausstellung.html" "Mozilla/4.0 (compatible; MSIE 8.0; Windows NT 5.1; Trident/4.0; .NET CLR 1.1.4322; .NET CLR 2.0.50727; .NET CLR 3.0.4506.2152; .NET CLR 3.5.30729)"

194.232.79.193 - - [29/Jul/2010:10:27:23 +0200] "GET /Bilder/Ausstellung_weisses_haus_wien_esel_fotos/eSeL_UBERMORGEN_asylabwehramt_dasweissehaus_507_thumb.jpg HTTP/1.1" 200 40356 "http://www.asylabwehramt.at/Seiten/Bilder_Ausstellung.html" "Mozilla/4.0 (compatible; MSIE 8.0; Windows NT 5.1; Trident/4.0; .NET CLR 1.1.4322; .NET CLR 2.0.50727; .NET CLR 3.0.4506.2152; .NET CLR 3.5.30729)"

194.232.79.193 - - [29/Jul/2010:10:27:24 +0200] "GET /Bilder/Ausstellung_weisses_haus_wien_esel_fotos/eSeL_UBERMORGEN_asylabwehramt_dasweissehaus_526_thumb.jpg HTTP/1.1" 200 47873 "http://www.asylabwehramt.at/Seiten/Bilder_Ausstellung.html" "Mozilla/4.0 (compatible; MSIE 8.0; Windows NT 5.1; Trident/4.0; .NET CLR 1.1.4322; .NET CLR 2.0.50727; .NET CLR 3.0.4506.2152; .NET CLR 3.5.30729)"

194.232.79.193 - - [29/Jul/2010:10:27:25 +0200] "GET /Seiten/Links.html HTTP/1.1" 200 19139 "http://www.asylabwehramt.at/Seiten/Bilder_Ausstellung.html" "Mozilla/4.0 (compatible; MSIE 8.0; Windows NT 5.1; Trident/4.0; .NET CLR 1.1.4322; .NET CLR 2.0.50727; .NET CLR 3.0.4506.2152; .NET CLR 3.5.30729)"

194.232.79.193 - - [29/Jul/2010:10:27:29 +0200] "GET /Seiten/Press.html HTTP/1.1" 200 12374 "http://www.asylabwehramt.at/Seiten/Links.html" "Mozilla/4.0 (compatible; MSIE 8.0; Windows NT 5.1; Trident/4.0; .NET CLR 1.1.4322; .NET CLR 2.0.50727; .NET CLR 3.0.4506.2152; .NET CLR 3.5.30729)"
194.232.79.193 - - [29/Jul/2010:10:27:39 +0200] "GET /DEFFENTLICHKEIT/07062010d.pdf HTTP/1.1" 200 333788 "http://www.asylabwehramt.at/Seiten/Press.html" "Mozilla/4.0 (compatible; MSIE 8.0; Windows NT 5.1; Trident/4.0; .NET CLR 1.1.4322; .NET CLR 2.0.50727; .NET CLR 3.0.4506.2152; .NET CLR 3.5.30729)"
```

```
194.232.79.193 - - [29/Jul/2010:10:30:13 +0200] "GET /index.html HTTP/1.1" 200 11992 "http://www.
asylabwehramt.at/Seiten/Aktuelles.html" "Mozilla/4.0 (compatible; MSIE 8.0; Windows NT 5.1; Tride
nt/4.0; .NET CLR 1.1.4322; .NET CLR 2.0.50727; .NET CLR 3.0.4506.2152; .NET CLR 3.5.30729)"
194.232.79.193 - - [29/Jul/2010:10:32:10 +0200] "GET /Seiten/Impressum.html HTTP/1.1" 200 11939 "
http://www.asylabwehramt.at/Seiten/Press.html" "Mozilla/4.0 (compatible; MSIE 8.0; Windows NT 5.1
; Trident/4.0; .NET CLR 1.1.4322; .NET CLR 2.0.50727; .NET CLR 3.0.4506.2152; .NET CLR 3.5.30729)
"
194.232.79.193 - - [29/Jul/2010:10:33:31 +0200] "GET /Seiten/Orgstrukt.html HTTP/1.1" 200 14119 "
http://www.asylabwehramt.at/Seiten/Impressum.html" "Mozilla/4.0 (compatible; MSIE 8.0; Windows NT
5.1; Trident/4.0; .NET CLR 1.1.4322; .NET CLR 2.0.50727; .NET CLR 3.0.4506.2152; .NET CLR 3.5.30
729)"
62.154.194.53 - - [30/Jul/2010:06:29:49 +0200] "GET / HTTP/1.1" 200 11992 "-" "Mozilla/4.0 (compa
tible; MSIE 5.5; Windows NT 5.0)"
80.120.179.10 - - [02/Aug/2010:14:40:47 +0200] "GET / HTTP/1.1" 200 11992 "-" "Mozilla/4.0 (compa
tible; MSIE 6.0; Windows NT 5.1; SV1; .NET CLR 1.1.4322; MS-RTC LM 8)"
194.138.12.170 - - [02/Aug/2010:14:52:50 +0200] "GET / HTTP/1.1" 200 11992 "-" "Mozilla/5.0 (Wind
ows; U; Windows NT 5.1; de; rv:1.9.0.19) Gecko/2010031422 Firefox/3.0.19 (.NET CLR 3.5.30729)"
194.138.12.170 - - [02/Aug/2010:14:52:53 +0200] "GET /favicon.ico HTTP/1.1" 302 336 "-" "Mozilla/
5.0 (Windows; U; Windows NT 5.1; de; rv:1.9.0.19) Gecko/2010031422 Firefox/3.0.19 (.NET CLR 3.5.3
0729)"
194.138.12.170 - - [02/Aug/2010:14:53:16 +0200] "GET /Seiten/Impressum.html HTTP/1.1" 200 11939 "
http://asylabwehramt.at/" "Mozilla/5.0 (Windows; U; Windows NT 5.1; de; rv:1.9.0.19) Gecko/201003
1422 Firefox/3.0.19 (.NET CLR 3.5.30729)"
213.208.144.130 - - [03/Aug/2010:15:37:42 +0200] "GET / HTTP/1.0" 200 11992 "-" "Mozilla/4.0 (com
patible; MSIE 7.0; Windows NT 5.2; .NET CLR 1.1.4322; InfoPath.1; .NET CLR 2.0.50727; .NET CLR 3.
0.4506.2152; .NET CLR 3.5.30729)"
80.120.179.10 - - [06/Aug/2010:11:22:19 +0200] "GET / HTTP/1.1" 200 11992 "http://www.google.at/u
rl?sa=t&source=web&cd=1&ved=0CBUQFjAA&url=http%3A%2F%2Fwww.asylabwehramt.at%2F&rct=j&q=asyl%20abw
```

ehramt&ei=R9RbTOXILoGQOPDsnaUP&usg=AFQjCNEy1zWClvnxkLlPAGifRc344_0U4Q" "Mozilla/4.0 (compatible; MSIE 8.0; Windows NT 5.1; Trident/4.0; .NET CLR 1.1.4322; .NET CLR 2.0.50727; .NET CLR 3.0.04506.30; .NET CLR 3.0.04506.648; InfoPath.2; .NET CLR 3.0.4506.2152; .NET CLR 3.5.30729; MS-RTC LM 8)"

80.120.179.10 - - [09/Aug/2010:12:58:30 +0200] "GET / HTTP/1.1" 200 11992 "http://www.google.at/search?hl=de&source=hp&q=asyl+abwehramt&aq=3s&aqi=g3g-s1g6&aql=&oq=asyl&gs_rfai=" "Mozilla/4.0 (compatible; MSIE 7.0; Windows NT 5.1; .NET CLR 1.1.4322; .NET CLR 2.0.50727; InfoPath.2)"

80.120.179.10 - - [09/Aug/2010:12:59:58 +0200] "GET /Seiten/Bilder.html HTTP/1.1" 200 10364 "http://www.asylabwehramt.at/" "Mozilla/4.0 (compatible; MSIE 7.0; Windows NT 5.1; .NET CLR 1.1.4322; .NET CLR 2.0.50727; InfoPath.2)"

80.120.179.10 - - [09/Aug/2010:13:00:27 +0200] "GET /Seiten/Aktuelles.html HTTP/1.1" 200 14343 "http://www.asylabwehramt.at/Seiten/Bilder.html" "Mozilla/4.0 (compatible; MSIE 7.0; Windows NT 5.1; .NET CLR 1.1.4322; .NET CLR 2.0.50727; InfoPath.2)"

80.120.179.10 - - [09/Aug/2010:13:00:53 +0200] "GET /Seiten/Rundzeichen.html HTTP/1.1" 200 8895 "http://www.asylabwehramt.at/Seiten/Aktuelles.html" "Mozilla/4.0 (compatible; MSIE 7.0; Windows NT 5.1; .NET CLR 1.1.4322; .NET CLR 2.0.50727; InfoPath.2)"

80.120.179.10 - - [09/Aug/2010:13:01:00 +0200] "GET /Seiten/Press.html HTTP/1.1" 200 12374 "http://www.asylabwehramt.at/Seiten/Rundzeichen.html" "Mozilla/4.0 (compatible; MSIE 7.0; Windows NT 5.1; .NET CLR 1.1.4322; .NET CLR 2.0.50727; InfoPath.2)"

80.120.179.10 - - [09/Aug/2010:13:01:11 +0200] "GET /Seiten/Links.html HTTP/1.1" 200 19139 "http://www.asylabwehramt.at/Seiten/Press.html" "Mozilla/4.0 (compatible; MSIE 7.0; Windows NT 5.1; .NET CLR 1.1.4322; .NET CLR 2.0.50727; InfoPath.2)"

80.120.179.10 - - [09/Aug/2010:17:01:32 +0200] "GET /favicon.ico HTTP/1.1" 302 340 "-" "Mozilla/4.0 (compatible; MSIE 7.0; Windows NT 5.1; .NET CLR 1.1.4322; .NET CLR 2.0.50727; .NET CLR 3.0.045 06.30; .NET CLR 3.0.04506.648; InfoPath.2; .NET CLR 3.0.4506.2152; .NET CLR 3.5.30729; MS-RTC LM 8)"

80.120.179.10 - - [09/Aug/2010:17:10:40 +0200] "GET /Seiten/Links_e.html HTTP/1.1" 200 19142 "http://www.asylabwehramt.at/Seiten/Bilder.html" "Mozilla/4.0 (compatible; MSIE 7.0; Windows NT 5.1; .NET CLR 1.1.4322; .NET CLR 2.0.50727; InfoPath.2)"

```
80.120.179.10 - - [10/Aug/2010:08:41:05 +0200] "GET / HTTP/1.1" 200 11992 "http://www.google.at/search?hl=de&source=hp&q=asyl+abwehramt&meta=&aq=0s&aqi=g-s1&aql=&oq=asylab&gs_rfai=" "Mozilla/4.0 (compatible; MSIE 6.0; Windows NT 5.1; SV1; .NET CLR 1.1.4322; .NET CLR 2.0.50727; .NET CLR 3.0.04506.30; .NET CLR 3.0.04506.648; InfoPath.2)"
80.120.179.10 - - [10/Aug/2010:08:41:13 +0200] "GET /Seiten/Bilder.html HTTP/1.1" 200 10364 "http://www.asylabwehramt.at/" "Mozilla/4.0 (compatible; MSIE 6.0; Windows NT 5.1; SV1; .NET CLR 1.1.4322; .NET CLR 2.0.50727; .NET CLR 3.0.04506.30; .NET CLR 3.0.04506.648; InfoPath.2)"
80.120.179.10 - - [10/Aug/2010:08:41:29 +0200] "GET /index.html HTTP/1.1" 200 11992 "http://www.asylabwehramt.at/Seiten/Bilder.html" "Mozilla/4.0 (compatible; MSIE 6.0; Windows NT 5.1; SV1; .NET CLR 1.1.4322; .NET CLR 2.0.50727; .NET CLR 3.0.04506.30; .NET CLR 3.0.04506.648; InfoPath.2)"
80.120.179.10 - - [10/Aug/2010:08:41:42 +0200] "GET /Seiten/Aktuelles.html HTTP/1.1" 200 14343 "http://www.asylabwehramt.at/index.html" "Mozilla/4.0 (compatible; MSIE 6.0; Windows NT 5.1; SV1; .NET CLR 1.1.4322; .NET CLR 2.0.50727; .NET CLR 3.0.04506.30; .NET CLR 3.0.04506.648; InfoPath.2)"
80.120.179.10 - - [10/Aug/2010:08:41:58 +0200] "GET /Seiten/Material.html HTTP/1.1" 200 17335 "http://www.asylabwehramt.at/Seiten/Aktuelles.html" "Mozilla/4.0 (compatible; MSIE 6.0; Windows NT 5.1; SV1; .NET CLR 1.1.4322; .NET CLR 2.0.50727; .NET CLR 3.0.04506.30; .NET CLR 3.0.04506.648; InfoPath.2)"
80.120.179.10 - - [10/Aug/2010:08:42:12 +0200] "GET /Seiten/Rundzeichen.html HTTP/1.1" 200 8895 "http://www.asylabwehramt.at/Seiten/Material.html" "Mozilla/4.0 (compatible; MSIE 6.0; Windows NT 5.1; SV1; .NET CLR 1.1.4322; .NET CLR 2.0.50727; .NET CLR 3.0.04506.30; .NET CLR 3.0.04506.648; InfoPath.2)"
80.120.179.10 - - [10/Aug/2010:08:42:21 +0200] "GET /Seiten/Links.html HTTP/1.1" 200 19139 "http://www.asylabwehramt.at/Seiten/Bilder.html" "Mozilla/4.0 (compatible; MSIE 6.0; Windows NT 5.1; SV1; .NET CLR 1.1.4322; .NET CLR 2.0.50727; .NET CLR 3.0.04506.30; .NET CLR 3.0.04506.648; InfoPath.2)"
80.120.179.10 - - [10/Aug/2010:08:44:45 +0200] "GET /Seiten/Press.html HTTP/1.1" 200 12374 "http://www.asylabwehramt.at/Seiten/Rundzeichen.html" "Mozilla/4.0 (compatible; MSIE 6.0; Windows NT 5.1; SV1; .NET CLR 1.1.4322; .NET CLR 2.0.50727; .NET CLR 3.0.04506.30; .NET CLR 3.0.04506.648; Inf
```

oPath.2)"

213.208.144.130 - - [10/Aug/2010:11:20:58 +0200] "GET / HTTP/1.0" 200 11992 "http://www.google.at/search?hl=de&source=hp&q=asyl+abwehramt&meta=&aq=9&aqi=g10&aql=&oq=asyl+&gs_rfai=" "Mozilla/4.0 (compatible; MSIE 6.0; Windows NT 5.0; InfoPath.1)"

80.120.179.10 - - [10/Aug/2010:14:20:13 +0200] "GET /index_e.html HTTP/1.1" 200 12025 "http://www.asylabwehramt.at/" "Mozilla/4.0 (compatible; MSIE 6.0; Windows NT 5.1; SV1; .NET CLR 1.1.4322; .NET CLR 2.0.50727; .NET CLR 3.0.04506.30; InfoPath.2; MS-RTC LM 8)"

80.120.179.10 - - [10/Aug/2010:14:20:14 +0200] "GET /Seiten/Latestnews.html HTTP/1.1" 200 14563 "http://www.asylabwehramt.at/index_e.html" "Mozilla/4.0 (compatible; MSIE 6.0; Windows NT 5.1; SV1; .NET CLR 1.1.4322; .NET CLR 2.0.50727; .NET CLR 3.0.04506.30; InfoPath.2; MS-RTC LM 8)"

80.120.179.10 - - [10/Aug/2010:14:20:30 +0200] "GET /Seiten/Bilder_Ausstellung.html HTTP/1.1" 200 16685 "http://www.asylabwehramt.at/Seiten/Aktuelles.html" "Mozilla/4.0 (compatible; MSIE 6.0; Windows NT 5.1; SV1; .NET CLR 1.1.4322; .NET CLR 2.0.50727; .NET CLR 3.0.04506.30; .NET CLR 3.0.04506.648; InfoPath.2; MS-RTC LM 8)"

80.120.179.10 - - [10/Aug/2010:14:20:31 +0200] "GET /Bilder/Ausstellung_weisses_haus_wien_esel_fotos/eSeL_UBERMORGEN_asylabwehramt_dasweissehaus_526_thumb.jpg HTTP/1.1" 200 47873 "http://www.asylabwehramt.at/Seiten/Bilder_Ausstellung.html" "Mozilla/4.0 (compatible; MSIE 6.0; Windows NT 5.1; SV1; .NET CLR 1.1.4322; .NET CLR 2.0.50727; .NET CLR 3.0.04506.30; .NET CLR 3.0.04506.648; InfoPath.2; MS-RTC LM 8)"

80.120.179.10 - - [10/Aug/2010:14:21:54 +0200] "GET /Material/Hotline_Deutsch.pdf HTTP/1.1" 200 489465 "http://www.asylabwehramt.at/Seiten/Material.html" "Mozilla/4.0 (compatible; MSIE 6.0; Windows NT 5.1; SV1; .NET CLR 1.1.4322; .NET CLR 2.0.50727; .NET CLR 3.0.04506.30; .NET CLR 3.0.04506.648; InfoPath.2; MS-RTC LM 8)"

80.120.179.10 - - [10/Aug/2010:14:22:12 +0200] "GET /Seiten/Links_e.html HTTP/1.1" 200 19142 "http://www.asylabwehramt.at/Seiten/Material.html" "Mozilla/4.0 (compatible; MSIE 6.0; Windows NT 5.1; SV1; .NET CLR 1.1.4322; .NET CLR 2.0.50727; .NET CLR 3.0.04506.30; .NET CLR 3.0.04506.648; InfoPath.2; MS-RTC LM 8)"

80.120.179.10 - - [10/Aug/2010:14:22:52 +0200] "GET /Bilder/Ladung.png HTTP/1.1" 200 114658 "http://www.asylabwehramt.at/Seiten/Material.html" "Mozilla/4.0 (compatible; MSIE 6.0; Windows NT 5.1; SV1; .NET CLR 1.1.4322; .NET CLR 2.0.50727; .NET CLR 3.0.04506.30; .NET CLR 3.0.04506.648; InfoPath.2; MS-RTC LM 8)"

80.120.179.10 - - [12/Aug/2010:13:12:29 +0200] "GET / HTTP/1.1" 200 11992 "http://www.google.at/search?hl=de&source=hp&q=asylabwehramt&meta=&aq=f&aqi=&aql=&oq=&gs_rfai=" "Mozilla/4.0 (compatible; MSIE 6.0; Windows NT 5.1; SV1; InfoPath.1; .NET CLR 1.1.4322; .NET CLR 2.0.50727; .NET CLR 3.0.04506.30; .NET CLR 3.0.04506.648; InfoPath.2; MS-RTC LM 8)"

80.120.179.10 - - [13/Aug/2010:13:01:43 +0200] "GET / HTTP/1.1" 200 11992 "http://www.zeit.de/20 10/28/A-Asylabwehramt" "Mozilla/4.0 (compatible; MSIE 8.0; Windows NT 5.1; Trident/4.0; .NET CLR 1.1.4322; .NET CLR 2.0.50727; .NET CLR 3.0.04506.30; .NET CLR 3.0.04506.648; InfoPath.2; MS-RTC LM 8)"

80.120.179.10 - - [13/Aug/2010:13:01:44 +0200] "GET /asyl.css HTTP/1.1" 200 860 "http://www.asylabwehramt.at/" "Mozilla/4.0 (compatible; MSIE 8.0; Windows NT 5.1; Trident/4.0; .NET CLR 1.1.4322; .NET CLR 2.0.50727; .NET CLR 3.0.04506.30; .NET CLR 3.0.04506.648; InfoPath.2; MS-RTC LM 8)"

80.120.179.10 - - [13/Aug/2010:13:01:58 +0200] "GET /Seiten/Material.html HTTP/1.1" 200 17335 "http://www.asylabwehramt.at/" "Mozilla/4.0 (compatible; MSIE 8.0; Windows NT 5.1; Trident/4.0; .NET CLR 1.1.4322; .NET CLR 2.0.50727; .NET CLR 3.0.04506.30; .NET CLR 3.0.04506.648; InfoPath.2; MS-RTC LM 8)"

80.120.179.10 - - [13/Aug/2010:13:02:23 +0200] "GET /Bilder/Ladung.png HTTP/1.1" 200 114658 "http://www.asylabwehramt.at/Seiten/Material.html" "Mozilla/4.0 (compatible; MSIE 8.0; Windows NT 5.1; Trident/4.0; .NET CLR 1.1.4322; .NET CLR 2.0.50727; .NET CLR 3.0.04506.30; .NET CLR 3.0.04506.64 8; InfoPath.2; MS-RTC LM 8)"

80.120.179.10 - - [13/Aug/2010:13:02:41 +0200] "GET /Seiten/Aktuelles.html HTTP/1.1" 200 14343 "http://www.asylabwehramt.at/Seiten/Material.html" "Mozilla/4.0 (compatible; MSIE 8.0; Windows NT 5 .1; Trident/4.0; .NET CLR 1.1.4322; .NET CLR 2.0.50727; .NET CLR 3.0.04506.30; .NET CLR 3.0.04506 .648; InfoPath.2; MS-RTC LM 8)"

80.120.179.10 - - [13/Aug/2010:13:02:42 +0200] "GET /Bilder/leistung_2.jpg HTTP/1.1" 200 4918 "ht

tp://www.asylabwehramt.at/Seiten/Aktuelles.html" "Mozilla/4.0 (compatible; MSIE 8.0; Windows NT 5
.1; Trident/4.0; .NET CLR 1.1.4322; .NET CLR 2.0.50727; .NET CLR 3.0.04506.30; .NET CLR 3.0.04506
.648; InfoPath.2; MS-RTC LM 8)"

80.120.179.10 - - [13/Aug/2010:13:03:24 +0200] "GET /index.html HTTP/1.1" 200 11992 "http://www.a
sylabwehramt.at/Seiten/Aktuelles.html" "Mozilla/4.0 (compatible; MSIE 8.0; Windows NT 5.1; Triden
t/4.0; .NET CLR 1.1.4322; .NET CLR 2.0.50727; .NET CLR 3.0.04506.30; .NET CLR 3.0.04506.648; Info
Path.2; MS-RTC LM 8)"

80.120.179.10 - - [13/Aug/2010:13:03:26 +0200] "GET /Seiten/Rundzeichen.html HTTP/1.1" 200 8895 "
http://www.asylabwehramt.at/index.html" "Mozilla/4.0 (compatible; MSIE 8.0; Windows NT 5.1; Tride
nt/4.0; .NET CLR 1.1.4322; .NET CLR 2.0.50727; .NET CLR 3.0.04506.30; .NET CLR 3.0.04506.648; Inf
oPath.2; MS-RTC LM 8)"

80.120.179.10 - - [13/Aug/2010:13:03:30 +0200] "GET /Seiten/Bilder.html HTTP/1.1" 200 10364 "http
://www.asylabwehramt.at/Seiten/Rundzeichen.html" "Mozilla/4.0 (compatible; MSIE 8.0; Windows NT 5
.1; Trident/4.0; .NET CLR 1.1.4322; .NET CLR 2.0.50727; .NET CLR 3.0.04506.30; .NET CLR 3.0.04506
.648; InfoPath.2; MS-RTC LM 8)"

80.120.179.10 - - [13/Aug/2010:13:03:38 +0200] "GET /Seiten/Bilder_Ausstellung.html HTTP/1.1" 200
16685 "http://www.asylabwehramt.at/Seiten/Bilder.html" "Mozilla/4.0 (compatible; MSIE 8.0; Windo
ws NT 5.1; Trident/4.0; .NET CLR 1.1.4322; .NET CLR 2.0.50727; .NET CLR 3.0.04506.30; .NET CLR 3.
0.04506.648; InfoPath.2; MS-RTC LM 8)"

80.120.179.10 - - [13/Aug/2010:13:05:08 +0200] "GET /Seiten/Links.html HTTP/1.1" 200 19139 "http:
//www.asylabwehramt.at/Seiten/Bilder.html" "Mozilla/4.0 (compatible; MSIE 8.0; Windows NT 5.1; Tr
ident/4.0; .NET CLR 1.1.4322; .NET CLR 2.0.50727; .NET CLR 3.0.04506.30; .NET CLR 3.0.04506.648;
InfoPath.2; MS-RTC LM 8)"

80.120.179.10 - - [14/Aug/2010:08:11:46 +0200] "GET / HTTP/1.1" 200 11992 "http://www.google.at/s
earch?hl=de&source=hp&q=asyl+abwehramt&aq=3s&aqi=g3g-s1g6&aql=&oq=asyl&gs_rfai=" "Mozilla/4.0 (co
mpatible; MSIE 7.0; Windows NT 5.1; SV1; InfoPath.1; .NET CLR 1.1.4322; .NET CLR 2.0.50727; InfoP
ath.2)"

80.120.179.10 - - [14/Aug/2010:08:12:34 +0200] "GET /Seiten/Links.html HTTP/1.1" 200 19139 "http:

215

/www.asylabwehramt.at/" "Mozilla/4.0 (compatible; MSIE 7.0; Windows NT 5.1; SV1; InfoPath.1; .NET CLR 1.1.4322; .NET CLR 2.0.50727; InfoPath.2)"

80.120.179.10 - - [14/Aug/2010:08:12:35 +0200] "GET /Bilder/dasweissehauslogo.png HTTP/1.1" 200 19920 "http://www.asylabwehramt.at/Seiten/Links.html" "Mozilla/4.0 (compatible; MSIE 7.0; Windows NT 5.1; SV1; InfoPath.1; .NET CLR 1.1.4322; .NET CLR 2.0.50727; InfoPath.2)"

80.120.179.10 - - [14/Aug/2010:08:13:21 +0200] "GET /Seiten/Material.html HTTP/1.1" 200 17335 "http://www.asylabwehramt.at/Seiten/Links.html" "Mozilla/4.0 (compatible; MSIE 7.0; Windows NT 5.1; SV1; InfoPath.1; .NET CLR 1.1.4322; .NET CLR 2.0.50727; InfoPath.2)"

80.120.179.10 - - [14/Aug/2010:08:13:28 +0200] "GET /Bilder/flyer_nigeria_Internet.pdf HTTP/1.1" 200 702826 "http://www.asylabwehramt.at/Seiten/Material.html" "Mozilla/4.0 (compatible; MSIE 7.0; Windows NT 5.1; SV1; InfoPath.1; .NET CLR 1.1.4322; .NET CLR 2.0.50727; InfoPath.2)"

195.69.193.12 [33] - - [17/Aug/2010:07:39:09 +0200] "GET / HTTP/1.1" 200 11992 "http://mail.oegb.at/mail/ptraschk.nsf/($Inbox)/2BEA27C7195872CAC12576CF000727F0/?OpenDocument&Form=s_MailMemoReadBodyContent" "Mozilla/4.0 (compatible; MSIE 7.0; Windows NT 5.1; .NET CLR 1.1.4322; .NET CLR 2.0.5072 7; .NET CLR 3.0.04506.30; .NET CLR 3.0.04506.2152; .NET CLR 3.5.30729)"

80.120.179.10 - - [17/Aug/2010:09:25:47 +0200] "GET / HTTP/1.1" 200 11992 "http://www.google.at/search?hl=de&source=hp&q=asyl+abwehramt&meta=&aq=0&aqi=g-s1&aql=&oq=asylabwehr&gs_rfai=" "Mozilla/4.0 (compatible; MSIE 6.0; Windows NT 5.1; SV1; .NET CLR 1.1.4322; .NET CLR 2.0.50727; .NET CLR 3.0.04506.648; InfoPath.2; .NET CLR 3.0.04506.2152; .NET CLR 3.5.30729; MS-RTC LM 8)"

80.120.179.10 - - [17/Aug/2010:09:26:35 +0200] "GET /Seiten/Bilder.html HTTP/1.1" 200 10364 "http://www.asylabwehramt.at/" "Mozilla/4.0 (compatible; MSIE 6.0; Windows NT 5.1; SV1; .NET CLR 1.1.4322; .NET CLR 2.0.50727; .NET CLR 3.0.04506.30; .NET CLR 3.0.04506.648; InfoPath.2; .NET CLR 3.0.4506.2152; .NET CLR 3.5.30729; MS-RTC LM 8)"

80.120.179.10 - - [17/Aug/2010:09:26:38 +0200] "GET /Bilder/Ausstellung_weisses_haus_wien_esel_fotos/eSeL_UBERMORGEN_asylabwehramt_dasweissehaus_453_thumb.jpg HTTP/1.1" 200 47504 "http://www.asy

[33] WHOIS record on page 309

```
labwehramt.at/Seiten/Bilder.html" "Mozilla/4.0 (compatible; MSIE 6.0; Windows NT 5.1; .NET C
LR 1.1.4322; .NET CLR 2.0.50727; .NET CLR 3.0.04506.30; .NET CLR 3.0.04506.648; InfoPath.2; .NET
CLR 3.0.4506.2152; .NET CLR 3.5.30729; MS-RTC LM 8)"
80.120.179.10 - - [17/Aug/2010:09:26:39 +0200] "GET /Bilder/SCREEN_AAbA_Edutainment_Video.jpg HTT
P/1.1" 200 29259 "http://www.asylabwehramt.at/Seiten/Bilder.html" "Mozilla/4.0 (compatible; MSIE
6.0; Windows NT 5.1; SV1; .NET CLR 1.1.4322; .NET CLR 2.0.50727; .NET CLR 3.0.04506.30; .NET CLR
3.0.04506.648; InfoPath.2; .NET CLR 3.0.4506.2152; .NET CLR 3.5.30729; MS-RTC LM 8)"
80.120.179.10 - - [17/Aug/2010:09:27:33 +0200] "GET /Seiten/Aktuelles.html HTTP/1.1" 200 14343 "h
ttp://www.asylabwehramt.at/Seiten/Bilder.html" "Mozilla/4.0 (compatible; MSIE 6.0; Windows NT 5.1
; SV1; .NET CLR 1.1.4322; .NET CLR 2.0.50727; .NET CLR 3.0.04506.30; .NET CLR 3.0.04506.648; Info
Path.2; .NET CLR 3.0.4506.2152; .NET CLR 3.5.30729; MS-RTC LM 8)"
80.120.179.10 - - [17/Aug/2010:09:27:34 +0200] "GET /Bilder/fitnesscenter_traiskirchen.jpg HTTP/1
.1" 200 5721 "http://www.asylabwehramt.at/Seiten/Aktuelles.html" "Mozilla/4.0 (compatible; MSIE 6
.0; Windows NT 5.1; SV1; .NET CLR 1.1.4322; .NET CLR 2.0.50727; .NET CLR 3.0.04506.30; .NET CLR 3
.0.04506.648; InfoPath.2; .NET CLR 3.0.4506.2152; .NET CLR 3.5.30729; MS-RTC LM 8)"
80.120.179.10 - - [17/Aug/2010:09:27:45 +0200] "GET /index.html HTTP/1.1" 200 11992 "http://www.a
sylabwehramt.at/Seiten/Bilder.html" "Mozilla/4.0 (compatible; MSIE 6.0; Windows NT 5.1; SV1; .NET
CLR 1.1.4322; .NET CLR 2.0.50727; .NET CLR 3.0.04506.30; .NET CLR 3.0.04506.648; InfoPath.2; .NE
T CLR 3.0.4506.2152; .NET CLR 3.5.30729; MS-RTC LM 8)"
80.120.179.10 - - [17/Aug/2010:09:28:22 +0200] "GET /Seiten/Links.html HTTP/1.1" 200 19139 "http:
//www.asylabwehramt.at/index.html" "Mozilla/4.0 (compatible; MSIE 6.0; Windows NT 5.1; SV1; .NET
CLR 1.1.4322; .NET CLR 2.0.50727; .NET CLR 3.0.04506.30; .NET CLR 3.0.04506.648; InfoPath.2; .NET
CLR 3.0.4506.2152; .NET CLR 3.5.30729; MS-RTC LM 8)"
80.120.179.10 - - [17/Aug/2010:09:28:23 +0200] "GET /Bilder/BMDI.png HTTP/1.1" 200 8268 "http://w
ww.asylabwehramt.at/Seiten/Links.html" "Mozilla/4.0 (compatible; MSIE 6.0; Windows NT 5.1; SV1; .
NET CLR 1.1.4322; .NET CLR 2.0.50727; .NET CLR 3.0.04506.30; .NET CLR 3.0.04506.648; InfoPath.2;
.NET CLR 3.0.4506.2152; .NET CLR 3.5.30729; MS-RTC LM 8)"
80.120.179.10 - - [17/Aug/2010:09:29:03 +0200] "GET /Seiten/Material.html HTTP/1.1" 200 17335 "ht
```

```
tp://www.asylabwehramt.at/Seiten/Bilder.html" "Mozilla/4.0 (compatible; MSIE 6.0; Windows NT 5.1;
SV1; .NET CLR 1.1.4322; .NET CLR 2.0.50727; .NET CLR 3.0.04506.30; .NET CLR 3.5.30729; MS-RTC LM 8)"

80.120.179.10 - - [17/Aug/2010:09:29:14 +0200] "GET /Bilder/Ladung.png HTTP/1.1" 200 114658 "http
://www.asylabwehramt.at/Seiten/Material.html" "Mozilla/4.0 (compatible; MSIE 6.0; Windows NT 5.1;
SV1; .NET CLR 1.1.4322; .NET CLR 2.0.50727; .NET CLR 3.0.4506.2152; .NET CLR 3.0.04506.30; InfoP
ath.2; .NET CLR 3.5.30729; MS-RTC LM 8)"

80.120.179.10 - - [17/Aug/2010:09:29:19 +0200] "GET /Material/Flyer_Volksschutz_Praevention_Aufkl
aerung_FP0E.pdf HTTP/1.1" 200 661529 "http://www.asylabwehramt.at/Seiten/Material.html" "Mozilla/
4.0 (compatible; MSIE 6.0; Windows NT 5.1; SV1; .NET CLR 1.1.4322; .NET CLR 2.0.50727; .NET CLR 3
.0.04506.30; .NET CLR 3.5.30729; MS-R
TC LM 8)"

80.120.179.10 - - [17/Aug/2010:09:29:27 +0200] "GET /Bilder/flyer_nigeria_Internet.pdf HTTP/1.1"
200 702826 "http://www.asylabwehramt.at/Seiten/Material.html" "Mozilla/4.0 (compatible; MSIE 6.0;
Windows NT 5.1; SV1; .NET CLR 1.1.4322; .NET CLR 2.0.50727; .NET CLR 3.5.30729; MS-RTC LM 8)"
04506.648; InfoPath.2; .NET CLR 3.0.

80.120.179.10 - - [17/Aug/2010:09:30:10 +0200] "GET /Seiten/Press.html HTTP/1.1" 200 12374 "http:
//www.asylabwehramt.at/" "Mozilla/4.0 (compatible; MSIE 6.0; Windows NT 5.1; SV1; .NET CLR 1.1.43
22; .NET CLR 2.0.50727; .NET CLR 3.0.04506.30; .NET CLR 3.0.04506.648; InfoPath.2; .NET CLR 3.0.4
506.2152; .NET CLR 3.5.30729; MS-RTC LM 8)"

80.120.179.10 - - [17/Aug/2010:09:30:21 +0200] "GET /Seiten/Rundzeichen.html HTTP/1.1" 200 8895 "
http://www.asylabwehramt.at/Seiten/Press.html" "Mozilla/4.0 (compatible; MSIE 6.0; Windows NT 5.1
; SV1; .NET CLR 1.1.4322; .NET CLR 2.0.50727; .NET CLR 3.0.04506.30; .NET CLR 3.0.04506.648; Info
Path.2; .NET CLR 3.0.4506.2152; .NET CLR 3.5.30729; MS-RTC LM 8)"

80.120.179.10 - - [17/Aug/2010:09:31:05 +0200] "GET /Seiten/Impressum.html HTTP/1.1" 200 11939 "h
ttp://www.asylabwehramt.at/index.html" "Mozilla/4.0 (compatible; MSIE 6.0; Windows NT 5.1; SV1; .
NET CLR 1.1.4322; .NET CLR 2.0.50727; .NET CLR 3.0.04506.30; .NET CLR 3.0.04506.648; InfoPath.2;
.NET CLR 3.0.4506.2152; .NET CLR 3.5.30729; MS-RTC LM 8)"
```

84.163.190.221 - - [18/Aug/2010:14:14:08 +0200] "GET /Seiten/Orgstrukt.html HTTP/1.1" 200 14119 " http://www.google.de/url?sa=t&source=web&cd=1&ved=0CBkQFjAA&url=http%3A%2F%2Fwww.asylabwehramt.at %2FSeiten%2F0rgstrukt.html&rct=j&q=asylantrag%20Formular%20f%C3%BCr%20Spanien&ei=M85rTJ-bPML-0an6 iVY&usg=AFQjCNFupGGPUoPKDe7UpjwYvDejEFC1yA" "Mozilla/4.0 (compatible; MSIE 8.0; Windows NT 5.1; T rident/4.0; GTB0.0; InfoPath.2)"

217.13.180.202 - - [18/Aug/2010:14:36:11 +0200] "GET / HTTP/1.1" 200 11992 "http://www.google.at/ url?sa=t&source=web&cd=1&ved=0CBoQFjAA&url=http%3A%2F%2Fwww.asylabwehramt.at%2F&rct=j&q=asylabweh ramt&ei=t9NrTLvOIMyZOIPXnZMC&usg=AFQjCNEy1zWClvnxkLlPAGifRc344_0U4Q" "Mozilla/4.0 (compatible; MS IE 8.0; Windows NT 5.2; Trident/4.0; .NET CLR 2.0.50727; .NET CLR 3.0.4506.215 2; .NET CLR 3.5.30729)"

217.13.180.202 - - [18/Aug/2010:14:36:12 +0200] "GET /asyl.css HTTP/1.1" 200 860 "http://www.asyl abwehramt.at/" "Mozilla/4.0 (compatible; MSIE 8.0; Windows NT 5.2; Trident/4.0; .NET CLR 1.1.4322 ; .NET CLR 2.0.50727; .NET CLR 3.0.4506.2152; .NET CLR 3.5.30729)"

217.13.180.202 - - [18/Aug/2010:14:36:21 +0200] "GET / HTTP/1.1" 304 - "http://www.asylabwehramt. at/" "Mozilla/4.0 (compatible; MSIE 8.0; Windows NT 5.2; Trident/4.0; .NET CLR 1.1.4322; .NET CLR 2.0.50727; .NET CLR 3.0.4506.2152; .NET CLR 3.5.30729)"

217.13.180.202 - - [18/Aug/2010:14:39:19 +0200] "GET /Seiten/Aktuelles.html HTTP/1.1" 200 14343 " http://www.asylabwehramt.at/" "Mozilla/4.0 (compatible; MSIE 8.0; Windows NT 5.2; Trident/4.0; .N ET CLR 1.1.4322; .NET CLR 2.0.50727; .NET CLR 3.0.4506.2152; .NET CLR 3.5.30729)"

217.13.180.202 - - [18/Aug/2010:14:39:20 +0200] "GET /asyl.css HTTP/1.1" 304 - "http://www.asylab wehramt.at/Seiten/Aktuelles.html" "Mozilla/4.0 (compatible; MSIE 8.0; Windows NT 5.2; Trident/4.0 ; .NET CLR 1.1.4322; .NET CLR 2.0.50727; .NET CLR 3.0.4506.2152; .NET CLR 3.5.30729)"

217.13.180.202 - - [18/Aug/2010:14:40:12 +0200] "GET /Seiten/Rundzeichen.html HTTP/1.1" 200 8895 "http://www.asylabwehramt.at/Seiten/Aktuelles.html" "Mozilla/4.0 (compatible; MSIE 8.0; Windows N T 5.2; Trident/4.0; .NET CLR 1.1.4322; .NET CLR 2.0.50727; .NET CLR 3.0.4506.2152; .NET CLR 3.5.3 0729)"

217.13.180.202 - - [18/Aug/2010:14:40:17 +0200] "GET /Seiten/Bilder.html HTTP/1.1" 200 10364 "htt

```
p://www.asylabwehramt.at/Seiten/Rundzeichen.html" "Mozilla/4.0 (compatible; MSIE 8.0; Windows NT 5.2; Trident/4.0; .NET CLR 2.0.50727; .NET CLR 1.1.4322; .NET CLR 3.0.4506.2152; .NET CLR 3.5.307 29)"
217.13.180.202 - - [18/Aug/2010:14:40:31 +0200] "GET /Seiten/Press.html HTTP/1.1" 200 12374 "http ://www.asylabwehramt.at/Seiten/Bilder.html" "Mozilla/4.0 (compatible; MSIE 8.0; Windows NT 5.2; T rident/4.0; .NET CLR 2.0.50727; .NET CLR 3.0.4506.2152; .NET CLR 3.5.30729)"
217.13.180.202 - - [18/Aug/2010:14:40:43 +0200] "GET /Seiten/Links.html HTTP/1.1" 200 19139 "http ://www.asylabwehramt.at/Seiten/Press.html" "Mozilla/4.0 (compatible; MSIE 8.0; Windows NT 5.2; Tr ident/4.0; .NET CLR 1.1.4322; .NET CLR 2.0.50727; .NET CLR 3.0.4506.2152; .NET CLR 3.5.30729)"
217.13.180.202 - - [18/Aug/2010:14:41:02 +0200] "GET /index.html HTTP/1.1" 200 11992 "http://www. asylabwehramt.at/Seiten/Links.html" "Mozilla/4.0 (compatible; MSIE 8.0; Windows NT 5.2; Trident/4 .0; .NET CLR 1.1.4322; .NET CLR 2.0.50727; .NET CLR 3.0.4506.2152; .NET CLR 3.5.30729)"
217.13.180.202 - - [18/Aug/2010:14:44:41 +0200] "GET / HTTP/1.1" 200 11992 "-" "Mozilla/4.0 (comp atible; MSIE 8.0; Windows NT 5.2; Trident/4.0; .NET CLR 2.0.50727; .NET CLR 3. 0.4506.2152; .NET CLR 3.5.30729)"
217.13.180.202 - - [18/Aug/2010:14:44:42 +0200] "GET /asyl.css HTTP/1.1" 200 860 "http://www.asyl abwehramt.at/" "Mozilla/4.0 (compatible; MSIE 8.0; Windows NT 5.2; Trident/4.0; .NET CLR 1.1.4322 ; .NET CLR 2.0.50727; .NET CLR 3.0.4506.2152; .NET CLR 3.5.30729)"
217.13.180.202 - - [18/Aug/2010:14:45:07 +0200] "GET /Seiten/Orgstrukt.html HTTP/1.1" 200 14119 " http://www.asylabwehramt.at/" "Mozilla/4.0 (compatible; MSIE 8.0; Windows NT 5.2; Trident/4.0; .N ET CLR 1.1.4322; .NET CLR 2.0.50727; .NET CLR 3.0.4506.2152; .NET CLR 3.5.30729)"
217.13.180.202 - - [18/Aug/2010:14:45:41 +0200] "GET /Seiten/Aktuelles.html HTTP/1.1" 200 14343 " http://www.asylabwehramt.at/Seiten/Orgstrukt.html" "Mozilla/4.0 (compatible; MSIE 8.0; Windows NT 5.2; Trident/4.0; .NET CLR 2.0.50727; .NET CLR 3.0.4506.2152; .NET CLR 3.5.30 729)"
217.13.180.202 - - [18/Aug/2010:14:46:00 +0200] "GET /Seiten/Links.html HTTP/1.1" 200 19139 "http ://www.asylabwehramt.at/Seiten/Aktuelles.html" "Mozilla/4.0 (compatible; MSIE 8.0; Windows NT 5.2 ; Trident/4.0; .NET CLR 1.1.4322; .NET CLR 2.0.50727; .NET CLR 3.0.4506.2152; .NET CLR 3.5.30729)"
```

"

217.13.180.202 - - [18/Aug/2010:14:46:58 +0200] "GET / HTTP/1.1" 200 11992 "-" "Mozilla/4.0 (comp
atible; MSIE 8.0; Windows NT 5.2; Trident/4.0; .NET CLR 1.1.4322; .NET CLR 2.0.50727; .NET CLR 3.
0.4506.2152; .NET CLR 3.5.30729)"
217.13.180.202 - - [18/Aug/2010:14:46:59 +0200] "GET /asyl.css HTTP/1.1" 200 860 "http://www.asyl
abwehramt.at/" "Mozilla/4.0 (compatible; MSIE 8.0; Windows NT 5.2; Trident/4.0; .NET CLR 1.1.4322
; .NET CLR 2.0.50727; .NET CLR 3.0.4506.2152; .NET CLR 3.5.30729)"
217.13.180.202 - - [18/Aug/2010:14:47:00 +0200] "GET /favicon.ico HTTP/1.1" 302 340 "-" "Mozilla/
4.0 (compatible; MSIE 8.0; Windows NT 5.2; Trident/4.0; .NET CLR 1.1.4322; .NET CLR 2.0.50727; .N
ET CLR 3.0.4506.2152; .NET CLR 3.5.30729)"
217.13.180.202 - - [18/Aug/2010:15:23:55 +0200] "GET / HTTP/1.1" 200 11992 "-" "Mozilla/4.0 (comp
atible; MSIE 8.0; Windows NT 5.2; Trident/4.0; .NET CLR 1.1.4322; .NET CLR 2.0.50727; .NET CLR 3.
0.4506.2152; .NET CLR 3.5.30729)"
217.13.180.202 - - [18/Aug/2010:15:23:56 +0200] "GET /asyl.css HTTP/1.1" 200 860 "http://www.asyl
abwehramt.at/" "Mozilla/4.0 (compatible; MSIE 8.0; Windows NT 5.2; Trident/4.0; .NET CLR 1.1.4322
; .NET CLR 2.0.50727; .NET CLR 3.0.4506.2152; .NET CLR 3.5.30729)"
217.13.180.202 - - [18/Aug/2010:16:28:50 +0200] "GET / HTTP/1.1" 200 11992 "-" "Mozilla/4.0 (comp
atible; MSIE 8.0; Windows NT 5.2; Trident/4.0; .NET CLR 1.1.4322; .NET CLR 2.0.50727; .NET CLR 3.
0.4506.2152; .NET CLR 3.5.30729)"
80.120.179.10 - - [19/Aug/2010:10:07:33 +0200] "GET / HTTP/1.1" 200 11992 "http://www.google.at/s
earch?hl=de&source=hp&q=asyl+abwehramt&meta=&aq=f&aqi=&aql=&oq=&gs_rfai=" "Mozilla/4.0 (compatibl
e; MSIE 6.0; Windows NT 5.1; SV1; .NET CLR 1.1.4322; .NET CLR 2.0.50727; .NET CLR 3.0.04506.30; .
NET CLR 3.0.04506.648; InfoPath.2; MS-RTC LM 8)"
80.120.179.10 - - [19/Aug/2010:10:07:59 +0200] "GET /index_e.html HTTP/1.1" 200 12025 "http://www
.asylabwehramt.at/" "Mozilla/4.0 (compatible; MSIE 6.0; Windows NT 5.1; SV1; .NET CLR 1.1.4322; .
NET CLR 2.0.50727; .NET CLR 3.0.04506.30; .NET CLR 3.0.04506.648; InfoPath.2; MS-RTC LM 8)"
80.120.179.10 - - [19/Aug/2010:10:08:03 +0200] "GET /Seiten/Aktuelles.html HTTP/1.1" 200 14343 "h
ttp://www.asylabwehramt.at/" "Mozilla/4.0 (compatible; MSIE 6.0; Windows NT 5.1; SV1; .NET CLR 1.

```
1.4322; .NET CLR 2.0.50727; .NET CLR 3.0.04506.30; .NET CLR 3.0.04506.648; InfoPath.2; MS-RTC LM
8)"
80.120.179.10 - - [19/Aug/2010:10:08:15 +0200] "GET /Seiten/Material.html HTTP/1.1" 200 17335 "ht
tp://www.asylabwehramt.at/Seiten/Aktuelles.html" "Mozilla/4.0 (compatible; MSIE 6.0; Windows NT 5
.1; SV1; .NET CLR 1.1.4322; .NET CLR 2.0.50727; .NET CLR 3.0.04506.30; .NET CLR 3.0.04506.648; In
foPath.2; MS-RTC LM 8)"
217.13.180.202 - - [23/Aug/2010:09:26:49 +0200] "GET / HTTP/1.1" 200 11992 "-" "Mozilla/4.0 (comp
atible; MSIE 8.0; Windows NT 5.2; Trident/4.0; .NET CLR 1.1.4322; .NET CLR 2.0.50727; .NET CLR 3.
0.4506.2152; .NET CLR 3.5.30729)"
217.13.180.202 - - [23/Aug/2010:09:26:50 +0200] "GET / HTTP/1.1" 304 - "-" "Mozilla/4.0 (compatib
le; MSIE 8.0; Windows NT 5.2; Trident/4.0; .NET CLR 1.1.4322; .NET CLR 2.0.50727; .NET CLR 3.0.45
06.2152; .NET CLR 3.5.30729)"
80.120.179.10 - - [23/Aug/2010:14:52:34 +0200] "GET / HTTP/1.1" 200 11992 "http://www.google.at/u
rl?sa=t&source=web&cd=82&ved=0CCgQFjABOFA&url=http%3A%2F%2Fwww.asylabwehramt.at%2F&rct=j&q=Terror
ismus%20Asylrecht&ei=Am9yTPKcPNDOswahx8G5Bg&usg=AFQjCNEy1zWC1vnxkLlPAGifRc344_0U4Q" "Mozilla/4.0
(compatible; MSIE 8.0; .NET CLR 3.0.04506.30; .NET CLR 1.1.4322; .NET CLR 2.0.50727; .NET C
LR 3.0.04506.30; Windows NT 5.1; Trident/4.0; .NET CLR 3.0.04506.648; InfoPath.2)"
85.158.226.103 - - [26/Aug/2010:10:34:30 +0200] "GET / HTTP/1.1" 200 11992 "-" "Mozilla/4.0 (comp
atible; MSIE 8.0; Windows NT 6.0; Trident/4.0; SLCC1; .NET CLR 2.0.50727; InfoPath.2; .NET CLR 3.
5.30729; .NET CLR 3.0.30729)"
85.158.226.103 - - [26/Aug/2010:10:34:31 +0200] "GET /favicon.ico HTTP/1.1" 302 340 "-" "Mozilla/
4.0 (compatible; MSIE 8.0; Windows NT 6.0; Trident/4.0; SLCC1; .NET CLR 2.0.50727; InfoPath.2; .N
ET CLR 3.5.30729; .NET CLR 3.0.30729)"
85.158.226.103 - - [26/Aug/2010:10:34:49 +0200] "GET /Seiten/Links.html HTTP/1.1" 200 19139 "http
://www.asylabwehramt.at/" "Mozilla/4.0 (compatible; MSIE 8.0; Windows NT 6.0; Trident/4.0; SLCC1;
.NET CLR 2.0.50727; InfoPath.2; .NET CLR 3.5.30729; .NET CLR 3.0.30729)"
85.158.226.103 - - [26/Aug/2010:10:35:52 +0200] "GET /index.html HTTP/1.1" 200 11992 "http://www.
asylabwehramt.at/Seiten/Links.html" "Mozilla/4.0 (compatible; MSIE 8.0; Windows NT 6.0; Trident/4
```

```
.0; SLCC1; .NET CLR 2.0.50727; InfoPath.2; .NET CLR 3.5.30729; .NET CLR 3.0.30729)"
85.158.226.103 - - [26/Aug/2010:10:36:27 +0200] "GET /Seiten/Material.html HTTP/1.1" 200 17335 "http://www.asylabwehramt.at/index.html" "Mozilla/4.0 (compatible; MSIE 8.0; Windows NT 6.0; Trident/4.0; SLCC1; .NET CLR 2.0.50727; InfoPath.2; .NET CLR 3.5.30729; .NET CLR 3.0.30729)"
85.158.226.103 - - [26/Aug/2010:10:36:46 +0200] "GET /Seiten/Orgstrukt.html HTTP/1.1" 200 14119 "http://www.asylabwehramt.at/Seiten/Material.html" "Mozilla/4.0 (compatible; MSIE 8.0; Windows NT 6.0; Trident/4.0; SLCC1; .NET CLR 2.0.50727; .NET CLR 3.5.30729; .NET CLR 3.0.30729)"
80.120.179.10 - - [26/Aug/2010:11:23:06 +0200] "GET /index.html HTTP/1.1" 200 11992 "-" "Mozilla/4.0 (compatible; MSIE 6.0; Windows NT 5.1; SV1; .NET CLR 1.1.4322; .NET CLR 2.0.50727; .NET CLR 3.0.04506.648; InfoPath.2; .NET CLR 3.0.04506.30; .NET CLR 3.0.4506.2152; .NET CLR 3.5.30729; MS-RTC LM 8)"
80.120.179.10 - - [26/Aug/2010:14:26:39 +0200] "GET / HTTP/1.1" 200 11992 "http://www.bing.com/search?q=asylabwehramt&FORM=IE8SRC" "Mozilla/4.0 (compatible; MSIE 8.0; Windows NT 5.1; Trident/4.0; .NET CLR 1.1.4322; .NET CLR 2.0.50727; .NET CLR 3.5.30729; .NET CLR 3.0.4506.2152; .NET CLR 3.0.04506.648; InfoPath.2; MS-RTC LM 8)"
80.120.179.10 - - [26/Aug/2010:14:27:36 +0200] "GET /Seiten/Aktuelles.html HTTP/1.1" 200 14343 "http://www.asylabwehramt.at/" "Mozilla/4.0 (compatible; MSIE 8.0; Windows NT 5.1; Trident/4.0; .NET CLR 1.1.4322; .NET CLR 2.0.50727; .NET CLR 3.0.04506.30; .NET CLR 3.0.04506.648; InfoPath.2; .NET CLR 3.0.4506.2152; .NET CLR 3.5.30729; MS-RTC LM 8)"
80.120.179.10 - - [26/Aug/2010:14:27:40 +0200] "GET /Seiten/Press.html HTTP/1.1" 200 12374 "http://www.asylabwehramt.at/Seiten/Aktuelles.html" "Mozilla/4.0 (compatible; MSIE 8.0; Windows NT 5.1; Trident/4.0; .NET CLR 1.1.4322; .NET CLR 2.0.50727; .NET CLR 3.0.04506.30; .NET CLR 3.0.04506.648; InfoPath.2; .NET CLR 3.0.4506.2152; .NET CLR 3.5.30729; MS-RTC LM 8)"
80.120.179.10 - - [26/Aug/2010:14:27:48 +0200] "GET /Seiten/Material.html HTTP/1.1" 200 17335 "http://www.asylabwehramt.at/Seiten/Press.html" "Mozilla/4.0 (compatible; MSIE 8.0; Windows NT 5.1; Trident/4.0; .NET CLR 1.1.4322; .NET CLR 2.0.50727; .NET CLR 3.5.30729; .NET CLR 3.0.04506.30; .NET CLR 3.5.30729; MS-RTC LM 8)"
```

194.107.234.50[34] - - [30/Aug/2010:11:14:58 +0200] "GET / HTTP/1.1" 200 11992 "http://oe1.orf.at/ar
tikel/246521" "Mozilla/4.0 (compatible; MSIE 7.0; Windows NT 6.0; SLCC1; .NET CLR 2.0.50727; .NE
T CLR 3.5.30729; .NET CLR 3.0.30618; MS-RTC LM 8)"
194.107.234.50 - - [30/Aug/2010:11:14:59 +0200] "GET /favicon.ico HTTP/1.1" 302 340 "-" "Mozilla/
4.0 (compatible; MSIE 7.0; Windows NT 6.0; SLCC1; .NET CLR 2.0.50727; .NET CLR 3.5.30729; .NET CL
R 3.0.30618; MS-RTC LM 8)"
194.107.234.50 - - [30/Aug/2010:11:15:30 +0200] "GET /Seiten/Aktuelles.html HTTP/1.1" 200 14343 "
http://www.asylabwehramt.at/" "Mozilla/4.0 (compatible; MSIE 7.0; Windows NT 6.0; SLCC1; .NET CLR
2.0.50727; .NET CLR 3.5.30729; .NET CLR 3.0.30618; MS-RTC LM 8)"
194.107.234.50 - - [30/Aug/2010:11:15:58 +0200] "GET /Seiten/Impressum.html HTTP/1.1" 200 11939 "
http://www.asylabwehramt.at/Seiten/Aktuelles.html" "Mozilla/4.0 (compatible; MSIE 7.0; Windows NT
6.0; SLCC1; .NET CLR 2.0.50727; .NET CLR 3.5.30729; .NET CLR 3.0.30618; MS-RTC LM 8)"
79.225.128.243 - - [01/Sep/2010:18:19:18 +0200] "GET /Seiten/Orgstrukt.html HTTP/1.1" 304 - "http
://www.google.at/search?hl=de&source=hp&q=asylantrag+%C3%B6sterreich+formular&aq=f&aqi=&oq=&
gs_rfai=" "Mozilla/4.0 (compatible; MSIE 7.0; Windows NT 5.1; .NET CLR 1.1.4322; InfoPath.1)"
80.120.179.10 - - [02/Sep/2010:15:17:55 +0200] "GET / HTTP/1.1" 200 11992 "-" "Mozilla/4.0 (compa
tible; MSIE 8.0; Windows NT 5.1; Trident/4.0; InfoPath.1; .NET CLR 2.0.50727;
MS-RTC LM 8; .NET4.0C)"
80.120.179.10 - - [02/Sep/2010:15:18:00 +0200] "GET /Seiten/Bilder.html HTTP/1.1" 200 10364 "http
://www.asylabwehramt.at/" "Mozilla/4.0 (compatible; MSIE 8.0; Windows NT 5.1; Trident/4.0; InfoPa
th.1; .NET CLR 1.1.4322; .NET CLR 2.0.50727; MS-RTC LM 8; .NET4.0C)"
80.120.179.10 - - [09/Sep/2010:10:14:49 +0200] "GET / HTTP/1.1" 200 11992 "-" "Mozilla/4.0 (compa
tible; MSIE 6.0; Windows NT 5.1; SV1; .NET CLR 1.1.4322; MS-RTC LM 8)"
80.120.179.10 - - [09/Sep/2010:10:14:50 +0200] "GET /asyl.css HTTP/1.1" 200 860 "http://www.asyla
bwehramt.at/" "Mozilla/4.0 (compatible; MSIE 6.0; Windows NT 5.1; SV1; .NET CLR 1.1.4322; MS-RTC
LM 8)"

---

[34]WHOIS record on page 314

213.208.144.130 - - [13/Sep/2010:11:32:22 +0200] "GET / HTTP/1.0" 200 11992 "http://www.google.at/search?hl=de&source=hp&q=asylabwehramt &aq=f&aql=g-s1&aql=&oq=&gs_rfai=" "Mozilla/4.0 (compatible; MSIE 7.0; Windows NT 5.2; .NET CLR 1.1.4322; InfoPath.1; .NET CLR 2.0.50727; .NET CLR 3.0.4506.2152; .NET CLR 3.5.30729)"

80.120.179.10 - - [17/Sep/2010:16:27:50 +0200] "GET / HTTP/1.1" 200 11992 "http://www.google.at/search?num=50&hl=de&newwindow=1&q= asyl+abwehramt &meta=&aq=3s&aql=g3g-s1g6&aql=&oq=asyl&gs_rfai=" Mozilla/4.0 (compatible; MSIE 6.0; Windows NT 5.1; SV1; .NET CLR 1.1.4322; .NET CLR 2.0.50727; .NET CLR 3.0.4506.2152; .NET CLR 3.5.307 ET CLR 3.0.04506.30; .NET CLR 3.0.04506.648; InfoPath.2; .NET CLR 3.0.4506.2152; .NET CLR 3.5.307 29; MS-RTC LM 8)"

80.120.179.10 - - [17/Sep/2010:16:31:34 +0200] "GET /Seiten/Bilder.html HTTP/1.1" 200 10364 "http ://www.asylabwehramt.at/" "Mozilla/4.0 (compatible; MSIE 6.0; Windows NT 5.1; SV1; .NET CLR 1.1.4 322; .NET CLR 2.0.50727; .NET CLR 3.0.04506.30; .NET CLR 3.0.04506.648; InfoPath.2; .NET CLR 3.0. 4506.2152; .NET CLR 3.5.30729; MS-RTC LM 8)"

80.120.179.10 - - [17/Sep/2010:16:32:36 +0200] "GET /Seiten/Material.html HTTP/1.1" 200 17335 "ht tp://www.asylabwehramt.at/Seiten/Bilder.html" "Mozilla/4.0 (compatible; MSIE 6.0; Windows NT 5.1; SV1; .NET CLR 1.1.4322; .NET CLR 2.0.50727; .NET CLR 3.0.04506.30; .NET CLR 3.0.04506.648; InfoP ath.2; .NET CLR 3.0.4506.2152; .NET CLR 3.5.30729; MS-RTC LM 8)"

80.120.179.10 - - [17/Sep/2010:16:34:01 +0200] "GET /Seiten/Rundzeichen.html HTTP/1.1" 200 8895 " http://www.asylabwehramt.at/Seiten/Bilder.html" "Mozilla/4.0 (compatible; MSIE 6.0; Windows NT 5. 1; SV1; .NET CLR 1.1.4322; .NET CLR 2.0.50727; .NET CLR 3.0.04506.30; .NET CLR 3.0.04506.648; Inf oPath.2; .NET CLR 3.5.30729; MS-RTC LM 8)"

80.120.179.10 - - [17/Sep/2010:16:34:09 +0200] "GET /index.html HTTP/1.1" 200 11992 "http://www.a sylabwehramt.at/Seiten/Rundzeichen.html" "Mozilla/4.0 (compatible; MSIE 6.0; Windows NT 5.1; SV1; .NET CLR 1.1.4322; .NET CLR 2.0.50727; .NET CLR 3.0.04506.2152; .NET CLR 3.5.30729; MS-RTC LM 8)" ; .NET CLR 3.0.4506.2152; .NET CLR 3.5.30729; MS-RTC LM 8)"

80.120.179.10 - - [17/Sep/2010:16:34:28 +0200] "GET /Seiten/Press.html HTTP/1.1" 200 12374 "http: //www.asylabwehramt.at/index.html" "Mozilla/4.0 (compatible; MSIE 6.0; Windows NT 5.1; SV1; .NET CLR 1.1.4322; .NET CLR 2.0.50727; .NET CLR 3.0.04506.30; .NET CLR 3.0.04506.648; InfoPath.2; .NET

```
CLR 3.0.4506.2152; .NET CLR 3.5.30729; MS-RTC LM 8)"
80.120.179.10 - - [17/Sep/2010:16:34:32 +0200] "GET /OEFFENTLICHKEIT/07062010d.pdf HTTP/1.1" 200
333788 "http://www.asylabwehramt.at/Seiten/Press.html" "Mozilla/4.0 (compatible; MSIE 6.0; Window
s NT 5.1; SV1; .NET CLR 1.1.4322; .NET CLR 2.0.50727; .NET CLR 3.0.04506.30; .NET CLR 3.0.04506.6
48; InfoPath.2; .NET CLR 3.0.4506.2152; .NET CLR 3.5.30729; MS-RTC LM 8)"
80.120.179.10 - - [17/Sep/2010:16:34:52 +0200] "GET /OEFFENTLICHKEIT/media/ZEIT.pdf HTTP/1.1" 200
484489 "http://www.google.at/search?num=50&hl=de&newwindow=1&q=asyl+abwehramt&meta=&aq=3s&aqi=g3
g-s1g6&aql=&oq=asyl&gs_rfai=" "Mozilla/4.0 (compatible; MSIE 6.0; Windows NT 5.1; SV1; .NET CLR 1
.1.4322; .NET CLR 2.0.50727; .NET CLR 3.0.04506.30; .NET CLR 3.0.04506.648; InfoPath.2; .NET CLR
3.0.4506.2152; .NET CLR 3.5.30729; MS-RTC LM 8)"
217.13.180.202 - - [20/Sep/2010:18:14:08 +0200] "GET / HTTP/1.1" 200 11992 "http://www.google.at/
search?hl=de&source=hp&q=asylabwehramt&aq=f&aqi=g-s1&aql=&oq=&gs_rfai=&fp=83689be276ae7af" "Mozil
la/5.0 (Windows; U; Windows NT 5.2; de; rv:1.9.1.5) Gecko/20091102 Firefox/3.5.5"
217.13.180.202 - - [20/Sep/2010:18:14:12 +0200] "GET /Bilder/Header_AAbA_anim.gif HTTP/1.1" 200 1
9997 "http://www.asylabwehramt.at/" "Mozilla/5.0 (Windows; U; Windows NT 5.2; de; rv:1.9.1.5) Gec
ko/20091102 Firefox/3.5.5"
217.13.180.202 - - [20/Sep/2010:18:14:15 +0200] "GET /favicon.ico HTTP/1.1" 302 340 "-" "Mozilla/
5.0 (Windows; U; Windows NT 5.2; de; rv:1.9.1.5) Gecko/20091102 Firefox/3.5.5"
217.13.180.202 - - [20/Sep/2010:18:14:25 +0200] "GET /Seiten/Rundzeichen.html HTTP/1.1" 200 8895
"http://www.asylabwehramt.at/" "Mozilla/5.0 (Windows; U; Windows NT 5.2; de; rv:1.9.1.5) Gecko/20
091102 Firefox/3.5.5"
80.120.179.10 - - [24/Sep/2010:12:08:42 +0200] "GET / HTTP/1.1" 200 11992 "-" "Mozilla/4.0 (compa
tible; MSIE 8.0; Windows NT 5.1; Trident/4.0; .NET CLR 1.1.4322; InfoPath.1; .NET CLR 2.0.50727;
.NET CLR 3.0.04506.648; .NET CLR 3.5.21022)"
80.120.179.10 - - [27/Sep/2010:11:56:12 +0200] "GET / HTTP/1.1" 200 11992 "http://www.abacho.at/s
uche/?q=asylabwehramt" "Mozilla/4.0 (compatible; MSIE 8.0; Windows NT 5.1; Trident/4.0; .NET CLR
1.1.4322; .NET CLR 2.0.50727; .NET CLR 3.0.04506.30; .NET CLR 3.0.04506.648; InfoPath.2; .NET CLR
3.0.4506.2152; .NET CLR 3.5.30729; MS-RTC LM 8)"
```

```
80.120.179.10 - - [27/Sep/2010:11:57:00 +0200] "GET /Seiten/Bilder.html HTTP/1.1" 200 10364 "http://www.asylabwehramt.at/" "Mozilla/4.0 (compatible; MSIE 8.0; Windows NT 5.1; Trident/4.0; .NET CLR 1.1.4322; .NET CLR 2.0.50727; .NET CLR 3.0.04506.30; .NET CLR 3.0.04506.648; InfoPath.2; .NET CLR 3.0.4506.2152; .NET CLR 3.5.30729; MS-RTC LM 8)"
193.171.152.33 - - [04/Oct/2010:12:13:09 +0200] "GET / HTTP/1.1" 200 11992 "http://www.google.at/search?hl=de&source=hp&q=asylabwehramt&meta=&aq=f&aqi=g-s1&aql=&oq=&gs_rfai=" "Mozilla/4.0 (compatible; MSIE 6.0; Windows NT 5.1; SV1; InfoPath.1; .NET CLR 1.1.4322; .NET CLR 2.0.50727)"
193.171.152.33 - - [04/Oct/2010:12:13:48 +0200] "GET /index.html HTTP/1.1" 200 11992 "http://www.asylabwehramt.at/" "Mozilla/4.0 (compatible; MSIE 6.0; Windows NT 5.1; SV1; InfoPath.1; .NET CLR 1.1.4322; .NET CLR 2.0.50727)"
193.171.152.33 - - [04/Oct/2010:12:18:46 +0200] "GET /index_e.html HTTP/1.1" 200 12025 "http://www.asylabwehramt.at/" "Mozilla/4.0 (compatible; MSIE 6.0; Windows NT 5.1; SV1; InfoPath.1; .NET CLR 1.1.4322; .NET CLR 2.0.50727)"
193.171.152.33 - - [04/Oct/2010:12:18:47 +0200] "GET /Seiten/Latestnews.html HTTP/1.1" 200 14563 "http://www.asylabwehramt.at/index_e.html" "Mozilla/4.0 (compatible; MSIE 6.0; Windows NT 5.1; SV1; InfoPath.1; .NET CLR 1.1.4322; .NET CLR 2.0.50727)"
193.171.152.33 - - [04/Oct/2010:12:18:48 +0200] "GET /Bilder/leistung_2.jpg HTTP/1.1" 200 4918 "http://www.asylabwehramt.at/Seiten/Latestnews.html" "Mozilla/4.0 (compatible; MSIE 6.0; Windows NT 5.1; SV1; InfoPath.1; .NET CLR 1.1.4322; .NET CLR 2.0.50727)"
193.171.152.33 - - [04/Oct/2010:12:19:08 +0200] "GET /Seiten/Aktuelles.html HTTP/1.1" 200 14343 "http://www.asylabwehramt.at/index.html" "Mozilla/4.0 (compatible; MSIE 6.0; Windows NT 5.1; SV1; InfoPath.1; .NET CLR 1.1.4322; .NET CLR 2.0.50727)"
193.171.152.33 - - [04/Oct/2010:12:19:43 +0200] "GET /Seiten/Material.html HTTP/1.1" 200 17335 "http://www.asylabwehramt.at/Seiten/Aktuelles.html" "Mozilla/4.0 (compatible; MSIE 6.0; Windows NT 5.1; SV1; InfoPath.1; .NET CLR 1.1.4322; .NET CLR 2.0.50727)"
193.171.152.33 - - [04/Oct/2010:12:19:49 +0200] "GET /Seiten/Rundzeichen.html HTTP/1.1" 200 8895 "http://www.asylabwehramt.at/Seiten/Material.html" "Mozilla/4.0 (compatible; MSIE 6.0; Windows NT
```

```
5.1; SV1; InfoPath.1; .NET CLR 1.1.4322; .NET CLR 2.0.50727)"
193.171.152.33 - - [04/Oct/2010:12:19:58 +0200] "GET /Seiten/Bilder.html HTTP/1.1" 200 10364 "htt
p://www.asylabwehramt.at/Seiten/Rundzeichen.html" "Mozilla/4.0 (compatible; MSIE 6.0; Windows NT
5.1; SV1; InfoPath.1; .NET CLR 1.1.4322; .NET CLR 2.0.50727)"
193.171.152.33 - - [04/Oct/2010:12:20:26 +0200] "GET /Seiten/Bilder_Ausstellung.html HTTP/1.1" 20
0 16685 "http://www.asylabwehramt.at/Seiten/Bilder.html" "Mozilla/4.0 (compatible; MSIE 6.0; Wind
ows NT 5.1; SV1; InfoPath.1; .NET CLR 1.1.4322; .NET CLR 2.0.50727)"
193.171.152.33 - - [04/Oct/2010:12:20:27 +0200] "GET /Bilder/Ausstellung_weisses_haus_wien_esel_f
otos/eSeL_UBERMORGEN_asylabwehramt_dasweissehaus_484_thumb.jpg HTTP/1.1" 200 48099 "http://www.as
ylabwehramt.at/Seiten/Bilder_Ausstellung.html" "Mozilla/4.0 (compatible; MSIE 6.0; Windows NT 5.1
; SV1; InfoPath.1; .NET CLR 1.1.4322; .NET CLR 2.0.50727)"
193.171.152.33 - - [04/Oct/2010:12:20:28 +0200] "GET /Bilder/Ausstellung_weisses_haus_wien_esel_f
otos/eSeL_UBERMORGEN_asylabwehramt_dasweissehaus_481_thumb.jpg HTTP/1.1" 200 25101 "http://www.as
ylabwehramt.at/Seiten/Bilder_Ausstellung.html" "Mozilla/4.0 (compatible; MSIE 6.0; Windows NT 5.1
; SV1; InfoPath.1; .NET CLR 1.1.4322; .NET CLR 2.0.50727)"
193.171.152.33 - - [04/Oct/2010:12:20:29 +0200] "GET /Bilder/Ausstellung_weisses_haus_wien_esel_f
otos/eSeL_UBERMORGEN_asylabwehramt_dasweissehaus_476_thumb.jpg HTTP/1.1" 200 46505 "http://www.as
ylabwehramt.at/Seiten/Bilder_Ausstellung.html" "Mozilla/4.0 (compatible; MSIE 6.0; Windows NT 5.1
; SV1; InfoPath.1; .NET CLR 1.1.4322; .NET CLR 2.0.50727)"
193.171.152.33 - - [04/Oct/2010:12:20:30 +0200] "GET /Bilder/Ausstellung_weisses_haus_wien_esel_f
otos/eSeL_UBERMORGEN_asylabwehramt_dasweissehaus_507_thumb.jpg HTTP/1.1" 200 40356 "http://www.as
ylabwehramt.at/Seiten/Bilder_Ausstellung.html" "Mozilla/4.0 (compatible; MSIE 6.0; Windows NT 5.1
; SV1; InfoPath.1; .NET CLR 1.1.4322; .NET CLR 2.0.50727)"
193.171.152.33 - - [04/Oct/2010:12:20:39 +0200] "GET /Bilder/Ausstellung_weisses_haus_wien_esel_f
otos/eSeL_UBERMORGEN_asylabwehramt_dasweissehaus_453.jpg HTTP/1.1" 200 298009 "http://www.asylabw
ehramt.at/Seiten/Bilder_Ausstellung.html" "Mozilla/4.0 (compatible; MSIE 6.0; Windows NT 5.1; SV1
; InfoPath.1; .NET CLR 1.1.4322; .NET CLR 2.0.50727)"
193.171.152.33 - - [04/Oct/2010:12:22:33 +0200] "GET /Seiten/Links.html HTTP/1.1" 200 19139 "http
```

://www.asylabwehramt.at/Seiten/Bilder.html" "Mozilla/4.0 (compatible; MSIE 6.0; Windows NT 5.1; S
V1; InfoPath.1; .NET CLR 1.1.4322; .NET CLR 2.0.50727)"
193.171.152.33 - - [04/Oct/2010:12:22:43 +0200] "GET /Seiten/Press.html HTTP/1.1" 200 12374 "http
://www.asylabwehramt.at/Seiten/Links.html" "Mozilla/4.0 (compatible; MSIE 6.0; Windows NT 5.1; SV
1; InfoPath.1; .NET CLR 1.1.4322; .NET CLR 2.0.50727)"
193.171.152.33 - - [04/Oct/2010:12:22:51 +0200] "GET /Seiten/Orgstruct.html HTTP/1.1" 200 14226 "
http://www.asylabwehramt.at/Seiten/Press.html" "Mozilla/4.0 (compatible; MSIE 6.0; Windows NT 5.1
; SV1; InfoPath.1; .NET CLR 1.1.4322; .NET CLR 2.0.50727)"
80.122.134.190 - - [08/Oct/2010:12:01:48 +0200] "GET /Seiten/Orgstrukt.html HTTP/1.1" 200 14119 "
http://www.google.at/url?sa=t&source=web&cd=6&ved=0CCoQFjAF&url=http%3A%2F%2Fwww.asylabwehramt.at
%2FSeiten%2FOrgstrukt.html&rct=j&q=asylantrag%20formular%20%C3%B6sterreich&ei=iuuuTKLwAdSO4Aan5YX
-Bg&usg=AFQjCNFupGGPUoPKDe7UpjwYvDejEFClyA" "Mozilla/5.0 (Windows; U; Windows NT 5.1; de; rv:1.9.
2.10) Gecko/20100914 Firefox/3.6.10 (.NET CLR 3.5.30729)"
78.41.144.41 - - [12/Oct/2010:09:25:42 +0200] "GET / HTTP/1.0" 200 11992 "http://www.google.at/ur
l?url=http://www.asylabwehramt.at/&rct=j&sa=U&ei=ZQ20TNyKOoaJsgba2IGjDA&ved=0CBkQFjAA&q=asyl+abwe
hramt&usg=AFQjCNE2gNZvjXlWMDEoXGh7SPdh_ftukg" "Mozilla/4.0 (compatible; MSIE 8.0; Windows NT 5.1;
Trident/4.0; .NET CLR 2.0.50727; .NET CLR 1.1.4322; .NET CLR 3.0.04506.30; .NET CLR 3.0.04506.64
8; .NET CLR 3.0.4506.2152; .NET CLR 3.5.30729)"
78.41.144.41 - - [12/Oct/2010:09:25:43 +0200] "GET /Bilder/Header_AAbA_anim.gif HTTP/1.0" 200 199
97 "http://www.asylabwehramt.at/" "Mozilla/4.0 (compatible; MSIE 8.0; Windows NT 5.1; Trident/4.0
; .NET CLR 2.0.50727; .NET CLR 1.1.4322; .NET CLR 3.0.04506.30; .NET CLR 3.0.04506.648; .NET CLR
3.0.4506.2152; .NET CLR 3.5.30729)"
78.41.144.41 - - [12/Oct/2010:09:26:32 +0200] "GET /Seiten/Aktuelles.html HTTP/1.0" 200 14343 "ht
tp://www.asylabwehramt.at/" "Mozilla/4.0 (compatible; MSIE 8.0; Windows NT 5.1; Trident/4.0; .NET
CLR 2.0.50727; .NET CLR 1.1.4322; .NET CLR 3.0.04506.30; .NET CLR 3.0.04506.648; .NET CLR 3.0.45
06.2152; .NET CLR 3.5.30729)"
78.41.144.41 - - [12/Oct/2010:09:27:39 +0200] "GET /Seiten/Material.html HTTP/1.0" 200 17335 "htt

```
p://www.asylabwehramt.at/Seiten/Aktuelles.html" "Mozilla/4.0 (compatible; MSIE 8.0; Windows NT 5.1; Trident/4.0; .NET CLR 2.0.50727; .NET CLR 1.1.4322; .NET CLR 3.0.04506.30; .NET CLR 3.0.04506.648; .NET CLR 3.0.4506.2152; .NET CLR 3.5.30729)"
78.41.144.41 - - [12/Oct/2010:09:28:11 +0200] "GET /Seiten/Rundzeichen.html HTTP/1.0" 200 8895 "http://www.asylabwehramt.at/Seiten/Material.html" "Mozilla/4.0 (compatible; MSIE 8.0; Windows NT 5.1; Trident/4.0; .NET CLR 2.0.50727; .NET CLR 1.1.4322; .NET CLR 3.0.04506.30; .NET CLR 3.0.04506.648; .NET CLR 3.0.4506.2152; .NET CLR 3.5.30729)"
78.41.144.41 - - [12/Oct/2010:09:28:20 +0200] "GET /Seiten/Bilder.html HTTP/1.0" 200 10364 "http://www.asylabwehramt.at/Seiten/Rundzeichen.html" "Mozilla/4.0 (compatible; MSIE 8.0; Windows NT 5.1; Trident/4.0; .NET CLR 2.0.50727; .NET CLR 1.1.4322; .NET CLR 3.0.04506.30; .NET CLR 3.0.04506.648; .NET CLR 3.0.4506.2152; .NET CLR 3.5.30729)"
85.158.226.1 - - [15/Oct/2010:06:36:44 +0200] "GET /Bilder/SCREEN_AbA_Edutainment_Video.jpg HTTP/1.1" 200 29259 "http://forum.geizhals.at/t562009,6159863.html" "Mozilla/4.0 (compatible; MSIE 7.0; Windows NT 5.1; Trident/4.0; .NET CLR 1.1.4322; .NET CLR 2.0.50727; .NET CLR 3.0.4506.2152; .NET CLR 3.5.30729)"
128.250.5.246[35] - - [18/Oct/2010:03:00:05 +0200] "GET /OEFFENTLICHKEIT/media/ZEIT.pdf HTTP/1.0" 200 484489 "http://www.google.com.au/search?hl=en&rls=com.microsoft%3Aen-au%3AIE-SearchBox&q=asylbewerber+problem+schlingensief&aq=f&aqi=&aql=&oq=&gs_rfai=" "Mozilla/4.0 (compatible; MSIE 8.0; Windows NT 6.1; WOW64; Trident/4.0; SLCC2; .NET CLR 2.0.50727; .NET CLR 3.5.30729; .NET CLR 3.0.30729; Media Center PC 6.0; MDDC; InfoPath.2; .NET4.0C; MDDC)"
128.250.5.245[36] - - [18/Oct/2010:03:00:16 +0200] "GET /OEFFENTLICHKEIT/media/ZEIT.pdf HTTP/1.0" 200 484489 "http://www.google.com.au/search?hl=en&rls=com.microsoft%3Aen-au%3AIE-SearchBox&q=asylbewerber+problem+schlingensief&aq=f&aqi=&aql=&oq=&gs_rfai=" "Mozilla/4.0 (compatible; MSIE 8.0; Windows NT 6.1; WOW64; Trident/4.0; SLCC2; .NET CLR 2.0.50727; .NET CLR 3.5.30729; .NET CLR 3.0.30729; Media Center PC 6.0; MDDC; InfoPath.2; .NET4.0C; MDDC)"
```

[35] WHOIS record on page 288
[36] WHOIS record on page 286

84.20.184.170 - - [19/Oct/2010:13:29:12 +0200] "GET /Seiten/Impressum.html HTTP/1.1" 200 11939 "http://www.google.at/url?sa=t&source=web&cd=10&ved=0CEEQFjAJ&url=http%3A%2F%2Fwww.asylabwehramt.at%2FSeiten%2FImpressum.html&rct=j&q=asylantrag%20formular%20%C3%B6sterreich%20doc&ei=74C9TK-vGI_0sgaL9cXQDQ&usg=AFQjCNHF7HP6dxpY82GEXb1PQnRvP4GW7g&sig2=T2jHY2Hgf65BZlLtkercwQ" "Mozilla/5.0 (Windows; U; Windows NT 6.1; de; rv:1.9.2.10) Gecko/20100914 Firefox/3.6.10"

80.120.179.10 - - [20/Oct/2010:08:53:50 +0200] "GET /OEFFENTLICHKEIT/media/ZEIT.pdf HTTP/1.1" 200 484489 "http://www.google.at/search?hl=de&cr=countryAT&tbs=ctr%3AcountryAT&q=kunstprojekt+asylamt&aq=f&aqi=&aql=&oq=&gs_rfai=" "Mozilla/4.0 (compatible; MSIE 7.0; Windows NT 5.1; .NET CLR 1.1.4322; .NET CLR 2.0.50727; .NET CLR 3.0.04506.30; .NET CLR 3.0.04506.648; InfoPath.2; .NET CLR 3.0.4506.2152; .NET CLR 3.5.30729; MS-RTC LM 8)"

80.120.179.10 - - [20/Oct/2010:08:55:55 +0200] "GET / HTTP/1.1" 200 12092 "-" "Mozilla/4.0 (compatible; MSIE 7.0; Windows NT 5.1; .NET CLR 1.1.4322; .NET CLR 2.0.50727; .NET CLR 3.0.04506.30; .NET CLR 3.0.04506.648; InfoPath.2; .NET CLR 3.0.4506.2152; .NET CLR 3.5.30729; MS-RTC LM 8)"

80.120.179.10 - - [20/Oct/2010:08:56:13 +0200] "GET /Seiten/Impressum.html HTTP/1.1" 200 11939 "http://asylabwehramt.at/" "Mozilla/4.0 (compatible; MSIE 7.0; Windows NT 5.1; .NET CLR 1.1.4322; .NET CLR 2.0.50727; .NET CLR 3.0.04506.30; .NET CLR 3.0.4506.2152; .NET CLR 3.5.30729; MS-RTC LM 8)"

80.120.179.10 - - [20/Oct/2010:08:56:41 +0200] "GET /Seiten/Orgstrukt.html HTTP/1.1" 200 14119 "http://asylabwehramt.at/Seiten/Impressum.html" "Mozilla/4.0 (compatible; MSIE 7.0; Windows NT 5.1; .NET CLR 1.1.4322; .NET CLR 2.0.50727; .NET CLR 3.0.04506.30; .NET CLR 3.0.04506.648; InfoPath.2; .NET CLR 3.0.4506.2152; .NET CLR 3.5.30729; MS-RTC LM 8)"

80.120.179.10 - - [20/Oct/2010:08:56:51 +0200] "GET /index.html HTTP/1.1" 200 12092 "http://asylabwehramt.at/Seiten/Orgstrukt.html" "Mozilla/4.0 (compatible; MSIE 7.0; Windows NT 5.1; .NET CLR 1.1.4322; .NET CLR 2.0.50727; .NET CLR 3.0.04506.30; .NET CLR 3.0.4506.2152; .NET CLR 3.5.30729; MS-RTC LM 8)"

80.120.179.10 - - [20/Oct/2010:08:56:54 +0200] "GET /Seiten/Aktuelles.html HTTP/1.1" 200 14343 "http://asylabwehramt.at/index.html" "Mozilla/4.0 (compatible; MSIE 7.0; Windows NT 5.1; .NET CLR 1

```
.1.4322; .NET CLR 2.0.50727; .NET CLR 3.5.30729; MS-RTC LM 8)"
3.0.4506.2152; .NET CLR 3.5.30729; MS-RTC LM 8)"
80.120.179.10 - - [20/Oct/2010:08:56:58 +0200] "GET /Seiten/Material.html HTTP/1.1" 200 17335 "ht
tp://asylabwehramt.at/Seiten/Aktuelles.html" "Mozilla/4.0 (compatible; MSIE 7.0; Windows NT 5.1;
.NET CLR 1.1.4322; .NET CLR 2.0.50727; .NET CLR 3.5.30729; MS-RTC LM 8)"
.NET CLR 3.0.4506.2152; .NET CLR 3.0.04506.30; .NET CLR 3.0.04506.648; InfoPath.2;
80.120.179.10 - - [20/Oct/2010:08:57:00 +0200] "GET /Seiten/Rundzeichen.html HTTP/1.1" 200 8895 "
http://asylabwehramt.at/Seiten/Material.html" "Mozilla/4.0 (compatible; MSIE 7.0; Windows NT 5.1;
.NET CLR 1.1.4322; .NET CLR 2.0.50727; .NET CLR 3.0.04506.30; .NET CLR 3.0.04506.648; InfoPath.2
; .NET CLR 3.0.4506.2152; .NET CLR 3.5.30729; MS-RTC LM 8)"
80.120.179.10 - - [20/Oct/2010:08:57:01 +0200] "GET /Seiten/Bilder.html HTTP/1.1" 200 10364 "http
://asylabwehramt.at/Seiten/Rundzeichen.html" "Mozilla/4.0 (compatible; MSIE 7.0; Windows NT 5.1;
.NET CLR 1.1.4322; .NET CLR 2.0.50727; .NET CLR 3.0.04506.30; .NET CLR 3.0.04506.648; InfoPath.2;
.NET CLR 3.0.4506.2152; .NET CLR 3.5.30729; MS-RTC LM 8)"
80.120.179.10 - - [20/Oct/2010:08:57:15 +0200] "GET /Seiten/Links.html HTTP/1.1" 200 19139 "http:
//asylabwehramt.at/Seiten/Bilder.html" "Mozilla/4.0 (compatible; MSIE 7.0; Windows NT 5.1; .NET C
LR 1.1.4322; .NET CLR 2.0.50727; .NET CLR 3.0.04506.30; .NET CLR 3.0.04506.648; InfoPath.2; .NET
CLR 3.0.4506.2152; .NET CLR 3.5.30729; MS-RTC LM 8)"
80.120.179.10 - - [20/Oct/2010:08:57:52 +0200] "GET / HTTP/1.1" 200 12092 "http://www.google.at/s
earch?hl=de&q=asylabwehramt&meta=cr%3DcountryAT&aq=f&aqi=g-s1&oq=&gs_rfai=" "Mozilla/4.0 (co
mpatible; MSIE 6.0; Windows NT 5.1; SV1; .NET CLR 1.1.4322; .NET CLR 2.0.50727; .NET CLR 3.0.0450
6.30; .NET CLR 3.0.04506.648; InfoPath.2)"
80.120.179.10 - - [20/Oct/2010:08:58:09 +0200] "GET /Seiten/Impressum.html HTTP/1.1" 200 11939 "h
ttp://www.asylabwehramt.at/" "Mozilla/4.0 (compatible; MSIE 6.0; Windows NT 5.1; SV1; .NET CLR 1.
1.4322; .NET CLR 2.0.50727; .NET CLR 3.0.04506.30; .NET CLR 3.0.04506.648; InfoPath.2)"
80.120.179.10 - - [20/Oct/2010:08:58:16 +0200] "GET /Seiten/Links_e.html HTTP/1.1" 200 19142 "htt
p://asylabwehramt.at/Seiten/Impressum.html" "Mozilla/4.0 (compatible; MSIE 7.0; Windows NT 5.1; .
NET CLR 1.1.4322; .NET CLR 2.0.50727; .NET CLR 3.0.04506.30; .NET CLR 3.0.04506.648; InfoPath.2;
```

.NET CLR 3.0.4506.2152; .NET CLR 3.5.30729; MS-RTC LM 8)"

80.120.179.10 - - [20/Oct/2010:09:00:11 +0200] "GET /Material/AABA_MATERIAL.zip HTTP/1.1" 200 983
48161 "http://asylabwehramt.at/Seiten/Links_e.html" "Mozilla/4.0 (compatible; MSIE 7.0; Windows N
T 5.1; .NET CLR 1.1.4322; .NET CLR 2.0.50727; .NET CLR 3.0.04506.30; .NET CLR 3.0.04506.648; Info
Path.2; .NET CLR 3.0.4506.2152; .NET CLR 3.5.30729; MS-RTC LM 8)"

80.120.179.10 - - [20/Oct/2010:13:38:46 +0200] "GET /favicon.ico HTTP/1.1" 302 340 "-" "Mozilla/4
.0 (compatible; MSIE 8.0; Windows NT 5.1; Trident/4.0; .NET CLR 1.1.4322; .NET CLR 2.0.50727; .NE
T CLR 3.0.04506.30; .NET CLR 3.0.04506.648; InfoPath.2; MS-RTC LM 8; .NET CLR 3.5.21022)"

78.41.144.41 - - [20/Oct/2010:13:42:48 +0200] "GET /Seiten/Links.html HTTP/1.0" 200 19139 "http:/
/www.google.at/url?sa=t&source=web&cd=22&ved=0CBcQFjABOBQ&url=http%3A%2F%2Fwww.asylabwehramt.at%2
FSeiten%2FLinks.html&rct=j&q=`%C3%B6sterreichisches%20Asylverfahren%20Download`&ei=ntW-TNXuE0EOqyZ
mVQ&usg=AFQjCNF-wWPeHYAHlkODAQIJUoowWXj_Jg" "Mozilla/4.0 (compatible; MSIE 8.0; Windows NT 5.1; T
rident/4.0; .NET CLR 2.0.50727; .NET CLR 1.1.4322; .NET CLR 3.0.04506.30; .NET CLR 3.0.04506.648;
.NET CLR 3.0.4506.2152; .NET CLR 3.5.30729)"

78.41.144.41 - - [20/Oct/2010:13:44:09 +0200] "GET /index.html HTTP/1.0" 200 12092 "http://www.as
ylabwehramt.at/Seiten/Links.html" "Mozilla/4.0 (compatible; MSIE 8.0; Windows NT 5.1; Trident/4.0
; .NET CLR 2.0.50727; .NET CLR 1.1.4322; .NET CLR 3.0.04506.30; .NET CLR 3.0.04506.648; .NET CLR
3.0.4506.2152; .NET CLR 3.5.30729)"

78.41.144.41 - - [20/Oct/2010:13:44:20 +0200] "GET /Seiten/Aktuelles.html HTTP/1.0" 200 14343 "ht
tp://www.asylabwehramt.at/index.html" "Mozilla/4.0 (compatible; MSIE 8.0; Windows NT 5.1; Trident
/4.0; .NET CLR 2.0.50727; .NET CLR 1.1.4322; .NET CLR 3.0.04506.30; .NET CLR 3.0.04506.648; .NET
CLR 3.0.4506.2152; .NET CLR 3.5.30729)"

78.41.144.41 - - [20/Oct/2010:13:45:02 +0200] "GET /Seiten/Material.html HTTP/1.0" 200 17335 "htt
p://www.asylabwehramt.at/Seiten/Aktuelles.html" "Mozilla/4.0 (compatible; MSIE 8.0; Windows NT 5.
1; Trident/4.0; .NET CLR 2.0.50727; .NET CLR 1.1.4322; .NET CLR 3.0.04506.30; .NET CLR 3.0.04506.
648; .NET CLR 3.0.4506.2152; .NET CLR 3.5.30729)"

78.41.144.41 - - [20/Oct/2010:13:45:11 +0200] "GET /Bilder/Ladung.png HTTP/1.0" 200 114658 "http:
//www.asylabwehramt.at/Seiten/Material.html" "Mozilla/4.0 (compatible; MSIE 8.0; Windows NT 5.1;

```
Trident/4.0; .NET CLR 2.0.50727; .NET CLR 1.1.4322; .NET CLR 3.0.04506.648
; .NET CLR 3.0.4506.2152; .NET CLR 3.5.30729)"
78.41.144.41 - - [20/Oct/2010:13:45:37 +0200] "GET /Bilder/IOM-Kosovo-Broschuere_Internet.pdf HTT
P/1.0" 200 728811 "http://www.asylabwehramt.at/Seiten/Material.html" "Mozilla/4.0 (compatible; MS
IE 8.0; Windows NT 5.1; Trident/4.0; .NET CLR 2.0.50727; .NET CLR 1.1.4322; .NET CLR 3.0.04506.30
; .NET CLR 3.0.04506.648; .NET CLR 3.0.4506.2152; .NET CLR 3.5.30729)"
78.41.144.41 - - [20/Oct/2010:13:45:38 +0200] "GET /Bilder/IOM-Kosovo-Broschuere_Internet.pdf HTT
P/1.0" 206 4096 "-" "Mozilla/4.0 (compatible; MSIE 8.0; Windows NT 5.1; Trident/4.0; .NET CLR 2.0
.50727; .NET CLR 1.1.4322; .NET CLR 3.0.04506.30; .NET CLR 3.0.04506.648; .NET CLR 3.0.4506.2152;
.NET CLR 3.5.30729)"
78.41.144.41 - - [20/Oct/2010:13:45:39 +0200] "GET /Bilder/IOM-Kosovo-Broschuere_Internet.pdf HTT
P/1.0" 206 363971 "-" "Mozilla/4.0 (compatible; MSIE 8.0; Windows NT 5.1; Trident/4.0; .NET CLR 2
.0.50727; .NET CLR 1.1.4322; .NET CLR 3.0.04506.30; .NET CLR 3.0.04506.648; .NET CLR 3.0.4506.215
2; .NET CLR 3.5.30729)"
78.41.144.41 - - [20/Oct/2010:13:46:25 +0200] "GET /Seiten/Aktuelles.html HTTP/1.0" 304 - "http:/
/www.asylabwehramt.at/index.html" "Mozilla/4.0 (compatible; MSIE 8.0; Windows NT 5.1; Trident/4.0
; .NET CLR 2.0.50727; .NET CLR 1.1.4322; .NET CLR 3.0.04506.30; .NET CLR 3.0.04506.648; .NET CLR
3.0.4506.2152; .NET CLR 3.5.30729)"
78.41.144.41 - - [20/Oct/2010:13:46:26 +0200] "GET /Seiten/Links.html HTTP/1.0" 304 - "http://www
.google.at/url?sa=t&source=web&cd=22&ved=0CBcQFjABOBQ&url=http%3A%2F%2Fwww.asylabwehramt.at%2FSei
ten%2FLinks.html&rct=j&q="%C3%B6sterreichisches%20Asylverfahren%20Download&ei=ntW-TNXuEcOE0qyZmVQ&
usg=AFQjCNF-wWPeHYAHlkODAQIJUoowWXj_Jg" "Mozilla/4.0 (compatible; MSIE 8.0; Windows NT 5.1; Tride
nt/4.0; .NET CLR 2.0.50727; .NET CLR 1.1.4322; .NET CLR 3.0.04506.30; .NET CLR 3.0.04506.648; .NE
T CLR 3.0.4506.2152; .NET CLR 3.5.30729)"
pc216-26.ftmeade.army.mil - - [20/Oct/2010:20:44:38 +0200] "GET /Seiten/Links.html HTTP/1.
1" 200 19139 "http://www.google.com/imgres?imgurl=http://www.asylabwehramt.at/Bilder/BMI.png&img
refurl=http://www.asylabwehramt.at/Seiten/Links.html&usg=_XkgYoQjCp8P3lzCYNfBOdVy0hmg=&h=488&w=2
```

```
000&sz=55&hl=en&start=21&zoom=1&um=1&itbs=1&tbnid=-J4hmZ76_kG4vM:&tbnh=37&tbnw=150&prev=/images%3
Fq%3DAsylabwehramt%26start%3D20%26um%3D1%26hl%3Den%26safe%3Dactive%26sa%3DN%26rls%3Dcom.microsoft
:en-us%26ndsp%3D20%26tbs%3Disch:1" "Mozilla/4.0 (compatible; MSIE 7.0; Windows NT 5.1; InfoPath.
1)"
pc216-26.ftmeade.army.mil - - [20/Oct/2010:20:44:39 +0200] "GET /asyl.css HTTP/1.1" 200 86
0 "http://www.asylabwehramt.at/Seiten/Links.html" "Mozilla/4.0 (compatible; MSIE 7.0; Windows NT
5.1; InfoPath.1)"
pc216-26.ftmeade.army.mil - - [20/Oct/2010:20:44:40 +0200] "GET /favicon.ico HTTP/1.1" 302
340 "-" "Mozilla/4.0 (compatible; MSIE 7.0; Windows NT 5.1; InfoPath.1)"
pc216-26.ftmeade.army.mil - - [20/Oct/2010:20:44:47 +0200] "GET /asyl.css HTTP/1.1" 200 86
0 "http://www.asylabwehramt.at/Seiten/Links.html" "Mozilla/4.0 (compatible; MSIE 7.0; Windows NT
5.1; InfoPath.1)"
pc216-26.ftmeade.army.mil - - [20/Oct/2010:20:44:48 +0200] "GET /Bilder/frontex.png HTTP/1
.1" 200 22383 "http://www.asylabwehramt.at/Seiten/Links.html" "Mozilla/4.0 (compatible; MSIE 7.0;
Windows NT 5.1; InfoPath.1)"
80.120.179.10 - - [22/Oct/2010:10:44:49 +0200] "GET / HTTP/1.1" 200 12092 "http://www.google.de/s
earch?hl=de&source=hp&q=asylabwehramt&meta=&aq=f&aqi=&aql=&oq=&gs_rfai=" "Mozilla/4.0 (compatible
; MSIE 6.0; Windows NT 5.1; SV1; .NET CLR 1.1.4322; .NET CLR 2.0.50727; .NET CLR 3.0.04506.30; .N
ET CLR 3.0.04506.648; InfoPath.2; .NET CLR 3.0.4506.2152; .NET CLR 3.5.30729; MS-RTC LM 8)"
80.120.179.10 - - [22/Oct/2010:10:44:56 +0200] "GET /Seiten/Aktuelles.html HTTP/1.1" 200 14343 "h
ttp://www.asylabwehramt.at/" "Mozilla/4.0 (compatible; MSIE 6.0; Windows NT 5.1; SV1; .NET CLR 1.
1.4322; .NET CLR 2.0.50727; .NET CLR 3.0.04506.30; .NET CLR 3.0.04506.648; InfoPath.2; .NET CLR 3
.0.4506.2152; .NET CLR 3.5.30729; MS-RTC LM 8)"
80.120.179.10 - - [22/Oct/2010:10:44:57 +0200] "GET /Bilder/fitnesscenter_traiskirchen.jpg HTTP/1
.1" 200 5721 "http://www.asylabwehramt.at/Seiten/Aktuelles.html" "Mozilla/4.0 (compatible; MSIE 6
.0; Windows NT 5.1; SV1; .NET CLR 1.1.4322; .NET CLR 2.0.50727; .NET CLR 3.0.04506.30; .NET CLR 3
.0.04506.648; InfoPath.2; .NET CLR 3.0.4506.2152; .NET CLR 3.5.30729; MS-RTC LM 8)"
```

80.120.179.10 - - [22/Oct/2010:10:45:26 +0200] "GET /Seiten/Latestnews.html HTTP/1.1" 200 14563 "
http://www.asylabwehramt.at/Seiten/Aktuelles.html" "Mozilla/4.0 (compatible; MSIE 6.0; Windows NT
5.1; SV1; .NET CLR 1.1.4322; .NET CLR 2.0.50727; .NET CLR 3.0.04506.30; .NET CLR 3.0.04506.648;
InfoPath.2; .NET CLR 3.0.4506.2152; .NET CLR 3.5.30729; MS-RTC LM 8)"
80.120.179.10 - - [22/Oct/2010:10:45:33 +0200] "GET /Seiten/Rundzeichen.html HTTP/1.1" 200 8895 "
http://www.asylabwehramt.at/Seiten/Latestnews.html" "Mozilla/4.0 (compatible; MSIE 6.0; Windows N
T 5.1; SV1; .NET CLR 1.1.4322; .NET CLR 2.0.50727; .NET CLR 3.0.04506.30; .NET CLR 3.0.04506.648;
InfoPath.2; .NET CLR 3.0.4506.2152; .NET CLR 3.5.30729; MS-RTC LM 8)"
193.186.185.101 - - [29/Oct/2010:09:30:40 +0200] "GET /Seiten/Links.html HTTP/1.1" 200 19139 "ht
tp://www.google.at/imgres?imgurl=http://www.asylabwehramt.at/Bilder/omvlogo_3c.jpg&imgrefurl=http
://www.asylabwehramt.at/Seiten/Links.html&usg=__jdCrP4GOHW8huU2g2KevTO6SyY0=&h=452&w=582&sz=23&hl
=de&start=1&zoom=1&tbnid=V7dn_zg9i3iCDM:&tbnh=104&tbnw=134&prev=/images%3Fq%3Domv%26um%3D1%26hl%3
Dde%26sa%3DN%26tbs%3Disch:1&um=1&itbs=1" "Mozilla/4.0 (compatible; MSIE 6.0; Windows NT 5.1; SV1
; InfoPath.1; .NET CLR 1.1.4322; .NET CLR 2.0.50727; .NET CLR 3.0.04506.30; .NET CLR 3.0.4506.215
2; .NET CLR 3.5.30729)"
193.186.185.101 - - [29/Oct/2010:09:30:48 +0200] "GET /Bilder/omvlogo_3c.jpg HTTP/1.1" 304 - "-"
"Mozilla/4.0 (compatible; MSIE 6.0; Windows NT 5.1; InfoPath.1; .NET CLR 1.1.4322; .NET CLR
2.0.50727; .NET CLR 3.0.04506.30; .NET CLR 3.0.4506.2152; .NET CLR 3.5.30729)"
81.217.158.113 - - [31/Oct/2010:00:19:03 +0200] "GET /OEFFENTLICHKEIT/media/ZEIT.pdf HTTP/1.1" 20
0 484489 "http://search.conduit.com/Results.aspx?q=meine%20zweite%20sagt%20mir%2C%20das%
20mein%20gef%C3%BChl%20nicht%20start=10&ctid=CT2269050&SearchSourceOrigin=10" "Mozilla/4.0 (comp
atible; MSIE 8.0; Windows NT 6.1; WOW64; Trident/4.0; GTB6.6; SLCC2; .NET CLR 2.0.50727; .NET CLR
3.5.30729; .NET CLR 3.0.30729; Media Center PC 6.0)"
193.186.185.101 - - [02/Nov/2010:13:19:40 +0100] "GET /Bilder/omvlogo_3c.jpg HTTP/1.1" 200 22855
"http://www.google.at/imgres?imgurl=http://www.asylabwehramt.at/Bilder/omvlogo_3c.jpg&imgrefurl=
http://www.asylabwehramt.at/Seiten/Links.html&usg=__jdCrP4GOHW8huU2g2KevTO6SyY0=&h=452&w=582&sz=2

```
3&hl=de&start=1&zoom=1&tbnid=V7dn_zg9i3iCDM:&tbnh=104&tbnw=134&prev=/images%3Fq%3Domv%26um%3D1%26
hl%3Dde%26sa%3DN%26tbs%3DDisch:1&um=1&itbs=1" "Mozilla/4.0 (compatible; MSIE 6.0; Windows NT 5.1;
SV1; InfoPath.1; .NET CLR 1.1.4322; .NET CLR 2.0.50727; .NET CLR 3.0.4506.2152; .NET CLR 3.5.307
29; MS-RTC LM 8)"

91.32.188.242 - - [08/Nov/2010:01:55:05 +0100] "GET /OEFFENTLICHKEIT/media/ZEIT.pdf HTTP/1.1" 200
484489 "http://www.google.de/url?sa=t&source=web&cd=9&ved=0CD4QFjAI&url=http%3A%2F%2Fasylabwehra
mt.at%2FOEFFENTLICHKEIT%2Fmedia%2FZEIT.pdf&rct=j&q=liebt%20mich%20mein%20nigeria%20freund&ei=nOPX
TMX9CYWSDq60u00J&usg=AFQjCNGV1D_w7_ftdD3VaxechL6E_oPsnQ" "Mozilla/5.0 (Windows; U; Windows NT 6.0
; de; rv:1.9.2.12) Gecko/20101026 Firefox/3.6.12 ( .NET CLR 3.5.30729)"

80.120.179.10 - - [08/Nov/2010:15:54:57 +0100] "GET / HTTP/1.1" 200 12092 "-" "Mozilla/4.0 (compa
tible; MSIE 6.0; Windows NT 5.1; SV1; .NET CLR 1.1.4322; .NET CLR 2.0.50727; .NET CLR 3.0.04506.3
0; .NET CLR 3.0.04506.648; InfoPath.2; MS-RTC LM 8; .NET CLR 3.5.21022)"

80.120.179.10 - - [08/Nov/2010:15:56:49 +0100] "GET /Seiten/Aktuelles.html HTTP/1.1" 200 14343 "h
ttp://www.asylabwehramt.at" "Mozilla/4.0 (compatible; MSIE 6.0; Windows NT 5.1; SV1; .NET CLR 1.1
.4322; .NET CLR 2.0.50727; .NET CLR 3.0.04506.30; .NET CLR 3.0.04506.648; InfoPath.2; MS-RTC LM 8
; .NET CLR 3.5.21022)"

80.120.179.10 - - [08/Nov/2010:15:58:01 +0100] "GET /Seiten/Material.html HTTP/1.1" 200 17335 "ht
tp://www.asylabwehramt.at/Seiten/Aktuelles.html" "Mozilla/4.0 (compatible; MSIE 6.0; Windows NT 5
.1; SV1; .NET CLR 1.1.4322; .NET CLR 2.0.50727; .NET CLR 3.0.04506.30; .NET CLR 3.0.04506.648; In
foPath.2; MS-RTC LM 8; .NET CLR 3.5.21022)"

80.120.179.10 - - [08/Nov/2010:15:58:05 +0100] "GET /Bilder/Ladung.png HTTP/1.1" 200 114658 "http
://www.asylabwehramt.at/Seiten/Material.html" "Mozilla/4.0 (compatible; MSIE 6.0; Windows NT 5.1;
SV1; .NET CLR 1.1.4322; .NET CLR 2.0.50727; .NET CLR 3.0.04506.30; .NET CLR 3.0.04506.648; InfoP
ath.2; MS-RTC LM 8; .NET CLR 3.5.21022)"

80.120.179.10 - - [08/Nov/2010:15:58:17 +0100] "GET /Bilder/flyer_nigeria_Internet.pdf HTTP/1.1"
200 702826 "http://www.asylabwehramt.at/Seiten/Material.html" "Mozilla/4.0 (compatible; MSIE 6.0;
Windows NT 5.1; SV1; .NET CLR 1.1.4322; .NET CLR 2.0.50727; .NET CLR 3.0.04506.30; .NET CLR 3.0.
```

04506.648; InfoPath.2; MS-RTC LM 8; .NET CLR 3.5.21022)"

188.22.65.4 - - [08/Nov/2010:20:00:32 +0100] "GET /Seiten/Orgstrukt.html HTTP/1.1" 200 14119 "htt
p://www.google.at/search?hl=de&client=firefox-a&hs=vxC&rls=org.mozilla%3Ade%3Aofficial&channel=s&
q=asylantrag+formular+%C3%B6sterreich&aq=0&aqi=g2&aql=&oq=asylantrag+formular+&gs_rfai=" "Mozilla
/5.0 (Windows; U; Windows NT 5.1; de; rv:1.9.2.12) Gecko/20101026 Firefox/3.6.12"

193.186.185.101 - - [12/Nov/2010:04:44:42 +0100] "GET /Seiten/Links_e.html HTTP/1.1" 200 19142 "
http://www.google.at/imgres?imgurl=http://www.asylabwehramt.at/Bilder/omvlogo_3c.jpg&imgrefurl=ht
tp://www.asylabwehramt.at/Seiten/Links_e.html&usg=__Aps-FaXNYsM-lavZWvwu8M6D8Kc=&h=452&w=582&sz=2
3&hl=de&start=2&zoom=1&tbnid=V7dn_zg9i3iCDM:&tbnh=104&tbnw=134&prev=/images%3Fq%3Domv%26um%3D1%26
hl%3Dde%26sa%3DN%26tbs%3DDisch:1&um=1&itbs=1" "Mozilla/4.0 (compatible; MSIE 6.0; Windows NT 5.1;
SV1; .NET CLR 1.1.4322; Badongo 2.0.0; .NET CLR 2.0.50727; InfoPath.1; .NET CLR 3.0.4506.2152; .
NET CLR 3.5.30729)"

193.186.185.101 - - [12/Nov/2010:04:44:47 +0100] "GET /Bilder/omvlogo_3c.jpg HTTP/1.1" 304 - "-"
"Mozilla/4.0 (compatible; MSIE 6.0; Windows NT 5.1; SV1; .NET CLR 1.1.4322; Badongo 2.0.0; .NET C
LR 2.0.50727; InfoPath.1; .NET CLR 3.0.4506.2152; .NET CLR 3.5.30729)"

193.186.185.101 - - [12/Nov/2010:04:55:41 +0100] "GET /Bilder/Header_AAbA_anim.gif HTTP/1.1" 200
19997 "http://www.asylabwehramt.at/Seiten/Links_e.html" "Mozilla/4.0 (compatible; MSIE 6.0; Windo
ws NT 5.1; SV1; .NET CLR 1.1.4322; Badongo 2.0.0; .NET CLR 2.0.50727; InfoPath.1; .NET CLR 3.0.45
06.2152; .NET CLR 3.5.30729)"

80.120.179.10 - - [14/Nov/2010:22:32:21 +0100] "GET /OEFFENTLICHKEIT/media/ZEIT.pdf HTTP/1.1" 200
484489 "http://www.google.at/search?q=haslinger+peter&hl=de&cr=countryAT&prmd=o&ei=P1XgTKGqLYOVO
oXT4eI0&start=40&sa=N" "Mozilla/4.0 (compatible; MSIE 6.0; Windows NT 5.1; SV1; .NET CLR 1.1.4322
; .NET CLR 2.0.50727; .NET CLR 3.0.04506.648; InfoPath.2; .NET CLR 3.5.210
22)"

78.41.144.41 - - [19/Nov/2010:14:46:17 +0100] "GET / HTTP/1.0" 200 12092 "http://www.google.at/ur
l?sa=t&source=web&cd=1&ved=0CBkQhgIwAA&url=http%3A%2F%2Fwww.asylabwehramt.at%2F&rct=j&q=asylabweh

r &ei=pn_mTLH9K4ubOogtLsK&usg=AFQjCNEy1zwClvnxklIPAGifRc344_OU4Q&sig2=6pZ_dz-lbtX_mpv4SbrxCQ" "Mozilla/4.0 (compatible; MSIE 8.0; Windows NT 5.1; Trident/4.0; .NET CLR 2.0.50727; .NET CLR 1.1.43 22; .NET CLR 3.0.04506.30; .NET CLR 3.0.4506.648; .NET CLR 3.0.4506.2152; .NET CLR 3.5.30729)"

78.41.144.41 - - [19/Nov/2010:14:46:26 +0100] "GET /Seiten/Aktuelles.html HTTP/1.0" 200 14343 "http://www.asylabwehramt.at/" "Mozilla/4.0 (compatible; MSIE 8.0; Windows NT 5.1; Trident/4.0; .NET CLR 2.0.50727; .NET CLR 1.1.4322; .NET CLR 3.0.45 06.2152; .NET CLR 3.5.30729)"

78.41.144.41 - - [19/Nov/2010:14:46:47 +0100] "GET /Seiten/Material.html HTTP/1.0" 200 17335 "http://www.asylabwehramt.at/Seiten/Aktuelles.html" "Mozilla/4.0 (compatible; MSIE 8.0; Windows NT 5.1; Trident/4.0; .NET CLR 2.0.50727; .NET CLR 1.1.4322; .NET CLR 3.0.04506.30; .NET CLR 3.0.04506.648; .NET CLR 3.0.04506.2152; .NET CLR 3.5.30729)"

78.41.144.41 - - [19/Nov/2010:14:47:01 +0100] "GET /Seiten/Bilder.html HTTP/1.0" 200 10364 "http://www.asylabwehramt.at/Seiten/Material.html" "Mozilla/4.0 (compatible; MSIE 8.0; Windows NT 5.1; Trident/4.0; .NET CLR 2.0.50727; .NET CLR 1.1.4322; .NET CLR 3.0.04506.30; .NET CLR 3.0.04506.648 ; .NET CLR 3.0.04506.2152; .NET CLR 3.5.30729)"

78.41.144.41 - - [19/Nov/2010:14:47:13 +0100] "GET /Seiten/Press.html HTTP/1.0" 200 12374 "http://www.asylabwehramt.at/Seiten/Bilder.html" "Mozilla/4.0 (compatible; MSIE 8.0; Windows NT 5.1; Tri dent/4.0; .NET CLR 2.0.50727; .NET CLR 1.1.4322; .NET CLR 3.0.04506.30; .NET CLR 3.0.04506.648; . NET CLR 3.0.4506.2152; .NET CLR 3.5.30729)"

85.158.226.32 - - [29/Nov/2010:14:56:47 +0100] "GET /Seiten/Orgstrukt.html HTTP/1.1" 200 14119 "h ttp://www.google.at/search?hl=de&q=asylantrag+formular+at&btnG=Suche&aq=f&aql=&oq=&gs_rfai=" "Mozilla/4.0 (compatible; MSIE 7.0; Windows NT 5.1; .NET CLR 1.1.4322; .NET CLR 2.0.50727; .NET CLR 3.0.4506.2152; .NET CLR 3.5.30729; .NET4.0C; .NET4.0E)"

85.158.226.32 - - [29/Nov/2010:14:57:05 +0100] "GET /index.html HTTP/1.1" 200 12092 "http://www.a sylabwehramt.at/Seiten/Orgstrukt.html" "Mozilla/4.0 (compatible; MSIE 7.0; Windows NT 5.1; .NET C LR 1.1.4322; .NET CLR 2.0.50727; .NET CLR 3.0.4506.2152; .NET CLR 3.5.30729; .NET4.0C; .NET4.0E)"

78.41.144.41 - - [01/Dec/2010:18:14:25 +0100] "GET /index.html HTTP/1.0" 200 12092 "Mozilla/4 .0 (compatible; MSIE 8.0; Windows NT 5.1; Trident/4.0; .NET CLR 1.1.4322; .NE

```
T CLR 3.0.04506.30; .NET CLR 3.0.04506.648; .NET CLR 3.0.4506.2152; .NET CLR 3.5.30729)"
78.41.144.41 - - [01/Dec/2010:18:14:31 +0100] "GET /Seiten/Aktuelles.html HTTP/1.0" 200 14343 "ht
tp://www.asylabwehramt.at/index.html" "Mozilla/4.0 (compatible; MSIE 8.0; Windows NT 5.1; Trident
/4.0; .NET CLR 2.0.50727; .NET CLR 1.1.4322; .NET CLR 3.0.04506.30; .NET CLR 3.0.04506.648; .NET
CLR 3.0.4506.2152; .NET CLR 3.5.30729)"
78.41.144.41 - - [01/Dec/2010:18:14:32 +0100] "GET /Bilder/220px-Schengenzone.svg.png HTTP/1.0" 2
00 40785 "http://www.asylabwehramt.at/Seiten/Aktuelles.html" "Mozilla/4.0 (compatible; MSIE 8.0;
Windows NT 5.1; Trident/4.0; .NET CLR 2.0.50727; .NET CLR 1.1.4322; .NET CLR 3.0.04506.30; .NET C
LR 3.0.04506.648; .NET CLR 3.0.4506.2152; .NET CLR 3.5.30729)"
194.107.234.50 - - [06/Dec/2010:09:27:57 +0100] "GET /favicon.ico HTTP/1.1" 302 340 "-" "Mozilla/
4.0 (compatible; MSIE 7.0; Windows NT 6.0; SLCC1; .NET CLR 2.0.50727; .NET CLR 3.5.30729; .NET CL
R 3.0.30618; MS-RTC LM 8)"
194.107.234.50 - - [06/Dec/2010:09:27:58 +0100] "GET /Bilder/Header_AAbA_anim.gif HTTP/1.1" 200 1
9997 "http://www.asylabwehramt.at/" "Mozilla/4.0 (compatible; MSIE 7.0; Windows NT 6.0; SLCC1; .N
ET CLR 2.0.50727; .NET CLR 3.5.30729; .NET CLR 3.0.30618; MS-RTC LM 8)"
193.171.152.33 - - [06/Dec/2010:14:26:45 +0100] "GET /Bilder/SCREEN_AAbA_Edutainment_Video.jpg HT
TP/1.1" 200 29259 "http://forum.geizhals.at/topic.jsp?id=562009&m=-1" "Mozilla/4.0 (compatible;
MSIE 6.0; Windows NT 5.1; InfoPath.1)"
85.158.226.32 - - [09/Dec/2010:10:01:07 +0100] "GET /index_e.html HTTP/1.1" 200 12169 "http://www
.google.at/search?hl=de&source=hp&q=National+defence+agency+austria&rlz=1R2ADFA_deAT366&aq=f&aqi=
&aql=&oq=&gs_rfai=" "Mozilla/4.0 (compatible; MSIE 7.0; Windows NT 5.1; GTB6; .NET CLR 1.1.4322;
.NET CLR 2.0.50727; .NET CLR 3.0.4506.2152; .NET CLR 3.5.30729; .NET4.0C; .NET4.0E)"
85.158.226.32 - - [09/Dec/2010:10:01:16 +0100] "GET /Seiten/Forms_and_Infos.html HTTP/1.1" 200 16
472 "http://www.asylabwehramt.at/index_e.html" "Mozilla/4.0 (compatible; MSIE 7.0; Windows NT 5.1
; GTB6; .NET CLR 1.1.4322; .NET CLR 2.0.50727; .NET CLR 3.0.4506.2152; .NET CLR 3.5.30729; .NET4.
0C; .NET4.0E)"
85.158.226.32 - - [09/Dec/2010:10:01:26 +0100] "GET /index.html HTTP/1.1" 200 12092 "http://www.a
sylabwehramt.at/Seiten/Forms_and_Infos.html" "Mozilla/4.0 (compatible; MSIE 7.0; Windows NT 5.1;
```

GTB6; .NET CLR 1.1.4322; .NET CLR 2.0.50727; .NET CLR 3.0.4506.2152; .NET CLR 3.5.30729; .NET CLR 3.0.4506.2152; .NET CLR 3.5.30729; .NET4.0C; .NET4.0C; .NET4.0E)"

85.158.226.32 - - [09/Dec/2010:10:01:32 +0100] "GET /Seiten/Rundzeichen.html HTTP/1.1" 200 8895 "http://www.asylabwehramt.at/index.html" "Mozilla/4.0 (compatible; MSIE 7.0; Windows NT 5.1; GTB6; .NET CLR 1.1.4322; .NET CLR 2.0.50727; .NET CLR 3.0.4506.2152; .NET CLR 3.5.30729; .NET4.0C; .NET4.0E)"

85.158.226.32 - - [09/Dec/2010:10:01:46 +0100] "GET /Seiten/favicon.ico HTTP/1.1" 302 340 "-" "Mozilla/4.0 (compatible; GoogleToolbar 6.1.1715.1442; Windows XP 5.1; MSIE 7.0.5730.13)"

78.41.144.41 - - [09/Dec/2010:11:00:20 +0100] "GET / HTTP/1.0" 200 12092 "http://www.google.at/url?sa=t&source=web&cd=1&ved=0CBcQFjAA&url=http%3A%2F%2Fwww.asylabwehramt.at%2F&rct=j&q=asylabwehramt&ei=nKgATYvtPIWn8QPu9aWbCA&usg=AFQjCNEy1zWClvnxkLlPAGifRc344_OU4Q" "Mozilla/4.0 (compatible; MSIE 8.0; Windows NT 5.1; Trident/4.0; .NET CLR 2.0.50727; .NET CLR 1.1.4322; .NET CLR 3.0.04506.30; .NET CLR 3.0.04506.648; .NET CLR 3.0.4506.2152; .NET CLR 3.5.30729)"

78.41.144.41 - - [09/Dec/2010:11:00:30 +0100] "GET /Seiten/Images.html HTTP/1.0" 200 10519 "http://www.asylabwehramt.at/" "Mozilla/4.0 (compatible; MSIE 8.0; Windows NT 5.1; Trident/4.0; .NET CLR 2.0.50727; .NET CLR 1.1.4322; .NET CLR 3.0.04506.30; .NET CLR 3.0.04506.648; .NET CLR 3.0.4506.2152; .NET CLR 3.5.30729)"

78.41.144.41 - - [09/Dec/2010:11:00:31 +0100] "GET /asyl.css HTTP/1.0" 304 - "http://www.asylabwehramt.at/Seiten/Images.html" "Mozilla/4.0 (compatible; MSIE 8.0; Windows NT 5.1; Trident/4.0; .NET CLR 2.0.50727; .NET CLR 1.1.4322; .NET CLR 3.0.04506.30; .NET CLR 3.0.04506.648; .NET CLR 3.0.4506.2152; .NET CLR 3.5.30729)"

78.41.144.41 - - [09/Dec/2010:11:00:42 +0100] "GET / HTTP/1.0" 304 - "http://www.google.at/url?sa=t&source=web&cd=1&ved=0CBcQFjAA&url=http%3A%2F%2Fwww.asylabwehramt.at%2F&rct=j&q=asylabwehramt&ei=nKgATYvtPIWn8QPu9aWbCA&usg=AFQjCNEy1zWClvnxkLlPAGifRc344_OU4Q" "Mozilla/4.0 (compatible; MSIE 8.0; Windows NT 5.1; Trident/4.0; .NET CLR 2.0.50727; .NET CLR 1.1.4322; .NET CLR 3.0.04506.30; .NET CLR 3.0.4506.2152; .NET CLR 3.5.30729)"

78.41.144.41 - - [09/Dec/2010:11:00:45 +0100] "GET /Seiten/Latestnews.html HTTP/1.0" 200 14563 "http://www.asylabwehramt.at/" "Mozilla/4.0 (compatible; MSIE 8.0; Windows NT 5.1; Trident/4.0; .NE

```
T CLR 2.0.50727; .NET CLR 1.1.4322; .NET CLR 3.0.04506.30; .NET CLR 3.0.04
506.2152; .NET CLR 3.5.30729)"
78.41.144.41 - - [09/Dec/2010:11:01:22 +0100] "GET /Seiten/Press.html HTTP/1.0" 200 12374 "http:/
/www.asylabwehramt.at/Seiten/Latestnews.html" "Mozilla/4.0 (compatible; MSIE 8.0; Windows NT 5.1;
Trident/4.0; .NET CLR 2.0.50727; .NET CLR 1.1.4322; .NET CLR 3.0.04506.64
8; .NET CLR 3.0.4506.2152; .NET CLR 3.5.30729)"
78.41.144.41 - - [09/Dec/2010:11:01:47 +0100] "GET /Seiten/Links_e.html HTTP/1.0" 200 19142 "http
://www.asylabwehramt.at/Seiten/Press.html" "Mozilla/4.0 (compatible; MSIE 8.0; Windows NT 5.1; Tr
ident/4.0; .NET CLR 2.0.50727; .NET CLR 1.1.4322; .NET CLR 3.0.04506.30; .NET CLR 3.0.04506.648;
.NET CLR 3.0.4506.2152; .NET CLR 3.5.30729)"
78.41.144.41 - - [09/Dec/2010:11:02:49 +0100] "GET /index.html HTTP/1.0" 200 12092 "http://www.as
ylabwehramt.at/Seiten/Links_e.html" "Mozilla/4.0 (compatible; MSIE 8.0; Windows NT 5.1; Trident/4
.0; .NET CLR 2.0.50727; .NET CLR 1.1.4322; .NET CLR 3.0.04506.30; .NET CLR 3.0.04506.648; .NET CL
R 3.0.4506.2152; .NET CLR 3.5.30729)"
78.41.144.41 - - [09/Dec/2010:11:02:52 +0100] "GET /Seiten/Forms_and_Infos.html HTTP/1.0" 200 164
72 "http://www.asylabwehramt.at/index.html" "Mozilla/4.0 (compatible; MSIE 8.0; Windows NT 5.1; T
rident/4.0; .NET CLR 2.0.50727; .NET CLR 1.1.4322; .NET CLR 3.0.04506.30; .NET CLR 3.0.04506.648;
.NET CLR 3.0.4506.2152; .NET CLR 3.5.30729)"
213.208.144.130 - - [14/Dec/2010:10:43:31 +0100] "GET / HTTP/1.0" 200 13966 "http://www.google.at
/search?hl=de&source=hp&q=asylabwehramt&aq=f&aqi=&aql=&oq=&gs_rfai=" "Mozilla/4.0 (compatible; MS
IE 7.0; Windows NT 5.1; .NET CLR 2.0.50727; InfoPath.1; .NET CLR 1.1.4322; .NET CLR 3.0.4506.2152
; .NET CLR 3.5.30729)"
213.208.144.130 - - [14/Dec/2010:10:44:38 +0100] "GET /Seiten/Aktuelles.html HTTP/1.0" 200 14343
"http://www.asylabwehramt.at/" "Mozilla/4.0 (compatible; MSIE 7.0; Windows NT 5.1; .NET CLR 1.1.4
322; InfoPath.1; .NET CLR 2.0.50727; .NET CLR 3.0.4506.2152; .NET CLR 3.5.30729)"
213.208.144.130 - - [14/Dec/2010:10:44:39 +0100] "GET /Bilder/56.jpg HTTP/1.0" 200 4494 "http://w
ww.asylabwehramt.at/Seiten/Aktuelles.html" "Mozilla/4.0 (compatible; MSIE 7.0; Windows NT 5.1; .N
ET CLR 1.1.4322; InfoPath.1; .NET CLR 2.0.50727; .NET CLR 3.5.30729)"
```

213.208.144.130 - - [14/Dec/2010:10:45:56 +0100] "GET /Seiten/Bilder.html HTTP/1.0" 200 10364 "ht
tp://www.asylabwehramt.at/Seiten/Aktuelles.html" "Mozilla/4.0 (compatible; MSIE 7.0; Windows NT 5
.1; .NET CLR 1.1.4322; InfoPath.1; .NET CLR 2.0.50727; .NET CLR 3.0.4506.2152; .NET CLR 3.5.30729
)"

213.208.144.130 - - [14/Dec/2010:10:46:25 +0100] "GET /Seiten/Material.html HTTP/1.0" 200 17335 "
http://www.asylabwehramt.at/Seiten/Bilder.html" "Mozilla/4.0 (compatible; MSIE 7.0; Windows NT 5.
1; .NET CLR 1.1.4322; InfoPath.1; .NET CLR 2.0.50727; .NET CLR 3.0.4506.2152; .NET CLR 3.5.30729)
"

213.208.144.130 - - [14/Dec/2010:10:46:40 +0100] "GET /Bilder/flyer_nigeria_Internet.pdf HTTP/1.0
" 200 702826 "http://www.asylabwehramt.at/Seiten/Material.html" "Mozilla/4.0 (compatible; MSIE 7.
0; Windows NT 5.1; .NET CLR 1.1.4322; InfoPath.1; .NET CLR 2.0.50727; .NET CLR 3.0.4506.2152; .NE
T CLR 3.5.30729)"

213.208.144.130 - - [14/Dec/2010:10:47:00 +0100] "GET /Bilder/flyer_nigeria_Internet.pdf HTTP/1.0
" 206 566427 "-" "Mozilla/4.0 (compatible; MSIE 7.0; Windows NT 5.1; .NET CLR 1.1.4322; InfoPath.
1; .NET CLR 2.0.50727; .NET CLR 3.0.4506.2152; .NET CLR 3.5.30729)"

88.70.36.241 - - [20/Dec/2010:18:49:43 +0100] "GET / HTTP/1.1" 200 13966 "http://www.google.de/ur
l?sa=t&source=web&cd=2&ved=0CCAQFjAB&url=http%3A%2F%2Fwww.asylabwehramt.at%2F&rct=j&q=Tschechisch
e%20Republik%20Messinstrument%20Penis%20Asylbewerber&ei=IJcPTea-O5C18QP-ruCEBw&usg=AFQjCNEy1zWClv
nxkLIPAGifRc344_0U4Q" "Mozilla/5.0 (Windows; U; Windows NT 6.1; en-US) AppleWebKit/534.10 (KHTML,
like Gecko) Chrome/8.0.552.224 Safari/534.10"

217.116.64.48[37] - - [21/Dec/2010:15:20:45 +0100] "GET /Seiten/Impressum.html HTTP/1.0" 200 11939 "h
ttp://www.google.at/url?sa=t&source=web&cd=20&ved=0CFcQFjAJOAo&url=http%3A%2F%2Fwww.asylabwehramt
.at%2FSeiten%2FImpressum.html&rct=j&q=asylantrag%20formular%20%C3%B6sterreich&ei=rLcQTev3Gcei8QPi
1bWHBw&usg=AFQjCNHF7HP6dxpY82GEXb1PQnRvP4GW7g" "Mozilla/4.0 (compatible; MSIE 8.0; Windows NT 5.1
; Trident/4.0; .NET CLR 2.0.50727; .NET CLR 3.0.4506.2152; .NET CLR 3.5.30729; InfoPath.1; .NET C
LR 1.1.4322)"

---

[37] WHOIS record on page 304

243

194.153.217.248 - - [29/Dec/2010:14:12:05 +0100] "GET /Bilder/SCREEN_AAbA_Edutainment_Video.jpg H
TTP/1.1" 200 29259 "http://forum.geizhals.at/t562009,-1.html" "Mozilla/5.0 (Windows; U; Windows
NT 5.1; de; rv:1.9.1) Gecko/20090624 Firefox/3.5"
83.215.85.200 - - [31/Dec/2010:18:49:40 +0100] "GET /Seiten/Impressum.html HTTP/1.1" 200 11939 "h
ttp://www.google.at/search?q=asylantrag+%C3%B6sterreich+formular&hl=de&rlz=1R2ADFA_deAT410&biw=16
55&bih=786&source=lnms&ei=1BceTeLTA8Wk8Q0qoNWHBw&sa=X&oi=mode_link&ct=mode&ved=0CCcQ_AU" "Mozilla
/4.0 (compatible; MSIE 8.0; Windows NT 6.1; Trident/4.0; GTB6.6; SLCC2; .NET CLR 2.0.50727; .NET
CLR 3.5.30729; .NET CLR 3.0.30729; Media Center PC 6.0; InfoPath.2; MAMD; Media Center PC 5.0; Of
ficeLiveConnector.1.4; OfficeLivePatch.1.3; SLCC1; .NET4.0C)"
192.164.72.10[38] - - [03/Jan/2011:16:51:47 +0100] "GET /Seiten/Impressum.html HTTP/1.1" 200 11939 "h
ttp://www.google.at/search?hl=de&q=asylantrag+%C3%B6sterreich+formular&aq=f&aqi=&aql=&oq=&gs_rfai
=" "Mozilla/4.0 (compatible; MSIE 7.0; Windows NT 5.1; .NET CLR 2.0.50727; .NET CLR 3.0.04506.30;
.NET CLR 3.0.4506.2152; .NET CLR 3.5.30729)"
195.230.168.36[39] - - [04/Jan/2011:11:21:32 +0100] "GET /Seiten/Orgstrukt.html HTTP/1.1" 200 14119 "
http://www.google.at/url?sa=t&source=web&cd=6&ved=0CC4QFjAF&url=http%3A%2F%2Fwww.asylabwehramt.at
%2FSeiten%2FOrgstrukt.html&rct=j&q=Formular%20Asylantrag%20%C3%96sterreich&ei=0PMiTdvWPMP5sgaB6oz
IDA&usg=AFQjCNFupGGPUoPKDeTUpjWvDejEFC1yA" "Mozilla/4.0 (compatible; MSIE 7.0; Windows NT 5.1; T
rident/4.0; .NET CLR 2.0.50727; .NET CLR 3.0.04506.30)"
195.230.168.36 - - [04/Jan/2011:11:21:35 +0100] "GET /asyl.css HTTP/1.1" 200 860 "http://www.asyl
abwehramt.at/Seiten/Orgstrukt.html" "Mozilla/4.0 (compatible; MSIE 7.0; Windows NT 5.1; Trident/4
.0; .NET CLR 2.0.50727; .NET CLR 3.0.04506.30)"
213.142.120.132 - - [06/Jan/2011:12:03:52 +0100] "GET /Seiten/Impressum.html HTTP/1.1" 200 11939
"http://www.google.at/url?sa=t&source=web&cd=4&ved=0CCoQFjAD&url=http%3A%2F%2Fwww.asylabwehramt.a
t%2FSeiten%2FImpressum.html&rct=j&q=asylantrag%20%20%C3%B6sterreich%20formular&ei=iqELTfHIDI-p8QPVra
mEAw&usg=AFQjCNHF7HP6dxpY82GEXb1PQnRvP4GW7g" "Mozilla/5.0 (Windows; U; Windows NT 6.0; de; rv:1.9

---

[38]WHOIS record on page 292
[39]WHOIS record on page 302

```
.0.19) Gecko/2010031422 AskTbSTC/3.9.1.14019 Firefox/3.0.19 (.NET CLR 3.5.30729)"
193.171.152.33 - - [07/Jan/2011:07:56:37 +0100] "GET /Bilder/SCREEN_AñbA_Edutainment_Video.jpg HT
TP/1.1" 200 29259 "http://forum.geizhals.at/t562009.html" "Mozilla/4.0 (compatible; MSIE 8.0; W
indows NT 6.1; Trident/4.0; SLCC2; .NET CLR 2.0.50727; .NET CLR 3.5.30729; .NET CLR 3.0.30729; Me
dia Center PC 6.0; Tablet PC 2.0; .NET4.0C)"
80.120.179.10 - - [08/Jan/2011:07:21:44 +0100] "GET /Seiten/Aktuelles.html HTTP/1.1" 200 14343 "
http://www.google.at/imgres?imgurl=http://www.asylabwehramt.at/Bilder/Asylabwehramt_Seal_800x800.
png&imgrefurl=http://www.asylabwehramt.at/Seiten/Aktuelles.html&usg=__M1_BYRGGagCVCEyu8bUgbxKgv54
=&h=800&w=800&sz=263&hl=de&start=6&zoom=1&tbnid=pX5pGoQcyxGCaM:&tbnh=143&tbnw=143&prev=/images%3F
q%3DGrundsiegel%26um%3D1%26hl%3Dde%26sa%3DN%26tbs%3Disch:1&um=1&itbs=1" "Mozilla/4.0 (compatible;
MSIE 6.0; Windows NT 5.1; SV1; .NET CLR 1.1.4322; .NET CLR 2.0.50727; .NET CLR 3.0.04506.30; .NE
T CLR 3.0.04506.648; InfoPath.2; .NET CLR 3.0.4506.2152; .NET CLR 3.5.30729; MS-RTC LM 8)"
195.248.32.227[40] - - [12/Jan/2011:09:45:41 +0100] "GET /Seiten/Links.html HTTP/1.1" 200 19139 "http
://www.google.at/imgres?imgurl=http://www.asylabwehramt.at/Bilder/raiffeisen.jpg&imgrefurl=http:/
/www.asylabwehramt.at/Seiten/Links.html&usg=__S9CyHZWxZ30Jf0S7SpSR3RfkSQQ=&h=1315&w=742&sz=79&hl=
de&start=22&zoom=1&tbnid=1_gXJ25FdnKZ6M:&tbnh=158&tbnw=89&prev=/images%3Fq%3Draiffeisen%2Binterna
tional%26um%3D1%26hl%3Dde%26client%3Dfirefox-a%26sa%3DX%26rls%3Dorg.mozilla:en-GB:official%26chan
nel%3Ds%26biw%3D1280%26bih%3D867%26tbs%3Disch:1,isz:10%2C943&um=1&itbs=1&iact=rc&dur=469&ei=M2otT
c_X04W6hAe3wLnWCQ&oei=J2otTemWMcyU0sf4uLwJ&esq=8&page=2&ndsp=23&ved=1t:429,r:16,s:22&tx=17&ty=48&
biw=1280&bih=867" "Mozilla/5.0 (Windows; U; Windows NT 5.1; en-GB; rv:1.9.2.10) Gecko/20100914 Fi
refox/3.6.10 ( .NET CLR 3.5.30729)"
195.248.32.227 - - [12/Jan/2011:09:45:44 +0100] "GET /favicon.ico HTTP/1.1" 302 340 "-" "Mozilla/
5.0 (Windows; U; Windows NT 5.1; en-GB; rv:1.9.2.10) Gecko/20100914 Firefox/3.6.10 ( .NET CLR 3.5
.30729)"
195.248.32.227 - - [12/Jan/2011:09:46:05 +0100] "GET /index.html HTTP/1.1" 200 13966 "http://www.
```

---

[40] WHOIS record on page 315

```
asylabwehramt.at/Seiten/Links.html" "Mozilla/5.0 (Windows; U; Windows NT 5.1; en-GB; rv:1.9.2.10)
Gecko/20100914 Firefox/3.6.10 ( .NET CLR 3.5.30729)"
195.248.32.227 - - [12/Jan/2011:09:46:56 +0100] "GET /Seiten/Impressum.html HTTP/1.1" 200 11939 "
http://www.asylabwehramt.at/index.html" "Mozilla/5.0 (Windows; U; Windows NT 5.1; en-GB; rv:1.9.2
.10) Gecko/20100914 Firefox/3.6.10 ( .NET CLR 3.5.30729)"
195.248.32.227 - - [12/Jan/2011:09:47:31 +0100] "GET / HTTP/1.1" 200 13966 "http://www.google.at/
search?q=asylabwehramt&ie=utf-8&oe=utf-8&aq=t&rls=org.mozilla:en-GB:official&client=firefox-a" "M
ozilla/5.0 (Windows; U; Windows NT 5.1; en-GB; rv:1.9.2.10) Gecko/20100914 Firefox/3.6.10 ( .NET
CLR 3.5.30729)"
78.41.144.41 - - [13/Jan/2011:10:40:43 +0100] "GET / HTTP/1.0" 200 13966 "http://www.ubermorgen.
com/2010/index.html" "Mozilla/4.0 (compatible; MSIE 8.0; Windows NT 5.1; Trident/4.0; .NET CLR 2
.0.50727; .NET CLR 1.1.4322; .NET CLR 3.0.04506.30; .NET CLR 3.0.4506.648; .NET CLR 3.0.4506.215
2; .NET CLR 3.5.30729)"
193.17.232.2 - - [18/Jan/2011:15:46:00 +0100] "GET / HTTP/1.0" 200 13966 "http://www.google.de/se
arch?hl=de&client=firefox-a&hs=icD&rls=org.mozilla%3Ade%3Aofficial&q=sexfilme+bei+einb%C3%BCrgeru
ng&aq=f&aqi=&aql=&oq=" "Mozilla/5.0 (Windows; U; Windows NT 5.1; de; rv:1.9.2.12) Gecko/20101026
Firefox/3.6.12"
80.120.179.10 - - [20/Jan/2011:14:36:15 +0100] "GET /Seiten/Links.html HTTP/1.1" 200 19139 "http
://www.google.at/imgres?imgurl=http://www.asylabwehramt.at/Bilder/BMI.png&imgrefurl=http://www.as
ylabwehramt.at/Seiten/Links.html&usg=_XkgYoQjCp8P3lzCYNfB0dVy0hmg=&h=488&w=2000&sz=55&hl=de&star
t=23&zoom=1&tbnid=-J4hmZ76_kG4vM:&tbnh=37&tbnw=150&ei=TDo4TeqkONGv8QPArMGrCA&prev=/images%3Fq%3DB
M.i%26start%3D20%26um%3D1%26hl%3Dde%26sa%3DN%26tbs%3Disch:1&um=1&itbs=1" "Mozilla/4.0 (compatibl
e; MSIE 6.0; Windows NT 5.1; SV1; .NET CLR 1.1.4322; .NET CLR 2.0.50727; .NET CLR 3.0.04506.30; .
NET CLR 3.0.04506.648; InfoPath.2; .NET CLR 3.0.4506.2152; .NET CLR 3.5.30729; MS-RTC LM 8)"
80.120.179.10 - - [20/Jan/2011:14:36:16 +0100] "GET /Bilder/Header_AAbA_anim.gif HTTP/1.1" 200 19
997 "http://www.asylabwehramt.at/Seiten/Links.html" "Mozilla/4.0 (compatible; MSIE 6.0; Windows N
```

T 5.1; SV1; .NET CLR 1.1.4322; .NET CLR 2.0.50727; .NET CLR 3.0.04506.30; .NET CLR 3.0.04506.648; InfoPath.2; .NET CLR 3.0.4506.2152; .NET CLR 3.5.30729; MS-RTC LM 8)"

86.32.69.77 - - [22/Jan/2011:16:39:49 +0100] "GET /OEFFENTLICHKEIT/media/ZEIT.pdf HTTP/1.1" 200 484489 "http://www.google.at/search?hl=de&source=hp&q=welche+Frau+sorgt+in+Wien+um+Asylanten&rlz=1W1MEDB_de&aq=f&aqi=&oq=" "Mozilla/4.0 (compatible; MSIE 7.0; Windows NT 6.0; GTB6.6; Embedded Web Browser from: http://bsalsa.com/; SLCC1; .NET CLR 2.0.50727; Media Center PC 5.0; .NET CLR 3.5.30729; .NET CLR 3.0.30618; .NET4.0C)"

91.115.92.121 - - [24/Jan/2011:19:36:31 +0100] "GET /Seiten/Orgstrukt.html HTTP/1.1" 200 14119 "http://www.google.at/url?sa=t&source=web&cd=25&ved=0CDQQFjAEOBQ&url=http%3A%2F%2Fwww.asylabwehramt.at%2FSeiten%2FOrgstrukt.html&rct=j&q=asylantrag%20formular&ei=TsY9TcTCF4TMswaRwrHzBg&usg=AFQjCNFupGPUoPKDe7UpjwYvDejEFClyA" "Mozilla/4.0 (compatible; MSIE 8.0; Windows NT 6.1; Trident/4.0; SLCC2; .NET CLR 2.0.50727; .NET CLR 3.5.30729; .NET CLR 3.0.30729; MAAU; OfficeLiveConnector.1.3; OfficeLivePatch.0.0; MAAU)"

193.228.104.102 [41] - - [26/Jan/2011:08:08:59 +0100] "GET / HTTP/1.0" 200 13966 "http://www.google.at/search?hl=de&source=hp&q=asylantrag+test&aq=f&aqi=&oq=" "Mozilla/4.0 (compatible; MSIE 7.0; Windows NT 5.1; .NET CLR 1.1.4322; .NET CLR 2.0.50727; InfoPath.1; .NET CLR 3.0.04506.648; .NET CLR 3.5.21022; MS-RTC LM 8)"

193.186.185.101 - - [28/Jan/2011:13:22:26 +0100] "GET /Bilder/omvlogo_3c.jpg HTTP/1.1" 200 22855 "http://www.bing.com/images/search?q=OMV+IMAGES&view=detail&id=F9F1978144E5659FE70FCC53F1ABE20C2E15C9E7&first=1&FORM=IDFRIR&qpvt=OMV+IMAGES" "Mozilla/4.0 (compatible; MSIE 8.0; Windows NT 5.1; Trident/4.0; InfoPath.1; .NET CLR 1.1.4322; .NET CLR 2.0.50727; MS-RTC LM 8)"

193.186.185.101 - - [28/Jan/2011:13:22:32 +0100] "GET /Seiten/Links.html HTTP/1.1" 200 19139 "http://www.bing.com/images/search?q=OMV+IMAGES&view=detail&id=F9F1978144E5659FE70FCC53F1ABE20C2E15C9E7&first=1&FORM=IDFRIR&qpvt=OMV+IMAGES" "Mozilla/4.0 (compatible; MSIE 8.0; Windows NT 5.1; Trident/4.0; InfoPath.1; .NET CLR 1.1.4322; .NET CLR 2.0.50727; MS-RTC LM 8)"

80.122.180.78 - - [28/Jan/2011:14:30:44 +0100] "GET /Seiten/Links.html HTTP/1.1" 200 19139 "http

---

[41] WHOIS record on page 328

```
://www.google.at/imgres?imgurl=http://www.asylabwehramt.at/Bilder/BMI.png&imgrefurl=http://www.as
ylabwehramt.at/Seiten/Links.html&usg=__XkgYoQjCp8P3lzCYNfBOdVyOhmg=&h=488&w=2000&sz=55&hl=de&star
t=21&zoom=1&tbnid=-J4hmZ76_kG4vM:&tbnh=37&tbnw=150&ei=d8RCTYmtGIabOr-A8bwB&prev=/images%3Fq%3Dbm.
i/%26hl%3Dde%26rlz%3D1G1ACAW_DEAT385%26biw%3D1899%26bih%3D895%26output%3Dimages_json%26tbs%3Disch:
11%2CO&itbs=1&bih=1899&bih=895"  "Mozilla/4.0 (compatible; MSIE 8.0; Windows NT 6.1; WOW64; Tride
nt/4.0; SLCC2; .NET CLR 2.0.50727; .NET CLR 3.5.30729; .NET CLR 3.0.30729; Media Center PC 6.0; e
SobiSubscriber 2.0.4.16)"

80.122.180.78 - - [28/Jan/2011:14:30:45 +0100] "GET /Bilder/Header_AAbA_anim.gif HTTP/1.1" 200 19
997 "http://www.asylabwehramt.at/Seiten/Links.html" "Mozilla/4.0 (compatible; MSIE 8.0; Windows N
T 6.1; WOW64; Trident/4.0; SLCC2; .NET CLR 2.0.50727; .NET CLR 3.5.30729; .NET CLR 3.0.30729; Med
ia Center PC 6.0; eSobiSubscriber 2.0.4.16)"

80.122.180.78 - - [28/Jan/2011:14:31:21 +0100] "GET /Bilder/BMI.png HTTP/1.1" 200 55823 "-" "Mozi
lla/4.0 (compatible; MSIE 7.0; Windows NT 6.1; WOW64; Trident/4.0; SLCC2; .NET CLR 2.0.50727; .NE
T CLR 3.5.30729; .NET CLR 3.0.30729; Media Center PC 6.0; eSobiSubscriber 2.0.4.16; MSOffice 12)"

80.122.180.78 - - [28/Jan/2011:14:31:45 +0100] "GET /favicon.ico HTTP/1.1" 302 340 "-" "Mozilla/4
.0 (compatible; MSIE 8.0; Windows NT 6.1; WOW64; Trident/4.0; SLCC2; .NET CLR 2.0.50727; .NET CLR
3.5.30729; .NET CLR 3.0.30729; Media Center PC 6.0; eSobiSubscriber 2.0.4.16)"

80.122.180.78 - - [28/Jan/2011:14:32:18 +0100] "GET /asyl.css HTTP/1.1" 200 860 "-" "Mozilla/4.0
(compatible; MSIE 7.0; Windows NT 6.1; WOW64; Trident/4.0; SLCC2; .NET CLR 2.0.50727; .NET CLR 3.
5.30729; .NET CLR 3.0.30729; Media Center PC 6.0; eSobiSubscriber 2.0.4.16; MSOffice 12)"

80.122.180.78 - - [28/Jan/2011:14:33:51 +0100] "GET /asyl.css HTTP/1.1" 304 - "-" "Mozilla/4.0 (c
ompatible; MSIE 7.0; Windows NT 6.1; WOW64; Trident/4.0; SLCC2; .NET CLR 2.0.50727; .NET CLR 3.5.
30729; .NET CLR 3.0.30729; Media Center PC 6.0; eSobiSubscriber 2.0.4.16; MSOffice 12)"

78.41.144.41 - - [02/Feb/2011:13:44:54 +0100] "GET / HTTP/1.0" 200 13966  "http://www.facebook.co
m/l.php?u=http%3A%2F%2Fwww.asylabwehramt.at%2F&h=0fdcd"  "Mozilla/4.0 (compatible; MSIE 8.0; Wind
ows NT 5.1; Trident/4.0; .NET CLR 2.0.50727; .NET CLR 3.0.04506.30; .NET CLR 3.0.04506.648; .NET
```

CLR 3.5.21022; .NET CLR 3.0.4506.2152; .NET CLR 3.5.30729; .NET CLR 3.5.30729; .NET4.0C; .NET4.0E)"
80.121.255.186 - - [02/Feb/2011:22:11:36 +0100] "GET /Seiten/Impressum.html HTTP/1.1" 200 11939 "http://www.google.at/url?sa=t&source=web&cd=6&ved=0CDkQFjAF&url=http%3A%2F%2Fwww.asylabwehramt.at%2FSeiten%2FImpressum.html&rct=j&q=asylantrag%20%C3%B6sterreich%20formular&ei=5MZJTaHuBsKb8QP10dCbDw&usg=AFQjCNHF7HP6dxpY82GEXb1PQnRvP4GW7g" "Mozilla/4.0 (compatible; MSIE 8.0; Windows NT 6.1; WOW64; Trident/4.0; SLCC2; .NET CLR 2.0.50727; .NET CLR 3.5.30729; .NET CLR 3.0.30729; Media Center PC 6.0; InfoPath.2; .NET4.0C)"
188.21.98.198[42] - - [04/Feb/2011:13:29:44 +0100] "GET / HTTP/1.1" 200 13966 "-" "-" "Mozilla/5.0 (Windows; U; Windows NT 5.1; de; rv:1.9.2.13) Gecko/20101203 Firefox/3.6.13"
188.21.98.198 - - [04/Feb/2011:13:29:45 +0100] "GET /asyl.css HTTP/1.1" 200 860 "http://www.asylabwehramt.at/" "Mozilla/5.0 (Windows; U; Windows NT 5.1; de; rv:1.9.2.13) Gecko/20101203 Firefox/3.6.13"
188.21.98.198 - - [04/Feb/2011:13:29:48 +0100] "GET /favicon.ico HTTP/1.1" 302 340 "-" "Mozilla/5.0 (Windows; U; Windows NT 5.1; de; rv:1.9.2.13) Gecko/20101203 Firefox/3.6.13"
188.21.98.198 - - [04/Feb/2011:13:30:16 +0100] "GET /Seiten/Orgstrukt.html HTTP/1.1" 200 14119 "http://www.asylabwehramt.at/" "Mozilla/5.0 (Windows; U; Windows NT 5.1; de; rv:1.9.2.13) Gecko/20101203 Firefox/3.6.13"
188.21.98.198 - - [04/Feb/2011:13:30:35 +0100] "GET /Seiten/Links.html HTTP/1.1" 200 19139 "http://www.asylabwehramt.at/Seiten/Orgstrukt.html" "Mozilla/5.0 (Windows; U; Windows NT 5.1; de; rv:1.9.2.13) Gecko/20101203 Firefox/3.6.13"
188.21.98.198 - - [04/Feb/2011:13:31:00 +0100] "GET /Seiten/Impressum.html HTTP/1.1" 200 11939 "http://www.asylabwehramt.at/Seiten/Links.html" "Mozilla/5.0 (Windows; U; Windows NT 5.1; de; rv:1.9.2.13) Gecko/20101203 Firefox/3.6.13"
188.21.98.198 - - [04/Feb/2011:13:32:55 +0100] "GET /Seiten/Bilder.html HTTP/1.1" 200 10364 "http://www.asylabwehramt.at/Seiten/Impressum.html" "Mozilla/5.0 (Windows; U; Windows NT 5.1; de; rv:1.9.2.13) Gecko/20101203 Firefox/3.6.13"

---

[42] WHOIS record on page 323

```
188.21.98.198 - - [04/Feb/2011:13:33:11 +0100] "GET /Seiten/Ausseneinsaetze.html HTTP/1.1" 200 93
81 "http://www.asylabwehramt.at/Seiten/Bilder.html" "Mozilla/5.0 (Windows; U; Windows NT 5.1; de;
rv:1.9.2.13) Gecko/20101203 Firefox/3.6.13"
188.21.98.198 - - [04/Feb/2011:13:33:12 +0100] "GET /Bilder/inventur.png HTTP/1.1" 200 848668 "ht
tp://www.asylabwehramt.at/Seiten/Ausseneinsaetze.html" "Mozilla/5.0 (Windows; U; Windows NT 5.1;
de; rv:1.9.2.13) Gecko/20101203 Firefox/3.6.13"
188.21.98.198 - - [04/Feb/2011:13:33:18 +0100] "GET /Seiten/Press.html HTTP/1.1" 200 12374 "http:
//www.asylabwehramt.at/Seiten/Ausseneinsaetze.html" "Mozilla/5.0 (Windows; U; Windows NT 5.1; de;
rv:1.9.2.13) Gecko/20101203 Firefox/3.6.13"
188.21.98.198 - - [04/Feb/2011:13:33:52 +0100] "GET /OEFFENTLICHKEIT/07062010d.pdf HTTP/1.1" 200
333788 "http://www.asylabwehramt.at/Seiten/Press.html" "Mozilla/5.0 (Windows; U; Windows NT 5.1;
de; rv:1.9.2.13) Gecko/20101203 Firefox/3.6.13"
188.21.98.198 - - [04/Feb/2011:13:34:11 +0100] "GET /Seiten/Rundzeichen.html HTTP/1.1" 200 8895 "
http://www.asylabwehramt.at/Seiten/Press.html" "Mozilla/5.0 (Windows; U; Windows NT 5.1; de; rv:1
.9.2.13) Gecko/20101203 Firefox/3.6.13"
78.41.149.241[43] - - [08/Feb/2011:11:21:37 +0100] "GET /Bilder/BMI.png HTTP/1.1" 200 55823 "http://w
ww.google.at/imgres?imgurl=http://www.asylabwehramt.at/Bilder/BMI.png&imgrefurl=http://www.asylab
wehramt.at/Seiten/Links.html&usg=__XkgYoQjCp8P3lzCYNfB0dVy0hmg=&h=488&w=2000&sz=55&hl=de&start=28
&zoom=1&tbnid=-J4hmZ76_kG4vM:&tbnh=52&tbnw=212&ei=LxlRTeer0cWwhAfE1_HTCA&prev=/images%3Fq%3Dlogo%
2Bbundesministerium%2Bf%25C3%25BCr%2BInneres%2B%25C3%25B6sterreich%26hl%3Dde%26sa%3DX%26biw%3D165
9%26bih%3D865%26tbs%3Disch:1,isz:10%2C389&itbs=1&iact=hc&vpx=269&vpy=518&dur=1201&hovh=111&hovw=4
55&tx=241&ty=73&oei=LBlRTf2h0YSCswahz-ndBg&esq=2&page=2&ndsp=28&ved=1t:429,r:1,s:28&biw=1659&bih=
865" "Mozilla/4.0 (compatible; MSIE 8.0; Windows NT 6.1; Trident/4.0; SLCC2; .NET CLR 2.0.50727;
.NET CLR 3.5.30729; .NET CLR 3.0.30729; Media Center PC 6.0; .NET4.0C; .NET4.0E; InfoPath.3; MS-R
TC LM 8; .NET CLR 1.1.4322)"
78.41.149.241 - - [08/Feb/2011:11:21:38 +0100] "GET /asyl.css HTTP/1.1" 200 860 "http://www.asyla
```

---

[43]WHOIS record on page 318

bwehramt.at/Seiten/Links.html" "Mozilla/4.0 (compatible; MSIE 8.0; Windows NT 6.1; Trident/4.0; SLCC2; .NET CLR 2.0.50727; .NET CLR 3.5.30729; .NET CLR 3.0.30729; Media Center PC 6.0; .NET4.0C; .NET4.0E; InfoPath.3; MS-RTC LM 8; .NET CLR 1.1.4322)"

89.186.150.239 - - [08/Feb/2011:17:20:05 +0100] "GET /Seiten/Material.html HTTP/1.1" 200 17335 "http://www.google.de/search?q=asylantrag+%C3%B6sterreich+formular&num=1&hl=de&ndsp=20&ie=UTF-8&sa=N&tab=iw" "Mozilla/5.0 (Windows; U; Windows NT 5.1; de; rv:1.9.2.13) Gecko/20101203 Firefox/3.6.13"

193.41.228.76 - - [09/Feb/2011:13:09:59 +0100] "GET / HTTP/1.1" 200 13966 "-" "Mozilla/4.0 (compatible; MSIE 8.0; Windows NT 5.1; Trident/4.0; .NET CLR 2.0.50727; .NET CLR 3.0.04506.648; .NET CLR 3.5.21022; InfoPath.1; .NET CLR 3.0.4506.2152; .NET CLR 3.5.30729)"

193.41.228.76 - - [09/Feb/2011:13:10:27 +0100] "GET /Seiten/Orgstrukt.html HTTP/1.1" 200 14119 "http://www.asylabwehramt.at/" "Mozilla/4.0 (compatible; MSIE 8.0; Windows NT 5.1; Trident/4.0; .NET CLR 2.0.50727; .NET CLR 3.0.04506.648; .NET CLR 3.5.21022; InfoPath.1; .NET CLR 3.0.4506.2152; .NET CLR 3.5.30729)"

193.41.228.76 - - [09/Feb/2011:13:10:52 +0100] "GET /Seiten/Rundzeichen.html HTTP/1.1" 200 8895 "http://www.asylabwehramt.at/Seiten/Orgstrukt.html" "Mozilla/4.0 (compatible; MSIE 8.0; Windows NT 5.1; Trident/4.0; .NET CLR 2.0.50727; .NET CLR 3.0.04506.648; .NET CLR 3.5.21022; InfoPath.1; .NET CLR 3.0.4506.2152; .NET CLR 3.5.30729)"

193.41.228.76 - - [09/Feb/2011:13:11:03 +0100] "GET /Seiten/Bilder.html HTTP/1.1" 200 10364 "http://www.asylabwehramt.at/Seiten/Rundzeichen.html" "Mozilla/4.0 (compatible; MSIE 8.0; Windows NT 5.1; Trident/4.0; .NET CLR 2.0.50727; .NET CLR 3.0.04506.648; .NET CLR 3.5.21022; InfoPath.1; .NET CLR 3.0.4506.2152; .NET CLR 3.5.30729)"

193.41.228.76 - - [09/Feb/2011:13:11:16 +0100] "GET /Seiten/Bilder_Ausstellung.html HTTP/1.1" 200 16685 "http://www.asylabwehramt.at/Seiten/Bilder.html" "Mozilla/4.0 (compatible; MSIE 8.0; Windows NT 5.1; Trident/4.0; .NET CLR 2.0.50727; .NET CLR 3.0.04506.648; .NET CLR 3.5.21022; InfoPath.1; .NET CLR 3.5.30729)"

193.41.228.76 - - [09/Feb/2011:13:13:06 +0100] "GET /Seiten/Material.html HTTP/1.1" 200 17335 "http://www.asylabwehramt.at/Seiten/Bilder_Ausstellung.html" "Mozilla/4.0 (compatible; MSIE 8.0; Win

```
dows NT 5.1; Trident/4.0; .NET CLR 2.0.50727; .NET CLR 3.0.4506.2152; .NET CLR 3.5.21022; InfoPat
h.1; .NET CLR 3.0.4506.2152; .NET CLR 3.5.30729)"
193.41.228.76 - - [09/Feb/2011:13:13:15 +0100] "GET /Bilder/Ladung.png HTTP/1.1" 200 114658 "http
://www.asylabwehramt.at/Seiten/Material.html" "Mozilla/4.0 (compatible; MSIE 8.0; Windows NT 5.1;
Trident/4.0; .NET CLR 2.0.50727; .NET CLR 3.0.04506.648; .NET CLR 3.5.21022; InfoPath.1; .NET CL
R 3.0.4506.2152; .NET CLR 3.5.30729)"
193.41.228.76 - - [09/Feb/2011:13:13:43 +0100] "GET /Material/Flyer_Volksschutz_Praevention_Aufkl
aerung_FPOE.pdf HTTP/1.1" 200 661529 "http://www.asylabwehramt.at/Seiten/Material.html" "Mozilla/
4.0 (compatible; MSIE 8.0; Windows NT 5.1; Trident/4.0; .NET CLR 2.0.50727; .NET CLR 3.0.04506.64
8; .NET CLR 3.5.21022; InfoPath.1; .NET CLR 3.0.4506.2152; .NET CLR 3.5.30729)"
193.41.228.76 - - [09/Feb/2011:13:13:44 +0100] "GET /Material/Flyer_Volksschutz_Praevention_Aufkl
aerung_FPOE.pdf HTTP/1.1" 206 368049 "-" "Mozilla/4.0 (compatible; MSIE 8.0; Windows NT 5.1; Trid
ent/4.0; .NET CLR 2.0.50727; .NET CLR 3.0.04506.648; .NET CLR 3.5.21022; InfoPath.1; .NET CLR 3.0
.4506.2152; .NET CLR 3.5.30729)"
193.41.228.76 - - [09/Feb/2011:13:14:08 +0100] "GET /Bilder/flyer_nigeria_Internet.pdf HTTP/1.1"
200 702826 "http://www.asylabwehramt.at/Seiten/Material.html" "Mozilla/4.0 (compatible; MSIE 8.0;
Windows NT 5.1; Trident/4.0; .NET CLR 2.0.50727; .NET CLR 3.0.04506.648; .NET CLR 3.5.21022; Inf
oPath.1; .NET CLR 3.0.4506.2152; .NET CLR 3.5.30729)"
193.41.228.76 - - [09/Feb/2011:13:14:09 +0100] "GET /Bilder/flyer_nigeria_Internet.pdf HTTP/1.1"
206 4096 "-" "Mozilla/4.0 (compatible; MSIE 8.0; Windows NT 5.1; Trident/4.0; .NET CLR 2.0.50727;
.NET CLR 3.0.04506.648; .NET CLR 3.5.21022; InfoPath.1; .NET CLR 3.0.4506.2152; .NET CLR 3.5.307
29)"
193.41.228.76 - - [09/Feb/2011:13:15:36 +0100] "GET /Material/Hotline_Deutsch.pdf HTTP/1.1" 200 4
89465 "http://www.asylabwehramt.at/Seiten/Material.html" "Mozilla/4.0 (compatible; MSIE 8.0; Wind
ows NT 5.1; Trident/4.0; .NET CLR 2.0.50727; .NET CLR 3.0.04506.648; .NET CLR 3.5.21022; InfoPath
.1; .NET CLR 3.0.4506.2152; .NET CLR 3.5.30729)"
193.41.228.76 - - [09/Feb/2011:13:16:28 +0100] "GET /Material/Hotline_Franzoesisch.PDF HTTP/1.1"
200 515416 "http://www.asylabwehramt.at/Seiten/Material.html" "Mozilla/4.0 (compatible; MSIE 8.0;
```

Windows NT 5.1; Trident/4.0; .NET CLR 2.0.50727; .NET CLR 3.0.4506.2152; .NET CLR 3.5.21022; InfoPath.1; .NET CLR 3.0.4506.2152; .NET CLR 3.5.30729)"

193.41.228.76 - - [09/Feb/2011:13:16:45 +0100] "GET /Material/AABA_MATERIAL.zip HTTP/1.1" 200 98348161 "http://www.asylabwehramt.at/Seiten/Material.html" "Mozilla/4.0 (compatible; MSIE 8.0; Windows NT 5.1; Trident/4.0; .NET CLR 2.0.50727; .NET CLR 3.0.04506.648; .NET CLR 3.5.21022; InfoPath.1; .NET CLR 3.0.4506.2152; .NET CLR 3.5.30729)"

193.41.228.76 - - [09/Feb/2011:13:17:05 +0100] "GET /Seiten/Links.html HTTP/1.1" 200 19139 "http://www.asylabwehramt.at/Seiten/Material.html" "Mozilla/4.0 (compatible; MSIE 8.0; Windows NT 5.1; Trident/4.0; .NET CLR 2.0.50727; .NET CLR 3.0.04506.648; .NET CLR 3.5.21022; InfoPath.1; .NET CLR 3.0.4506.2152; .NET CLR 3.5.30729)"

193.41.228.76 - - [09/Feb/2011:13:17:06 +0100] "GET /Bilder/frontex.png HTTP/1.1" 200 22383 "http://www.asylabwehramt.at/Seiten/Links.html" "Mozilla/4.0 (compatible; MSIE 8.0; Windows NT 5.1; Trident/4.0; .NET CLR 2.0.50727; .NET CLR 3.0.04506.648; .NET CLR 3.5.21022; InfoPath.1; .NET CLR 3.0.4506.2152; .NET CLR 3.5.30729)"

193.41.228.76 - - [09/Feb/2011:13:19:08 +0100] "GET /Seiten/Press.html HTTP/1.1" 200 12374 "http://www.asylabwehramt.at/Seiten/Links.html" "Mozilla/4.0 (compatible; MSIE 8.0; Windows NT 5.1; Trident/4.0; .NET CLR 2.0.50727; .NET CLR 3.0.04506.648; .NET CLR 3.5.21022; InfoPath.1; .NET CLR 3.0.4506.2152; .NET CLR 3.5.30729)"

193.41.228.76 - - [09/Feb/2011:13:19:19 +0100] "GET /OEFFENTLICHKEIT/07062010d.pdf HTTP/1.1" 200 333788 "http://www.asylabwehramt.at/Seiten/Press.html" "Mozilla/4.0 (compatible; MSIE 8.0; Windows NT 5.1; Trident/4.0; .NET CLR 2.0.50727; .NET CLR 3.0.04506.648; .NET CLR 3.5.21022; InfoPath.1; .NET CLR 3.0.4506.2152; .NET CLR 3.5.30729)"

193.41.228.76 - - [09/Feb/2011:13:21:49 +0100] "GET /favicon.ico HTTP/1.1" 302 340 "-" "Mozilla/4.0 (compatible; MSIE 8.0; Windows NT 5.1; Trident/4.0; .NET CLR 2.0.50727; .NET CLR 3.0.04506.648; .NET CLR 3.5.21022; InfoPath.1; .NET CLR 3.0.4506.2152; .NET CLR 3.5.30729)"

193.41.228.76 - - [09/Feb/2011:13:22:33 +0100] "GET /Seiten/Aktuelles.html HTTP/1.1" 200 14343 "http://www.asylabwehramt.at/Seiten/Press.html" "Mozilla/4.0 (compatible; MSIE 8.0; Windows NT 5.1; Trident/4.0; .NET CLR 2.0.50727; .NET CLR 3.0.04506.648; .NET CLR 3.5.21022; InfoPath.1; .NET CL

```
R 3.0.4506.2152; .NET CLR 3.5.30729)"
193.41.228.76 - - [09/Feb/2011:13:27:34 +0100] "GET /Seiten/Ausseneinsaetze.html HTTP/1.1" 200 93
81 "http://www.asylabwehramt.at/Seiten/Bilder.html" "Mozilla/4.0 (compatible; MSIE 8.0; Windows N
T 5.1; Trident/4.0; .NET CLR 2.0.50727; .NET CLR 3.0.04506.648; .NET CLR 3.5.21022; InfoPath.1; .
NET CLR 3.0.4506.2152; .NET CLR 3.5.30729)"
193.41.228.76 - - [09/Feb/2011:13:27:35 +0100] "GET /Bilder/inventur.png HTTP/1.1" 200 848668 "ht
tp://www.asylabwehramt.at/Seiten/Ausseneinsaetze.html" "Mozilla/4.0 (compatible; MSIE 8.0; Window
s NT 5.1; Trident/4.0; .NET CLR 2.0.50727; .NET CLR 3.0.04506.648; .NET CLR 3.5.21022; InfoPath.1
; .NET CLR 3.0.4506.2152; .NET CLR 3.5.30729)"
193.41.228.76 - - [09/Feb/2011:13:27:56 +0100] "GET /Seiten/Bilder_Ausstellung_2.html HTTP/1.1" 2
00 20902 "http://www.asylabwehramt.at/Seiten/Bilder.html" "Mozilla/4.0 (compatible; MSIE 8.0; Win
dows NT 5.1; Trident/4.0; .NET CLR 2.0.50727; .NET CLR 3.0.04506.648; .NET CLR 3.5.21022; InfoPat
h.1; .NET CLR 3.0.4506.2152; .NET CLR 3.5.30729)"
193.41.228.76 - - [09/Feb/2011:13:27:57 +0100] "GET /Bilder/Ausstellung_weisses_Haus_fotos_ubermo
rgen/DSC_0030_AAbA_ubermorgen_thumb.jpg HTTP/1.1" 200 346801 "http://www.asylabwehramt.at/Seiten/
Bilder_Ausstellung_2.html" "Mozilla/4.0 (compatible; MSIE 8.0; Windows NT 5.1; Trident/4.0; .NET
CLR 2.0.50727; .NET CLR 3.0.04506.648; .NET CLR 3.5.21022; InfoPath.1; .NET CLR 3.0.4506.2152; .N
ET CLR 3.5.30729)"
193.41.228.76 - - [09/Feb/2011:13:27:58 +0100] "GET /Bilder/Ausstellung_weisses_Haus_fotos_ubermo
rgen/DSC_0173_AAbA_ubermorgen_thumb.jpg HTTP/1.1" 200 358713 "http://www.asylabwehramt.at/Seiten/
Bilder_Ausstellung_2.html" "Mozilla/4.0 (compatible; MSIE 8.0; Windows NT 5.1; Trident/4.0; .NET
CLR 2.0.50727; .NET CLR 3.0.04506.648; .NET CLR 3.5.21022; InfoPath.1; .NET CLR 3.0.4506.2152; .N
ET CLR 3.5.30729)"
193.41.228.76 - - [09/Feb/2011:13:28:05 +0100] "GET /Bilder/Ausstellung_weisses_Haus_fotos_ubermo
rgen/DSC_0017.jpg HTTP/1.1" 200 1130855 "http://www.asylabwehramt.at/Seiten/Bilder_Ausstellung_2.
html" "Mozilla/4.0 (compatible; MSIE 8.0; Windows NT 5.1; Trident/4.0; .NET CLR 2.0.50727; .NET C
LR 3.0.04506.648; .NET CLR 3.5.21022; InfoPath.1; .NET CLR 3.0.4506.2152; .NET CLR 3.5.30729)"
193.41.228.76 - - [09/Feb/2011:13:31:11 +0100] "GET /Bilder/Ausstellung_weisses_Haus_fotos_ubermo
```

```
rgen/DSC_0036_AAbA_ubermorgen_thumb.jpg HTTP/1.1" 200 304658 "http://www.asylabwehramt.at/Seiten/
Bilder_Ausstellung_2.html" "Mozilla/4.0 (compatible; MSIE 8.0; Windows NT 5.1; Trident/4.0; .NET
CLR 2.0.50727; .NET CLR 3.0.04506.648; .NET CLR 3.5.21022; InfoPath.1; .NET CLR 3.0.4506.2152; .N
ET CLR 3.5.30729)"
193.41.228.76 - - [09/Feb/2011:13:31:12 +0100] "GET /Bilder/Ausstellung_weisses_Haus_fotos_ubermo
rgen/DSC_0173_AAbA_ubermorgen_thumb.jpg HTTP/1.1" 200 358713 "http://www.asylabwehramt.at/Seiten/
Bilder_Ausstellung_2.html" "Mozilla/4.0 (compatible; MSIE 8.0; Windows NT 5.1; Trident/4.0; .NET
CLR 2.0.50727; .NET CLR 3.0.04506.648; .NET CLR 3.5.21022; InfoPath.1; .NET CLR 3.0.4506.2152; .N
ET CLR 3.5.30729)"
193.246.50.2[44] - - [10/Feb/2011:08:39:49 +0100] "GET / HTTP/1.1" 200 13966 "http://www.ubermorgen.
com/2010/index.html" "Mozilla/5.0 (Windows; U; Windows NT 5.1; de; rv:1.9.2.4) Gecko/20100611 Fi
refox/3.6.4 ( .NET CLR 3.5.30729)"
193.246.50.2 - - [10/Feb/2011:08:39:52 +0100] "GET /favicon.ico HTTP/1.1" 302 340 "-" "Mozilla/5.
0 (Windows; U; Windows NT 5.1; de; rv:1.9.2.4) Gecko/20100611 Firefox/3.6.4 ( .NET CLR 3.5.30729)
"
193.246.50.2 - - [10/Feb/2011:08:43:59 +0100] "GET /favicon.ico HTTP/1.1" 302 340 "-" "Mozilla/5.
0 (Windows; U; Windows NT 5.1; de; rv:1.9.2.4) Gecko/20100611 Firefox/3.6.4 ( .NET CLR 3.5.30729)
"
193.246.50.2 - - [10/Feb/2011:08:44:24 +0100] "GET /Seiten/Aktuelles.html HTTP/1.1" 200 14343 "ht
tp://www.asylabwehramt.at/" "Mozilla/5.0 (Windows; U; Windows NT 5.1; de; rv:1.9.2.4) Gecko/20100
611 Firefox/3.6.4 ( .NET CLR 3.5.30729)"
193.246.50.2 - - [10/Feb/2011:08:44:41 +0100] "GET /Seiten/Material.html HTTP/1.1" 200 17335 "htt
p://www.asylabwehramt.at/Seiten/Aktuelles.html" "Mozilla/5.0 (Windows; U; Windows NT 5.1; de; rv:
1.9.2.4) Gecko/20100611 Firefox/3.6.4 ( .NET CLR 3.5.30729)"
193.246.50.2 - - [10/Feb/2011:08:44:52 +0100] "GET /Material/Hotline_Russisch.pdf HTTP/1.1" 200 2
39827 "http://www.asylabwehramt.at/Seiten/Material.html" "Mozilla/5.0 (Windows; U; Windows NT 5.1
```

---

[44] WHOIS record on page 296

255

```
; de; rv:1.9.2.4) Gecko/20100611 Firefox/3.6.4 ( .NET CLR 3.5.30729)"
193.246.50.2 - - [10/Feb/2011:08:44:55 +0100] "GET /Material/Hotline_Russisch.pdf HTTP/1.1" 206 2
07281 "-" "Mozilla/5.0 (Windows; U; Windows NT 5.1; de; rv:1.9.2.4) Gecko/20100611 Firefox/3.6.4
( .NET CLR 3.5.30729)"
193.246.50.2 - - [10/Feb/2011:08:45:15 +0100] "GET /Bilder/flyer_nigeria_Internet.pdf HTTP/1.1" 2
00 702826 "http://www.asylabwehramt.at/Seiten/Material.html" "Mozilla/5.0 (Windows; U; Windows NT
5.1; de; rv:1.9.2.4) Gecko/20100611 Firefox/3.6.4 ( .NET CLR 3.5.30729)"
193.246.50.2 - - [10/Feb/2011:08:45:16 +0100] "GET /Bilder/flyer_nigeria_Internet.pdf HTTP/1.1" 2
06 637611 "-" "Mozilla/5.0 (Windows; U; Windows NT 5.1; de; rv:1.9.2.4) Gecko/20100611 Firefox/3.
6.4 ( .NET CLR 3.5.30729)"
178.191.167.158 - - [13/Feb/2011:16:12:08 +0100] "GET / HTTP/1.1" 200 13966 "http://www.google.co
m/url?sa=t&source=web&cd=6&sqi=2&ved=0CDYQFjAF&url=http%3A%2F%2Fwww.asylabwehramt.at%2F&rct=j&q=t
schechien%20fl%C3%BCchtlinge%20%20penis%20 &ei=c_RXTbLlB9CwhQeAw7z9DA&usg=AFQjCNEy1zWClvnxkLlPAGif
Rc344_0U4Q" "Mozilla/5.0 (Macintosh; U; Intel Mac OS X 10_6_6; de-de) AppleWebKit/533.19.4 (KHTML
, like Gecko) Version/5.0.3 Safari/533.19.4"
194.138.12.170 - - [14/Feb/2011:04:32:26 +0100] "GET /Bilder/SCREEN_AAbA_Edutainment_Video.jpg HT
TP/1.1" 200 29259 "http://forum.geizhals.at/t562009,-1.html" "Mozilla/4.0 (compatible; MSIE 8.0
; Windows NT 5.2; WOW64; Trident/4.0; .NET CLR 1.0.3705; .NET CLR 2.0.50727; .NET CLR 3.0.04506.3
0; .NET CLR 1.1.4322; InfoPath.1; .NET CLR 3.0.4506.2152; .NET CLR 3.5.30729; MS-RTC LM 8; .NET4.
0C; .NET4.0E)"
193.186.185.101 - - [18/Feb/2011:07:34:05 +0100] "GET /Seiten/Links.html HTTP/1.1" 200 19139 "ht
tp://www.google.at/imgres?imgurl=http://slopeships.com/burns/pics/Fingertips.jpg&imgrefurl=http:/
/www.asylabwehramt.at/Seiten/Links.html&usg=__lhNBx6OD3bsoraY2vFIB3_uJ7A8=&h=924&w=1056&sz=66&hl=
de&start=65&zoom=1&tbnid=30e_S_Vc1QpBWM:&tbnh=146&tbnw=167&ei=2BJeTeGHHJkD5Aa38PzjCQ&prev=/images
%3Fq%3DOMV%2BOTS%26um%3D1%26hl%3Dde%26sa%3DN%26rlz%3D1R2GFRE_deAT391%26biw%3D1259%26bih%3D791%26t
bs%3Disch:10%2C1898&um=1&itbs=1&iact=hc&vpx=332&vpy=237&dur=250&hovw=240&tx=122&ty=130&o
```

ei=yhJeTa-IEcPp4galjtTVCQ&page=4&ndsp=23&ved=1t:429,r:1,s:65&biw=1259&bih=791" "Mozilla/4.0 (com
patible; MSIE 8.0; Windows NT 5.1; Trident/4.0; GTB6.5; InfoPath.1; .NET CLR 1.1.4322; .NET CLR 2
.0.50727; MS-RTC LM 8)"

193.186.185.101 - - [18/Feb/2011:07:34:06 +0100] "GET /asyl.css HTTP/1.1" 200 860 "http://www.asy
labwehramt.at/Seiten/Links.html" "Mozilla/4.0 (compatible; MSIE 8.0; Windows NT 5.1; Trident/4.0;
GTB6.5; InfoPath.1; .NET CLR 1.1.4322; .NET CLR 2.0.50727; MS-RTC LM 8)"

193.186.185.101 - - [18/Feb/2011:07:34:11 +0100] "GET /favicon.ico HTTP/1.1" 302 340 "-" "Mozilla
/4.0 (compatible; MSIE 8.0; Windows NT 5.1; Trident/4.0; GTB6.5; InfoPath.1; .NET CLR 1.1.4322; .
NET CLR 2.0.50727; MS-RTC LM 8)"

195.78.53.127[45] - - [21/Feb/2011:12:38:17 +0100] "GET / HTTP/1.1" 200 13966 "-" "Mozilla/4.0 (compa
tible; MSIE 8.0; Windows NT 6.1; Trident/4.0; SLCC2; .NET CLR 2.0.50727; .NET CLR 3.5.30729; .NET
CLR 3.0.30729; Media Center PC 6.0; InfoPath.2; Tablet PC 2.0; .NET4.0C)"

195.78.53.127 - - [21/Feb/2011:12:38:19 +0100] "GET /favicon.ico HTTP/1.1" 302 340 "-" "Mozilla/4
.0 (compatible; MSIE 8.0; Windows NT 6.1; Trident/4.0; SLCC2; .NET CLR 2.0.50727; .NET CLR 3.5.30
729; .NET CLR 3.0.30729; Media Center PC 6.0; InfoPath.2; Tablet PC 2.0; .NET4.0C)"

195.78.53.127 - - [21/Feb/2011:12:59:25 +0100] "GET /Seiten/Aktuelles.html HTTP/1.1" 200 14343 "h
ttp://www.asylabwehramt.at/" "Mozilla/4.0 (compatible; MSIE 8.0; Windows NT 6.1; Trident/4.0; SLC
C2; .NET CLR 2.0.50727; .NET CLR 3.5.30729; .NET CLR 3.0.30729; Media Center PC 6.0; InfoPath.2;
Tablet PC 2.0; .NET4.0C)"

195.78.53.127 - - [21/Feb/2011:13:00:11 +0100] "GET /Seiten/Rundzeichen.html HTTP/1.1" 200 8895 "
http://www.asylabwehramt.at/Seiten/Aktuelles.html" "Mozilla/4.0 (compatible; MSIE 8.0; Windows NT
6.1; Trident/4.0; SLCC2; .NET CLR 2.0.50727; .NET CLR 3.5.30729; .NET CLR 3.0.30729; Media Cente
r PC 6.0; InfoPath.2; Tablet PC 2.0; .NET4.0C)"

195.78.53.127 - - [21/Feb/2011:13:00:22 +0100] "GET /Seiten/Links.html HTTP/1.1" 200 19139 "http:
//www.asylabwehramt.at/Seiten/Rundzeichen.html" "Mozilla/4.0 (compatible; MSIE 8.0; Windows NT 6.
1; Trident/4.0; SLCC2; .NET CLR 2.0.50727; .NET CLR 3.0.30729; Media Center P

---

[45]WHOIS record on page 300

```
C 6.0; InfoPath.2; Tablet PC 2.0; .NET4.0C)"
195.78.53.127 - - [21/Feb/2011:13:00:46 +0100] "GET /Seiten/Press.html HTTP/1.1" 200 12374 "http://www.asylabwehramt.at/Seiten/Links.html" "Mozilla/4.0 (compatible; MSIE 8.0; Windows NT 6.1; Trident/4.0; SLCC2; .NET CLR 2.0.50727; .NET CLR 3.5.30729; .NET CLR 3.0.30729; Media Center PC 6.0; InfoPath.2; Tablet PC 2.0; .NET4.0C)"
193.171.152.33 - - [21/Feb/2011:14:34:57 +0100] "GET /Bilder/SCREEN_AAbA_Edutainment_Video.jpg HTTP/1.1" 200 29259 "http://forum.geizhals.at/t562009.html" "Mozilla/5.0 (compatible; MSIE 9.0; Windows NT 6.1; Trident/5.0)"
195.78.53.127 - - [21/Feb/2011:14:39:26 +0100] "GET /Seiten/Bilder.html HTTP/1.1" 200 10364 "http://www.asylabwehramt.at/" "Mozilla/4.0 (compatible; MSIE 8.0; Windows NT 6.1; Trident/4.0; SLCC2; .NET CLR 2.0.50727; .NET CLR 3.5.30729; .NET CLR 3.0.30729; Media Center PC 6.0; InfoPath.2; Tablet PC 2.0; .NET4.0C)"
193.5.216.100 - - [23/Feb/2011:07:08:36 +0100] "GET /OEFFENTLICHKEIT/media/ZEIT.pdf HTTP/1.0" 200 484489 "http://www.ubermorgen.com/2010/index.html" "Mozilla/4.0 (compatible; MSIE 8.0; Windows NT 5.1; Trident/4.0; .NET CLR 1.1.4322; .NET CLR 2.0.50727; .NET CLR 3.0.4506.2152; .NET CLR 3.5.30729; EIE6)"
88.116.224.102 - - [24/Feb/2011:10:39:42 +0100] "GET / HTTP/1.1" 200 13966 "-" "Mozilla/5.0 (X11; U; Linux i686; de; rv:1.9.2.13) Gecko/20101206 Ubuntu/9.10 (karmic) Firefox/3.6.13"
88.116.224.102 - - [24/Feb/2011:10:39:45 +0100] "GET /favicon.ico HTTP/1.1" 302 340 "-" "Mozilla/5.0 (X11; U; Linux i686; de; rv:1.9.2.13) Gecko/20101206 Ubuntu/9.10 (karmic) Firefox/3.6.13"
88.116.224.102 - - [24/Feb/2011:10:40:10 +0100] "GET /Seiten/Bilder.html HTTP/1.1" 200 10364 "http://www.asylabwehramt.at/" "Mozilla/5.0 (X11; U; Linux i686; de; rv:1.9.2.13) Gecko/20101206 Ubuntu/9.10 (karmic) Firefox/3.6.13"
88.116.224.102 - - [24/Feb/2011:10:41:49 +0100] "GET /Seiten/Bilder_Ausstellung.html HTTP/1.1" 200 16685 "http://www.asylabwehramt.at/Seiten/Bilder.html" "Mozilla/5.0 (X11; U; Linux i686; de; rv:1.9.2.13) Gecko/20101206 Ubuntu/9.10 (karmic) Firefox/3.6.13"
88.116.224.102 - - [24/Feb/2011:10:41:50 +0100] "GET /Bilder/Ausstellung_weisses_haus_wien_esel_f
```

```
88.116.224.102 - - [24/Feb/2011:10:41:51 +0100] "GET /Bilder/Ausstellung_weisses_haus_wien_esel_fotos/eSeL_UBERMORGEN_asylabwehramt_dasweissehaus_456_thumb.jpg HTTP/1.1" 200 28685 "http://www.asylabwehramt.at/Seiten/Bilder_Ausstellung.html" "Mozilla/5.0 (X11; U; Linux i686; de; rv:1.9.2.13) Gecko/20101206 Ubuntu/9.10 (karmic) Firefox/3.6.13"
88.116.224.102 - - [24/Feb/2011:10:41:53 +0100] "GET /Bilder/Ausstellung_weisses_haus_wien_esel_fotos/eSeL_UBERMORGEN_asylabwehramt_dasweissehaus_467_thumb.jpg HTTP/1.1" 200 40316 "http://www.asylabwehramt.at/Seiten/Bilder_Ausstellung.html" "Mozilla/5.0 (X11; U; Linux i686; de; rv:1.9.2.13) Gecko/20101206 Ubuntu/9.10 (karmic) Firefox/3.6.13"
88.116.224.102 - - [24/Feb/2011:10:41:54 +0100] "GET /Bilder/Ausstellung_weisses_haus_wien_esel_fotos/eSeL_UBERMORGEN_asylabwehramt_dasweissehaus_468_thumb.jpg HTTP/1.1" 200 32572 "http://www.asylabwehramt.at/Seiten/Bilder_Ausstellung.html" "Mozilla/5.0 (X11; U; Linux i686; de; rv:1.9.2.13) Gecko/20101206 Ubuntu/9.10 (karmic) Firefox/3.6.13"
88.116.224.102 - - [24/Feb/2011:10:42:02 +0100] "GET /Bilder/Ausstellung_weisses_haus_wien_esel_fotos/eSeL_UBERMORGEN_asylabwehramt_dasweissehaus_476_thumb.jpg HTTP/1.1" 200 46505 "http://www.asylabwehramt.at/Seiten/Bilder_Ausstellung.html" "Mozilla/5.0 (X11; U; Linux i686; de; rv:1.9.2.13) Gecko/20101206 Ubuntu/9.10 (karmic) Firefox/3.6.13"
88.116.224.102 - - [24/Feb/2011:10:42:04 +0100] "GET /Bilder/Ausstellung_weisses_haus_wien_esel_fotos/eSeL_UBERMORGEN_asylabwehramt_dasweissehaus_478_thumb.jpg HTTP/1.1" 200 54914 "http://www.asylabwehramt.at/Seiten/Bilder_Ausstellung.html" "Mozilla/5.0 (X11; U; Linux i686; de; rv:1.9.2.13) Gecko/20101206 Ubuntu/9.10 (karmic) Firefox/3.6.13"
88.116.224.102 - - [24/Feb/2011:10:42:07 +0100] "GET /Bilder/Ausstellung_weisses_haus_wien_esel_fotos/eSeL_UBERMORGEN_asylabwehramt_dasweissehaus_481_thumb.jpg HTTP/1.1" 200 25101 "http://www.asylabwehramt.at/Seiten/Bilder_Ausstellung.html" "Mozilla/5.0 (X11; U; Linux i686; de; rv:1.9.2.13) Gecko/20101206 Ubuntu/9.10 (karmic) Firefox/3.6.13"
88.116.224.102 - - [24/Feb/2011:10:42:08 +0100] "GET /Bilder/Ausstellung_weisses_haus_wien_esel_fotos/eSeL_UBERMORGEN_asylabwehramt_dasweissehaus_507_thumb.jpg HTTP/1.1" 200 40356 "http://www.asylabwehramt.at/Seiten/Bilder_Ausstellung.html" "Mozilla/5.0 (X11; U; Linux i686; de; rv:1.9.2.13) Gecko/20101206 Ubuntu/9.10 (karmic) Firefox/3.6.13"
88.116.224.102 - - [24/Feb/2011:10:42:08 +0100] "GET /Bilder/Ausstellung_weisses_haus_wien_esel_f
```

```
otos/eSeL_UBERMORGEN_asylabwehramt_dasweissehaus_512_thumb.jpg HTTP/1.1" 200 40860 "http://www.as
ylabwehramt.at/Seiten/Bilder_Ausstellung.html" "Mozilla/5.0 (X11; U; Linux i686; de; rv:1.9.2.13)
Gecko/20101206 Ubuntu/9.10 (karmic) Firefox/3.6.13"
88.116.224.102 - - [24/Feb/2011:10:42:09 +0100] "GET /Bilder/Ausstellung_weisses_haus_wien_esel_f
otos/eSeL_UBERMORGEN_asylabwehramt_dasweissehaus_516_thumb.jpg HTTP/1.1" 200 43027 "http://www.as
ylabwehramt.at/Seiten/Bilder_Ausstellung.html" "Mozilla/5.0 (X11; U; Linux i686; de; rv:1.9.2.13)
Gecko/20101206 Ubuntu/9.10 (karmic) Firefox/3.6.13"
88.116.224.102 - - [24/Feb/2011:10:42:11 +0100] "GET /Bilder/Ausstellung_weisses_haus_wien_esel_f
otos/eSeL_UBERMORGEN_asylabwehramt_dasweissehaus_518_thumb.jpg HTTP/1.1" 200 72634 "http://www.as
ylabwehramt.at/Seiten/Bilder_Ausstellung.html" "Mozilla/5.0 (X11; U; Linux i686; de; rv:1.9.2.13)
Gecko/20101206 Ubuntu/9.10 (karmic) Firefox/3.6.13"
88.116.224.102 - - [24/Feb/2011:10:42:12 +0100] "GET /Bilder/Ausstellung_weisses_haus_wien_esel_f
otos/eSeL_UBERMORGEN_asylabwehramt_dasweissehaus_526_thumb.jpg HTTP/1.1" 200 47873 "http://www.as
ylabwehramt.at/Seiten/Bilder_Ausstellung.html" "Mozilla/5.0 (X11; U; Linux i686; de; rv:1.9.2.13)
Gecko/20101206 Ubuntu/9.10 (karmic) Firefox/3.6.13"
88.116.224.102 - - [24/Feb/2011:10:42:18 +0100] "GET /Bilder/Ausstellung_weisses_haus_wien_esel_f
otos/eSeL_UBERMORGEN_asylabwehramt_dasweissehaus_514_thumb.jpg HTTP/1.1" 200 58758 "http://www.as
ylabwehramt.at/Seiten/Bilder_Ausstellung.html" "Mozilla/5.0 (X11; U; Linux i686; de; rv:1.9.2.13)
Gecko/20101206 Ubuntu/9.10 (karmic) Firefox/3.6.13"
88.116.224.102 - - [24/Feb/2011:10:43:28 +0100] "GET /Bilder/ausseneinsatz.png HTTP/1.1" 206 5911
08 "http://www.asylabwehramt.at/Seiten/Bilder.html" "Mozilla/5.0 (X11; U; Linux i686; de; rv:1.9.
2.13) Gecko/20101206 Ubuntu/9.10 (karmic) Firefox/3.6.13"
88.116.224.102 - - [24/Feb/2011:10:43:37 +0100] "GET /Seiten/Bilder_Ausstellung_2.html HTTP/1.1"
200 20902 "http://www.asylabwehramt.at/Seiten/Bilder.html" "Mozilla/5.0 (X11; U; Linux i686; de;
rv:1.9.2.13) Gecko/20101206 Ubuntu/9.10 (karmic) Firefox/3.6.13"
88.116.224.102 - - [24/Feb/2011:10:43:38 +0100] "GET /Bilder/Ausstellung_weisses_Haus_fotos_uberm
orgen/DSC_0036_AAbA_ubermorgen_thumb.jpg HTTP/1.1" 200 304658 "http://www.asylabwehramt.at/Seiten
/Bilder_Ausstellung_2.html" "Mozilla/5.0 (X11; U; Linux i686; de; rv:1.9.2.13) Gecko/20101206 Ubu
```

```
ntu/9.10 (karmic) Firefox/3.6.13"
88.116.224.102 - - [24/Feb/2011:10:44:33 +0100] "GET /Bilder/Ausstellung_weisses_Haus_fotos_uberm
orgen/DSC_0037_AAbA_ubermorgen_thumb.jpg HTTP/1.1" 200 283193 "http://www.asylabwehramt.at/Seiten
/Bilder_Ausstellung_2.html" "Mozilla/5.0 (X11; U; Linux i686; de; rv:1.9.2.13) Gecko/20101206 Ubu
ntu/9.10 (karmic) Firefox/3.6.13"
88.116.224.102 - - [24/Feb/2011:10:44:38 +0100] "GET /Bilder/Ausstellung_weisses_Haus_fotos_uberm
orgen/DSC_0040_AAbA_ubermorgen_thumb.jpg HTTP/1.1" 200 356912 "http://www.asylabwehramt.at/Seiten
/Bilder_Ausstellung_2.html" "Mozilla/5.0 (X11; U; Linux i686; de; rv:1.9.2.13) Gecko/20101206 Ubu
ntu/9.10 (karmic) Firefox/3.6.13"
88.116.224.102 - - [24/Feb/2011:10:44:39 +0100] "GET /Bilder/Ausstellung_weisses_Haus_fotos_uberm
orgen/DSC_0041_AAbA_ubermorgen_thumb.jpg HTTP/1.1" 200 336354 "http://www.asylabwehramt.at/Seiten
/Bilder_Ausstellung_2.html" "Mozilla/5.0 (X11; U; Linux i686; de; rv:1.9.2.13) Gecko/20101206 Ubu
ntu/9.10 (karmic) Firefox/3.6.13"
88.116.224.102 - - [24/Feb/2011:10:44:41 +0100] "GET /Bilder/Ausstellung_weisses_Haus_fotos_uberm
orgen/DSC_0043_AAbA_ubermorgen_thumb.jpg HTTP/1.1" 200 370306 "http://www.asylabwehramt.at/Seiten
/Bilder_Ausstellung_2.html" "Mozilla/5.0 (X11; U; Linux i686; de; rv:1.9.2.13) Gecko/20101206 Ubu
ntu/9.10 (karmic) Firefox/3.6.13"
88.116.224.102 - - [24/Feb/2011:10:44:45 +0100] "GET /Bilder/Ausstellung_weisses_Haus_fotos_uberm
orgen/DSC_0051_AAbA_ubermorgen_thumb.jpg HTTP/1.1" 200 300193 "http://www.asylabwehramt.at/Seiten
/Bilder_Ausstellung_2.html" "Mozilla/5.0 (X11; U; Linux i686; de; rv:1.9.2.13) Gecko/20101206 Ubu
ntu/9.10 (karmic) Firefox/3.6.13"
88.116.224.102 - - [24/Feb/2011:10:45:06 +0100] "GET /Bilder/Ausstellung_weisses_Haus_fotos_uberm
orgen/DSC_0052_AAbA_ubermorgen_thumb.jpg HTTP/1.1" 200 114861 "http://www.asylabwehramt.at/Seiten
/Bilder_Ausstellung_2.html" "Mozilla/5.0 (X11; U; Linux i686; de; rv:1.9.2.13) Gecko/20101206 Ubu
ntu/9.10 (karmic) Firefox/3.6.13"
88.116.224.102 - - [24/Feb/2011:10:45:28 +0100] "GET /Bilder/Ausstellung_weisses_Haus_fotos_uberm
orgen/DSC_0054_AAbA_ubermorgen_thumb.jpg HTTP/1.1" 200 73675 "http://www.asylabwehramt.at/Seiten/
Bilder_Ausstellung_2.html" "Mozilla/5.0 (X11; U; Linux i686; de; rv:1.9.2.13) Gecko/20101206 Ubun
```

```
88.116.224.102 - - [24/Feb/2011:10:45:30 +0100] "GET /Bilder/Ausstellung_weisses_Haus_fotos_ubermorgen/DSC_0055_AAbA_ubermorgen_thumb.jpg HTTP/1.1" 200 309196 "http://www.asylabwehramt.at/Seiten/Bilder_Ausstellung_2.html" "Mozilla/5.0 (X11; U; Linux i686; de; rv:1.9.2.13) Gecko/20101206 Ubuntu/9.10 (karmic) Firefox/3.6.13"
88.116.224.102 - - [24/Feb/2011:10:45:38 +0100] "GET /Bilder/Ausstellung_weisses_Haus_fotos_ubermorgen/DSC_0057_AAbA_ubermorgen_thumb.jpg HTTP/1.1" 200 413997 "http://www.asylabwehramt.at/Seiten/Bilder_Ausstellung_2.html" "Mozilla/5.0 (X11; U; Linux i686; de; rv:1.9.2.13) Gecko/20101206 Ubuntu/9.10 (karmic) Firefox/3.6.13"
88.116.224.102 - - [24/Feb/2011:10:45:42 +0100] "GET /Bilder/Ausstellung_weisses_Haus_fotos_ubermorgen/DSC_0058_AAbA_ubermorgen_thumb.jpg HTTP/1.1" 200 263348 "http://www.asylabwehramt.at/Seiten/Bilder_Ausstellung_2.html" "Mozilla/5.0 (X11; U; Linux i686; de; rv:1.9.2.13) Gecko/20101206 Ubuntu/9.10 (karmic) Firefox/3.6.13"
88.116.224.102 - - [24/Feb/2011:10:45:46 +0100] "GET /Bilder/Ausstellung_weisses_Haus_fotos_ubermorgen/DSC_0060_AAbA_ubermorgen_thumb.jpg HTTP/1.1" 200 305781 "http://www.asylabwehramt.at/Seiten/Bilder_Ausstellung_2.html" "Mozilla/5.0 (X11; U; Linux i686; de; rv:1.9.2.13) Gecko/20101206 Ubuntu/9.10 (karmic) Firefox/3.6.13"
88.116.224.102 - - [24/Feb/2011:10:45:49 +0100] "GET /Bilder/Ausstellung_weisses_Haus_fotos_ubermorgen/DSC_0061_AAbA_ubermorgen_thumb.jpg HTTP/1.1" 200 435014 "http://www.asylabwehramt.at/Seiten/Bilder_Ausstellung_2.html" "Mozilla/5.0 (X11; U; Linux i686; de; rv:1.9.2.13) Gecko/20101206 Ubuntu/9.10 (karmic) Firefox/3.6.13"
88.116.224.102 - - [24/Feb/2011:10:45:57 +0100] "GET /Bilder/Ausstellung_weisses_Haus_fotos_ubermorgen/DSC_0063_AAbA_ubermorgen_thumb.jpg HTTP/1.1" 200 345962 "http://www.asylabwehramt.at/Seiten/Bilder_Ausstellung_2.html" "Mozilla/5.0 (X11; U; Linux i686; de; rv:1.9.2.13) Gecko/20101206 Ubuntu/9.10 (karmic) Firefox/3.6.13"
88.116.224.102 - - [24/Feb/2011:10:46:32 +0100] "GET /Bilder/Ausstellung_weisses_Haus_fotos_ubermorgen/DSC_0064_AAbA_ubermorgen_thumb.jpg HTTP/1.1" 200 693171 "http://www.asylabwehramt.at/Seiten/Bilder_Ausstellung_2.html" "Mozilla/5.0 (X11; U; Linux i686; de; rv:1.9.2.13) Gecko/20101206 Ubuntu/9.10 (karmic) Firefox/3.6.13"
```

```
ntu/9.10 (karmic) Firefox/3.6.13"
88.116.224.102 - - [24/Feb/2011:10:46:33 +0100] "GET /Bilder/Ausstellung_weisses_Haus_fotos_uberm
orgen/DSC_0065_AAbA_ubermorgen_thumb.jpg HTTP/1.1" 200 359596 "http://www.asylabwehramt.at/Seiten
/Bilder_Ausstellung_2.html" "Mozilla/5.0 (X11; U; Linux i686; de; rv:1.9.2.13) Gecko/20101206 Ubu
ntu/9.10 (karmic) Firefox/3.6.13"
88.116.224.102 - - [24/Feb/2011:10:46:44 +0100] "GET /Bilder/Ausstellung_weisses_Haus_fotos_uberm
orgen/DSC_0066_AAbA_ubermorgen_thumb.jpg HTTP/1.1" 200 367175 "http://www.asylabwehramt.at/Seiten
/Bilder_Ausstellung_2.html" "Mozilla/5.0 (X11; U; Linux i686; de; rv:1.9.2.13) Gecko/20101206 Ubu
ntu/9.10 (karmic) Firefox/3.6.13"
88.116.224.102 - - [24/Feb/2011:10:47:02 +0100] "GET /Bilder/Ausstellung_weisses_Haus_fotos_uberm
orgen/DSC_0075_AAbA_ubermorgen_thumb.jpg HTTP/1.1" 200 330516 "http://www.asylabwehramt.at/Seiten
/Bilder_Ausstellung_2.html" "Mozilla/5.0 (X11; U; Linux i686; de; rv:1.9.2.13) Gecko/20101206 Ubu
ntu/9.10 (karmic) Firefox/3.6.13"
88.116.224.102 - - [24/Feb/2011:10:47:20 +0100] "GET /Bilder/Ausstellung_weisses_Haus_fotos_uberm
orgen/DSC_0078_AAbA_ubermorgen_thumb.jpg HTTP/1.1" 200 290879 "http://www.asylabwehramt.at/Seiten
/Bilder_Ausstellung_2.html" "Mozilla/5.0 (X11; U; Linux i686; de; rv:1.9.2.13) Gecko/20101206 Ubu
ntu/9.10 (karmic) Firefox/3.6.13"
88.116.224.102 - - [24/Feb/2011:10:47:21 +0100] "GET /Bilder/Ausstellung_weisses_Haus_fotos_uberm
orgen/DSC_0084_AAbA_ubermorgen_thumb.jpg HTTP/1.1" 200 308189 "http://www.asylabwehramt.at/Seiten
/Bilder_Ausstellung_2.html" "Mozilla/5.0 (X11; U; Linux i686; de; rv:1.9.2.13) Gecko/20101206 Ubu
ntu/9.10 (karmic) Firefox/3.6.13"
88.116.224.102 - - [24/Feb/2011:10:47:51 +0100] "GET /Bilder/Ausstellung_weisses_Haus_fotos_uberm
orgen/DSC_0087_AAbA_ubermorgen_thumb.jpg HTTP/1.1" 200 295472 "http://www.asylabwehramt.at/Seiten
/Bilder_Ausstellung_2.html" "Mozilla/5.0 (X11; U; Linux i686; de; rv:1.9.2.13) Gecko/20101206 Ubu
ntu/9.10 (karmic) Firefox/3.6.13"
88.116.224.102 - - [24/Feb/2011:10:48:03 +0100] "GET /Bilder/Ausstellung_weisses_Haus_fotos_uberm
orgen/DSC_0094_AAbA_ubermorgen_thumb.jpg HTTP/1.1" 200 373390 "http://www.asylabwehramt.at/Seiten
/Bilder_Ausstellung_2.html" "Mozilla/5.0 (X11; U; Linux i686; de; rv:1.9.2.13) Gecko/20101206 Ubu
```

```
88.116.224.102 - - [24/Feb/2011:10:48:20 +0100] "GET /Bilder/Ausstellung_weisses_Haus_fotos_uberm
orgen/DSC_0115_AAbA_ubermorgen_thumb.jpg HTTP/1.1" 200 383960 "http://www.asylabwehramt.at/Seiten
/Bilder_Ausstellung_2.html" "Mozilla/5.0 (X11; U; Linux i686; de; rv:1.9.2.13) Gecko/20101206 Ubu
ntu/9.10 (karmic) Firefox/3.6.13"
88.116.224.102 - - [24/Feb/2011:10:48:22 +0100] "GET /Bilder/Ausstellung_weisses_Haus_fotos_uberm
orgen/DSC_0125_AAbA_ubermorgen_thumb.jpg HTTP/1.1" 200 356220 "http://www.asylabwehramt.at/Seiten
/Bilder_Ausstellung_2.html" "Mozilla/5.0 (X11; U; Linux i686; de; rv:1.9.2.13) Gecko/20101206 Ubu
ntu/9.10 (karmic) Firefox/3.6.13"
88.116.224.102 - - [24/Feb/2011:10:48:24 +0100] "GET /Bilder/Ausstellung_weisses_Haus_fotos_uberm
orgen/DSC_0126_AAbA_ubermorgen_thumb.jpg HTTP/1.1" 200 392451 "http://www.asylabwehramt.at/Seiten
/Bilder_Ausstellung_2.html" "Mozilla/5.0 (X11; U; Linux i686; de; rv:1.9.2.13) Gecko/20101206 Ubu
ntu/9.10 (karmic) Firefox/3.6.13"
88.116.224.102 - - [24/Feb/2011:10:48:50 +0100] "GET /Bilder/Ausstellung_weisses_Haus_fotos_uberm
orgen/DSC_0129_AAbA_ubermorgen_thumb.jpg HTTP/1.1" 200 340215 "http://www.asylabwehramt.at/Seiten
/Bilder_Ausstellung_2.html" "Mozilla/5.0 (X11; U; Linux i686; de; rv:1.9.2.13) Gecko/20101206 Ubu
ntu/9.10 (karmic) Firefox/3.6.13"
88.116.224.102 - - [24/Feb/2011:10:49:01 +0100] "GET /Bilder/Ausstellung_weisses_Haus_fotos_uberm
orgen/DSC_0131_AAbA_ubermorgen_thumb.jpg HTTP/1.1" 200 371116 "http://www.asylabwehramt.at/Seiten
/Bilder_Ausstellung_2.html" "Mozilla/5.0 (X11; U; Linux i686; de; rv:1.9.2.13) Gecko/20101206 Ubu
ntu/9.10 (karmic) Firefox/3.6.13"
88.116.224.102 - - [24/Feb/2011:10:49:22 +0100] "GET /Bilder/Ausstellung_weisses_Haus_fotos_uberm
orgen/DSC_0133_AAbA_ubermorgen_thumb.jpg HTTP/1.1" 200 373173 "http://www.asylabwehramt.at/Seiten
/Bilder_Ausstellung_2.html" "Mozilla/5.0 (X11; U; Linux i686; de; rv:1.9.2.13) Gecko/20101206 Ubu
ntu/9.10 (karmic) Firefox/3.6.13"
88.116.224.102 - - [24/Feb/2011:10:49:39 +0100] "GET /Bilder/Ausstellung_weisses_Haus_fotos_uberm
orgen/DSC_0136_AAbA_ubermorgen_thumb.jpg HTTP/1.1" 200 391844 "http://www.asylabwehramt.at/Seiten
/Bilder_Ausstellung_2.html" "Mozilla/5.0 (X11; U; Linux i686; de; rv:1.9.2.13) Gecko/20101206 Ubu
ntu/9.10 (karmic) Firefox/3.6.13"
```

```
ntu/9.10 (karmic) Firefox/3.6.13"
88.116.224.102 - - [24/Feb/2011:10:49:42 +0100] "GET /Bilder/Ausstellung_weisses_Haus_fotos_uberm
orgen/DSC_0142_AAbA_ubermorgen_thumb.jpg HTTP/1.1" 200 393968 "http://www.asylabwehramt.at/Seiten
/Bilder_Ausstellung_2.html" "Mozilla/5.0 (X11; U; Linux i686; de; rv:1.9.2.13) Gecko/20101206 Ubu
ntu/9.10 (karmic) Firefox/3.6.13"
88.116.224.102 - - [24/Feb/2011:10:49:46 +0100] "GET /Bilder/Ausstellung_weisses_Haus_fotos_uberm
orgen/DSC_0144_AAbA_ubermorgen_thumb.jpg HTTP/1.1" 200 380728 "http://www.asylabwehramt.at/Seiten
/Bilder_Ausstellung_2.html" "Mozilla/5.0 (X11; U; Linux i686; de; rv:1.9.2.13) Gecko/20101206 Ubu
ntu/9.10 (karmic) Firefox/3.6.13"
88.116.224.102 - - [24/Feb/2011:10:49:53 +0100] "GET /Bilder/Ausstellung_weisses_Haus_fotos_uberm
orgen/DSC_0151_AAbA_ubermorgen_thumb.jpg HTTP/1.1" 200 404705 "http://www.asylabwehramt.at/Seiten
/Bilder_Ausstellung_2.html" "Mozilla/5.0 (X11; U; Linux i686; de; rv:1.9.2.13) Gecko/20101206 Ubu
ntu/9.10 (karmic) Firefox/3.6.13"
88.116.224.102 - - [24/Feb/2011:10:50:06 +0100] "GET /Bilder/Ausstellung_weisses_Haus_fotos_uberm
orgen/DSC_0164_AAbA_ubermorgen_thumb.jpg HTTP/1.1" 200 606516 "http://www.asylabwehramt.at/Seiten
/Bilder_Ausstellung_2.html" "Mozilla/5.0 (X11; U; Linux i686; de; rv:1.9.2.13) Gecko/20101206 Ubu
ntu/9.10 (karmic) Firefox/3.6.13"
88.116.224.102 - - [24/Feb/2011:10:50:34 +0100] "GET /Bilder/Ausstellung_weisses_Haus_fotos_uberm
orgen/DSC_0165_AAbA_ubermorgen_thumb.jpg HTTP/1.1" 200 335964 "http://www.asylabwehramt.at/Seiten
/Bilder_Ausstellung_2.html" "Mozilla/5.0 (X11; U; Linux i686; de; rv:1.9.2.13) Gecko/20101206 Ubu
ntu/9.10 (karmic) Firefox/3.6.13"
88.116.224.102 - - [24/Feb/2011:10:50:52 +0100] "GET /Bilder/Ausstellung_weisses_Haus_fotos_uberm
orgen/DSC_0169_AAbA_ubermorgen_thumb.jpg HTTP/1.1" 200 722902 "http://www.asylabwehramt.at/Seiten
/Bilder_Ausstellung_2.html" "Mozilla/5.0 (X11; U; Linux i686; de; rv:1.9.2.13) Gecko/20101206 Ubu
ntu/9.10 (karmic) Firefox/3.6.13"
88.116.224.102 - - [24/Feb/2011:10:50:55 +0100] "GET /Bilder/Ausstellung_weisses_Haus_fotos_uberm
orgen/DSC_0171_AAbA_ubermorgen_thumb.jpg HTTP/1.1" 200 371771 "http://www.asylabwehramt.at/Seiten
/Bilder_Ausstellung_2.html" "Mozilla/5.0 (X11; U; Linux i686; de; rv:1.9.2.13) Gecko/20101206 Ubu
```

```
ntu/9.10 (karmic) Firefox/3.6.13"
88.116.224.102 - - [24/Feb/2011:10:51:02 +0100] "GET /Bilder/Ausstellung_weisses_Haus_fotos_uberm
orgen/DSC_0173_AAbA_ubermorgen_thumb.jpg HTTP/1.1" 200 358713 "http://www.asylabwehramt.at/Seiten
/Bilder_Ausstellung_2.html" "Mozilla/5.0 (X11; U; Linux i686; de; rv:1.9.2.13) Gecko/20101206 Ubu
ntu/9.10 (karmic) Firefox/3.6.13"
88.116.224.102 - - [24/Feb/2011:10:51:10 +0100] "GET /Bilder/Ausstellung_weisses_Haus_fotos_uberm
orgen/DSC_0176_AAbA_ubermorgen_thumb.jpg HTTP/1.1" 200 353336 "http://www.asylabwehramt.at/Seiten
/Bilder_Ausstellung_2.html" "Mozilla/5.0 (X11; U; Linux i686; de; rv:1.9.2.13) Gecko/20101206 Ubu
ntu/9.10 (karmic) Firefox/3.6.13"
88.116.224.102 - - [24/Feb/2011:10:51:34 +0100] "GET /Bilder/Ausstellung_weisses_Haus_fotos_uberm
orgen/DSC_0178_AAbA_ubermorgen_thumb.jpg HTTP/1.1" 200 413101 "http://www.asylabwehramt.at/Seiten
/Bilder_Ausstellung_2.html" "Mozilla/5.0 (X11; U; Linux i686; de; rv:1.9.2.13) Gecko/20101206 Ubu
ntu/9.10 (karmic) Firefox/3.6.13"
88.116.224.102 - - [24/Feb/2011:10:51:53 +0100] "GET /Bilder/Ausstellung_weisses_Haus_fotos_uberm
orgen/DSC_0185_AAbA_ubermorgen_thumb.jpg HTTP/1.1" 200 778291 "http://www.asylabwehramt.at/Seiten
/Bilder_Ausstellung_2.html" "Mozilla/5.0 (X11; U; Linux i686; de; rv:1.9.2.13) Gecko/20101206 Ubu
ntu/9.10 (karmic) Firefox/3.6.13"
88.116.224.102 - - [24/Feb/2011:10:51:55 +0100] "GET /Bilder/Ausstellung_weisses_Haus_fotos_uberm
orgen/DSC_0050_AAbA_ubermorgen_thumb.jpg HTTP/1.1" 200 327203 "http://www.asylabwehramt.at/Seiten
/Bilder_Ausstellung_2.html" "Mozilla/5.0 (X11; U; Linux i686; de; rv:1.9.2.13) Gecko/20101206 Ubu
ntu/9.10 (karmic) Firefox/3.6.13"
88.116.224.102 - - [24/Feb/2011:10:52:44 +0100] "GET /Bilder/ausseneinsatz.png HTTP/1.1" 206 5263
41 "http://www.asylabwehramt.at/Seiten/Bilder.html" "Mozilla/5.0 (X11; U; Linux i686; de; rv:1.9.
2.13) Gecko/20101206 Ubuntu/9.10 (karmic) Firefox/3.6.13"
88.116.224.102 - - [24/Feb/2011:10:52:51 +0100] "GET /Seiten/Ausseneinsaetze.html HTTP/1.1" 200 9
381 "http://www.asylabwehramt.at/Seiten/Bilder.html" "Mozilla/5.0 (X11; U; Linux i686; de; rv:1.9
.2.13) Gecko/20101206 Ubuntu/9.10 (karmic) Firefox/3.6.13"
88.116.224.102 - - [24/Feb/2011:10:53:22 +0100] "GET /Bilder/ausseneinsatz.png HTTP/1.1" 206 2143
```

58 "http://www.asylabwehramt.at/Seiten/Bilder.html" "Mozilla/5.0 (X11; U; Linux i686; de; rv:1.9.2.13) Gecko/20101206 Ubuntu/9.10 (karmic) Firefox/3.6.13"

88.116.224.102 - - [24/Feb/2011:10:53:32 +0100] "GET /Seiten/Aktuelles.html HTTP/1.1" 200 14343 "http://www.asylabwehramt.at/Seiten/Bilder.html" "Mozilla/5.0 (X11; U; Linux i686; de; rv:1.9.2.13) Gecko/20101206 Ubuntu/9.10 (karmic) Firefox/3.6.13"

88.116.224.102 - - [24/Feb/2011:10:53:33 +0100] "GET /Bilder/fitnesscenter_traiskirchen.jpg HTTP/1.1" 200 5721 "http://www.asylabwehramt.at/Seiten/Aktuelles.html" "Mozilla/5.0 (X11; U; Linux i686; de; rv:1.9.2.13) Gecko/20101206 Ubuntu/9.10 (karmic) Firefox/3.6.13"

88.116.224.102 - - [24/Feb/2011:10:54:22 +0100] "GET /Seiten/Press.html HTTP/1.1" 200 12374 "http://www.asylabwehramt.at/Seiten/Aktuelles.html" "Mozilla/5.0 (X11; U; Linux i686; de; rv:1.9.2.13) Gecko/20101206 Ubuntu/9.10 (karmic) Firefox/3.6.13"

88.116.224.102 - - [24/Feb/2011:10:54:52 +0100] "GET /Seiten/Links.html HTTP/1.1" 200 19139 "http://www.asylabwehramt.at/Seiten/Press.html" "Mozilla/5.0 (X11; U; Linux i686; de; rv:1.9.2.13) Gecko/20101206 Ubuntu/9.10 (karmic) Firefox/3.6.13"

88.116.224.102 - - [24/Feb/2011:10:57:38 +0100] "GET /index.html HTTP/1.1" 200 13966 "http://www.asylabwehramt.at/Seiten/Press.html" "Mozilla/5.0 (X11; U; Linux i686; de; rv:1.9.2.13) Gecko/2010 1206 Ubuntu/9.10 (karmic) Firefox/3.6.13"

88.116.224.102 - - [24/Feb/2011:10:57:41 +0100] "GET /Seiten/Orgstrukt.html HTTP/1.1" 200 14119 "http://www.asylabwehramt.at/index.html" "Mozilla/5.0 (X11; U; Linux i686; de; rv:1.9.2.13) Gecko/20101206 Ubuntu/9.10 (karmic) Firefox/3.6.13"

88.116.224.102 - - [24/Feb/2011:10:59:10 +0100] "GET /Seiten/Rundzeichen.html HTTP/1.1" 200 8895 "http://www.asylabwehramt.at/Seiten/Orgstrukt.html" "Mozilla/5.0 (X11; U; Linux i686; de; rv:1.9.2.13) Gecko/20101206 Ubuntu/9.10 (karmic) Firefox/3.6.13"

88.116.224.102 - - [24/Feb/2011:10:59:19 +0100] "GET /Seiten/Material.html HTTP/1.1" 200 17335 "http://www.asylabwehramt.at/Seiten/Rundzeichen.html" "Mozilla/5.0 (X11; U; Linux i686; de; rv:1.9.2.13) Gecko/20101206 Ubuntu/9.10 (karmic) Firefox/3.6.13"

```
203.172.248.174[46] - - [25/Feb/2011:05:38:36 +0100] "GET /Seiten/Aktuelles.html HTTP/1.0" 200 14343 "http://www.myskyshoes.com/" "Mozilla/5.0 (Windows; U; Windows NT 5.1; en-US; rv:1.9.0.14) Gecko/2009082707 Firefox/3.0.14 (.NET CLR 3.5.30729)"

80.122.180.78 - - [01/Mar/2011:10:22:43 +0100] "GET /Seiten/Links_e.html HTTP/1.1" 200 19142 "http://www.google.at/imgres?imgurl=http://www.asylabwehramt.at/Bilder/BMI.png&imgrefurl=http://www.asylabwehramt.at/Seiten/Links_e.html&usg=__LTPcsjfoUI418a5pnKpA96gV4Pw=&h=488&w=2000&sz=55&hl=de&start=0&zoom=1&tbnid=-J4hmZ76_kG4vM:&tbnw=35&tbnh=144&ei=3bpsTf7UDI2R4gaulvWBBA&prev=/images%3Fq%3DBMI%26um%3D1%26hl%3Dde%26biw%3D1920%26bih%3D887%26tbs%3Disch:1&um=1&itbs=1&iact=rc&dur=293&oei=3bpsTf7UDI2R4gaulvWBBA&page=1&ndsp=77&ved=1t:429,r:33,s:0&tx=32&ty=19" "Mozilla/5.0 (Windows; U; Windows NT 6.1; de; rv:1.9.2.13) Gecko/20101203 Firefox/3.6.13"

80.122.180.78 - - [01/Mar/2011:10:22:44 +0100] "GET /Bilder/IBM.png HTTP/1.1" 200 8413 "http://www.asylabwehramt.at/Seiten/Links_e.html" "Mozilla/5.0 (Windows; U; Windows NT 6.1; de; rv:1.9.2.13) Gecko/20101203 Firefox/3.6.13"

80.122.180.78 - - [01/Mar/2011:10:22:50 +0100] "GET /favicon.ico HTTP/1.1" 302 340 "-" "Mozilla/5.0 (Windows; U; Windows NT 6.1; de; rv:1.9.2.13) Gecko/20101203 Firefox/3.6.13"

80.122.180.78 - - [01/Mar/2011:10:22:53 +0100] "GET /favicon.ico HTTP/1.1" 302 340 "-" "Mozilla/5.0 (Windows; U; Windows NT 6.1; de; rv:1.9.2.13) Gecko/20101203 Firefox/3.6.13"

62.47.213.0 - - [03/Mar/2011:19:08:44 +0100] "GET /Seiten/Impressum.html HTTP/1.1" 200 11939 "http://www.google.at/search?hl=de&q=asylantrag+%C3%B6sterreich+formular&aq=0&aqi=g2&aql=&oq=asylantrag+%C3%B6sterreich+" "Mozilla/5.0 (Windows; U; Windows NT 6.0; en-US) AppleWebKit/534.10 (KHTML, like Gecko) Chrome/8.0.552.215 Safari/534.10"

144.65.158.38[47] - - [04/Mar/2011:12:00:10 +0100] "GET /Material/Flyer_Volksschutz_Praevention_Aufklaerung_FPOE.pdf HTTP/1.1" 200 661529 "http://sosheimat.wordpress.com/2011/03/04/mein-erlebnis-be
```

[46] WHOIS record on page 314

[47] WHOIS record on page 324

`i-der-wgkk/` "Mozilla/4.0 (compatible; MSIE 8.0; Windows NT 6.1; WOW64; Trident/4.0; SLCC2; .NET CLR 2.0.50727; .NET CLR 3.5.30729; .NET CLR 3.0.30729; Media Center PC 6.0; InfoPath.2)"

144.65.158.38 - - [04/Mar/2011:12:00:11 +0100] "GET /Material/Flyer_Volksschutz_Praevention_Aufkl aerung_FP0E.pdf HTTP/1.1" 206 4096 "-" "Mozilla/4.0 (compatible; MSIE 8.0; Windows NT 6.1; WOW64; Trident/4.0; SLCC2; .NET CLR 2.0.50727; .NET CLR 3.5.30729; .NET CLR 3.0.30729; Media Center PC 6.0; InfoPath.2)"

144.65.158.38 - - [04/Mar/2011:12:00:49 +0100] "GET / HTTP/1.1" 200 13966 "-" "Mozilla/4.0 (compa tible; MSIE 8.0; Windows NT 6.1; WOW64; Trident/4.0; SLCC2; .NET CLR 2.0.50727; .NET CLR 3.5.3072 9; .NET CLR 3.0.30729; Media Center PC 6.0; InfoPath.2)"

144.65.158.38 - - [04/Mar/2011:12:03:06 +0100] "GET /Seiten/Bilder.html HTTP/1.1" 200 10364 "http ://www.asylabwehramt.at/" "Mozilla/4.0 (compatible; MSIE 8.0; Windows NT 6.1; WOW64; Trident/4.0; SLCC2; .NET CLR 2.0.50727; .NET CLR 3.5.30729; .NET CLR 3.0.30729; Media Center PC 6.0; InfoPath .2)"

144.65.158.38 - - [04/Mar/2011:12:03:20 +0100] "GET /index.html HTTP/1.1" 200 13966 "http://www.a sylabwehramt.at/Seiten/Bilder.html" "Mozilla/4.0 (compatible; MSIE 8.0; Windows NT 6.1; WOW64; Tr ident/4.0; SLCC2; .NET CLR 2.0.50727; .NET CLR 3.5.30729; .NET CLR 3.0.30729; Media Center PC 6.0 ; InfoPath.2)"

144.65.158.38 - - [04/Mar/2011:12:03:21 +0100] "GET / HTTP/1.1" 304 - "http://www.asylabwehramt.a t/index.html" "Mozilla/4.0 (compatible; MSIE 8.0; Windows NT 6.1; WOW64; Trident/4.0; SLCC2; .NET CLR 2.0.50727; .NET CLR 3.5.30729; .NET CLR 3.0.30729; Media Center PC 6.0; InfoPath.2)"

144.65.158.38 - - [04/Mar/2011:12:03:24 +0100] "GET /Seiten/Aktuelles.html HTTP/1.1" 200 14343 "h ttp://www.asylabwehramt.at/" "Mozilla/4.0 (compatible; MSIE 8.0; Windows NT 6.1; WOW64; Trident/4 .0; SLCC2; .NET CLR 2.0.50727; .NET CLR 3.5.30729; .NET CLR 3.0.30729; Media Center PC 6.0; InfoP ath.2)"

144.65.158.38 - - [04/Mar/2011:12:03:52 +0100] "GET /Seiten/Rundzeichen.html HTTP/1.1" 200 8895 " http://www.asylabwehramt.at/Seiten/Aktuelles.html" "Mozilla/4.0 (compatible; MSIE 8.0; Windows NT 6.1; WOW64; Trident/4.0; SLCC2; .NET CLR 2.0.50727; .NET CLR 3.5.30729; .NET CLR 3.0.30729; Medi a Center PC 6.0; InfoPath.2)"

```
144.65.158.38 - - [04/Mar/2011:12:05:43 +0100] "GET /Seiten/Orgstrukt.html HTTP/1.1" 200 14119 "h
ttp://www.asylabwehramt.at/Seiten/Bilder.html" "Mozilla/4.0 (compatible; MSIE 8.0; Windows NT 6.1
; WOW64; Trident/4.0; SLCC2; .NET CLR 2.0.50727; .NET CLR 3.5.30729; .NET CLR 3.0.30729; Media Ce
nter PC 6.0; InfoPath.2)"
144.65.158.38 - - [04/Mar/2011:12:06:11 +0100] "GET /Seiten/Bilder.html HTTP/1.1" 304 - "http://w
ww.asylabwehramt.at/Seiten/Rundzeichen.html" "Mozilla/4.0 (compatible; MSIE 8.0; Windows NT 6.1;
WOW64; Trident/4.0; SLCC2; .NET CLR 2.0.50727; .NET CLR 3.5.30729; .NET CLR 3.0.30729; Media Cent
er PC 6.0; InfoPath.2)"
144.65.158.38 - - [04/Mar/2011:12:06:12 +0100] "GET /Seiten/Rundzeichen.html HTTP/1.1" 304 - "htt
p://www.asylabwehramt.at/Seiten/Aktuelles.html" "Mozilla/4.0 (compatible; MSIE 8.0; Windows NT 6.
1; WOW64; Trident/4.0; SLCC2; .NET CLR 2.0.50727; .NET CLR 3.5.30729; .NET CLR 3.0.30729; Media C
enter PC 6.0; InfoPath.2)"
144.65.158.38 - - [04/Mar/2011:12:06:13 +0100] "GET /Seiten/Aktuelles.html HTTP/1.1" 304 - "http:
//www.asylabwehramt.at/" "Mozilla/4.0 (compatible; MSIE 8.0; Windows NT 6.1; WOW64; Trident/4.0;
SLCC2; .NET CLR 2.0.50727; .NET CLR 3.5.30729; .NET CLR 3.0.30729; Media Center PC 6.0; InfoPath.
2)"
144.65.158.38 - - [04/Mar/2011:12:06:14 +0100] "GET / HTTP/1.1" 304 - "http://www.asylabwehramt.a
t/index.html" "Mozilla/4.0 (compatible; MSIE 8.0; Windows NT 6.1; WOW64; Trident/4.0; SLCC2; .NET
CLR 2.0.50727; .NET CLR 3.5.30729; .NET CLR 3.0.30729; Media Center PC 6.0; InfoPath.2)"
144.65.158.38 - - [04/Mar/2011:12:06:16 +0100] "GET /Material/Flyer_Volksschutz_Praevention_Aufkl
aerung_FPOE.pdf HTTP/1.1" 206 254769 "-" "Mozilla/4.0 (compatible; MSIE 8.0; Windows NT 6.1; WOW6
4; Trident/4.0; SLCC2; .NET CLR 2.0.50727; .NET CLR 3.5.30729; .NET CLR 3.0.30729; Media Center P
C 6.0; InfoPath.2)"
194.153.217.248 - - [08/Mar/2011:15:37:32 +0100] "GET / HTTP/1.1" 200 14285 "-" "Mozilla/5.0 (Win
dows; U; Windows NT 5.1; de; rv:1.9.2.15) Gecko/20110303 Firefox/3.6.15"
194.153.217.248 - - [08/Mar/2011:15:37:35 +0100] "GET /favicon.ico HTTP/1.1" 404 536 "-" "Mozilla
/5.0 (Windows; U; Windows NT 5.1; de; rv:1.9.2.15) Gecko/20110303 Firefox/3.6.15"
```

80.120.182.178 [48] - - [08/Mar/2011:17:38:01 +0100] "GET /Seiten/Material.html HTTP/1.1" 200 6514 "http://www.google.at/url?sa=t&source=web&cd=5&ved=0CDYQFjAE&url=http%3A%2F%2Fwww.asylabwehramt.at%2FSeiten%2FMaterial.html&rct=j&q=asylantrag%20%C3%B6sterreich%20formular &ei=QFt2TefVOYnKswaauJD9BA&usg=AFQjCNFyFHsiSQXaEJ5RVynwkdksptioPQ" "Mozilla/4.0 (compatible; MSIE 8.0; Windows NT 5.1; Trident/4.0; .NET CLR 1.1.4322)"

80.122.56.230 [49] - - [11/Mar/2011:08:08:37 +0100] "GET / HTTP/1.1" 200 5955 "http://www.google.com/search?q=www.asylabwehramt &rls=com.microsoft:de-at:IE-Address&ie=UTF-8&oe=UTF-8&sourceid=ie7&rlz=1I7ADBR_de" "Mozilla/4.0 (compatible; MSIE 8.0; Windows NT 5.1; Trident/4.0; GTB6.6; .NET CLR 2.0.50727; .NET CLR 3.0.4506.2152; .NET CLR 3.5.30729; InfoPath.1)"

80.122.56.230 - - [11/Mar/2011:08:11:48 +0100] "GET /Seiten/Bilder.html HTTP/1.1" 200 4129 "http://www.asylabwehramt.at/" "Mozilla/4.0 (compatible; MSIE 8.0; Windows NT 5.1; Trident/4.0; GTB6.6; .NET CLR 2.0.50727; .NET CLR 3.0.4506.2152; .NET CLR 3.5.30729; InfoPath.1)"

80.122.56.230 - - [11/Mar/2011:08:11:49 +0100] "GET /Bilder/ausseneinsatz.png HTTP/1.1" 200 12412 "http://www.asylabwehramt.at/Seiten/Bilder.html" "Mozilla/4.0 (compatible; MSIE 8.0; Windows NT 5.1; Trident/4.0; GTB6.6; .NET CLR 2.0.50727; .NET CLR 3.0.4506.2152; .NET CLR 3.5.30729; InfoPath.1)"

80.122.56.230 - - [11/Mar/2011:08:11:57 +0100] "GET /favicon.ico HTTP/1.1" 404 507 "-" "Mozilla/4.0 (compatible; MSIE 8.0; Windows NT 5.1; Trident/4.0; GTB6.6; .NET CLR 2.0.50727; .NET CLR 3.0.4506.2152; .NET CLR 3.5.30729; InfoPath.1)"

80.122.56.230 - - [11/Mar/2011:08:12:45 +0100] "GET /Seiten/Material.html HTTP/1.1" 200 6514 "http://www.asylabwehramt.at/Seiten/Bilder.html" "Mozilla/4.0 (compatible; MSIE 8.0; Windows NT 5.1; Trident/4.0; GTB6.6; .NET CLR 2.0.50727; .NET CLR 3.0.4506.2152; .NET CLR 3.5.30729; InfoPath.1)"

80.122.56.230 - - [11/Mar/2011:08:12:53 +0100] "GET /Bilder/flyer_nigeria_Internet.pdf HTTP/1.1" 200 148104 "http://www.asylabwehramt.at/Seiten/Material.html" "Mozilla/4.0 (compatible; MSIE 8.0; Windows NT 5.1; Trident/4.0; GTB6.6; .NET CLR 2.0.50727; .NET CLR 3.0.4506.2152; .NET CLR 3.5.30729

[48] WHOIS record on page 316
[49] WHOIS record on page 327

729; InfoPath.1)"
80.122.56.230 - - [11/Mar/2011:08:12:55 +0100] "GET /Bilder/flyer_nigeria_Internet.pdf HTTP/1.1"
206 4454 "-" "Mozilla/4.0 (compatible; MSIE 8.0; Windows NT 5.1; Trident/4.0; GTB6.6; .NET CLR 2.
0.50727; .NET CLR 3.0.4506.2152; .NET CLR 3.5.30729; InfoPath.1)"
206 605576 "-" "Mozilla/4.0 (compatible; MSIE 8.0; Windows NT 5.1; Trident/4.0; GTB6.6; .NET CLR
2.0.50727; .NET CLR 3.0.4506.2152; .NET CLR 3.5.30729; InfoPath.1)"
80.122.56.230 - - [11/Mar/2011:08:12:56 +0100] "GET /Bilder/flyer_nigeria_Internet.pdf HTTP/1.1"
80.122.56.230 - - [11/Mar/2011:08:13:43 +0100] "GET /Seiten/Rundzeichen.html HTTP/1.1" 200 3676 "
http://www.asylabwehramt.at/Seiten/Material.html" "Mozilla/4.0 (compatible; MSIE 8.0; Windows NT
5.1; Trident/4.0; GTB6.6; .NET CLR 2.0.50727; .NET CLR 3.0.4506.2152; .NET CLR 3.5.30729; InfoPat
h.1)"
80.122.56.230 - - [11/Mar/2011:08:14:03 +0100] "GET /Seiten/Aktuelles.html HTTP/1.1" 200 5423 "ht
tp://www.asylabwehramt.at/Seiten/Rundzeichen.html" "Mozilla/4.0 (compatible; MSIE 8.0; Windows NT
5.1; Trident/4.0; GTB6.6; .NET CLR 2.0.50727; .NET CLR 3.0.4506.2152; .NET CLR 3.5.30729; InfoPa
th.1)"
80.122.56.230 - - [11/Mar/2011:08:17:13 +0100] "GET /Seiten/Links.html HTTP/1.1" 200 5874 "http:/
/www.asylabwehramt.at/Seiten/Aktuelles.html" "Mozilla/4.0 (compatible; MSIE 8.0; Windows NT 5.1;
Trident/4.0; GTB6.6; .NET CLR 2.0.50727; .NET CLR 3.0.4506.2152; .NET CLR 3.5.30729; InfoPath.1)"
80.122.56.230 - - [11/Mar/2011:08:18:54 +0100] "GET /Seiten/Press.html HTTP/1.1" 200 4677 "http:/
/www.asylabwehramt.at/Seiten/Links.html" "Mozilla/4.0 (compatible; MSIE 8.0; Windows NT 5.1; Trid
ent/4.0; GTB6.6; .NET CLR 2.0.50727; .NET CLR 3.0.4506.2152; .NET CLR 3.5.30729; InfoPath.1)"
80.122.56.230 - - [11/Mar/2011:08:19:57 +0100] "GET /OEFFENTLICHKEIT/07062010d.pdf HTTP/1.1" 200
334092 "http://www.asylabwehramt.at/Seiten/Press.html" "Mozilla/4.0 (compatible; MSIE 8.0; Window
s NT 5.1; Trident/4.0; GTB6.6; .NET CLR 2.0.50727; .NET CLR 3.0.4506.2152; .NET CLR 3.5.30729; In
foPath.1)"
80.122.56.230 - - [11/Mar/2011:08:54:35 +0100] "GET /Seiten/Bilder.html HTTP/1.1" 304 213 "http:/
/www.asylabwehramt.at/Seiten/Press.html" "Mozilla/4.0 (compatible; MSIE 8.0; Windows NT 5.1; Trid
ent/4.0; GTB6.6; .NET CLR 2.0.50727; .NET CLR 3.0.4506.2152; .NET CLR 3.5.30729; InfoPath.1)"

```
80.122.56.230 - - [11/Mar/2011:08:59:54 +0100] "GET /Seiten/Rundzeichen.html HTTP/1.1" 304 213 "h
ttp://www.asylabwehramt.at/Seiten/Bilder.html" "Mozilla/4.0 (compatible; MSIE 8.0; Windows NT 5.1
; Trident/4.0; GTB6.6; .NET CLR 2.0.50727; .NET CLR 3.0.4506.2152; .NET CLR 3.5.30729; InfoPath.1
)"
80.122.56.230 - - [11/Mar/2011:08:59:59 +0100] "GET /Seiten/Bilder.html HTTP/1.1" 304 212 "http:/
/www.asylabwehramt.at/Seiten/Rundzeichen.html" "Mozilla/4.0 (compatible; MSIE 8.0; Windows NT 5.1
; Trident/4.0; GTB6.6; .NET CLR 2.0.50727; .NET CLR 3.0.4506.2152; .NET CLR 3.5.30729; InfoPath.1
)"
80.122.56.230 - - [11/Mar/2011:09:00:04 +0100] "GET /Seiten/Links.html HTTP/1.1" 304 212 "http://
www.asylabwehramt.at/Seiten/Bilder.html" "Mozilla/4.0 (compatible; MSIE 8.0; Windows NT 5.1; Trid
ent/4.0; GTB6.6; .NET CLR 2.0.50727; .NET CLR 3.0.4506.2152; .NET CLR 3.5.30729; InfoPath.1)"
80.122.56.230 - - [11/Mar/2011:09:02:06 +0100] "GET /Seiten/Links_e.html HTTP/1.1" 200 5823 "http
://www.asylabwehramt.at/Seiten/Links.html" "Mozilla/4.0 (compatible; MSIE 8.0; Windows NT 5.1; Tr
ident/4.0; GTB6.6; .NET CLR 2.0.50727; .NET CLR 3.0.4506.2152; .NET CLR 3.5.30729; InfoPath.1)"
80.122.56.230 - - [11/Mar/2011:09:02:07 +0100] "GET /Bilder/frontex.png HTTP/1.1" 304 189 "http:/
/www.asylabwehramt.at/Seiten/Links_e.html" "Mozilla/4.0 (compatible; MSIE 8.0; Windows NT 5.1; Tr
ident/4.0; GTB6.6; .NET CLR 2.0.50727; .NET CLR 3.0.4506.2152; .NET CLR 3.5.30729; InfoPath.1)"
80.122.56.230 - - [11/Mar/2011:09:02:54 +0100] "GET /Seiten/Links.html HTTP/1.1" 304 213 "http://
www.asylabwehramt.at/Seiten/Bilder.html" "Mozilla/4.0 (compatible; MSIE 8.0; Windows NT 5.1; Trid
ent/4.0; GTB6.6; .NET CLR 2.0.50727; .NET CLR 3.0.4506.2152; .NET CLR 3.5.30729; InfoPath.1)"
80.122.56.230 - - [11/Mar/2011:09:02:56 +0100] "GET /index.html HTTP/1.1" 200 5954 "http://www.as
ylabwehramt.at/Seiten/Links.html" "Mozilla/4.0 (compatible; MSIE 8.0; Windows NT 5.1; Trident/4.0
; GTB6.6; .NET CLR 2.0.50727; .NET CLR 3.0.4506.2152; .NET CLR 3.5.30729; InfoPath.1)"
193.171.152.33 - - [11/Mar/2011:14:53:10 +0100] "GET /favicon.ico HTTP/1.1" 404 508 "-" "Mozilla/
5.0 (X11; U; Linux i686; de; rv:1.9.2.13) Gecko/20101206 Ubuntu/10.10 (maverick) Firefox/3.6.13"
193.171.152.33 - - [11/Mar/2011:14:53:13 +0100] "GET /favicon.ico HTTP/1.1" 404 507 "-" "Mozilla/
5.0 (X11; U; Linux i686; de; rv:1.9.2.13) Gecko/20101206 Ubuntu/10.10 (maverick) Firefox/3.6.13"
193.171.152.33 - - [11/Mar/2011:14:53:22 +0100] "GET /Seiten/Aktuelles.html HTTP/1.1" 200 5422 "h
```

ttp://www.asylabwehramt.at/" "Mozilla/5.0 (X11; U; Linux i686; de; rv:1.9.2.13) Gecko/20101206 Ub
untu/10.10 (maverick) Firefox/3.6.13"
193.171.152.33 - - [11/Mar/2011:14:54:33 +0100] "GET /Seiten/Press.html HTTP/1.1" 200 4677 "http:
//www.asylabwehramt.at/Seiten/Aktuelles.html" "Mozilla/5.0 (X11; U; Linux i686; de; rv:1.9.2.13)
Gecko/20101206 Ubuntu/10.10 (maverick) Firefox/3.6.13"
193.171.152.33 - - [11/Mar/2011:14:54:35 +0100] "GET /Seiten/Presse.html HTTP/1.1" 200 4644 "http
://www.asylabwehramt.at/Seiten/Press.html" "Mozilla/5.0 (X11; U; Linux i686; de; rv:1.9.2.13) Gec
ko/20101206 Ubuntu/10.10 (maverick) Firefox/3.6.13"
193.171.152.33 - - [11/Mar/2011:14:55:15 +0100] "GET /Seiten/Images.html HTTP/1.1" 200 4187 "http
://www.asylabwehramt.at/Seiten/Orgstrukt.html" "Mozilla/5.0 (X11; U; Linux i686; de; rv:1.9.2.13)
Gecko/20101206 Ubuntu/10.10 (maverick) Firefox/3.6.13"
193.171.152.33 - - [11/Mar/2011:14:55:55 +0100] "GET /Seiten/Latestnews.html HTTP/1.1" 200 5509 "
http://www.asylabwehramt.at/Seiten/Images.html" "Mozilla/5.0 (X11; U; Linux i686; de; rv:1.9.2.13
) Gecko/20101206 Ubuntu/10.10 (maverick) Firefox/3.6.13"
62.47.197.199 - - [14/Mar/2011:11:08:42 +0100] "GET /Seiten/Material.html HTTP/1.1" 200 6514 "htt
p://www.google.at/url?sa=t&source=web&cd=5&ved=0CDoQFjAE&url=http%3A%2F%2Fwww.asylabwehramt.at%2F
Seiten%2FMaterial.html&rct=j&q=`asylantrag%20%C3%B6sterreich%20formular`&ei=h-h9TbmqEI-1hAeGj7DpgBg&
usg=AFQjCNFyFHsiSQXaEJ5RVynwkdksptioPQ" "Mozilla/4.0 (compatible; MSIE 8.0; Windows NT 6.1; WOW64
; Trident/4.0; SLCC2; .NET CLR 2.0.50727; .NET CLR 3.5.30729; .NET CLR 3.0.30729; .NET4.0C; .NET4
.0E)"
`195.110.213.194`[50] - - [14/Mar/2011:18:09:08 +0100] "GET /OEFFENTLICHKEIT/media/ZEIT.pdf HTTP/1.1" 2
00 484793 "http://www.google.de/search?hl=de&lr=&as_qdr=all&sa=X&ei=1kB-TcLmM5Sz8Q0x-unKAw&ved=0C
CUQBSgA&q=`Ausreise+w%C3%A4hrend+Asylverfahren+Site%3A.at`&spell=1" "Mozilla/4.0 (compatible; MSIE
8.0; Windows NT 6.1; Trident/4.0; SLCC2; .NET CLR 2.0.50727; .NET CLR 3.5.30729; .NET CLR 3.0.307
29; Media Center PC 6.0; .NET4.0C)"
195.110.213.194 - - [14/Mar/2011:18:12:11 +0100] "GET / HTTP/1.1" 200 5955 "http://www.bing.com/s

---

[50]WHOIS record on page 299

earch?q=asylabwehramt&src=IE-SearchBox&FORM=IE8SRC" "Mozilla/4.0 (compatible; MSIE 8.0; Windows N
T 6.1; Trident/4.0; SLCC2; .NET CLR 2.0.50727; .NET CLR 3.5.30729; .NET CLR 3.0.30729; Media Cent
er PC 6.0; .NET4.0C)"

195.110.213.194 - - [14/Mar/2011:18:12:12 +0100] "GET /favicon.ico HTTP/1.1" 404 507 "-" "Mozilla
/4.0 (compatible; MSIE 8.0; Windows NT 6.1; Trident/4.0; SLCC2; .NET CLR 2.0.50727; .NET CLR 3.5.
30729; .NET CLR 3.0.30729; Media Center PC 6.0; .NET4.0C)"

195.110.213.194 - - [14/Mar/2011:18:12:19 +0100] "GET /favicon.ico HTTP/1.1" 404 507 "-" "Mozilla
/4.0 (compatible; MSIE 8.0; Windows NT 6.1; Trident/4.0; SLCC2; .NET CLR 2.0.50727; .NET CLR 3.5.
30729; .NET CLR 3.0.30729; Media Center PC 6.0; .NET4.0C)"

195.110.213.194 - - [14/Mar/2011:18:12:55 +0100] "GET /Seiten/Links.html HTTP/1.1" 200 5874 "http
://www.asylabwehramt.at/" "Mozilla/4.0 (compatible; MSIE 8.0; Windows NT 6.1; Trident/4.0; SLCC2;
.NET CLR 2.0.50727; .NET CLR 3.5.30729; .NET CLR 3.0.30729; Media Center PC 6.0; .NET4.0C)"

195.110.213.194 - - [14/Mar/2011:18:13:12 +0100] "GET /index.html HTTP/1.1" 200 5955 "http://www.
asylabwehramt.at/Seiten/Links.html" "Mozilla/4.0 (compatible; MSIE 8.0; Windows NT 6.1; Trident/4
.0; SLCC2; .NET CLR 2.0.50727; .NET CLR 3.5.30729; .NET CLR 3.0.30729; Media Center PC 6.0; .NET4
.0C)"

195.110.213.194 - - [14/Mar/2011:18:13:30 +0100] "GET /Seiten/Material.html HTTP/1.1" 200 6514 "h
ttp://www.asylabwehramt.at/index.html" "Mozilla/4.0 (compatible; MSIE 8.0; Windows NT 6.1; Triden
t/4.0; SLCC2; .NET CLR 2.0.50727; .NET CLR 3.5.30729; Media Center PC 6.0; .N
ET4.0C)"

195.110.213.194 - - [15/Mar/2011:14:11:06 +0100] "GET /Bilder/flyer_nigeria_Internet.pdf HTTP/1.1
" 200 249612 "http://www.asylabwehramt.at/Seiten/Material.html" "Mozilla/4.0 (compatible; MSIE 8.
0; Windows NT 6.1; Trident/4.0; SLCC2; .NET CLR 2.0.50727; .NET CLR 3.5.30729; .NET CLR 3.0.30729
; Media Center PC 6.0; .NET4.0C)"

195.110.213.194 - - [15/Mar/2011:14:11:09 +0100] "GET /Bilder/flyer_nigeria_Internet.pdf HTTP/1.1
" 206 4454 "-" "Mozilla/4.0 (compatible; MSIE 8.0; Windows NT 6.1; Trident/4.0; SLCC2; .NET CLR 2
.0.50727; .NET CLR 3.5.30729; .NET CLR 3.0.30729; Media Center PC 6.0; .NET4.0C)"

195.110.213.194 - - [15/Mar/2011:14:11:19 +0100] "GET /Seiten/Orgstrukt.html HTTP/1.1" 200 5531 "

```
http://www.asylabwehramt.at/Seiten/Material.html" "Mozilla/4.0 (compatible; MSIE 8.0; Windows NT
6.1; Trident/4.0; SLCC2; .NET CLR 2.0.50727; .NET CLR 3.5.30729; .NET CLR 3.0.30729; Media Center
PC 6.0; .NET4.0C)"
195.110.213.194 - - [15/Mar/2011:14:11:20 +0100] "GET /asyl.css HTTP/1.1" 304 211 "http://www.asy
labwehramt.at/Seiten/Orgstrukt.html" "Mozilla/4.0 (compatible; MSIE 8.0; Windows NT 6.1; Trident/
4.0; SLCC2; .NET CLR 2.0.50727; .NET CLR 3.5.30729; .NET CLR 3.0.30729; Media Center PC 6.0; .NET
4.0C)"
193.171.152.33 - - [16/Mar/2011:12:38:25 +0100] "GET /Bilder/STRABAG.jpg HTTP/1.1" 200 39336 "ht
tp://www.google.at/imgres?imgurl=http://www.asylabwehramt.at/Bilder/STRABAG.jpg&imgrefurl=http://
www.asylabwehramt.at/Seiten/Links.html&usg=__KCMOwP1t4abQOSNeYgXjxHawsYM=&h=495&w=1203&sz=39&hl=d
e&start=0&zoom=1&tbnid=5J_pvbNz4bFe4M:&tbnh=83&tbnw=201&ei=2KCATf25CY-Mswa38_z7Bg&prev=/images%3F
q%3Dstrabag%26hl%3Dde%26sa%3DG%26biw%3D1276%26bih%3D823%26gbv%3D2%26tbs%3Disch:1&itbs=1&iact=hc&v
px=92&vpy=153&dur=2515&hovh=144&hovw=350&tx=91&ty=168&oei=2KCATf25CY-Mswa38_z7Bg&page=1&ndsp=21&v
ed=1t:429,r:0,s:0" "Mozilla/4.0 (compatible; MSIE 7.0; Windows NT 5.1; Trident/4.0; InfoPath.1;
.NET CLR 2.0.50727; .NET CLR 3.0.4506.2152; .NET CLR 3.5.30729)"
193.171.152.33 - - [16/Mar/2011:12:38:26 +0100] "GET /asyl.css HTTP/1.1" 200 828 "http://www.asyl
abwehramt.at/Seiten/Links.html" "Mozilla/4.0 (compatible; MSIE 7.0; Windows NT 5.1; Trident/4.0;
InfoPath.1; .NET CLR 2.0.50727; .NET CLR 3.0.4506.2152; .NET CLR 3.5.30729)"
193.171.152.33 - - [16/Mar/2011:12:38:37 +0100] "GET /favicon.ico HTTP/1.1" 404 507 "-" "Mozilla/
4.0 (compatible; MSIE 8.0; Windows NT 5.1; Trident/4.0; InfoPath.1; .NET CLR 2.0.50727; .NET CLR
3.0.4506.2152; .NET CLR 3.5.30729)"
193.171.152.33 - - [16/Mar/2011:12:39:08 +0100] "GET /favicon.ico HTTP/1.1" 404 508 "-" "Mozilla/
4.0 (compatible; MSIE 8.0; Windows NT 5.1; Trident/4.0; InfoPath.1; .NET CLR 2.0.50727; .NET CLR
3.0.4506.2152; .NET CLR 3.5.30729)"
200.195.74.221 - - [25/Mar/2011:17:57:49 +0100] "GET /Seiten/?pg=http://www.sic.gov.co/recursos_u
ser/imagenes/forms.gif?? HTTP/1.1" 200 5964 "-" "Mozilla/4.7C-CCK-MCD C-UDP; EBM-APPLE (Macinto
```

```
sh; I; PPC)"
200.195.74.221 - - [25/Mar/2011:17:57:53 +0100] "GET /?pg=http://www.sic.gov.co/recursos_user/ima
genes/forms.gif?? HTTP/1.1" 200 14247 "-" "Mozilla/4.7C-CCK-MCD C-UDP; EBM-APPLE (Macintosh; I;
PPC)"
41.188.192.57 - - [26/Mar/2011:22:01:45 +0100] "GET /Material/border-wars-and-asylum-crimes.pdf H
TTP/1.0" 200 92672 "http://scholar.google.co.za/scholar?hl=en&q=beware+of+the+goths&btnG=Search&a
s_sdt=0%2C5&as_ylo=&as_vis=0" "Mozilla/5.0 (Windows; U; Windows NT 5.1; en-US; rv:1.9.2.13) Gecko
/20101203 Firefox/3.6.13 (.NET CLR 3.5.30729)"
41.188.192.57 - - [26/Mar/2011:22:01:46 +0100] "GET /favicon.ico HTTP/1.0" 200 1190 "-" "Mozilla/
5.0 (Windows; U; Windows NT 5.1; en-US; rv:1.9.2.13) Gecko/20101203 Firefox/3.6.13 (.NET CLR 3.5.
30729)"
41.188.192.57 - - [26/Mar/2011:22:07:52 +0100] "GET /Material/border-wars-and-asylum-crimes.pdf H
TTP/1.0" 200 220096 "http://scholar.google.co.za/scholar?hl=en&q=beware+of+the+goths&btnG=Search&
as_sdt=0%2C5&as_ylo=&as_vis=0" "Mozilla/5.0 (Windows; U; Windows NT 5.1; en-US; rv:1.9.2.13) Geck
o/20101203 Firefox/3.6.13 (.NET CLR 3.5.30729)"
41.188.192.57 - - [26/Mar/2011:22:08:09 +0100] "GET /Material/border-wars-and-asylum-crimes.pdf H
TTP/1.0" 200 540104 "http://scholar.google.co.za/scholar?hl=en&q=beware+of+the+goths&btnG=Search&
as_sdt=0%2C5&as_ylo=&as_vis=0" "Mozilla/5.0 (Windows; U; Windows NT 5.1; en-US; rv:1.9.2.13) Geck
o/20101203 Firefox/3.6.13 (.NET CLR 3.5.30729)"
41.188.192.57 - - [26/Mar/2011:22:08:28 +0100] "GET /Material/border-wars-and-asylum-crimes.pdf H
TTP/1.0" 200 852872 "http://scholar.google.co.za/scholar?hl=en&q=beware+of+the+goths&btnG=Search&
as_sdt=0%2C5&as_ylo=&as_vis=0" "Mozilla/5.0 (Windows; U; Windows NT 5.1; en-US; rv:1.9.2.13) Geck
o/20101203 Firefox/3.6.13 (.NET CLR 3.5.30729)"
41.188.192.57 - - [26/Mar/2011:22:08:42 +0100] "GET /Material/border-wars-and-asylum-crimes.pdf H
TTP/1.0" 206 1089646 "-" "Mozilla/5.0 (Windows; U; Windows NT 5.1; en-US; rv:1.9.2.13) Gecko/2010
1203 Firefox/3.6.13 (.NET CLR 3.5.30729)"
41.188.192.57 - - [26/Mar/2011:22:09:01 +0100] "GET /Material/border-wars-and-asylum-crimes.pdf H
```

```
41.188.192.57 - - [26/Mar/2011:22:09:02 +0100] "GET /Material/border-wars-and-asylum-crimes.pdf HTTP/1.0" 206 1971 "-" "Mozilla/5.0 (Windows; U; Windows NT 5.1; en-US; rv:1.9.2.13) Gecko/20101203 Firefox/3.6.13 (.NET CLR 3.5.30729)"
41.188.192.57 - - [26/Mar/2011:22:09:03 +0100] "GET /Material/border-wars-and-asylum-crimes.pdf HTTP/1.0" 206 8339 "-" "Mozilla/5.0 (Windows; U; Windows NT 5.1; en-US; rv:1.9.2.13) Gecko/20101203 Firefox/3.6.13 (.NET CLR 3.5.30729)"
41.188.192.57 - - [26/Mar/2011:22:09:05 +0100] "GET /Material/border-wars-and-asylum-crimes.pdf HTTP/1.0" 206 45055 "-" "Mozilla/5.0 (Windows; U; Windows NT 5.1; en-US; rv:1.9.2.13) Gecko/20101203 Firefox/3.6.13 (.NET CLR 3.5.30729)"
41.188.192.57 - - [26/Mar/2011:22:09:07 +0100] "GET /Material/border-wars-and-asylum-crimes.pdf HTTP/1.0" 206 21563 "-" "Mozilla/5.0 (Windows; U; Windows NT 5.1; en-US; rv:1.9.2.13) Gecko/20101203 Firefox/3.6.13 (.NET CLR 3.5.30729)"
41.188.192.57 - - [26/Mar/2011:22:09:09 +0100] "GET /Material/border-wars-and-asylum-crimes.pdf HTTP/1.0" 206 14896 "-" "Mozilla/5.0 (Windows; U; Windows NT 5.1; en-US; rv:1.9.2.13) Gecko/20101203 Firefox/3.6.13 (.NET CLR 3.5.30729)"
41.188.192.57 - - [26/Mar/2011:22:09:11 +0100] "GET /Material/border-wars-and-asylum-crimes.pdf HTTP/1.0" 206 26610 "-" "Mozilla/5.0 (Windows; U; Windows NT 5.1; en-US; rv:1.9.2.13) Gecko/20101203 Firefox/3.6.13 (.NET CLR 3.5.30729)"
41.188.192.57 - - [26/Mar/2011:22:09:13 +0100] "GET /Material/border-wars-and-asylum-crimes.pdf HTTP/1.0" 206 22417 "-" "Mozilla/5.0 (Windows; U; Windows NT 5.1; en-US; rv:1.9.2.13) Gecko/20101203 Firefox/3.6.13 (.NET CLR 3.5.30729)"
41.188.192.57 - - [26/Mar/2011:22:09:13 +0100] "GET /Material/border-wars-and-asylum-crimes.pdf HTTP/1.0" 206 13307 "-" "Mozilla/5.0 (Windows; U; Windows NT 5.1; en-US; rv:1.9.2.13) Gecko/20101203 Firefox/3.6.13 (.NET CLR 3.5.30729)"
41.188.192.57 - - [26/Mar/2011:22:09:15 +0100] "GET /Material/border-wars-and-asylum-crimes.pdf HTTP/1.0" 206 25969 "-" "Mozilla/5.0 (Windows; U; Windows NT 5.1; en-US; rv:1.9.2.13) Gecko/20101203 Firefox/3.6.13 (.NET CLR 3.5.30729)"
41.188.192.57 - - [26/Mar/2011:22:09:16 +0100] "GET /Material/border-wars-and-asylum-crimes.pdf HTTP/1.0" 206 24699 "-" "Mozilla/5.0 (Windows; U; Windows NT 5.1; en-US; rv:1.9.2.13) Gecko/20101203 Firefox/3.6.13 (.NET CLR 3.5.30729)"
```

```
03 Firefox/3.6.13 (.NET CLR 3.5.30729)"
41.188.192.57 - - [26/Mar/2011:22:09:18 +0100] "GET /Material/border-wars-and-asylum-crimes.pdf H
TTP/1.0" 206 30475 "-" "Mozilla/5.0 (Windows; U; Windows NT 5.1; en-US; rv:1.9.2.13) Gecko/201012
03 Firefox/3.6.13 (.NET CLR 3.5.30729)"
41.188.192.57 - - [26/Mar/2011:22:09:21 +0100] "GET /Material/border-wars-and-asylum-crimes.pdf H
TTP/1.0" 206 1106 "-" "Mozilla/5.0 (Windows; U; Windows NT 5.1; en-US; rv:1.9.2.13) Gecko/2010120
3 Firefox/3.6.13 (.NET CLR 3.5.30729)"
41.188.192.57 - - [26/Mar/2011:22:11:13 +0100] "GET /Material/border-wars-and-asylum-crimes.pdf H
TTP/1.0" 200 666080 "http://scholar.google.co.za/scholar?hl=en&q=beware+of+the+goths&btnG=Search&
as_sdt=0%2C5&as_ylo=&as_vis=0" "Mozilla/5.0 (Windows; U; Windows NT 5.1; en-US; rv:1.9.2.13) Geck
o/20101203 Firefox/3.6.13 (.NET CLR 3.5.30729)"
41.188.192.57 - - [26/Mar/2011:22:11:52 +0100] "GET /Material/border-wars-and-asylum-crimes.pdf H
TTP/1.0" 200 457568 "http://scholar.google.co.za/scholar?hl=en&q=beware+of+the+goths&btnG=Search&
as_sdt=0%2C5&as_ylo=&as_vis=0" "Mozilla/5.0 (Windows; U; Windows NT 5.1; en-US; rv:1.9.2.13) Geck
o/20101203 Firefox/3.6.13 (.NET CLR 3.5.30729)"
41.188.192.57 - - [26/Mar/2011:22:12:12 +0100] "GET /Material/border-wars-and-asylum-crimes.pdf H
TTP/1.0" 200 550240 "http://scholar.google.co.za/scholar?hl=en&q=beware+of+the+goths&btnG=Search&
as_sdt=0%2C5&as_ylo=&as_vis=0" "Mozilla/5.0 (Windows; U; Windows NT 5.1; en-US; rv:1.9.2.13) Geck
o/20101203 Firefox/3.6.13 (.NET CLR 3.5.30729)"
41.188.192.57 - - [26/Mar/2011:22:12:36 +0100] "GET /Material/border-wars-and-asylum-crimes.pdf H
TTP/1.0" 200 515488 "http://scholar.google.co.za/scholar?hl=en&q=beware+of+the+goths&btnG=Search&
as_sdt=0%2C5&as_ylo=&as_vis=0" "Mozilla/5.0 (Windows; U; Windows NT 5.1; en-US; rv:1.9.2.13) Geck
o/20101203 Firefox/3.6.13 (.NET CLR 3.5.30729)"
41.188.192.57 - - [26/Mar/2011:22:13:16 +0100] "GET /Material/border-wars-and-asylum-crimes.pdf H
TTP/1.0" 200 482184 "http://scholar.google.co.za/scholar?hl=en&q=beware+of+the+goths&btnG=Search&
as_sdt=0%2C5&as_ylo=&as_vis=0" "Mozilla/5.0 (Windows; U; Windows NT 5.1; en-US; rv:1.9.2.13) Geck
o/20101203 Firefox/3.6.13 (.NET CLR 3.5.30729)"
```

```
41.188.192.57 - - [26/Mar/2011:22:13:39 +0100] "GET /Material/border-wars-and-asylum-crimes.pdf H
TTP/1.0" 200 1601488 "http://scholar.google.co.za/scholar?hl=en&q=beware+of+the+goths&btnG=Search
&as_sdt=0%2C5&as_ylo=&as_vis=0" "Mozilla/5.0 (Windows; U; Windows NT 5.1; en-US; rv:1.9.2.13) Gec
ko/20101203 Firefox/3.6.13 (.NET CLR 3.5.30729)"
41.188.192.57 - - [26/Mar/2011:22:14:10 +0100] "GET /Material/border-wars-and-asylum-crimes.pdf H
TTP/1.0" 206 677550 "-" "Mozilla/5.0 (Windows; U; Windows NT 5.1; en-US; rv:1.9.2.13) Gecko/20101
203 Firefox/3.6.13 (.NET CLR 3.5.30729)"
41.188.192.57 - - [26/Mar/2011:22:14:24 +0100] "GET /Material/border-wars-and-asylum-crimes.pdf H
TTP/1.0" 206 1681 "-" "Mozilla/5.0 (Windows; U; Windows NT 5.1; en-US; rv:1.9.2.13) Gecko/2010120
3 Firefox/3.6.13 (.NET CLR 3.5.30729)"
41.188.192.57 - - [26/Mar/2011:22:14:25 +0100] "GET /Material/border-wars-and-asylum-crimes.pdf H
TTP/1.0" 206 1971 "-" "Mozilla/5.0 (Windows; U; Windows NT 5.1; en-US; rv:1.9.2.13) Gecko/2010120
3 Firefox/3.6.13 (.NET CLR 3.5.30729)"
41.188.192.57 - - [26/Mar/2011:22:14:28 +0100] "GET /Material/border-wars-and-asylum-crimes.pdf H
TTP/1.0" 206 7678 "-" "Mozilla/5.0 (Windows; U; Windows NT 5.1; en-US; rv:1.9.2.13) Gecko/2010120
3 Firefox/3.6.13 (.NET CLR 3.5.30729)"
81.223.187.210[51] - - [28/Mar/2011:11:14:11 +0200] "GET /Seiten/Aktuelles.html HTTP/1.1" 200 5423 "h
ttp://www.google.at/search?client=firefox-a&rls=org.mozilla%3Ade%3Aofficial&channel=s&hl=de&sourc
e=hp&q=wesentliche+punkte+%C3%B6sterreichischer+asylpolitik&meta=&btnG=Google-Suche" "Mozilla/5.0
(Windows; U; Windows NT 5.1; de; rv:1.9.1.3) Gecko/20090824 Firefox/3.5.3"
81.223.187.210 - - [28/Mar/2011:11:14:12 +0200] "GET /asyl.css HTTP/1.1" 200 828 "http://www.asyl
abwehramt.at/Seiten/Aktuelles.html" "Mozilla/5.0 (Windows; U; Windows NT 5.1; de; rv:1.9.1.3) Gec
ko/20090824 Firefox/3.5.3"
81.223.187.210 - - [28/Mar/2011:11:14:14 +0200] "GET /Bilder/STRABAG.jpg HTTP/1.1" 200 39336 "htt
p://www.asylabwehramt.at/Seiten/Aktuelles.html" "Mozilla/5.0 (Windows; U; Windows NT 5.1; de; rv:
1.9.1.3) Gecko/20090824 Firefox/3.5.3"
```

---

[51]WHOIS record on page 313

81.223.187.210 - - [28/Mar/2011:11:14:15 +0200] "GET /favicon.ico HTTP/1.1" 200 1189 "-" "Mozilla/5.0 (Windows; U; Windows NT 5.1; de; rv:1.9.1.3) Gecko/20090824 Firefox/3.5.3"

81.223.187.210 - - [28/Mar/2011:11:15:05 +0200] "GET /index.html HTTP/1.1" 200 5955 "http://www.asylabwehramt.at/Seiten/Aktuelles.html" "Mozilla/5.0 (Windows; U; Windows NT 5.1; de; rv:1.9.1.3) Gecko/20090824 Firefox/3.5.3"

81.223.187.210 - - [28/Mar/2011:11:15:33 +0200] "GET / HTTP/1.1" 200 5955 "http://ecosia.org/search.php?q=asyl%20abwehramt&source=forestle" "Mozilla/5.0 (Windows; U; Windows NT 5.1; de; rv:1.9.1.3) Gecko/20090824 Firefox/3.5.3"

193.171.152.33 - - [29/Mar/2011:13:07:46 +0200] "GET / HTTP/1.1" 200 14285 "http://www.google.at/search?as_q=pornofilm+landesverteidigung+wien&as_epq=&as_oq=&as_eq=&hl=de&num=100&lr=&cr=&as_ft=i&as_filetype=&as_qdr=all&as_occt=any&as_dt=i&as_sitesearch=&as_rights=&safe=images&btnG=Google-Suche" "Mozilla/4.0 (compatible; MSIE 6.0; Windows NT 5.1; SV1)"

193.171.152.33 - - [29/Mar/2011:13:08:17 +0200] "GET /Seiten/Orgstrukt.html HTTP/1.1" 200 14438 "http://www.asylabwehramt.at/" "Mozilla/4.0 (compatible; MSIE 6.0; Windows NT 5.1; SV1)"

193.171.152.33 - - [29/Mar/2011:13:08:37 +0200] "GET /index.html HTTP/1.1" 200 14285 "http://www.asylabwehramt.at/Seiten/Orgstrukt.html" "Mozilla/4.0 (compatible; MSIE 6.0; Windows NT 5.1; SV1)"

41.188.192.57 - - [31/Mar/2011:11:01:06 +0200] "GET /Material/border-wars-and-asylum-crimes.pdf HTTP/1.0" 200 15928 "-" "Mozilla/5.0 (Windows; U; Windows NT 5.1; en-US) AppleWebKit/534.12 (KHTML, like Gecko) Chrome/9.0.587.0 Safari/534.12"

41.188.192.57 - - [31/Mar/2011:11:01:07 +0200] "GET /favicon.ico HTTP/1.0" 200 1190 "-" "Mozilla/5.0 (Windows; U; Windows NT 5.1; en-US) AppleWebKit/534.12 (KHTML, like Gecko) Chrome/9.0.587.0 Safari/534.12"

41.188.192.57 - - [31/Mar/2011:11:01:10 +0200] "GET /Material/border-wars-and-asylum-crimes.pdf HTTP/1.0" 206 593680 "http://www.asylabwehramt.at/Material/border-wars-and-asylum-crimes.pdf" "Mozilla/5.0 (Windows; U; Windows NT 5.1; en-US) AppleWebKit/534.12 (KHTML, like Gecko) Chrome/9.0.58 7.0 Safari/534.12"

193.5.216.100 - - [01/Apr/2011:10:25:05 +0200] "GET / HTTP/1.0" 200 5917 "http://www.google.de/search?q=asylabwehramt" "Mozilla/4.0 (compatible; MSIE 7.0; Windows NT 5.1; .NET CLR 1.1.4322; .NET

```
CLR 2.0.50727; .NET CLR 3.0.4506.2152; .NET CLR 3.5.30729)"
193.5.216.100 - - [01/Apr/2011:10:25:06 +0200] "GET /asyl.css HTTP/1.0" 200 791 "http://www.asyla
bwehramt.at/" "Mozilla/4.0 (compatible; MSIE 7.0; Windows NT 5.1; .NET CLR 1.1.4322; .NET CLR 2.0
.50727; .NET CLR 3.0.4506.2152; .NET CLR 3.5.30729)"
193.5.216.100 - - [01/Apr/2011:10:25:09 +0200] "GET /Seiten/Presse.html HTTP/1.0" 200 4607 "http:
//www.asylabwehramt.at/" "Mozilla/4.0 (compatible; MSIE 7.0; Windows NT 5.1; .NET CLR 1.1.4322; .
NET CLR 2.0.50727; .NET CLR 3.0.4506.2152; .NET CLR 3.5.30729)"
46.57.52.51 - - [01/Apr/2011:15:18:33 +0200] "GET /Seiten/Material.html HTTP/1.1" 200 6514 "http:
//www.google.at/url?sa=t&source=web&cd=5&ved=0CD0QFjAE&url=http%3A%2F%2Fwww.asylabwehramt.at%2FSe
iten%2FMaterial.html&rct=j&q=asylantrag%20%C3%B6sterreich%20formular &ei=7c-VTY3mM4XusgaOp-m7CA&us
g=AFQjCNFyFHsiSQXaEJ5RVynwkdksptioPQ" "Mozilla/4.0 (compatible; MSIE 8.0; Windows NT 6.0; Trident
/4.0; SLCC1; .NET CLR 2.0.50727; .NET CLR 1.1.4322; .NET CLR 3.5.30729; .NET CLR 3.0.30729; .NET4
.0C; OfficeLiveConnector.1.5; OfficeLivePatch.1.3)"
vpn-vie01.bmi.gv.at - - [03/Apr/2011:20:37:35 +0200] "GET / HTTP/1.1" 200 14285 "-" "Mozil
la/4.0 (compatible; MSIE 6.0; Windows NT 5.1; SV1; InfoPath.1; .NET CLR 1.1.4322; .NET CLR 2.0.50
727; MS-RTC LM 8; .NET CLR 3.0.04506.648; .NET CLR 3.5.21022)"
vpn-vie01.bmi.gv.at - - [03/Apr/2011:20:39:23 +0200] "GET /Seiten/Bilder.html HTTP/1.1" 20
0 10683 "http://www.asylabwehramt.at/" "Mozilla/4.0 (compatible; MSIE 6.0; Windows NT 5.1; SV1; I
nfoPath.1; .NET CLR 1.1.4322; .NET CLR 2.0.50727; MS-RTC LM 8; .NET CLR 3.0.04506.648; .NET CLR 3
.5.21022)"
vpn-vie01.bmi.gv.at - - [03/Apr/2011:20:39:24 +0200] "GET /Bilder/Ausstellung_weisses_haus
_wien_esel_fotos/eSeL_UBERMORGEN_asylabwehramt_dasweissehaus_453_thumb.jpg HTTP/1.1" 200 47800 "h
ttp://www.asylabwehramt.at/Seiten/Bilder.html" "Mozilla/4.0 (compatible; MSIE 6.0; Windows NT 5.1
; SV1; InfoPath.1; .NET CLR 1.1.4322; .NET CLR 2.0.50727; MS-RTC LM 8; .NET CLR 3.0.04506.648; .N
ET CLR 3.5.21022)"
78.41.149.241 - - [06/Apr/2011:10:04:27 +0200] "GET /Seiten/Aktuelles.html HTTP/1.1" 200 14662 "h
ttp://www.google.at/search?hl=de&cr=countryAT&tbs=ctr:countryAT&sa=X&ei=yh2cTdvaPIfxsgaWh4W9Bg&ve
```

d=0CEAQBSgA&q=asyl+luftweg&spell=1" "Mozilla/4.0 (compatible; MSIE 8.0; Windows NT 5.1; Trident/4.0; InfoPath.1; .NET CLR 1.1.4322; .NET CLR 2.0.50727; .NET CLR 3.0.04506.648; .NET CLR 3.5.21022)"

78.41.149.241 - - [06/Apr/2011:10:05:26 +0200] "GET /Seiten/Material.html HTTP/1.1" 200 17654 "http://www.asylabwehramt.at/Seiten/Aktuelles.html" "Mozilla/4.0 (compatible; MSIE 8.0; Windows NT 5.1; Trident/4.0; InfoPath.1; .NET CLR 1.1.4322; .NET CLR 2.0.50727; .NET CLR 3.0.04506.648; .NET CLR 3.5.21022)"

78.41.149.241 - - [06/Apr/2011:10:05:43 +0200] "GET /Bilder/Ladung.png HTTP/1.1" 200 114956 "http://www.asylabwehramt.at/Seiten/Material.html" "Mozilla/4.0 (compatible; MSIE 8.0; Windows NT 5.1; Trident/4.0; InfoPath.1; .NET CLR 1.1.4322; .NET CLR 2.0.50727; .NET CLR 3.0.04506.648; .NET CLR 3.5.21022)"

78.41.149.241 - - [06/Apr/2011:10:05:58 +0200] "GET /Material/Flyer_Volksschutz_Praevention_Aufklaerung_FPOE.pdf HTTP/1.1" 200 661832 "http://www.asylabwehramt.at/Seiten/Material.html" "Mozilla/4.0 (compatible; MSIE 8.0; Windows NT 5.1; Trident/4.0; InfoPath.1; .NET CLR 1.1.4322; .NET CLR 2.0.50727; .NET CLR 3.0.04506.648; .NET CLR 3.5.21022)"

78.41.149.241 - - [06/Apr/2011:10:06:50 +0200] "GET /Material/Hotline_Albanisch.PDF HTTP/1.1" 200 644942 "http://www.asylabwehramt.at/Seiten/Material.html" "Mozilla/4.0 (compatible; MSIE 8.0; Windows NT 5.1; Trident/4.0; InfoPath.1; .NET CLR 1.1.4322; .NET CLR 2.0.50727; .NET CLR 3.0.04506.648; .NET CLR 3.5.21022)"

78.41.149.241 - - [06/Apr/2011:10:07:03 +0200] "GET /Material/Hotline_Englisch.PDF HTTP/1.1" 200 473662 "http://www.asylabwehramt.at/Seiten/Material.html" "Mozilla/4.0 (compatible; MSIE 8.0; Windows NT 5.1; Trident/4.0; InfoPath.1; .NET CLR 1.1.4322; .NET CLR 2.0.50727; .NET CLR 3.0.04506.648; .NET CLR 3.5.21022)"

78.41.149.241 - - [06/Apr/2011:10:07:38 +0200] "GET /Seiten/Orgstrukt.html HTTP/1.1" 200 14438 "http://www.asylabwehramt.at/Seiten/Aktuelles.html" "Mozilla/4.0 (compatible; MSIE 8.0; Windows NT 5.1; Trident/4.0; InfoPath.1; .NET CLR 1.1.4322; .NET CLR 2.0.50727; .NET CLR 3.0.04506.648; .NET CLR 3.5.21022)"

193.171.152.33 - - [07/Apr/2011:14:59:22 +0200] "GET /Bilder/SCREEN_AAbA_Edutainment_Video.jpg HT

```
TP/1.1" 200 29556 "http://forum.geizhals.at/t562009.html" "Mozilla/5.0 (compatible; MSIE 9.0; W
indows NT 6.1; Trident/5.0)"
188.22.71.175 - - [09/Apr/2011:21:27:42 +0200] "GET /Seiten/Material.html HTTP/1.1" 200 6514 "htt
p://www.google.at/url?sa=t&source=web&cd=3&ved=0CCkQFjAC&url=http%3A%2F%2Fwww.asylabwehramt.at%2F
Seiten%2FMaterial.html&rct=j&q=asylantrag%20formular%20auf%20persisch&ei=V7KgTaiqFNHBswadjriBAg&u
sg=AFQjCNFyFHsiSQXaEJ5RVynwkdksptioPQ" "Mozilla/5.0 (Windows; U; Windows NT 6.1; de; rv:1.9.2.16)
 Gecko/20110319 AskTbIMB/3.11.3.15590 Firefox/3.6.16"
213.227.184.134 - - [11/Apr/2011:14:15:05 +0200] "GET /Seiten/Orgstrukt.html HTTP/1.0" 200 5531 "
http://www.google.at/url?sa=t&source=web&cd=7&ved=0CEkQFjAG&url=http%3A%2F%2Fwww.asylabwehramt.at
%2FSeiten%2FOrgstrukt.html&rct=j&q=asylantrag%20formular%20%C3%B6sterreich&ei=v--iTa0kDsSd0unWgTU
&usg=AFQjCNFupGGPUoPKDe7UpjwYvDejEFC1yA" "Mozilla/5.0 (Windows; U; Windows NT 5.1; de; rv:1.9.1.7
) Gecko/20091221 Firefox/3.5.7"
```

2 WHOIS Records

```
80.122.180.78
```

% This is the RIPE Database query service.
% The objects are in RPSL format.
%
% The RIPE Database is subject to Terms and Conditions.
% See http://www.ripe.net/db/support/db-terms-conditions.pdf

% Note: this output has been filtered.
%   To receive output for a database update, use the "-B" flag.

% Information related to '80.122.180.76 - 80.122.180.79'

```
inetnum:       80.122.180.76 - 80.122.180.79
netname:       VERE-HWY-AT
descr:         Verein Menschenrechte OEsterreich
descr:         Alser Strasse 20/21
descr:         1090 Wien
country:       AT
admin-c:       HMH25-RIPE
tech-c:        HMH25-RIPE
status:        ASSIGNED PA
mnt-by:        AS8447-MNT
mnt-lower:     AS8447-MNT
source:        RIPE # Filtered
```

% Information related to '80.120.0.0/14AS8447'

```
route:         80.120.0.0/14
descr:         HIGHWAY194
origin:        AS8447
remarks:       ==========================================
remarks:       please report abuse incidents (eg network
remarks:       scanning, spam originating, etc.) to
remarks:       abuse@aon.at
remarks:       ==========================================
```

```
mnt-by:          AS8447-MNT
source:          RIPE # Filtered
```

```
128.250.5.245
```

```
% [whois.apnic.net node-2]
% Whois data copyright terms    http://www.apnic.net/db/dbcopyright.h
```

```
inetnum:         128.250.0.0 - 128.250.255.255
netname:         UNIMELB
descr:           The University of Melbourne
country:         AU
admin-c:         MM620-AP
tech-c:          SD4-AP
status:          ALLOCATED PORTABLE
notify:          abuse@unimelb.edu.au
mnt-by:          APNIC-HM
mnt-lower:       MAINT-AU-UNIMELB
changed:         hm-changed@apnic.net 20040318
changed:         hm-changed@apnic.net 20041214
changed:         hm-changed@apnic.net 20060127
source:          APNIC
```

```
person:          Mark Munro
nic-hdl:         MM620-AP
e-mail:          mcm@unimelb.edu.au
address:         Department of Information Infrastrucure
address:         The University of Melbourne
address:         Victoria 3010
address:         Australia
phone:           +61-3-83447477
fax-no:          +61-3-83445537
country:         AU
changed:         mcm@unimelb.edu.au 20051223
mnt-by:          MAINT-NEW
source:          APNIC
```

```
person:          Sasha Dangubic
nic-hdl:         SD4-AP
e-mail:          dangubic@unimelb.edu.au
address:         The University of Melbourne
address:         Victoria 3010
address:         Australia
phone:           +61 3 8344 4855
```

```
fax-no:        +61 3 9347 4803
country:       AU
changed:       dangubic@unimelb.edu.au 20030916
mnt-by:        MAINT-NEW
source:        APNIC
```

193.186.185.101

```
% This is the RIPE Database query service.
% The objects are in RPSL format.
%
% The RIPE Database is subject to Terms and Conditions.
% See http://www.ripe.net/db/support/db-terms-conditions.pdf

% Note: this output has been filtered.
%          To receive output for a database update, use the "-B" flag.

% Information related to '193.186.184.0 - 193.186.187.255'

inetnum:       193.186.184.0 - 193.186.187.255
netname:       OEMV-NET
descr:         OEMV AG
country:       AT
admin-c:       AOA9-RIPE
tech-c:        AOA9-RIPE
status:        ASSIGNED PI
mnt-by:        OMV-MNT
mnt-routes:    OMV-MNT
mnt-domains:   OMV-MNT
mnt-by:        AS12878-MNT
mnt-routes:    AS12878-MNT
mnt-domains:   AS12878-MNT
mnt-by:        RIPE-NCC-HM-PI-MNT
mnt-lower:     RIPE-NCC-HM-PI-MNT
source:        RIPE # Filtered

% Information related to '193.186.184.0/22AS25069'

route:         193.186.184.0/22
descr:         OMV-NET
origin:        AS25069
mnt-by:        OMV-MNT
mnt-by:        AS12878-MNT
source:        RIPE # Filtered
```

```
 193.134.242.12
```

% This is the RIPE Database query service.
% The objects are in RPSL format.
%
% The RIPE Database is subject to Terms and Conditions.
% See http://www.ripe.net/db/support/db-terms-conditions.pdf

% Note: this output has been filtered.
%   To receive output for a database update, use the "-B" flag.

% Information related to '193.134.240.0 - 193.134.247.255'

```
inetnum:        193.134.240.0 - 193.134.247.255
netname:        UNHCR
descr:          United Nations High Commissioner for Refugees
descr:          Geneva, Switzerland
country:        CH
tech-c:         GM256-RIPE
admin-c:        MB54-RIPE
status:         ASSIGNED PI
mnt-by:         CH-UNISOURCE-MNT
source:         RIPE # Filtered
```

% Information related to '193.134.240.0/21AS43189'

```
route:          193.134.240.0/21
descr:          Route_Object_unhcr
origin:         AS43189
mnt-by:         COLT-CH-MNT
source:         RIPE # Filtered
```


```
 128.250.5.246
```

% [whois.apnic.net node-2]
% Whois data copyright terms   http://www.apnic.net/db/dbcopyright.

```
inetnum:        128.250.0.0 - 128.250.255.255
netname:        UNIMELB
descr:          The University of Melbourne
country:        AU
admin-c:        MM620-AP
```

```
tech-c:        SD4-AP
status:        ALLOCATED PORTABLE
notify:        abuse@unimelb.edu.au
mnt-by:        APNIC-HM
mnt-lower:     MAINT-AU-UNIMELB
changed:       hm-changed@apnic.net 20040318
changed:       hm-changed@apnic.net 20041214
changed:       hm-changed@apnic.net 20060127
source:        APNIC

person:        Mark Munro
nic-hdl:       MM620-AP
e-mail:        mcm@unimelb.edu.au
address:       Department of Information Infrastrucure
address:       The University of Melbourne
address:       Victoria 3010
address:       Australia
phone:         +61-3-83447477
fax-no:        +61-3-83445537
country:       AU
changed:       mcm@unimelb.edu.au 20051223
mnt-by:        MAINT-NEW
source:        APNIC

person:        Sasha Dangubic
nic-hdl:       SD4-AP
e-mail:        dangubic@unimelb.edu.au
address:       The University of Melbourne
address:       Victoria 3010
address:       Australia
phone:         +61 3 8344 4855
fax-no:        +61 3 9347 4803
country:       AU
changed:       dangubic@unimelb.edu.au 20030916
mnt-by:        MAINT-NEW
source:        APNIC
```

`188.21.224.34`

```
% This is the RIPE Database query service.
% The objects are in RPSL format.
%
% The RIPE Database is subject to Terms and Conditions.
% See http://www.ripe.net/db/support/db-terms-conditions.pdf
```

```
% Note: this output has been filtered.
%         To receive output for a database update, use the "-B" flag.

% Information related to '188.21.224.32 - 188.21.224.35'

inetnum:        188.21.224.32 - 188.21.224.35
netname:        HOCHWARTSUSA-HWY-AT
descr:          Susanne Hochwarter
descr:          Wollzeile
descr:          1010 Wien
country:        AT
admin-c:        HMH25-RIPE
tech-c:         HMH25-RIPE
status:         ASSIGNED PA
mnt-by:         AS8447-MNT
mnt-lower:      AS8447-MNT
source:         RIPE # Filtered

% Information related to '188.20.0.0/14AS8447'

route:          188.20.0.0/14
descr:          HIGHWAY194
origin:         AS8447
remarks:        ===========================================
remarks:        please report abuse incidents (eg network
remarks:        scanning, spam originating, etc.) to
remarks:        abuse@aon.at
remarks:        ===========================================
mnt-by:         AS8447-MNT
source:         RIPE # Filtered
```

`195.245.92.74`

```
% This is the RIPE Database query service.
% The objects are in RPSL format.
%
% The RIPE Database is subject to Terms and Conditions.
% See http://www.ripe.net/db/support/db-terms-conditions.pdf

% Note: this output has been filtered.
%         To receive output for a database update, use the "-B" flag.

% Information related to '195.245.92.0 - 195.245.93.255'
```

```
inetnum:          195.245.92.0 - 195.245.93.255
netname:          ALLIANZ-AT-NET
descr:            Allianz Elementar Versicherungs AG
country:          AT
org:              ORG-AA83-RIPE
admin-c:          TS634-RIPE
tech-c:           PG2153-RIPE
status:           ASSIGNED PI
mnt-by:           ALLIANZ-AT-MNT
mnt-by:           AS1764-MNT
mnt-by:           RIPE-NCC-END-MNT
mnt-lower:        RIPE-NCC-END-MNT
mnt-routes:       ALLIANZ-AT-MNT
mnt-routes:       AS1764-MNT
mnt-domains:      ALLIANZ-AT-MNT
mnt-domains:      AS1764-MNT
source:           RIPE # Filtered

% Information related to '195.245.92.0/23AS29429'

route:            195.245.92.0/23
descr:            ALLIANZ-AT-NET
origin:           AS29429
mnt-by:           ALLIANZ-AT-MNT
mnt-by:           AS1764-MNT
source:           RIPE # Filtered
```

194.138.12.171

```
% This is the RIPE Database query service.
% The objects are in RPSL format.
%
% The RIPE Database is subject to Terms and Conditions.
% See http://www.ripe.net/db/support/db-terms-conditions.pdf

% Note: this output has been filtered.
%        To receive output for a database update, use the "-B" flag.

% Information related to '194.138.0.0 - 194.138.255.255'

inetnum:          194.138.0.0 - 194.138.255.255
netname:          SIEMENS-EURO
descr:            Siemens AG
```

```
descr:           world headquarter
descr:           Wittelsbacherplatz 2
descr:           DE-80333
descr:           Munich
descr:           sites in Europe
org:             ORG-SNIC1-RIPE
country:         DE
admin-c:         SNIC1-RIPE
tech-c:          SNIC1-RIPE
status:          ASSIGNED PI
mnt-by:          SAG-MNT
mnt-lower:       SAG-MNT
mnt-routes:      SAG-MNT
source:          RIPE # Filtered
```

% Information related to '194.138.12.0/24AS8971'

```
route:           194.138.12.0/24
descr:           Siemens AT
origin:          AS8971
remarks:         Siemens AG
remarks:         main web server
mnt-by:          AS8971-MNT
mnt-by:          SAG-MNT
source:          RIPE # Filtered
```

`192.164.72.10`

% This is the RIPE Database query service.
% The objects are in RPSL format.
%
% The RIPE Database is subject to Terms and Conditions.
% See http://www.ripe.net/db/support/db-terms-conditions.pdf

% Note: this output has been filtered.
%   To receive output for a database update, use the "-B" flag.

% Information related to '192.164.72.0 - 192.164.79.255'

```
inetnum:         192.164.72.0 - 192.164.79.255
netname:         OEAMTC-NET
org:             ORG-OAMu1-RIPE
descr:           Oesterreichischer Automobil Motorrad und Touring Clu
descr:           OEAMTC
```

```
country:          AT
admin-c:          OA481-RIPE
tech-c:           OA481-RIPE
status:           ASSIGNED PI
mnt-by:           AS1901-MNT
mnt-lower:        OEAMTC-MNT
mnt-routes:       OEAMTC-MNT
mnt-domains:      OEAMTC-MNT
source:           RIPE # Filtered
```

% Information related to '192.164.72.0/21AS16381'

```
route:            192.164.72.0/21
descr:            OEAMTC-AT-NET
origin:           AS16381
mnt-by:           OEAMTC-MNT
source:           RIPE # Filtered
```

```
193.247.39.154
```

% This is the RIPE Database query service.
% The objects are in RPSL format.
%
% The RIPE Database is subject to Terms and Conditions.
% See http://www.ripe.net/db/support/db-terms-conditions.pdf

% Note: this output has been filtered.
%   To receive output for a database update, use the "-B" flag.

% Information related to '193.247.39.152 - 193.247.39.159'

```
inetnum:          193.247.39.152 - 193.247.39.159
netname:          OIM-NET
descr:            Organisation Internationale pour les Migrations
descr:            1218 Le Grand-Saconnex
country:          CH
admin-c:          GC5264-RIPE
tech-c:           GC5264-RIPE
status:           ASSIGNED PA
mnt-by:           CH-UNISOURCE-MNT
source:           RIPE # Filtered
```

% Information related to '193.247.36.0/22AS3303'

```
route:          193.247.36.0/22
descr:          NET-193-PA
origin:         AS3303
mnt-by:         CH-UNISOURCE-MNT
source:         RIPE # Filtered
```

193.171.152.33

```
% This is the RIPE Database query service.
% The objects are in RPSL format.
%
% The RIPE Database is subject to Terms and Conditions.
% See http://www.ripe.net/db/support/db-terms-conditions.pdf
```

```
% Note: this output has been filtered.
%          To receive output for a database update, use the "-B" flag.
```

```
% Information related to '193.171.152.0 - 193.171.154.255'
```

```
inetnum:        193.171.152.0 - 193.171.154.255
netname:        BMLV-HDVA
descr:          Bundesministerium fuer Landesverteidigung
descr:          Heeres-Datenverarbeitungsamt
country:        AT
admin-c:        LS37-RIPE
tech-c:         HHZ1-RIPE
remarks:        rev-srv:        ns1.univie.ac.at
remarks:        rev-srv:        ns1.bmlv.gv.at
status:         ASSIGNED PA
mnt-by:         ACONET-LIR-MNT
source:         RIPE # Filtered
remarks:        rev-srv attribute deprecated by RIPE NCC on 02/09/20
```

```
irt:            IRT-ACONET-CERT
address:        Vienna University Computer Center
address:        Universitaetsstrasse 7
address:        A-1010 Wien
address:        Austria
phone:          +43 1 427714045
fax-no:         +43 1 42779140
abuse-mailbox:  cert@aco.net
signature:      PGPKEY-800559FB
encryption:     PGPKEY-800559FB
admin-c:        TI123-RIPE
```

```
tech-c:           TI123-RIPE
auth:             PGPKEY-800559FB
remarks:          This is a TI accredited CSIRT/CERT
remarks:          emergency phone number +43 1 427714045
remarks:          timezone GMT+01 (GMT+02 with DST)
remarks:          https://www.trusted-introducer.org/teams/aconet-cert.html
remarks:          RFC-2350 service definition:
remarks:          http://www.aco.net/rfc2350.html
irt-nfy:          cert@aco.net
mnt-by:           TRUSTED-INTRODUCER-MNT
source:           RIPE # Filtered


% Information related to '193.170.0.0/15AS1853'

route:            193.170.0.0/15
descr:            ACOnet, Provider Local Registry Block
origin:           AS1853
mnt-by:           AS1853-MNT
source:           RIPE # Filtered
```

`194.153.217.248`

```
% This is the RIPE Database query service.
% The objects are in RPSL format.
%
% The RIPE Database is subject to Terms and Conditions.
% See http://www.ripe.net/db/support/db-terms-conditions.pdf

% Note: this output has been filtered.
%       To receive output for a database update, use the "-B" flag.

% Information related to '194.153.217.0 - 194.153.217.255'

inetnum:          194.153.217.0 - 194.153.217.255
netname:          SOZVERS-NET
descr:            Society of Austrian social insurance carriers
country:          AT
admin-c:          HK576-RIPE
tech-c:           HK576-RIPE
status:           ASSIGNED PI
mnt-by:           RIPE-NCC-HM-PI-MNT
source:           RIPE # Filtered

% Information related to '194.153.217.0/24AS16099'
```

```
route:          194.153.217.0/24
descr:          SOZVERS-NET
origin:         AS16099
mnt-by:         SOZVERS-MNT
source:         RIPE # Filtered
```

`85.158.226.103`

```
% This is the RIPE Database query service.
% The objects are in RPSL format.
%
% The RIPE Database is subject to Terms and Conditions.
% See http://www.ripe.net/db/support/db-terms-conditions.pdf

% Note: this output has been filtered.
%          To receive output for a database update, use the "-B" flag.

% Information related to '85.158.226.64 - 85.158.226.127'

inetnum:        85.158.226.64 - 85.158.226.127
netname:        CNBMWA
descr:          Corporate Network Austria
descr:          Bundesministerium fuer Wirtschaft und Arbeit
country:        AT
admin-c:        NM441-RIPE
tech-c:         HCGD1-RIPE
status:         ASSIGNED PA
mnt-by:         BRZ-MNT
source:         RIPE # Filtered

% Information related to '85.158.224.0/21AS8692'

route:          85.158.224.0/21
descr:          CNA-AT
origin:         AS8692
mnt-by:         AS8692-MNT
source:         RIPE # Filtered
```

`193.246.50.2`

```
% This is the RIPE Database query service.
% The objects are in RPSL format.
```

```
%
% The RIPE Database is subject to Terms and Conditions.
% See http://www.ripe.net/db/support/db-terms-conditions.pdf

% Note: this output has been filtered.
%         To receive output for a database update, use the "-B" flag.

% Information related to '193.246.50.0 - 193.246.50.31'

inetnum:       193.246.50.0 - 193.246.50.31
netname:       SWISS-OLYMPIC-ASSOCIATION-NET
descr:         Swiss Olympic Association
descr:         3006 Bern
country:       CH
admin-c:       CV643-RIPE
tech-c:        CV643-RIPE
status:        ASSIGNED PA
mnt-by:        CH-UNISOURCE-MNT
source:        RIPE # Filtered

% Information related to '193.246.50.0/24AS3303'

route:         193.246.50.0/24
descr:         NET-193-PA
origin:        AS3303
mnt-by:        CH-UNISOURCE-MNT
source:        RIPE # Filtered
```

`213.208.144.130`

```
% This is the RIPE Database query service.
% The objects are in RPSL format.
%
% The RIPE Database is subject to Terms and Conditions.
% See http://www.ripe.net/db/support/db-terms-conditions.pdf

% Note: this output has been filtered.
%         To receive output for a database update, use the "-B" flag.

% Information related to '213.208.144.128 - 213.208.144.191'

inetnum:       213.208.144.128 - 213.208.144.191
netname:       CARITAS-NET
descr:         Caritas der Erzdioezese Wien
```

```
descr:          1160
descr:          Wien
country:        AT
admin-c:        SH144-RIPE
tech-c:         SH144-RIPE
tech-c:         RG2284-RIPE
status:         ASSIGNED PA
mnt-by:         AS1764-MNT
source:         RIPE # Filtered
```

% Information related to '213.208.128.0/19AS1764'

```
route:          213.208.128.0/19
descr:          Provider Local Registry Block
descr:          next layer Telekommunikationsdienstleistungs- GmbH
origin:         AS1764
mnt-by:         AS1764-MNT
source:         RIPE # Filtered
```

78.41.144.41

% This is the RIPE Database query service.
% The objects are in RPSL format.
%
% The RIPE Database is subject to Terms and Conditions.
% See http://www.ripe.net/db/support/db-terms-conditions.pdf

% Note: this output has been filtered.
%   To receive output for a database update, use the "-B" flag.

% Information related to '78.41.144.0 - 78.41.144.255'

```
inetnum:        78.41.144.0 - 78.41.144.255
netname:        BKA-NET-VIE
descr:          Bundeskanzleramt Wien
country:        AT
admin-c:        TG6940-RIPE
tech-c:         BN746-RIPE
status:         ASSIGNED PA
mnt-by:         BKA-MNT
source:         RIPE # Filtered
```

% Information related to '78.41.144.0/24AS42685'

```
route:          78.41.144.0/24
descr:          BKA-NET-VIE
origin:         AS42685
mnt-by:         BKA-MNT
source:         RIPE # Filtered
```

% Information related to '78.41.144.0/23AS42685'

```
route:          78.41.144.0/23
descr:          BKA-NET
origin:         AS42685
mnt-by:         BKA-MNT
source:         RIPE # Filtered
```

195.110.213.194

% This is the RIPE Database query service.
% The objects are in RPSL format.
%
% The RIPE Database is subject to Terms and Conditions.
% See http://www.ripe.net/db/support/db-terms-conditions.pdf

% Note: this output has been filtered.
%   To receive output for a database update, use the "-B" flag.

% Information related to '195.110.213.192 - 195.110.213.199'

```
inetnum:        195.110.213.192 - 195.110.213.199
netname:        AT-LANSKY-NET
descr:          Lansky und Partner
country:        AT
admin-c:        GL840-RIPE
tech-c:         AE45-RIPE
status:         ASSIGNED PA
mnt-by:         AS12971-MNT
source:         RIPE # Filtered
```

% Information related to '195.110.192.0/19AS12971'

```
route:          195.110.192.0/19
descr:          B.I.O.S
descr:          PROVIDER
descr:          BIOS Internet Handels- und Dienstleistungs GmbH
remarks:        http://www.biosnet.at
```

```
origin:          AS12971
mnt-by:          BIOSNET-MNT
mnt-routes:      BIOSNET-MNT
source:          RIPE # Filtered
```

193.41.228.76

```
% This is the RIPE Database query service.
% The objects are in RPSL format.
%
% The RIPE Database is subject to Terms and Conditions.
% See http://www.ripe.net/db/support/db-terms-conditions.pdf

% Note: this output has been filtered.
%         To receive output for a database update, use the "-B" flag.

% Information related to '193.41.228.0 - 193.41.228.255'

inetnum:         193.41.228.0 - 193.41.228.255
netname:         SBGLAND-NET
descr:           Amt der Salzburger Landesregierung
country:         AT
admin-c:         SNOC2-RIPE
tech-c:          SNOC2-RIPE
status:          ASSIGNED PI
mnt-by:          RIPE-NCC-HM-PI-MNT
mnt-lower:       RIPE-NCC-HM-PI-MNT
mnt-by:          SALZBURG-MNT
mnt-routes:      SALZBURG-MNT
mnt-domains:     SALZBURG-MNT
source:          RIPE # Filtered

% Information related to '193.41.228.0/24AS8445'

route:           193.41.228.0/24
descr:           Route Object fuer das Land Salzburg
origin:          AS8445
mnt-by:          SALZBURG-MNT
source:          RIPE # Filtered
```

195.78.53.127

```
% This is the RIPE Database query service.
```

```
% The objects are in RPSL format.
%
% The RIPE Database is subject to Terms and Conditions.
% See http://www.ripe.net/db/support/db-terms-conditions.pdf

% Note: this output has been filtered.
%        To receive output for a database update, use the "-B" flag.

% Information related to '195.78.52.0 - 195.78.53.255'

inetnum:        195.78.52.0 - 195.78.53.255
netname:        CSCAT-NET
descr:          CSC Computer Sciences Consulting Austria GmbH
org:            ORG-CAA3-RIPE
country:        AT
admin-c:        aAG27-RIPE
tech-c:         aTG7-RIPE
status:         ASSIGNED PI
mnt-by:         RIPE-NCC-END-MNT
mnt-by:         CSC-AT-MNT
mnt-lower:      RIPE-NCC-END-MNT
mnt-routes:     CSC-AT-MNT
mnt-domains:    CSC-AT-MNT
source:         RIPE # Filtered

% Information related to '195.78.52.0/23AS28857'

route:          195.78.52.0/23
descr:          CSC Austria AG
origin:         AS28857
mnt-by:         CSC-AT-MNT
source:         RIPE # Filtered
```

`194.232.79.100`

```
% This is the RIPE Database query service.
% The objects are in RPSL format.
%
% The RIPE Database is subject to Terms and Conditions.
% See http://www.ripe.net/db/support/db-terms-conditions.pdf

% Note: this output has been filtered.
%        To receive output for a database update, use the "-B" flag.
```

% Information related to '194.232.79.96 - 194.232.79.127'

```
inetnum:        194.232.79.96 - 194.232.79.127
netname:        DiePresseNet
descr:          Local Area Network of Die PResse
country:        AT
admin-c:        KB2467-RIPE
tech-c:         AN6666-RIPE
status:         ASSIGNED PA
mnt-by:         AS5403-MNT
source:         RIPE # Filtered
```

% Information related to '194.232.0.0/16AS5403'

```
route:          194.232.0.0/16
descr:          AT-APA-960125
origin:         AS5403
mnt-by:         AS5403-MNT
org:            ORG-AAPA1-RIPE
source:         RIPE # Filtered
```

`195.230.168.36`

% This is the RIPE Database query service.
% The objects are in RPSL format.
%
% The RIPE Database is subject to Terms and Conditions.
% See http://www.ripe.net/db/support/db-terms-conditions.pdf

% Note: this output has been filtered.
%   To receive output for a database update, use the "-B" flag.

% Information related to '195.230.168.32 - 195.230.168.47'

```
inetnum:        195.230.168.32 - 195.230.168.47
netname:        LANDBGLD-NET
descr:          Amt der burgenlaendischen Landesregierung
descr:          Eisenstadt
country:        AT
admin-c:        FT1245-RIPE
tech-c:         WA527-RIPE
status:         ASSIGNED PA
mnt-by:         AS8559-MNT
source:         RIPE # Filtered
```

% Information related to '195.230.160.0/19AS8559'

```
route:          195.230.160.0/19
descr:          Well.COM
origin:         AS8559
mnt-by:         AS8559-MNT
source:         RIPE # Filtered
```

91.204.193.192

% This is the RIPE Database query service.
% The objects are in RPSL format.
%
% The RIPE Database is subject to Terms and Conditions.
% See http://www.ripe.net/db/support/db-terms-conditions.pdf

% Note: this output has been filtered.
%   To receive output for a database update, use the "-B" flag.

% Information related to '91.204.192.0 - 91.204.195.255'

```
inetnum:        91.204.192.0 - 91.204.195.255
netname:        REDBULL-SBG-NET
descr:          Red Bull GmbH
country:        AT
org:            ORG-RBG2-RIPE
admin-c:        BL2066-RIPE
tech-c:         BL2066-RIPE
status:         ASSIGNED PI
mnt-by:         RIPE-NCC-END-MNT
mnt-lower:      RIPE-NCC-END-MNT
mnt-by:         REDBULL-MNT
mnt-routes:     REDBULL-MNT
mnt-domains:    REDBULL-MNT
source:         RIPE # Filtered
```

% Information related to '91.204.192.0/22AS48151'

```
route:          91.204.192.0/22
descr:          Route Object Red Bull GmbH
origin:         AS48151
mnt-by:         REDBULL-MNT
source:         RIPE # Filtered
```

% Information related to '91.204.193.0/24AS48151'

```
route:          91.204.193.0/24
descr:          Route Object Red Bull GmbH
origin:         AS48151
mnt-by:         REDBULL-MNT
source:         RIPE # Filtered
```

`85.158.226.32`

% This is the RIPE Database query service.
% The objects are in RPSL format.
%
% The RIPE Database is subject to Terms and Conditions.
% See http://www.ripe.net/db/support/db-terms-conditions.pdf

% Note: this output has been filtered.
%   To receive output for a database update, use the "-B" flag.

% Information related to '85.158.226.32 - 85.158.226.63'

```
inetnum:        85.158.226.32 - 85.158.226.63
netname:        CNJ
descr:          Corporate Network Austria
descr:          Bundesministerium fuer Justiz
country:        AT
admin-c:        NM441-RIPE
tech-c:         HCGD1-RIPE
status:         ASSIGNED PA
mnt-by:         BRZ-MNT
source:         RIPE # Filtered
```

% Information related to '85.158.224.0/21AS8692'

```
route:          85.158.224.0/21
descr:          CNA-AT
origin:         AS8692
mnt-by:         AS8692-MNT
source:         RIPE # Filtered
```

`217.116.64.48`

% Information related to '217.116.64.0 - 217.116.67.63'

```
inetnum:        217.116.64.0 - 217.116.67.63
netname:        KAV-IT
descr:          KAV Internet
descr:          Wiener Krankenanstaltenverbund, KAV-IT
country:        AT
admin-c:        FH396-RIPE
tech-c:         SGE2-RIPE
tech-c:         NAB6-RIPE
tech-c:         WIW1-RIPE
tech-c:         LUA1-RIPE
status:         ASSIGNED PA
mnt-by:         KAV-MNT
mnt-lower:      KAV-MNT
mnt-routes:     KAV-MNT
source:         RIPE # Filtered
```

% Information related to '217.116.64.0/20AS16314'

```
route:          217.116.64.0/20
descr:          KAV Internet
origin:         AS16314
mnt-by:         KAV-MNT
source:         RIPE # Filtered
```

`193.104.125.4`

```
%        To receive output for a database update, use the "-B" flag.

% Information related to '193.104.125.0 - 193.104.125.255'

inetnum:        193.104.125.0 - 193.104.125.255
netname:        FMA-Financial-Market-Authority
descr:          Finanzmarktaufsicht
country:        AT
org:            ORG-FFMA1-RIPE
admin-c:        HS320-RIPE
tech-c:         HS320-RIPE
status:         ASSIGNED PI
mnt-by:         RIPE-NCC-END-MNT
mnt-by:         AS12878-MNT
mnt-lower:      RIPE-NCC-END-MNT
mnt-routes:     AS12878-MNT
mnt-domains:    AS12878-MNT
source:         RIPE # Filtered

% Information related to '193.104.125.0/24AS50143'

route:          193.104.125.0/24
descr:          FINANZMARKTAUFSICHT-AT-NET
origin:         AS50143
mnt-by:         AS12878-MNT
source:         RIPE # Filtered
```

195.190.15.10

```
% This is the RIPE Database query service.
% The objects are in RPSL format.
%
% The RIPE Database is subject to Terms and Conditions.
% See http://www.ripe.net/db/support/db-terms-conditions.pdf

% Note: this output has been filtered.
%        To receive output for a database update, use the "-B" flag.

% Information related to '195.190.15.0 - 195.190.15.255'

inetnum:        195.190.15.0 - 195.190.15.255
netname:        NEWS-AT-NET
descr:          NEWS VerlagsgesmbH
country:        AT
```

```
org:            ORG-NV4-RIPE
tech-c:         GK2072-RIPE
admin-c:        WW804-RIPE
status:         ASSIGNED PI
mnt-by:         RIPE-NCC-HM-PI-MNT
mnt-lower:      RIPE-NCC-HM-PI-MNT
mnt-by:         AS12878-MNT
mnt-routes:     AS12878-MNT
mnt-domains:    AS12878-MNT
source:         RIPE # Filtered
```

% Information related to '195.190.15.0/24AS47130'

```
route:          195.190.15.0/24
descr:          Verlagsgruppe NEWS GmbH
origin:         AS47130
mnt-by:         AS12878-MNT
source:         RIPE # Filtered
```

88.116.224.102

% This is the RIPE Database query service.
% The objects are in RPSL format.
%
% The RIPE Database is subject to Terms and Conditions.
% See http://www.ripe.net/db/support/db-terms-conditions.pdf

% Note: this output has been filtered.
%   To receive output for a database update, use the "-B" flag.

% Information related to '88.116.224.100 - 88.116.224.103'

```
inetnum:        88.116.224.100 - 88.116.224.103
netname:        BMF-HWY-AT
descr:          BM f. Landesverteidigung
descr:          Hetzgasse 2
descr:          1030 Wien
country:        AT
admin-c:        HMH25-RIPE
tech-c:         HMH25-RIPE
status:         ASSIGNED PA
mnt-by:         AS8447-MNT
mnt-lower:      AS8447-MNT
source:         RIPE # Filtered
```

```
% Information related to '88.116.0.0/15AS8447'

route:          88.116.0.0/15
descr:          HIGHWAY194
origin:         AS8447
remarks:        ==========================================
remarks:        please report abuse incidents (eg network
remarks:        scanning, spam originating, etc.) to
remarks:        abuse@aon.at
remarks:        ==========================================
mnt-by:         AS8447-MNT
source:         RIPE # Filtered
```

`193.187.212.100`

```
% This is the RIPE Database query service.
% The objects are in RPSL format.
%
% The RIPE Database is subject to Terms and Conditions.
% See http://www.ripe.net/db/support/db-terms-conditions.pdf

% Note: this output has been filtered.
%          To receive output for a database update, use the "-B" flag.

% Information related to '193.187.212.0 - 193.187.243.255'

inetnum:        193.187.212.0 - 193.187.243.255
netname:        RZPOST-NET
descr:          Postrechenzentrum
country:        AT
admin-c:        PA622-RIPE
tech-c:         PA622-RIPE
tech-c:         PA622-RIPE
status:         ASSIGNED PI
mnt-by:         AS8447-MNT
mnt-by:         RIPE-NCC-HM-PI-MNT
mnt-lower:      RIPE-NCC-HM-PI-MNT
mnt-routes:     AS8447-MNT
source:         RIPE # Filtered

% Information related to '193.187.212.0/22AS8447'

route:          193.187.212.0/22
```

```
descr:          RZPOST-NET
origin:         AS8447
remarks:        =============================================
remarks:        please report abuse incidents (eg network
remarks:        scanning, spam originating, etc.) to
remarks:        abuse@aon.at
remarks:        =============================================
mnt-by:         AS8447-MNT
source:         RIPE # Filtered
```

195.69.193.12

```
% This is the RIPE Database query service.
% The objects are in RPSL format.
%
% The RIPE Database is subject to Terms and Conditions.
% See http://www.ripe.net/db/support/db-terms-conditions.pdf

% Note: this output has been filtered.
%          To receive output for a database update, use the "-B" flag.

% Information related to '195.69.192.0 - 195.69.195.255'

inetnum:        195.69.192.0 - 195.69.195.255
netname:        OEBB-NET
descr:          OeBB Infrastruktur AG
country:        AT
admin-c:        OEBB1-RIPE
tech-c:         OEBB1-RIPE
status:         ASSIGNED PI
mnt-by:         RIPE-NCC-END-MNT
mnt-by:         AUSTRIAN-RAILWAYS-MNT
mnt-lower:      RIPE-NCC-END-MNT
mnt-routes:     AUSTRIAN-RAILWAYS-MNT
source:         RIPE # Filtered

% Information related to '195.69.192.0/22AS25011'

route:          195.69.192.0/22
descr:          Oesterreichische Bundesbahnen
origin:         AS25011
mnt-by:         AUSTRIAN-RAILWAYS-MNT
mnt-by:         AS1901-MNT
source:         RIPE # Filtered
```

62.154.194.53

```
% This is the RIPE Database query service.
% The objects are in RPSL format.
%
% The RIPE Database is subject to Terms and Conditions.
% See http://www.ripe.net/db/support/db-terms-conditions.pdf

% Note: this output has been filtered.
%          To receive output for a database update, use the "-B" flag.

% Information related to '62.154.194.48 - 62.154.194.63'

inetnum:        62.154.194.48 - 62.154.194.63
netname:        DBB-NET
descr:          Deutscher Beamtenbund und Tarifunion
country:        DE
admin-c:        FH1531-RIPE
tech-c:         FH1531-RIPE
status:         ASSIGNED PA
mnt-by:         DTAG-NIC
source:         RIPE # Filtered

% Information related to '62.154.0.0/15AS3320'

route:          62.154.0.0/15
descr:          Deutsche Telekom AG, Internet service provider
origin:         AS3320
member-of:      AS3320:RS-PA-TELEKOM
mnt-by:         DTAG-RR
source:         RIPE # Filtered
```

194.232.11.80

```
% This is the RIPE Database query service.
% The objects are in RPSL format.
%
% The RIPE Database is subject to Terms and Conditions.
% See http://www.ripe.net/db/support/db-terms-conditions.pdf

% Note: this output has been filtered.
%          To receive output for a database update, use the "-B" flag.
```

```
% Information related to '194.232.0.0 - 194.232.20.255'

inetnum:        194.232.0.0 - 194.232.20.255
netname:        TTZ-NET
descr:          Tiroler Tageszeitung (Moser Holding)
country:        AT
admin-c:        AN6666-RIPE
tech-c:         AN6666-RIPE
status:         ASSIGNED PA
mnt-by:         AS5403-MNT
source:         RIPE # Filtered

% Information related to '194.232.0.0/16AS5403'

route:          194.232.0.0/16
descr:          AT-APA-960125
origin:         AS5403
mnt-by:         AS5403-MNT
org:            ORG-AAPA1-RIPE
source:         RIPE # Filtered
```

91.112.214.67

```
% This is the RIPE Database query service.
% The objects are in RPSL format.
%
% The RIPE Database is subject to Terms and Conditions.
% See http://www.ripe.net/db/support/db-terms-conditions.pdf

% Note: this output has been filtered.
%       To receive output for a database update, use the "-B" flag.

% Information related to '91.112.214.64 - 91.112.214.79'

inetnum:        91.112.214.64 - 91.112.214.79
netname:        BUNDESMINIST-HWY-AT
descr:          Bundesministerium fuer Landesverteidigung
descr:          Rossauer Laende
descr:          1090 Wien
country:        AT
admin-c:        HMH25-RIPE
tech-c:         HMH25-RIPE
status:         ASSIGNED PA
```

```
mnt-by:          AS8447-MNT
mnt-lower:       AS8447-MNT
source:          RIPE # Filtered
```

% Information related to '91.112.0.0/14AS8447'

```
route:           91.112.0.0/14
descr:           HIGHWAY194
origin:          AS8447
remarks:         ==========================================
remarks:         please report abuse incidents (eg network
remarks:         scanning, spam originating, etc.) to
remarks:         abuse@aon.at
remarks:         ==========================================
mnt-by:          AS8447-MNT
source:          RIPE # Filtered
```

`194.232.11.100`

% This is the RIPE Database query service.
% The objects are in RPSL format.
%
% The RIPE Database is subject to Terms and Conditions.
% See http://www.ripe.net/db/support/db-terms-conditions.pdf

% Note: this output has been filtered.
%   To receive output for a database update, use the "-B" flag.

% Information related to '194.232.0.0 - 194.232.20.255'

```
inetnum:         194.232.0.0 - 194.232.20.255
netname:         TTZ-NET
descr:           Tiroler Tageszeitung (Moser Holding)
country:         AT
admin-c:         AN6666-RIPE
tech-c:          AN6666-RIPE
status:          ASSIGNED PA
mnt-by:          AS5403-MNT
source:          RIPE # Filtered
```

% Information related to '194.232.0.0/16AS5403'

```
route:           194.232.0.0/16
descr:           AT-APA-960125
```

```
origin:           AS5403
mnt-by:           AS5403-MNT
org:              ORG-AAPA1-RIPE
source:           RIPE # Filtered
```

`81.223.187.210`

```
% Note: this output has been filtered.
%           To receive output for a database update, use the "-B" flag.


% Information related to '81.223.187.208 - 81.223.187.223'

inetnum:          81.223.187.208 - 81.223.187.223
netname:          Modellschule-Graz
descr:
descr:            Modellschule Grazprivates Realgymnasium
descr:            Brigitte Brunsteiner
descr:            Graz
country:          AT
admin-c:          AH10082-RIPE
tech-c:           AH10082-RIPE
status:           ASSIGNED PA
mnt-by:           AT-INODE-DOM
source:           RIPE # Filtered


% Information related to '81.223.0.0/16AS8514'

route:            81.223.0.0/16
descr:            inode Internet
origin:           AS8514
mnt-by:           AT-INODE-DOM
source:           RIPE # Filtered


% Information related to '81.223.128.0/17AS6830'

route:            81.223.128.0/17
descr:            UPC Austria GmbH
origin:           AS6830
```

```
mnt-by:            AS6830-MNT
source:            RIPE # Filtered
```

203.172.248.174

```
% [whois.apnic.net node-4]
% Whois data copyright terms     http://www.apnic.net/db/dbcopyright.

inetnum:           203.172.192.0 - 203.172.255.255
netname:           MOE-NET
descr:             Static IP for schools and offices under administrati
descr:             Ministry of Education Network Operation Center
country:           th
admin-c:           CL3-AP
tech-c:            MS2-AP
status:            assigned non-portable
mnt-by:            MAINT-TH-MOE-EDNET
changed:           apipolg@tot.co.th 20100226
source:            APNIC
```

194.107.234.50

```
% This is the RIPE Database query service.
% The objects are in RPSL format.
%
% The RIPE Database is subject to Terms and Conditions.
% See http://www.ripe.net/db/support/db-terms-conditions.pdf

% Note: this output has been filtered.
%         To receive output for a database update, use the "-B" flag.

% Information related to '194.107.232.0 - 194.107.247.255'

inetnum:           194.107.232.0 - 194.107.247.255
netname:           WK-NET
descr:             Wirtschaftskammer Oesterreich
country:           AT
org:               ORG-WO16-RIPE
admin-c:           SB12558-RIPE
tech-c:            AP12441-RIPE
mnt-by:            RIPE-NCC-HM-PI-MNT
mnt-lower:         RIPE-NCC-HM-PI-MNT
mnt-by:            WKO-MNT
```

```
mnt-routes:        WKO-MNT
mnt-routes:        i3B-MNT
mnt-domains:       WKO-MNT
status:            ASSIGNED PI
source:            RIPE # Filtered


% Information related to '194.107.232.0/21AS39912'

route:             194.107.232.0/21
descr:             WKO Inhouse GmbH
origin:            AS39912
remarks:           --------------------------------------------
remarks:           for routing issues with this prefix you can
remarks:           contact core@ascus.at
remarks:           --------------------------------------------
mnt-by:            WKO-MNT
source:            RIPE # Filtered
```

```
195.248.32.227
```

```
% This is the RIPE Database query service.
% The objects are in RPSL format.
%
% The RIPE Database is subject to Terms and Conditions.
% See http://www.ripe.net/db/support/db-terms-conditions.pdf

% Note: this output has been filtered.
%        To receive output for a database update, use the "-B" flag.

% Information related to '195.248.32.0 - 195.248.32.255'

inetnum:           195.248.32.0 - 195.248.32.255
netname:           RZB-WIEN
descr:             Raiffeisen Zentralbank
descr:             Am Stadtpark 9
descr:             A-1030 Wien
country:           AT
tech-c:            UI01-RIPE
admin-c:           UI01-RIPE
status:            ASSIGNED PA
mnt-by:            AS8437-MNT
source:            RIPE # Filtered

% Information related to '195.248.32.0/24AS8437'
```

```
route:          195.248.32.0/24
descr:          Tele2 Telecommunication GmbH
descr:          Donaucitystrasse 11
descr:          A-1220 Vienna
origin:         AS8437
mnt-by:         AS8437-MNT
member-of:      RS-UTA
remarks:        ====================================================
remarks:        UTA - Network Operation Center
remarks:
remarks:        mail:  service@uta.at
remarks:        phone: +43 1 9009 3333 or 0800-882 662
remarks:        fax:   +43 1 9009 3599
remarks:
remarks:        Abuse contact: abuse@uta.at
remarks:        ====================================================
source:         RIPE # Filtered
```

% Information related to '195.248.32.0/19AS8437'

```
route:          195.248.32.0/19
descr:          Tele2 Telecommunication GmbH
descr:          Donaucitystrasse 11
descr:          A-1220 Vienna
origin:         AS8437
mnt-by:         AS8437-MNT
member-of:      RS-UTA
remarks:        ====================================================
remarks:        UTA - Network Operation Center
remarks:
remarks:        mail:  service@uta.at
remarks:        phone: +43 1 9009 3333 or 0800-882 662
remarks:        fax:   +43 1 9009 3599
remarks:
remarks:        Abuse contact: abuse@uta.at
remarks:        ====================================================
source:         RIPE # Filtered
```

`80.120.182.178`

% This is the RIPE Database query service.
% The objects are in RPSL format.
%

% Information related to '80.120.182.176 - 80.120.182.179'

```
inetnum:        80.120.182.176 - 80.120.182.179
netname:        HOTE-HWY-AT
descr:          Hotel Roemischer Kaiser
descr:          Annagasse 16
descr:          1010 Wien
country:        AT
admin-c:        GJ345-RIPE
tech-c:         GJ345-RIPE
status:         ASSIGNED PA
mnt-by:         AS8447-MNT
mnt-lower:      AS8447-MNT
source:         RIPE # Filtered
```

% Information related to '80.120.0.0/14AS8447'

```
route:          80.120.0.0/14
descr:          HIGHWAY194
origin:         AS8447
remarks:        =========================================
remarks:        please report abuse incidents (eg network
remarks:        scanning, spam originating, etc.) to
remarks:        abuse@aon.at
remarks:        =========================================
mnt-by:         AS8447-MNT
source:         RIPE # Filtered
```

193.17.232.2

% Information related to '193.17.232.0 - 193.17.247.255'

```
inetnum:        193.17.232.0 - 193.17.247.255
netname:        BUNDESTAG
descr:          Deutscher Bundestag
descr:          11011 Berlin
country:        DE
admin-c:        MK3064-RIPE
tech-c:         MO687-RIPE
status:         ASSIGNED PI
mnt-by:         DFN-LIR-MNT
mnt-by:         RIPE-NCC-HM-PI-MNT
mnt-lower:      RIPE-NCC-HM-PI-MNT
mnt-routes:     DFN-MNT
mnt-routes:     WCOM-EMEA-RICE-MNT
mnt-domains:    DFN-HM-MNT
source:         RIPE # Filtered
```

% Information related to '193.17.232.0/22AS702'

```
route:          193.17.232.0/22
descr:          Deutscher Bundestag
descr:          205031.00001
origin:         AS702
member-of:      AS702:RS-DE,
                AS702:RS-DE-PI,
                AS702:RS-DE-PULLUP
inject:         upon static
mnt-by:         WCOM-EMEA-RICE-MNT
source:         RIPE # Filtered
```

`78.41.149.241`

% This is the RIPE Database query service.
% The objects are in RPSL format.
%
% The RIPE Database is subject to Terms and Conditions.
% See http://www.ripe.net/db/support/db-terms-conditions.pdf

% Note: this output has been filtered.
%   To receive output for a database update, use the "-B" flag.

% Information related to '78.41.149.0 - 78.41.149.255'

```
inetnum:          78.41.149.0 - 78.41.149.255
netname:          BMI-IV-NET
descr:            Bundesministerium fuer Inneres, Sektion IV
country:          AT
admin-c:          KMW7-RIPE
tech-c:           BGER1-RIPE
status:           ASSIGNED PA
mnt-by:           BKA-MNT
source:           RIPE # Filtered
```

% Information related to '78.41.149.0/24AS47515'

```
route:            78.41.149.0/24
descr:            BMI-IV-NET
origin:           AS47515
mnt-by:           BKA-MNT
source:           RIPE # Filtered
```

`194.232.79.193`

% This is the RIPE Database query service.
% The objects are in RPSL format.
%
% The RIPE Database is subject to Terms and Conditions.
% See http://www.ripe.net/db/support/db-terms-conditions.pdf

% Note: this output has been filtered.
%   To receive output for a database update, use the "-B" flag.

% Information related to '194.232.79.192 - 194.232.79.223'

```
inetnum:          194.232.79.192 - 194.232.79.223
netname:          BMA-LAN
descr:            BMEIA
org:              ORG-Bfeu1-RIPE
country:          AT
admin-c:          HW1080-RIPE
admin-c:          JL7010-RIPE
tech-c:           AN6666-RIPE
status:           ASSIGNED PA
mnt-by:           AS5403-MNT
source:           RIPE # Filtered
```

% Information related to '194.232.0.0/16AS5403'

```
route:          194.232.0.0/16
descr:          AT-APA-960125
origin:         AS5403
mnt-by:         AS5403-MNT
org:            ORG-AAPA1-RIPE
source:         RIPE # Filtered
```

`80.120.179.10`

% This is the RIPE Database query service.
% The objects are in RPSL format.
%
% The RIPE Database is subject to Terms and Conditions.
% See http://www.ripe.net/db/support/db-terms-conditions.pdf

% Note: this output has been filtered.
%   To receive output for a database update, use the "-B" flag.

% Information related to '80.120.179.0 - 80.120.179.63'

```
inetnum:        80.120.179.0 - 80.120.179.63
netname:        BMI-GV-AT
descr:          Bundesministerium fuer Inneres
country:        AT
admin-c:        CF678-RIPE
tech-c:         CF678-RIPE
status:         ASSIGNED PA
mnt-by:         AS8447-MNT
mnt-lower:      AS8447-MNT
source:         RIPE # Filtered
```

% Information related to '80.120.0.0/14AS8447'

```
route:          80.120.0.0/14
descr:          HIGHWAY194
origin:         AS8447
remarks:        =========================================
remarks:        please report abuse incidents (eg network
remarks:        scanning, spam originating, etc.) to
remarks:        abuse@aon.at
remarks:        =========================================
mnt-by:         AS8447-MNT
```

source: RIPE # Filtered

% This is the RIPE Database query service.
% The objects are in RPSL format.
%
% The RIPE Database is subject to Terms and Conditions.
% See http://www.ripe.net/db/support/db-terms-conditions.pdf

% Note: this output has been filtered.
%   To receive output for a database update, use the "-B" flag.

% Information related to '194.138.0.0 - 194.138.255.255'

```
inetnum:       194.138.0.0 - 194.138.255.255
netname:       SIEMENS-EURO
descr:         Siemens AG
descr:         world headquarter
descr:         Wittelsbacherplatz 2
descr:         DE-80333
descr:         Munich
descr:         sites in Europe
org:           ORG-SNIC1-RIPE
country:       DE
admin-c:       SNIC1-RIPE
tech-c:        SNIC1-RIPE
status:        ASSIGNED PI
mnt-by:        SAG-MNT
mnt-lower:     SAG-MNT
mnt-routes:    SAG-MNT
source:        RIPE # Filtered
```

% Information related to '194.138.12.0/24AS8971'

```
route:         194.138.12.0/24
descr:         Siemens AT
origin:        AS8971
remarks:       Siemens AG
remarks:       main web server
mnt-by:        AS8971-MNT
mnt-by:        SAG-MNT
source:        RIPE # Filtered
```

```
217.13.180.202
```

% This is the RIPE Database query service.
% The objects are in RPSL format.
%
% The RIPE Database is subject to Terms and Conditions.
% See http://www.ripe.net/db/support/db-terms-conditions.pdf

% Note: this output has been filtered.
%   To receive output for a database update, use the "-B" flag.

% Information related to '217.13.180.192 - 217.13.180.255'

```
inetnum:      217.13.180.192 - 217.13.180.255
netname:      RI-BEV
descr:        Bundesamt fuer Eich- und Vermessungswesen
descr:        www.bev.gv.at
country:      AT
admin-c:      ET1089-RIPE
tech-c:       ET1089-RIPE
status:       ASSIGNED PA
remarks:      -------------------------------
remarks:      For notifying SPAM or ABUSE,
remarks:      send inquiries to ET1089-RIPE
remarks:      -------------------------------
mnt-by:       AS24864-MNT
source:       RIPE # Filtered
```

% Information related to '217.13.176.0/20AS24864'

```
route:        217.13.176.0/20
descr:        [company] Raiffeisen Informatik GmbH
              [street] Lilienbrunngasse 7-9
              [postal code] A-1020
              [city] Vienna
              [country] Austria
              http://raiffeiseninformatik.at
origin:       AS24864
mnt-by:       AS24864-MNT
source:       RIPE # Filtered
```

```
85.158.227.72
```

% This is the RIPE Database query service.
% The objects are in RPSL format.
%
% The RIPE Database is subject to Terms and Conditions.
% See http://www.ripe.net/db/support/db-terms-conditions.pdf

% Note: this output has been filtered.
%   To receive output for a database update, use the "-B" flag.

% Information related to '85.158.227.24 - 85.158.227.255'

```
inetnum:        85.158.227.24 - 85.158.227.255
netname:        CNAx-AT
descr:          Corporate Network Austria next generation
descr:          Bundesrechenzentrum GmbH
country:        AT
admin-c:        NM441-RIPE
tech-c:         HCGD1-RIPE
status:         ASSIGNED PA
mnt-by:         BRZ-MNT
source:         RIPE # Filtered
```

% Information related to '85.158.224.0/21AS8692'

```
route:          85.158.224.0/21
descr:          CNA-AT
origin:         AS8692
mnt-by:         AS8692-MNT
source:         RIPE # Filtered
```

`188.21.98.198`

% This is the RIPE Database query service.
% The objects are in RPSL format.
%
% The RIPE Database is subject to Terms and Conditions.
% See http://www.ripe.net/db/support/db-terms-conditions.pdf

% Note: this output has been filtered.
%   To receive output for a database update, use the "-B" flag.

% Information related to '188.21.98.196 - 188.21.98.199'

```
inetnum:        188.21.98.196 - 188.21.98.199
```

```
netname:        ASYLKOORDINA-HWY-AT
descr:          Asylkoordination Oesterreich
descr:          Laudongasse
descr:          1080 Wien
country:        AT
admin-c:        HMH25-RIPE
tech-c:         HMH25-RIPE
status:         ASSIGNED PA
mnt-by:         AS8447-MNT
mnt-lower:      AS8447-MNT
source:         RIPE # Filtered
```

% Information related to '188.20.0.0/14AS8447'

```
route:          188.20.0.0/14
descr:          HIGHWAY194
origin:         AS8447
remarks:        =========================================
remarks:        please report abuse incidents (eg network
remarks:        scanning, spam originating, etc.) to
remarks:        abuse@aon.at
remarks:        =========================================
mnt-by:         AS8447-MNT
source:         RIPE # Filtered
```

`144.65.158.38`

% This is the RIPE Database query service.
% The objects are in RPSL format.
%
% The RIPE Database is subject to Terms and Conditions.
% See http://www.ripe.net/db/support/db-terms-conditions.pdf

% Note: this output has been filtered.
%   To receive output for a database update, use the "-B" flag.

% Information related to '144.65.0.0 - 144.65.255.255'

```
inetnum:        144.65.0.0 - 144.65.255.255
netname:        BMWFNET
descr:          Austrian Federal Ministry of Science and Research
descr:          Minoritenplatz 5
descr:          Vienna, A 1014
country:        AT
```

```
admin-c:        KU4-RIPE
tech-c:         JS8207-RIPE
tech-c:         KU4-RIPE
status:         EARLY-REGISTRATION
mnt-by:         AT-GV-BMWF-MNT
mnt-lower:      AT-GV-BMWF-MNT
mnt-routes:     AT-GV-BMWF-MNT
source:         RIPE # Filtered


person:         Klemens Urban
address:        Austrian Federal Ministry of Science and Research
address:        Minoritenplatz 5
address:        1014 Vienna
address:        Austria
phone:          +43-1-53120-9720
phone:          +43-664-6109147
fax-no:         +43-1-53120-999720
e-mail:         klemens.urban@bmwf.gv.at
nic-hdl:        KU4-RIPE
mnt-by:         AT-GV-BMWF-MNT
source:         RIPE # Filtered


person:         Joerg Steiner
address:        Austrian Federal Ministry of Science and Research
address:        Minoritenplatz 5
address:        1014 Vienna
address:        Austria
phone:          +43-1-53120-9716
fax-no:         +43-1-53120-819716
e-mail:         Joerg.Steiner@bmwf.gv.at
nic-hdl:        JS8207-RIPE
mnt-by:         AT-GV-BMWF-MNT
source:         RIPE # Filtered


% Information related to '144.65.0.0/16AS1853'

route:          144.65.0.0/16
descr:          BMWFNET
origin:         AS1853
mnt-by:         AS1853-MNT
source:         RIPE # Filtered
```

193.5.216.100

% This is the RIPE Database query service.
% The objects are in RPSL format.
%
% The RIPE Database is subject to Terms and Conditions.
% See http://www.ripe.net/db/support/db-terms-conditions.pdf

% Note: this output has been filtered.
%   To receive output for a database update, use the "-B" flag.

% Information related to '193.5.216.0 - 193.5.223.255'

```
inetnum:        193.5.216.0 - 193.5.223.255
netname:        KOMBV
descr:          Swiss Federal Government
descr:          Berne, Switzerland
country:        CH
org:            ORG-SFrb1-RIPE
admin-c:        MH2447-RIPE
tech-c:         BIT1-RIPE
status:         ASSIGNED PI
mnt-by:         CH-BIT-MNT
source:         RIPE # Filtered
```

% Information related to '193.5.216.0/21AS33845'

```
route:          193.5.216.0/21
descr:          SWISSGOV
origin:         AS33845
mnt-by:         CH-BIT-MNT
source:         RIPE # Filtered
```

`85.158.226.1`

% This is the RIPE Database query service.
% The objects are in RPSL format.
%
% The RIPE Database is subject to Terms and Conditions.
% See http://www.ripe.net/db/support/db-terms-conditions.pdf

% Note: this output has been filtered.
%   To receive output for a database update, use the "-B" flag.

% Information related to '85.158.226.0 - 85.158.226.31'

```
inetnum:        85.158.226.0 - 85.158.226.31
netname:        CNF
descr:          Corporate Network Austria
descr:          Bundesministerium fuer Finanzen
country:        AT
admin-c:        NM441-RIPE
tech-c:         HCGD1-RIPE
status:         ASSIGNED PA
mnt-by:         BRZ-MNT
source:         RIPE # Filtered


% Information related to '85.158.224.0/21AS8692'

route:          85.158.224.0/21
descr:          CNA-AT
origin:         AS8692
mnt-by:         AS8692-MNT
source:         RIPE # Filtered
```

80.122.56.230

```
% This is the RIPE Database query service.
% The objects are in RPSL format.
%
% The RIPE Database is subject to Terms and Conditions.
% See http://www.ripe.net/db/support/db-terms-conditions.pdf

% Note: this output has been filtered.
%        To receive output for a database update, use the "-B" flag.

% Information related to '80.122.56.228 - 80.122.56.231'

inetnum:        80.122.56.228 - 80.122.56.231
netname:        BUND-HWY-AT
descr:          Bundesministerium fuer Landesverteidigung
descr:          Garnisonstrasse 36/3
descr:          4020 Linz
country:        AT
admin-c:        HMH25-RIPE
tech-c:         HMH25-RIPE
status:         ASSIGNED PA
mnt-by:         AS8447-MNT
mnt-lower:      AS8447-MNT
source:         RIPE # Filtered
```

% Information related to '80.120.0.0/14AS8447'

```
route:          80.120.0.0/14
descr:          HIGHWAY194
origin:         AS8447
remarks:        ===========================================
remarks:        please report abuse incidents (eg network
remarks:        scanning, spam originating, etc.) to
remarks:        abuse@aon.at
remarks:        ===========================================
mnt-by:         AS8447-MNT
source:         RIPE # Filtered
```

193.228.104.102

% This is the RIPE Database query service.
% The objects are in RPSL format.
%
% The RIPE Database is subject to Terms and Conditions.
% See http://www.ripe.net/db/support/db-terms-conditions.pdf

% Note: this output has been filtered.
%   To receive output for a database update, use the "-B" flag.

% Information related to '193.228.104.0 - 193.228.107.255'

```
inetnum:        193.228.104.0 - 193.228.107.255
netname:        LENZING-NET
descr:          Lenzing AG
country:        AT
admin-c:        AIJ-RIPE
tech-c:         AIJ-RIPE
status:         ASSIGNED PI
mnt-by:         LENZING-MNT
mnt-by:         RIPE-NCC-HM-PI-MNT
mnt-lower:      RIPE-NCC-HM-PI-MNT
source:         RIPE # Filtered
```

% Information related to '193.228.104.0/22AS30739'

```
route:          193.228.104.0/22
descr:          LENZING-NET
origin:         AS30739
```

```
mnt-by:        LENZING-MNT
source:        RIPE # Filtered

% Information related to '193.228.104.0/24AS30739'

route:         193.228.104.0/24
descr:         LENZING-NET
origin:        AS30739
mnt-by:        LENZING-MNT
source:        RIPE # Filtered
```

3 Epilog

English

The project Asylum Defense Agency was developed in 2010 for an exhibition at the posh off-space "das Weisse Haus" in Vienna as a net.art project as well as a large-scale installation. It was subsequently shown in museums in Holland, Switzerland, England, Korea and China. The project installtion itself is a bastard hybrid, a melange of a counterintelligence bureau (situated within the Ministry of Defense) and a federal asylum agency (part of the Ministry of the Interior) within 4 rooms in an exhibition space of 400 square meters. The installation was aesthetically modeled to work as a perfect copy of a functional federal office. It offered the user (visitor) the possibility to slip into the job of an official of the Asylum Defense Agency: sifting through paper or computer documents of asylum seekers and special agents employed by the agency as well as accessing other relevant real-life objects and watching edutainment videos in order to conduct private research into the matters of the Asylum Defence Agency.

In the entrance area of the installation we find a classic waiting room, its walls covered with governmental print-outs that were originally planned as "artefakes" (fake facts), but due to the now more than surreal reality in the field of European immigration and asylum policy, we were able to use actual artefacts from diverse government agencies as well as NGOs. The information on these leaflets was extremely reactionary & dadaistic and worked perfectly in confusing the hell out of visitors of the exhibition - the content provided a perverse authenticity and the slightly uncomfortable feeling that one expects to experience in an government office. Passive aggressive, stuffy and bleak but also beautiful, well-lit and familiar. Secure.

The "AABA logfile" published here is the core of the website Asylabwehramt.at. Just like in any nautical, aeronautical and space travel log, this book shows line by line all movement registered in the webserver logs. No digital twitching, no errors, no search goes undedected. The logfile begins on 4 June 2010 and ends on 11 April 2011. The WHOIS section is the most revealing and most exciting part of the book, here one can find resolved IP addresses, revealing the people and/or institution behind the query or server request. The entire logfile is a pool of raw data in chronological order but not necessarily to be read in a linear fashion. You will find no additional texts is in this book apart from this one.

If you think this publication is violating privacy rights of users of the website, then we would like to point out chapter 231, first paragraph (3) letter (j) of our user agreement which grants the operators of the website the irrevocable right to use all data collected for their own purposes and for any publication. After all, if you have never been a bad citizin, you got nothing to hide, right?

UBERMORGEN.COM, Wien, Juli 2011

Deutsch

Das Projekt Asylabwehramt wurde 2010 fuer eine Ausstellung im "das Weisse Haus" Wien als net.art Projekt und als Grossrauminstallation entwickelt und in der Folge in Museen in Holland, Schweiz, England, Korea und China gezeigt. Es entstand ein Hybrid aus dem im Verteidigungsministerium beheimateten Abwehramt und dem zum Innenministerium gehoerigen Asylamt auf 400m2 Ausstellungflaeche. Die Installation war aesthetisch zu 100% einem funktionellen Buero nachempfunden und bot dem User (Visitor) die Moeglichkeit, sich selbst an den Arbeitsplatz eines Beamten des Asylabwehramtes zu setzen und dort einerseits auf Papier oder im Computer Dokumente zu durchforsten und durchzuarbeiten und andererseits einschlägige Objekte anzusehen, Edutainment Videos anzuschauen oder auch selbst Recherche zu betreiben.

Im Eingangsbereich der Installation befindet sich ein klassischer Warteraum, die dort affichierten Ausdrucke waren urspruenglich als Artefakes (gefaelschte

Tatsachen) geplant, wurden dann aber aufgrund der mittlerweile schon mehr als surrealen Realitaet im Bereich der europaeischen Immigrations- und Asylpolitik durch Artefakte ersetzt, die die Besucher der Ausstellung aufgrund der ueberaus reaktionaeren und dadaistischen Inhalte dermassen verwirren, dass sich sogleich eine perverse Authentizitaet und auch die bekannte leicht unangenehme Stimmung einer Amtsstube einstellte. Passiv-aggressiv, miefig und duester aber auch schoen, lichtdurchflutet und vertraut. Sicher.

Mit dem "AAbA Logfile" wird der wichtigste Herzstueck der Asylabwehramt.at Website, das Logfile, publiziert. Wie in der Raumfahrt oder der Seefahrt wird in diesem "Buch" Zeile fuer Zeile jegliche Bewegung auf dem Webserver registriert und detailliert aufgeschrieben. Kein digitales Zucken, keine Errors, kein Suchbegriff entgehen dem aufmerksamen Auge. Das hier abgedruckte Logfile beginnt am 4. Juni 2010 und endet am 11. April 2011. Die WHOIS Sektion ist der aufschlussreichste Teil des Buches: hier sind IP Adressen aufgeloest und damit die Person oder Institution hinter der Suchanfrage,/Serveranfrage sichtbar. Das ganze Logfile ist ein chronologisch aber nicht notwendigerweise linear zu lesendes Pool an Rohdaten. Bis auf diesen Text gibt es in diesem Buch keine publizierten Informationen.

Wenn Sie denken, wir verstossen mit dieser Publikation gegen die Persoenlichkeitsrechte der User der Website, dann möchten wir Sie an unsere AGBs, im besonderen Paragraph 231 Absatz (3) Buchstabe (j) erinnern, der den Betreibern der Website das unwiderrufliche Recht gibt, alle erhaltenen Daten zum eigenen Zwecke und zu jedweder Veroeffentlichung zu nutzen. Wer eine weisse Weste hat, hat ja schliesslich nichts zu verstecken.

UBERMORGEN.COM, Wien, Juli 2011

4 Asylabwehramt

Das Asylabwehramt (AAbA) ist dem Abwehramt (AbwA) und dem Bundeasylamt übergeordnet und untersteht dem Bundesministerium fuer Landesverteidigung und Sport (BMLVS). Die teilanonyme und teilautonome Behörde ist zuständig fuer Prävention, Asylgesuchstellung im Ausland, Anonymisierung des Asylverfahrens, Aufklärung des Schlepperwesens, Immigrationsdiversion, Abwehr von überzähligen Flüchtlingen und AsylbewerberInnen, Selektion (Wirtschaftsflüchtlinge, Einbürgerungen), geheime Abschiebungen (kontrollierte Ausreisen), Migrationsanalysen, Automatisierung des Asylwesens, Volksschutz, Vermeidung von Retraumatisierung und dem Ausbau bürokratischer Hindernisse.

Das Amt verfügt über eine eigene schnelle Eingreiftruppe und beschäftigt private Sicherheitsdienste die im In- und Ausland taetig sind. Das Abwehramt dient dem Eigenschutz des Landes und der Bevölkerung, d.h. es soll Invasion und Unterminierung durch ungewollte Immigrationssubjekte und Terror durch ebensolche Personen und Gruppen in Österreich und in den Herkunftsländern aufklären und präventiv und/oder mit/ohne Gewalt verhindern (IMMINTEL). Das Asylabwehramt verfügt sowohl über bürokratische Instrumente (administrativ - judikativ) als auch über Weisungskompetenz bei den exekutiven Diensten (Eingreiftruppen, Fremdenpolizei, Militär, private Sicherheitsdienste) und verfügt über legale aktive und passive Gewaltinstrumente wie Folter, unterlassene Hilfestellung und Tötung.

Desweiteren gibt es beim AAbA bei OMV/Strabag/Frontex angesiedelte, gesicherte und anonyme Anlaufstellen für freiwillig Ausreisende (ausgelagerte Servicestelle PATSEC: Expatriation/Rueckführung). Damit steht der gesicherten Rückkehr in die Heimat nichts mehr im Wege (RueckkehrServiceHotline 0800 20 30 40). Hierzu stehen den Flüchtlingen und AsylbewerberInnen kompetente Mitar-

Asylabwehramt*

beiter zur Verfügung die individuell über die Zukunftsperspektiven in den Zielländern aufklären.

Im Rahmen des österreichischen Rechtsschutzsystems hat das Asylabwehramt die Aufgabe, das verwaltungsbehördliche Handeln der ersten Instanz im Asylverfahren (die Bescheide des Bundesasylamts) auf rechtmäßigen und ordnungsgemäßen Vollzug der einschlägigen Bestimmungen, durch glaubhafte anonyme Gutachter zu überprüfen.

Das Wiener Büro des Asylabwehramtes gliedert sich auf in einen Empfangsraum, Sachbearbeiter- und Chefbüro mit angeschlossenem Screeningraum fuer Videokonferenzen mit den jeweiligen Aussenstellen, audiovisuelle Dokumentationen und Unterhaltung.

Mit den besten Grüßen,
(elektronisch gefertigt)
OARat Dr. Andreas Bichelbauer
http://www.asylabwehramt.at

5 Asylum Defence Agency

The Asylum Defence Agency (Asylabwehramt, AAbA) is superordinated to the Defence Office (Abwehramt, AbwA) as well as the Federal Asylum Office and subordinated to the Federal Ministry of National Defence and Sports.

This semi-anonymous and semi-autonomic Agency is responsible for anonymization of asylum proceedings, stopping human trafficking, immigration diversion, and for defending against surplus refugees and asylum seekers. The Agency also takes action in the fields of imigration pre-selection (economic refugees, naturalization), secret deportation, migration analysis for national protection as well as in prevention of re-traumatization and the expansion of bureaucratic barriers.

The Agency disposes of its own intervention force and employs a private security agency which operates both nationally and internationally. The Defense Agency serves the country's and people's self-protection. Subsequently, the Agency takes part in resolving as well as preventing and/or with/without violence the invasion and the undermining of unwanted immigration subjects and the terror occurred through them and through groups in Austria as well as in their countries of origin (IMMINTEL). The Asylum Defense Agency possesses bureaucratic instruments (administrative – adjudicative) as well as instruction competence in the executive ministries (deployment force, immigration authorities, military, private security services) as well as an expanded expertise covering affairs such as torture, denial of assistance and homicides.

Furthermore there are externally located, secured and anonymous centres for people leaving a country deliberately (service point for expatriation/repatriation - PATSEC, outsourced to the leading oil and building construction corporations OMV, Frontex and STRABAG). This service ensures a safe travel back home (ServiceHotline 0800 20 30 40). Our competent employees offer assistance to all refugees in opening up new perspectives for the refugee's future options in the respective destination country.

The Asylum Defence Agency is also the authority charged with the enforcement of adminstrative acts in all asylum proceedings (first instance verdicts of the Federal Asylum Office). Core to its activities in this field are trustworthy anonymous experts and their respective reports, which are vital in scrutinising any affidavits and reports given by individual refugees and witnesses.

The Office of the Asylum Defence Agency in Vienna consists of a lobby, an adminsitrative office and a head office with an adjacent screening room equipped for video-conferencing with the Agency's international satellite offices, as well as audiovisual documentations and entertainment.

Sincerely yours,
(digitally signed)
OARat Dr. Andreas Bichelbauer
http://www.asylabwehramt.at

6 ADDENDUM: Die ZEIT: "Asyl? Nicht mit uns!"

Eine neue Behörde organisiert die Verteidigung der Heimat gegen Flüchtlinge und Schlepperkriminalität. Ihr Auftrag sorgt für Irritationen – genau das wollen die Künstler.

Sandra Baierl mag es eher streng. Die Beine korrekt übereinandergeschlagen, sitzt die 36-Jährige mit durchgestrecktem Rücken an ihrem Schreibtisch. Eng taillierter Businessanzug, ordentliche Ponyfrisur, eisige Augen. Die Sachbearbeiterin ist abwehrbereit. Und das von Amts wegen. Schließlich arbeitet sie in einer Behörde, die Tag für Tag im Kampf gegen Flüchtlinge, Überfremdung und Schlepperkriminalität steht: dem Asylabwehramt (AAbA).

Die Behörde operiert in einem politisch hochsensiblen Bereich, auf Publicity wird naturgemäß wenig Wert gelegt. Doch im Schatten der grassierenden Debatte um die Abschiebung der Flüchtlingsfamilie Zogaj gelang es derZEIT erstmals, Einblick in die Arbeit des klandestinen Diensts zu gewinnen. »Wir sind bestrebt, die Invasion und Unterminierung der Republik durch ungewollte Immigrationssubjekte zu verhindern«, beschreibt Baierl den Auftrag des AAbA. »In erster Linie geht es um den Volksschutz. Wir sind aber auch dafür da, Abschiebeorgane bei Fragen zu kontrollierten Ausreisen von Schüblingen zu unterstützen. Wenn's da zu Problemen kommt, sind ja die Kollegen immer mit Anschuldigungen der Presse konfrontiert«, weiß die Beamtin. Ihr Kollege Peter Haslinger, ein massiger Mittdreißiger mit glatt rasiertem Schädel, nickt stumm. Hinter seinen dicken Brillengläsern schwimmt ein argwöhnischer Blick. »Aber damit ist nun Schluss«, poltert der Ex-Security-Mitarbeiter plötzlich, und seine volle Stimme hallt von den Wänden der Amtsräume.

Seit Kurzem residieren die Staatsdiener in der Wollzeile, einer noblen Adresse in der Wiener City. Nur ein schlichtes Metallschild mit dem Amtswappen verweist darauf, dass im vierten Stock des unscheinbaren Hauses die Verteidigung der Heimat gegen Asylmissbrauch und illegale Einwanderung organisiert wird. Wer bis hierher vordringt, wird sofort mit der effizientesten Waffe des Beamtenstaates konfrontiert: dem Wartezimmer. Einige abgewetzte Holzstühle möblieren den Raum, die Wände sind mit in Klarsichtfolie gehüllten Aushängen gepflastert. Darauf preist etwa das Innenministerium die Vorteile einer raschen Rückkehr eines Asylwerbers in die Heimat an. »Planen Sie aktiv Ihre Zukunft«, steht auf dem Papier, darunter eine Gratishotline-Nummer. In unzähligen Sprachen wird über die freiwillige Ausreise informiert, dazwischen hängt in roter Fettschrift ein Hinweis in eigener Sache: »Warten! Sie werden abgeholt!«

Eine Tür weiter verrichtet Frau Baierl gemeinsam mit einem Bürolehrling ihre Arbeit. Hinter hohen Aktenstapeln tippen die beiden eifrig auf ihren Computertastaturen. Herr Haslinger schlichtet mit feierlicher Miene Asylanträge. Die Kaffeemaschine gluckert, im Radio dudelt leise Ö3. An der Wand kleben bunte Urlaubskarten von den Kollegen – man liebt die Ferne, so sie einem nicht zu nahe kommt. Auf eine seltsame Art gemütlich wirkt dieser mit persönlichem Tinnef behübschte Raum, wie ein aus der Zeit gefallenes Passamt. Wenn da nicht die Packung Einweghandschuhe auf Frau Baierls Schreibtisch wäre.

Gediegener, nachgerade feudal hat es sich hingegen Oberamtsrat Andreas Bichelbauer in seinem Büro eingerichtet: Auf dem opulenten Holzschreibtisch thront eine repräsentative Messinglampe, neobarocke Fauteuils harren der Besucher. »Der Herr Oberamtsrat weilt zurzeit auf Weiterbildung in den USA«, sagt der Bürolehrling mit devot gesenkter Stimme. Sein Aufbruch dürfte überstürzt erfolgt sein: In der halb geöffneten Schreibtischschublade liegt noch seine Dienstpistole, eine Glock 26, in Fachkreisen als Baby Glock bekannt.

Bloß ein dezenter Hinweisgeber, dass hier der Obrigkeitsstaat den Kettenhund losgelassen hat. Zum Bundesministerium für Landesverteidigung ressortierend, steht der Apparat hierarchisch über dem Abwehramt, dem militärischen Inlandsnachrichtendienst als auch dem Bundesasylamt. Auf der »Heimseite« der Behörde gibt die »teilanonyme und teilautonome« Einrichtung darüber Auskunft, wie sie diese Machtfülle einzusetzen gedenkt: »Das Amt verfügt sowohl über bürokratische Instrumente und über die Weisungskompetenz bei den exekutiven Diensten als auch über legale aktive und passive Gewaltinstrumente wie Folter, unterlassene Hilfestellung und Tötung«, steht da geschrieben.

Nicht weniger als 350 Mitarbeiter in 34 auf der ganzen Welt verstreuten Außenstellen sorgen dafür, dass bereits vor Ort potenzielle Asylsuchende von ihrem Vorhaben abgebracht werden. Aber auch im Inland greift man auf die Dienste des AAbA zurück. »Wir sind ein Schnittstellenamt für andere Behörden«, betont Sandra Baierl stolz. »Praktisch ist, dass wir über eine eigene Eingreiftruppe verfügen. So wie die Cobra. Vor allem in afrikanischen Ländern wie Nigeria oder Somalia ist die Arbeit für sie sehr angenehm, weil die Gesetzeslage vor Ort einfacher ist.« Kollege Haslinger drückt sich weniger diplomatisch aus: »Asylanten sollten generell kriminalisiert werden«, meint er knapp. Für diese Aussage wurde er übrigens noch nie verklagt. Für etwa 15 seiner Aktionen sind hingegen juristische Verfahren anhängig. Denn Peter Haslinger ist im richtigen Leben der Medienkünstler Hans Bernhard. Er und seine Partnerin – Sandra Baierl hört auf den Künstlernamen LIZ VLX – sind nur anlässlich eines bis zum 17. Juli laufenden Kunstprojekts in die Rolle der strengen Sachbearbeiter geschlüpft. Weder das »Asylabwehramt« noch dessen kruden Auftrag gibt es tatsächlich – nur einige zu Behördenbüros umfunktionierte Räume des Kunstvereins Das weiße Haus in der Wollzeile und eine gekonnt gefälschte Website des Verteidigungsministeriums. Bundesadler, Rundwappen und umständliches Beamtendeutsch vermitteln trügerische Authentizität. Vor allem, weil die Website in Links und Download-Seiten von existierenden Behörden und Institutionen eingebunden ist. Informationen mehrerer Ministerien, aber auch von honorigen Non-Profit-Organisationen sind nur einen Klick entfernt. Bei der angegebenen Hotline-Nummer hebt übrigens tatsächlich eine freundliche Dame ab: Nur berät sie für European Homecare, jenes Unternehmen, das im Auftrag des Innenministeriums für die Asylbetreuung zuständig ist.

Bei der Ausstattung des Amtes wurde gleichfalls auf Authentizität Wert gelegt: Gewissenhaft hat man in dreiwöchiger Kleinarbeit Formblätter und Anträge aus heimischen Behörden zusammengetragen. »Wir haben sogar unsere Arbeitstreffen in Warteräumen durchgeführt, um ein Gefühl für die Stimmung dort zu bekommen«, erzählt Bernhard.

Seit 1995 operieren der Schweizer und die Wienerin LIZ VLX unter dem NamenUbermorgen.com in der Grauzone zwischen Realität und Fiktion. »Forged Original« nennen sie ihre meist satirischen Wirklichkeitskonstruktionen. Mitunter darf ihre Kunst aber auch das Leben verändern: jener Skinheads zumindest, die 2001 im Rahmen eines etwas anderen Resozialisierungsprogramms für Christoph Schlingensiefs Inszenierung vonHamlet am Zürcher Schauspielhaus gecastet wurden. Das Vorhaben, ehemaligen Nazis als Schauspielern eine zweite Chance zu geben, sorgte für einige Aufregung – kein Vergleich jedoch zu den Irritationen, die das auf »Media-Hacking« spezialisierte Duo während des US-Präsidentschaftswahlkampfs im Jahr 2000 ausgelöst hatte.

Damals entwickelten sie mit Voteauction.com eine Homepage, auf der sie Wählern die Möglichkeit gaben, ihr Stimmrecht an den meistbietenden Kandidaten zu verkaufen. Die Aktion löste ein weltweites Echo aus: Von derNew York Times über die Frankfurter Allgemeine Zeitung bis hin zu Boulevardblättern wurde über den Coup der Kommunikationsguerilleros berichtet. Nur die US-Wahlbehörden waren nicht begeistert. Seitdem ist eine Strafzahlung im fünfstelligen Bereich anhängig. Die aktuelle Aktion kommt da vergleichsweise günstig. »Wegen des Missbrauchs des Hoheitszeichens auf der Website rechne ich mit 750 Euro Strafe«, meint Bernhard und zuckt mit den Schultern. Mehr Kopfzerbrechen bereitete den Künstlern das Projekt während der Vorbereitung. »Es fiel uns relativ schwer, die restriktive Asylpolitik in diesem Land noch zu überzeichnen«, erzählt LIZ VLX. »Manchmal hat man das Gefühl, dass die Realität jegliche Fiktion überholt.«

Ohne Genehmigung, Die ZEIT, 9.7.2010, Druckausgabe

http://www.zeit.de/2010/28/A-Asylabwehramt/seite-1

7 ADDENDUM: Service Formulare / Service Forms

 REPUBLIK ÖSTERREICH
BUNDESMINISTERIUM FÜR INNERES
SEKTION III-RECHT

A keni pytje për një shanc të re në vendlindje?

Ne shpresojm se puntoret tanë prej ditës së parë në Austri ju kan ndihmuar.
Nje shërbim kujdesësh e re ju ofron ende këshillime:

Telefoni hotline për kthimin vullnetarisht është:
Na thirrni neve □pa pagesë nga tërë Austrija!

Telefoni gratis: 0800-20 30 40

Të hënën deri të premten prej 9.00 deri 17.00

Dobija juaj gjat kthimit vullnerarisht në vendllndje do të jëtë:
- ☐ Mu pa përsëri me te afërmit të juaj, me antarët familiar dhe shoqërine
- ☐ Kthimi me avion pa pagesë
- ☐ Kontaktin telefonik me familjen e juaj e keni falas
- ☐ Dokumentet për udhtimin i pregaditim ne
- ☐ Vendëqëndrimi juaj gjatë ketij organizimi do te eshte Traiskirchen
- ☐ Më ketë merr fund pasigurija
- ☐ Plani□kone ju aktivisht të ardhmën e juaj-informime nga vendlindja juaj
- ☐ Ne ju ndihmojme □hanciarisht për një shanc te dyt në vendlindjen e juaj

Ne ju këshillojm juve individualisht dhe ne besim edhe për perspektiva

Ne thirrni pa pagesë nga tërë Austrija-Telefoni: 0800-20 30 40
Kthimi vullnetarisht-një shanc e re për një □lim në atdhe

Albanisch

آیا خواهان معلومات درباره یک اغاز جدید در زادگاه خویش هستید؟

ما امیدواریم که همکاران ما در زمان اقامت شما با ما به شما کمک و رسیده گی لازم کرده باشند.

یک مرجع جدید کمک و همکاری هنوز هم در خدمت شما قرار دارد.

عودت داوطلبانه به کشور

شماره مجانی معلومات :   0800203040

شما میتوانید توسط شماره داده شده از دوشنبه ها تا جمعه ها از ساعت 9 صبح الی 5 عصر به صورت رایگان با ما در تماس شوید.

فواید عودت دوباره به وطن:

- طرح ریزی برای یک اینده خوب در وطن.

- بدست اوردن کمک های در نظر گرفته شده برای یک اغاز جدید در کشور.

- جلوگیری از یک دوره انتظار نامعلوم و بی نتیجه.

- امکانات صحبت تیلیفونی مجانی با اقارب و خویشاوندان تان در وطن.

- امکانات فراهم اوری اسناد ضروری و پاسپورت از سفارتخانه های مربوط.

- فراهم اوری تکت طیاره با بلت هواپیما به صورت مجانی.

- فراهم اوری زمینه بود و باش و سکونت تان در لاگر تراپزگیرخن تا به تاریخ عودت تان به کشور.

شما می توانید در صورت لزوم و با مشکلات از مشوره های ما مستفید شوید.

با ما در تماس شوید. به صورت رایگان و از تمام نقاط اتریش.

شماره تلفون مجانی ما: 0800203040

Farsi, Dari (Persisch)

345

REPUBLIK ÖSTERREICH
BUNDESMINISTERIUM FÜR INNERES
SEKTION III–RECHT

Haben Sie Fragen über eine neue Chance in der Heimat?

Wir hoffen, dass unsere MitarbeiterInnen Ihnen während der ersten Tage in Österreich behilflich waren.
Ein neues Betreuungsservice steht Ihnen auch weiterhin zur Verfügung:

Freiwillige Rückkehr - Telefon Hotline
Rufen Sie uns an – k o s t e n l o s aus ganz Österreich!
Gratis-Telefon: 0800 – 20 30 40
Rückkehrberatung HOTLINE
Mo – Fr 9.00 – 17.00 Uhr

Vorteile der freiwilligen Rückkehr in Ihre Heimat:
o Wiedersehen mit Ihren Verwandten, Bekannten und Freunden
o Keine Kosten für den Rückflug
o Kostenlose Kontaktaufnahme mit Ihren Verwandten in der Heimat
o Besorgung aller Reisedokumente
o Rückkehr nach Traiskirchen zur Vorbereitung Ihrer Rückkehr
o Ende des Wartens mit ungewissem Ausgang
o Planen Sie aktiv Ihre Zukunft – Information über Ihr Heimatland
o Finanzielle Starthilfe für Ihre zweite Chance in der Heimat
Wir beraten Sie individuell und vertrauensvoll über Ihre Perspektiven.

Rufen Sie an – gratis – Tel. 0800 20 30 40
Freiwillige Rückkehr – Eine Chance für einen neuen Start in der Heimat!

Do You Have Questions About Returning Home?

We hope that our staff could be of help during your days in the Refugee Initial Care Center Traiskirchen. Here is some information on a new service, you may use from anywhere in Austria:

Voluntary Return - Telephone Hotline
Call us – t o l l f r e e from anywhere in Austria!

Gratis-Telephone: 0800 – 20 30 40
Voluntary Return HOTLINE
Mo – Fr **9.00 – 17.00**

Benefits of returning home voluntarily:
- o   Reunite with your family and friends
- o   No costs for your travel (f.i. airplane) back home
- o   Call your family before going home
- o   We will get the travel documents for you
- o   Return back to Traiskirchen to prepare for your travel home
- o   Put an end to the endless waiting with unknown result
- o   Plan your future actively with information about your home country
- o   Financial help for your start

We provide individual and confidential counselling on returning home voluntarily!

Call Us – Toll Free – Tel. 0800 20 30 40
Voluntary Return – A Chance For A New Start Back Home!

Englisch

347

REPUBLIK ÖSTERREICH
BUNDESMINISTERIUM FÜR INNERES
SEKTION III-RECHT

Aves vous des questions concernant unne nouveau Chanse dans votre patrie ?

Nous espérons que nos collaborateurs ont bien pu vous assister durant vos premiers jours en Autriche.
Un nouveau service d'assistance continue à être à votre disposition :

Retour volontaire-Telefon Hotline
Appelez-nous gratuitement depuis toute l'Autriche au :
Telefon : 0800-20 30 40
Lu à Ve **9.00 – 17.00** heures

Les avantages du retour volontaire dans votre patrie :
- vous reverrez vos proches et vos amis
- nous nous chargeons des frais du voyage
- mise en contact gratuite avec vos proches dans votre pays
- on vous procure tous les papiers pour le voyage
- retour àTraiskirchen pour preparer votre retour
- plus d'attente sans connaître l'issue des démarches.
- préparez activement votre avenir- information concernant votre pays
- une aide financiére pour votre deuzieme chance dans votre patrie

Nous vous conseillerons en toute confiance et discrétion

Appelez le numéro-gratuit –Tel.0800 20 30 40
Retour volontaire-unne chance pour un nouveau start dans votre patrie!

Französisch

ايا غواړی چی د يو نوي پيل لپاره په خپل کلي او کور کی معلومات پيدا کړی؟

مونږ هيله مند يو چی زمونږ کارمندانو ستاسو د استوګني په وخت کی زمونږ په کمپ کی ستاسو سره پوره مرسته کړي وي٠

زمونږ د مرستو د يوي نوي شعبي درواري ستاسو په مخ هميشه خلاصي دي٠

وطن ته خپل په خوښنه بيرته ستنيدل

تاسو کولای شی زمونږ سره د ټول اتريش نه په لاندي نمره په وريا توګه وعربيزي؛

0800203040

تاسو کولای شی چی له دی نمري له لاري زمونږ سره د دوشنبي نه تر جمعي پوري دسهار د نه بجو نه د ماښام د پنځه بجو پوري په وريا توګه تماس ونيسي٠

وطن ته د بيرته ورتګ ګټي؛

- د يو سوکاله راتلونکي دپاره په خپل وطن کي د کار پيل٠
- د يو نوي ژوند د پيل په هدف د مرستو د لاسته راورل٠
- د يو ناخرګنده وخت لپاره يو ناخرګنده خواب ته د انتظار نه ده ده .
- د خپلوانو سره د بيرته ستنيدو په هدف زمونږ د تلفون په واسطه وريا خبري کول٠
- ستاسو د مربوط سفارت نه تاسو سره د پاسپورت نه په لاس ته راورلو کي مرسته٠
- د الوتکي وريا تکت٠
- ستاسو د بيرته تګ پوري ستاسو د اوسيدو بندوبست د ترايسکيربنن په کمپ کي٠
- تاسو کولايشی زمونږ دمشورو نه ګټه واخلی٠
- زمونږ سره تماس ونيسی٠٠٠٠ په وريا توګه٠٠٠٠ د ټول اتريش نه

زمونږ تلفون؛   0800203040

Paschtu (Afghanistan und Pakistan)

Aveti intrebari referitoare la posibilitatea de reintoarcere in tara?

Speram ca angajatii nostrii v-au fost de folos in perioada in care a-ti locuit in lagar.

Un nou serviciu de consiliere va sta in continuare la dispozitie:

Linie telefonica gratuita – Repatriere voluntara
Sunati-ne –GRATIS-din orice parte a Austriei!
TELEFON: 0800-20 30 40 vorbim romaneste
De Luni pina Vineri intre orele 9.00-17.00

Avantajele repatrierii voluntare:

- o Revederea cu familia, prietenii si cunoscutii dvs.
- o Noi va platim biletul de avion
- o Puteti telefona gratis cu familia
- o Noi va procuram toate documentele necesare ptr. Repatriere
- o Puteti locui in lagar pina la plecare
- o Terminati cu asteptarea unui raspuns nesigur
- o Primiti un ajutor financia

Repatriere voluntara cea mai buna sansa pentru un nou inceput!

Sunati-ne – gratis – Tel. 0800-20 30 40

Rumänisch

перед Вами стоит вопрос: безысходность, а может быть вернуться на Родину?   Мы сможем Вам в этом помочь!

Надеемся, что наши сотрудники смогли помочь Вам в Ваши первые дни в Австрии. Вам придётся многие проблемы решать самим, но мы оставляем Вам возможность остаться с нами в контакте:

добровольное возвращение на Родину- горячая линия

Вы можете звонить нам бесплатно по всей территории Австрии
тел: 0800-20 30 40
консультации проводятся с понедельника по пятницу с **9.00** до **17.00**

преимущества для тех, кто хочет вернутьсна Родину:
* ощутить запах Отчизны,всретиться вновь с родными, близкими и друзьями;
* бесплатный телефонный контакт с Вашими родными на Родине;
* оплата всех расходов за проезд домой;
* оформление и получение проездных документов;
* планирование Вашего будущего на Родине;
* стартовая финансовая поддержка для нового начала на Родине;
* окончание ожидания неизвестности, и возможности, как туристу вернуться домой, но обязательным условием ,во время подготовительной процедуры отправления домой, является проживание в лагере Трайскирхен

Вам будет оказана доверительная, квалифицированная помощь на Вашем родном языке

Звоните бесплатно-тел. 0800 20 30 40
добровольное возвращение - лучший шанс начать всё сначала на Родине

Russisch

BM.I REPUBLIK ÖSTERREICH
BUNDESMINISTERIUM FÜR INNERES
SEKTION III-RECHT

Memleketinizde yeni şans için sorularınız var mı?

Umariz, işarkadaşlarımız avusturyada ilk günleriniz esnasında yardımcı olmuşlardir. Yeni bir yardım hizmetimiz bundan başka emrinize hazırbulunuyor:

Gönüllü dönüş - Telefon hattı
Bizi ücretsiz tüm avusturyadan araya bilirsiniz!
Ücretsiz Telefon: 0800 – 20 30 40
Dönüş-danışma hattı
Pazartesi - cuma **09.00 – 17.00**

Memlektinize gönüllü dönüşün avatajları:

*   akrabalarınızı, tanıdıklarınızı ve arkadaşlarınızı tekrar görmek
*   ücretsiz dönüş-uçuşu
*   Yolculuk belgeriniz tedarik edilecek
*   Vatana dönüşünüze hazırlanmak için Traiskirchen´e dönüş
*   belirsiz sonucları beklemenize son verilecek
*   geleceğinizi aktiv planlamak - memleketiniz hakkında bilgiler
*   memleketinizde ikinci şans için ilk mali yardımı

Biz size gelecek imkanlarınız hakkında ferdi ve güvenli suret´de istişare ederiz.

Bizi ücretsiz arayın – tel: **0800 20 30 40**

Gönüllü dönüş – Vatan´da yeni bir başlangıç için şans!

Türkisch

8 ADDENDUM: Code

```python
# "Cut" line-length for better formatting, and emphasise
# interesting pieces of information in the webserver log

from optparse import OptionParser
import socket

parser = OptionParser()
parser.add_option("-i", "--infile", dest="filename",
                  help="logfile to parse", metavar="FILE")

(options, args) = parser.parse_args()

lineW = ''
lineF = ''

for line in open(options.filename).read().split("\n"):
  try:
    referrer = line.split(' ')[2]
    if not referrer.startswith("http://www.asyl") and \
    not referrer.startswith("http://asyl") \
    and len(referrer) > 4 and "q=" not in referrer:
      line = ' '.join(line.split(' ')[:2]) + ' "$%s "' % \
      line.split(' ')[2].replace('"', '$"') + \
      ' '.join(line.split(' ')[3:])
  except:
    pass
  try:
    socket.inet_aton(line.split(" ")[0])
  except:
    if (len(line) > 0):
      line = "\high{%s" % line
      line = line.replace(" ", "} ", 1)
  while len(line) > 97:
```

```
    lineW += "%s|||||||||" % line[:97]
    line = line[97:]
  lineW += "%s\n" % line

def high(match, end, line):
  variations = [match]
  for i in range(1, len(variations)+1):
    variations.append(match[:i] + "|||||||||" + match[i:])
  for variation in variations:
      if variation in line and end in line:
        line = line.split(variation)
        return "%s%s\\high{%s}%s%s\n" % \
        (line[0], variation,
         line[1].split(end)[0].replace("|||||||||",
                              "}|||||||||\high{"),
         end, end.join(line[1].split(end)[1:]))
      elif variation in line and '"' in line:
        line = line.split(variation)
        return "%s%s\\high{%s}%s%s\n" % \
        (line[0], variation,
         line[1].split('"')[0].replace("|||||||||",
                              "}|||||||||\high{"),
         '"', '"'.join(line[1].split('"')[1:]))

  return None

for line in lineW.split("\n"):
  if high("&q=", "&", line):
    lineF += high("&q=", "&", line)
  elif high("?q=", "&", line):
    lineF += high("?q=", "&", line)
  elif high('"$', '$"', line):
    lnt = high('"$', '$"', line).replace('"$', ' "')
    lineF += lnt.replace('$"', '" ')
  else:
    lineF += "%s\n" % line

print "\n".join(lineF.split("|||||||||"))
```

`ipshostnames.py`

```
# Filter IPs for WHOIS queries
```

```python
import socket

log = open("sorted").read().split("\n")

ips = []

for line in log:
  ip = line.split(" ")[0]
  try:
    socket.inet_aton(ip)
    ip = "whois -r %s > %s.txt" % (ip, ip)
    if ip not in ips: ips.append(ip)
  except:
    pass

print "; ".join(ips[:-1])
```

latexifywhoisrecords.py

```python
# Link first appearance of an IP in the log to its
# respective WHOIS record in a footnote

from glob import glob

whoisrs = ""
ips = []

for record in glob("whoisrecords/*.txt"):
  ip = ".".join(record.split("/")[1].split(".")[:-1])
  ips.append(ip)
  whoisrs += "\high{%s}\phantomsection\label{%s}\n\n" % \
             (ip, ip)
  whoisrs += open(record).read()

print whoisrs

l = open("sortedcut").read()

for ip in ips:
  l = l.replace("%s" % ip, "\high{%s}\\footnote{WHOIS" + \
                " record on page \pageref{%s}}" % \
                (ip, ip), 1)
```

```
open("sortedcutfns", 'w').write(l)
```

```
sortlog.py
```

```python
# Sort webserver access log by date/time

from time import strptime
from optparse import OptionParser

parser = OptionParser()
parser.add_option("-i", "--infile", dest="filename",
                  help="logfile to parse", metavar="FILE")

(options, args) = parser.parse_args()

class TimedLine(object):
  def __init__(self, line, time):
    self.line = line
    self.time = time

  def __cmp__(self,other):
    return cmp(self.time, other.time)

timedlines = []

for li in open(options.filename).read().split("\n"):
  try:
    lic = li.split("- [")[1].split('] "')[0].split(" ")[0
    liti = strptime(lic, "%d/%b/%Y:%H:%M:%S")
    current = TimedLine(li, liti)
    if not current in timedlines:
      timedlines.append(TimedLine(li, liti))
  except:
    pass

timedlines.sort()

for timedline in timedlines:
  print timedline.line
```

Asylabwehramt

OESTERREICH

Dem Menschen zum Schutze

P/834752390 PGH

www.ingramcontent.com/pod-product-compliance
Lightning Source LLC
LaVergne TN
LVHW042331060326
832902LV00006B/101